Understanding
Mass Communi

SEVENTH EDITION

Understanding Mass Communication

A Liberal Arts Perspective

Melvin L. DeFleur
BOSTON UNIVERSITY

Everette E. Dennis
FORDHAM UNIVERSITY

HOUGHTON MIFFLIN COMPANY

BOSTON   NEW YORK

Sponsoring Editor: Adam P. Forrand
Assistant Editor: Kristen Desmond
Editorial Associate: Brigitte Maser
Senior Project Editor: Kathryn Dinovo
Senior Cover Design Coordinator: Deborah Azerrad Savona
Senior Manufacturing Coordinator: Marie Barnes
Marketing Manager: Barbara LeBuhn

Cover image: Bruce Rogovin, Stone Images

Printed in the U.S.A.

Library of Congress Control Number: 2001131488

ISBN: 0-618-12857-3

3456789-CRK-05 04 03

Brief Contents

Contents

Chapter 1
Mass Communication and Mass Media 2

Part One
PUBLISHING 27

Chapter 2
Books: The First and Most Respected Mass Medium 28

Chapter 3
Newspapers, News, and the News Media 58

Chapter 4
Magazines: Voices for Many Interests 98

Part Two
ELECTRONIC AND VISUAL MEDIA 125

Chapter 5
Motion Pictures: The Great Entertainer 126

Chapter 6
Radio: The First Broadcast Medium 160

Chapter 7
Television: The Most Influential Medium 188

Chapter 8
The New Media: Communication for the Digital Age 214

Part Three
MEDIA AUDIENCES, SERVICES, AND SUPPORT 239

Chapter 9
International Communication and Global Media 240

Chapter 10
Popular Culture: Entertainment, Sports, and Music 256

Chapter 11
Advertising: Using Media in the Marketplace 290

Chapter 16
Ethics: Assessing Content and Behavior of the Media   460

Introduction

This book is written at the dawn of a digital age when interactive media and all that they portend make uncertain the very concept of mass communication. Still in the midst of massive economic, technological, and regulatory changes, mass communication as a *field of study* and as *media industries* warrants attention and understanding more than ever before. Always important in the modern age, the media and the processes that shape and direct them have grown in influence as linchpins of the new economy in which technology and communication have joined forces to create an information society, one that now overshadows the industrial and agricultural sectors. This has given the media a greater societal impact—vital to institutions of all kinds and to virtually every individual.

From its beginning, this book has uniquely linked research and intellectual inquiry with industry and professional experience. This approach creates a useful portrait of the functions of communication generally as well as their applications across the several distinct media industries, now often combined under large corporate umbrellas. In times past, media were the handiwork of individuals and their families, then of small or large companies, and more recently multinational, multimedia firms that are international or global in scope.

The book takes up the basic functions of communication, most often described as *information, opinion, entertainment,* and *advertising/marketing* as they have evolved across different media in different generations. We look at mass communication as a system, both in the United States and on the international scene. Against a backdrop of *historical development* and attention to *media economies, technology,* and *policy* considerations, we treat the several separable media industries both as social institutions themselves and as part of multimedia enterprises, both large and small.

Beginning with an assessment of media and communication as products *of* society and culture as well as an influence on them, we look at books, newspapers, magazines, motion pictures, radio, television, new online media, and the yield of popular culture, namely various entertainment forms including music and sports. Considering these industries and media first in the U.S. context, we follow these chapters with a look at the global scene. Our portrait would not be complete without considering advertising and public relations as functional activities and as industries in themselves, both linked to the communication sector in the broadest sense. And no discussion of media as institutions can be truly satisfying without a look at the audiences—important as users of media and as powerful factors in their development. Moving on to what we call controls—the politics, policies, and economic forces that guide and shape media, we also treat the influences and impact of media on individuals, society, and culture in a chapter on effects. We conclude with ethics, an all-pervasive concern, especially for the behavior and contents of media.

Stepping back, the readers see that they have journeyed through the country of media and communication, including the realms of information, opinion, entertainment, and outreach as well as through the vital links to the economic, technological, and social factors. We have thus looked at the media landscape from afar as well as inside and close-up. Beyond that, we consider the consequences of mass communication in relation to other institutions, social forces, and influences.

This book is the result of a longstanding conversation between the authors as we ourselves have come to know and understand the media, the communication process, and the ideas that best explain and interpret them. This we have done by continuously examining research, again from many sources, as well as offering our own observations of and experience with media industries on the inside from the highest-ranking corporate officers to entry-level employees. While respecting the yield of information from the academy and the industry, we also have benefited from commentary and criticism by people outside the media industries and the academy, including critics, institutional leaders, and others. Our study is based both in the United States and in some fifty countries abroad where we have lived, worked, researched, and taught. We have benefited enormously from scores of people "who know what they are talking about," in the words of the writer Nelson Algren. Unlike some texts that simply synthesize and represent the work of others, we have introduced new theoretical perspectives from our own work as well as other scholarship, observation, and analysis based on original studies we have conducted, research we have commissioned, and proprietary material from industry experts with whom we have worked. For this effort by us and by others, we received the highest accolade from a respected professor who also worked as an executive in several of the media. He wrote our publisher with these words: "This is a book for people who respect their students—and for students who appreciate more than a superficial look at one of the most complex, fascinating, fun, exasperating and perplexing fields of human endeavor."

This book has evolved over several decades and is informed by a long and current view of the literature of communication, media studies, and related fields, as well as personal participation in hundreds of industry, professional, and scholarly meetings on nearly every continent. Cognizant of the changing contours of knowledge and understanding, we have benefited from the work of visionary thinkers and the services of forecasting firms—all aimed at a book that appreciates the past, understands the current scene, and speculates with evidence about the probable future. Interactive long before the digital age, when the computerization of almost everything reordered the world, we are nonetheless impressed that this is a time of truly profound mass media and communication transformation and hope our work contributes to thoughtful understanding of a great social force whose imprint is evident everywhere.

Preface

This seventh edition of *Understanding Mass Communication* has been significantly changed from previous editions. New chapters have been added, existing ones have been extensively modified, and those retained from the earlier editions have been updated in terms of their data about the media and their references to published works. Important new features have been added to the book to make it easier for the student to understand the nature and functions of contemporary communication and mass media as well as the influences that they have on us as individuals and as a society.

FOCUS OF THE BOOK

Understanding Mass Communication amply covers the nuts and bolts of media content and how it is processed and delivered to a variety of audiences who selectively attend to it. Considerable attention is given to the ways in which professional communicators function within each media setting. However, *Understanding Mass Communication* differs from many of its competitors in that it is organized around three broad questions that go well beyond what a beginner's survey needs to include. These questions place each of the media within a broad *liberal arts perspective*. That perspective draws on concepts and conclusions, derived from many disciplines, that have helped us to understand the process and effects of mass communications. The three fundamental questions this book addresses are:

1. *How have the mass media come to be organized in the way they are?* What historical, demographic, economic, political, and technological factors have shaped our nation's privately owned, profit-oriented mass media in such a way that they attract wide audiences mainly by presenting popular culture and entertainment?

2. *How do the mass media actually function?* How do professional communicators in each of the major media decide on the content they select, modify it, and present it in various ways, using a variety of technologies so as to reach specific kinds of audiences?

3. *What effect does this flow of information from media to audiences have on us, both individually and collectively?* Does it have only minor influences on our thoughts and behavior as individuals and does it modify our culture and society in only limited ways? Or, is mass communication a powerful force that shapes both individual conduct and our nation's history?

NEW TO THE SEVENTH EDITION

This edition of *Understanding Mass Communication* has new chapters and distinctive features that are not found in earlier versions of this text or in similar books. We have strengthened old chapters and added new ones, compressed some material and expanded our discussion on related information. We have added considerable new material on digital applications and new media, not just in a reworked chapter, but throughout the text. We have expanded our treatment of news in the context of newspapers as well as other news and information media. Music, sports, and entertainment media have been integrated into a broader discussion of popular culture. As always, we have buttressed our exposition and discussion with new data, some of it made available to us by research services as the book went to press. Our own original work on "Trends in Media Use," including curves of adoption, has been updated and extended. A special new feature is "Insights from Media Leaders" in several chapters that includes interviews we have conducted with key media executives and others who are in positions both to help students understand how they themselves got started in their respective fields, but also to provide a current assessment of specific industries and their likely futures.

Important in the seventh edition is the unique feature "Explaining Media Effects." Prepared by Professor Margaret H. DeFleur, and included with her permission, are eighteen theory inserts, each of which explains an important aspect of how the media function or the nature of one of their influences. Some summarize existing theories that will be familiar to media scholars. Others are new, having recently been prepared by Professor DeFleur. Each is stated in a set of interlinked formal propositions—the format advocated be media researchers and theorists, but which has not been accomplished before in any competing text.

INSIGHTS FROM MEDIA LEADERS: A NEW FEATURE FOR THE SEVENTH EDITION

From its inception, *Understanding Mass Communication* has attempted to capture the current state and likely future of media and communications industries against the backdrop of their theoretical underpinnings, history, economics, legal status, technology, social context, and other factors. Adding texture and a "real-time" perspective to that mix are a series of original interviews with notable media leaders conducted by the authors exclusively for this book. The authors have long maintained close relations with media industry executives and professionals from chief executive officers of leading companies and network anchors to midcareer and younger professionals.

Some of the flavor of those important links are reflected in the "Insights from Media Leaders" feature in chapters 2–8 and 10–13. Here, students will find the stories of notable owners, executives, and top managers—how they got to their present positions, their insider perspectives on how individual industries work and survive, the probable future of their field, as well as its rewards and difficulties.

Published here for the first time are interviews with eleven media leaders:

 • Books: Peter Osnos, Publisher and Chief Executive, Public Affairs Press, New York, New York

 • Magazines: Myrna Blyth, Editor in Chief, *Ladies Home Journal* and Senior Vice President, Meredith Corporation, New York, New York

 • Radio: Alfred C. Liggins III, Chief Executive Officer, Radio One, Inc., Lanham, Maryland

 • New Media: James Kinsella, Member of the Board of Directors and Former Chief Executive Officer, Tiscali, Milan, Italy

 • Advertising: John Zweig, Chief Executive Officer, WWP Group plc, New York, New York

 • Opinion Research: Humphrey Taylor, Chairman, Harris Poll (Harris Interactive), New York, New York

 • Newspapers: Jay T. Harris, Chairman and Publisher, *San Jose Mercury News,* San Jose, California (resigned March 2001)

 • Motion Pictures: David Brown, Film Producer, New York, New York

 • Television: Mark Walton, Managing Director, Onyx Media Group, New York, New York

 • Recorded Music: Lia Vollack, Executive Vice President, Music, Columbia Pictures, Los Angeles, California

 • Public Relations: Richard D. Jernstedt, Chief Executive Officer, Golin/Harris, Chicago, Illinois

Many of the individuals interviewed are located in the heart of the media industries—New York, Los Angeles, Chicago, and other key locations—while others have international billets; and almost all engage in national and global connections. Some are heads of their firms, some are in the top executive ranks, while others lead editorial or content divisions of their respective companies. A great editor, Tom Winship of the *Boston Globe*, once remarked that media leadership is explained in three words: "genes, romance, and nepotism." All three of these factors—sheer ability, marriage, and family connections—are part of the story you will find in these profiles.

ACKNOWLEDGMENTS

Our thanks to the chairman, president, and chief executive officer of Houghton Mifflin Company, Nader Darehshori, who has been enormously supportive of every edition of this book, and his able colleagues, especially our editor, Adam Forrand, as well as the several busy persons who have served as readers and critics of this book including the prerevision reviewers:

Kevin Kawamoto, *University of Washington*

Elizabeth M. Perse, *University of Delaware*

Mark Poindexter, *Central Michigan University*

Hoyt Purvis, *University of Arkansas*

Melissa M. Spirek, *Bowling Green State University*

And, of course, our thanks to the thousands of students who have used this book in more than two hundred colleges and universities over two decades. A special service for this edition was rendered by Erik Ugland of the University of Minnesota, who prepared the instructor's manual. Other preparatory work was done by Christine Kuehbeck and Mario J. Panlilio, Jr., in New York.

TO THE STUDENT

This book has been prepared by its two authors as a tool for you. Our goal has been to help you understand the increasingly important part played by mass communications in our society as part of your personal intellectual development. We sincerely hope that you find the book interesting and that it serves you well. If it does not, we will have to share part of the blame. For that reason, if you find any part of this book difficult to understand, if we have failed to touch on matters that you feel are important, or if we have dwelled too long on issues that do not deserve such extensive treatment, we would like to hear from you. In fact, we would be delighted if you would offer any suggestions as to how we can make this book better. To that end, after you have finished any chapter or the whole book, we invite you to write or send us an e-mail message and offer any kind of criticism or comment that you feel is important. You will have our full attention!

Melvin L. DeFleur
College of Communication
Boston University
640 Commonwealth Avenue
Boston, MA 02215
e-mail: defleur@bu.edu

Everette E. Dennis
Graduate School of Business
Fordham University at Lincoln Center
113 West 60th Street
New York, NY 10023
e-mail: dennis@fordham.edu

April 2001

Understanding
Mass Communication

Chapter 1

MASS COMMUNICATION AND MASS MEDIA

TODAY, THE MASS MEDIA ARE PRESENT IN ONE FORM OR ANOTHER IN VIRTUALLY EVERY SOCI-ETY. THERE REMAIN ONLY A FEW POCKETS OF population in remote areas where one can find people who have no access to mass communications. In modern societies, television, radio, newspapers, and the Internet provide citizens with rapid access to news, entertainment, and other content all day, every day. The size of audiences who attend to media content in some cases almost defies the imagination. Perhaps the viewing audience reached an all-time high in November 2000 when billions of people around the globe were glued to their television sets viewing the unfolding drama of the American presidential election. National polls conducted at the time indicated that an astonishing 90 percent of the American population was following the unfolding election contest on their TV sets for several days following the voting. Additional billions of people in Europe, Asia, and Latin America heard reports about it via their media.

The billboard or outdoor advertising harkens to one of the oldest communication forms—the simple sign presented for public inspection and information.

Even the humble soap opera draws huge audiences. More people view a single episode of a popular daytime serial than have even seen one of Shakespeare's plays performed on a stage since they were written in the late 1500s. About 60 million in America will read a newspaper today. A popular first-run movie will be seen by tens of millions—and later by additional millions on videocassette or television. With such massive numbers attending to the media, it is little wonder that many thoughtful people are concerned about how readers, listeners, and viewers are influenced by what they see and hear.

MASS COMMUNICATION IN CONTEMPORARY SOCIETY

The media provide many categories of information, including news, entertainment, advertising, practical advice, education, and much more. However, most of the content of the mass media is designed to *entertain* audiences. This is particularly true in countries where profit-making organizations compete for the attention of audiences to advertising messages. As will be explained in later chapters, even the news media in many modern societies have a substantial focus on entertainment. That is, stories are often selected not so much for what they may offer to enlighten their audiences, but because those who gather and prepare them believe that they will be interesting or entertaining in some way.

PROBLEMS POSED BY THE MEDIA

Most people spend little time worrying about the effects of mass communication on society, or even on their own behavior. If they criticize the media, it is with complaints such as they cannot find enough of their favorite type of TV program, they did not like the last movie they saw, or they are bored by the news. However, a more thoughtful segment of the public realizes how deeply embedded the media are in modern life and is concerned about *how their content influences us both individually*

More than ever before, communicators in a digital environment choose from a multiplicity of media and communication methods as they target and bombard individuals with messages. This Web site for a Sacramento, California, advertising agency outlines these choices.

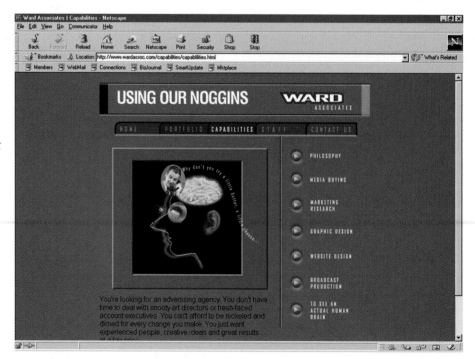

and collectively. An important question, then, is whether the influences of mass communication are beneficial, harmless, or hazardous. Thoughtful citizens want to understand how our media *operate,* what *influences* they have on both children and adults, whether they are *ethical and responsible* in what they present, and how much *control* we as a society actually have over their content. In particular, citizens are concerned about such issues as the portrayal of violence, excessive sexual depictions, and the use of vulgar language. They want to know if such content will affect their children and whether it causes unwanted behavior forms in society.

While answers and explanations are sorely needed, there are no quick and easy solutions. Questions concerning the influences of the media are complex. Increasingly, however, research findings and other information are being accumulated by communication researchers, media scholars, and social scientists—information providing important perspectives on the functioning and influences of the mass media in American society. Just as the physical and biological sciences have developed understandings and explanations of the aspects of nature that they study, so have media researchers and scholars made discoveries in the study of mass communication. It is a major goal of this book to provide explanations of the process and effects of mass communication—information that can lead to a better understanding of our contemporary mass media. To provide that understanding, this book addresses three important questions:

(1) *How were our present media shaped by the events, trends, policies, and characteristics of the American society?* That is, what took place in earlier years as these media were developing that have structured them as they are today? That is a very important question. Reviewing what took place in the past is the only way we can understand what we have at present.

(2) *How do our media function today to select, process, and disseminate various categories of content?* That is, who makes the decisions and why concerning what is presented to audiences by those who design and transmit the content of books, newspapers, magazines, movies, radio and television programs, and what appears on the Internet? An adequate understanding of mass communication—both in terms of its processes and effects—cannot be achieved without addressing this question.

(3) *What assumptions and forecasts can we make about the media we will have in the future, and what they will offer to their audiences in the years ahead?* Obviously, many of the factors that have had an influence on our media in the past will play a part in changing them in the future. Thus, understanding the past provides insight into the present. Understanding both the past and the present provides a basis for trying to look ahead into the future.

EXPLAINING THE PROCESSES AND EFFECTS OF THE MASS MEDIA

To explain the processes and effects of mass communication as they are understood today, this book will introduce a number of *theories.* Theories are the basis of all explanation and they are in many ways *the most practical of all forms of knowledge.* That is true whether one is dealing with the physical, biological, or social world. Each of us makes use of many kinds of theories that have provided practical solutions every day in a multitude of ways. If you drive a car, feel comfortable in an air-conditioned or centrally heated room, eat a meal without serious health consequences, read at night using electricity, go to a movie, watch television, take medication, use a computer, or engage in hundreds of other routine daily activities, you are receiving the benefits of theories. They were developed by a host of researchers and scientists who found

The Nature and Uses of Theory

explaining
MEDIA EFFECTS

Theories are developed in all fields that seek to understand their subject matter, so that the implications of what is being studied can be understood. Simply put, *theories explain how things work.*

Most people think of a theory as something developed in physics, chemistry, or the biological sciences. Obviously, those fields have made remarkable achievements. However, the methods and logic of scientific investigation are now being applied to the younger field of mass communication as well, and a number of important theories have been developed in recent decades. Thus, the logic and methods of science have been adapted to the study of the processes and effects of mass communication to develop theories explaining how consequences occur.

Theories are not just vague speculations. They are, first of all, systematic *descriptions* of what prior conditions bring about what consequences. Such a description usually consists of a set of *assumptions* about the relationships between clearly stated prior conditions and a "therefore" statement describing the process or effects that they bring about. In simpler terms, theories are precise sets of statements about what causes are assumed to bring about what outcomes.

Statements about what causes what provide *explanations.* Thus, theories explain why certain effects occur as a result of prior conditions that are both necessary and sufficient to bring about those consequences.

To learn how things work, scientists (including those who study the media) conduct careful and extensive research. In fact, theories are usually initially proposed when researchers think that, as a result of studies they have conducted, they have discovered some cause-effect connection between some set of prior conditions and some consequence. If that is the case, they put together an initial (tentative) version of a theory that might explain what they have uncovered. Thus, a third feature of theories is that they are *products of research* that uncover possi-

ble causal connections between prior conditions and their consequences.

When such potential relationships have been identified, the tentative theory is set forth as a set of statements or propositions that logically predict what effects should be observable *if the prior conditions actually do cause the consequences.* Thus, a fourth feature of a well-developed theory is that it provides a prediction of what should be found by further careful observation—assuming that the theory is a correct description of what prior conditions cause what consequences.

Such logical predictions are then checked by careful research to see if the theory's prediction is accurate or not. Thus, a fifth feature of a theory is that it provides a *guide for relevant research* to check whether it has made a valid logical prediction. If the research shows that the prediction is correct, the theory has received positive support. If not, it needs to be modified and tested again, or even abandoned. Theories, then, have the following features and functions:

1. Theories are *sets of interrelated propositions,* derived from research, that provide descriptions about how things work.

2. Theories provide *explanations* about what prior conditions bring about what consequences.

3. Theories provide *logical predictions,* that is, guides to research, about what should be found by further careful observation.

4. Theories are supported when their predictions are found by research to be *accurate.* If not, they must be revised and retested or simply rejected.

solutions as to how things work. They conducted systematic research to develop theories that describe and explain *what events or factors bring about, result in, or cause some sort of consequence.* Once these causal sequences were known—in a vast list of fields—clever people invented ways to use that knowledge in practical ways.

Exactly the same principles apply to the study of mass communication. Although it is a young field that has conducted systematic research for less than a century, a number of theories that explain various aspects of the process and consequences of mass communication have been developed. A number of them will be presented in brief form in the chapters of this book.

As noted previously, the media as they exist today have been shaped by a number of social, political, economic, and cultural influences from the past. Furthermore, the media will continue to be shaped, not only by what they are today, but by future social, political, economic, and cultural changes in our society as they continue to unfold. These two basic principles constitute a guide for the organization of chapters related to each of our media.

Obviously, some of our media are older than others. Bound books have been around since Roman times, and scrolls were in existence even before that. Newspapers and magazines, on the other hand, are much more recent developments; they were not possible until the technology of printing became available. As mass media, they came into their own during the 1800s when steam presses made it possible to produce printed pages quickly and in large numbers. More modern media—the movies, radio, television, and the Internet—were all developed during the 1900s. In each case, these media were introduced into the society as *innovations*—cultural items that had not been present earlier. None were instantly *adopted*—taken up to be used—by the majority of the population. In each case, a few persons started using these media, then their use became more common as they were adopted by larger and larger proportions of the population.

Social scientists Everett Rogers and F. Floyd Shoemaker have developed a very useful theory that describes and explains the process of the *adoption of innovation*.[1] It applies not only to the pattern by which a new medium of communication comes into use within a population, but also to almost any kind of new cultural item that is either invented within the society or adopted from some outside source (e.g., the electric light, the pizza, the automobile, the refrigerator, the computer, the wristwatch, the cigarette, and the hamburger). All of the above are examples of cultural items that followed a more or less similar *curve of adoption*. The adoption pattern of each of the major media will be presented in the chapters that follow.

But where does one begin when tracing the development of mass communication and the adoption of the several media in the American society? One answer is to start by looking closely at the *fundamental process of human communication as it takes place between human beings at the interpersonal level.* Mediated communication is, after all, interpersonal communication aided by a sophisticated technology that conquers both time and distance. The media are simply devices that bring messages quickly from communicators to multitudes—rather than to an audience of a single person. Looking at the fundamental process of interpersonal communication, then, reveals insights that help place mass communication in perspective.

THE INTERPERSONAL COMMUNICATION PROCESS

Language and its use are at the heart of the process by which mass communication takes place. To understand that process more fully, we must first look at how human communication takes place in the *absence* of media. That is, what are the fundamentals of face-to-face human communication? With that analysis as a basis for comparison, we will take a close look at mass communication. This, in turn, will permit a comparison of the two and a fuller understanding of the advantages, limitations, and effects of communicating using our contemporary media.

Human beings communicate in ways that are very different from those of any other species on our planet. Specifically, we communicate with some form of learned and shared verbal and nonverbal language that is part of a culture that has accumulated and

Adoption of Innovation Theory

In a changing society there is a constant flow of new technical products, solutions to problems, interpretations, language, clothing styles, and other kinds of innovations. They can range from the trivial, such as a new dance step, to the profound, such as a new political philosophy (like communism or democracy).

Sometimes the origin of an innovation is *well-known.* Specific persons invent something at a particular time, as when Thomas Edison invented the phonograph on July 18, 1877. At other times, the origins of an innovation are *unknown.* For example, it is entirely unclear who first invented the humble hamburger.

Many innovations are adopted by a population after having been *invented elsewhere.* For example, many in the world eagerly adopted the powered aircraft after Orville and Wilbur Wright first flew one in 1903. Other borrowed innovations are adopted by people in a society by a far less obvious process. For example, the now-popular pizza was virtually unknown in most parts of the United States before about 1945.

But whether invented internally or abroad, every innovation that is taken up by people in a particular society is adopted in a *regular and predictable process.*

The adoption of innovation theory is important for the study of mass communication for two reasons. First, each of our major mass media was *originally an innovation* that had yet to be adopted and widely used. Examples are the mass newspaper (which began in New York in 1834), the motion picture (beginning about 1900), home radio (the early 1920s), television as a mass medium (post–World War II), and so on.

A second way in which adoption theory is important to the study of mass communication is that the media are often responsible for bringing new items to the *attention of people* who will eventually adopt them.

Some innovations spread swiftly through a society and are taken up by virtually everyone. Others spread slowly and are eventually adopted by only a fraction of the population. An accumulative plot of the proportion of the population who have adopted at any given time starts upward slowly as a few people acquire the item. It then rises quickly as more people take it up. Finally, it flattens out as it is acquired by fewer and fewer late adopters. Thus, most (but not all) follow a characteristic *S-shaped pattern of adoption* that results from the process described in the following set of propositions:

1. The adoption process begins with an *awareness stage* in which those who will eventually adopt a particular innovation learn of its existence (often from the mass media) but lack detailed information.

2. Awareness is followed by an *interest stage* during which those who contemplate possible adoption will devote increasing attention to the innovation and seek additional information about it. (The media often provide this information.)

3. In an *assessment stage,* which follows, potential adopters use the information they have obtained to evaluate the applicability of the innovation to their anticipated uses and situations.

4. In a *trial stage,* which is next, a small number of potential adopters acquire and use the innovation on a small scale (or temporarily) to determine its utility for their purposes.

5. **Therefore,** in the *final adoption stage,* a few innovators and early adopters acquire and use the innovation on a full scale. After that, increasing numbers adopt it, and the accumulation of new users follows a characteristic *S-shaped curve.*

grown increasingly complex over time. Other species communicate with signs and signals in ways that have changed little since the dawn of their existence. In spite of romantic ideas about whales, porpoises, and other animals that supposedly "talk," animals do not use languages based on culturally shared systems of symbols, grammar, and meanings. Animals clearly do communicate with each other, sometimes in relatively sophisticated ways. However, they do so with behavioral systems that are in most cases inherited, and in some cases learned, but that are never part of a culture in the true sense. In other words, no matter how one looks at it, in any realistic sense, only human beings communicate with language based on shared cultural rules.[2]

THE DEVELOPMENT OF LANGUAGE

If we count a human generation as about thirty years on average, we need go back only about two thousand grandmothers ago to come to a time when our prehistoric ancestors did not use language as we know it. Early human beings, such as *Australopithecus, Homo habilis,* and *Homo erectus,* clearly did not speak. In fact, they *could not* because the structure of their voice boxes was like that of modern apes and chimpanzees.[3] They could make vocal noises, as do their anthropoid counterparts today, but the human anatomy of the time did not permit them the delicate control over vocal sounds that are required for speech.

That anatomical limitation continued even through the more recent era of the Neanderthal *(Homo sapiens neanderthalensis),* who inhabited wide areas of our planet starting about 150 to 125 thousand years ago. The Neanderthal apparently were able to communicate reasonably well, but they had to do so with gestures, body movements, and a limited number of sounds that they were capable of making. Between about ninety and thirty-five thousand years ago, the Neanderthal were replaced by a very different type of human being. These were the Cro-Magnon *(Homo sapiens sapiens),* our direct ancestors. If dressed in modern clothes, they would be virtually indistinguishable from people today. Because they had the same larynx, voice box, tongue, and lip structures as do modern people, the Cro-Magnon were able to generate and control voice sounds in intricate ways.[4] This made it possible for them to speak and develop language. Thus, the use of complex languages began sometime around forty thousand years ago, give or take a few thousand years. This was a relatively recent development in the several millions of years of the evolutionary history of our species.[5] It was the first great communication revolution.

The subsequent development of increasingly efficient and flexible systems for storing, recovering, and disseminating information through the use of various media provided additional revolutions. At first, each step took thousands of years. Few people today are even aware of that long history, or of the great breakthroughs that each step required—first language, then writing, the alphabet, portable media,

An early "writing" form or pictograph has a twenty-first–century descendant—information signage that uses a commonly understood, international code.

figure1.1

Early Forms of Communication

books, print, newspapers, telegraph, film, radio, television in various forms, computers, and the rest. But with those media in place today, human beings can use language and media together to conquer time and distance in ways that would have defied even the wildest imagination of people only a few generations back.

SHARING MEANING WITH VERBAL AND NONVERBAL SYMBOLS

In our current age of mass communications, we still communicate, whether face-to-face or through media, by using verbal and nonverbal *symbols*. A symbol is a word, an action, or an object that "stands for" and arouses standardized internal meanings in people within a given language community. By an established *convention* (a well-established rule), each symbol—such as "dog," "child," or even complex terms like "carcinogen" and "biodegradable"—is supposed to arouse similar internal meaning experiences in everyone who uses it. In a similar way, actions, such as gestures and facial expressions, can be governed by meaning conventions. The same is true of certain objects, such as a cross, a star of David, or a wedding ring.

Language also includes rules for putting symbols together in patterns that arouse meanings. The familiar rules of *grammar* establish standard ways for linking and modifying classes of symbols (like verbs, pronouns, and adjectives) to give more precision and flexibility to their use in complex messages. Another common category of rules, called *syntax,* provides for ordering symbols to make the mean-

Much of the public's concern and fear about the mass media focuses on their possible impact on children, whether that involves violence, sex, or other objectionable content.

ings clear. For example, syntax determines whether you say "the ball struck the man" or "the man struck the ball." Other familiar rules are those for *pronunciation*— socially accepted ways to make the sounds for words.

A BASIC MODEL OF HUMAN COMMUNICATION

While each of us converses with other people many times every day, few of us step back from the process and ask exactly how it works. It is only in recent years that this question has been addressed in a theoretical way. One of the earliest attempts to develop a "model" of human communication—that is, a simple but accurate representation with either graphics or verbal propositions—came from the laboratories of Bell Telephone Company. Claude E. Shannon, working with Warren Weaver, was faced with the task of trying to determine how to improve physical signals, carried by a medium such as a telephone line, so that there was less chance of error when the messages being transmitted were received. The theory developed by Shannon and Weaver was a complex mathematical formulation.[6] However, it contained some very basic and simple ideas that were seen as helpful by scholars trying to portray the process of language communication. Using Shannon and Weaver's depiction of the communication process, they developed a *model* that gives us a *representation* of the human communication process in very simple and linear terms.

The simple and linear view of human communication that was developed from Shannon and Weaver's work became a fairly standard way of describing the process.[7] Many similar verbal and graphic versions of this basic formulation can be found in communication textbooks. What the basic linear model did not include was the idea that communication has an *effect*. That is, people transmit messages that have some influence when they are received and interpreted. That idea can be added, and the following list of stages describes, in a simple way, what happens when one person communicates a message to another:

1. The act of human communication begins with a "sender" who decides to *initiate* a message that expresses a specific set of intended meanings.
2. That sender *encodes* the intended meanings by selecting specific words and gestures with conventionalized interpretations that the receiver will presumably understand.
3. The message is then *transmitted*—spoken or written so as to cross the space between sender and receiver as a signal of patterned information.

explaining
MEDIA EFFECTS

Shannon and Weaver's Information Theory

During the late 1940s, Dr. Claude E. Shannon, a physicist working in Bell Telephone Laboratories with Warren Weaver, developed a mathematical theory to describe physical events in the accuracy of transmission of information in a mechanical communication system—such as a telephone line or radio system. One of its basic concepts was the idea of *entropy*. It referred to *inefficiency* in a system. The greater the entropy in the system, the less the efficiency.[8]

At first, the theory focused only on the technical problem of transmitting physical signals along a medium. Later it was expanded to a more general theory describing the accuracy of transmitting patterned signals used to send and receive language. The more the randomness in a message, the more difficult it is for a receiving person to "make sense" out of it when trying to decode the signals being transmitted.

These concepts were adopted by early media theorists to use as a simple model, a model that shaped thinking about mass communication for decades. That is, the *higher the entropy factor, the more difficult it is to achieve accuracy between the sender and the receiver of a message.*

These media theorists described the act of communication as a movement of information by a medium from a *source* to a *destination*. The source selects a desired message (written or spoken words) that a *transmitter* encodes into patterned signals that can be sent over a *channel* (that is a medium, or even just over air as in interpersonal communication). The *receiver* reverses the process of the transmitter and *decodes* the patterned signals back into a message that can be understood by the destination.

Shannon and Weaver recognized that things could always go wrong at virtually any point in the communication process. To describe problems between source and destination, they used the term "noise," which refers to any category of events, whether physical or behavioral, that *increases* rather than *decreases* entropy (thereby reducing the accuracy of the message as understood by the destination).

A graphic *representation* helps to explain their concepts in simple linear terms. Information moves from a starting point at the source through the transmitter via the channel to the receiver to be decoded at the final destination:

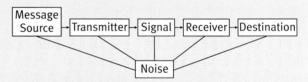

In verbal terms, Shannon and Weaver's theory can be expressed in the following way:

1. Human communication begins with a *source* who selects a desired message that he or she wants to send to one or more other people.

2. The source makes use of a *transmitter* to encode this message into physical signals—corresponding to words and other symbols that the sender believes will arouse the intended meanings on the part of a destination person or persons.

3. The patterned signals are transmitted over a channel capable of moving the physical information across the intervening space to a *receiver*.

4. The receiver *decodes* the patterned signals back into a message of words or other symbols that can be interpreted and understood.

5. Various kinds of physical or semantic *noise* can limit accuracy by distorting the reception and interpretation of the message.

4. The "receiver," the individual to whom the message is directed, attends to and *perceives* the incoming patterned information, identifying it as a specific language message.

5. The receiver then *decodes* the message by constructing his or her own interpretations of the conventionalized meanings of the symbols.

6. As a result of interpreting the message, the receiver is *influenced* in some way. That is, the communication has some effect, which can range from trivial to profound.

Almost all scholars today agree that this *basic linear model* of the human communication process greatly oversimplifies what actually takes place. The human conversations that we engage in with people around us are *transactional* (not linear)—each party encodes and decodes messages at the same time and is alert to all kinds of cues from the other person.[9]

In spite of its simplicity and obvious limitations, the basic linear model is useful for *analyzing the communication process*—breaking it down into its distinct stages in order to understand what happens at each. Also, those stages are at the heart of the complex transactions of any conversation. That is, even if both parties are simultaneously encoding, transmitting, and decoding, they are still serving as senders and receivers, initiating and receiving messages. In other words, the six stages noted above are *embedded* within the complexities of simultaneous transactional communication. Thus, the basic linear model simplifies the task of looking carefully at each stage of the process separately so as to see exactly how people use symbols and conventions of meaning to accomplish the act of human communication.

Common sense tells us that often meanings may not match! One person may fail to understand what another person is saying, even with a simple message, because there are various sources of inaccuracy that are difficult to control. Thus, Shannon and Weaver were right in saying that *noise* can enter the process at virtually any stage.

Moreover, as we have suggested, communication is a simultaneous back-and-forth, or *interactive,* process. People are not merely passive and linear senders and receivers. They respond to the content of others' meanings, ask for clarification, and indicate agreement. Thus, each person shifts roles to become a sender at one moment and a receiver at another.

Finally, we normally put words together into sentences, paragraphs, and various constructions using accepted rules of *grammar* and *syntax.* These patterns themselves introduce meanings that go beyond those associated with each of the words used. For example, the pattern "the boy killed the snake" implies a meaning totally different from the pattern "the snake killed the boy," even though the words are identical. However, these patterns pose no serious problem in understanding human communication. We learn the patterns and their associated meanings as part of our language, just as we learn the meanings of each word.

COMMUNICATING ACCURATELY

As suggested above, the meanings intended by communicators and those interpreted by receivers may not be perfectly parallel. In that case, the communication has suffered a loss of *accuracy.* In fact, a perfect match between the meanings of both parties is unlikely, perhaps with the exception of trivial messages. In a common-sense way, then, loss of accuracy can be defined as any reduction in the correspondence between the details of the sender's intended message and those of the receiver's interpreted message.

The accuracy principle. There can be many causes of a loss of accuracy between meanings as a result of *noise*. It can result from dim light, poor acoustics, disruptive sounds, or any other physical condition that interferes with the transfer of information. Limited accuracy can also result from memory failure, faulty perception, or unfamiliarity with the language. Or, it may happen when the sender and receiver do not share the same cultural rules for the use of language—a common problem in a multicultural society. In other words, inaccuracy can arise from any physical, psychological, social, or cultural condition that reduces similarities between the intended meanings of the sender and the interpreted meanings of the receiver.

If accuracy suffers, for whatever reasons, the communication will be less effective in achieving the goals of the communicator. That can be a problem in interpersonal communication, and as will be made clear, it can be devastating in mass communication. This conclusion regarding accuracy and its consequences can be stated more formally as a rather common-sense generalization, which we can call the *accuracy principle:*

> The lower the level of correspondence between the intended meanings of the sender and the interpreted meanings of the receiver, the less effective an act of communication will be in achieving either mutual understanding or an intended influence.

Clearly, then, it is important for both the sender and the receiver to strive for accuracy if they are to achieve either goal of understanding or influence. But how, aside from careful selection of words and thoughtful organization of a message, can communication be made more accurate? Actually, in interpersonal communication there are two very effective ways: One is by the receiver's providing *feedback,* and the other by the sender's engaging in *role-taking.* As we will see, these two ideas have profound implications for understanding the differences between face-to-face and mass communication.

The feedback principle. Usually, interpersonal communication is an ongoing process that goes back and forth between the parties. For example, you start to explain something to a friend and at some point your friend may frown or shrug as you are talking. Seeing this, you sense that he or she may not have understood very well. So, you try to explain that point in a different way or provide a brief example as you continue with your account. Your friend then nods and you conclude that you have clearly made your point. In such a face-to-face situation, the sender is ever alert to observable verbal and nonverbal signals coming back from the receiver. These cues provide *feedback*—essentially a reverse communication by the receiver back to the communicator that indicates whether the message is getting through. In face-to-face communication, the receiver usually provides both verbal and nonverbal feedback on an ongoing basis to influence the communicator's selection of words, gestures, and meanings. Thus, the two parties alternately become both sender and receiver as the messages of one stimulates feedback from the other.

Feedback may be deliberate or not. In any event, the communicator takes feedback into account to try to increase communication accuracy. This is a very important idea. Stated simply, feedback leads to greater accuracy in communication. Conversely, without feedback, accuracy is likely to suffer. This can be stated as a second important generalization, which we can call the *feedback principle:*

> If ongoing and immediate feedback is provided by the receiver, accuracy will be increased. That is, the intended meanings of the communicator have a better chance of being similar to those constructed by the receiver.

The role-taking principle. When a sender correctly interprets feedback cues from the intended receiver and adjusts the message in order to increase accuracy, the communicator is figuratively placing himself or herself in the receiver's shoes. Stated in another way, mentally, the sender tries to *be* the receiver in order to understand how he or she is likely to respond to the message being transmitted. This process is called *role-taking*. That is, the sender tries to understand how the message looks from the other person's point of view and to modify it where needed to increase accuracy. Thus, role-taking can be defined as the sender's use of feedback to judge which words and nonverbal cues will work best to arouse the intended meanings in the receiver.

Some people are better at role-taking than others. Also, some situations are better suited for it than others. Role-taking can be most effective in close, personal, and intimate situations where the communicating parties know each other well. It is most limited and ineffective in interpersonal situations where strangers are trying to communicate. These considerations lead to a third generalization, which we can call the *role-taking principle:*

> In communication situations where the sender can engage in sensitive role-taking, accuracy is increased. That is, meanings intended by the sender more closely match those constructed by the receiver.

In summary, these three principles tell us that: (1) Face-to-face communication is accurate to the extent that adequate feedback cues are provided by the receiver. (2) Accuracy depends on the extent to which the communicator uses role-taking

figure1.2 **Significant Transitions in Human Communication**

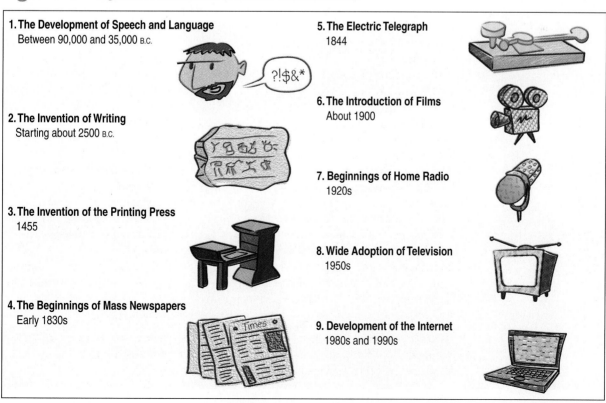

1. **The Development of Speech and Language**
   Between 90,000 and 35,000 B.C.

2. **The Invention of Writing**
   Starting about 2500 B.C.

3. **The Invention of the Printing Press**
   1455

4. **The Beginnings of Mass Newspapers**
   Early 1830s

5. **The Electric Telegraph**
   1844

6. **The Introduction of Films**
   About 1900

7. **Beginnings of Home Radio**
   1920s

8. **Wide Adoption of Television**
   1950s

9. **Development of the Internet**
   1980s and 1990s

appropriately to formulate the message in terms that are likely to be well understood by the receiver. These principles governing the relationship between feedback, role-taking, and accuracy in the case of interpersonal communication need to be kept in mind as we turn to and analyze the nature of mass communication. As will be discussed, it is with respect to these issues that the two kinds of communication differ considerably.

THE MASS COMMUNICATION PROCESS

In mass communication, the first three stages of the linear model are much more complex than in face-to-face interpersonal communication. Professional communicators formulate, encode, and transmit messages of many kinds for a multitude of purposes to a great variety of receivers.

Communicating with media is not something new. Human beings have used various technologies to preserve messages in time or to send them over distances for thousands of years. In spite of their speed and audience size, today's mass media perform the same functions as their more primitive predecessors. Like the stone walls on which hieroglyphics were carved, the smoke signals of Native Americans, or the jungle drums of earlier times, modern media move *information* across either time or space. Information consists of *a patterned physical signal corresponding to a message.* Such information should not be confused with the meaning of the message. One example of information is the patterned sound waves we can hear when people speak to us. Both the speaker and the receiver must construct their own meanings of those physical signals, using memories of their shared language. In more complex and contemporary media, information is transmitted as particular patterns of electronic radiations, as in radio, or as in the light waves we use to read, watch television, or view a movie. Only human beings can transform meanings in their heads into such signals, or as receivers, decode them back into a similar internal experience.

Using media that can reach huge audiences more or less simultaneously adds additional complexities. To help in discussing and clarifying the nature of the mass communication process making use of such media, it will be helpful to develop a formal definition of mass communication. At first glance, this may seem unnecessary. After all, we are already familiar with such media as movies, newspapers, and television sets. But when we use film, print, or broadcasting to communicate with large audiences, what is actually happening? Do all the media operate according to the same underlying principles of communication or is each medium unique in some way? And in what ways are the principles underlying mass communication different from those for a face-to-face conversation between two people? These questions are critical to understanding the nature of mass communication.

The TV news director is representative of the many professional communicators who generate and encode messages that lead to content transmitted by the media. The "encoding" process involves selecting from among many choices, a process that can affect what people perceive and how they are influenced.

We cannot define mass communication in a quick and simple way in just a sentence or two because each medium includes its own special kinds of communicators, technologies, groups, content, audiences, and effects. To develop a good definition of mass communication we must take all these aspects into account and proceed one step at a time, describing each of the major features before pulling them together. In the sections that follow, that is exactly our strategy. We shall look at each "stage" in the mass communication process before combining all the stages into an overall basic definition. The first step is to explain how and why mass communication is a *linear process*.

DEVELOPING A CONCISE DEFINITION

Mass communication can be conceptualized within an expanded version of the same linear model that helps (at least in part) to explain face-to-face communication—a formulation that has its roots in Shannon and Weaver's information theory. While each progressive stage is far more complex, as can be seen, the basic stages are similar in many ways:

1. Mass communication begins with senders who are "professional communicators." They *decide on the nature and goals of a message* to be presented to an audience via their particular medium. (That message may be a news report, an advertising campaign, a movie, or some other media presentation.)
2. The *intended meanings are encoded* by production specialists (a news team, a film company, a magazine staff, etc.). The encoding process includes not only the selection of verbal and nonverbal symbols, but the special effects that are possible with a particular medium (sound, graphics, color, etc.).
3. The *message is transmitted* as information through the use of specialized media technologies characteristic of print, film, or broadcasting to disseminate it as widely as possible.
4. *Large and diverse* (mass) *audiences* of individual receivers attend to the media and *perceive* the incoming information, decoding it into a message of conventionalized verbal and nonverbal symbols.
5. *Individual receivers* selectively construct interpretations of the message in such a way that they experience subjective *meanings* that are to at least some degree parallel to those intended by the professional communicators.

6. As a result of experiencing these meanings, *receivers are influenced in some way* in their feelings, thoughts, or actions. That is, the communication has some effect.

These six stages provide not only a basic identification of what takes place in the process of mass communication but also a convenient framework for defining it carefully. Using these stages, we can formulate a definition of mass communication that enables us to separate it clearly from other forms.

Each of the six stages we have described must be part of a succinct definition of mass communication. With these stages in mind, we can define the process in the following terms:

> Mass communication is a process in which professional communicators design and use media to disseminate messages widely, rapidly, and continuously in order to arouse intended meanings in large, diverse, and selectively attending audiences in attempts to influence them in a variety of ways.

With this definition in mind, we must ask which media really are (or are not) mass media. This is not an idle question because it sets *boundaries* on what needs to be studied under the general heading "mass communication."

WHICH MEDIA ARE MASS MEDIA?

Is the telephone a mass medium? How about a fax machine or personal computers linked in a network? What about a large museum? Should we include rock concerts, theatrical performances, church services, or even parades in our study of mass communication? After all, each of these human activities is a form of communication. For our purposes, whether or not they are mass media depends on whether they can carry out the process of mass communication we have just defined.

To be true to our definition, we would have to conclude that talking on the telephone is *not* really mass communication because the audience is not large and diverse; usually there is only one person at each end of the line. Furthermore, telephone users usually are not "professional communicators." The same is true of the use of a fax machine with phone lines, or even two personal computers used to exchange messages between individuals. (The Internet and the World Wide Web do qualify as mass media for some usages.) A museum does not participate in mass communication because it does not provide "rapid dissemination" with "media." Neither does a rock concert qualify, because it does not disseminate messages "over distance"; it is a form of direct communication to audiences. Similarly, no situation in which live performers and an audience can see each other directly—in a theater or church, at a sports event, or parade—is an example of mediated communication. Large-scale advertising by direct mail might qualify, except that it is not really "continuous." Thus, our definition turns out to be relatively rigorous. It enables us to set definite boundaries on what can be included and studied as a medium of mass communication. By definition, none of the activities listed above is such a medium, although all of them can arouse specific meanings and influence people.

Similarly, although people often speak of "the news media," this expression is misleading. News is a special form of content produced by media organizations that present their products to the public through the use of the same mass media that bring us communications about drama, music, and sports (as we will see in Chapter 4). Thus, we will treat the gathering and distribution of news not as a distinct mass medium in itself but as an important *process* dependent on the print, broadcast and online media.

Compositors in printing shops traditionally locked up mechanical elements made of lead, a process dating to Johannes Gutenberg, but used less today as printing processes have advanced.

By exercising the criteria set forth in our definition, then, we can identify precisely what we consider to be mass media in the present text. The major mass media are print (including books, magazines, and newspapers), film (principally commercial motion pictures), and broadcasting (mainly radio and television but also several associated forms such as cable television and videocassettes). Today, the Internet (and particularly its World Wide Web) functions in some ways as a mass medium that fits the above definition. Although other kinds of media are worthy of study, the focus of our attention will be on those that closely fit our definition of mass communication.

COMPARING FACE-TO-FACE AND MASS COMMUNICATION

Having examined the nature of both face-to-face and mass communication, we can now ask how these two processes differ from each other. Our starting point is that mass communication (1) depends on mechanical or electronic media and (2) addresses a large, diverse audience. We can ask, then, do these two characteristics alter the communication process in some fundamental way? Or is mass communication just like any other form of human communication? More simply: What difference does the use of media make?

THE CONSEQUENCES OF USING ANY MEDIUM

While human communication, whether with a medium or not, depends on verbal and nonverbal symbols and all the stages discussed in our basic linear model, introducing a medium into communication between two people clearly alters the process. One major consequence is the *loss of direct and immediate feedback*. A second is *severe limitation on effective role-taking* because of that loss.

Lack of immediate feedback. As was suggested earlier, when we communicate with another person and have a medium intervening between, we cannot perceive the rich nonverbal cues that are available when we converse face-to-face. Even when using the phone in direct interpersonal communication we cannot detect visual, nonverbal messages such as a puzzled look, raised eyebrows, a smile—or even subtle tones of voice or small changes of pitch and emphasis that may not come through the system. Exchanges of messages by fax machine or by personal computer using e-mail are even more limited. Neither the fax paper nor the computer monitor shows visual, nonverbal signs or signals, and they both are unable to convey nuances of pronunciation and timing. All these cues help us know how our message is being received in face-to-face interpersonal communication—or indeed, whether it is being received at all.

Inability to engage in effective role-taking. Limitations on simultaneous feedback in virtually all mediated communication reduce our ability to understand how well our message is being understood by the person or persons toward whom it is directed. Because of these limitations, accuracy when using a medium is less attainable than in the direct, face-to-face, interpersonal mode. This, in turn, reduces communication effectiveness—a point that most people understand very well. Each of us has at some time told a friend, "Let's not try to settle this over the telephone. Let's get together and talk it over."

Still, talking on the telephone, typing messages to each other with computers, or sending fax documents is clearly human communication, because each depends on learned patterns of meaning, labeling with language symbols, transmission of information over distance, perception by the receiver, and the construction of reasonably similar meanings by the sender and the receiver. In short, while communication through virtually any medium follows the same stages as face-to-face communication, using a medium definitely does alter the process.

Loss of accuracy. As the foregoing indicates, the big difference between face-to-face and any form of mediated communication is a loss of accuracy due to limitations on feedback and role-taking. Stated more formally:

1. The use of a medium *reduces the richness of feedback and limits the process of role-taking.*
2. Both of these limitations *increase the possibility of inaccuracy between meanings of senders and receivers.*
3. When meanings between sender and receiver are dissimilar, *accuracy is reduced and mutual understanding is limited.*
4. A decrease in the accuracy of communication *reduces the probability that the message will influence receivers.*

These limitations certainly apply to mass communication. Indeed, they are even more important when communication takes place via a medium such as a newspaper, a movie, or television. In mass communication, a large, diverse audience is at the receiving end. There is no realistic way for the communicator to engage in any role-taking during the process of transmitting a message, or for the audience to provide immediate and ongoing feedback while transmission is taking place.

These limitations are well understood by professional communicators. Dan Rather or Tom Brokaw can never place themselves mentally in your personal shoes as you view the evening news, thus, they are unable to understand and predict accurately how you personally will receive and interpret the broadcast. By extension, there is no way that such newscasters can modify their ongoing presentation on the basis of your feedback in order to make you understand more fully. The same situation applies to any professional communicator, whether the medium is a newspaper, a movie, a radio broadcast, and so on.

At the same time, professional communicators have some knowledge of the audience in a collective sense. To provide a kind of *a priori* form of feedback, large communication corporations (for example, the major television networks) conduct extensive research on audience characteristics and behavior. The results of such research provide guidelines concerning the likely tastes and interests of at least the majority of their audience at a particular time. The researchers study many categories of people to give an overall picture.

The information obtained from such research is the basis for certain necessary assumptions about audiences, and it has to replace individual-by-individual role-taking. However, that approach has serious limitations because assumptions can be inaccurate. The failure of hundreds of magazines, newspapers, films, and television programs over the years, despite extensive "market research," testifies to how imperfect such role-taking assumptions can be.

Feedback is similarly limited. Indeed, for all intents and purposes it does not exist. Audience members cannot interrupt what they see as a confusing or infuriating television reporter, or gain immediate access to a newspaper editorial writer. Even though mass media often invite letters or phone calls, this kind of reverse flow provides only a delayed trickle of feedback information from the few people who are motivated enough to go to the trouble.

Thus, by comparison with face-to-face communication, mass communication is essentially a *rigidly linear process.* Communicators try to guess how their messages will be received, with only indirect, delayed feedback in the form of advertising revenues, research findings, a few telephone calls, occasional letters, movie reviews, and box-office receipts. This delayed feedback may help them shape future communications, but it provides no basis for altering a message while it is being disseminated. As a consequence, accuracy to and influence on any particular member of the audience are significantly limited compared to what can be accomplished in face-to-face communication.

THE CONSEQUENCES OF LARGE AND DIVERSE AUDIENCES

Mass communication differs from face-to-face communication and from mediated interpersonal communication not only because it involves more complex media but also because the audience is *large* and *diverse.* Still, whether there is one receiver or there are a million receivers, the basic activities of sender and receiver are the same. Even if the sender is a professional and the audience is immense, the act of communication still depends on messages composed of verbal and nonverbal symbols linked to meanings by cultural conventions of grammar and syntax and all the rest. Thus, we can conclude that mass communication is not a process that depends on some exotic or unique principles of communication. It is a special form of mediated communication that is limited in accuracy and influence because simultaneous role-taking and feedback are difficult or impossible.

However, the existence of a large and diverse audience can pose still other significant limitations on the content, accuracy, and influences of the messages transmitted by a mass medium. Inevitably, much mass media content—perhaps most of it—is designed for the tastes and presumed intellectual level of "the average citizen" or, often, for the average member of a specialized category of people who are assumed to share some common taste or interest (for instance, all fishing enthusiasts, football fans, or fashion-conscious men). In forming appropriate message content, assumptions must be made about such audiences. In fact, most professional communicators tend to assume that the majority in their audiences:

1. has a *limited attention span,*
2. prefers to be *entertained rather than enlightened,* and
3. quickly *loses interest in any subject that makes intellectual demands.*

With no intention of being either critical or elitist, it seems clear that in large part these assumptions are correct. Well-educated people with sophisticated tastes and high intellectual capacity are a relatively minor part of the population. Just over 30 percent have graduated from college. Even among that category, not all are either affluent or urbane. Those who are will probably not attend to the majority of content presented by the American mass media. However, this is not really a problem in a profit-oriented media system. This is because those cultivated citizens who are in short supply constitute a very small segment of *purchasing consumers.* Therefore, in attempting to maximize profits, professional communicators who prepare media content can safely ignore them. It is much more profitable to reach the much larger numbers of *intellectually undemanding receivers whose aggregate purchasing power is immense.* In other words, as we will show in later chapters, reaching large numbers of exactly the right kind of people is critically important in the advertising-driven and profit-oriented American system of mass communication. Thus, all of the factors discussed above work together in a kind of system that *encourages media content that is high in entertainment value and low in intellectual demand.*

It is important to understand the conditions and principles that fit together to produce the above consequence, because they explain a great deal about why our

Big Bird and his puppet cohorts on TV's "Sesame Street" demonstrate the importance of easily understood characters and concepts important in communicating with large audiences, especially audiences of children.

media function as they do. Furthermore, we can then more readily understand why the media inevitably attract the attention of deeply concerned critics who have generated a long list of charges and complaints supporting the idea that the media are both trivial and harmful in some way.[10]

The fact is that there is indeed much to criticize regarding what the system delivers. From the outset of mass communication, the content of American media has prompted thoughtful people to object to its generally shallow nature. We do not wish to imply that all media content is superficial, or that it caters only to the interests of limited-capacity audiences. There certainly are books, newspaper analyses, magazines, radio programs, and television shows for the educated and sophisticated as well as for those of less-developed capacities and tastes. Undeniably, however, most media content is of limited aesthetic or intellectual merit. Early in the twentieth century, critics focused on "yellow journalism" and the emphasis on crime in newspapers. Today's low-brow content includes such forms as quiz shows, paperback thrillers, violent portrayals, personal-interest "news," soap operas, game shows, explicit sexual depictions, dirty language, popular music, unsophisticated sit-coms, ball games, wrestling, and telemarketing.

The critics want different content. They urge the media to inform, enlighten, and uplift—to provide information in depth as a basis for intelligent political decision-making, arts appreciation,

Palm Pilots and MP3 players are among the latest in receiving devices for communication messages. Whether used for personal messaging or for receiving content from media organizations, both are technological innovations processing information, as telephones and radio receivers had done before them.

and improvement in moral standards. These are commendable goals, which no thoughtful person can seriously dispute. At the same time, the environment in which the media operate makes it very unlikely that these goals will ever be fully achieved—not because greedy people will always control the media, but because our society has defined mass communication as part of the *private enterprise system.* However, when pressed, few critics of the American media would exchange our system for one such as those found in China, North Korea, or Cuba, where content remains tightly controlled by authoritarian governments.

The remaining chapters of the present text address in some detail the many ways that American society has shaped its media. The factors to be considered are the development of technology, the influence of a growing population with a multicultural composition, a democratic political system, and a profit-oriented economic system in which private ownership is valued. The chapters devoted to specific media focus on the unique features of each. They discuss how each operates to disseminate its particular kind of information. Included for each medium is information describing its pattern of adoption by the American population. Finally, a unique feature of this book is the seventeen theory summaries that help explain various aspects of the processes and effects of mass communication.[11]

Chapter Review

- Human communication differs sharply from the processes used by other species. It depends on systems of learned and shared verbal and nonverbal symbols, their meanings, and conventionalized rules for their use.

- The basic act of human communication can be analyzed in terms of a linear model that includes six major steps: deciding on a message, encoding the message by linking symbols and meanings, transmitting information to span distance, perceiving the incoming information patterns, perceiving the message and constructing its meanings. As a result, receivers experience some effect.

- In face-to-face communication, feedback and role-taking are important principles related to accuracy.

- Mass communication is also a linear process in which professional communicators encode and transmit various kinds of messages to present to different segments of the public for a variety of purposes. Through the use of mass media, those messages are disseminated to large and diverse audiences who attend to the messages in selective ways.

- Members of the audience interpret the message selectively, and the meanings they construct may or may not be parallel to those intended by the communicator.

- Mass communication and face-to-face communication differ in important ways. Because of feedback and role-taking, interpersonal transactions can be flexible and influential. Mass communication lacks these features and is largely a one-way, relatively inflexible process.

- In an advertising-driven and profit-oriented system, media content must be tailored to the majority, whose collective purchasing power is huge, but whose intellectual level and tastes are not sophisticated. This tailoring of content results in many criticisms.

- The study of mass communication must include attention to three broad sets of issues: (1) The many ways in which a society's history, values, and economic and political realities have influenced its media; (2) The unique features of each medium in the system that make it different from the other media; and (3) The kinds of influences that media have on us as individuals and on our society and culture.

Notes and References

1. Everett M. Rogers and F. Floyd Shoemaker, *Communication of Innovations: A Cross-Cultural Approach* (New York: The Free Press, 1971).
2. For an extended discussion of the basic nature of human face-to-face communication, see "Verbal Communication," Chapter 2 in Melvin L. DeFleur, Patricia Kearney, and Timothy G. Plax, *Fundamentals of Human Communication* (Mountain View, Calif.: Mayfield Publishing Company, 1993), pp. 33–62.
3. Phillip Lieberman, "The Evolution of Human Speech: The Fossil Record," Chapter 12 in *The Biology and Evolution of Language* (Cambridge, Mass.: Harvard University Press, 1984), pp. 287–329.
4. The full range of the incredibly flexible human voice comes through especially in opera. Anyone listening to the pronunciation required by Gilbert and Sullivan's *Mikado* or the range of sounds produced by Luciano Pavarotti singing the major role in *I Pagliacci* can appreciate how different our voice box, larynx, tongue, and lip structures are from those of the greater apes, who can make only a limited range of sounds.
5. For a more detailed explanation of these and other changes in human communication, see Melvin L. DeFleur and Sandra Ball Rokeach, "A Theory of Transitions," Chapter 1 in *Theories of Mass Communication,* 5th ed. (White Plains, N.Y.: Longman, 1989), pp. 7–26.
6. Claude E. Shannon and Warren Weaver, *The Mathematical Theory of Communication* (Urbana, Ill.: University of Illinois Press, 1949).
7. Shannon and Weaver, *The Mathematical Theory.*

8. DeFleur, Kearney, and Plax, *Fundamentals of Human Communication,* pp. 33–62.

9. For a discussion of a simultaneous transactional model of human communication, see DeFleur, Kearney, and Plax, *Fundamentals of Human Communication,* pp. 21–25.

10. Marshall McLuhan and Eric McLuhan, *Law of the Media* (Toronto: University of Toronto Press, 1989).

11. These seventeen summaries of mass communication theories, set forth in propositional form, were prepared by Margaret H. DeFleur. While drawn from many cases from social science and communication literature, the systematic propositional form of each is set forth in her forthcoming book, *Fundamentals of Mass Communication Theory: Explaining Media Processes and Effects* (anticipated publication date 2002). As set forth in this book, they are her intellectual property and cannot be reproduced in any form without her written consent. They are used in this book with her permission.

Part One

PUBLISHING

Chapter 2

BOOKS: THE FIRST AND MOST RESPECTED MASS MEDIUM

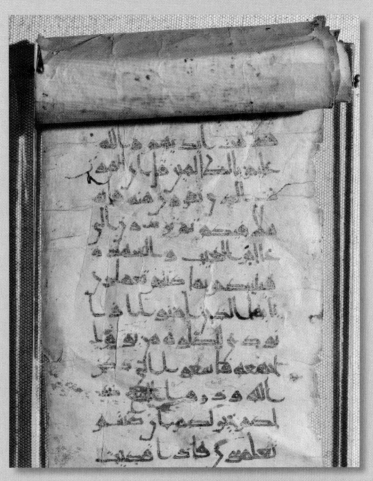

Hand-lettered and printed scrolls, among the earliest forms of books, originally brought religious texts such as this fragment from the Koran to expanding audiences.

BOOKS CAME FIRST AMONG OUR CURRENT MEDIA, AND THEY REMAIN OUR CHOICE FOR SERIOUS TOPICS AS WELL AS FOR THOUGHTFUL entertainment. Before books could be printed, however, early people had to develop the art of writing, which took thousands of years. With writing systems and portable media on which to record graphic symbols both available, a first transition in the development of books took place. Lengthy scrolls could be produced for storing extensive information. These were the earliest books. Later, a second transition took place when the Romans gave us the book form as we know it—with bound pages and hard covers. A third transition occurred in the mid-1400s when Johannes Gutenberg invented moveable type and perfected a printing press that could make large numbers of identical copies. These great transitions took place over more than five thousand years. Today, a fourth transition appears to be developing as books are being downloaded from the Internet and other electronic sources to be read on special machines developed specifically for that purpose. But whatever its physical form, the book is our oldest and most respected medium, without which civilization as we know it could not have developed.

Americans love books in their traditional form, and they are currently buying them in numbers never thought possible in earlier years. Since the middle of the recently concluded twentieth century, the number of titles being published in the United States has soared by more than 500 percent (see Figure 2.1, page 44). In 1999 alone, 70,000 titles of all kinds were sold to people of all ages and backgrounds.

Today, a number of technological futurists claim that the days of the traditional book are numbered, and that within a few years the computer screen will completely replace the printed paper page. They maintain that books will be obtained online to be read on a screen. As one such analyst puts it:

> As a common item of communication . . . the physical object consisting of bound dead trees in a shiny wrapper is headed for the antique heap. Its replacement will be a lightning-quick injection of digital bits into a handheld device with an ultrasharp display. Culture vultures and bookworms might cringe at the prospect, but it's as inevitable as page two's following page one. Books are goners, at least as far as being the dominant form of reading.[1]

Others are skeptical about such forecasts. Certainly, they feel, such changes may come, but they will not take place soon. It is difficult, they say, to curl up in bed with one's computer and read what is on the screen—having to restart the program after every interruption. Book enthusiasts also maintain that computer screens, at least in their present form, are inappropriate when one is sitting under a tree, on the patio, riding a bus or train to work, relaxing in a chair before the fireplace, or getting a tan at the beach. For a very long time, books printed on paper have been regularly read in such circumstances, and they indicate one of the great advantages that the traditional book has always enjoyed compared to more complex electronic media.

However, the technological advances of the last half of the twentieth century and their prospects for the future may ultimately challenge how we obtain and read lengthy documents. It does seem likely that advances in technology also will be witnessed in the use of books, just as has been the case in virtually every other form of communication. A more serious question is *whether* or *how soon* books in their traditional form will disappear.

The answer to that question depends on the time perspective one takes. As this chapter will explain, books have changed greatly at least three times over the centuries since they first appeared in the form of handwritten scrolls of papyrus or parchment. Because books are so commonly used in their present form, any radical transformation within a short time seems unlikely. But half a century or more from now, who knows? Certainly remarkable changes are already taking place in book retailing, and a fourth great transition—from traditional book to electronic form—appears to be beginning.

At present, books printed on paper have singular advantages over existing forms of computerized reading devices: Books are simple, portable, relatively inexpensive, and permanent. They require no batteries or power supply, no complex software, no period of waiting until a machine warms up, and no special skills to open them or leaf through their pages. A book can be picked up or put down in an instant, or it can reside on a shelf unchanged for decades. As technology advances, the advantages of the traditional book form may compare less favorably, but that remains to be seen.

What is clear is that for hundreds of years books in their traditional form have been the most important means by which we preserve our culture, transmit it to the next generation, and communicate important new ideas to millions of readers. For those reasons, and whatever their future, books need to be understood in terms of where they came from, the form in which they exist today, and what they may be like in the decades ahead.

THE EVOLUTION OF WRITTEN DOCUMENTS

But where did books come from? Most people realize that they have been around for a long time, and that their development took place over an extended period. They also know that hand-lettered books *(manu scripti)* were available long before the printing press became a reality. Perhaps less well-understood is that extended booklike documents in the form of scrolls were produced before that. However, neither scrolls nor hand-copied books were a mass medium, easily acquired and read by many people. That transition would not take place until relatively modern times. How, then, did this medium become a part of our common culture? The sections that follow summarize the highlights in the development of the book throughout history into the form that we recognize today and the ways it may develop in the future. It is an incredible story that reveals how much we owe to a number of creative geniuses of earlier centuries.

These ancient cave drawings, our links to early civilizations, were found in Mali, West Africa.

FROM CAVE PAINTINGS TO ALPHABETS

The first step in understanding books and our other contemporary print media is to examine the origins of writing. The graphic representation of ideas, unlike speaking, requires a *medium.* Thus, the development of writing and the evolution of media are part of the same process. A medium can be defined very simply. It is *a device by which a sender can move physical information (graphic symbols; sound, light, radio waves, etc.) through time or space in such a way that one or more others can receive the information and decipher the sender's intended meanings.* A medium can be any object or arrangement of objects used to accomplish those goals so as to enable human beings to record, transmit, receive, and interpret messages.

Representing ideas with graphic symbols. Media used in writing depend on some *physical representation* of thoughts and ideas, either by using pictures or other kinds of graphic symbols placed on a surface. A "symbol" is simply a carved, written, or printed mark, picture, character, or letter associated with a culturally agreed-upon meaning. Even physical objects can be used as symbols (e.g, a cross, a flag, a wedding ring, etc.).

The earliest known attempts to represent ideas with pictures—the first step toward the development of writing—were cave paintings. Fifteen to twenty thousand years ago, unknown artists painted hundreds of dramatic murals on the walls of caves in what is now southern Europe. Well-known examples are found in Lascaux, France, and Altamira, Spain. These paintings show bison, reindeer, wild horses—even extinct animals—and the men who hunted them. The artists' tools were bones, sticks, and primitive brushes used to color their images. The pigments were made of animal fat mixed with charcoal and powdered earth of several bright colors.[2]

As artistic products, the prehistoric paintings are large, vivid, dramatic, and surprisingly contemporary in appearance. Certainly, they show a grasp of the complex principles of pictorial representation equaling that of modern artists. Picasso himself, after seeing the great cave at Altamira, is said to have remarked that artists today have learned nothing (about color and composition) beyond what those prehistoric painters knew. However, for all their artistic merits, such paintings are extremely limited as a way of communicating ideas. Their meaning to the people who made them, and the reasons for which they were done, remain unknown.

Nevertheless, representing something *graphically* was a significant step beyond oral description of the objects and events being portrayed. Even if they were only mnemonic devices—serving loosely as memory stimulators—depictions such as cave paintings could help a storyteller provide a more detailed and accurate account, compared with unaided recall. In fact, this illustrates one major purpose of writing. In all its forms, writing is a tool for preserving ideas that were expressed earlier. In other words (to borrow from today's computer jargon), writing is a system for *information storage.* Just as we seek more and more storage capacity in computers, primitive people sought systems of graphic representation of ideas to free themselves from the limitations and inaccuracies of human memory.

Writing must also serve another purpose. Ideally, it permits people who did not record the ideas originally to recover accurately the meanings and implications of those who did. In this sense (to borrow again from contemporary computer usage), writing is a means of *information exchange.* Thus, the development of picture drawing was not enough. Only the original artist could recall accurately the intended meanings represented. The next step was to *standardize* both the depictions and the rules for interpreting their meaning. That advance took more than ten thousand years!

Even before writing was developed, people of the time were using many complex nonverbal communication systems—just as we do today. They communicated with hairstyles, clothing, tattoos, scars, jewelry, crowns, and other objects and ornaments. They used these to signify rank, status, power, marital condition, achievement, occupation, family membership, and dozens of additional meanings that were vital to life in their societies. However, it was not until about 4000 B.C.—six thousand years ago—that people began to leave records in the form of codified writing that can be understood today. They left graphic representations on many surfaces—stone, baked clay, baskets, sticks, cloth, animal skins, bark, and even leaves. On these media they rendered a rich variety of signs, symbols, drawings, and decorative motifs to convey socially important ideas.

Standardizing meanings with cultural conventions. At some unknown point between 5000 and 4000 B.C., people in several areas of the Near East began to use drawings to represent ideas in a somewhat more uniform way.[3] Most were agricultural people, and their early attempts at writing grew out of their need to keep accurate accounts so as to record land ownership, boundaries, crop sales, and the like. Some were traders who needed reliable records of cargoes, profits, and commercial transactions.

Generally, these peoples' symbols were pictures of what they knew—birds, the sun, a bundle of grain, a boat, the head of a bull, or parts of the human body. Writing in a technical sense began to emerge when such graphic depictions came to represent *standardized meanings that were agreed upon by cultural conventions*— rules for interpretation established among a given people. Thus, for those who understood the rules, a simplified drawing of a human form could mean "a man"; a crudely drawn rising sun might be "one day"; a stylized human foot, "walking"; and a wavy line, "water."

The use of such standardized graphic representations was a true form of writing. Each symbol was understood by both senders and receivers in the same way— because of the rule that assigned one and only one agreed-upon meaning to it. When strung together such symbols could tell a story. For example, the stylized drawings discussed above, when arranged in a sequence, might mean "A man walked for a day along a river."

Such a system is called *ideographic* or "thought writing", because it associates specific whole thoughts or meanings with pictures in a standardized way. It is also sometimes called *pictographic* writing. This style of writing links carefully drawn, often highly stylized (abstract) representations of objects to ideas, rather than to specific sounds. Well-known ideographic systems of writing were those developed independently by the early Egyptians, the Chinese, and the Maya of the New World.

Actually, ideographic writing works quite well—given enough ideographs. A separate picture is needed for each idea or thought that is to be recorded. One limitation is that as a society and its culture become increasingly complex, more new ideas or concepts need to have their own pictures, symbols, or characters. Eventually, in a sophisticated society, thousands may be needed. This increases the complexity of writing by requiring a larger and larger number of standardized ideographs.

In fact, in a truly complex society, the number of characters required in a system of ideographic writing can eventually become staggering. To illustrate this, the *hieroglyphic* (sacred carving) system used during the early Egyptian dynasties required only about seven hundred different ideographs. Learning those was difficult enough. In a simple Chinese farming village today, only about fifteen hundred are needed. But in contrast, highly educated Chinese literary scholars today may need to know up to fifty thousand different characters!

Thus, "thought language," or ideographic systems can be very difficult to learn and use. Historically, where such systems have been used, the majority of the population remained illiterate. The ability to read and write was regarded with awe. Even powerful rulers were often illiterate, and like others, they had to rely on professional scribes. Because of their importance and skill, scribes often enjoyed high status and impressive financial rewards.

Representing sound in written form. A much simpler system of writing is to link graphic symbols not to ideas or thoughts, but to *sounds*. Here, instead of ideographs, simpler *phonograms* are all that are needed. A phonogram is a graphic symbol linked to a specified sound by a cultural convention or rule that prevails among those who speak a particular language. An example is the letter "b," which English speakers pronounce with a pursing of the lips, a throat-generated sound, and expelling of air. The common *alphabet* that we use every day has twenty-six variations of orally produced sounds that we easily combine to pronounce the sounds of thousands of words. Our contemporary alphabet comes to us from ancient sources. Even its name reveals its origins—*alpha* and *beta* are the first two letters of the ancient Greek version.

The development of alphabets, like books and printing, ranks as one of the great human achievements. Alphabets made reading and writing—often a hideously complex activity with ideographic systems—literally "child's play." All of us, when we first tackled our ABCs as children, learned the consonant and vowel sounds uniquely linked to each of the twenty-six letters. Along with our numbers and numerals, plus a scattering of additional symbols representing punctuation, contractions, and so on, we can transform into spoken pronunciation virtually any set of written words that need to be orally expressed in our language (or vice versa).

It took over two thousand years after the earliest attempts at writing to develop the incredibly efficient alphabet that you are now using to read these passages. We inherited our current alphabet from the Romans. They had refined the one that they obtained from the Etruscans, who had copied most of theirs from the Greeks. But the Greeks did not invent the underlying idea (linking sounds to individual letters). They refined their alphabet from origins leading back through time to the Phoenicians, the Assyrians, the Babylonians, and finally the Sumerians (who probably did invent the process).

Apparently, our phonetic system of writing originated when the Sumerians began to use *cuneiform* writing as a means to make records.[4] The Sumerians were an agricultural people who lived from about 3000 to around 1700 B.C. in the so-called Fertile Crescent—a region that now includes parts of Iraq, between the Tigris and Euphrates rivers, and portions of present-day Israel, Jordan, Syria, Turkey, and Iran. This was the part of the ancient world where the earliest known literate civilizations developed.

The Sumerians found that a pad of wet clay held in a small flat box made an excellent medium, at least compared to stone. They made little drawings on the surface with a sharpened stick to represent ideas in pictographic form. It took a lot of time and skill to make realistic drawings, so they soon simplified the pictures into more stylized forms. Before long, their drawings evolved into abstract ideographs that were unrecognizable as representations of actual objects. To be efficient, their writers sharpened their sticks to a wedgelike *(cuneiform)* shape at the end. They could very quickly imprint their characters on the clay pad using this instrument.

What the Sumerians eventually hit upon was the idea of letting a particular graphic symbol *stand for a sound*. In their system, sounds were usually what we would call whole syllables, rather than the much simpler sound elements that we use in our alphabet. However, even though it was complex by comparison with today's alphabets, the Sumerian cuneiform system, using phonograms to represent *sounds*, and combinations of characters to represent ideas, was a major breakthrough. It was an innovation that other societies would soon improve upon and simplify.[5]

Beginning about 500 B.C., the Greeks developed a remarkably efficient alphabet (including vowels) out of many versions that had been developed earlier. Standardizing their alphabet greatly enriched Greek culture. For example, in 403 B.C., Athens passed a law making one version (the Ionian alphabet) *compulsory* in official documents. This simplified alphabet promoted increased literacy, formal education, and learning. Because they had a written language that could easily be read during their time, and even today, much of Greek culture was passed on to become an important base of contemporary Western civilization.

FROM STONE AND CLAY TO PORTABLE MEDIA

Phonetic writing using a standardized alphabet was not the only innovation that enabled the Greeks to develop a rich culture. Another factor was that portable media were in wide use by their time. While the clay tablets of the Sumerians could be carried around, they were still heavy and bulky. As early as 3000 B.C., the Egyptians had

Egyptians produced a beautiful form of ideographic writing between 5000 and 4000 B.C. Their hieroglyphs were ideograms, with each symbol representing a separate idea. Later, they introduced photograms in their system for consonants, but did not provide for vowel sounds, which makes it impossible for us to pronounce their ancient language today.

developed a much more portable medium—*papyrus* (from which, incidentally, we get our modern word "paper"). Actually, papyrus is a tall reed common to marshy areas of the Nile. Its stalks, up to two inches thick, were sliced thin and laid out in two layers at right angles to each other. When pounded together, pressed, and dried, papyrus yielded a paperlike surface suitable for writing on with a brush or a reed pen. The sheets were sometimes joined together at the ends and rolled up on a stick to produce *scrolls*—extended documents that were in fact an early type of book. Thus, a first great transition in the form of books was from stone and clay to more portable media.

Papyrus was a great technological solution. However, because it was controlled by the Egyptians (and later the Romans), it was often difficult to obtain and was in perpetually short supply. As the use of writing spread, alternatives had to be devised. One important writing surface that was used until relatively modern times was *parchment,* which is the tanned skin of a sheep or goat. Another was *vellum,* which resembled parchment but was prepared from the skin of a young calf. These media were very expensive. A single animal skin produced only a few pages. However, such skin surfaces were very durable, which helped some ancient scrolls survive into later centuries.

EARLY TRANSITIONS IN THE EVOLUTION OF BOOKS

Throughout the time that writing, alphabets, and portable media were being developed, societies themselves were undergoing great changes. Their cultures were becoming increasingly complex and sophisticated. The term *culture* refers to a society's entire way of life—its shared beliefs, its rules for acceptable behavior, its language, technology, and all other ways in which its problems of living are handled. Centuries before the time of Christ, great urban centers had been established; techniques of agriculture had been refined; technologies of war and conquest were well developed; and the pace of trade and contact between unlike peoples had quickened. Above all, great empires rose as a result of military conquest. An example was the huge Roman Empire, which brought together virtually the entire known Western world under a single government administration. Communicating to administer this vast political system was a constant challenge. This was one reason lengthy and portable documents were developed.

BOOKS AS SCROLLS: THE FIRST TRANSITION

There were other changes in human society and culture that led to the need for long documents for recording lengthy and complex ideas. Hundreds of years before biblical times, thinkers were debating complex and perplexing questions: What is the true nature of reality and how do people know it? What supernatural forces exist, and what part do they play in people's lives? What is a just social order? What are those bright bodies in the sky, and why do they move in such regular patterns? How do animals differ from human beings? What happens to us after death?

Increasingly, then, human curiosity and intelligence led to the search for answers and knowledge about the physical, social, and religious world. As answers accumulated, a need arose to record lengthy discussions and teachings as well as short messages—such as edicts, land claims, and administrative commands. For example, one of the great problems for all who governed was how to stabilize the social order and make it work more justly. Ancient *codes of law* were developed to provide formal guidelines for behavior and to specify punishments for deviance. A classic example is the system of 282 laws developed by the Babylonian King Hammurabi almost four thousand years ago. His laws covered everything from the regulation of commerce and military affairs to the practice of medicine and the treatment of children. In the absence of books, he had his laws carved on huge *stellae*—blocks of basalt eight feet square—that he had set up in the center of each major city in his empire. But it was a terribly cumbersome system. Portable media were far more efficient. Books and libraries were sorely needed, and by the time of Christ, the Romans were using books to store their famous legal codes.

The rise of great religious systems also created a need to record lengthy sacred writings. The Old Testament of Judaism is an outstanding example of a long and complex set of ideas that could not have been passed on accurately in oral form over many generations. Later, Christians began to record the revelations, testimony, and injunctions of their scriptures. Islam soon followed with the teachings of the sacred Koran.

The scroll, consisting of a handwritten document on parchment or papyrus, often of considerable length, and rolled up with a stick at each end, solved the problem. Such scrolls were essentially the first books. Libraries in which these important documents could be stored were developed in Egypt, Rome, and Greece. Unfortunately, relatively few survive. Most ancient libraries were destroyed by invaders or the scrolls did not withstand the ravages of time. But the few that remain, such as the famous Dead Sea Scrolls, provide insights of immense importance into the beliefs and cultures of earlier people.

BOOKS WITH BOUND PAGES: THE SECOND TRANSITION

With alphabetical writing well developed, and with the availability of efficient portable media, such as papyrus, parchment, and vellum, it was not a difficult step for the Romans to move beyond the relatively cumbersome scroll to the more easily stored bound book with cut pages of uniform size. It was they who developed the book into the form that we know today.[6] They gave us pages with writing on both sides, bound at the edge between boards or covers.

The Romans did far more than just develop the physical form of the medium. They also produced many innovations that shaped the *formats* we use in preparing books. For example, they greatly refined the alphabet and originated much of the grammatical structure of sentences that we follow today. They brought us the idea of *paragraphs,* and they standardized systems of *punctuation,* much as we use them now. Their *majuscule* letters, used extensively on their monuments, became our capital letters, just as they are used on the present page. Their smaller *minuscule* letters (refined under the influence of Charlemagne in the eighth century as Carolingian scripts) became the lowercase letters that you see on the present page. (However, the terms *uppercase* and *lowercase* actually came from early printers, who stored majuscule and minuscule type in separate trays—upper- and lowercases—for easy access.)

Saving the art of producing manu scripti. Beginning not long after the birth of Christ, illiterate tribes (the Germanic Visigoths and Vandals) began to invade parts of Rome. Within a relatively short time, Rome was eventually completely overrun. By A.D. 476, the last Emperor was deposed and the great empire that had dominated the world for nearly a thousand years came to an inglorious end. The Roman alphabet and the art of hand-lettered book production were all but lost as the Western world entered the so-called Dark Ages—which would last for another seven centuries. However, within the Christian monasteries the precious knowledge of alphabetical writing and hand-copied books was preserved and improved. Using the Roman alphabet and letter forms (sometimes modified in various ways) and the Latin language, diligent monks hand-copied thousands upon thousands of *manu scripti*—a term we still use.[7]

Most of the books produced in the monasteries were merely working documents used for practical purposes in churches and schools. However, some were exquisite works of art, "illuminated" (decorated) with elaborate letters and drawings. Perhaps the most beautiful book ever produced is the extraordinary *Book of Kells,* created by

Producing a *manu scriptus* was a demanding and laborious process carried out by monks in monasteries in which books were copied letter by letter on parchment or vellum. From the end of the Roman civilization until the fifteenth century when printing was invented, this process preserved written records and human memory.

monks around A.D. 800 in a remote monastery in the western part of Ireland. Written and illuminated using gold, ground jewels, and other precious materials gathered from all parts of the world then known, the *Book of Kells* was prepared as an act of deep religious devotion. It survives intact today as a great national treasure of Ireland, carefully preserved at Trinity College in Dublin.

As Europe slowly emerged from the Dark Ages, interest in books and writing began to grow. It was no longer only monks who were copying books by hand. In many urban centers, commercial establishments called *scriptoria* manufactured and sold books. One factor that encouraged this type of book production was the growing proportion of the population that was literate. During the thirteenth century, universities were established in the major cities in Europe as centers of learning and the arts. Many books were produced for teaching. The wealthy student could buy books already copied by professional scribes from the official texts. The poor student had to rent textbooks, one chapter at a time, and laboriously hand-copy each page. For the most part, Latin remained the language of the learned. But more and more, as the thirteenth century progressed, some scribes wrote in the local "vulgar" (or *vernacular*) languages common to the people, such as English, French, German, and Italian.

Paper becomes available. One of the technologies that would become critically important in the development of all print media was the manufacture of *paper*. The Chinese had developed paper and used it extensively as early as the second century A.D.[8] Later, during the middle of the eighth century, Persian soldiers captured a group of Chinese papermakers, who either taught the process to their captors or revealed it under torture (depending on whose version of the story one believes). In any case, the Islamic world had paper long before Europeans. However, it was brought to Spain by the Moors in the twelfth century.

The production and use of paper caught on quickly, and within a century it was being skillfully manufactured in all parts of Europe. Some papermakers became truly skilled craftsmen, and they made beautiful silklike papers from linen rags. Some of the paper produced in the 1400s and 1500s rivals the best seen today. Most, however, was crude but *cheap* (by comparison with sheep and goat skins). Most important, it was *available*. It would be a long time, however, before parchment and vellum were entirely replaced by paper for the best-quality books.

PRINTED BOOKS: THE THIRD TRANSITION

The development of printing technology did not, as we will see, come out of nowhere. Many of the prerequisites—paper, literacy, the need for lengthy documents, and a sophisticated format for books—were already a part of Western culture. Nevertheless, the invention of a practical and efficient press marked one of those occasions when the ideas of a single person made a great difference. Furthermore, once it became available, printing with "movable" type was immediately recognized as a truly extraordinary technological advance. The influence of that advance on Western civilization rivaled the influence of computers during the last decades of the twentieth century.

Gutenberg's remarkable machine. Johannes Gutenberg was the son of a goldsmith who lived in Mainz, in what is now Germany. He studied metalworking and developed great skill in shaping various kinds of steel and brass, and in melting and casting various kinds of alloys in molds. It was these skills that would aid him in developing a practical printing system.

Printing as such was not really unknown by Gutenberg's time.[9] The Chinese had begun making inked impressions from elaborately carved wooden blocks shortly after A.D. 175, when they first developed paper. Whole books, printed in this manner by the Koreans and Japanese during the eighth century, survive today. The Koreans had even cast individual letters in metal, although very crudely, more than a century before Gutenberg perfected the process. Printing with wooden blocks, however, was extremely difficult and inefficient. To print from a block, an entire page of characters had to be carved (in reverse) on a single slab of hard wood. Ink was applied to the carved face, and a sheet of paper was pressed onto the surface. A roller or brush was passed over the paper, and an impression resulted. Sometimes the characters did not reproduce very clearly because the wood did not take razor-sharp edges. Also, the process was very laborious. Even if all went well, only a limited number of copies (perhaps a hundred or so) could be printed by this technique before the wood became too worn.

While all of these forerunners had been around for centuries, Gutenberg made a truly significant technological advance. He eventually managed to cast *individual letters in molten metal* in such a way that they would be as clear and sharp as those on this page. The individual letters (movable type) could be set up in lines, one letter at a time, as needed and they could be used over and over without wearing out quickly.

It took Gutenberg about twenty years to develop just the right process for making the letters and arranging them in a suitable press, developing the right inks, and bringing all the components together into a practical system. First, he made hard steel punches with the letters engraved in relief on the end. Then he used the punch to strike the letters individually into suitable pieces of softer brass. The brass impression was then surrounded by a clay mold. With the help of a special melted metal alloy of his own formula, he was able to cast crisp letters individually and to make many identical copies of each one. He also developed an ink made from lamp black (a soft soot) ground in a linseed oil–based varnish.[10] These techniques were so simple and practical that they remained in use for hundreds of years.

Some historians say the most significant development in modern human communication was the invention of moveable type in 1455 by Johannes Gutenberg. He worked many years perfecting his invention, worrying that mechanical (rather than hand-copying) reproduction would never be accepted.

Gutenberg also worked out a superior system for pressing the blank pages against the inked type. It was essentially a screw-type press, much like those used for centuries for making wine. Even his press required many years' experimentation to get just the right pressure on the parchment or paper. He experimented with many techniques, toiling to produce beautiful examples of printed copy so that when he was ready, his products would have a market among the rich. But he was filled with doubts. Would people buy what he was going to produce? He was not at all sure that mechanical printing would ever catch on. He feared that many people would still want their books copied by hand.

Unfortunately, just before he was ready to produce his first great book—the famous forty-line Bible—he ran out of money. To continue his project, he borrowed heavily from his lawyer, Johannes Fust (whose son-in-law Peter Schoffer was the foreman in the print shop). Eventually, in 1455, Gutenberg was ready for his first great success. He designed, set the type for, and printed two hundred copies of all the pages needed for his Bible. All that was needed was the binding. It was, and still is, one of the world's most beautiful examples of the printer's art.

The work was intended for an elite and wealthy market. He even managed to use his press to produce "illuminated" letters complete with colors. But before the copies were ready for binding and final sale, Fust demanded repayment of the loan. Gutenberg did not have the money, so the lawyer took him to court. With his assistant Schoffer testifying against him at the trial, Gutenberg was stripped of his press, type, Bible, and even legal claim to his inventions. The lawyer and his son-in-law took over everything and left Gutenberg financially ruined.

The poor man lost his eyesight and remained destitute until, toward the end of his life, a nobleman named Adolph von Nassau took pity on him and made him a member of his court, providing him with a yearly allowance of cloth, grain, and wine. Gutenberg, whose work changed the world and enriched the lives of billions of people in later centuries, died in 1468 at age seventy, blind and without any recognition of his timeless contribution to humanity. Even today, little or no mention is made of his contributions in college and university history texts (printed by the process he invented).[11]

The rapid adoption of printing. The number of books available simply exploded as the printing press quickly spread throughout Europe. During the *incunabula* (the period between 1455 and 1501—not even a half century), a tidal wave of books printed in popular languages passed into the hands of increasingly eager populations. No one knows how many were published during the period, but estimates range between 8 and 20 million copies.[12] (The average press run was only about five hundred copies per book, so these figures represent a very large number of titles.)

Because more and more of these books appeared in the vernacular, printing greatly accelerated developments in science, philosophy, and religion. Knowledge of many topics became available to almost anyone who was literate in a common language and had enough money to purchase a book. They were still expensive but much cheaper than the older *manu scripti*. It is very likely that even before Columbus's departure for the New World (about thirty-six years after Gutenberg's first press run), more books were printed than the accumulated total of all the *manu scripti* that had been copied during the previous thousand years since the fall of Rome. As presses and printing technology were improved during the 1600s and 1700s, and as paper became increasingly available, the number of books printed each year grew sharply.

Printing in the New World began very early. In 1539 (approximately a century before the Pilgrims arrived at Plymouth Rock), Juan Pablo set up a press in Mexico

City and printed the first book in the Americas, a religious work entitled *Breve y Mass Compendiosa Doctrina Cristiana*. This book, like many others that followed, was printed under the authority of the Spanish archbishop of Mexico.

The development of education in many countries contributed greatly to the growth in book publishing. More universities were established every year until, by the sixteenth century, they were common in all parts of western Europe. Religious changes (primarily the rise of Protestantism) brought a considerable demand for Bibles and other religious works. In addition, the Renaissance, with its expansion of art, science, philosophy, and literature, contributed to the demand for more and more books. Gutenberg had unleashed a powerful medium indeed.

At first, books were not recognized as a political force. But as soon as those in authority realized that printing could be used to circulate ideas contrary to those of the ruling powers, presses came under strong regulation. In 1529, for example, Henry VIII of England established a list of prohibited books and a system of licensing printers. In spite of these measures, many documents expressing political opinions were circulated. Nevertheless, the Tudors, who controlled the Crown in the mid-1500s, were effective censors of England's presses. This suppression was to last more than a century.[13]

Book publishing in the American colonies. Book publishing was slow to start in North America. The early settlers were not avid readers. In September 1620, one hundred and one passengers, along with forty-eight crew members and a number of chickens and pigs, left England on the Mayflower. Nearly two months later they landed on Cape Cod, where they spent a rather miserable eight weeks before moving to the mainland. There they quickly laid out a road up from the shore and began constructing shelters. Within two years, they had a small village of simple homes that they had named New Plymouth. The houses they built were small and compactly arranged on each side of the road, each with its own garden plot.

The people in the new community worked hard all day but had very little to do after sunset other than talk with their families and friends. There were religious services on the Sabbath and daily family prayers, but the strict codes of the Pilgrims did not permit frivolous activities. Aside from the family Bible, there was nothing to read in most of the houses. Even if there had been, the majority could neither read nor write. Even for the few who could, it was difficult. After dark, tallow candles, crude lamps, and the fireplace provided barely enough light to move around. Thus, by comparison with today, the citizens of New Plymouth led a life almost free of any form of communication other than talking.[14]

Others soon came to the new colonies, and within a short time an early press was established at the newly founded Harvard College in Cambridge, Massachusetts. This is where the first book in New England was published in 1640. It was a religious work entitled the *Whole Booke of Psalmes* (most often called the *Bay Psalm Book*). The college controlled the press until 1662, when the Massachusetts legislature took it over.

Book publishing on any scale was slow to develop in the North American colonies, partly because of restrictions imposed by the Crown. However, growing political dissent before the Revolution stimulated all forms of publishing—books, early newspapers, and political pamphlets. These played a significant part in motivating the separation from England. In the decades following the Revolution, New York, Boston, and Philadelphia became established as centers of a budding publishing industry. Books published early in America's history included religious works and almanacs as well as political and social treatises.

Before the 1800s, only a small proportion of the American population was able to read. After the turn of the nineteenth century, however, the new democratic political system spurred an increasing interest in reading and writing. Following a plan devised in the 1830s by Horace Mann, of the Massachusetts legislature, tax-supported public schools were established to teach all children to read and write. Democracy required an informed citizenry if it was to survive as its architects had hoped. Mann's plan made school attendance mandatory and it was quickly adopted by other states.

By the 1840s, a growing audience for books existed in America. In addition to textbooks and scholarly and religious works, cheap paperback reprints of popular books appeared, including sensational fiction. By 1855, the United States far surpassed England in the number of books sold. That year saw the first publication of Whitman's *Leaves of Grass,* Longfellow's *Hiawatha,* and Bartlett's *Familiar Quotations,* which remains a basic reference source even today. Probably no other book in American history had as much impact on its time as one published during this period: Harriet Beecher Stowe's antislavery novel, *Uncle Tom's Cabin.* Thus, as the nineteenth century progressed, book publishing in the United States became well established as a business, a mass medium, and a shaper of American culture.[15]

BOOKS AS A CONTEMPORARY MEDIUM

Because they are so common and familiar, it may be difficult for people today to appreciate the truly remarkable nature of books and to grasp easily the irreplaceable services they provide to individuals and society. The fact that they have not only survived for so many centuries, but also prospered in the face of increasingly sophisticated competing media, is one indicator of their importance. They remain a medium of entertainment, the principal repository of our culture, guides to our technical knowledge, the source of teachings on many subjects, and our basic reference to religious doctrines.

BOOKS AS MASS MEDIUM

Books as they exist today fit our definition of a mass medium. Their "messages" are prepared and encoded by professional communicators and are normally transmitted to relatively large and diverse audiences. Because books (such as the present text) often take a year or more to produce—even after the author gives the finished manuscript to the publisher—they are less timely than newspapers and magazines. In addition, like each of the mass media, they have distinctive characteristics that set them apart from the others. They differ from newspapers and magazines in that they are bound and covered and are consecutive from beginning to end. Nevertheless, books represent an important and popular mass medium, widely used for a variety of purposes in contemporary society.

One obvious difference between books and other media is that, like movies, they are not heavily supported by advertising. Books have to earn profits for their producers on the basis of their sale as content and as physical objects. Moreover, books are made to last longer than any other print medium, and this feature lends itself to in-depth, durable exploration and development of topics and ideas.

These characteristics suit the book for a special role among our contemporary media mix. Most books sell only a few thousand copies. Even a national runaway best seller will probably sell no more than 10 million copies over its effective years of life—less than the audience for some soap operas during a single day of televi-

The rise of book megastores, which are now found in almost every community, has spurred the sales of books to eager consumers, but at the same time has eroded the market for small, independent bookstores. The megastores provide expert information about books and easy access to inventories and other advantages as with this Border's store in Costa Mesa, California, where customers interact with employees.

sion! Yet, the social importance of books can hardly be overestimated. Books often persuade the influential, bringing new policies and solutions to problems. They can have a readership and influence far beyond their actual sales. Thus, in addition to serving as a major channel for transmitting the cultural heritage, they can promote powerful ideas and inspire great changes—even revolutions.

THE BOOK PUBLISHING INDUSTRY: AN OVERVIEW

Between the authors who prepare the content of a book and the public who reads it is the publishing company. The publisher's role is threefold: (1) to *select* and help shape what will be published; (2) to *produce* the book as a physical artifact; and (3) to *advertise and distribute* the book to receivers—which are usually retail book stores that sell it for a profit. While authors prepare the actual content of a book, publishers take the risks involved in investing the money required to convert a manuscript into a book, and to promote and distribute it to consumers. Because most publishers are privately owned businesses, they have a clear necessity to earn a profit. In recent years, the industry's changing economics have influenced the way publishers carry out their other roles.

Growing numbers of books published. Figure 2.1 shows the changes in the output of book publishers in the United States during the twentieth century. Clearly, book publishing is a growing industry, with more titles being produced in recent years than at any time in our nation's history. There are several reasons for this. During the first half of the century, book publishing took an important turn toward *commercialism.* What it offered the public was determined more and more by a sharp focus on profits. Many kinds of books were found to be profitable, and the number published rose steadily. In the 1920s, the Book-of-the-Month Club and the Literary Guild were founded, expanding the market for novels and other works by reaching those who lived far from bookstores. Following World War II, more and more Americans pursued higher education. Demand for textbooks soared as returning veterans, helped by the GI Bill, filled colleges and universities. And, with the postwar baby boom more children entered school than ever before. Today, the children of those baby boomers are overflowing primary and secondary schools, and have already begun attending colleges and universities. Once again, the demand for textbooks is increasing.

One of the important innovations in book publishing in the United States was the introduction of the now-familiar small *paperback*. Even during the nineteenth century, following the development of cheap paper and high-speed presses, paperback "dime" novels were widely available and an important part of American publishing. However, until well into the present century, more "serious" books were always published in hardcover. In Europe, less expensive paperbound books came into wide use well before World War II, but they did not catch on in the United States. However, when cheaper printing and binding processes were introduced during the 1950s, the small paperback format made it possible for all kinds of books to reach much larger audiences than ever before. The dollars Americans spent for books increased massively from the mid-twentieth century to the present. For example, total sales went from just over $435 million in 1947 to more than $40 billion in 2000! Even after taking inflation into account, that is a truly significant change.

Emphasis on profits.   These trends were accompanied by noteworthy changes within the industry. Book publishing prior to World War II was always something of a dignified "gentlemen's" profession. It had not been the place to find either "big money" or shrewd business practices. Much of the industry had consisted of family-owned enterprises passed on from one generation to the next. To take advantage of the new opportunities for growth, however, publishers needed new resources, so they "went public." This means that they sold stock in their companies. That was an important turning point. Banks and other profit-oriented investors began to buy the stock. This increased the demand for a good return on investment. The bottom line, rather than the intellectual satisfaction of publishing important books, became the driving force, and it remains so today.

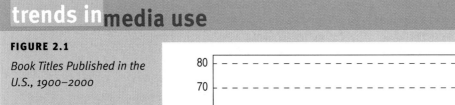

FIGURE 2.1

Book Titles Published in the U.S., 1900–2000

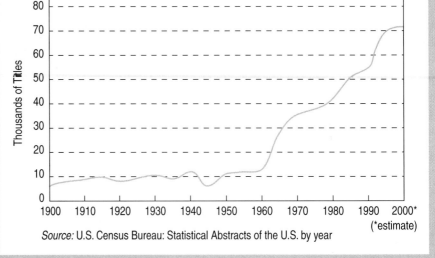

Source: U.S. Census Bureau: Statistical Abstracts of the U.S. by year

Consolidation of ownership. Another trend is a consolidation of ownership—a factor common to all American media. Since the 1960s, and particularly in recent years, many publishers merged or were acquired by communications corporations and conglomerates. As a result of such buyouts and consolidations, publishing firms gained financial resources along with more sophisticated business and marketing skills.

> Some industry observers point to 1998 as the year when everything got crazy. In that year alone, there were fifteen acquisition deals worth more than $11 billion. Bertelsmann grabbed the biggest headlines for its estimated $1.4 billion purchase of Random House, a move that merged the largest U.S. publishing company with Bantam Doubleday Dell, which the German media conglomerate already owned. As one company, Bertelsmann now controls anywhere from 11 to 35% of the American adult trade market, depending on whom you ask.[16]

The book-buying public paid a cost in these consolidations. Many publishers lost autonomy in decision-making. More and more, they had to show constant profits for their stockholders and new owners. Publishing was no longer a dignified club but an objective business. Today, mergers and sales of companies continue to take place at a dizzying pace. Large publishing companies are now no different from other large businesses, being subject to buyouts, takeovers, and above all, concern about annual earnings as opposed to producing a quality product that may sell in only modest amounts.

These economic changes forced publishers to alter the ways that they acquired, produced, and sold books. Until recent decades, publishers ran their own printing plants, binderies, and bookstores. Now they conduct market research to make decisions about what to publish. They "out-place" much of what they once did "in-house." They contract with freelancers outside the company to design the appearance of the book, edit the manuscript, provide photos, draw illustrations, proofread copy, prepare indexes, and do many of the other tasks that are part of the process of producing books. The completed manuscript then goes to independent printers and bookbinders who manufacture the finished product.

Today, few book publishers are likely to express interest in noteworthy but unprofitable manuscripts. Instead, they are more likely to consider themselves simply as entrepreneurs, little different in principle from producers of beer, soap, or soup. Their aim is to manufacture a product that they can persuade consumers to buy, regardless of its other qualities. Thus, publishing today looks less like a craft or an intellectual enterprise and more like any other modern industry. Critics fear that neither the meticulous craftsmanship of the traditional publishing industry nor intellectual standards will survive, and that in their place we will soon find only "conformity to the median of popular tastes."[17]

THE PUBLISHING PROCESS

In addition to publishers, the key people in the production and distribution of books are authors, editors, book manufacturers, bookstores, and sales personnel. Naturally, many kinds of specialists and technicians have supporting roles. Since nonemployees now do so much of the work of developing a book, to a great extent contemporary publishers have become orchestrators—hiring and coordinating the work of many outside suppliers.

TYPES OF PUBLISHERS AND TYPES OF BOOKS

Like theatrical producers, publishers (to some extent, at least) have styles and reputations. In part, these come from how they organize the publishing process, how they deal with authors, and the physical appearance of their books. In spite of the press for profits, a few publishers are still known for their craftsmanship, producing books of high quality. The majority, however, produce books as quickly and cheaply as possible. A few publish "instant" books shortly after news events. During recent years, books came on the market almost overnight on such topics as the Oklahoma City bombing, several airline crashes, and various natural disasters such as earthquakes. Others focused on events that captured widespread interest, such as O.J. Simpson's and President Bill Clinton's problems. Such books take advantage of headlines while they are still freshly in mind.

A more important consideration is content area. That is, many companies focus on a general topic—for example, science, fiction, fine arts, medicine, law, or religion. There are other bases of specialization among publishers, such as nonfiction, high school texts, and so on. Table 2.1 shows a classification of types of books according to audience and function.

Books can also be classified in terms of their share of the market. As Figure 2.2 shows, trade books account for the largest share of books sold by publishers, making up nearly half of publishers' total sales—and that share is rising.[18]

Included in the trade book category are books published by university presses, but their output is a very small part of the overall business. However, university presses, associated with and often subsidized by a particular educational institution, are often far more important than their dollar sales would suggest. Their books are aimed primarily at scholars and scientists. However, in recent years many university presses have also become more profit-oriented and have been expanding their lists to include topics of popular interest.

Table 2.1	Types of Books
Type	**Description**
Trade	Includes literature, biography, and all fiction and nonfiction books for general reading. These books are usually handled by retail bookstores.
Textbooks	Includes books for elementary and high schools, colleges, and universities. These books are usually sold through educational institutions or college bookstores, but publishers make their sales pitches to state or local school boards or faculty members.
Children's	Sold through bookstores or to schools and libraries.
Reference	Includes dictionaries, encyclopedias, atlases, and similar books. These require long and expensive preparation.
Technical and Scientific	Includes manuals, original research, and technical reports.
Law	Involves the codification of legal materials and constant updating.
Medical	Also requires frequent updating.

Source: Datus C. Smith Jr., *Guide to Book Publishing* (1989), pp. 128–129; used by permission of University of Washington Press

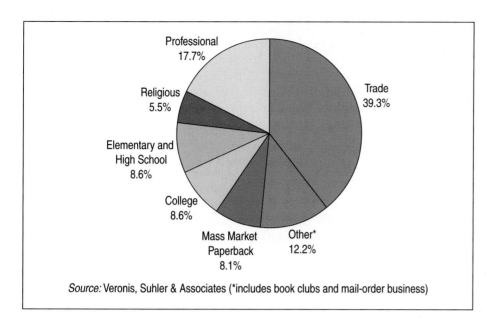

figure2.2

**Estimated Book Sales
by Category, 2000**

Professional
17.7%

Religious
5.5%

Elementary and
High School
8.6%

College
8.6%

Mass Market
Paperback
8.1%

Other*
12.2%

Trade
39.3%

Source: Veronis, Suhler & Associates (*includes book clubs and mail-order business)

FROM TYPED MANUSCRIPT TO FINISHED BOOK

Since the time of Plato, whose *Republic* is the earliest surviving book-length work in philosophy, books have had their first stirrings of life as ideas in the heads of their authors. However, authors are in a very real sense "outsiders" in the publishing world—that is, they are rarely employees of the publisher. Nonetheless, because publishing is a competitive business, the author represents an important resource. Publishers must have a continuing flow of new manuscripts to process and sell, and therefore, authors are key players in book publishing.

Beginning novelists may have a difficult time getting their works read by a publisher, but once a work is accepted, and especially if an author has previously produced successful works, things get better. The fiction author often receives a substantial advance (against royalties) from the publisher, ranging from a few thousand dollars (for a beginner) up to several million dollars or more (for a well-known writer). Royalties are some agreed-upon small percentage of the publisher's earnings from selling books to retailers. If the book is successful, a novelist may receive huge additional income from paperback contracts and even movie or television rights.

In the trade book world, authors normally use *literary agents* to represent them. The agent ferrets out book ideas, identifies authors whose works are likely to be of interest to publishers, contacts publishing houses and particular editors who may be interested in what an author is working on, and negotiates a contract with the publisher for the author. The agent receives a percentage (usually 15 percent) of the author's share from a book's earnings.

Either an author, an agent, or an editor may initiate the idea for a trade book. As publishers have increased their use of market research, the editor's role in initiating or reshaping the idea for a book has grown. For example, Time, Inc., sometimes sends prospective readers elaborate brochures describing a proposed book or series of books and eliciting responses. The replies received may lead editors to cancel the project or to change its proposed content, format, and/or promotion.

On the textbook side, the relationship between publishers and authors is different. Textbook authors are often sought out and asked to undertake a work that the publisher feels will sell. They are offered contracts before writing the book on the basis of

Much of the book industry's financial growth in the late 1990s and early 2000s was due to the mass marketing of a single book series—the Harry Potter children's books—written by author J. K. Rowling, shown here at a London book launch in 2000.

a detailed outline and perhaps a draft of a chapter. However, textbook authors must be specialists in the field in which they are writing, and publishers must carefully screen prospects. The financial incentives are also different. Textbook authors usually command lower (or no) advances compared to novelists or writers of other trade books. However, a good textbook can often go through several editions, providing a continuous if modest source of income for both the writer and the publisher.

Clearly, publishers are risk-takers. Editor Dan Lacy, commenting on the "essence of publishing as entrepreneurship," notes, "The publisher pays the costs and assumes the risks of issuing each book, and hence he occupies a highly speculative position."[19] Of course, authors also take a risk. Writing a successful novel or a complex textbook can take years. While the author may receive advances from the publisher before book publication, almost all the money will come much later from royalties. If the book does well, the author gets paid; if it does not, he or she has toiled a very long time for very little.

Once the publisher receives the author's original manuscript, several kinds of editors work on it. Publishing companies have many specialized editors, often with impressive-sounding titles, who are responsible for such activities as bringing in manuscripts, analyzing and editing them, and preparing the final copy for the typesetter. One kind is an *acquisitions* editor, whose work may be devoted mainly to generating ideas for books and finding able and willing authors. Other editors may evaluate the quality of manuscripts and their sales potential. Some work directly with the author as *developmental* editors to organize the book effectively and help make it the most effective statement of its topic. There are also *copy* editors, whose main task is to check the spelling, syntax, and grammar of a manuscript, and to check "proofs" (preliminary printed versions of pages). Other specialists develop illustrations and design the print style, cover, and format of the book. As noted earlier, today many of these tasks may be done by freelancers on a contract basis.

To set the manuscript into type for printing, publishers hire outside companies called *compositors.* The publisher also contracts with printers and binders. Sales representatives from the publishing company persuade independent booksellers to carry the company's books, school boards to adopt them, or college and university faculty members to assign them. A few publishers also run chains of bookstores of their own.

Thus, the publisher is a sort of *impresario*—a manager who brings together and coordinates a complex team including authors, editors, designers, compositors, printers, and booksellers. Through the various stages of bookmaking, publishers try to control the costs, schedule, and quality of the work. Their role, in publishing executive Lacy's words, is "somewhat analogous to that of a theater producer, or an independent film producer."[20]

THE PUBLISHER AS ENTREPRENEUR

The mainstream of American publishing is found in the large publishing houses, many of which are located in New York City. In fact, just 2 percent of the nation's publishers account for about 75 percent of book sales.[21] However, small publishing houses flourish across the country, producing more specialized books. A publishing company can begin with only one or two people and little equipment, hiring outside suppliers on a book-by-book basis. Unlike the small radio or TV station, the small book publisher needs no federal license, and unlike a small newspaper, the enterprise is not limited to a local audience. Through selective promotion, direct-mail, and Web site advertising a new firm can command national attention and sales. Book publishers can thus begin with limited capital, publishing only a few titles until they begin to show a profit.

In view of what we have said up to now, it may seem surprising that many books—perhaps most—*never turn a profit!* It is very difficult to forecast whether a book will succeed, so the publishers are forced to gamble. However, publishers survive because the earnings for a good seller can be high enough to pay for other books that lose money or barely break even. Moreover, if a book at least breaks even it keeps a highly skilled staff in place and working until the really hot seller comes along. If that does happen, that staff is sorely needed.

A continuing debate centers on the quality of contemporary books. As a profit-oriented industry, often owned by large conglomerates concerned mainly with the bottom line, many critics feel that the book industry has lost important qualities that it once had:

> Of late, books and book publishing have come under fire not only as a doomed medium, but as a once-great institution fallen to schlock and profit mongering. Publishing houses have turned into houses of ill repute, the critics sniff, charging that the bottom line and market-oriented decision making has resulted in such a lowering of quality that book publishers, if not doomed by illiteracy and competition, should be nonetheless put out of their low-brow misery.[22]

The contemporary book industry uses a variety of marketing techniques. Included are direct mail, telephone marketing, Web sites, professional meeting displays, book clubs, and magazine ads. Publishers sometimes offer a reduced rate for buying the book in advance of the publication date. Virtually every promotional device used to market other products has been tried. However, traditionally, publishers have tiny advertising budgets compared with other consumer product industries. Perhaps more than other forms of print, books depend on other media. For example, they depend on magazines and newspapers to promote books through reviews as well as paid advertising. Fiction authors frequently appear as guests on television and radio talk shows, where they promote their books.

The *New York Times* bestseller list continues to be the dominant rating of the success of fiction and nonfiction books, based on a sample drawn from bookstores and electronic services. The list is regarded as prestigious by authors and publishers.

THE DIGITAL FUTURE OF BOOKS:
THE FOURTH TRANSITION

At this moment in time, the future looks quite bright for this venerable medium. As this chapter has shown, books in their traditional form are currently more popular than ever. There are, however, reasons to expect that over the long term another major transition will take place in the ways in which books are *produced, stored, distributed, sold,* and *read.* While it is unlikely that in the near future books printed on paper will become obsolete, the Internet and developing computer technology will introduce new ways for readers to obtain and read books and for vendors to sell them. That transition is already starting.

New technologies now becoming available for publishing books may allow us to forecast what will happen to books over the decades ahead. Such predictions are difficult at best, but a number of recent developments provide some clues. Certainly, interesting ways of *selling* books have been developed that were not a part of retailing even a decade or so ago. In addition, the ways in which books are transmitted from those who sell them to those who read them are already showing signs of change. Specifically, the Internet is becoming a source for downloading books from venders, and computer-like devices, specifically designed for reading books stored in digital files, are now appearing on the market.

RECENT CHANGES IN RETAILING

Buying a traditional book today is not as difficult as it was ten years ago. For one thing, the places where books can be bought have undergone change. "Mom and pop" bookstores and small ones in shopping malls, both with limited inventories, are rapidly being replaced by huge stores operated by national chains. As author Bridget Kinsella notes, "Ten years ago these superstores did not exist."[23] These megastores have hundreds of thousands of titles—a book for every reading level, interest, and taste. Even though some critics mourn the loss of the personal attention they claim to have received in the smaller stores, the "mom and pop" enterprise is not likely to make a comeback.

The development of book retailing via the World Wide Web has already simplified book purchasing for those who are online. With organizations such as Amazon.com retailing books over the Internet, purchasers no longer have to drive to a "brick-and-mortar" establishment, find a place to park, walk through the store, and search through the shelves hoping to find what they want. The computer literate can buy a book of their choice with a few clicks of a mouse, and within a short time it will be delivered to their home.

ELECTRONIC PUBLISHING AND READING

But what does the longer-range future hold? Will books in their traditional form eventually be replaced altogether? As was noted at the beginning of this chapter, pundits are predicting the death of books as they now exist—printed on paper, bound between covers, sold in bookstores, and stored on shelves in libraries. It would be much more efficient, such futurists maintain, to place books online, where users can download them from the Internet.

There are grounds for the belief that, in the truly long range, the nature of books will undergo some sort of transformation along those lines. Books, as has been

Amazon.com became one of the best-known Internet "brands" and is now a universally known site for the selling of books, videos, and other products.

explained, have changed their form at least three times: We noted earlier that they started as scrolls on papyrus and parchment. Later, the Romans developed them as bound *manu scripti* with multiple pages. Gutenberg changed them a third time, through the invention of the printing press, which allowed multiple exact copies to be mechanically printed on paper. The modern power press decreased the time it takes to produce books, but it did not change their basic form, which is still in use today. Taking a truly long-range perspective, the Internet may bring about a fourth significant transition: *books acquired on demand* and *books in digital form* downloaded from the Internet. There are already two visible ways in which this is beginning.

Printed books on demand via the Internet. One way in which consumers in some areas can already obtain printed books via the Internet is at a local bookstore (that has the service). Instead of a bookstore employee going to a shelf, or to a stored inventory, the bookstore will call up the title that the customer wishes to buy from its central database on the Internet. A customer can either select the title while at the store or phone in the order from a different location. The book's content will be swiftly downloaded at the store and printed on the spot for the customer. The resulting book is printed on paper, with a cover, and the customer reads it in that form. Thus, in this system, it is the process of production, storage, and delivery that has changed—not end use.

   This method of acquiring books represents only a tiny fraction of books sold today, but there will be a number of advantages associated with the system if it is expanded. For one thing, book retailers need only maintain an electronic database, rather than a warehouse of printed books. If that is the case, a number of so-called "middlemen" costs will be eliminated by the process. There will be no need for shipping to the retailer, stocking a large inventory, and absorbing losses on unsold books. Presumably, as these costs are reduced, the retail price of a book will also drop. Furthermore, books no longer available in print can be stored in electronic form to be obtained in this way.

Publishers like Houghton Mifflin maintain active Web sites to promote their books with special attention to booksellers, the media, teachers, and other consumers.

A problem with such a system, some point out, is that it neglects the "browser." Many people find large bookstores very attractive. They can stroll among the shelves, look at the actual physical book, perhaps read a few pages, and decide whether they want to buy it. Electronic online book purveyors do not accommodate this type of consumer, which may be a factor that limits their share of the market.

Direct downloading from the Internet. A somewhat different version of books via the Internet goes much further. Currently in its infancy, in this system book venders maintain no brick-and-mortar store, or even a warehouse in the usual sense. They only maintain a Web site and a server, via which they can be contacted directly by their customers. Such venders maintain a database of book titles that can be transmitted quickly and downloaded directly to the customer's computer and then to a dedicated device specially designed for reading these types of books.

There are already such Web sites as well as dedicated reading devices. Examples of such Web sites are Powell's Books (www.powells.com), ecampusbooks (www.ecampus.com), and Barnes & Noble (www.bn.com). Some companies, such as Glassbook (www.glassbook.com), offer free software and even free books in some cases as an inducement to purchase others later. Normally, however, the customer pays a fee and downloads (onto a personal computer) a file containing the complete book. If it is to be read on a dedicated reading device, or reader, it must be downloaded again to the device via a special cable.

Several readers are already on the market. For example, the Rocket ebook (from NuvoMedia, Inc.) is a rather flat device about the size and thickness of a large paperback book. Downloading the book onto such a reader is done in a way in which the recipient cannot reproduce it, pass it on to a friend, or even print it. In some cases, the file may even have a time limit after which the file will be erased from the customer's computer or reader. However, once loaded onto the reader, the user can then "turn" through the pages with the use of simple buttons. The reading device is not a computer and it does not accept new information—other than "electronic" bookmarks and similar aids. The machine can hold a number of books (or files) and a dictionary. Its battery lasts up to twenty hours before it has to be recharged.

On the down side, the liquid crystal diode (LCD) screens on such devices are not as bright as those on a standard computer and can be a bit difficult to read—especially under certain light conditions. They have a current pricetag of about $200 for the cheapest model and run much higher for fancier models. The book files themselves can also be expensive. A recent novel by a well-known author can cost over $20. Obviously, also, such devices require that the reader be able to use a computer and the Internet to download the book files from the source.

In spite of these limitations, the emerging technology is intriguing. Obviously, there are many improvements that need to be made in both cost and complexity. However, the vision for the future includes the idea that libraries and even large bookstores with hard copies will no longer be needed. They are expected to be replaced by large databases of electronic books. One possible thought is to supplement libraries, which can have limited holdings or out-of-date materials, with such systems so that their users can have access to the most current of all forms of information. This would be a boon to many local school libraries, whose holdings are often hopelessly out of date.

With rapid access to electronic books, people traveling on business or vacation need not lug along heavy hard copies in their luggage. They can get what they need at any time over almost any telephone line. In a very long-range sense, there is the tantalizing possibility that individuals in countries that have few libraries and book retailers would be able to obtain virtually any kind of book that they desire via this system—thereby increasing their level of literacy and cultural sophistication.

Generally, then, given the remarkable progress in computer systems that has taken place over the last twenty years, it seems likely that at some point in the future, new technologies will be developed that will produce a fourth transition in the nature of books.[24]

However, even if all these technological changes take place, will bookstores and libraries all go out of business? At present, that does not seem likely. What is more likely is that both systems—paper and electronic—will coexist, with businesses and libraries handling both forms. If that is the case, our current book publishing industry will undergo significant reconfiguration to produce and distribute e-books. In the short term, however, a number of scholars and observers of the book publishing industry foresee the following trends happening:

- Books printed on paper will be with us for the foreseeable future. Their replacement by online forms as discussed previously will probably occur in the years ahead but not in any revolutionary way.
- For books on paper, because of escalating production costs, hardcover versions may be an increasingly small proportion of what is produced as publishers find it increasingly difficult to compete in today's mass market in both trade and text publishing.
- Highly diversified small publishing houses and university presses with far lower marketing and distribution costs will flourish, while big, labor-intensive commercial houses may continue to consolidate to remain competitive.
- Because of rising costs, direct-mail and, especially, online sales of conventional books to customers will slowly begin to intrude upon traditional retail marketing. Traditional retailers that do survive will be those that both operate stores with huge inventories of titles in hard copy and also develop effective online systems for selling books.

Peter Osnos
Publisher and Chief Executive
Public Affairs Press
New York, New York

insights from
MEDIA LEADERS

A respected leader in book publishing since the 1980s, Peter Osnos is regarded by insiders as the "hottest editor" in the business. His reputation rests on his work with sought-after authors including U.S. presidents and first ladies as well as other world leaders, politicians, sports heroes, and media celebrities. At Random House from 1984 to 1996, he served as vice president and associate publisher as well as publisher of the Times Books imprint. Before that, he spent twenty years at the *Washington Post* as a foreign correspondent and editor and was also a commentator for National Public Radio. He founded Public Affairs Press in 1997 and has published authors ranging from Vladimir Putin to Andy Rooney. He attended Brandeis University and received a master's degree in journalism from Columbia University.

Q. How did you initially get involved in the book publishing field?

A. While I had been involved in several book projects as a correspondent and editor at the *Washington Post,* my real entry into book publishing came in 1984 when the then-chairman of Random House, Robert Bernstein, recruited me. He wanted to expand their line of serious, long-form books. At that time, books by writers like David Halberstam and Bob Woodward had become the "gold standard" of long-form journalism.

Q. How relevant was this new assignment to your experience as a foreign correspondent, newspaper reporter, and radio commentator?

A. Quite. In many ways it was a natural progression for me. As a rule, newspaper people *get* the story and put it in the paper. In book publishing you do that, but you also have to *sell* the story. While exciting and comfortable, my move from journalism to publishing required some new skills. My work at the *Post* gave

me a sense of wanting to write for an audience. As a foreign correspondent (unlike most reporters on a given beat) you could sometimes write for various sections of the paper ranging from public affairs news to business and sports. In publishing, you can do the same thing but on a larger scale. You can edit and publish books that reflect a broader sense of your interests—cutting across different fields. For me, journalism was an excellent preparation for doing big autobiographies and other serious books. In acquiring and shaping those books, I had to learn how to elicit lively and interesting stories from people as different as Tip O'Neil and Boris Yeltsin.

Q. What have been the main influences that have led you to high-level positions in book publishing?

A. Number one is impact. Of course, it is important in publishing to make a judgment that *impact* is different from *business success.* If you were only concerned about financial success that would mean publishing only a certain kind of book. You have to determine how to afford to publish books of enormous consequence and significant impact if they are not going to sell very many copies. The analogy I like to use is NPR and C-SPAN. Both are enormously influential but not expensive to run. They are *not* predicated on financial success. If NPR, for example, were valued monetarily, it would be worth billions. Remember that AOL only had 21 million subscribers when it bought Time Warner. The trick for book publishers is to have strong core audiences and to keep expenses in check. As Esther Tyson has said, "We've moved from the information age to the attention age." That's a very smart analysis and quite relevant to book publishing where attention is critical. The most important problem today is getting people's attention. Yes, you must collect and galvanize information, but publishing requires a whole different set

Overall, then, the outlook for books remains positive. The content that they provide—whatever the forms in which we purchase and read them—is essential to our civilization. With expanding markets, new retailing systems, vigorous publishers, and increasingly user-friendly technology for downloading and reading them, books will continue to be important in the future—just as they have been in the past.

of skills than those of the solitary writer, alone in a garret. One needs to be willing to engage the work in a marketing and PR sense, but to produce something that has credibility. But just remember that the media and entertainment companies have skewed values these days. That's reflected in the fact that the sum of the salaries of the three top network anchors is more than the entire annual budget of C-SPAN.

Q. What do you think will be the long-term impact of digital media and e-commerce on book publishing?

A. Well, I analogize books to music. Music begins with the composer and the function of the composer has never changed. That's the person who writes the music, just as an author writes the book. What has changed is the way music is disseminated. A piece of music can be consumed by you in many different ways, from CDs and cassettes to radio with commercials, radio without commercials, an orchestra, or in reading sheet music. If you think about books, they too are disseminated in a variety of ways—hard cover, paperback, talking books, the e-book, and in ways not yet thought of. I do not believe the e-book will replace the printed book any more than videos from a video store will replace going to the movies. They are just two different ways of having the same experience. You are still watching the movie, or in this case, reading the book. The future of books will depend on developing reasonable economic models for various ways of creating and selling the book.

Q. What is the best pathway to a successful and satisfying career in this field?

A. I'm surrounded by wonderful young people who had a range of job choices, but they chose books and book publishing. When people ask me about preparation for book publishing, I tell them to think of going to work for a publishing house in the same way they think about going to graduate school, whether in business, law, journalism, or whatever. In graduate school, you *pay* tuition, but don't earn any money. If you go into publishing in an entry-level job, you get *paid* and you'll get a professional education. But make no mistake; there is a big difference between going to school and going to work. In this business an A minus does not count. You have to pay attention to detail, to complete every task as truly as it can be, and you must absolutely be on time, always meeting deadlines.

Q. Based on job satisfaction, compensation, and long-term prospects, how would you rate this field as a career choice?

A. Well, I like the old adage that it is not *what you eat* that matters, but *what is eating you.* If your primary goal is financial, there are many ways to make more money. But publishing is a very good career. The pay at the beginning is modest compared with other professional fields, but it pays as well as other professional fields as you move to the middle and top ranks of the business. It is not a path to riches, but you can make a respectable living—and you can do things that are significant at the same time. For the right person who values doing this kind of work, it is a very satisfying career choice.

Q. What is the most satisfying aspect of this field? The least?

A. I think the least satisfying aspect of the field these days is the tendency of many publishers toward making business judgments that aren't appropriate to books. For example, the values and profit margins that the big entertainment companies insist on simply cannot apply to books that are only going to sell twenty thousand or thirty thousand copies. Some publishers accept this reasoning, but it is not right. The most satisfying? I'd say the intellectual stimulation of it all, being involved in things that matter, producing books that have lasting value.

Chapter Review

■ Books began after writing and portable media were developed. They have undergone at least three significant transformations over the last six centuries.

- Cave paintings were human beings' first attempts to represent ideas graphically. Such efforts represent a transition from purely oral description to the graphic depiction of ideas.

- Ideographic systems based on pictographs began about 4000 B.C. Improvements occurred gradually over about two thousand years until phonograms came into use. Eventually writing was greatly simplified when alphabets were invented. Our alphabet is based on early forms that were standardized by the Greeks and passed on to the Romans.

- When portable media replaced stone, longer documents and even libraries of scrolls became possible. The Romans made the first books with letters on both sides of cut and bound pages and end boards or covers. They also developed many of the written language formats that we still use in books and other printed material.

- The skills of writing and manuscript preparation were kept alive during the Dark Ages by the Christian monasteries, but after the twelfth and thirteenth centuries, they passed into lay hands as well. Meanwhile, paper had come into use, and the stage was set for print.

- A great technological advance came when Johannes Gutenberg developed both a workable press and cast-metal type. His invention was enormously important and quickly spread throughout the Western world.

- Book publishing came late to North America, but when it caught on books had a powerful influence on the spread of literacy and on popular opinions and ideas.

- A publishing house processes the content of a book from author's manuscript to finished product. The publishers, who risk capital, hoping to make a return on their investment, fill the role of bringing together individuals with diverse talents to create an end product, somewhat in the manner of a movie or theater producer.

- Publishers are entrepreneurs who use different strategies to make a profit on what they produce. Many books published do not make a profit, and the ones that do have to support those that do not.

- Books printed on paper are likely to survive in the near future due to their portability, permanence, and cost-effectiveness. However, as technology continues to develop, major changes lie ahead in the ways in which books are produced, stored, distributed, purchased, and read. Electronic systems, currently in their infancy, may bring about a fourth transition in the form of this venerable medium. Nevertheless, books, whatever their physical form, will remain our most respected medium and essential to our civilization.

Notes and References

1. Steven Levy, "It's Time to Turn the Last Page," *Newsweek,* January 1, 2000, p. 96.
2. Miguel Angel Garcia Guinea, *Altamira: and Other Cantabrian Caves* (Madrid: Silex, 1979), p. 4.
3. The sections on writing, the alphabet, early books, and the invention of printing are based on the following sources: Albertine Gaur, *A History of Writing* (London: Scribner's, 1984); Joseph Naveh, *Early History of the Alphabet* (Jerusalem: Magnes, 1982); Donald

Jackson, *The Story of Writing* (New York: Taplinger, 1981); and Douglas McMurtrie, *The Book: A History of Printing and Book-Making* (New York: Oxford University Press, 1943).

4. Hendrik D. L. Vervliet, ed., *Through Five Thousand Years* (London: Phaidon, 1972), p. 18.

5. The Egyptians, who were very powerful during the same period, worked out a similar idea. However, they did not want to give up the beautiful pictograms that made up their earlier hieroglyphics, so they tried to mix an ideographic system with phonograms. It was not an effective solution. Furthermore, a serious shortcoming of their system was that they had no symbols to represent vowels. For example, the Egyptians would write (the equivalent of) the word *foot* as *ft,* or *beetle* as *btl.* Occasionally, we do this today with such words as *boulevard* and other "contractions." Unfortunately for the Egyptians, the pronunciation of missing sounds was lost over the centuries and their language died out.

6. McMurtrie, *The Book,* pp. 76–77.

7. Francis Falconer Madan, *Books in Manuscript: A Short Introduction to Their Study and Use,* 2nd ed. (Oxford: Oxford University Press, 1920).

8. Robert Hamilton Clapper, *Paper, An Historical Account of Its Making by Hand from the Earliest Times Down to the Present Day* (Oxford: Oxford University Press, 1934).

9. James Moran, *Printing Presses: History and Development from the Fifteenth Century to Modern Times* (Berkeley and Los Angeles: University of California Press, 1973), p. 17.

10. Moran, *Printing Presses,* p. 18.

11. David Stebenne, Seth Rachlin, and Martha FitzSimon, *Coverage of the Media in College Textbooks* (New York: Freedom Forum Media Studies Center, 1992).

12. The actual number will forever remain elusive. But it was clearly a great communication revolution, rivaling that which has occurred in the twentieth century. For a detailed analysis of the implications of that revolution, see Elizabeth Eisenstein, *The Printing Press as an Agent of Change,* vols. 1 and 2 (Cambridge: Cambridge University Press, 1979).

13. Frederick Seibert, *Freedom of the Press in England, 1476–1622* (Urbana, Ill.: University of Illinois Press, 1952), chaps. 1–3.

14. See John E. Ponfret, *Founding the American Colonies: 1583–1660* (New York: Harper and Row, 1970).

15. John Tebbel, *The Media in America* (New York: Crowell, 1974).

16. Bridget Kinsella, "Publishing 2000," *Fiction Writer,* February 2000, p. 16.

17. Charles A. Madison, *Book Publishing in America* (New York: McGraw-Hill, 1966), p. 402. See also Benjamin M. Compaine, *The Book Industry in Transition* (White Plains, N.Y.: Knowledge Industry, 1978).

18. There is a considerable lag in the process of gathering and reporting such figures because publishers are often reluctant to disclose current sales trends. Therefore, completely current unit and dollar sales are not always available. The figures for trade and college text publishing in this chapter were obtained from the 2000 Veronis Suhler Media Merchant Bank's *Communications Industry Forecast,* an annual industry information publication.

19. Dan Lacy, "The Economics of Publishing, or Adam Smith and Literature," *The American Reading Public* (New York: Bowker, 1965), based on an issue of *Daedalus.*

20. Lacy, "Economics of Publishing."

21. See *Books in Print* (New York: R. R. Bowker, Inc., 1991).

22. Everette E. Dennis, Craig Lamay, and Edward C. Pease, eds., *Publishing Books* (New Brunswick, N.J.: Transaction, 1997), p. xiv. Two excellent recent books on publishing are Jason Epstein, *Book Business: Past, Present, and Future* (New York: Random House, 2001) and André Schiffrin, *The Business of Books: How the International Conglomerates Took Over Publishing and Changed the Way We Read* (New York: Verso Books, 2000).

23. Kinsella, "Publishing 2000," p. 16.

24. For a summary of the state of electronic publishing as of the end of 1999, see Steven Zeitchek, "Pixel Power," *Publisher's Weekly,* December 20, 1999, pp. 38–44.

Chapter 3

NEWSPAPERS, NEWS, AND THE NEWS MEDIA

Newspapers of the colonial period in the U.S. often emphasized news of commerce and government, as with this 1770 issue of *The Boston Gazette & Country Journal.*

ALMOST EVERYONE KNOWS THAT A NEWSPA-PER IS A PRINTED PRODUCT CONTAINING NEWS AND OTHER CONTENT THAT IS PREPARED AND disseminated daily or weekly. Newspapers, the oldest of the mass media, are still highly visible in their traditional form and they remain profoundly important—even in an era of interactive media. Just what they are, what they do, and how they do it—once considered settled issues—are now less than clear at the dawn of a digital age. Some contemporary critics say that newspapers are simply "platforms," or the technical means of packaging information in an ink-on-paper form, that contain news, articles of opinion, advertising, and other material—some of it entertainment. Some "newspapers" do not use paper or ink at all and are instead delivered online in electronic form. Clearly newspapers, once lone sentinels delivering news about both government and the private sector, are now part of a multimedia mix of magazines, radio, network television, cable television, digital communication, and other means of storing, packaging, and delivering information. Thus, today, newspapers are part of the *news media.* But in spite of many changes, they continue to play a leading role in the creation of content.

In the eyes of many, those who produce newspapers are still the most prestigious and serious of all journalists. The majority are high-caliber people devoted to the gathering, processing, and disseminating of reports on current situations and events. Some say that they provide a "gold standard" for news offered by other media. There are some grounds for such a characterization because newspapers do play an extremely important role in shaping the news; therefore, they are in the business of portraying society.

Moreover, some of the news seen or heard via other media is actually drawn from newspapers because of their large and often superior capacity for assembling information. Having been a part of America, and indeed the world, for over two centuries, newspapers are said to have *gravitas,* that is, intellectual and cultural weight in the functions they perform in society.

While they contain many other kinds of content, news is the primary concern of newspapers and it is offered in more depth and greater detail than anywhere else. That remains true no matter what form the medium takes—print or electronic. The same cannot really be said for most other media, even if they do offer news to their readers, viewers, listeners, and users.

NEWSPAPERS: A MEDIUM FOR THE MASS SOCIETY

Essentially, the story of newspapers begins with Gutenberg's press. Soon after it was invented, printed descriptions of important events began to appear. These brief documents were the forerunners of newspapers, and they were sent relatively quickly to distant places. For example, the story of the voyage and discoveries of Christopher Columbus spread through Spain in the form of printed copies of his own accounts within a few months of his return. From there, by word of mouth and private correspondence, descriptions of what was found (often grossly exaggerated) traveled relatively swiftly to all the major cities in Europe.

Enterprising "newsboys"— some of whom were girls— began to sell papers on the streets in the 1830s as part of the penny press proprietors' efforts to reach large audiences faster than conventional mail service would allow. Street selling of newspapers by children, still common in some countries, has virtually disappeared in the U.S., though house-to-house distribution continues.

THE FIRST NEWSPAPERS

Even during its earliest years, the printing press was used in a variety of ways to provide news on a regular basis. For example, in the mid-1500s, leaders in Venice regularly made available to the public printed news sheets about the war in Dalmatia. To receive a copy, Venetians had to pay a *gazetta*, a small coin. (The term "gazette," so frequently used in newspaper titles, comes from that source.) An obscure forerunner of what we would now call newspapers was apparently printed in Germany beginning in 1609, but not much is known about it. Better known is the *coranto* of the same period (from which we get the term "courant," which is also often used in the titles of modern newspapers. The coranto was a brief printed news sheet whose form originated in Holland. During the early 1600s, corantos were being published periodically for the commercial community in several countries. The oldest surviving example, printed in 1602, is shown on page 59. It could be regarded as the first newspaper printed in English, although it lacks certain features of true newspapers as we define them today.[1]

Newspapers of more modern times have seven important characteristics that distinguish them from other media. That is, a true newspaper of general circulation: (1) is published at least *weekly*, (2) is produced on paper by a *mechanical printing process* or *"delivered" online in digital form*, (3) is available (free or for a price) to *people of all walks of life*, (4) prints *news of general interest* rather than items on specialized topics such as religion or business, (5) is readable by *people of ordinary literacy*, (6) is *timely*, and (7) is *stable over time*.[2]

By this definition, the first true newspaper was the *Oxford Gazette* (later called the *London Gazette*). First published in 1665 under the authority of King Charles II, the *Gazette* appeared twice a week and continued publication well into the twentieth century. This was an "authorized" newspaper, which means that its content was controlled and pre-screened by the Crown.

The first *daily* newspaper in English, the *Daily Courant* (from *coranto*), began publication on London on March 11, 1702. A newspaper of high quality and considerable integrity, the *Courant* was not really a "mass" medium, in the contemporary sense of being read by a large and anonymous audience. It maintained a sophisticated literary style and appealed primarily to an affluent and well-educated elite. Its readers paid an annual subscription fee, but like the more popular newspapers that would come in the 1800s, it recovered some of its costs from advertising.[3]

After the late 1600s, censorship was rarely enforced in England. However, it was a different story in the American colonies. The colonial press remained tightly controlled by the Crown. It was thought that a newspaper could arouse *dissent*, and insurrection was always regarded as a possibility in Great Britain's remote colonies. Thus, control of printing presses continued, and it was wielded by the governor appointed by the Crown in each of the colonies. In spite of those efforts, however, colonial governments soon faced lively and independent newspapers.

THE PRESS IN THE AMERICAN COLONIES

It was the colonial press that established many of the features that characterize American newspapers of today. The growth of newspapers in the American colonies was tied closely to the cultural, economic, and political circumstances that existed at the time. Both the population and the commerce in the colonies grew steadily, creating a market for news of shipping and trading as well as a need for a limited amount of advertising. At the same time, political tensions in the colonies grew over such issues as taxes and control of trade. These widespread feelings were *news,* and the colonial papers began to write about them and to publish criticisms of the Crown's policies.

One of the more significant criticisms of the Crown appeared in Boston on September 25, 1690—in the first (and last) issue of a paper titled *Publick Occurrences Both Foreign and Domestick.* This four-page paper was the work of Benjamin Harris, a printer who had previously fled to Boston from London, where the authorities first jailed him and later seized one of his publications. In *Publick Occurrences,* Harris managed to insult both the Native Americans, who were allies of the British, and the French King. The Governor of Massachusetts immediately banned Harris's paper on the grounds that it was published "without authority" (prior to review by the Crown's representatives) and that it contained material that was disapproved of by the government.

While it survived only a single issue, *Publick Occurrences* was important, not only because it was the first paper printed in the colonies, but also because it *spoke out against the government.* However, since it was not published continuously, it does not really fit our definition of a newspaper. The honor of being the first that fits the definition began publishing in April 1804. It was the *Boston News-Letter*—a dull paper that was "published by authority," in April 1704. John Campbell, the publisher, was also the postmaster of Boston. As postmaster he was able to mail the paper without postal charges. For early colonial papers, a connection with a post office was almost indispensable because there really was no other way to distribute the paper. In fact, until the advent of steam engines and railroads, delivery beyond a local area would remain a problem.

ESTABLISHING TRADITIONS IN AMERICAN JOURNALISM

The conditions in which the American press operates today are very different from those of the colonial period. Newspapers are protected by the First Amendment's provision for *freedom of the press* and by a body of law developed over more than two centuries. Those protections are the result of a long chain of events that started during colonial times. As the 1700s progressed, colonial governors continued to suppress articles that criticized the government. However, their control was gradually subverted by rather bold printers and publishers in a long struggle marked by numerous conflicts and harsh repressions.[4]

The press as watchdog of the public interest. In 1721, James Franklin—an older brother of Benjamin Franklin—started his own paper, the *New England Courant.* It was something of a departure from the restrictive colonial tradition because it was not "published by authority." Moreover, it had no connection with a post office. The paper was aimed at a well-educated and prosperous elite. It appealed mainly to those who liked literary essays and controversial political opinions, but it also contained practical information, such as the shipping reports and news from nearby towns.

The *Courant* was the first newspaper in the colonies to "crusade" on, what the editor defined as, a public issue. During an outbreak of smallpox in Boston, it argued strongly against the newly invented medical procedure of smallpox inoculation. From a medical standpoint, its position turned out to be wrong. Nevertheless, using the newspaper to *speak out* against a situation seen as harmful to the public began an important tradition. Increasingly, American newspapers would become *watchdogs of the public interest,* a role that they vigorously maintain today.

The principle of freedom of the press. Another truly significant tradition of the American press began to develop early in the 1700s. It grew out of a court trial that pitted editor John Peter Zenger against William Cosby, Governor of New York. The outcome helped to establish the principle of freedom of the press in the American colonies. Zenger was persuaded (and funded) by a group of businessmen to establish a newspaper, the *New York Weekly Journal.* Their purpose was to have a paper in opposition to the officially authorized *New York Gazette.* Zenger began publishing the *Journal* in 1734, and his paper ran articles openly critical of the Governor and his policies. That was too much for Governor Cosby, and he had Zenger clapped in jail on a charge of *seditious libel.* The legal definition of *sedition* is to promote disaffection with government, that is, to incite people to revolt against constituted authority. *Libel,* in legal terms, means deliberately "publishing" (making public) untruths about a person. However, under British law at the time, it was seditious intent that was considered the major offense and the central issue of the case. It really did not matter whether or not the material published by the defendant was true.

Zenger was brought to trial in 1735 before a jury of his fellow colonials. Technically, the Governor's case seemed *airtight.* Zenger had, in fact, broken the existing law. Defending Zenger was Andrew Hamilton, a distinguished attorney provided by Zenger's backers. Hamilton's strategy was unique; he freely admitted that Zenger had published articles criticizing the government. However, he argued with great conviction that the articles were *true,* and that in spite of what the law said, *no one should be punished for printing the truth.*

Hamilton's argument convinced the jury that they should ignore the judge's instructions to convict Zenger. They declared him not guilty. It was a stunning upset and the Governor was furious. Zenger's trial did not change the law, but it established an important principle: *The press should be allowed to criticize government.* That idea would eventually find its way into the First Amendment to the Constitution of the United States, which would be formulated a half-century later.

In retrospect, the colonial papers were small and limited in many ways. Their news was seldom up to date, they were published infrequently, and they were slow to reach subscribers. They were also limited by existing technology. The hand press used by Benjamin Franklin and others in the late 1700s was little different from the one used by Johannes Gutenberg in the mid-1400s. Paper was still made from rags, not wood, and was both expensive and always in short supply. Compounding the problem, literacy rates were low by comparison with later centuries. We noted earlier that advertising is an important source of financial support for newspapers. However, before the Industrial Revolution and the resulting rise in consumerism, there really was not a great need for advertising.

Another limiting factor was that the colonial papers were aimed at comparatively well-educated and relatively affluent subscribers, who made up only a small part of society. The colonial papers were very expensive, which made them *unavailable to the common people.* Around the time of the American Revolution, a newspaper might cost between $6 and $10 a year—about as much as a worker's salary for one or two weeks. In today's terms, that would be like paying several hundred dollars for a year's subscription. Few people would be willing to pay that much. However, in spite of these many limitations, the colonial press played a vital role in establishing a number of traditions in journalism that were to become an important part of the emerging American press.

NEWSPAPERS FOR THE COMMON PEOPLE

By the early 1800s, the Industrial Revolution had started. Innovators were beginning to solve the technological and other problems of printing—including price and distribution—in order to provide widely circulated newspapers for the public. It was a time when all kinds of new machines were being driven by steam power to accomplish tasks with astonishing rapidity and uniformity. The printing press was no exception. With the old screw-type press, a well-trained team of two printers working full speed could put out only a few hundred sheets per day at best. By 1830, steam-powered rotary presses were introduced. They were a truly significant advance in technology. Even the earliest could produce four thousand sheets *per hour,* printed on both sides.[5]

THE EMERGENCE OF THE PENNY PRESS

On September 3, 1833, a strange little newspaper appeared on the streets of New York City. It was published by Benjamin Day and called the *New York Sun.* Its masthead carried the slogan "It Shines for All." That slogan was somewhat misleading. The *Sun* was not designed to appeal to everyone, but specifically to the *less sophisticated.* Day offered his readers a different kind of news—the incidental happenings of New York life. The *Sun* was filled with human-interest items about common people. In its first issue, on page one, Day declared: "The object of the paper is to lay before the public, at a price within the means of everyone, all the news of the day, and at the same time afford an advantageous medium for advertising."

Day began an important newspaper tradition when he hired the very first salaried *reporter,* who went to the local courts each morning and wrote lively stories about local happenings, with an emphasis on crime, human interest, accidents, and humorous anecdotes. (The term "reporter" is derived from those who record court proceedings.) Another feature of this new paper was its *mode of delivery.* It was sold on the streets by newsboys for only a penny. This method worked well. These *newsboys* (some of whom apparently were girls dressed as boys) bought the papers in lots of a hundred for sixty-seven cents. If they sold the entire hundred, they earned thirty-three cents, which was quite a profit for a youngster at the time.

One of the most important features of the *Sun* was the way it made a profit. The penny that buyers paid for their copy did not even recover the costs of production. The *Sun* made its profit by *selling advertising space* for a great variety of products and services. This was possible at the time because the new factories were producing a greater variety of goods, and new retail establishments were selling to larger and larger markets.

The paper was an instant success. Soon it was selling more than eight thousand copies per day. From there its sales doubled, and within three years it was selling an astonishing thirty thousand copies daily! Other journalists were astounded; they scrambled to imitate Day's model and within a few months the Sun had competitors. The mass press became reality. Together, all the competing newspapers that adopted Day's basic formula were known as the *penny press.*

The penny papers had very distinctive characteristics that made them completely different from the colonial press. They were vulgar, sensational, and trivial in many respects. However, publishers soon began to provide increasing amounts of basic economic and political news as well as editorial viewpoints regarding public matters. As they developed, then, the penny newspapers brought at least some sig-

During the Civil War, newspapers sent hundreds of reporters to the fields of action where they lived and traveled with military forces. Top: Reporters gather at the *New York Herald's* field headquarters. Below: A few photographers, notably Matthew Brady, captured the grimmer side of the war in their vivid photographs, but newspapers lacked the mechanical processes to reproduce photos. It was not until decades later that photos were commonly used in newspapers, thanks to the zinc engraving. Nonetheless, Brady and others provided a gripping documentary record for the archives and later use.

nificant firsthand information and ideas to large numbers of people who had not been readers of newspapers up to that time.

THE IMPACT OF SOCIETY ON THE GROWTH OF NEWSPAPERS

During the 1800s, three great changes took place in American society that had significant influences on the growth of the nation's newspaper industry. One was the *rapid expansion of the population.* The second change was the remarkable *evolution of technology,* which increased enormously the ability of journalists to gather, transmit, print, and distribute news. The third was the influence of the *Civil War,* which stimulated a great demand for news and the development of increasingly efficient systems for getting it to newspapers and from there to subscribers.

The rate of population growth in the United States during the nineteenth century was unprecedented in history. During the two decades preceding the Civil War (1840–1860), millions of people arrived, especially from northern Europe. Most settled in the eastern states and the Great Lakes region. At the same time, steady streams of internal migrants moved westward, settling along a continuously

Newspaper editors have been depicted as mythic figures in some artistic works, which calls attention to their seminal role as information agenda-setters and opinion leaders, as seen in Thomas Hart Benton's 1946 painting, "New England Editor."

The Hayden Collection.
Charles Henry Fund
Courtesy, Museum of Fine Arts, Boston.

expanding frontier, establishing new towns and cities where newspapers were needed. Even higher levels of immigration, especially from southern and eastern Europe, came during the last half of the century. People were needed to occupy the vast lands that had been acquired from France, Mexico, and the Native Americans. As these new residents learned to read English, they subscribed in ever-increasing numbers to daily newspapers.

As the century progressed, the industrial and mechanical arts flourished at a remarkable pace. Beginning about 1839, ever larger and more elaborate steam-powered rotary presses could print, cut, and fold thousands of finished newspapers per hour. Cheap paper to feed these presses was being made from wood as early as 1867. In another great advance in technology, telegraph wires along the rail lines linked major cities and made possible the rapid transmission of news stories to editors' desks. Soon *wire services* would be established and newspapers in all parts of the country would begin to receive a flow of stories from the "lightening lines." The rapid expansion of the railroads and steamboat lines also promoted the growth of newspapers. Now daily papers printed in the city could be delivered across substantial distances so that people in surrounding communities could receive the news in a timely manner. The ancient dream of conquering both time and distance with an effective medium of communication was becoming a reality.

The Civil War enormously stimulated the development of newspapers. Its battles resulted in terrible slaughter—the most devastating loss of life our country has ever known. People on both sides of the conflict were desperate for reports of the battles and news about the fate of their loved ones. The hundreds of reporters in the field often devised ingenious methods to get their reports out ahead of their competitors. Faster and faster steam presses across the nation churned out millions of copies daily.

By the end of the 1800s, the newspaper was a technologically sophisticated and complex mass medium. Newspaper publishers had at their disposal a rapid telegraphic news-gathering system, cheap paper, linotype, color printing, cartoons, electric presses, and, above all, a corps of *skilled journalists.* The newspaper had settled into more or less standard format, very much like the one that exists today. Its features included not only domestic and foreign news but also a financial page, letters to the editor, sports news, society reports, "women's pages," classified sections, and advice to the lovelorn. Newspapers were complex, extremely competitive, and very popular. Furthermore, they had *no competition* from other media.

NEWSPAPERS AS CULTURAL INNOVATION

Scholars who study patterns of social and cultural change in societies have noted that inventions introduced into a society, or items borrowed from other societies, follow a typical pattern as they are taken up—that is, adopted and used. Specifically, when the proportion of the population in a society who begin to use a particular innovation is plotted against time, a *curve of adoption* is described. Figure 3.1 shows the adoption curve for newspapers in terms of the proportion of U.S. households who subscribed to a daily paper over succeeding decades. The classic curve of adoption is an S-shaped pattern that starts slowly, rises swiftly, and then levels off. As Figure 3.1 shows, after a slow start during the early 1800s, subscriptions to daily newspapers per household did grow sharply during the last decades of that century, reaching a peak early in the 1900s and lasting until about the time of World War I.

The curve of adoption shows that by the time of World War I, circulation had grown to a point where many households in the United States were subscribing to both a morning and an afternoon paper. Thus, during the early decades of the new century, newspapers enjoyed a kind of *golden age.* But, as the curve indicates, it would not last. Once newer media arrived, newspapers entered a decline in subscriptions per household—a trend that continues to this day. As a consequence of declining subscriptions, there has been a corresponding pattern of decline in the *number* of daily newspapers published in the United States. During the 1800s, as more and more states were admitted to the union, and as the population grew—along with the number of towns and cities—the number of newspapers continued to grow. But, as Figure 3.2 shows, after 1910, when the country had over 2,200 English-language and nearly 400 foreign-language dailies, the number of papers actually *started to decline.* Some papers merged; some dailies became weeklies; others suspended publication completely. Since then, the U.S. Census reports that the number of daily newspapers that are still published declined from 2,042 in 1920 to just over 1,500 in 2000.[6]

As Figure 3.1 shows, the *golden age of the newspaper* was between 1910 and 1930. Subscriptions per household were twice what they are today. The great decline was a consequence of two major factors: After 1930, the *costs of news gathering* and all other aspects of publishing began to increase. Furthermore, *competition for advertising dollars* from radio, and eventually television, rose relentlessly. Consequently, papers began to fail financially or were purchased by their rivals to consolidate production and other facilities. These trends have continued to the present time and are likely to persist into the future. The result is fewer newspapers that have fewer readers.

TYPES OF CONTEMPORARY NEWSPAPERS

Contemporary American newspapers come in many types and sizes. But most, past and present, have shared at least one characteristic: They are very *local* in their orientation and coverage. Although most American dailies cover national and international news, they emphasize community and regional events with local news and

trends in media use

FIGURE 3.1

The Curve of Adoption of Daily Newspapers in the U.S., 1850–2000

Subscriptions to daily newspapers rose at an increasing pace during the last half of the nineteenth century. Newspaper usage peaked around the time of World War I. It was the medium's golden age. Later, radio, magazines, and television offered competition and subscriptions declined steadily.

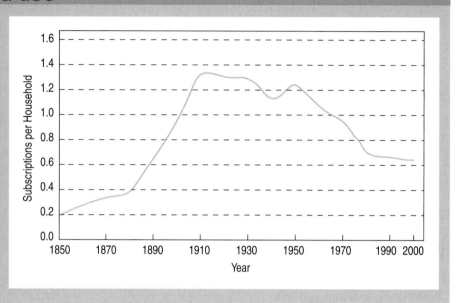

concerns. The United States does have a few national newspapers—for example, *USA Today,* the *Christian Science Monitor,* and the *Wall Street Journal.* In addition, the *New York Times,* and to some extent, the *Washington Post* are read nationwide, although both depend on their respective cities for most of their readers. Both carry at least some news of their city on the front page and devote a section to their region. Other large American papers, such as the *Boston Globe* and the *Seattle Times,* are regional papers with a distinctive local stamp.

We can divide almost all of America's thousands of newspapers into two very broad categories—*general-news* papers intended for readers within their area, and *specialized-news* papers aimed at a particular kind of reader. These types of papers are aimed at readers of specific minority groups, those of a particular religious faith, and/or people with a well-focused interest. Both categories of papers can be further classified in terms of how *often* they publish (daily, weekly, etc.) and their *circulations*—that is, how many people they reach. Using these criteria, most of America's newspapers fall into one of the following categories.

Metropolitan dailies. Newspapers in the nation's largest cities have circulations (copies sold) that usually exceed 250,000 and a potential readership several times larger. Most metropolitan newspapers are printed full size—usually fourteen by twenty-two inches with six or seven columns—and they usually publish seven days a week. Their Sunday editions typically devote considerable space to books, travel, the arts, personalities, and similar topics. Examples are the *Chicago Tribune* and the *Los Angeles Times.* Such papers reach readers not only within their metropolitan area but also across a large, multistate area. Others, such as the *Kansas City Star,* serve a more limited region around their cities. Still others, like the *Emporia* (Kan.) *Gazette,*

trends in media use

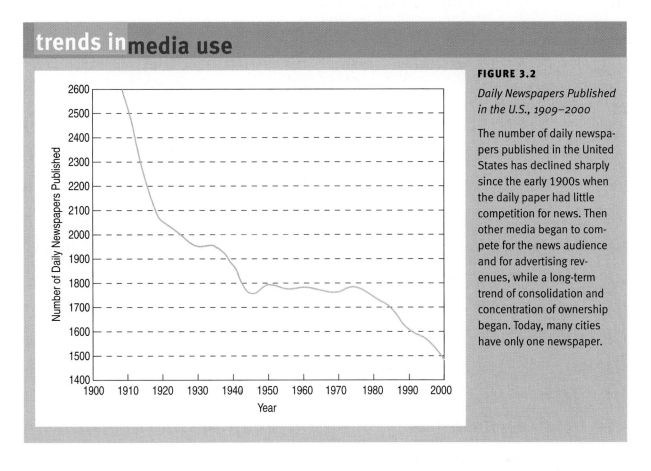

FIGURE 3.2

Daily Newspapers Published in the U.S., 1909–2000

The number of daily newspapers published in the United States has declined sharply since the early 1900s when the daily paper had little competition for news. Then other media began to compete for the news audience and for advertising revenues, while a long-term trend of consolidation and concentration of ownership began. Today, many cities have only one newspaper.

have a primarily local readership. All, however, are distributed house-to-house by carriers, on the street in coin boxes or newsstands, and occasionally by mail.

The major dailies include news, features, entertainment, sports, and opinion. They rely on the wire services for much of their national staffs (usually based in Washington, D.C.) and foreign correspondents in important cities around the world. Several have set up special investigative teams, such as the Spotlight Team of the *Boston Globe*, who put together detailed analyses of local or even national issues, problems, or scandals. Much of the content of the major dailies originates from syndicates.

Some metropolitan dailies are *tabloids*. Technically, the term refers mainly to a special size—twelve by sixteen inches, with five columns. At one time a tabloid newspaper was one of low quality and sensational content. The big-city tabloids were usually splashy, designed to capture attention and high street sales with large bold headlines. Today, the distinctions are less clear because tabloids (in the sense of size and format) include papers that mix sensationalism and professionalism (*New York Post* and *Boston Herald*) as well as the more sedate *Christian Science Monitor*.

Quite another category of tabloids are those displayed and sold at the check-out counter in supermarkets, and that feature unusual and bizarre stories often defying the imagination. Examples are the *National Enquirer,* the *Star,* and the even more extreme *Weekly World News.* Despite their tasteless content, these tabloids earn a great deal of money.

The *USA Today* newsroom in Arlington, Virginia, pioneered satellite links to news sources and printing plants, and continues to be a model newsroom in the digital age.

Medium-sized and small dailies. Newspapers in this category have more modest circulations (50,000–100,000), but are often physically hefty. They may have fewer of their own editorial resources than the major dailies, but they use wire service news and subscribe to syndicates that provide much of their feature material.

Small dailies have a circulation under 50,000. They are even more locally focused than medium-sized dailies and sometimes are meant to be read along with a larger nearby regional paper. They are usually small, relative to other dailies, and use less material from external sources.

Non-daily newspapers. Sometimes called *community* or *grassroots* press, the weeklies were once exclusively rural or suburban publications. They ranged from suburban papers that featured lifestyle stories (for example, on apartment living or how to fund day-care centers) to small country papers dominated by local events and country correspondence. During the 1980s, an increasing number of new urban weeklies were founded. Some concentrate on their neighborhood; others are sophisticated, cosmopolitan publications that review such topics as politics and the arts. Urban weeklies like New York City's *Village Voice,* Chicago's *Reader,* and San Francisco's *Bay Guardian* are mainly supplementary reading for people who are already informed about news and public affairs from other media.

Free-distribution newspapers. Papers that were originally called "shoppers" by the commercial press have been published for decades. Beginning in the 1980s, many of these papers took a more aggressive stance in competing with traditional daily and weekly newspapers. They added more news and entertainment material as well as calendars of local events and various features. Many have been willing to print publicity material for local organizations and groups without much editing. These papers, once dismissed by the mainstream press, have become formidable *competitors for advertising.* Indeed, a number of conventional papers have begun their own free-distribution papers. By 2000, free-circulation dailies, often distributed in conjunction with subway and other public transport systems, were being developed.

The ethnic press. During those periods of our history when massive numbers of immigrants were pouring into the United States, the *foreign-language press* was substantial. In colonial times, French papers were common. During the late nineteenth century, German and Scandinavian papers prospered. But as the older immigrant groups assimilated into the general population, foreign-language papers tended to die out.

Today, both foreign-language papers and papers written in English—but aimed at a particular ethnic group—make up the ethnic press. Because of continuing immigration from Mexico and Latin American countries, the number of Spanish papers is increasing. However, many of the papers serving racial and cultural minorities are now published in English rather than in other languages.

The African-American press began in the nineteenth century. Today, the United States has several black-oriented newspapers, including the *Baltimore Afro-American,* New York City's *Amsterdam News,* and the *Chicago Defender.* Most of these newspapers emerged because of segregation in the white press, which virtually ignored African-American people and their concerns. For many years it was difficult for blacks to get jobs within the mainstream media. By and large, the press itself took steps to reverse this situation. Many industry and professional newspaper organizations have developed special programs for recruiting and training minorities, although many fall short of their goals. There has also been greater emphasis on reporting on the minority community, although many media critics consider this coverage inconsistent.

The urban newsstand offers an array of international and ethnic newspapers, although online Web sites maintained by the papers also make them more easily accessible.

Other specialized papers. The list of specialized papers can go on and on, including industrial and commercial newspapers, labor newspapers, religious newspapers, and those serving environmental interests, people pursuing unconventional lifestyles, special hobbyists, members of voluntary associations, and of course college students. There are even prison newspapers. Some of these specialized papers are supported not by advertising but by membership fees or an organization's profits.

DEVELOPMENTS THAT SHAPED TODAY'S NEWSPAPERS

Three important developments began in the 1800s that helped shape today's newspapers. One was the development of *wire services,* mentioned earlier, that bring to local newspapers a daily flow of news reports from beyond their community. The second is made up of a number of *syndicates*—commercial groups that contract with publishers to provide a great many of the features that make up the content of today's newspapers. A third is the changing *pattern of ownership* that characterized American newspapers all during the 1900s.

THE GROWTH OF WIRE SERVICES AND SYNDICATES

Two kinds of national organizations supply newspapers with much of their daily content. These are the *wire services* and various *feature syndicates.* If you doubt the extent to which modern papers depend on these sources, take your local newspaper, clip all the stories that come from wire services and the material provided by feature syndicates, and set the clippings aside. You will probably be left with only stories from your local community, a lot of advertisements, and little more. Thus, even though most newspapers are still geographically local, they depend on the wire services to bring them regional, national, and international news. They also depend on syndicates to provide cartoons, comic strips, columns, crossword puzzles, and other familiar features of the daily paper.

A major advantage of these two kinds of services is *lower cost.* For example, the cost of supporting reporters in many cities would be prohibitive. And hiring a full-time comic-strip artist would be well beyond the means of most small newspapers and even some large ones. But a wire-service reporter can send stories to many papers, greatly cutting the costs to the papers. A syndicate can employ a comic-strip artist and sell the strip to papers all across the country, also greatly reducing the amount each paper is charged.

CHANGING PATTERNS OF OWNERSHIP

A major trend that has shaped today's newspapers is the *consolidation of their ownership.* This has occurred for several reasons. One is the fact that—even though they continue to earn a great deal of money—newspapers have lost the enviable position they held earlier as the *only* source of news. They now compete for advertising dollars with other media. Although newspaper profits are almost *twice* what is being earned per dollar of investment in the nation's five hundred leading corporations, their subscriptions are shrinking.

The growth of chains.   The profitability of American papers is due largely to the buying up of individual papers. Like the disappearance of the "mom and pop" hamburger stand (and the spread of the golden arches), the independently owned newspaper is very close to extinction. Economic forces—soaring costs in labor, material, and services—have led to a great expansion of chain ownership of newspapers. For example, by 2000 the Gannett Corporation owned daily newspapers as well as television and radio stations in the United States, Guam, and the Virgin Islands. Gannett, which owns *USA Today,* one of the nation's largest newspapers, also owns *Sports Weekly, Sunday Magazine,* a printing company, "new (or digital) media," offset-printing firms, and other holdings. Such media empires also own other kinds of businesses.

Determining the relative size and scope of a newspaper chain or group is more difficult than it may seem. Some critics are fond of counting the number of newspapers owned, whereas others look more to circulation figures. What is easier to assess is the pattern of change over time. Going back to 1920, during the period when newspapers were enjoying a virtual monopoly on the news industry, there were only 31 chains or newspaper groups in the United States, and each owned on the average fewer than 5 newspapers. By 1960, there were 109 chains and they controlled an average of 5 newspapers each. By 1986, the number of chains had risen to 127 with an average of 9 dailies per chain. Looked at another way, the number of actual papers owned by chains rose from 153 in 1920 to just over 1,200 by 1990. Today, chains own about 75 percent of all the daily newspapers published in the United States.[7]

The implications of concentrated ownership.   For many critics, the change in newspaper ownership has ominous implications. As Richard McCord points out, those who established the chains often used dubious practices and harsh means.[8] Moreover, chain ownership implies an ability on the part of the group to control the news and thereby (potentially) shape how readers think about events. Another troublesome factor is that most communications enterprises have in the past been owned by companies that specialize in communications, although other corporations have moved into the field. Media critics warn that in a few years a handful of corporate conglomerates might have a stranglehold on the nation's newspapers.

There are three reasons why control by such *absentee owners* is more alarming than dominance by large communication industries. One is that absentee owners, with far-flung and diverse economic interests, have *little commitment* to the local communities that the newspapers serve. Second, they are not likely to continue the practice of expensive but critical journalistic *watchdog traditions.* And third, a conglomerate is designed primarily to make profits on "products," and news may come to be defined as only *one of many products* in a conglomerate's portfolio.

When all is said and done, however, the big question is whether the trend toward consolidation of newspaper ownership will actually restrict debate and robust discussion of issues in such a way that it will change the *missions* and *quality* of the American press. In the days of William Randolph Hearst, the corporate offices in New York City dominated his chain's papers. His move into yellow journalism *did* change his papers' mission and quality. Today, however, only a few newspaper groups issue direct orders to local editors about editorial policies. However, they do firmly control finances and have generally high expectations about local newspapers' profits.

Overall, the implications of chain ownership remain an *open question.* At some point in the future, Americans may find that the papers they read have about as much local autonomy in what they print as does a Kentucky Fried Chicken franchise in what it cooks. On the other hand, as we have seen, the search in the past decades has not been for ways to dominate reader's opinions regarding political or moral positions. Their search instead has focused on ways to *maximize profits* by giving readers more of what *they* want and think they need. In other words, newspaper content in a profit-oriented economic system is *audience-driven.* Although that may limit corporate control of news, it may also mean that, in the search for greater profits, the focus on entertainment will increase at the expense of providing information to the public.

GATHERING, SELECTING, PROCESSING, AND PRESENTING THE NEWS

Defining what is news can be complex. Hundreds of definitions have been advanced since scholars began writing about the topic. For our purposes, however, we can define news in a very simple way: *News is current or fresh knowledge about an event or subject that is gathered, processed, and disseminated via a medium to a significant number of interested people.* That act of gathering, processing, and disseminating such fresh information can be called *the news process.* One key to understanding newspapers—and indeed all of the news media that compete with them—is to examine the news process in some detail.

The news process begins with *surveillance* of the news environment. Reporters and others monitor key people and places where newsworthy events are likely to take place. The news process continues when initial accounts of what happened arrive at the newsroom. There, the first thing that happens is that they are sorted and selected by a process called *gatekeeping.* That is, some reports are immediately discarded, while others are retained for further consideration. Those retained will be carefully edited to make sure that they can be understood by the public and are factually correct. Whether they actually are retained in the final selection will depend on whether they are judged to be either *important* or *interesting* to the readers, and whether there is enough space available. At this selection stage, *news values* play a key role.

When all stories have been edited and judged for their importance and interest, the final arrangement of news stories and other content in the day's edition is designed. Some stories thought to be important or of the most interest to the audience will be placed on the front page with a large headline. Others receive less prominent postioning. This pattern is also used in the sports section, financial pages, and so on. In each section, stories judged not to be very important are assigned very little space and are positioned toward the end. In broadcast or online news much the same happens. The *lead* stories come first in the broadcast or on the Web site and are allotted more time or space. In online media, news values play a role that is similar to those in the case of traditional newspapers.

Thus, in all of "the press", the same basic news process is used for deciding what information will be presented daily to the public. The *agenda-setting process,* in which decisions are made about the final format of the paper or broadcast, has important implications for how readers, viewers, and listeners, as well as policymakers, judge the significance of daily news accounts. Therefore, the agenda-setting process will be discussed in greater detail in a later section of this chapter.

THE SURVEILLANCE FUNCTION

A broad idea that places the news process in perspective is the *surveillance function* of the medium. The main idea here is that news providers keep an eye on what is going on, and through the use of the steps of the news process described previously, newspapers give reliable reports about what is deemed to be important. Thus, citizens supposedly have *trustworthy information* enabling them to make *informed decisions* about events and issues that are of significance to them as individuals and to society as a whole. This idealized interpretation of the function of the press in our democracy is the justification for, according to news media, special protections and privileges not extended to other kinds of profit-making businesses.

If the news process works well—that is, if the information presented is reasonably *complete* and *accurate* as a representation of reality—the public gets a valid picture of what is actually going on. However, as this chapter will make clear, there are many reasons to believe that the news presented by the press has only a *limited correspondence* with what is actually happening in the real world.

Recognizing the limitations of the news process, as we do in this chapter, is not the same as condemning it. To show that the reports about what is going on are not entirely complete and accurate is not to say that journalists and our news media *deliberately* set out to mislead us. The press may deserve criticism in many cases, but the fact is that such distortions are an *inevitable* and *unintended product* of the forces, factors, and conditions that all of the news media must operate within to survive. A major purpose of this section, therefore, is to examine the news process impartially in order to provide a better understanding of how well, or how poorly, it actually performs its surveillance function, and why.

Categories for surveillance. Reality, of course, is the ultimate source of all news. The problem is reality's mind-boggling complexity. In the words of the philosopher William James, the world is a great "blooming and buzzing confusion." Thus, each day's news is drawn from a reality made up of an enormous variety of issues, events, conflicts, trends, and a host of other happenings. But whatever the perplexing nature of reality, the first steps in the news process are that it must be *observed, understood, interpreted,* and *recorded* by reporters whose task is to prepare initial comprehensible descriptions for public consumption.

To understand this initial stage of the news process, we need first to look at how practicing journalists reduce the complex world to a limited number of *categories* so as to divide up the task of surveillance into an orderly division of labor. A brief look at each of these categories will help in understanding the initial stage of news gathering. The resulting division of labor has grown out of the practical experience of journalists over many years.

One important set of categories is the somewhat natural division of *geographic territories.*[9] Thus, facts for news stories come from events that are *local, regional, national,* or *international.* Each of these rather imprecise territorial definitions refers to rather different types of facts that hold different levels of interest for particular segments of the public. These preferences have become well understood by professional journalists, who balance their news reports to meet the needs of these different audiences.

Within each territory there are additional well-understood classifications based on *specialized topics.* Typical of such topics are politics, the economy, science, health, education, sports, fashions, weather, entertainment, space, crime, and so on. These topics play a key role in structuring the nature of the surveillance engaged in by the various media. In a digital world, the geographic boundaries of news merge with those that are topical or specialized. It is possible now to reach people everywhere who are interested in almost any narrow subject.

Still another broad category has to do with the *organizations* from where facts for developing new stories are often obtained. Thus, at a national level, reporters are specifically assigned to cover the White House, the Pentagon, or Congress. Assignments at the local level may be the police department, city hall, or the local university. Each category and subcategory represents a different focus of attention in the ongoing activities of society, and each represents a different subject matter and degree of interest to various segments of the population. Using categories and subcategories as the basis for division of labor in a news organization allows reporters to become specialized and thereby *expert* in one or more categories. Thus, some reporters confine themselves to international affairs—or even to a particular area of the world. Others focus exclusively on a particular topic or kind of activity, such as fashion, science, or education. This kind of specialization helps reporters develop unique skills and perspectives in locating, understanding, and writing about the important facts that are central to the territory, activity, or organization over which they exercise surveillance.

A rather different kind of distinction among news stories can be made, within any of the previously mentioned categories, on the basis of the *extension of the story through time.* Some news happenings are of short duration and are essentially

Jay T. Harris, Chairman and Publisher, *San Jose Mercury News*, San Jose, California*

Jay T. Harris is an acknowledged leader in the newspaper industry, his picture having graced the cover of *Editor & Publisher* in September 2000. His leadership in the respected Knight Ridder newspaper group has included a stint as assistant to the chairman, editor of the *Philadelphia Daily News,* and publisher of the highly successful and award-winning *San Jose Mercury News.* He also served as assistant dean of the Medill School of Journalism at Northwestern University from which he has a master's degree in journalism.

Q. How did you first get involved in the newspaper field?

A. That was in the late 1960s when I was a college student at Lincoln University in Pennsylvania. I was editor of my college paper, but really got involved in the first place because the campus paper was not doing the job it needed to in covering campus political activism during those years. The summer following my junior year I had a reporting internship at the *Wilmington* (Del.) *News-Journal* papers. I continued working there—even though the paper was twenty-five miles from campus—on weekends and holidays 'til I graduated. Then, they hired me as a general assignment reporter.

Q. Once you got this job, what else inspired your continued interest and inspiration for journalism and newspapers?

*Resigned March 2001

insights from
MEDIA LEADERS

A. As a young reporter at the *News-Journal,* I was ultimately and permanently captured by the realization that through newspapers I could help improve the lives of people and the health of our communities and nation.

Q. What have been the main influences that have led you to your current position in San Jose, the Knight Ridder Company, and the industry generally?

A. Well, there are personal and professional influences. Personally, my career has been bolstered by the support and understanding of my family, willingness to work hard and to take risks in the pursuit of professional growth. And, of course, a lust for new ideas and insights. Professionally, I've had some influential mentors and role models including Bill Cole, the longtime dean of the Medill School of Journalism; Bob Maynard, a distinguished journalist who was editor and publisher of the *Oakland* (Calif.) *Tribune;* Gerald Sass, a foundation executive at the former Gannett Foundation and Freedom Forum; Zack Stalberg, editor of the *Philadelphia Daily News;* and two leaders at Knight Ridder—the late former chairman and CEO James Batten and his successor, Tony Ridder.

Q. What is your take on the current state and probable future of newspapers?

A. As a general proposition they are better journalistically than they have ever been. And those that are in

one-time events. For example, at the local level, a house may burn down or an explosion may occur. Such events provide *spot news*—a staple of the industry. Spot stories have no history. The event occurs; it provides facts for a news story; the account is prepared; it is disseminated to the public; and that is the end.

Other time-linked stories can be classified as *developing.* They occur in stages, like the acts of a play, and new stories are generated periodically as the action or situation unfolds. Eventually, however, each story comes to an end and is no longer newsworthy to the same degree. An example at the national level was the highly publicized case of Elian Gonzalez, the six-year-old Cuban boy who was rescued off the coast of Florida in 1999 and became the subject of a legal and political tug of war in 2000. One aspect or another of what began as a simple rescue mission made developing news for months as fresh information became available. The story that began as spot news dragged on as developing news for months. Some commentators say that it

economically healthy or noncompetitive markets are doing quite well as businesses. But the competition newspapers face—for the time of readers and the business of advertisers—is more intense than ever. Periodically, newspapers that are part of public companies face cost-reduction pressures as those companies work to produce the earnings growth the markets and shareholders require. *For the foreseeable future, newspapers will remain an important and vital part of the communications industry.*

Q. The "death of print" is occasionally predicted, which raises questions about the long-term future of the newspaper. Will we likely see newspapers on the scene by the year 2020?

A. Yes, newspapers will definitely be part of the news and information arena in 2020 and for years thereafter. Increasingly, I believe, they will be:

- part of a larger array of news and information services offered by publishing companies;

- tailored to serve the needs, interests, and preferences of individual readers or groups of readers;

- used more for context, depth, and analysis;

- used less as a source for static information such as stock prices and sports scores.

Q. Given this optimistic assessment, what, in your opinion, is the best pathway for a satisfying and successful career in newspaper work?

A. Come to the profession with a broad, liberal education and a commitment to continuing intellectual growth. Work your way to an aspect of newspaper work that you find personally and professionally fulfilling. Know what you value and what professional and personal values are most important to you. These will be your most useful and reliable guides throughout your career.

Q. How would you rate newspaper publishing as a career choice based on job satisfaction, compensation, and long-term prospects?

A. Newspaper work—like other creative careers—should be entered because it offers something you *want* to do. That said, for those who are successful, a career in newspapers can provide enormous personal and professional satisfaction. It pays relatively well and can be the foundation for a fulfilling career.

Q. What is the most satisfying aspect of work in this field?

A. The most satisfying aspects of newspaper work are the satisfaction to be derived from working as part of a team of creative professionals and the influence newspapers can wield in the pursuit of public good.

played a role in the 2000 presidential election when George W. Bush narrowly defeated Al Gore in Florida, winning the contest—after a Supreme Court ruling.

A rather different time-related category is *continuing* news. Here, there is no clear beginning or end, but only an ongoing series of related happenings. Each time some related event occurs, stories can be generated about the ongoing process. A good example is the issue of abortion. Protests, counterprotests, court cases, and political debates about the right of women to have abortions have provided a continuing theme around which stories have been developed for more than a decade. As the issue of the "abortion pill" came to the United States, it seemed clear that the story would unlikely come to an end any time soon.

Another category that is somewhat time-related can be seen in the distinction between *hard news* and *soft news*. The former is what most ordinary people think of as news. Something actually happens on a particular day—a bank is robbed, a murder is

Gatekeeping Theory

explaining
MEDIA EFFECTS

This theory addresses the question of how particular news stories come to be included in the daily newspaper or newscast, while others are rejected or ignored. Basically, it comes down to decisions made by editors or others whose responsibility it is to define and design what will be included in today's newspaper or broadcast.

The need to select a particular lineup of stories from those available begins with the fact that reporters, stringers, or other newsgatherers constantly feed into editorial offices or newsrooms huge numbers of accounts and stories of what is happening in the community, region, society, and world. Far more stories are generated than can be included. Therefore, some system for *screening, decision-making,* and *selecting* must be in place to sort out what should (or should not) be reported to the public. That process has come to be known as *gatekeeping.*

The term "gatekeeping" was first used to label screening, decision-making, and selecting as a result of a study conducted for the government during World War II. With some 15 million men and women in uniform, this huge military force consumed a large portion of the country's meats. Consequently, systems of food rationing were imposed on the civilian population. With meats in short supply, it was important to persuade civilians to switch to using such meat cuts as kidneys, liver, and hearts—which are high in nutritional value but not eaten very much by Americans. By persuading people to buy and cook such organ meats, the more traditional cuts could be reserved for those in the military service.

The federal government sponsored a research project designed to determine how that goal might be achieved. Kurt Lewin, a distinguished social psychologist, conducted a study of how decisions were made by housewives to select specific kinds of meats. He used the analogy of a *gate,* that is letting certain products through to the family table and keeping others out. Lewin found that knowing who the *gatekeepers* were, and the *criteria* they used in making their selections, enabled him to design persuasive campaigns to increase the selection and consumption of organ meats—while maintaining the nutrition of the civilian population. In time, the term "gatekeeping" came to be applied to a variety of decision-making functions, including the selection of news stories. Essentially, the theory states this:

1. In exercising its "surveillance" function, every news medium, whether newspaper, radio, television, or other, has a *very large number* of news stories brought to its attention daily by "wire" services, reporters, and other sources.

2. Due to a variety of practical considerations, only a *limited amount of time or space* is available in any medium for its daily presentation of the news to its audience.

3. Within any news organization, there exists a *complex set of criteria* for judging a particular news story—criteria based on organizational policy, personal preferences, definitions of newsworthiness, conceptions of the nature of the relevant audience, and fourth-estate obligations.

4. Those complex criteria are used by editors, news directors, and other personnel who *select a limited number* of news stories for presentation to the public and encode them in ways so that the needs of the medium are met.

5. **Therefore,** personnel in the news organization become *gatekeepers,* letting some stories pass through the system but keeping others out, thus limiting and controlling the public's knowledge of the actual events occurring.

committed, or a bridge collapses. Time is an important consideration in such stories—they happen, and then they are over. That is, they are news precisely because they are today's fresh happenings, and must be reported to the public as rapidly as possible. Soft news, on the other hand, is not as time-critical. It focuses on situations, people, or events that have *human interest.* Such stories are seldom based on events that are restricted to a particular day, and can be used in the news whenever they are needed.

The problem of flawed surveillance. One of the initial problems that can result in the unintended distortion of the news is *flawed surveillance.* Perhaps the source of news facts that most readily comes to mind is *direct observation.* Such "on-the-spot" coverage of events or situations presumably gives the news gatherer the most complete access to the facts. A related source, which is very traditional in news-gathering, is the *report of witnesses,* who themselves have directly observed an event and who in interviews can provide "eyewitness" accounts. Another related source is the *expert,* who may not have observed the particular event in question, but who is knowledgeable about the general topic. The problem here is the human processes of *perception, memory,* and *recall.* No human being—whether reporter, witness, or expert—is a perfect observation, recording, or remembering machine. Each of us is *selective* in what we observe, remember, and retell. Because this is the case, a reporter's version of what happened may contain a number of unintended flaws.

Many less personal sources are also used. One is the *news release*—a prepared and often biased handout provided to reporters by an organization (such as the Pentagon or a major corporation) to summarize the organization's "official" version of an event or situation. Another impersonal source of facts used by news gatherers is the many published *documents* stored in libraries or databases, such as reports of business, educational, or governmental groups; technical journals; census reports; or summaries of economic trends. Finally, *public records*—court, tax agency, or property ownership records—are widely used as sources of facts.

Although professional standards prevailing among news gatherers demand a high degree of accuracy in observing and assembling facts, much evidence suggests that unwitting errors, biases, and misrepresentations of reality are inevitable when *any* of the previously mentioned sources are used. That is not to say that reporters or others in the news industries deliberately falsify the accounts they prepare. On the contrary, the majority try very hard to be factually accurate but distortions often occur.

Too many stories arrive in the newsroom. That is, the newspaper, or in much the same way, the TV report, radio news, or Internet site, can handle only what its space and time will allow. Therefore, some stories are rejected immediately and never become part of the daily edition or broadcast. This selection process is called *gate-keeping.* Various criteria (described above) are used to let a particular story "in" or keep it "out." In that sense the system works like a gate—one that opens for some stories but remains closed for others.

Once a story has been admitted, however, it must undergo an exhaustive process of examination, pruning, and editing before it finds its place in the daily edition, newscast, etc. There are a host of considerations that dictate just how the facts of the story will be put together. Putting them together in just the way that is best for both the news medium and the audience is called *encoding.* There are a number of encoding strategies that are used.

ENCODING STRATEGIES FOR PACKAGING THE NEWS

A major stage in the news process occurs as selected stories are transformed within news organizations into versions deemed suitable to be received by the public in their particular medium, whether it be print, radio, television, or computer dissemination. Quite obviously, encoding is somewhat different for each medium. Nevertheless, modifications and repackaging of news stories occur at this stage in all media for a variety of reasons.

One encoding strategy is based on the need to emphasize certain *news values* when stories are selected, in order to make the report interesting enough to capture and hold the attention of the audience. Another encoding strategy is based on the need to *format* news stories, so as to organize the pattern or sequences within which its facts are presented. Finally, encoding strategies must fit with the *journalistic style*

Reporter David Willman of the *Los Angeles Times* won the 2001 Pulitzer Prize for investigative reporting "for his pioneering expose of seven unsafe prescription drugs (including Rezulin) that had been approved by the Federal Food and Drug Administration and for an analysis of policy reforms that had reduced the agency's effectiveness." This is in the tradition of investigative journalism that serves as a watchdog on government.

preferred by a particular newspaper, magazine, broadcasting group, or online service. Each of these encoding strategies is discussed below in more detail.

A second consideration in encoding arises from the ways in which the news media organize their daily list of stories into an *agenda* that is actually transmitted to the public. Stories received from reporters are positioned in the paper, in the broadcast, or on the Web site along with advertising and other content. The position may be more or less *prominent* or *obscure*. A particular story may be placed on the front page or in the back near the obituaries, at the beginning of a broadcast, or following the weather report, and so on. All of these decisions influence the way people interpret a story.

For many understandable reasons, then, as distinguished journalist Walter Lippmann aptly said many years ago, *news and truth are not the same thing.* In addition to the problems of selective perception, many kinds of judgments must be made by editors, news directors, and others in the chain of command—judgments about story size, content, location, balance with other reports, ethical status, ideological slant, and general suitability for the particular medium. The result of this processing by the organization is that the medium's news stories may present versions of reality to the public that are far removed from the actual events that actually happened.

Traditional news values. Journalists have developed convenient criteria for judging the *newsworthiness,* (that is, potential interest level) of stories. If the audience finds it either dull or too complex, communication will fail. These criteria are called *news values,* and the account prepared must incorporate as many of them as possible. Both print, broadcast, and online journalists use a number of considerations to judge the general newsworthiness of a story. These criteria have been derived over a long period and represent a kind of historically distilled wisdom as to what the public wants to read, hear about, or view in news presentations. Such news values are of considerable importance to reporters when they initially decide what is worth covering and when they prepare their initial accounts of what happened. News values also guide editors and news directors in making final decisions about what to print, put on the air, or put online.

At least seven major criteria can be applied in assessing a particular story as an attractive candidate for presentation to the public. Few stories fit all. And, of course, some stories may be of great importance even if they fulfill none. Nevertheless, in a practical sense, the news values listed below provide important guidelines for judging the newsworthiness of any particular story:

(1) The *impact* of a story is important. This criterion refers to the number of people whose lives will be influenced in some way by the subject of the story. For example, if workers in a local bakery decide to strike, it may have only a minor impact on the majority of the community. There may be some inconvenience, but

AND NOW FOR SOME LATE-BREAKING SPECULATION—

9/7/97

most people will not be greatly affected. However, if a telephone system fails almost everyone will feel its impact; thus, a news report about a bakery strike will have less impact than one about a telecommunications failure.

(2) *Timeliness* is a news value. One of the most important features of a news story is that it should be presented to the public while it is still fresh. News that is stale has less appeal. Thus, stories of recent events have higher news value than those about earlier happenings. Of particular value are the stories brought to the public ahead of the competition. An older term for such a story is a "scoop." Journalists like to claim, "You read it (heard it, or viewed it) here first."

(3) A third value is *prominence*. Stories about people who are in the public eye have much higher news value than those about obscure people, even if the occurrences are the same. Thus, a story about a well-known football or basketball star who has a major problem would be more newsworthy than one about some unknown individual with a similar difficulty. An example in recent years was the intense attention paid to the O. J. Simpson trial, or to the death of John F. Kennedy, Jr., in 1999. If they had been ordinary citizens, their tragedies would not have commanded the attention of news media.

(4) *Proximity* is an important consideration. Stories about events and situations in one's home community are more newsworthy than events that take place far away. A rather grim hypothetical example often used by journalists to illustrate the point is to equate the news value of various numbers of deaths at various distances. If a thousand people drown in a flood in a faraway country, the story has about the same news value as one describing how a hundred people drowned in a distant part of the United States. That event, in turn, has about the same news value as a story concerning ten flood victims in one's own state. And finally, a story about those ten has about the same value as one describing a flood that drowns a single person in one's local community.

(5) A time-honored news value is *the bizarre*. An example that illustrates this criterion well is the oft-quoted definition of news attributed to John B. Bogart, who was the city editor of the *Sun* in New York during the 1880s: "When a dog bites a man," Bogart is purported to have said, "that's not news, because it happens so often. But if a man bites a dog, that is news." In any case, odd or peculiar events have

always seemed more newsworthy than those of a routine nature. For that reason, the news media can usually be counted on to give space or time to sightings of Bigfoot, the appearance of a likeness of Mother Teresa on a cinnamon bun, reports of UFOs, or disappearances of ships and planes in the Bermuda Triangle.

(6) *Conflict* in a story always has value. The rule here is that harmony is dull, but strife is newsworthy. Stories that describe such events as messy divorces or child custody battles, rebellions, personal vendettas, and other kinds of clashes are high in news value. Thus, what transpired at a meeting of an organization devoted to promoting lasting peace might make dull news. However, if a fistfight broke out that would be newsworthy.

(7) Finally, an important news value is *currency*. More value is attributed to stories pertaining to issues or topics that are in the spotlight of public concern than to those about which people care less. Thus, in the late 1990s, President Bill Clinton's problems involving Monica Lewinsky were high on the public's agenda of concern and led to his impeachment hearing in the U.S. Congress. Subsequently, later scandals concerning pardons and other matters after he left the White House took front row center seats: eventually these were replaced with more current concerns in the ever-changing list of news stories covered by the media.

Essentially, then, the news industry prefers stories that their accumulated wisdom identifies as those in which the public will be most *interested*. The cost of relying on such criteria to define newsworthiness is that many stories will be ignored that are in fact truly significant from other points of view but boring for the public. For example, discoveries in scientific research may be of historic importance, contribute to the betterment of the human condition, and advance the frontiers of knowledge. However, they may be judged as dull. If so, they are likely to be found in the back pages or in the last part of the newscast (if they appear at all). Thus breakthroughs in human genome research are likely to get less coverage than a celebrated murder or a sex scandal.

Story formats. Another major encoding consideration is that the story itself must be packaged in one of the *story formats* that prevail in the relevant news medium. This is done to ensure that it will be understandable while maintaining or even increasing its interest. Over many decades, journalists have worked out effective ways of organizing news stories that will accomplish those objectives.

(1) The "five Ws" provide one format. By tradition, a well-written newspaper story is one that tells *Who* did *What, Where, When,* and *Why.* This basic format is learned by every beginning journalism student. In large part, the Ws encompass the way working journalists package most of their stories. This inventory for story organization is used to some extent in all news media, but the requirements of radio, television, and the Internet can be quite different from those of print and can allow enhancements to the standard print format.

(2) The *inverted pyramid* is a traditional story format. Using one or more of the five Ws, news stories are organized so that the most important ideas appear first. It has been said that this style grew out of telegraphed news. It permitted editors to chop the end off of a story if further details took too much space. The main ideas came early in the transmission. Journalists also learned long ago that many people read only the headlines. Others stop after reading the "lead" sentence, or perhaps the first paragraph or two, and then go on to the next story. Thus, the important ideas need to be set forth at the beginning, and overall the account should both be interesting and make few intellectual demands. Journalists have little confidence in the willingness of the aver-

age citizen to linger over complex details or sophisticated analyses. Many maintain that in writing stories they observe the KISS (Keep It Simple, Stupid) system.

Broadcast journalists, of course, must also use formats. Radio and television news stories tend to follow the criteria of news values, the five Ws, and the pyramid. However, as a radio or television newscast has much greater flexibility and can draw upon many variations to maintain audience interest; they organize to be seen or heard, rather than read. Radio news, for instance, can incorporate the "actualities"—of sound effects, such as the noise of a log being sawed in a news report on a lumber mill.

Television is even more flexible. The simplest format for a TV newscast is the *word story,* where the anchorperson is shown behind a desk telling what happened. A variant is to provide a graphic that appears in the upper corner of the screen, with an identifying phrase keyed to the story. Another TV format is the VOT (voice-over-tape), in which the viewer first sees the anchorperson, but is then switched to a videotape with the anchor's voice over the ongoing picture. Another is the *stand-up,* in which the anchor switches to a reporter in the field who comments on the scene. The *stand-up with package* is similar, with the reporter interviewing someone at the scene. Several versions of such formats are regularly used in producing TV news in an effort to create audience interest and to provide richer information. All of these have the possibility of introducing meanings into a story that modify it in selective ways.

Alternative journalistic styles. Finally, while the ideals of fairness, objectivity, and accuracy continue to be approved by the news industry, a number of alternative *journalistic styles* have come into use at one time or another. These, too, are encoding strategies that can reshape meanings. Styles are based on the idea that a particular set of facts can be combined into a news story in a variety of ways. Some of these styles are far more widely used than others, but each has had its period of popularity, and each has left its mark on the contemporary news industries. Moreover, each presents the story within a different framework of meaning.

(1) The *sensational or tabloid journalism* style characterized the press from the late 1800s to about 1920. It stressed shocking details, bizarre events, and sometimes appalling transgressions of the social norms. The newspapers of the time thrived on implications of scandal and sin in high places. If a murder had been committed, the crime was described with special attention to the appearance of the corpse, the look of the blood, suggestions of illicit sex, and the insidious nature of the killer. Facts in such accounts were of secondary importance. The sensational style is alive and well in such tabloids as the *National Enquirer* and similar publications sold chiefly in supermarkets.

(2) The "*objective*" or *impartial journalism* style replaced sensationalism and generally prevailed well into the twentieth century. By 1950, Alan Barth of the *Washington Post* wrote with pride, "The tradition of objectivity is one of the principal glories of American journalism."[10] In reality, that opinion was not universally held. As an examination of contemporary trade journals quickly shows, objectivity had been under fire for generations. For a few years, however, there was almost complete consensus among journalists and consumers that objectivity was a vast improvement over the sensational journalism that characterized the earlier American press.

Generally speaking, objectivity is a style that has traditionally been characterized by three aims: (1) separating *fact from opinion,* (2) presenting an *emotionally detached view* of the news, and (3) striving for *fairness and balance,* giving both sides an opportunity to reply in a way that provides full information to the audience. By world standards, American reporters have long been (and still are) relatively objective. That is they are not ideological in a partisan political sense. For decades their aim has been to use this style in their reports—keeping factual accounts in the news columns and opinion on the editorial page.

Beginning in the 1960s, this style was challenged. Critics have increasingly claimed that no human being is capable of complete objectivity. The challenge to objectivity occurred in part because critics had come to feel that American journalism was lifeless—unemotional and incapable of dealing with great social problems. There is much to be said for this view. During the 1960s and 1970s, the press was criticized with a vigor it had rarely encountered before. In this fate it had much company, during the same period most American institutions were challenged by widespread distrust and a search for new approaches.

The outcome was that several alternative styles for presenting news stories emerged, and although they did not revolutionize the press, they have influenced contemporary journalism. To understand how, we can examine a few of these alternatives more closely. They included the *new journalism*, along with *advocacy* and *precision journalism*. Today, objectivity is still dominant, but these newer styles are currently used to some extent in both the print and broadcast media, although because of government regulation, most of them are more difficult to implement in broadcasting.

(3) The *advocacy style* is another alternative to objectivity. Here, the reporter and the story identify with and "advocate"—that is, try to promote—a cause or position. Unlike editorial writing, advocacy journalism appears in news columns and not as a simple statement of opinion. In a sense, it is a kind of hybrid news story that promotes a particular point of view, departing from traditional journalism.

(4) A very different style that is becoming increasingly important is *precision journalism*. It makes use of the research procedures of the social sciences to gather and report quantitative information for the purposes of developing a news story. Reporters can either conduct such surveys and polls themselves—as is sometimes done—or they can make use of existing reports on such research available from government agencies, universities, or private firms.

The basic goal of precision journalists is to present to the public understandable analyses based on accurate quantitative information relevant to significant issues in the news. For example, traditional journalists often interview people selected casually or conveniently so as to portray the opinions of "people in the street" concerning a forthcoming bond issue to build a new convention center or some other project. The precision journalist would interview a number of citizens, selected according to the rules of scientific random sampling, to obtain a more representative summary of the views shared in the community.

A variation of precision journalism is *computer-assisted reporting* (CAR). Quantitative or other data are obtained from government or other sources in the form of computer-usable information. They can then be analyzed to obtain the facts needed for a story. Often, the Freedom of Information Act must be used to request copies of the tapes on which such information is recorded. Such legislation was passed during the 1980s not only at the federal level, but also by nearly all of the states.

A more recent story format is *civic* or *public journalism*. This style developed in the 1990s and its chief characteristic is that it usually involves projects aimed at diagnosing and helping solve community problems. It is a journalistic effort to promote and achieve a "civil society"—voluntary efforts that improve the quality of life for the public. It moves beyond simply relating the news into attempts to revive civic life and to improve public dialogue.

Widely practiced by today's newspapers and some television stations, civic journalism's goal is to keep the press grounded in the concerns of ordinary people, rather than in those of the elite. Essentially, this form of journalism first identifies problems to be solved, such as a high crime rate in the community, political corruption, or taxes that are imposed unevenly in different neighborhoods, then attempts to assist in their solution. The newspaper or TV station reports on citizens' meetings, assemblies, and other cooperative efforts where problems are aired, often taking sides in controversies.[11]

Advocates of this approach argue that traditional journalism is no longer trusted by the public and that civic journalism can restore confidence. Journalism needs a rebirth, they maintain, as a more democratic profession concerned with the problems of ordinary people. Critics warn that it moves journalism away from its traditional impartial and disinterested stance to that of political activists pushing a particular agenda. They reject the notion that social problems can be fixed through journalism by having news columns take sides in local disputes. Such efforts are seen as inappropriate, or even arrogant.

Encoding consequences of the profit motive. The ways in which journalists encode their stories is influenced by the profit motive. Real people as shareholders invest real dollars in newspapers, magazines, broadcasting stations, cable, and online systems. Logically enough, they expect to make real profits. What critics protest is not so much the idea that media owners make a return on investment, but *what the owners do* to maximize their profits. However, Americans value a profit-driven market economy—so much so that we now avidly support its development in all parts of the world. There is no denying that the profit motive will continue to exert powerful influences on what the public receives as news.

Nowhere is the problem better illustrated than in the case of network television news. In the past, network television's newsgathering and broadcasting were supported by all of the other programming offered by the networks. The news programs themselves were not expected to show a profit. Their ratings were not as high as those of entertainment programming, and advertisers did not flock to news programs as a context for their commercials. Subsidizing the news was seen as similar to the system in newspapers. The news part of the paper is not expected to operate profitably on its own. The revenues from the newspaper as a whole provide funding for newsgathering, editorial functions, printing, and the like.

However, when use of cable TV and the VCR began to eat into audience shares for network television, new corporate leadership took over and news policies changed significantly. The new policies declared that the news *had to earn its own keep.* The leadership had to develop ways of offering the news that would increase ratings in order to make news broadcasts more attractive to advertisers. Under these new policies, the networks sharply pared down news teams to cut costs. Even cameras were automated to save labor costs.

Far more important, however, were corporate decisions to define news program content in different ways. It had to be more fun to watch, so as to bring in more viewers. Less funding was to be available for such frills as investigative reporting, on-the-spot coverage, camera teams in foreign lands, or opinion and analysis. Instead, new kinds of programming were designed, sometimes even "staging" or "recreating" news events. The relationship of such programs to news in a traditional sense is remote. Indeed, critics used the term "trivialization" of the news to describe such programming. Quite clearly, such news was "not truth."

Out of these transformations of news substance originated the concept of *infotainment*—a merging of information and entertainment—now an important criterion for gatekeeping. From all that is available to news directors and editors, many selections of stories appear to be made for their entertainment value, rather than because of their newsworthiness or their essential importance to society.

A Theory of Unintentional News Distortion

Walter Lippmann (1889–1974) was a distinguished American journalist and political philosopher who wrote extensively about the relationship between the "press" (newspapers in his time), public opinion, and the democratic process. His explanations remain central to our understanding of this relationship today.

Essentially, Lippmann's theory explains how the news media *unintentionally distort reality* in the stories they present to the public—even though journalists strive for accuracy and want their reports to reflect the facts. Inevitably, however, Lippmann said, "News is not truth."

One factor limiting what the press can report is that there is just *too much going on* in the world. Every day, hundreds of reports are received by "wire" services and from reporters at various locations. Editors must select from this sea of stories those that they feel readers will *find interesting,* and those that seem important for the public to understand.

In addition, newspapers (and other modern media) have *limited resources* with which to cover any story. Their deadlines limit their time; their budgets cannot support exhaustive investigation or extensive manpower. Thus, the stories they prepare often *leave out important details and background information.*

When citizens form their political opinions on the basis of such flawed reports, those opinions *cannot reflect the detailed truth* of whatever situation or event is being reported. At the same time, Lippmann said, the function of the press in society is to provide for us "pictures in our heads of the world outside." Because of the limitations of time and resources, plus the need to focus on "newsworthy" events (as opposed to important ones that may make dull reading), citizens' ideas about the world outside become a "pseudoreality." In other words, the "pictures in their heads" formed from news reports do not provide citizens with a sound basis for responding to political issues and candidates.

The political establishment, however, is always anxious to please voters—even though this may result in a distorted grasp of what is taking place in the real world. Thus, many of the policies formed may be based on faulty foundations.

Lippmann's theory can be summed up in the following propositions:

1. The press systematically *monitors* events, people, and situations occurring in the physical and social environment to identify potential news stories (the "surveillance function").

2. To prepare the news that it will report, the press selects from the abundance of possible stories that come to its attention—an *agenda* consisting of those reports that the news personnel believe will be of importance or of interest to the populations of readers that they serve.

3. Many factors beyond the control of those in charge (time, money, technology, and opportunity) *limit the ability* of the press to investigate, describe, and transmit full details of all events and situations that come to its attention.

4. Due to these factors (in proposition 3), news reports are often characterized by *selectivity, omissions,* and *distortions* in spite of efforts by the press to be objective, fair, and factual.

5. **Therefore,** when audiences construct their own meanings from the daily agenda of news reports, the "pictures in their heads" constitute a pseudoenvironment in that they often have *limited correspondence* with the facts that occurred in reality ("the world outside"). This can lead people to respond to events in unrealistic ways and to flawed policymaking by leaders.

To a greater or lesser degree, pressures toward trivialization exist in all of the news media, but it is a special problem for the television networks. As the emphasis on infotainment has gradually become the television standard, most thoughtful analysts feel that the nation is being poorly served. Indeed, the question can be raised as to whether the reasons for protecting TV news media with the First Amendment and with a body of shield laws and other legislation unique to this category of business make sense any more.

There is an overall lesson that emerges from the previous review of the ways in which journalists in all of the news media monitor, select or reject, edit, format, polish, and arrange an agenda of news stories so that in their minds their reports will accomplish their complex goals. The lesson is that Lippmann's comment that *news is not truth* has considerable validity. As he noted, the distortion of the facts that results is by no means intentional. Nevertheless, what readers, listeners, viewers, or surfers come away with is a distorted version "in their heads" of what is really going on in the "world outside."

CONTRASTING CONCEPTIONS OF THE NATURE AND FUNCTION OF NEWS

Individual newspapers and broadcasters vary in how they resolve the conflict between the obligation to inform the public fully and the need to be profitable. The choice involved can be very well illustrated by comparing two almost completely opposite prevailing conceptions of the nature and functions of news. One conception of the nature of news is the *marketing approach,* which avidly pursues the goal of maximizing profits by selling news as a product (like soap, shoes, or soup) and thereby sharply limiting public service. Another conception is the *adversarial approach,* which is closer to the earlier traditions of the colonial press. This conception sees news as information needed by the public and it emphasizes the watchdog functions of the press—but often at the expense of profits. That these strategies coexist in sharp contrast shows the two very different paths our nation's press may follow in carrying out its surveillance function in the future.

THE MARKETING APPROACH: NEWS AS A PRODUCT

A news organization that uses the marketing approach devotes considerable resources to the task of understanding what the audience wants to find in a news medium. Then it makes certain that it serves those interests. The idea is to market its product, that is, the news, in much the same way as is any other commercial commodity—like beer, hot dogs, or breakfast cereal.

This approach begins with extensive *market research* that assembles statistical data on the interests, media habits, and concerns of the audience. These data are then used as guidelines in determining what material will be offered in news reports, and especially, in what manner. Thus, both the content of news stories and the style in which they are offered to the public are selected on the basis of research findings that define what the audience wants most.

Of course, for decades newspaper editors and publishers have been concerned with what will and will not sell papers. The same is true of those in other news media. The marketing approach, however, takes this concern a giant step further. News organizations using this strategy invest a great deal of time and money to find out what the public wants to read about, listen to, or view and what formats and styles they like best. The organizations then apply the answers methodically to shape their products. Thus, the marketing approach institutionalizes concern with the audience so as to enhance revenues, and it gives this concern priority in the process of selecting and encoding the news. Whether or not the resulting news accurately portrays the "world outside" is a secondary concern.

Marketing the news is not a new idea. For many years, the marketing approach was used heavily by broadcasters. Newspapers were actually slow to adopt methods that broadcast stations had used routinely to calibrate their product to their audience. Indeed, the marketing approach had been applied to television news almost from its beginning, with changes in format and style made to attract a larger audience. For years, print journalists tended to treat these practices with contempt. But in the 1970s and 1980s, managers and owners of metropolitan daily newspapers were appalled by their declining circulations per household (Figure 3.1), and soon print journalists had their own "news doctors." There seemed to be many causes for the declining circulation; competition from television, the growth of the suburbs, new life styles, and a lack of relevance in the content of the papers were all blamed. The newspapers responded with market research designed to diagnose the "ills" that were causing the decline.

To end declines in newspaper circulation, the market research experts prescribed *change,* advising the newspapers to add new sections on topics such as lifestyles, entertainment, gardening, and housing—sections that help readers "use" their communities and their environment. Such sections are hardly "news." They are edited and written for audience interest and approval—infotainment.

In some ways these new sections represent extended and repackaged coverage of topics that have always been in the paper. For example, many newspapers covered real estate for years, but as a result of the marketing approach, some renamed the section "Shelter" or "Home" and began to treat the topic from the consumer's point of view, adding personal stories about how to find an apartment or remodel a house. Similarly, in their lifestyles sections the newspapers print advice from "experts" on how people can solve their everyday problems—from how to get rid of stubborn stains to how to deal with a sullen child or a spouse's infidelity.

The best-known example of a newspaper that relies heavily on the marketing approach is the nationally circulated *USA Today.* It was designed on the basis of market research and continues to make heavy use of research findings that indicate audience interests. *USA Today* not only selects its topics of coverage on the basis of guidelines from research, but has also pioneered the use of color, new styles of graphic presentation, and brevity (some say superficiality) in writing. In spite of the critics, many other newspapers have followed *USA Today's* style and approach.

THE ADVERSARIAL APPROACH: WATCHDOGS OF THE PUBLIC INTEREST

The role of the press as an adversary of government is the one most honored in the traditions of journalism. In this capacity the press has sometimes been called the *fourth estate.* Thomas Carlyle (1795–1881) attributed the phrase to Edmund Burke (1729–1797) who called the reporters' gallery in the English Parliament "a Fourth Estate more important by far" than the other three estates of Parliament—the Lords, Bishops, and Commons.

It was because the right to speak out freely acted as a check on government, holding it accountable, that the American founders nurtured the principles of freedom of speech and protection of the right to public dissent. Today, the adversarial approach makes a critical contribution to society by increasing accountability and by exposing unsatisfactory conditions in both government and the private sector.

Traditional investigative reporting.   Central to the adversarial approach is *investigative reporting.* This is a kind of newsgathering in which the reporter probes deeply into a situation and assembles evidence that discloses whether or not there is something unusual, unethical, illegal, or even outrageous going on. Although the fact-gathering may be done by a single reporter or a team of individuals working together, the decision to undertake such an investigation is made by editors who must provide the financial support and be ready to defend reports on what is uncovered. This can be expensive and cut into the profit margin.[12]

A professional organization, Investigative Reporters and Editors (IRE), defines such reporting in the following terms: *It is reporting, through one's own work product and initiative, matters of importance that some persons or organizations wish to keep secret.* The three basic elements in this definition are that (1) the investigation is made by someone else, (2) the subject of the story involves something of *reasonable importance* to the reader or viewer, and (3) others are attempting to *hide these matters* from the public.[13]

Investigative reporting started in the nineteenth century. Some view the first such investigation to have been conducted in the 1840s by James Gordon Bennett, the energetic publisher of the *New York Herald.* Dissatisfied with the usual ways of reporters covering the courts, he sought a way to provide more interesting accounts of serious crimes. Choosing the occasion of the spectacular murder of a young prostitute, he personally went to the "fancy house" where she had worked, interviewed the "madam," poked through the victim's personal papers, and even examined the unfortunate girl's remains. The resulting story, rich in details about the place and the people involved, made very interesting reading.

Investigative reporting reached dramatic heights late in the 1800s. An adventurous young woman, "Nellie Bly" (a *nom de plume;* her name was actually Elizabeth Cochrane), became famous as a result of her investigative report of Blackwell's Island, a mental institution in New York City. In an elaborate scheme, she posed as a mentally ill person and was committed to the asylum. There, continuing the deception, she saw firsthand how patients were treated. The doctors and staff had no idea that she was a reporter, and she received very bad treatment for about ten days. Fortunately, she had prearranged with her newspaper, Joseph Pulitzer's *New York World,* to extricate her. They did so, and her exposé of the hospital conditions gained worldwide attention.[14]

Early in the 1900s, the journalists of the muckraker tradition investigated many private and governmental institutions. They uncovered and exposed corruption, abuse, and crime that characterized both private industry and government at the time. The contribution of the muckrakers to American society was far more than just interesting reading matter. Their exposés led to reform and legislation that still affect us today.

American journalists have kept this great tradition alive. During the 1920s, they played an important part in exposing the Teapot Dome scandal, in which Secretary of the Interior Albert B. Fall leased drilling rights to federal oil reserves to private developers and received a large loan and gift in return. Fall was tried and convicted of receiving a bribe and was sentenced to a year in prison. Also implicated but never convicted was Harry M. Daugherty, U.S. Attorney General. The *New York Times* and other newspapers disclosed many details about the case and kept the affair public. Although President Warren G. Harding was apparently not directly involved, the affair broke his presidency. (He died soon after the extent of the scandal became known.) Upton Sinclair, a controversial Pulitzer Prize–winning novelist and one of the original muckrakers, wrote *Oil,* a book about the scandal.[15]

The young Joseph Pulitzer brought innovation and new standards to American journalism, beginning in St. Louis and extending to New York in the late nineteenth century. His name is among the most illustrious in the modern era because of his role in founding the Columbia Graduate School of Journalism in New York City and providing for the prestigious Pulitzer Prizes for journalistic and literary excellence.

Investigative reporter and author Bob Woodward, an editor at the *Washington Post,* appears regularly on TV news shows, whether to promote a new book or to serve as a news commentator.

An extraordinary example of investigative reporting during the 1970s was the disclosure of the Watergate scandal concerning the Nixon administration. Beginning in mid-1972 and continuing through 1973, the series of stories developed by investigative reporters Carl Bernstein and Robert Woodward of the *Washington Post* dominated American news media for months, exposing a conspiracy by the White House Staff, the CIA, and others to cover up a number of covert illegal activities carried out by White House aides during the 1972 presidential election. The ensuing congressional investigation eventually implicated the president and led to his resignation. Investigative reports, notably in *Newsweek,* played a key role in the investigation of President Clinton by Special Prosecutor Kenneth Starr in the late 1990s and eventually led to an impeachment trial in the U.S. Congress.

One of the most celebrated examples of investigative reporting in recent years is that of David L. Protess, a Northwestern University professor, and his students, who investigated the wrongful conviction of several convicted criminals. Their work led to the release of several men and inspired a television show in fall 2000. Professor Protess is the author of several books about investigative journalism, which he called "the journalism of outrage."

Today, investigative reporting seems to be on the increase in the American press. Although such reporting is expensive, new sources of information and new tools of analysis have become available. Advances in computer use for both data storage and information recovery permit reporters to develop stories based on a broader body of information than ever before.

Computer-Assisted Investigative Reporting. An important new form of investigative reporting is know as CAIR, which makes use of electronic records that are kept by federal, state, and local governments. Most government organizations have abandoned the older and cumbersome paper files for the ease of electronic files. As freedom of information laws opened such electronic files to journalists, investigative reporters with computer skills and statistical training were able to uncover important trends in the functioning of government, instances of mismanagement, and even wrongdoing, by careful analysis of recorded electronic government records. One study found misapplication of the income tax laws. Another, reported by Margaret DeFleur, revealed a long-term trend of increased plea-bargaining in the federal courts.[16]

An interesting example is the misuse of police officer time in Boston—a story prepared by the Spotlight Team of the *Boston Globe* and published on October 1, 2000. Massachusetts requires a police officer to be present at major road construction projects to direct traffic and perform other duties related to safety. Such work is paid for by the contractor; off-duty officers can earn large sums for performing such private work. With the use of computerized court records and other information, the investigative journalists discovered that many officers were performing such private work for high pay when they were supposed to appear in court to testify against people who had been arrested for crimes. Because the officers failed to appear in court, the wrongdoers often went free as there were no witnesses present to testify against them.

Computers play an important function today, not only in investigative reporting but in routine fact gathering for other kinds of stories. *Online data services,* operated by commercial vendors, are especially valuable for obtaining background material for the development of a story or an investigation. Starting in the 1970s, a few online information services became available. At first they were used mainly for bibliographic retrieval, allowing a user to find out from a database, who had published what in, say, scientific journals. Today, the thousands of different databases operating on a fee basis supply information ranging from stock-market prices and airline schedules to complete files of scientific articles on every conceivable topic. With a personal computer and a modem permitting access to large mainframe computers at remote sites, a user can retrieve vast amounts of information on virtually any subject.

THE AGENDA-SETTING FUNCTION OF THE PRESS

One important consequence of the continuous flow of news provided by the mass media is the influence on the kinds of public policies and laws that are passed by legislators—both at the national and local level. But how can this happen? It is a consequence of influencing people who, in turn, influence politicians.

It was explained earlier that the final stage in constructing the daily news is deciding *which stories* to present to the public and the degree of *prominence* they deserve. Communications scholars refer to this final part of the news process as *agenda setting.* It means deciding on where, within the newspaper or broadcast, the stories of the day should appear. Some, it will be decided, should be prominent. These will be on the front page and have a large headline. These stories may have a photo or be allowed many column inches. Others, which seem less important, will have a smaller headline, be short, have no photo, and will be relegated to back sections of the paper. In the case of broadcast news, some stories can appear early in the presentation, perhaps be given more time, be accompanied by some background information, and have some video footage taken on the scene. Others can be presented in less dramatic and simpler form toward the end of the broadcast.

In the final setting of their medium's agenda, those who make the decisions about content and prominence have already considered which news values to emphasize, what story or broadcasting formats will be used, and whether concerns over ethical, legal, or profit matters have been met. Thus, the final set of stories that appears in the newspaper or broadcast on any given day has undergone a very complex news process, beginning with the surveillance of the environment for story possibilities and ending with the decisions of what will be the actual content and positioning of each news story to be transmitted to the audience served by that particular medium.

Communication scholars and researchers have discovered that the agenda defined by news professionals, as just outlined, has a counterpart among the audiences that attend to their media. When people are asked about their personal ranking of importance of the news stories of the day, it has been found that their selections usually *reflect the degree of prominence* given those same stories in newspapers and broadcasts. Simply put, people believe that a story is important if it is given a position of prominence by the press.

This conclusion from research may seem hardly surprising, but it is an important issue. What it means is that those who set the agenda of the press have significant influence on the public in terms of what people believe to be important. That is exactly what catches the eye of politicians who want to be elected or stay in office. Thus, the agenda of the public, often influenced by the agenda of the press, becomes a major influence on the kinds of laws and policies that politicians formulate. Obviously, then, the agenda-setting function of the press is more than an interesting relationship uncovered by researchers. It can have profound influences on the direction the nation takes in developing its laws and policies.

THE FUTURE OF THE NEWSPAPER

Try to envision a boardroom in which a group of strategic planners are gathered around a large conference table at a major media company. They are speculating about plans for the "newspaper of the future." The newspaper of the first years of the twenty-first century, says one young executive, will be "a dinosaur, part of a dying breed and a dying industry." "Why?" asks another. The first replies: "It is expensive to produce, reaches a limited audience, doesn't last very long, and is not popular with young people." "The answer," a third participant says, "is to create an all-purpose *electronic newspaper*. It will be one that is interactive, offers as much information as anyone wants to click on instantly, and will be available at little or no cost."

This conversation, in one form or another, has been replayed in yearly corporate settings for two decades. For years, futurists have been predicting "the death of print." In spite of these forecasts, the print media, including the newspaper, have survived and succeeded despite their critics emphasizing their shortcomings. The reason that such forecasts have not come true is that newspapers in their traditional form have many valuable attributes that are often ignored as people rush to replace them by creating new Web sites and other digital media products.

To understand the survival of the newspaper, one needs to look back at the medium's history and development—as we have done—and the traditions of journalism that newspapers have developed over the past three centuries. One must also consider all of the modern articulations of the concept of *news*.

The newspaper was the first medium to organize and package the news in a coherent, systematic, and predictable manner. From the earliest times to the present, newspapers had visual rules and a *grammar of presentation*. World affairs were in one place, financial news was in another, and national and local affairs in still another. From editorial pages to sports pages and other special sections, newspapers created an *architecture* for the presentation of news—a framework for organizing news and information in a manner that appeals to people wanting to know what is going on. That news architecture is so deeply established in our culture—and so widely used in all news media—that it constantly brings people back for more.

But back to that boardroom, where the speakers are trying to figure out the reasons for the newspaper's continued success. They have agreed that whether the newspaper focuses more on entertainment than news, or the other way around, a newspaper is: (1) *Portable*. That is, it goes anywhere a person goes and needs no equipment, software, or plug-ins. (2) *Predictable*. Readers know what to expect—how it is organized and what is where. (3) *Accessible*. There is no mystery about where or how you get a newspaper. (4) *Cost effective*. A newspaper is cheap to purchase and the reader gets a lot for his or her money.

The Agenda-Setting Theory of the Press

A theory concerning the influence of the press on peoples' beliefs and evaluations of the topics reported in the news was first developed by Maxwell McCombs and Donald Shaw. Their initial version of the theory explains how individuals come to regard some events and situations that they encounter via news reports in print and broadcast media as *more important* than others. Thus, the original agenda-setting theory implies a relationship between the prominence of the placement of a story in a news report in newspapers, on television, or in radio news, and the *beliefs about its importance or significance* on the part of the news audience.

The theory came from a study of the presidential political campaign of 1968. Its authors observed how people decided which issues, among those receiving extended news attention, were important. As it turned out, the public developed a kind of ranking in their own minds about the importance of the different issues discussed in the news. The authors of the theory found a high level of correspondence between the amount and kind of attention paid to a particular political issue by the press and the level of importance assigned to that issue by people in the community who had received information about it from the press.

It was the press, therefore, that determined during a political campaign which issues people discussed among themselves and how much importance they attached to each. In other words, the press developed *its own agenda* concerning what issues were news and how much space and prominence to give them. Then the agenda of the press became the agenda *of those who followed the news of the campaign.* This does not imply that the press tells people what they should think and decide about the issues. However, it does imply that the press tells people what they should think about and what issues are important enough so that they should develop an opinion.

Later, it was realized that such public opinion was a basis for policy decisions by leaders and politicians. Thus, both the public agenda and the policy agenda were influenced by the press agenda. These basic ideas have been well verified by research. The theory is applicable mainly to the relationship between political issues and beliefs about their importance by those who follow campaigns in the news. Here are the theory's basic propositions:

explaining MEDIA EFFECTS

1. The print, broadcast, and digital media select a number of issues, topics, and events from their daily surveillance of the political and social environment to process and report as "the news."

2. Because of limited space and time, and because of journalists' convictions as to what is "newsworthy," many issues and topics are *ignored* and do not become part of the news.

3. The press gives each of the selected news stories greater or lesser *prominence* in its reports by assigning it more or less space and a particular position (e.g., front page versus back page in the newspaper, or lead or late position with more or less time in the news broadcast). This forms the daily *news agenda* of the press.

4. When the public attends to these reports, they will perceive the order of prominence assigned by the press in its agenda and will use it to decide on their *personal rankings of importance* of the issues and topics that make up the news.

5. **Therefore,** as politicians become aware of the public's ranking of importance concerning these issues, that ranking can influence the *policy-making agenda* of leaders and legislators.

There are some negatives: (1) Newspapers are *perishable* products—flimsy, difficult to store, and impossible to update. (2) They appeal mostly to middle-aged and older readers. (3) They cause smudges on your hands from the ink. Even so, what would breakfast be for millions of families without a newspaper to read?

As we noted, newspapers are slowly declining in terms of the percentage of the population who subscribe to them. They are also declining in terms of the share of the total amount of money spent by the nation's advertisers. Nevertheless, they remain quite profitable for their owners. Newspapers command the largest share of American advertising dollars that are spent by local businesses that advertise their goods and services to local customers. Moreover, newspapers remain a personal and local medium, where people find information about events, people, and illustrations relating to their own communities. Newspapers thus continue to serve needs that are difficult for any other medium to fulfill.

However, all is not positive. Three very different factors will probably continue to reduce both the proportions of Americans who read newspapers and their revenues in the future: (1) Many newspapers are owned by corporations that also own radio and television stations and that could result in a reduction of competitive efforts. (2) There are a finite number of advertising dollars available in our economy, and they are being chased by an increasing number of competitors (newspapers, radio, television, cable television, magazines, direct mail, as well as phone and Internet companies). In other words, newspapers are now getting a smaller slice of the advertising pie. (3) Media consultants maintain that consumers will spend only a certain constant percentage of their income on information and entertainment, no matter how many outlets and services are available. Thus, that revenue pie is also only so large, and as the number of media competitors increases, the pie will have to be cut into smaller and smaller pieces. Inevitably, these factors will decrease the profitability of newspapers. In spite of these problems, however, it seems clear that newspapers will survive for the foreseeable future. Their long-range prospects nonetheless are less than clear.

Interactive media and online newspapers may find increasing acceptance in the future. By 2000, virtually all large U.S. and international newspapers had an interactive or digital edition, and some online newspapers existed only on the Internet. In a 2000 study, researcher Leo Bogart reported that most newspaper Web sites in the United States and Canada were no more than five years old—and most were either breaking even or showing a profit.

The potential impact of Internet newspapers was noted by researcher Enrique Dans of the Institute of the Press in Madrid, Spain, who wrote:

> In the 450 years of existence, the written press has never faced a change with the intensity and consequences as those of the Internet. The decision of going online represents a set of opportunities and threats that publishers must carefully weigh. Once they have made the step, newspapers find themselves in a completely different competitive environment. They deal with different competitors, business models, customers and patterns of consumption.[17]

But, as Bogart noted, the Internet newspaper is not yet replacing the printed product. Online newspaper audiences are still small compared with those of printed newspapers, and "the typical newspaper site gets relatively few users in the course of a week, compared with the cumulative impact of its daily circulation."[18] The bigger the newspaper, however, the greater the impact of the Web edition. A look inside the Internet newspaper services was somewhat disappointing after learning that most had small staffs and a little more than one-third of them update material more than once a day. Thus, most were missing one of the greatest possible benefits of the Internet, the ability to constantly update posted information. A study by market researchers at Insight Express had more bad news in May 2000 when it reported that some 55 percent of online users are *not willing to pay* for online news.[19]

At present, however, scholars are by no means counting the Internet newspapers out. They do have a following. Their readers/users tend to be younger people, and online newspapers have an enormous capacity to handle classified advertising plus other, quick turnaround commercial transactions. Online editions also bring the traditional newspaper into the world of e-commerce (which we discuss in some detail in Chapter 8). Nevertheless, it is difficult to predict what will happen. In July 2000, a headline in the *Wall Street Journal* questioned newspapers' digital future:

"Newspapers Internet Stories Haven't Clicked With Investors" and noted that one of the industry's biggest boosters, Warren Buffett, a major investor in the Washington Post Company and the owner of a newspaper in upstate New York, joined other doomsayers in predicting the death of the medium. Efforts by newspapers to leverage their Internet assets to increase their value on the market and their profits had fallen short. The reason was the same one that other businesses often encounter when they try to embrace the new economy of the Internet. And also, newspapers still have the same industrial problems that have slowed newspapers for years— "shrinking circulation, rising newsprint prices, and the slow growth nature of their core businesses."[20]

Not only the Internet poses potential difficulties for the newspaper in its present form, but the print medium also faces threats within its own ranks. Many worry about the competition of new free-circulation dailies and weeklies, including some that are sponsored by local governments and distributed through transportation systems including buses and subways. A paper called *Metro* engaged in this in Philadelphia in 2000, and hoped to get a foothold in other cities. Already, there are free-circulation weeklies, including alternative news weeklies, that cut into entertainment and cultural advertising as well as job, real estate, and other classified ads. Newspapers suffer from high labor and newsprint prices as well as declining advertising revenues in the face of new media competition.[21]

In short, the future of the newspaper at this point cannot be predicted. Perhaps the best guess is that in its traditional form it will continue to survive. Newspapers are a formidable advertising medium for local businesses and the older generations use them much as they did in earlier times. However, as technology continues to advance, there is every possibility that new generations will show declining interest in the printed paper that is delivered to their door every morning.

Chapter Review

- Newspapers were slow in coming to the American colonies. The first to publish more than a single issue was the *Boston News-Letter* of 1704. A succession of small colonial newspapers followed, and a tradition of free expression was slowly established. The dramatic trial of Peter Zenger in 1734 was an important landmark in establishing the concept of a free press.

- The colonial papers were small, slow, aimed at affluent readers, and limited in coverage. Some were partisan papers published to express and support a particular political position; others were commercial papers of interest mainly to merchants and traders. Nevertheless, they established important traditions as guardians of the public interest and played a key role in spreading ideas that became important to the founding of the new nation.

- Newspapers for common people became increasingly possible as the Industrial Revolution brought new technologies, and as immigration, the growth of cities, and increased literacy led to larger potential audiences. In the *New York Sun,* Benjamin Day put together the necessary components of printing technology, advertising support, new content with wide popular appeal, and an effective distribution system. Quickly, the penny papers spread to America's other cities.

- A number of changes in American society spurred the growth of newspapers: Among these were rapid population growth through immigration, increasing literacy, and technological changes brought about by the steam press, telegraph, trains, and steamboats. Intense competition for readers among competing urban newspapers fostered an era of yellow journalism.

■ Early in the twentieth century, the newspaper was the nation's only mass medium, and was adopted by most American households. However, as other media arrived, its number of subscriptions per household declined. That downward trend continues today.

■ The functions of newspapers began to change with increased emphasis on corporate profits. The older function of informing readers is still there, but entertaining them has assumed growing importance. Newspapers increasingly emphasize their tradition of in-depth coverage and interpretation because of competition from radio and television, which get the news out much faster.

■ Newspapers are distinguishable from other media because they are portable, predictable, accessible, and cost-effective.

■ News, the main commodity delivered by newspapers and other news media, is current or fresh information about an event or subject that is gathered, processed, and disseminated via a medium to a significant number of people.

■ News is mainly concerned about surveillance of the environment, discerning new, useful, and important information for people. It is often geographic—local, national, or international—but is also increasingly demographic—that is, taking on topics of interest to particular segments of the audience such as those interested in economics, the environment, health, and other issues.

■ Certain social and human values influence and help structure the news. Among them are impact, timeliness, prominence, proximity, the bizarre, conflict, and currency.

■ News is often packaged in a fashion that reflects journalistic styles, standards, and trends, ranging from sensational tabloid journalism to fact-based "objective" coverage.

■ Newspapers, which began as ink-on-paper products, are becoming part of the digital world. They are increasingly dependent on computer hardware and software for all aspects of their operations.

■ As the future unfolds, new technologies may replace the newspaper altogether. However, the news process for gathering, processing, and shaping the news will by necessity remain a part of whatever media deliver the information to the public.

Notes and References

1. C. A. Giffard, "Ancient Rome's Daily Gazette," *Journalism History* 2, winter 1975–76, pp. 107–108.
2. Edwin Emery, *The Press in America,* 5th ed. (Englewood Cliffs, N.J.: Prentice-Hall, 1972), p. 3.
3. Marvin Rosenberg, "The Rise of England's First Daily Newspaper," *Journalism Quarterly* 30 (Winter 1953), pp. 3–14.
4. Emery, *The Press in America,* p. 31.
5. For an especially insightful history of newspaper and other media, see Hiley H. Ward, *Mainstreams of American Media History* (Boston: Allyn and Bacon, 1997).
6. See U.S. Bureau of Census, *Statistical Abstract of the United States* (Washington, D.C.: U.S. Government Printing Office, 1991–1996).
7. The sources for these various figures on trends in ownership are Lynch, Jones, and Ryan, Inc. and John Morton Research, Inc.
8. Richard McCord, *The Chain Gang: One Newspaper Versus the Gannett Empire* (Columbia, Mo.: The University of Missouri Press, 1996).
9. These classifications are based on a similar discussion in Gaye Tuchman, *Making News: A Study in the Construction of Reality* (New York: Free Press, 1978), pp. 23–31.
10. Alan Barth, quoted in Herbert Brucker, "What's Wrong with Objectivity," *Saturday Review,* October 11, 1969, p. 77.
11. For various views on civic journalism, see the following: Carl Sessions Stepp, "Public Journalism: Balancing the Scales," *American Journalism Review* (May 1996), pp. 28–40; Davis Merritt, *Public Journalism and Public Life: Why Telling the News Is Not Enough* (Mahwah, N.J.: Lawrence Erlbaum Associates, 1995); Jay Rosen, *What Are Journalists For?* (New Haven, Conn.: Yale University Press, 2000); Anthony J. Eksterowicz and Robert N. Roberts, eds., *Public Journalism and Public Knowledge* (Boston: Rowman and Littlefield, 2000); Everette Dennis, "Questions about Public Journalism," *Editor and Publisher,* July 29, 1995, p. 48; and Philip Meyer, "In Defense of the Marketing Approach," *Columbia Journalism Review* (January–February 1978), pp. 60–62.
12. See Margaret H. De Fleur, *Computer Assisted Investigative Reporting: Its Development and Methodology* (Mahwah, N.J.: Lawrence Erlbaum Associates, 1997).
13. John Ullman and Steve Honeyman, eds., *The Reporter's Handbook: An Investigator's Guide to Documents and Techniques* (New York: Twayne Publishers, 1974), pp. 59–92. Also see, Steve Weinberg, *The Reporter's Handbook* (New York: St. Martin's Press, 1995).
14. Iris Noble, *Nellie Bly: First Woman Reporter* (New York: Julian Messner, 1956), and Brooke Kroeger, *Nellie Bly: Daredevil, Reporter, Feminist* (New York: Crown, 1994).
15. See "The History of the Standard Oil Company" in Mary E. Tompkins, *Ida M. Tarbell* (New York: Twayne Publishers, 1974), pp. 59–92.
16. De Fleur, *Computer Assisted Investigative Reporting.*
17. Enrique Dans, "Internet Newspapers: Are Some More Equal Than Others?" *International Journal on Media Management,* spring 2000, p. 11.
18. Leo Bogart, "Web Realities: News Survey Documents, Profits and Pitfalls," *Presstime,* July/August 2000, p. 11.
19. Felicity Barringer, "Newspapers Bring Threat of Web Into Perspective," *New York Times,* May 15, 2000, p. C21.
20. Suzanne McGee and Mathew Rose, "Newspapers' Internet Stories Haven't Clicked With Investors," *Wall Street Journal,* July 11, 2000, C1, C4.
21. Bogart, "Web Realities," p. 11.

Chapter 4

MAGAZINES: VOICES FOR MANY INTERESTS

The myriad of magazines available on newsstands in airports, stores, and elsewhere showcase the specialized, targeted audience nature of this old and continuing medium.

MAGAZINES—MEMBERS OF THE PRINT MEDIA FAMILY—HAVE ENTERED THE TWENTY-FIRST CENTURY IN A STATE OF CONFUSION. ALTHOUGH they are still very much ink-on-paper products, magazines also reach people on Web sites, and some are exclusively available in digital form on the Internet. At the same time, the magazine format, with information organized by topic and theme in an entertaining manner, has been borrowed by television. Thus, the magazine is a media product, a medium of communication, and a communication format. Understanding what magazines are and how they have evolved from their beginnings in the eighteenth century is vital to understanding what they are today.

The word "magazine" entered the English language in the late 1500s, but it did not refer to a printed medium. The term comes originally from the Arabic *makhasin,* which means "storehouse." In ancient times the term magazine referred to a place containing a collection of items, usually military stores. We still use the word to describe many kinds of military enclosures where explosives are kept. In the 1700s, when the early printed periodicals began to appear, they eventually came to be called magazines because they were, in a sense, storehouses of writings about various topics.

Magazines depended on the same technological developments in movable type, presses, printing, and paper as did books and newspapers. However, magazines in their traditional form are not like other print media. Although they have some of the features of books and are published on some regular schedule like newspapers, they are a unique medium in their own right.

The first magazines were originally established in London, where they prospered in a great city inhabited by many urbane and educated residents. The rougher societal conditions prevailing in America all during the eighteenth century held back the development of periodicals on this side of the Atlantic. However, as the nation expanded, became urban, and developed improved transportation, magazines began to prosper in the United States. By the end of the nineteenth century, they were a serious and respected medium serving millions of readers.

During the early twentieth century, magazines played an important role in exposing unacceptable social conditions and stimulating social reform. Between the two world wars, before television became a household medium, they were one of the major mass media, advertising nationally distributed products. After World War II, the growth of television had a significant influence on the magazine industry. Large-circulation general magazines were severely hurt financially, but new kinds of magazines were founded to meet new demands, and the industry thrives today.

Magazines have always served specific functions in society that differ from those of either newspapers or books. Furthermore, those who subscribe to and read magazines constitute a distinct segment of U.S. society. The functions of magazines and the audiences they attract have a long and colorful history, and although both have changed greatly over time, at least some remain remarkably similar to what they were from their beginnings.

The history of the magazine began in London in 1704 with the first issue of a small periodical called the *Review*. In some ways this "little" publication resembled a newspaper of the time, in that it was printed on about four small pages, and (at first) was published weekly. Yet it was different from the early newspapers because it was much less concerned with news; it focused mainly on articles about domestic affairs and national policy.[1] In England at that time people could still be thrown in jail for writing and publishing material contrary to the Crown. As it happened, the founder of the *Review* had been doing precisely that just before his publication made its debut. The founder was the outspoken Daniel Defoe (who later wrote *Robinson Crusoe*), and he wrote the first issue while in Newgate Prison, where he was being held because of his critical writings denouncing certain policies of the Church of England.

The magazine was thus born as an instrument of politics. The *Review,* like many magazines that would follow it, was a vehicle for political commentary, and was intended to influence its readers' beliefs and opinions. At the same time, it was an instrument of entertainment—at least for sophisticated readers—in that it also contained essays on literature, manners, and morals. Both of these functions were central to the medium from the beginning, and for many magazines, they remain so today.

After his release, Defoe continued to produce the *Review* on a regular schedule about three times a week, until 1712. The significance of Defoe's "little" publication was that it was almost immediately imitated, and the idea of magazines as a separate kind of print medium began to catch on. By 1709, another writer Richard Steele, had begun publication of the *Tatler,* offering a mixture of news, poetry, political analyses, philosophical essays, and even coffee house gossip. Within a short time, Joseph Addison joined Steele and together they produced the *Spectator,* which quickly became a favorite of London's urbane elite, enjoying a circulation of several thousand.

Although seen as the first magazines, these early publications were not called that at the time. The term was not applied to printed works until 1731, when Edward Cave, a London printer, first published his monthly *Gentlemen's Magazine,* which was so successful that it eventually reached some fifteen thousand subscribers—truly a remarkable circulation for the time.

From the beginning these early magazines differed greatly from newspapers of the period in both their content and their authors. For one thing, the magazines became a medium for some of the ablest writers of the time. Their pages contained essays, stories, and entertaining commentaries by such figures as Samuel Johnson, Alexander Pope, and, as noted, Defoe, Addison, and Steele—among the most respected English writers of the eighteenth century.

As the form and substance of the new medium came together by the middle of the 1700s, the functions it was serving in society remained unique. The magazine was clearly designed to make a profit. It depended on subscription payments by its readers and, to a limited extent, on advertising revenues. It sought to attract readers with a mixture that was heavy on political commentary but it also included discussions of controversial topics and opinion-shaping essays. Its literary quality was high and its typical reader was a member of the affluent, well-educated elite. It was definitely not a medium for the masses.

By the middle of the century, a number of rival magazines were being published successfully in England, and the concept was spreading to other parts of the world. Thus, by the time of the American Revolution, hundreds of publications that we would recognize as magazines today were being produced in the major cities of Europe.

THE DEVELOPMENT OF AMERICAN MAGAZINES

Magazines were slow to develop in America. Although attempts to produce them started even before the American Revolution, they almost always ended in failure. The central reason for this was that the conditions of society needed to support this kind of publication did not exist in the United States until after the beginning of the nineteenth century. Then, as education, transportation, printing technology, and other conditions improved, many magazines were started, some of which were extraordinarily successful.

The first issue of the *Pennsylvania Magazine or American Monthly Museum* was published in Philadelphia in 1775 by Thomas Paine.

BARRIERS TO DEVELOPMENT IN THE EIGHTEENTH CENTURY

The magazines that had been established in England were impressive models. To some intellectuals it seemed like a great idea to begin publication of such a periodical in the colonies. In fact, Benjamin Franklin, ever the innovator, tried to get one started in 1741. It had the awesome title of *General Magazine, and Historical Chronicle, for All the British Plantations in America*. It even had a competitor with an equally awesome title, Andrew Bradford's *American Magazine, or A Monthly View of the Political State of the British Colonies*. Franklin's effort lasted only six issues; Bradford's failed after three.[2]

After that, attempts to produce a magazine were sporadic.[3] Several, including the *American Magazine and Historical Chronicle* and *Christian History*, also appeared during the 1740s. Neither lasted more than two or three years. Then a whole decade went by with no further attempt to publish in this form.

If Franklin, Bradford, and the others had been able to hire a modern market researcher, he or she could have looked carefully at colonial "demographics," as we say today, to try to determine if there was a realistic magazine market. It would not have taken much research to reveal why such projects were doomed before they started. There were four major conditions that created barriers to the successful establishment of magazines in America and caused their development to lag considerably behind that of their European counterparts: (1) the size and dispersion of the population, (2) the economics of publishing at the time, (3) the state of transportation and the postal system needed for delivery, and (4) the characteristics of the readers themselves.

The population factor. At the time Franklin and Bradford brought out their rival magazines, the population of the entire thirteen colonies was only about one million, and few people were village or city dwellers. During the colonial period, people were spread over a huge land area, about twelve hundred miles along the seacoast and just a few hundred miles inland. The majority of the colonists lived on farms, often in isolated locations. While there was some commerce, the principle industry was agriculture. There was no manufacturing of the kind that would later draw laborers to factory locations to form industrial cities, and there really was only a handful of communities of any appreciable size. By 1790, when the first official U.S. census was taken, only 3.9 million white and black people lived throughout the entire original thirteen states. And there were only twenty-four "urban places" (having more than twenty-five hundred inhabitants). Only Philadelphia and Boston had populations in excess of twenty-five thousand. Altogether, city dwellers made up only 3.5 percent of the entire American population.[4] As a consequence of these population conditions, no accessible market existed for a magazine in eighteenth-century America. If Franklin and Bradford and those who tried later to start magazines had understood how these factors were related to the success of their medium, they probably would not have even taken the trouble.

Obstacles to magazine delivery. Along with the country's sparse and dispersed population, colonial transportation retarded the development of magazines in America. Traveling from New York City to Boston today requires only minutes by air and just over four hours by car on the interstate highway. By contrast, in the middle of the eighteenth century, it was a rough eight- to ten-day trip by stagecoach, and just getting there was an accomplishment. Hauling goods (such as bundles of magazines) by wagon or pack animal was much slower. In many parts of the country, mud or snow made whatever rude tracks that existed as roads impassable during long periods of the year. Even near population centers such as Boston and Philadelphia, travel was difficult. In the less-settled areas there were few roads of any kind, and most travelers went by horseback, in sailing vessels, or even in canoes. In 1790, the steamboat was still decades away, and railroads would not link the nation's cities until after the 1840s.

Today we receive magazines in the mail routinely and reliably. Subscribers seldom think about postage because it is paid by the publisher (and is really quite inexpensive). Getting magazines to subscribers in the eighteenth century was a different matter. As early as 1710, a mail system had been established in the colonies by the Crown. It was mainly for letters that were carried by postal riders, and it was not available for bulky magazines. By the 1790s, the new U.S. Congress did allow magazines to be sent by post, but the fees were not practical because they were based on weight. Full letter postage was required, which made mailing heavy magazines prohibitively expensive. A few years later the Congress changed rates to a system based on the number of pages plus the distance required for delivery. This also did not work well because of the expense to people in remote areas. Postage, which had to be paid in advance by the subscriber, added 20 to 40 percent to the cost of the periodical.

It was not until 1852 that postal rates for magazines could be paid at the point of mailing by the publisher. By that time, roads had been greatly improved, and both steamship lines and railroads were operating on regular schedules to carry the mails quickly, cheaply, and efficiently. The lower costs led most publishers to absorb the postage as part of the subscription price.

The cost of subscribing. A magazine in the early days was a real luxury. It is difficult to try to convert coin and money systems of colonial America into today's dollars. However, the first magazines produced by Franklin and Bradford, for instance, sold for a shilling per issue in the currency of the time, which remained the going rate up until the time of the American Revolution. At that time in New England, a shilling was about half a day's wages for a farm laborer. A year's subscription would equal what a laborer could earn in about four or five days. Delivery was an additional cost, about another day's wages. Today, a laborer working for five or six days at $10 an hour would make at least $400. Few among us would be willing to pay that much for a magazine subscription.

Magazines were then, and were to remain for a substantial period, a medium for the well-to-do. They were just what was needed in European cities like London and Paris. The presence of affluent people made cities into centers not only of commerce and political power, but also of fashion, the arts, and literature—exactly the topics discussed in the magazines. In other words, the elite of the population centers made up a pool of potential subscribers, but the farmers and laborers of America, thinly scattered over a vast area, were not a potential market.

CATALYSTS FOR DEVELOPMENT IN THE NINETEENTH CENTURY

Although virtually every imaginable factor conspired against the development of magazines in America during the 1700s, the situation started to change significantly after the next century began. As noted, transportation improved greatly and changes came about in the postal system. In addition, printing technologies developed quickly, the population grew sharply, people were better educated, cities were expanding, and there were important issues about which the population urgently needed detailed information. These were just the conditions needed for a great flowering of magazines.[5]

Rapid population growth. A significant factor in the development of American magazines during the nineteenth century was the rapid growth in the population that helped the spread of newspapers. The first U.S. census (1790) counted only 3.9 million people. Ten years later the figure had increased to 5.3 million. Then, after only five decades, the population had soared to 23.2 million, which represents an increase of over 400 percent. By the end of the nineteenth century, due in large part to massive immigration, it had skyrocketed to 75.9 million. Few nations in history have ever recorded such an astonishing rate of population growth.

Population expansion remained a factor that helped to decide the fate of magazines well into the twentieth century. Massive immigration continued into the 1920s before it was slowed by legislation. Throughout the nineteenth century and into the twentieth, the birth rate was also high, adding to population growth. The rate finally dropped during the Great Depression of the 1930s but climbed sharply again after World War II when the "baby boom" generation was born. (Our population in 2001 reached over 283 million people.) The golden age of magazine growth during the nineteenth century would never have occurred without these long-term population trends. As we will see, population growth also characterized the first half of the twentieth century.

Urbanization. Not only did the population grow numerically, it also became more urban; that is, an increasing number of citizens lived in villages, towns, and cities rather than on farms. In part, this trend toward urban living arose from the spread of transportation networks that made it possible to move farm goods to domestic and foreign market centers. With construction starting in 1815, the great Erie Canal linking lakes, rivers, and a wide ditch between them was dug (without power machinery) across an incredible three hundred miles, connecting Albany on the Hudson River with Buffalo on Lake Erie. By this route, combining horse-drawn barges and Great Lakes steamboats, travelers and goods could journey cheaply along a network from New York City to the new city of Chicago and beyond.

As farm products and consumer goods moved over this great transportation system, hundreds of communities sprang up in the Midwest and in northern parts of Pennsylvania, New York, Indiana, and Ohio. Southward links allowed barge traffic to move from Lake Erie down the Miami River into Ohio and on into Mississippi. Thus, before the midcentury, one could travel by canal barge and paddle-wheel steamboat from New York City to New Orleans by way of the Great Lakes. New York City itself, at the eastern end of the system, grew into a great port for exports and imports. It also became the largest and most important city of the nation's emerging mass communication industries.

Between about 1840 and 1900, the railroads, too, had spread to most parts of the country, fostering their own share of towns and cities. The United States was developing into one of the most productive agricultural and industrial powers the world had ever known. Steel mills, factories, and hundreds of other kinds of production facilities were established by the end of the century, drawing more people into concentrated communities. Thus, while all segments of the population were growing, the mix was changing. Increasing proportions lived in towns and cities and earned salaries and wages. During the same period, smaller and smaller proportions were living on farms.

The growth of towns and cities meant more concentrated populations with larger cash incomes and higher levels of education. These were precisely the conditions required for an expanding market for magazines. To give some idea of the shift, in 1790 more than 95 percent of American families lived on farms. By 1820, this figure had dropped to 80 percent. At the time of the Civil War it was about 70 percent. The flow of people from farm to city continued and even accelerated in the twentieth century. By 1920, only half of the nation's families lived on farms. Today it is less than 2 percent. We truly are an urban nation. Over half of us live on only 1 percent of the landmass.

Vogue, **the magazine of fashion, has long been a leader in its genre of periodicals that appeal to the fashion-conscious. Once independent, it exists today under group ownership, still competing vigorously for the fashion audience.**

Increasing education.

Although sheer numbers and their concentrations are important, the quality of the population is also a factor shaping the market for a product like a magazine. In its early years, the United States was a nation whose citizens for the most part had received little or no formal instruction in reading. Even at the beginning of the nineteenth century, education beyond the rudiments was largely for the elite. Few ordinary people went to secondary school, and only the wealthy attended college.

Nevertheless, at the beginning of the nineteenth century, the idea of education for all citizens (at the time, that meant all white citizens) became remarkably and uniquely American. Here, after all, was a new kind of society, based on assumptions of personal freedom, equality, and participation in the political process. A literate

Table 4.1 The Growth of Education in the United States for Selected Periods from the Civil War to Modern Times	
Period	**School Enrollments*** **(percent)**
1869–1870	57.0
1889–1890	68.6
1909–1910	74.2
1929–1930	81.7
1949–1950	83.2
1969–1970	86.9
1977–1978	88.7
1987–1988	96.5
1997–1998	98.0

(*percent of population ages 5–17 enrolled in elementary and high school)

Source: U.S. Bureau of the Census; U.S. Department of Health, Education, and Welfare, Statistics of the School Systems, 1986–1987; U.S. Department of Education, Mini-Digest of Education Statistics: Enrollments, 1999

citizenry was essential to the system. Furthermore, as industrialization began, it became increasingly clear that reading, writing, and arithmetic were skills needed to improve a person's chances in life. Free public education was vigorously promoted, thanks to Horace Mann of Massachusetts, who by 1834 had persuaded his state's legislature to adopt a system of universal and mandatory education. Essentially, Mann's concept consisted of three basic principles: (1) *tuition-free* (that is, tax-supported) elementary and secondary schools should be available to all children, (2) teachers should receive *professional training* in special schools devoted to their education, (3) all children should be *required to attend* school (either public or private) to a minimum age.

In those conservative times, Mann's system was widely regarded as a wild and radical scheme and was vigorously opposed by large numbers of the wealthy and the propertied classes. They feared that universal education would foster too many critics of the prevailing system (which they for the most part controlled). Many religious leaders also fought it, holding that too much book learning would clearly lead to godlessness.

In spite of such controversy, the Massachusetts system for educating all citizens quickly spread to other states. In the 1860s, the Civil War greatly disrupted society, including educational development. But in the years that followed, the proportion of the nation's children enrolled in schools began to increase and this growth continued for more than a century. This great social change had profound implications for the development of magazine markets.[6]

The great issues. As population changes occurred during the 1800s, growing demands for specialized types of information played a part in the spread of the modern magazine. It was an instrument uniquely qualified for this special task. It was a medium that could present positions, details, opinions, and analyses in ways quite different from the newspaper, and in much greater depth. It was from the perspective of magazines that Americans began to learn about important trends, controversies, and significant issues affecting their society.

The entire century was marked by extraordinary events, sweeping changes, and truly significant movements in thought, politics, and religion. For example, there was no more important event for Americans during the nineteenth century than the Civil War, with its accompanying debates over slavery. Works like Harriet Beecher Stowe's *Uncle Tom's Cabin* were serialized in magazines and reached a reading public far exceeding the number who had access to the book.

Intellectual debates of monumental significance provided unique content for magazines. An example was the explosive issue of Charles Darwin's explanation of the origin of species. Magazines were an important forum in the debate over evolution versus creation. Magazines also delved into topics like financial panics and depressions, controversial discoveries in medicine, great religious revivals, and the continuously expanding frontier.

During the middle and later part of the century, no issue stirred the population more than the question of the proper place of women in society. Many magazines were aimed directly at women and provided stories and commentary on changes advocated by leaders of the growing women's movement. There was an emotionally charged debate between those who advocated, and those who wanted to prevent, women from voting (women's suffrage). Others believed that women should have the right to obtain credit, to get a mortgage, to initiate divorce, to wear more comfortable clothing, and even to work outside the home in jobs traditionally reserved for men. Magazines presented views on all aspects of these issues.[7]

AMERICAN MAGAZINE CHARACTERISTICS IN THE NINETEENTH CENTURY

With the catalysts noted earlier, the United States magazine industry flowered during the nineteenth century. It was a dynamic industry, constantly seeking new formats, new audiences, new appeals, and new ways to increase profits. Although thousands of magazines were started only to fail within a short time, some lasted for generations.

Numbers and circulations of magazines. The number of magazines published in the United States showed a remarkable pattern of growth over a seventy-five-year period as Figure 4.1 shows. In 1825 there were fewer than 100 magazines in circulation.[8] By 1850 there were 685 periodicals other than newspapers being regularly published. The Civil War held down magazine growth, but by 1870 the number had risen to 1,200. It then doubled in a single decade to 2,400. By the end of the century, 5,500 magazines were circulating.

Paralleling this rapid expansion in the number of magazines published was growth in circulation rates. Actual circulation amounts were not systematically recorded during the century, but various figures are available that show a sharply increasing trend. For example, during the late 1700s, a magazine would have been lucky to have 1,500 subscribers. Most had fewer. In contrast, the *Country Gentleman* in 1858 had 25,000 subscribers. Other magazines that year were within the same range. *Godley's Lady Book,* a very popular magazine for women, had 15,000 subscribers.

Within fifteen years circulation had risen sharply. In 1885 the *Youth's Companion* was the leader with 300,000 subscribers, and the more literary *Scribner's Monthly* had a respectable 200,000.

A magazine for every taste and interest. During the last years of the nineteenth century, magazine publishers came to understand their markets very well.

trends in media use

FIGURE 4.1

Increases in the Number of Magazine Titles Published in the U.S. During the Nineteenth Century

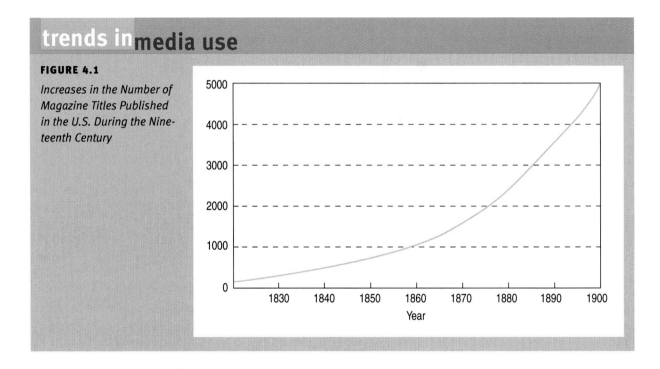

"Every interest had its own journal or journals—all the ideologies and movements, all the arts, all the schools of philosophy and education, all the sciences, all the trades and industries, all the professions and callings, all organizations of importance, all hobbies and recreations."[9] In other words, whereas newspapers provided their readers with a daily cafeteria of many different types of content, magazines zeroed in on specific categories—on people who shared an interest in a particular subject.

As the century came to a close, the world of magazines was varied indeed. In particular, the religious periodicals were thriving. In fact, by 1885 there were some 650 publications aimed at different groups, from the main denominations to those interested in every obscure religious taste and philosophy. Scores of magazines were also devoted to the arts, music, theater, and literature. Short stories, travel accounts, and virtually every other conceivable subject of interest were all served by some form of periodical. Many of what are now the nation's most prestigious professional and technical journals were started during the last years of the nineteenth century.

Generally, by the end of the 1800s, the magazine had become a mature and important medium. For many citizens, magazines supplied the major source of opinions and analyses concerning complex issues and topics that were not covered in depth by newspapers. For other people they offered amusement and trivial entertainment. Some read them to reinforce their religious views or to gain insight into complex political questions. Others subscribed to receive information about a particular hobby. Magazines were as varied as the country's interests and concerns.

MAGAZINES IN THE TWENTIETH CENTURY

Magazines gained additional respect early in the twentieth century, when a number of them became vehicles for exposing political corruption, social problems, and economic exploitation. During the first decade of the century, prestigious magazines took the lead in pricking the nation's social, moral, and political conscience as their writers, editors, and publishers probed into the country's economic and political life. As we will see, the conditions revealed during this period resulted in many needed reforms and corrective legislature.

Yet ultimately, magazines, like all other American mass media, were produced and distributed for the most part because they made a profit for their owners. It was also true that some were started because of some specific mission of communication—for example, to provide religious information to the faithful. Even so, revenues to support these enterprises had to be found. If none were available, they failed. Subscriptions were important, paying a considerable portion toward the costs of producing and distributing the publications. But the real profit, as in newspapers, was to be found in attracting advertisers.

As an advertising medium, the magazines of the nineteenth and early twentieth centuries were formidable. There were no other widely distributed media for touting wares to the national market; radio would not arrive as a household medium until the 1920s, and television would not be a reality for decades. Newspapers were local, and neither books nor movies were able to distribute national advertising in the same way. For the cost of the space, a magazine circulated nationwide could guarantee that potential customers all over the country would be exposed to the same message.

This advertising function led to the large-circulation general magazines of the first half of the twentieth century. These periodicals were aimed at a nationwide readership drawn from all walks of life, they truly were magazines in the original meaning of the term. They had something for everyone in every issue—fiction, biography, travel, humor, advice for the homemaker, a sprinkling of political commentary (but not too much), and sports. Magazines like *Collier's, Cosmopolitan, Liberty,* and the *Saturday Evening Post* would come to dominate the industry during the mid-twentieth century.

MAGAZINES AS A FORCE FOR SOCIAL REFORM

One of the most important periods in the history of magazines began just before the end of the nineteenth century and lasted until the end of World War I. It was a time when a limited number of magazines took the lead in what we would now call **investigative reporting.** At the time it was called **muckraking,** a term coined by President Theodore Roosevelt to characterize journalists who, instead of extolling the virtues of America, were determined to expose its dark and seamy side. Roosevelt compared such journalists to the "man with the muckrake" in John Bunyan's classic, *Pilgrim's Progress,* in which the central figure would not look up from the filth on the floor even when offered a glittering crown.

Particularly forceful in the muckraking movement were *McClure's,* the *North American Review, Forum,* the *Atlantic Monthly,* and even the *Saturday Evening Post.* These were national publications with a huge combined circulation. A number of their writer-investigators probed political, social, and economic conditions as part of the popular movement sweeping the country. These investigative writers were vigorous, relentless, and thorough. As early as the 1870s, *Harper's Weekly* campaigned to oust New York City's political dictator William Marcy "Boss" Tweed. Another nineteenth-century magazine, *Arena,* attacked slums, sweatshops, and prostitution, demanding sanitation laws, birth control, and socialized medicine. By the turn of the century, thorough exposés of corruption in the cities and abuses by industry had been published and widely read.

McClure's Magazine, the most important of the muckraking periodicals of the late nineteenth and early twentieth centuries, set a high standard for investigative journalism. Lincoln Steffens (top left), a great reporter, produced the famed "Shame of the Cities" series and wrote an influential biography. His colleague, Ida Tarbell, a journalist and biographer, is best known for her "History of the Standard Oil Company." These were two of the greatest journalistic exposés of all time.

With the new century, the movement to expose the unsatisfactory social conditions moved into even higher gear. Perhaps the best-known example of muckraking was a series in *McClure's* by Ida M. Tarbell on the giant Standard Oil Company. Tarbell was a remarkable woman, whose accomplishments illustrate the best traditions of journalism as the watchdog of society. The publisher Samuel S. McClure had confidence in Tarbell because she had already written very good biographies of Napoleon and Lincoln for him. She was an understanding writer and a thorough researcher, and McClure hired her as a staff writer to produce the series about Standard Oil, expecting a portrayal of the high achievements and efficiency of the American industry in producing and distributing an important product.

What he got turned out to be something very different. Tarbell spent five years preparing and writing seventeen articles about the giant trust. She dug into every public record she could find, interviewed people, and examined letters, court transcripts, and thousands of other documents. She did report that Standard Oil was superbly organized and that it achieved its objectives with great efficiency. But she also revealed, in merciless detail, how John D. Rockefeller and his corporation had used "bribery, fraud, violence, corruption of public officials and the railroads, and the wrecking of competitors by fair means and foul."[10] The public was outraged, and *McClure's* circulation soared. Tarbell's series gained worldwide recognition as an example of thorough investigative reporting.

The names of other reform-minded writers, like Lincoln Steffens and Ray Stannard Baker, also became household words. Steffens produced the widely praised

"Shame of the Cities" series, showing how corrupt governments worked in a number of American communities; Baker's "The Right to Work" was a series on the problems of workers and corruption in labor unions. These writers and dozens of others of the muckraking period made a tremendous impression on the public and became the conscience of the nation. Powerful political figures took up their cry for reform, and both federal and state governments acted to correct the political and economic abuses that were exposed.

Eventually, a great many magazines turned to this kind of material. Some did well, but others churned out poorly researched criticisms of virtually everything about which stories could be written. Eventually the public tired of this tidal wave of criticism, and magazines had to change. The muckraking period ended with World War I, but it may have been the high point in the social and political importance of magazines.

Some magazines tried to push social change in ways other than investigative reports. *Cosmopolitan* actually sent a correspondent to Spain to negotiate the purchase of Cuba during the Spanish-American War. The correspondent was ignored, but his dispatches made good copy. The magazine also sent "goodwill ambassadors" to foreign countries, asking that they be allowed to meet with heads of state. *Cosmopolitan* proposed an international language and an international congress, and even started a national correspondence university, complete with a campus. These quirky schemes all proved to be failures.

THE CHALLENGE OF TELEVISION

After interest in muckraking declined, new classes of magazines began to appear. One was the **newsmagazine,** a term coined by Henry Luce and Briton Hadden in 1923 when they founded *Time.* New concepts arose too (or more accurately, old concepts were revived), such as the **digest**—a collection of excerpts from other publications. Even today, *Reader's Digest* remains one of the most successful magazines of all time. The *New Yorker* was also founded in the 1920s. In 1936, the picture magazine *Life* was first published and met instant success. In 1945, the African-American picture magazine *Ebony* was founded. For almost thirty years, from the 1920s into the 1950s, large general-circulation magazines such as *Life, Look, Collier's,* and the *Saturday Evening Post* dominated the market. National circulations reached into the tens of millions. Magazines were far ahead of newspapers and books in the effective, sophisticated use of photographs and graphic design. They were beautifully printed, efficiently distributed, rewarding to read, great as an advertising medium, and enormously profitable for their owners. People loved them and they seemed to be a part of society that would last forever.

Then came television! As this new medium's popularity grew, the general large-circulation magazine found its subscriber pool shrinking and its advertising revenues dwindling. Television was its own kind of "magazine" and was much easier to use. Furthermore, it was free to the user. Those who were marketing products nationally began turning in droves to the networks and TV commercials. Within a few years, the magazine industry had to make major adjustments. As it turned out, most of the big general magazines with the "something for everyone" approach died. For example, *Collier's* and *American* were early casualties, succumbing to economic pressures in the 1950s. In the 1960s many others failed, including the large picture magazines *Life* and *Look.* Some, like *Life,* returned in the 1970s and 1980s, but in their new form they have smaller, more carefully targeted circulations.

There are still a few immensely popular magazines appealing to the general population, including *Reader's Digest* (circulation over 14 million), *TV Guide*

(13 million), and *National Geographic* (8.5 million). But most magazines today are directed not to a broad heterogeneous audience preferring a "storehouse" of mixed content; rather they aim toward a more defined group with distinct interests. In place of general, large-circulation magazines there are now thousands of more narrowly focused, special-interest publications. Some enjoy huge circulations, such as *Modern Maturity* (renamed *MM* in 2001 and accompanied by a new magazine called *My Generation* for people in their fifties), the publication of the American Association of Retired Persons (with a circulation of over 20.5 million). *People, Playboy, Skiing, PC* (for personal computer enthusiasts), and *Better Homes & Gardens* are some of the other best-known periodicals.

Meanwhile, the venerable newsmagazines like *Time, Newsweek,* and *U.S. News & World Report* are experiencing difficulties. Although their circulations have either held even or decreased only slightly, the demographic category at which they aim—college-educated readers between the ages of twenty-five and forty-four—has nearly trebled during the same period. Thus, they have lost a large share of their target group during a time when their circulations should have boomed. Whether this type of magazine can survive in today's competitive news and advertising environment remains to be seen.[11]

THE GROWTH OF SPECIALTY MAGAZINES

In 2000, there were more than eighteen thousand periodicals of all kinds in circulation in the United States, and as previously noted, most of them focused on special interests. There is currently a specialty magazine (in fact, there are often several) for every conceivable interest, hobby, and taste—from tennis, fly-fishing, and model trains to wine collecting and wooden boats. There is even one called *SUV Power Magazine* for devotees of these vehicles.[12]

Advertisers love specialized magazines because they are so effective in reaching precisely the categories of consumers who buy their kind of product. For example, no maker of expensive handcrafted bamboo fly rods would advertise those wares on national television, in a newspaper, or on local radio, because most people using those media would not be interested. The maker has a better chance of reaching relatively affluent buyers with a potential interest in such equipment, who are scattered all over the nation, and perhaps even in foreign countries, with a single ad placed in one or more magazines devoted to fly-fishing. Subscribers will see the ad, and the magazine will likely be passed on to other fly-fishing enthusiasts. Furthermore, such advertising is cheap by comparison with other media. It is because of these factors that so many narrowly focused magazines can make a profit today. By this pattern of targeting its market, the magazine industry has adapted to and survived the challenge posed by television.

THE MAGAZINE AS A TWENTY-FIRST–CENTURY MEDIUM

After reviewing the history of magazines over more than two centuries, it may seem idle now to ask just what a magazine is and how it differs from a newspaper. Actually, this is a necessary question, because in contemporary publishing it is sometimes difficult to distinguish between the two. Generally, a magazine is published less frequently than a newspaper. It is also manufactured in a different format—usually on better quality paper, bound rather than merely folded, and with some kind of cover. There are exceptions to all these characteristics, but for the most part they satisfactorily distinguish the form of magazines from that of newspapers. To these differences in form we can also add differences in audiences, content, functions, and influences of contemporary magazines.

We have already seen how magazines usually probe issues and situations more carefully than newspapers; however, with an increasing interest in investigative reporting on the part of today's larger newspapers, that is not always the case. What we do find in magazine content is less concern for the details of daily events and more for interpreting topics in a broad context. Historically, magazines have appealed to a regional or national audience and have been free of the fierce localism of newspapers. Theodore Peterson offered this succinct description of the modern magazine:

> Although the magazine lacked the immediacy of the broadcast media and the newspaper, it nevertheless was timely enough to deal with the flow of events. Its timeliness and continuity set it apart from the book. As a continuing publication, it could provide a form of discussion by carrying responses from its audience, could sustain campaigns for indefinite periods, and could work for cumulative rather than single impact. Yet its available space and the reading habits of its audience enabled it to give fairly lengthy treatment to the subjects it covered. Like the other print media it appealed more to the intellect than to the senses and emotions of its audience. It was not as transient as the broadcast media, nor did it require attention at a given time; it was not as soon discarded as the newspaper; its issues remained in readers' homes for weeks, for months, sometimes even for years. In short, the magazine by its nature met well the requirements for a medium of instruction and interpretation for the leisurely, critical reader.[13]

Magazines today, then, retain their traditional functions. They are a major medium of **surveillance,** often delivering information ahead of the rest of the media. Some magazines, like *Time,* are intended mainly to inform, and others, like *Playboy,* to entertain. However, among the various functions served by magazines in contemporary society, the most notable is still **correlation.** This refers to interpreting society and its parts, projecting trends, and explaining the meaning of the news by bringing together fragmented facts. Other print media also inform and entertain, but it is in performance of the correlation function that magazines stand out. Magazines, in other words, are the great *interpreters*.

The long-held distinction among newspapers, published magazines, and electronic magazines is becoming increasingly blurred. Indeed, when newspapers have made major changes in packaging and presentation, it is often said that they are adopting a "magazine format." Thus, newspapers have become more like magazines, both in marketing methods and in writing style. Even television has been influenced: CBS's *60 Minutes* and its current imitators call themselves "television magazine" shows.

The distinction in format between printed magazines and other media is increasingly ambiguous and likely to be more so in the future. With the spreading use of computers capable of connecting to the Internet and the World Wide Web, search engines and portals, like Yahoo!, MSN, Lycos, and others, people may eventually be able to create their own specialized magazines without benefit of paper or magazine editors. Currently, a few magazines are available only online. However, for the foreseeable future, most analysts think the magazine will continue to exist in its present form (though it may be supplemented by an Internet presence), because of its portability and its permanence.

THE MAGAZINE AS AN INDUSTRY

To reach their specialized audiences, magazine publishers sort potential readers into neat demographic categories with the help of computers; then they refine their products to match readers' interests. In other words, they target their content and tone to attract specific audiences, thereby appealing, as we have noted, to many advertisers, who direct their advertising to probable customers.

For magazines, as for other media, audience ratings and audience surveys are important in determining advertising rates. But as Philip Dougherty has pointed out, there is an interesting twist for magazines:

> If an editor creates a magazine that is so on target that subscribers refuse to part with it, that's bad. If, however, the editor puts out a magazine that means so little to each individual that it gets passed from hand to hand, that's good. Reason: the more the magazine is passed along, the higher the total audience figure will be. In that way, the ad agency rates will look more efficient to agency people, which would be more likely to put the magazine on their . . . schedule [for advertising].[14]

Thus, like all other media that are supported by advertising, a magazine must pay keen attention to its audience in order to survive. In fact, American magazines seem to be in a continual process of birth, adaptation, and death. Because magazine publishers rarely own their own printing presses, the initial investment needed to found a magazine is rather modest, and so starting a magazine is relatively easy. Maintaining it is much more difficult. Most leading observers agree that many magazines die because the publisher failed to strike a balance between revenue from circulation and revenue from advertising. Some magazines die because the publisher failed to fine-tune the product to meet changing fashion and interest. The most successful magazine publishers produce more than one magazine. If one magazine fails, they still have others to keep their company alive.

Types of magazines.   As noted, the American magazine industry today provides a periodical for just about every interest. Magazines also target categories defined by income, age, education, and occupation.

Although there are various ways to categorize magazines, the industry typically speaks of two broad categories: consumer magazines and business magazines. **Consumer magazines** are those readily available to the public by subscription—to be received through the mail—or by direct purchase at newsstands. **Business magazines,** on the other hand, cover particular industries, trades, and professions, and go mainly to persons in those fields.

Writer's Digest, a publication with a considerable focus on magazines, classifies them into only four major types: trade journals, such as *Nightclub & Bar* magazine or *International Boat Industry;* sponsored publications, such as *American Legion,* or *Harvard Magazine;* farm publications, like *National Hog Farmer;* and consumer magazines, such as *Vogue* and *Road and Track.* Table 4.2 describes the main types of consumer magazines and the leading business magazines.

Consumer magazines, like *McCall's* and *Ebony,* are also called "slicks," because of their coated paper. Many in this category are mass-circulation magazines, but a subcategory, the secondary consumer magazine, includes broadly circulated magazines that concentrate on a specialized topic or a specific interest—examples are *Private Pilot, Yachting,* and *Gourmet.*

During the 1990s, the number of consumer magazine titles grew from 14,000 in 1990 to nearly 18,000 in 2000, according to the Magazine Publishers Association.

Table 4.2   Types of Magazines
Consumer magazines: Periodicals purchased on newsstands or subscribed to by the general public for home delivery. Examples are *Reader's Digest, Life, Ebony, TV Guide,* and *Sports Illustrated.*
Trade journals: Magazines aimed at a particular trade or industry (also called the business paper press). Examples are *Editor & Publisher, Modern Machine Shop,* and *Publisher's Weekly.*
Sponsored publications: Internal publications of particular organizations, unions, and other groups, including college and university magazines, customers' publications, and employee magazines. Examples are *American Way, Elks Magazine, Foreign Affairs,* and *Consumer Report.*
Farm Publications: These magazines are given a category of their own because of their large number and the degree of specialization within the farm press. Examples are *Farm Journal* and *American Small Farm.*
Newsmagazines: Serving as national newspapers in America, newsmagazines include *Time,* which was once known for its strong Republican bias but is now more moderately political; *Newsweek,* a less doctrinaire publication, with a generally liberal bias; and *U.S. News & World Report,* with a strong business orientation.
City magazines: Publications such as *New York, San Diego,* the *Washingtonian,* and *Boston* exemplify city magazines, which tend to concentrate on the activities of a particular city or region. Most major cities (such as Columbus) and many smaller ones (for example, Albuquerque) now have city magazines that investigate public affairs and try to critique the local scene (especially entertainment and restaurants).
Sex magazines: These publications have substantial circulations and generate considerable revenues. They take pride in their fiction and nonfiction articles and interviews as well as their suggestive photographs. This group includes such general-interest sex magazines as *Playboy, Playgirl,* and *Penthouse.* Publications such as *Hustler* and *Screw* cater to people with explicit sexual appetites. There are sex magazines for gays, lesbians, and bisexuals as well as for heterosexuals.
Sports magazines: Americans are preoccupied with sports of all kinds, and there are scores of magazines to satisfy their interests, ranging from *Sports Illustrated* and *Sport,* which cover a variety of sports, to specialized magazines covering just one sport, such as *Golf, Racquetball,* and *Skiing.* A new sports fashion will quickly generate magazines. When racquetball gained enthusiasts in the 1980s, several racquetball magazines appeared. Skateboarding had the same effect in the 1990s. Sports magazines, like sex magazines, once seemed to be intended for men only; but women now make up more of the audience for general sports magazines, and some sports magazines are designed especially for women.
Opinion magazines: These include some of the oldest and most respected journals in the United States. They range from the liberal *Nation,* which has been published since the Civil War, to the *National Review,* a conservative magazine founded in the 1950s by columnist William F. Buckley and the *Weekly Standard,* an entry from the 1990s. Some others are the liberal *American Prospect, New Republic,* and the *Progressive.*
Intellectual magazines: These small-circulation publications are very similar to opinion magazines, but they usually have denser copy and are aimed at a more intellectual audience. Examples include *Commentary, American Scholar,* and *Tikkun.* Both opinion magazines and intellectual magazines pride themselves on "influencing the influential."

(continued on page 116)

Table 4.2   Types of Magazines (continued from page 115)
Quality magazines: Although these magazines are similar to opinion and intellectual magazines, they usually have larger circulations (perhaps as high as 500,000) and reach a more general audience. Some examples are *Atlantic Monthly, Harper's,* the *Smithsonian,* and the *New Yorker.*
Men's interest magazines: These publications, such as *Men's Health,* sometimes overlap with sex magazines and sports magazines. *Gentleman's Quarterly* and other similar magazines represent men's new preoccupation with fashion.
Women's interest magazines: Some of the most successful magazines in the country, with the highest circulations, are aimed at women. The first American magazine in the nineteenth century to have a circulation of more than 1 million was *Ladies' Home Journal,* which continues today. Other magazines in this class are *Vogue, Better Homes and Gardens, Good Housekeeping,* and *Rosie.*
Humor magazines: Taking hold in the 1870s with *Puck,* the *Comic Weekly,* humor magazines have been with us ever since and include *National Lampoon, the Onion,* and *Mad.* Related to humor magazines are comic books, forming an industry in themselves. Many of these publications are not humorous at all, but use cartoon-style artwork to present complex plots and characters, diverse views, and social commentary.
Business magazines: Few subjects are more compelling to the American audience than business. Among leading business magazines are *Business Week,* published by McGraw-Hill; *Fortune,* a Time-Warner publication; and *Forbes,* which uses the whimsical slogan "A Capitalist Tool." *Barron's* is published by Dow Jones & Company, which also produces the *Wall Street Journal.* Some business magazines offer broad-based news coverage; others are designed to advise their readers on the machinations of the stock market. There are also new economy magazines, especially those covering high technology and electronics, such as the *Industry Standard* and *Computer World* (in fact, the publishing industry has benefited a great deal from changes in technology; there are many new publications just on computers).

Typically, entrepreneurs who want to start a new magazine develop a business plan charting a course for the magazine and "proving" with statistics (on potential readership and related market research) that there is a niche (market) for the new publication. Then a staff is hired and offices are established. Typically, printing is contracted out, as are arrangements for distribution and circulation. Advertising space can be sold either by the magazine staff or by national advertising media representatives. Many new magazines start with high hopes, only to find that no significant niche exists to make the new publication profitable. Often, new magazines that do succeed are quickly sold to large-magazine and other media companies, whose economies of scale make it profitable to publish many different magazines under the same corporate roof.

The number of new magazines that appear each year has grown sharply in recent times and is now nothing short of phenomenal. Industry sources indicate that literally hundreds of new consumer magazines are introduced every year. However, on average, only two in ten of the newcomers are expected to survive for more than ten years. The Magazine Publishers Association regularly reports on growing magazines by categories as shown in Table 4.3.

The greatest increase in magazine publication from 1995 to 1996 was in sports (41 percent). For nearly a decade, sex was the leading category, with sports a close

Table 4.3 Top Ten Magazine Categories, 1988–1998				
	Category	**1988**	**1998**	**Growth in No. of Titles**
1.	Business and Industry	358	694	336
2.	Health	169	494	325
3.	Education	227	519	292
4.	Computers and Automation	338	605	267
5.	Travel	342	589	247
6.	Regional Interest	517	752	235
7.	Automotive	233	451	218
8.	Entertainment	127	328	201
9.	Lifestyle	158	336	178
10.	Women's	202	367	165

Note: Titles on this list may include Canadian and trade publications in addition to U.S. consumer magazines.

Source: National Directory of Magazines 1999, Oxbridge Communications

second. That changed in 1996, with sex dropping to fifth place. Some of the newcomers on the list were established by large publishing companies; others were low-budget projects begun by individuals.

Making a profit. Consumer magazines are the industry's major moneymakers. According to Veronis, Suhler & Associates (a media forecasting firm), revenues from magazine advertising and circulation will total $23 billion in 2001.

The vast majority of magazine sales are through mailed subscriptions. In fact, this number rose from 67.6 percent in 1980 to 83.9 percent in 2000. This statistic is important because about half of the total earnings of consumer magazines comes from subscriptions (and newsstand sales), and the other half comes from advertising. For business-to-business magazines, the revenue picture is radically different. In 2001, forecasters say, business magazine revenues will reach $16.3 billion, of which approximately 90 percent will come from advertising. Thus, subscriptions are not a significant part of the profit picture in the business magazine.

In fact, many business magazines are actually given away free; that is, they have what are called controlled nonpaying distributions. The magazines using this pattern of distribution can afford to do so because they literally blanket the relevant field or industry, which makes them especially attractive to advertisers. Magazines aimed directly at a given industry tend to be read by a large percentage of people in that field—exactly the people that the advertisers want to reach.

Successful magazines are often linked to writers and columnists associated with them, as is the case for *Elle* magazine columnist and author E. Jean Carroll (a.k.a. Jeannie Carroll).

Myrna Blyth, Editor in Chief, *Ladies' Home Journal* **and Senior Vice President,** *Meredith Corporation,* **New York, New York**

Myrna Blyth, a respected and innovative leader in the magazine industry, is a senior vice president of the Meredith Corporation, where she serves both as publishing director and editor in chief of the *Ladies' Home Journal,* where she has been since 1981. *LHJ* was the first magazine in America to garner circulation of one million, which it accomplished in the 1880s, and now, over one hundred years later, it is called "one of the hottest magazines in America" by *Ad Week* magazine. On her watch, *LHJ* has garnered many honors including the Clarion Award from Women in Communications. In 1998, she created *More,* a lifestyle magazine for women under forty. Blyth was herself honored with the Magazine Publishers Association's coveted Henry Johnson Fisher Award for lifetime achievement in the magazine industry.

Q. How did you first get actively involved in the magazine industry?

A. It was a natural development and an outgrowth of working on student newspapers and magazines from high school forward. I was editor of my college magazine at Bennington [in Vermont] and decided that magazines were for me. When I graduated, I went home to New York and got a job on a magazine. I've been with magazines ever since.

Q. What factors have sustained your continued interest and involvement, now and over your career?

A. Being successful and getting promoted in places where I worked. I liked to write and edit and was able to do both in magazines. Early on, I wrote two novels and found writing to be exciting and a wonderful outlet for creativity. To some degree, I moved from magazine to magazine and got assignments that were increasingly exciting. That certainly sustained my interest. I eventually moved into management where I oversee writers and editors. I love the process of creating and producing magazines.

Q. Reflecting on a highly successful and honored role as a leader in magazine publishing, how do you assess the current state and probable future of magazines?

A. There are more magazines than ever with more people reading them. That really says it all. Magazines have also proliferated to an enormous degree with some big magazine readerships splitting into niche markets. The industry is quite healthy. The magazine is a profitable, low-cost medium. Magazines have portability and provide hours of enjoyment through high-quality visual and intellectual material. They are a good, cost-effective medium for the reader and for the advertiser as well.

Q. Some critics persist in predicting the "death of print," though they have been wrong to date. Do you see magazines merging into a multimedia landscape or maintaining a clear role and identity for themselves?

A. Well, some Internet sites have actually produced spinoff print magazines, as have television and cable networks. While magazines are capable of using different platforms and outlets, I suspect that the ink-on-paper magazine will be with us for a long time. The Internet is simple and accessible for some written and visual material, but people really like a relaxing experience with magazines. They enjoy the aspirational nature of magazines, spending an hour

In recent years, magazine starts and failures have paralleled changes in the general economy. As America has moved from an economy based on heavy manufacturing and extractive industries (such as coal, iron, and oil) to one based on information, communication, and services; a corresponding decline has occurred in business publications serving the older industries, with an increase in magazines aimed at covering the computer, electronic, and financial services.

Like other media, magazines are creatures of the marketplace. Although they can be a powerful medium for precise, demographically defined advertising, they are also susceptible to fickle consumer demands. As Chapter 10 explains, media advertising is a complex and dynamic process that links together specific forms of advertising con-

or so reading and appreciating the written visual material. It is a pleasurable experience that the best of magazines provide.

Q. But aren't magazines generational and isn't that penchant for reading and relaxation likely to change?

A. Yes, they are generational, so that means magazines need to be sensitive to change and be ready to reinvent themselves for succeeding generations. The *Ladies' Home Journal* is now in its third century, yet it has always been contemporary, speaking to the lives of American women in a fashion that both reflects and empowers them. Some magazines are identified with a particular generation. For example, *People* reflects the interests of the baby boomers; *Rolling Stone* takes in a somewhat younger group, and so on. Magazines live or die by the way they relate to a particular generation and are able to bridge the gap to the next one. Sometimes they are supplanted by other media. For example, the *Saturday Evening Post, Life,* and some other onetime leaders couldn't survive television.

Q. What do you think are the best prospects—and pathways for achieving them—for people eager to work on magazines?

A. Well, one needs to be interested in magazines in the first place and to have some talent either in writing, editing, or design. A person also needs to go to a place where they can succeed—where the environment is good for them. Early in my career, I worked for an editor who liked my energy level and was on my wavelength. That made all the difference. Finding the right boss is important. That means that the chemistry is right for a strong personal and professional relationship to work. It is important to be the kind of person a company needs at a given moment—to have the right idea. If you are a highly energetic person, a static, staid magazine is not the place to be. As much as possible we all need to work in a place where we are appreciated, comfortable, and have a chance to grow.

Q. Do you recommend any specific or specialized training such as magazine courses in addition to liberal arts education?

A. I have had good experiences with graduates of magazine programs from schools like Syracuse, Columbia, Penn, and others, but that really isn't necessary. That kind of training doesn't hurt, but most magazine people don't come out of specialized programs or journalism schools for that matter. The main thing people need is ideas and a capacity to grow. In some instances, specialized training in fields like health, business, or law are helpful. For that matter, knowing something about the subject matter of the particular magazine, whether fashion or politics, is helpful. It is vital to have passion for what you are doing.

Q. What has been the most satisfying aspect of your work in magazine publishing? The least?

A. The most satisfying thing is that magazines are always interesting. There is the creativity of the articles and the excitement of putting together the whole package. As for the most frustrating aspect of magazine work these days, I'd say that is dealing with celebrities and their handlers. Putting celebrities on the covers of magazines affects everyone in this business and television too. The overwhelming presence of the celebrity culture is diminishing the power of editors.

tent, specific media, and consumer demands for particular products. Thus, when consumers demand change, advertising content in magazines moves up and down in volume, causing the magazine industry to prosper or decline accordingly.

To some, the way magazines court business may sound a bit crass. For example, an article in *Folio,* which serves the magazine industry, began as follows:

> That din you hear is the sound of media players fighting to be the publication, or the network, or the Web site to deliver any given advertiser's message to a potential customer . . . Any magazine publisher who wants to stand out from the crowd

has to understand how media buyers interact with the marketers they serve, and show how his or her magazine can help.[15]

And here is what advertising agency executives recommend to magazines that want to survive in an increasingly competitive market:

- Spend a lot of time creating your pitch,
- Customize your offerings to match clients' objectives,
- Impact the bottom line, and
- Research, reach, circ, and buzz—maximize chances with agencies.[16]

Magazines are very much creatures of the economy and especially sensitive to individual wealth since they deal largely with specialized topics that often require affluent readers. The high-flying new economy of the 1990s and the early twenty-first century, brought—at least temporarily—an infusion of magazine advertising that targeted the "smart" reader instead of the "elite" reader, according to *Advertising Age*.[17] An executive at *Esquire* explained that magazines are after "the new affluent reader" who is more *psychographic* than *demographic,* meaning that people with midrange incomes are also buying products like Gucci shoes and clothes by Ralph Lauren. Luxury advertisers marketing expensive cars, home furnishings, clothing, watches, and electronic toys often choose magazines for their media buys. Indeed, many new media and e-commerce companies also pick magazines aimed at the luxury market that is increasingly crossing income lines, lines that were once thought to be insurmountable barriers.

Ownership trends. Much that was said in chapters 2 and 3 about trends in media ownership also applies to magazines. Today, many are owned by chains. Large corporations and conglomerates regularly buy up successful beginners and incorporate them into their financial empires. The resulting concentration of magazine ownership, whether by multinational firms from abroad or by large media corporations in the United States, appears to be continuing unabated.

THE INFLUENCE AND IMPORTANCE OF MAGAZINES

As we have shown, magazines differ greatly in their circulations. However, size and power and importance are not the same; nor can total revenues be equated with power and influence. Under such an evaluation *TV Guide,* perhaps the nation's most financially successful publication, boasting the largest circulation, would seem more important than a magazine like *Foreign Affairs,* an influential quarterly with a very modest circulation. But whereas millions may read the former and only a few thousand the latter, the smaller magazine may influence a much more powerful audience.

Editor Hendrik Hertzberg addresses the issue of the relative importance and influence of magazines in this earthy comment:

> Browse through any newsstand and you will be obliged to conclude that journals of opinion occupy a laughingly piddling place even in that relative backwater of "the media" known as magazine publishing. General magazines of any kind—that is, magazines read for their own sake rather than adjuncts to cooking, masturbating, riding dirt bikes, wearing clothes, or collecting guns—take up less and less shelf space; and journals of opinion (never big sellers at the drug store to begin with) are a next-to-invisible subset. Yet, no student of American society and its power

relationships would dispute that *The Nation* (circulation 80,000) is somehow more important than *Self* (circulation 1.2 million), *National Review* (circulation 120,000) and *The New Republic* (circulation 96,000) are more important than *Weightwatchers* (circulation 950,000).[18]

While Hertzberg's analysis may seem elitist, he has a point. The journals of opinion exert influence far beyond their numbers. They are read by government officials, business leaders, educators, intellectuals, and others who affect public affairs more than does the average person. The opinion magazines set agendas, shape ideas, start trends, and offer labels for virtually everything (like "yuppies" and the "X generation"). Perhaps more important, they speak to what it is that magazines do better than almost any other medium. Clearly, magazines inform, but compared with the reach of television news or the immediacy and impact of daily newspapers, this function is modest in any overall assessment. The same is true for entertainment, where television and movies are champions. Even fiction, where magazines were once very important, accounts for little of their content today. In none of these is the magazine a strong contender. It is in the realm of *opinion* that magazines triumph. They have the luxury of expressing their biases, being openly liberal or conservative, and as grumpy or savage as they choose. Other media, trying to court larger audiences, could never accomplish this. Magazines also can make longer investigations and present their findings in equally lengthy form. For example, the *New Yorker,* a widely respected opinion magazine, can have lengthy articles that take up topics such as law and justice in a cerebral and philosophical sense, or it can present articles about the United Nations that severely challenge the moral authority of that institution. The *New Yorker* does this kind of thing in the context of an eighty-year history during which it has earned a high reputation for such analyses. As with other respected opinion magazines, when the *New Yorker* speaks on an issue people listen, and the ideas it presents are picked up and diffused by more popular magazines, newspapers, and even television to audiences far beyond its readership. Thus, a respected opinion magazine can have an influence far beyond what the number of its subscribers would suggest.

TV host and film star Oprah Winfrey introduces the inaugural issue of *O, The Oprah Magazine,* in New York City, 2000, which both extended her media interests from television, film, and books (which she promotes on TV) to magazines. Magazines named for their entrepreneurs have a long and ongoing history, from *Harper's Weekly* in the nineteenth century to *Rosie* and *Brill's Content* in the twenty-first century.

THE FUTURE OF MAGAZINES

Many of the same challenges faced by newspapers because of the development of multimedia computers and the World Wide Web also confront magazines. Changes are taking place very rapidly in this technological world and it is impossible to predict over the long run how they will influence any of the print media. Many people, however, are not ready to believe that electronic media will displace magazines in print form. Their demise has been predicted many times past, as Charles P. Daly and his colleagues note.

On more than one occasion in the past 250 years or so, someone has sounded the death knell for the American magazine. Improvements in the printing press and mail distribution in the late 1880s enabled some magazines to increase their circulations dramatically. That was bad news for one editor who gloomily predicted that magazines wouldn't be worth reading any more because large circulations could only mean mediocrity and conservatism.[19]

Of particular importance for the future are magazines that are on the Internet. New terms have been developed to label magazines that are available online. For example, the term **e-zines** has come into use to identify magazines available in this form. These range from highly specialized (sometimes crude) tracts to truly sophisticated electronic magazines. Web pages are easily found for subscribing to magazines, often at significant discounts. A number of pay-per-read sites provide full-text articles. Good sources for finding information about magazines on the World Wide Web is www.newslink.org or www.foliomag.com.

Whatever the relationship between their print and electronic forms in the future, magazines are not only likely to survive as a medium; they may also thrive in the decades ahead. In facing their many challenges over a long history, magazines have survived by adapting to an ever-changing system of mass communication. The great diversity to be found in the industry provides something for everyone—in a form that is current, portable, permanent, and presented at a level within the readers' capability. That is a formidable formula. So although the medium may have to adapt to a new mix in the media system over time, it seems at this point that Americans will continue to support magazines as a voice for their many interests.

Chapter Review

- Magazines as we know them today started in London, where there was a concentration of urbane, affluent, and literate people. The earliest magazines were mainly instruments of politics, both in England and in the United States.

- It was difficult to establish magazines in the American colonies because people were spread out, literacy was not widespread, and the population was not affluent. In addition, such factors as transportation and mail service were inconsistent at best.

- During the 1800s, societal changes encouraged the growth of magazines in the United States. The population grew, cities became larger, more citizens were educated, the mails became more reliable and less costly, and all forms of transportation improved. In addition, it was a century of great issues.

- The magazine flourished early in this century during the era of the "muckrakers." Prestigious magazines took the lead in exposing corruption in business and government and unacceptable social conditions. Magazines played a significant role in the reform movement that characterized the first decade of the 1900s.

- New kinds of magazines appeared in the 1920s. One category was the newsmagazine. Another was the large-circulation magazine containing something for everyone. Such magazines had huge circulations, making them important vehicles for national advertising. They were very successful, and it seemed that they would be a permanent feature of society.

- When television arrived it absorbed much of the advertising that had previously gone to the large general magazines, many of which failed as a consequence of this change. However, the industry adapted remarkably well by developing a host of specialty magazines aimed at markets with well-defined interests and characteristics.

- The magazine as a contemporary medium continues to serve surveillance functions—monitoring what is going on, transmitting the culture, and entertaining the population. Its most notable function, however, is correlation, that is, interpreting the society by bringing together diverse facts, trends, and sequences of events.

- The magazine business today is fiercely competitive and very dynamic. An impressive variety of magazines are published. Every year, many are started; and the majority fail. The two basic types are consumer and business magazines; of the two, the consumer predominates.

- Trends in American magazine ownership parallel other media; that is, most are owned by chains. Large conglomerates, with many kinds of businesses, buy magazines and add them to their diverse holdings. The consequence of such consolidation of ownership is difficult to predict.

- The sheer number of people who subscribe to or even read a magazine is no indicator of either its ability to make a profit or its influence. The most influential periodicals are the opinion magazines. Their circulations are small compared with more popular magazines, but the people who read such magazines tend more than others to occupy positions of power and leadership, where their decisions can markedly influence public affairs.

- Although the new computer technologies challenge magazines as well as newspapers, the magazine is likely to survive in its present form. It is a medium that presents material tailored for the interests of specific kinds of people. It is likely that Americans will be reading magazines for a long time to come.

Notes and References

1. Many of the details in this section concerning the first magazines were drawn from James P. Wood, *Magazines in the United States* (New York: Ronald, 1949), pp. 3–9.
2. Wood, *Magazines in the United States,* p. 10.
3. The details of these early American attempts to produce magazines are drawn from Frank Luther Mott, *A History of American Magazines, 1741–1850* (Cambridge, Mass.: Harvard University Press, 1930), vol. 1, pp. 13–72.
4. Melvin L. DeFleur, William V. D'Antonio, and Lois DeFleur, *Sociology* (Glenview, Ill.: Scott, Foresman, 1972), p. 279.
5. Frank Luther Mott, *A History of American Magazines,* vols. 3 and 4 (Cambridge, Mass.: The Belknap Press of Harvard University Press, 1957).
6. Paul S. Boyer, *Purity in Print: The Vice Society Movement and Book Censorship in America* (New York: Scribner's, 1968).
7. Theodore Peterson, *Magazines in the Twentieth Century* (Urbana, Ill.: University of Illinois Press, 1964). Two excellent contemporary sources on magazines are Sammye Johnson and Patricia Prijatel, *The Magazine Industry from Cover to Cover: Inside a Dynamic Industry* (New York: NTC Publishing Co., 2000) and Charles P. Daly et al., *The Magazine Publishing Industry* (Boston, Allyn and Bacon, 1996).

8. These various figures were painstakingly assembled from historical accounts and various early government documents by Mott in his five-volume *History of American Magazines.* As he notes, many are approximations. The present section is a compilation of figures from several of his volumes. A useful contemporary scorecard on magazines is Samir Husni's *New Guide to Consumer Magazines* (New York: Oxbridge Communications, 1997).

9. Mott, *History of American Magazines,* vol. 4, p. 10.

10. Wood, *Magazines in the United States,* p. 131.

11. Fleming Meeks, "God Is Not Providing," *Forbes,* October 30, 1989, pp. 151–158. See also Magazine Publishers Association (MPA) Fact Sheet on "Average Circulation for Top ABC Magazines, 1998." See also www.magazine.org.

12. See MPA Fact Sheet on "New and Noted Magazines, 1998."

13. Theodore Peterson, *Magazines in the Twentieth Century,* 2nd ed. (Urbana, Ill.: University of Illinois Press, 1964), p. 442.

14. Philip Dougherty "Saturday Review's New Drive," *New York Times,* April 2, 1979.

15. Susan Thea Posnock, "Inside Media Minds," *Folio,* May 2000, p. 14.

16. Posnock, "Inside Media Minds," p. 2

17. John Fire, "Luxury Surges to Magazines," *Advertising Age,* Aug. 11, 2000, p. 54.

18. Hendrik Hertzberg, "Journals of Opinion, an Historical Sketch," *Gannett Center Journal,* spring 1989, p. 61.

19. Charles P. Daly, Patrick Henry, and Ellen Ryder, *The Magazine Publishing Industry* (Boston: Allyn and Bacon, 1997), p. xii.

Part Two

ELECTRONIC AND VISUAL MEDIA

Chapter 5

MOTION PICTURES: THE GREAT ENTERTAINER

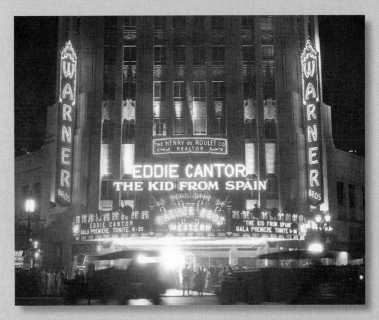

Ornate movie theaters of the 1920s and 1930s, like Warner's Western Theater in Los Angeles, here ablaze with lights for a premiere, have given way to smaller-screened multiplex and individual theaters.

THE MOTION PICTURE INDUSTRY, LIKE OTHER MEDIA INDUSTRIES, LIVES AND FUNCTIONS AMID NEW TECHNOLOGIES AND ALWAYS HAS. This is true today in the digital age. Movies are a medium of communication, an industry, and a form of popular culture as well as being cultural products themselves. Movies are sometimes an art form yet also a business. In the digital age, movies live within the new economy and are acquired by giant conglomerates that are themselves the products of technology and media. Inside the movie industry, digital technologies are nearly revolutionizing production and are changing content. And even in the world of movie distribution, from theaters to DVDs, the digital age is being seen and felt.

In superficial ways movies and television are alike. They both have moving images in color and sound. As mass media, however, the similarities end there. We have long had a dynamic, separate industry that makes films. It existed before television was even a dream in the minds of electronic engineers. By the 1920s, the motion picture was a fully developed form of popular entertainment with audiences in the millions, whereas television existed only crudely in early laboratory experiments. Today, although the motion picture medium has had to change in many ways to adjust to the influence of television, it remains a thriving and vital industry. Above all, the movies have left and continue to leave an indelible stamp on society and culture. To understand the nature, functions, and influences of movies today, it is necessary to see how they were shaped in the past.

The history of the motion picture is short, spanning just over a century. The events that led to motion pictures, however, go back to much earlier times. The first steps in this story involved solving a series of complex technical problems. A motion picture is, after all, a series of still pictures rapidly projected onto a screen in such a way that the viewer perceives smooth motion. To achieve this illusion of motion, problems in optics, chemistry, and even human physiology had to be overcome. Lenses, projectors, cameras, and roll film had to be invented. Only then were "the movies" born.

MAGIC SHADOWS ON THE WALL

The first problem to be solved was how to focus and project an image. Convex quartz lenses for magnifying and focusing the sun's rays were used as early as 600 B.C. Most of us as children experimented with magnifying glasses in which we tried to set a piece of paper on fire by concentrating the rays of the sun. That feature of lenses was understood long ago. In 212 B.C., Archimedes earned fame by frightening the Romans with a lens during the defense of Syracuse. It was said that on the wall of the city he mounted a large "burning glass" that could set fire to the Roman ships. The story may or may not be true, but it indicates that the ancients had begun to grapple with one of the main problems that would later be associated with cameras and projectors—how to use lenses to focus light.

The next major advance came nearly two thousand years later. A German priest, Athanasius Kircher, conducted experiments on projecting a visual image by passing light through a transparency. In 1645, he put on a "magic lantern show" for his fellow scholars at the Collegio Romano, using glass slides he had painted himself. His projected images of religious figures could barely be seen, but his show was a sensation. No one had ever seen anything like it. His light source was dim, so the images on the wall looked like ghosts. In fact, there were dark rumors that he was in league with the devil and was conjuring up spirits through the practice of "black arts."[1]

In the eighteenth century, the public became increasingly aware of the idea of the projected image. Traveling magicians and showmen entertained audiences with shadow plays and projected images of ghostlike figures. By the mid-1800s, improved lanterns with reflecting mirrors and condensing lenses provided fairly reliable sources of light. By the 1870s, the simple oil-burning lantern had been replaced by a powerful light that was produced by burning hydrogen gas and oxygen through a cylinder of hard lime. That form of illumination was widely used in the theater to spotlight acts and events. (Hence the expression *limelight*.) Ultimately, of course, electric lights provided the necessary illumination.

DEVELOPING THE TECHNOLOGY

Because movies focus so strongly on popular entertainment, it is easy to think of them in less than serious terms and to overlook the fact that they depend on a highly sophisticated base of scientific knowledge. The technological components in the motion picture are far more complex than those of print, and they were a very long time in coming. However, they all came together by the end of the nineteenth century.

Photography. The science of lenses and projection advanced earlier than that of photography. Until the nineteenth century, people could project images, but no one had been able to capture images to form a still picture. However, advances in chemistry in the late 1700s and early 1800s set the stage for the development of photography. Several experimenters worked to perfect a photographic process. However, it was two Frenchmen, an artist and inventor, Louis Daguerre, and a chemist, Joseph Niepce, who arrived at the best method after years of work. Niepce died shortly before success was achieved, but his partner, Daguerre, carried on.

In 1839, Daguerre announced the success of his work and showed examples of his sharp, clear photographs to the public. He called his process the **daguerreotype.** Each picture was made on a polished copper plate that had been coated with gleaming silver. In total darkness, the silver coated plate was exposed to iodine fumes, which formed a thin coating of light-sensitive silver iodide on its surface. When the well-protected plate was placed in a camera and then exposed briefly to a strongly lighted scene, the pattern of light and dark entering the lens of the camera altered the silver iodide. Chemical baths then fixed the image on the plate. Because Daguerre's pictures were much clearer and sharper than those of others (who tried to use paper), his process was rapidly adopted all over the world.[2]

Photography was received enthusiastically in the United States. By the time of the Civil War, there were daguerrotype studios in almost every major city. Everyone wanted their picture taken and photos of their loved ones. It was even common to photograph the recently deceased in their coffins so that the family could retain a final image. Itinerant photographers traveled the backcountry in wagons to meet the surging demand.

By the 1880s, as chemistry and technology improved, such pioneers as George Eastman transformed photography from an art practiced by trained technicians to a popular hobby. More than anything else, it was Eastman's development and marketing of flexible celluloid roll film and a simple box camera that made popular photography a success.[3] The availability of flexible film also made motion pictures technically feasible. Before they could become a reality, however, the development of photography had to be matched by progress in understanding visual processes and the perception of motion.

The illusion of motion. Motion pictures, of course, do not "move." They consist of a series of still pictures rapidly presented that capture the moving object in progressively different positions. When the stills are run through a projector at the correct speed, the viewer perceives an illusion of smooth motion. At the heart of this illusion is a process called visual lag or **visual persistence:** "The brain will persist in seeing an object when it is no longer before the eye itself."[4] We "see" an image for a fraction of a second after the thing itself has changed or disappeared. If we are presented with one image after the other, the visual persistence of the first image fills in the time lag between the two images, so they seem to be continuous.

The discovery of visual persistence by Dr. Peter Mark Roget in 1824 and its study by eminent scientists of the time led to widespread interest in the phenomenon. Toys and gadgets were produced that were based on visual lag. For example, a simple card with a string attached to each end can be wound up and then twirled. If a figure, say a bird, is drawn on one side of the card and a cage on the other, the bird will seem to be inside the cage when the device is spun. The reason for this is that both the bird and the cage are retained by the human retina for a brief period during the rotation. Today, for the same reason, children who rapidly rotate a Fourth of July "sparkler" see the entire pattern made by the moving point of light.

The quest for a machine to harness the principle of visual lag in order to create the illusion of motion occupied inventors through the last half of the nineteenth century. Inventions with odd names such as the phenakistoscope, mutascope, and zoetrope followed. All worked on the same principle, however—showing the viewer a series of still drawings that when seen in rapid sequence produced the illusion of motion. Developed by Émile Reynaud, the praxinoscope shown here astonished audiences with its displays of moving pictures.

By the middle of the century, the wheel of life (or *phenakistoscope,* as it came to be called) was highly developed. In various versions it consisted of a large disk on which was mounted a series of drawings showing a person or animal in progressively different positions. By rotating the disk and viewing the drawings through an aperture as the "wheel" turned, a person could "see" smooth motion. When elaborated and combined with the photography of things in motion, its principles provided the basis for movies.

Capturing and projecting motion with film.   During the closing decades of the nineteenth century, a number of people tried to photograph motion using a series of still cameras. One major advance was the result of a bet. In 1872, former Governor of California, Leland Stanford, and some of his friends made a large wager over whether a running horse ever had all its feet off the ground at once. To settle the bet, they hired an obscure photographer with an odd name, Eadweard Muybridge. In 1875, Muybridge photographed moving horses by setting up a bank of twenty-four still cameras, each of which was tripped by a thread as the horse galloped by. His photographs showed that at a full gallop a horse did indeed at times have all four feet off the ground at once.

The photographs created such interest that Muybridge took many more, refining his techniques by photographing people in motion. He eventually traveled to Europe to display his work and found that others had been making similar studies. Interest in the photography of motion became intense, but in 1890 no one had yet taken motion pictures as we do today. Further advances in both cameras and projectors were needed.

During the late 1880s and early 1890s, various crude motion picture cameras were under development, and a number of showmen were entertaining people with moving pictures based on serially projected drawings. Then, during the 1890s, applications of film and viewing procedures virtually exploded. By 1895, greatly impressed French audiences were seeing brief motion pictures projected on a screen by Auguste and Louis Lumière. Other applications of the new technology soon followed, and several individuals clamored for the title of "inventor of the motion picture." But it was William Dickson, assistant to Thomas Alva Edison, who developed the first practical motion picture camera.

Meanwhile, Edison and another assistant, Thomas Armat, developed a reliable projection system. Edison and Armat obtained U.S. patents and began to manufacture their projector, which they called the **Vitascope.** Edison also set up a studio to produce short films—mostly of vaudeville acts. Although it had many shortcomings, the Vitascope worked quite well. Its major flaw was that it projected at a wasteful forty-eight frames per second, whereas sixteen frames would have been enough to provide the illusion of smooth motion.

Because Edison, ever the penny pincher, declined to spend $150 to obtain foreign patents, his machines were quickly duplicated and patented in Europe. In fact, numerous improvements soon made Edison's original machines obsolete. Furious patent fights in the courts later threatened to kill the new medium.

Then Edison decided to exhibit his moving pictures in a peep-show device that he called the **Kinetoscope.** For a nickel, a single viewer could turn a crank, look inside the machine, and see a brief film on a small screen. This one-viewer-at-a-time approach, Edison thought, would bring a larger return on investment than projecting to many people at once. Edison's approach did not catch on; instead, in the end the industry developed along the lines of the traditional theater model. The Lumière brothers and others in Europe had seen clearly that this was the way to exhibit films. By 1896, however, Edison was projecting motion pictures for the first time in America to the public in New York City.

In general, by 1900, all the scientific and technological underpinnings of the motion picture were in place, and the new device was ready for mass use. Millions of people were eager to pay to be entertained. It was now a matter of developing the medium to present content that people wanted to see and to identify ways to maximize profits from the movies.

THE MOVIES BECOME A MEDIUM

The first few years of the fledgling medium in the new century were marked by experimentation. Many of the early films ran for only a minute or two. Yet just the sight of something moving on the screen could thrill an audience. Inevitably, however, the novelty wore off and patrons wanted something different. In response, the motion picture makers began to try longer films offering more interesting content. The fledgling medium developed at a rapid pace.

By 1903, both American and European producers were making "one-reelers" that lasted ten to twelve minutes and told a story. One-reel films were produced on every conceivable topic, from prizefights to religious plays, for exhibition at vaudeville halls, saloons, amusement parks, and even opera houses. Some have become classics, such as *A Trip to the Moon* (1902), *Life of an American Fireman* (1903), and *The Great Train Robbery* (1903). Many other one-reelers have been lost or perhaps were not believed to be worth preserving. By 1905, two-reelers were becoming increasingly common, lasting up to twenty-five minutes. These were more interesting for audiences, and as the popularity of the new movies increased, production and distribution of films expanded at an extraordinary pace.

The nickelodeons. The idea of renting films may seem to be of little significance, but it made the local motion picture theater possible as a small business venture. The required investment was modest and the profits could be high. One could rent a film and a vacant store, add some cheap decorations, install folding chairs, buy a projector, a piano, and a screen, and open the doors for business. In 1905, two entrepreneurs from Pittsburgh, Harry P. Davis and John P. Harris, did just that. They charged five cents for admission and called their theater "The Nickelodeon." In a week they made $1,000, playing to near-capacity houses. At the time, this was the next best thing to owning an Alaska gold mine.

The success of the first nickelodeon greatly impressed the entertainment world, and there was a stampede to set up others in cities across the nation. Within a year, one thousand were in operation, and by 1910, ten thousand were showing films! National gross receipts for 1910 have been estimated at $91 million.[5] The motion picture medium was skyrocketing to success.

Most of the early theaters were located in the hearts of industrial cities of the Northeast. Movies were made to order for that time and place. America had become a nation of immigrants, most of whom were newly arrived and many of whom lived in the larger urban centers. Many of these people spoke either no English or very little. Because the early movies were silent, language posed no barrier for an immigrant audience. Going to the movies was cheap, so they provided entertainment for people in the bottom stratum of society. Because of their near-universal appeal and modest price, the nickelodeons have been called "democracy's theaters." They showed stereotyped plots, overdramatized acting, and slapstick humor—the content that was needed to please their audiences at that time. Even the illiterate could understand a pie in the face, a wife's lover crawling out of a window as her husband came in the front door, or a mean boss.

The early movies proved to be popular beyond the wildest dreams of their pioneers. In New York City alone, more than a million patrons attended the nickelodeons each week in the early 1900s. Although the nickelodeons were associated with slums and ghettos, movies had become big business, and corporations were quickly formed to produce, distribute, and exhibit films.

Almost from the beginning, motion pictures have used posters, billboards, print— and later electronic media— advertisements to promote their wares. In time, posters like this one have become more than utilitarian promotional material, but collector's items as well.

This is the great picture upon which the famous comedian has worked a whole year.

6 reels of Joy.

Charles Chaplin IN

"THE KID"

Written and directed by Charles Chaplin

A First National ® Attraction

Movies for the middle class. Although the nickelodeons brought large numbers of the urban poor to the movies, the industry was anxious to lure other kinds of customers into the theaters— especially the huge mass of middle-class families. However, at first such people viewed movies as vulgar and trivial. The young medium not only bore the stigma of low taste but also was associated with the least prestigious elements of society. Even poor immigrant women were afraid to sit in the dark surrounded by strange men.

To shake this image and bring middle-class patrons to the box office, attractive theaters were built in better neighborhoods, and movie "palaces" opened in the business districts. Moviemakers produced longer, more sophisticated films to exhibit in such improved surroundings. While striving for a better product, producers discovered that they could increase attendance by giving prominent roles and media attention to particular actors and actresses. They hired "press agents" to publicize them as artists and important personalities. These early public relations specialists created masculine idols and love goddesses of the "silver screen" that were adored from afar by unsophisticated fans. Thus the "star" system was born—and gave a tremendous boost to the popularity of motion pictures.

By 1914, an estimated 40 million patrons attended movies every week, including an increasing number of women and children. The movies were being accepted by the middle class. Movie theaters had become respectable and the era of the tacky nickelodeon was over. Meanwhile, by the time Europe entered World War I, Hollywood had been established as the center of American moviemaking. The film industries in Europe had to close because of the war, leaving production and the world market to American filmmakers. They took swift advantage of the opportunity and a huge growth in film attendance occurred all over the globe. American films have been popular in the world market ever since.

The talkies. In the 1890s, inventors made their first attempts to combine the phonograph and the motion picture to produce movies with synchronized sound. Few of their early contraptions worked well. The sound was either weak and scratchy or poorly coordinated with the action in the film. The public soon tired of such experiments, and the moviemakers thought that talking pictures posed insurmountable technical problems.

However, the difficulties were overcome by the mid-1920s. American Telephone and Telegraph (AT&T) used enormous capital resources to produce a reliable sound system. Based on optical recording of sound incorporated directly into the actual film, it eliminated the problem of people being seen speaking with the sound coming earlier or later. Recently, controversies have arisen over who really invented the key devices, such as the vacuum light tube and the photoelectric cell, the inventions that made it possible to develop practical sound movies.[6] In any case, by 1926, Warner Brothers had signed an agreement with AT&T and the transition to sound was underway. The film company produced a new feature including sound for the 1927–1928 season. Starring Al Jolson, *The Jazz Singer* actually did not have a full soundtrack. It included a few songs and a few minutes of dialogue; the rest of the film was silent. It was an enormous success, however, and other talkies followed quickly.

Almost overnight the silent movie was obsolete; the motion picture with a full soundtrack became the norm. As technical quality, theaters, acting, and other aspects of the medium improved, motion pictures entered their maturity. Within little more than a decade, color would be possible and the movies as we know them today would be a reality.

The great silent film star Mary Pickford was among the first to command a large salary as actors became the most visible symbol of motion pictures in the minds of the public. Female and male stars—and sex symbols—continue to draw audiences today.

Portrayals of the fast life. The 1920s were a time of great transition. The old Victorian codes of morality simply crumbled following World War I. As the twenties progressed, there was a great emancipation from—some said deterioration of—the old rules. In the Victorian era women had been confined to lengthy dresses stretching from the chin to the ground, tight corsets, and long hair. Prim codes of conduct had made demure behavior and even chaperones mandatory for generations. By the mid-1920s, women could smoke in public, wear short dresses and cosmetics, cut their hair short, and even drink alcohol without being branded as harlots for life. It was a time of fast music, fast cars, "fast bucks," and, many thought, "fast women." These changes shocked the older generation but delighted the "flaming youth" of the twenties.

It is hard to say whether the movies of the time contributed to these changes in social norms or merely portrayed them as they developed. In any case, in its struggle for increased profits, the movie industry began to introduce subject matter that, for the time, was sexually frank and portrayed modes of behavior that were very clearly unacceptable by the standard of the older generation. Within a short time, major religious groups began actively to oppose portrayals in the movies of easy money, gangsterism, alcohol use, and sexual themes. These were powerful critics, and the industry was forced to take steps to police itself. As we will discuss later in more detail, in 1930, the industry adopted its first voluntary **code** for censoring films before exhibition.

The "golden age." During the thirties, the movies increasingly tried to appeal to entire families and become their major form of entertainment. In the process, the standards in the motion picture code became about as sinful as a Norman Rockwell painting. By the mid-1930s, for example, the code banned many words (that referred to sexual meanings) such as broad, hot, fairy, pansy, tart, and whore. Bedroom scenes always showed twin beds, with a table and a lamp placed in between and fully clad actors. The code was rigidly enforced, and by the 1940s, the movies had become a wholesome, if bland, form of family entertainment.

It was during this same period—from 1930 to the late 1940s—that American movies in many ways reached their peak. During those two decades movies were the most popular form of mass entertainment in America. In the thirties during the Great Depression, there really was not much else one could enjoy in the way of popular entertainment for so little money. The price of admission for adults was usually less than fifty cents. Children could get in for half price or less. A whole family could go to the movies together, have a snack afterward, and generally have what was regarded as a "swell time" while barely denting their hard-earned family resources. The golden age of movies had arrived, and people loved them. On average, for every household in America, between two and three tickets to the movies were sold each week.

The decline. Box office receipts held steady until the late 1940s. Movies were especially popular during the war years (1941–1945). By 1946, some 90 million tickets were being sold weekly. Then, with extraordinary rapidity, a new medium arrived and was adopted by the public in a way that had a devastating impact on motion picture theaters. It would also *alter the rigid standards that had been imposed by the industry*. With the rise of television, the movies in their traditional form underwent a precipitous decline. By 1960, after television had been widely adopted, only one-fourth as many tickets were being sold to American families as had been the case in 1948 (just before TV arrived).

To try to draw patrons back to the theaters, moviemakers turned to a variety of gimmicks and innovations. They tried increasing the use of color, escalating levels of violence, showing more explicit portrayals of spectacular special effects, and even occasional three-dimensional productions. None of those efforts really helped. Attendance at motion picture theaters has shown a downward trend ever since the arrival of television. It is clear, then, that on a per capita basis, movie attendance will never again be what it was before television. Movie exhibitors (those who own theaters and show films) continue to be plagued by a number of negative trends. Audiences today do not consist of entire families, as was the case in earlier decades, but consist mainly of young people for whom going to the movies can be a cheap date or a peer activity. Also, the older neighborhood theaters and drive-ins closed long ago, when TV became popular. And today, multiscreen cinemas, often located in or near malls, offer young viewers a range of films from which to choose.

In spite of these trends, the movie as a medium is here to stay. Fewer people may see movies by paying at the box office, but they see movies in other ways. The original social and cultural forces that drove the motion picture to heights of popularity are still in place. The United States is still an urban-industrial society in which people who work all day want to enjoy popular culture during evenings and weekends. In such a society there is an almost insatiable demand for popular entertainment that costs very little and makes few intellectual demands. Movies successfully fill that need. Many have no other options. Today, huge numbers of people want to sit back and have movies come to them. Thus, the industry has survived and prospered by producing movies for broadcast and cable television. The rapid growth in movie rentals for home VCR showings also has greatly improved the profit picture. Foreign markets add still another dimension.

The irony to this is that the motion picture has often faced the challenges of new technology, but not always with great vision. In 1982, Jack Valenti, President of the Motion Picture Association of America, appeared before a congressional committee

The gesticulating actor Orson Welles both starred in and directed *Citizen Kane,* a thinly veiled attack on newspaper mogul William Randolph Hearst. Many critics regard *Citizen Kane* as the best motion picture of all time.

and declared, "The growing and dangerous intrusion of this new technology threatens an entire industry's economic vitality and future security."[7] He was talking about the VCR and he was worried that home taping of movies would ruin the movie industry. Of course, that did not happen and instead videocassette rental became a whole new revenue stream for the movies. Currently, the motion picture industry is looking warily at DVDs, which, like videocassettes, can also be rented in video stores, but can be downloaded into a computer if one has hyperlinks to Web sites that contain encryption codes. In 2000, a lawsuit was filed to stop the Internet music service Napster from freely transmitting music files that people could download without paying those who owned the rights. While Napster and other music sites were constrained by the courts, the issue of ownership of intellectual property continued to evolve. In the case of DVDs, the encryption code is easily available on several web sites, and it is easier to obtain copies of movies this way than it was to make tapes using VCRs, since that process required two recorders. Once again, First Amendment arguments about the free flow of information run head on into the intellectual property rights of movie studios as creators of content. The VCR case went to the U.S. Supreme Court before it was settled, and perhaps current disputes will also be heard by the highest court in the United States.

FILM AS A CONTEMPORARY MEDIUM

Perhaps more than any other medium, the motion picture industry has attracted the popular imagination. Screaming supermarket tabloids, gushing movie magazines, and caustic television commentators pass on the latest Hollywood gossip and speculation to a fascinated public. The pictures themselves, from *The Birth of a Nation* to the latest "blockbuster" churned out by the industry, can be seen by tens of millions. The stars have always been in the public eye. Enthusiastic followers have been fascinated with the smallest details of their lives.

The movies are more than entertainment. They have played a long-term role in shaping our culture. Our nation's standards of female beauty and sexual attractiveness have for generations been derived in some part from movies. This influence started early in the twentieth century when Lillian Gish set the norms for the ideal female. It continued with the "vamps" of the 1920s and great beauties like Greta Garbo and Ingrid Bergman in the 1930s. By mid century "sex goddesses" such as Marilyn Monroe and Elizabeth Taylor served as models. Today, the definition of female sexual attractiveness is set by actresses such as Julia Roberts and Jennifer Lopez. Similarly, our conceptions of handsome manliness have been influenced by such figures as John Wayne, Clark Gable, and more recently Tom Cruise, Brad Pitt, and Denzel Washington. These standards can have a profound influence on the behavior of millions, in everything from applying cosmetics to forming criteria for selecting a mate.

All the publicity and popularity may do more to hinder than to help our understanding of movies. Behind the gossip and the glamour lie the complex realities of the industry as a mass medium. In addition to being a medium of communication and a social force, motion pictures are both a huge and diversified industry and an intricate art form. As art, film takes in the whole spectrum of forms that the term implies: it is a *performing* art, like theater and dance; it is *representational* art, like painting; and, like music, it is a *recording* art. Evaluating the artistic merit of films, however, is beyond the scope of this book.

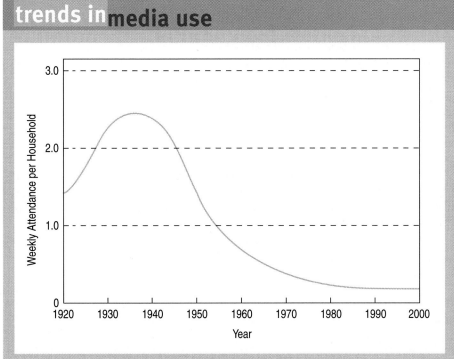

trends in media use

FIGURE 5.1

The Curve of the Adoption of the Motion Picture: Motion Picture Attendance per Household, 1920–2000

People began to purchase tickets to the early motion picture theaters before systematic data were collected by the U.S. Census or the motion picture industry. In 1922, systematic estimates became available. The peak period for paid movie attendance was between about 1930 and the end of World War II.

As a social force, film raises issues concerning the medium and the industry's presumed influences on morals, manners, beliefs, and behavior. We consider those issues in later chapters. In this section, we are most concerned with film as a contemporary medium of communication with different kinds of content that serve distinctive *functions*. Both the content and the functions are determined by professional communicators, the industry that produces the pictures, and their large and diverse audience.

THE FUNCTIONS OF FILM

For the people who make films, the medium provides an avenue for expression and an opportunity to practice a complex craft. It is also a means to wealth for some and simply a livelihood for others. The end product may be frivolous and diverting; it may provide information or training; it may make a social or political statement; or it may have important aesthetic qualities. Thus, a particular movie may seek to amuse or *entertain* by providing diversion and enjoyment; to *educate,* as many documentaries do; to *persuade* or influence (as in the case of wartime propaganda films); or (perhaps less frequently) to *enrich* our cultural experiences. Most often, a film will have combined functions. For the audience, the film may be informative, provide an escape, or deliver an engaging lesson in history, morality, or human relationships. For their producers, films are a source of profit. For directors and actors, films can be a means of supporting artistic values. For writers, films may be a way of raising consciousness about social causes.

Film's function is, of course, partly in the eye of the beholder. For example, most people consider vintage Walt Disney family films to be wholesome entertainment. Others interpret them as rigid ideological statements that praise an unrealistic image of America, showing artificial, antiseptic, white middle-class communities devoid of social problems. It is safe to say, however, that the main function of American films has been, throughout their history, to *entertain*. In this very important respect, movies differ from the print and broadcast media. We refer not to their obvious mechanical aspects, but to the traditional functions inherent in their origins. The origins of magazines and newspapers were related to the functions of providing information and influencing opinion, but films grew from the traditions of both theater and popular amusements. These traditions had far less to do with transmitting information and opinion; their central focus was always on entertainment. Today, films continue those traditions, and their principal function has always been to take their viewers away from the pressing issues and mundane details of everyday life, rather than to focus their attention on them.

THE DEVELOPMENT OF THEMES AND STYLES

The early movies looked to the established forms of drama (comedy, tragedy, and musicals) for their themes. Then and now they often turn to books for ideas and screenplays. Due to the nature of their audiences and the lack of sound, the early films relied on the art of *mime*. Soon, however, American films developed their own forms and traditions. In the silent period, Mack Sennett, Charlie Chaplin, Buster Keaton, Harold Lloyd, and others created their own forms of acting and storytelling; later, directors such as Erich von Stroheim and Cecil B. DeMille added their mark. These talented men from the past and filmmakers of today such as Spike Lee and Steven Spielberg, who create films with a distinctive style, are known as **auteurs.**

Eventually, film content and style were influenced as a dramatic form less by material from plays or books and more by film's own emerging traditions. The 1930s research of Edgar Dale provides a glimpse of those traditions. Dale analyzed the content of five hundred films that had been released by 1920, another five hundred released between 1921 and 1925, and still another five hundred between 1926 and 1930. He found that three major themes—crime, sex, and love—accounted for approximately three-fourths of the movies produced during the period.[8] In many ways, these are still the major themes of the industry.

In general, *directors* were the dominating force shaping films until the 1930s. Then, in the 1930s and 1940s, the *studios* became dominant. Several studios came to have recognizable styles. MGM was long known for its richly produced, glossy epics aimed at middlebrow tastes. Paramount was said to give its films a European sensibility. Warner Brothers often shot on location because creating the sets was too expensive, so the studio developed a reputation for realism.[9]

Today, these differences in production styles have disappeared as the influence of the major studios has declined. However, even in the heyday of the studios, some individuals—such as directors, actors, or cinematographers—marked their films with their own distinct stamp. Different members of filmmaking teams may dominate at any time and in any film. During the 1970s and 1980s, the director once again held sway as the king of film. Today, on the whole, there is a greater awareness of varying directorial styles. Although, movie stars still have on enormous influence on film because of their economic clout.

THE CONTENT OF AMERICAN FILMS

A film's content is almost always shaped by conflicting forces. The audience, technology, economics, and the filmmakers themselves all play a part. Producers look carefully at the balance sheet, continually worrying about audience interests. They ask: What is technically and economically possible and efficient, and what does the audience want? The search for efficiency led, for example, to standardized *lengths* for films, although those lengths have changed through the decades. The public wants and expects realistic *locations,* or settings, for films, whether in jungles, in cities, or on submarines. People enjoy *special effects* that seem realistic. The public wants and expects *coherent plot structures.* Old Westerns, for example, were usually melodramas with a hero, a villain, a beautiful girl, a sidekick, a handsome horse, and perhaps inaccurately portrayed Native Americans. The audience had particular expectations of what it would see, and plots usually conformed to those expectations. That principle still prevails.

However, old formulas can become trite. Over time audiences change, in terms of both their characteristics and what they want to see. Anxious to keep track of audience composition and tastes, studios hire the services of groups like the Opinion Research Institute of Princeton, which puts together a profile of moviegoers. Today, for example, more than half of those attending movies are under age thirty; and a very large part of the under-thirty group are teenagers. Fifteen percent are fifty years of age or older.[10] Making movies for the young, therefore, became a more certain way to make money than making them for mature audiences.

Still, the balance sheet is not the only factor that determines the shape of films. Directors, actors, and even producers may also want to put the mark of their own imagination on a film. According to one film historian, the workings of these opposing forces—bottom line versus personal expression—"drove the Hollywood cinema: the clash between the artist's sensibility and the classic mythic structure of the story types that were identified and popular."[11] Out of this clash came a broad range of films and film genres.

Genres. Balanced against the filmmaker's desire for individuality, then, is the need to give the audience a message it will understand and accept—the need for successful dream building. As a result of this need, plots become more or less standardized. Story types, or **genres,** develop—a category of films with the same basic kind of characters, settings, and plots. The gangster film is an example. Another is the war film. Still another is the slapstick comedy. Probably the most popular film genre of all time has been the Western. It was a completely American invention, with brave men and women living the rugged life on the range, or moving across the frontier where they met hardship in battle with the elements, Native Americans, and the law. (The Republic studio in particular made a large number of the early Westerns.)

Musicals were once immensely popular and some studios, such as Warner Brothers, virtually specialized in this genre. It was Warner Brothers that produced Busby Berkeley's elaborate, geometrically choreographed dance films of the 1930s, featuring group dancing with performers forming intricate patterns when photographed from overhead. Many of Berkeley's "dancers" knew nothing (and did not need to know anything) about genuine dance. All they had to do was to move precisely together in a few scenes. He used unusual camera angles and fast-paced editing to create spectacular effects.

Comedies have always attracted wide audiences. They have ranged from dry-witted, British-inspired parlor comedies to screwball films by the Marx Brothers, the Three Stooges, and Laurel and Hardy, to contemporary comics like Chevy Chase and Jim Carrey. Other genres include horror films, historical romances, and detective thrillers. Occasionally, public taste dictates development of a new genre, such as the science-fiction thrillers of the 1950s, the teen-horror movies of the 1960s, and action-thrillers in the 1990s. Today, with the use of computer technology, a new digital genre is developing.

Public attitudes and social conditions have often influenced (some would say dictated) the treatment of racial and ethnic minorities in film. For many years it was difficult for African-American and Hispanic or Asian actors to get good film roles. They were often depicted in subservient positions that reinforced racial stereotypes. In more recent years, there have been new images for minorities in screen roles. In the early 1970s, several major studios began to distribute films that portrayed the life, achievements, or problems of African Americans. Some, such as *Shaft* (1971) and *Superfly* (1972), starred heroes achieving victory over the white establishment. Others showed unity among blacks. Still others, such as *Glory* (1989), *Driving Miss Daisy* (1990), and *Waiting to Exhale* (1996), were sympathetic portrayals of the achievements, character, and problems of African Americans. However, despite their portrayals of African Americans and their themes, and even though African Americans such as Spike Lee often wrote, directed, and acted in these films, they were actually owned and distributed by white-run studios. In recent times, another ethnic genre appeared featuring comedians such as Eddie Murphy and Richard Pryor. Although such efforts have provided opportunities, black performers and artists still complain, justifiably, that there are not enough roles for them and for members of other racial minorities.

Films depicting women and women's issues have also gone through a number of phases. In the early films, women were usually melodramatic heroines—pretty girls threatened by evil villains and saved by virile heroes. However, in the 1930s and 1940s, actresses such as Bette Davis, Joan Crawford, and Barbara Stanwyck portrayed very strong women. In the 1950s, the "sexy blond" role, most prominently associated with Marilyn Monroe, brought a different and much weaker image of women. During the 1980s and 1990s, women returned in less-demeaning film roles. Indeed, a number of popular films took on clear feminist themes, with actresses

Actors such as Whitney Houston, Angela Bassett, Gregory Hines, and Wesley Snipes, in the 1995 film *Waiting to Exhale,* demonstrate a contrast from earlier times when almost all on-screen performers in significant roles were white, and African Americans were relegated to denigrating roles.

One of the most celebrated nonfiction documentaries of all time, Robert Flaherty's *Nanook of the North,* depicting Arctic life, set today's standard for this film genre. Then and now, documentaries are most often identified with the filmmaker instead of the topic or movie stars.

playing important roles that dealt with issues and problems of special interest to women. However, few female stars are as "bankable" as top male stars, who continue to get higher salaries and more multimillion-dollar deals.

Documentaries. Although the public overwhelmingly identifies "the movies" (both as an industry and as products for consumption) with the entertainment function, an important category of nonfiction films providing an educational function are *documentaries.* The term was first introduced by British filmmaker John Grierson, although his film was not the first of the category. His nonfiction film *The Drifters* (1929) depicted the lives of herring fishermen in the North Sea. In the documentary's purest form, the filmmaker intrudes as little as possible; the director, for example, does not direct actors or set up scenes.

From an intellectual perspective, documentaries can have a lasting importance, far exceeding entertainment films, as records of human culture in particular periods. In our flights of fancy we can imagine what we might see if someone at the time could have made documentaries of the ancient Egyptians building pyramids, of Johannes Gutenberg developing printing, or of the first encounters of Christopher Columbus with the people of the New World. At some point in the future, some of the documentaries produced in this century will have precisely that value. An example is the World War II documentary series, *Victory at Sea,* which recorded that global conflict for future generations. Another example is the film and video record of the first human beings on the moon. These are priceless records of human struggle and achievement that will have immense value to future generations far beyond that of the latest film produced for entertainment.

Through the years, documentaries have dealt with people at work, the efforts of nations at war, social problems, and other issues. Some are timeless and artful classics that are now intellectual treasures, like Robert Flaherty's *Nanook of the North* (1922), which depicted Eskimo life just before the native culture was transformed into a more contemporary form. Some documentaries take bits and pieces of a process and weld them into a film. For example, Emile de Antonio and Daniel Talbot's award-winning *Point of Order!* (1963) used sequences from the McCarthy hearings that others had filmed. The directors creatively put together the work of other filmmakers and of camera operators that had not been under their direction to produce an outstanding film. Documentaries often carry a powerful message, like Peter Davis's *Hearts and Minds* (1975), which traced the painful relationship between the United States and Vietnam.

By the late 1980s, documentaries began once again to reach audiences. Some were shown in movie theaters; others came via television. An outstanding example was the 1990 four-part documentary, *The Civil War,* based mainly on still pictures from the period. It electrified Americans when it was presented on public television. Nevertheless, there are ample reasons to question whether the documentary is becoming an endangered species. If it is on the wane, that is a loss to us all.

Public preferences. Many factors influence preferences: trends in morality, current fads, recent events, plus various styles and standards. The 1930s fostered stark realism and grim themes that came out of the Great Depression, as well as cheerful musicals that helped the public to escape from its troubles. Historical and patriotic themes as well as war films were popular during World War II and after, but so were light comedies. In the 1950s, films seemed to reflect the lighthearted mood of the country. Comedies and Westerns were increasingly popular, and sexual themes were becoming more explicit. In the late 1960s, during a period of dissatisfaction with prevailing standards and styles, some films successfully celebrated the antihero and began to take on controversial social topics. Films from the late 1960s to the early 2000s explored such themes as racism, drug use, feminism, and homosexuality. However, there was still time for the nonsense comedy and the lighthearted musical. Recent films have also explored international espionage and organized crime, as well as labor strikes, sports, and the supernatural.

THE MOVIE INDUSTRY

Above all, makers of motion pictures want profit. Art has never really been a prime mover of the industry. Charlie Chaplin, whose "Little Tramp" films are now regarded as art, put it bluntly in 1972: "I went into the business for money and the art grew out of it. If people are disillusioned by that remark, I can't help it. It's the truth."[12] There can be no doubt that filmmaking is a process in which money talks. To sketch a profile of this industry, we will look briefly at its organization—owners, studios, and employees—the source and size of its financial rewards, the number of its theater screens and films, and how many people watch films.

THE FILMMAKERS

By the late 1920s, the movies were a billion-dollar-a-year industry employing thousands and claiming a lion's share of America's entertainment dollar. Because of its benign weather and abundant sunshine for filming, the early studios of the 1920s chose southern California (specifically Hollywood) as the home for their huge dream factories. They established their studios on back "lots" that could be made into a Western town or a jungle paradise. However, as the industry matured, films were made in many locations. Hollywood became in some ways more of an administrative than a production capital. Nevertheless, it remained a symbol of glamour. As editor Peter Buckley wrote, "Hollywood was synonymous with everything that came out of the U.S. film industry, yet few films were actually made there . . . Hollywood was a wonderful, fanciful state of mind: the film capital that never really was."[13]

Owners and studios. The glamour myth of Hollywood overstated the geographic concentration of the film industry. From its beginnings, the industry forged financial links with Wall Street as well as artistic and production ties with European countries, and movies were often filmed at remote locations. Nevertheless, concentration of control and ownership was always part of the equation in American film. Major studios, such as the Big Five, have been the dominant force in Hollywood since its early days. The studios organized early and gained tight control over the whole production process, as well as over distribution and exhibition.

Founded by legendary motion picture moguls (such as Samuel Goldwyn and Louis B. Mayer), the studios ran their huge production companies in high gear. If you wanted to work in the movies in the heyday of the 1930s and 1940s, you worked for a studio, which had its own writers, directors, actors, and actresses all under contract, as well as its own technicians, equipment, and lots. Through a practice know as *block booking,* each studio forced theater owners to show its bad films if they wanted a chance to show the good ones. The studios even owned their own chains of theaters. Thus, they had an assured outlet for their films—good or bad—whereas other smaller producers found it difficult to have their movies exhibited. In short, the studios had control from idea to camera to box office. It was little wonder that smaller companies had difficulty breaking into the business.

Then the federal government stepped in. The courts ruled that major studios must stop block booking and give up their theaters. Because of this decision, filmmaking became a riskier business, and the major studios became less powerful.

In the 1960s, various corporations bought up studios and theaters, integrating these holdings with other kinds of investments. Large corporations bought up the old major studios. Gulf & Western bought Paramount. In the 1970s, the trend toward conglomerate ownership of studios abated in favor of emphasis on independent production companies, which continued into the 1990s. In the early 1990s, Columbia Pictures was purchased by Sony, the Japanese conglomerate. Warner Brothers was bought by Kinney National, which also owned funeral parlors, parking lots, and magazines, among other things. In the 1990s, the whole conglomerate became Time Warner, which was acquired by AOL in 2001, and Disney bought ABC Television. (America has also seen a corresponding rise in the number of cable system channels owned by other types of media companies.)

The mix keeps changing. The top motion picture studios today, such as Sony (Columbia-Tri Star), Buena Vista, MGM, Universal, and Twentieth Century Fox, dominate theatrical film distribution. Although the names of these studios have survived for many decades, they are no longer what they once were—the private empires of single movie moguls; they are now publicly held by numerous stockholders.[14] Thus, the movie industry is more diverse and scattered today than it was in the first half of the century, with independent producers making many films. The major studios continue to lead the industry, financing and distributing most films produced by independents as well as by their own companies. They collect more than 90 percent of the total income of movie distributors, although they share this income with the independent producers and directors whom they hire for particular services or assignments.

MOVIES AND MONEY—THE ECONOMICS OF THE BUSINESS

Like books, where most of what is published loses money and only a few bestsellers make profits, most movies also lose money. Of the six hundred to seven hundred films made each year in the United States, only about two hundred get the kind of favorable release that permits any financial return at all, let alone a profit. As film industry attorney Schuyler Moore has written, "The saving grace in the film industry is that when the rare blockbuster occurs, it can make up for the losses of a lot of other films."[15] Moore compares movies to wildcat oil drilling—a lot of capital is required to make enough films to produce a rare blockbuster. This system naturally favors the big studios that take care of their own distribution and have continuing relationships with theaters. Independent filmmakers farm their distribution out to third parties, a costly but necessary operation. Not surprisingly, over the years in this fiscally fragile field many independent filmmakers have gone out of business, while distribution companies have a longer life cycle. As *Variety's* editor in chief, Peter Bart, has written:

> A mere twenty years ago, it was common practice to open a movie in a few theaters across the country, build on word of mouth, adjust advertising strategies to audience response and then slowly expand to an ever broader audience. Today a movie is unveiled, not with a quietly orchestrated build, but with a cosmic paroxysm, a global spasm of hype involving giant marketing partners like McDonald's and profligate network ad buys on the Super Bowl or the Olympics. A new film is thus machine tooled to become either an instant blockbuster or an overnight flop. There is no room for adjustment or strategic change.[16]

The seemingly endless credits at the end of a motion picture are a cue to what a complex industry it really is. Understanding the movie business requires a look at the industry's creative and even arcane accounting practices. Like all industries, motion pictures have revenue-generating and revenue-consuming components. In a movie budget, the terms *above the line* and *below the line* have important meanings. There is actually a line in the budget that separate the costs of literary material, writers, producers, directors, and leading actors (above the line) from all the other costs(below the line), which include the actual production costs. A breakdown helps to focus this complex and variable industry where costs can soar because of superstar salaries and other demands that tend to drive up all of the other costs.

People Above the Line
- Producers
- Directors
- Actors
- Writers

People Below the Line
- Casting directors
- Production assistants
- Assistant directors
- Camera operators
- Gaffers and best boys
- Wardrobe coordinators
- Stunt coordinators
- Film editors

- Post production staff
- Composers and musicians
- Technical advisers
- and many others

Much has been written about the shady nature of the motion picture industry where tens of millions of dollars swirl around films that are often said to be unprofitable. Unlike other media companies and firms where there are owners and employees, the motion picture industry has many players who bring talent and financing to the table and also participate in the profits. As one recent book declares, "Motion pictures can illicit deep passion" and like oil gushers they "can create a flood of cash."[17] Some critics say that the participation system of the industry "amounts to nothing more than a price-fixing conspiracy by the major powers in a company town,"[18] while others "defend the fairness of the system with vigor."[19] Nevertheless, the motion picture industry is a lively and important part of the media industries generating considerable profits.

MAKING A MOVIE

Making movies is a communal process. Movies are not the product of one person but of many. As a result, according to film scholar John L. Fell:

> The substance of any particular production is likely to change appreciably between its early idea stages and the final release print. These changes may be dominated by some individual's vision, ordered by his own evolving understanding of what the movie is, but such a happy circumstance is never altogether the case, . . . even if most of the time someone pretends to be in charge.[20]

Moreover, every film requires the solution of both mechanical and aesthetic problems. The many people who are part of the team making the film must have different skills. Just consider the various unions involved in filmmaking: the Writers Guild of America, the American Cinema Editors, the Directors Guild of America, the Screen Actors Guild, and the International Association of Theatrical and Stage Employees. In other words, films are put together under chaotic conditions with a variety of artistic, technical, and organizational people.

Fell has identified seven stages or elements in the process of filmmaking:

1. *Conceptualization.* The idea for a film may come from any one of various people. Early directors often wrote their own scripts.
2. *Production.* To produce a film means to get the money together, organize all the people involved in the schedule, and continue supervising the process until the film is ready for distribution.
3. *Direction.* Once financial backing is secured and the script is acquired, then the director is chosen.
4. *Performance.* Actors must be chosen and their performances calibrated to the script and to other personnel involved in the film.
5. *Visualization.* The planning and execution of the actual filming involves cinematographers, lighting technicians, and others.
6. *Special effects.* Everything from camera trickery to monsters to stuntmen and stuntwomen comes under this heading.
7. *Editing.* This process involves choosing takes from all the film that has been shot and processing a finished film.

The producer is a key figure in putting all these elements together. In most cases he or she is part of a film studio that has the space, facilities, and personnel to complete the film. It is the producer who carries the responsibility for most of the central decisions, other than technical ones about acting, editing, and so on. The producer initiates the development of a film by acquiring a story or a script, or he or she may merely take an **option** on a story (that is, an agreement giving one the right to purchase at a later date) until he or she sees if the talent and the money are available to produce the film. If financial backing is available and suitable acting talent can be placed under contract, then the producer finds a director and assembles the rest of the filmmaking team. Directors are in charge of the shooting.

EMPLOYEES

Working for the studios is a host of specialists: electricians, makeup artists, property workers, grips, projectionists, studio teamsters, costumers, craftworkers, ornamental plasterers, script supervisors, actors, extras, film editors, writers, composers, musicians, camerapersons, sound technicians, directors, art directors, and set directors, not to mention the stars. Almost all the technical workers are unionized. Recently, the number of those employed in the motion picture industry has steadily increased. As Table 5.1 shows, most of these people are engaged in making films, or advertising and distributing them to exhibitors. Note that the number of people employed in movie theaters has declined steadily, because movie attendance has decreased while theaters have become smaller. Theaters have consolidated into multiscreen establishments and equipment has been automated.

Wages, of course, are only part of the cost of movies. By one estimate, the stars and other members of the acting cast account for only 20 percent of the costs, whereas sets and physical properties account for 35 percent.[21] The average cost of making a film in 2000 was $54.8 million. However, many films cost far more. Advertising and other costs were an additional $15 million per film on average. The money that the studios take in to balance such costs obviously depends on the number of films they distribute, the size of their audience, and the cost of admission. The industry took in $40.8 billion at the box office in 1999, a new all-time high. However, what accounts for the increase is not more people going to the movies but continuing inflation in the price of admission.

Table 5.1	Number of Persons Employed in the Motion Picture Industry, 1988–1999				
Year	Total	Production and Services	Theaters	Videocassette Rental	Other
1999	600.1	265.5	144.2	170.5	19.9
1998	564.8	240.2	133.5	171.9	19.2
1997	548.1	233.4	131.8	162.9	20.0
1996	524.7	222.5	123.9	155.1	23.2
1995	487.6	200.7	118.7	146.1	22.1
1994	441.2	169.6	113.4	138.8	19.4
1993	412.0	152.7	110.6	132.4	16.3
1992	400.9	148.8	110.2	127.1	14.8
1991	410.9	153.1	112.0	131.2	14.6
1990	407.7	147.8	112.1	133.7	14.1
1989	374.7	133.9	109.9	118.2	12.7
1988	340.9	113.7	108.0	103.3	15.9

Source: Motion Picture Association of America, 1999

THE MOVIE AUDIENCE

After the film is made, the next step is to distribute it in such a way that a maximum number of people will pay to see it. This boils down largely to renting it to exhibitors who operate theaters. Some are independent, but like newspapers, more and more are owned by chains. Deregulating media industries generally has benefited the motion picture industry. As a result, at least four of the major studios now own theaters or shares in companies that do.[22] To understand the current situation of distribution, we need to look at both the number of films being released and the number of theaters that show them to the public.

THEATERS AND COST OF ADMISSION

In the late 1940s, there were just over 20,000 (single-screen) theaters in the United States. By 2000, there were 37,396 (indoor and outdoor) screens. Although that looks like somewhat of an increase, keep in mind that the U.S. population expanded from about 150 million to approximately 283 million during the period, so that the per capita decline in moviegoing has been truly significant. Even the number of seats per theater has declined. Whereas in 1950 the average indoor movie theater had about 750 seats, by the late 1990s the average theater just had under 500.

The average weekly attendance at movies reached a peak of more than 90 million in the late 1940s; it was down to just over 18.5 million by 1992. The rate of decline leveled off during the 1990s, but there is little prospect that it will rise significantly again. Clearly, television has been the major factor in this precipitous decline, but the increasing price of admission may also have discouraged moviegoing. The price of attendance to a first-run picture (a single adult ticket) rose from an average of only twenty three cents in 1933 to more than $7.50 in most midsized and larger U.S. cities at a typical mall theater. In metropolitan areas admissions are even higher. For example, to attend a first-run picture in a major movie theater in New York City, the average price of admission in September 2000 was $8.50.

Overall, Americans are now spending more money on movies than ever before. However, in real terms the industry is attracting a much smaller part of the family entertainment dollar than before. For example, in 1943 Americans spent more than 25 percent of their recreational expenditures on movies. By 2000, this figure had dropped to less than 5 percent.

Who pays at the box office? As indicated earlier, movie theaters draw a youthful audience and appeal less to those who are older (see Table 5.2). The youthful vitality of the theater audience and its relative stability in makeup are an important force in keeping the industry alive and well. Most mass communication industries see young audiences as very desirable, because it is that portion of the population that in the future will buy goods and services and participate in the political process. For about twenty years, starting in about 1970, due to a declining number of births earlier, the young movie audience was slowly shrinking. By the mid-1990s, however, the number of teenagers in the population started an upward trend. Today, with the nation's grade schools and even high schools crammed with rising numbers of students, the young movie audience will increase steadily in the years ahead.

How often do people pay to see a movie in a theater? Not very frequently, according to national studies; but those who do, go frequently and pay quite often. So-called frequent moviegoers make up only about a fifth of the public over age

Age Group	Percent of Total Yearly Admissions					Percent of Resident Civilian Population as of Jan. 1999
	1995	1996	1997	1998	1999	
12–15	9%	11%	9%	10%	11%	7%
16–20	16%	16%	17%	18%	20%	9%
21–24	11%	11%	11%	9%	10%	6%
25–29	12%	11%	12%	10%	12%	8%
30–39	20%	18%	19%	17%	18%	19%
40–49	16%	16%	15%	16%	14%	18%
50–59	7%	8%	9%	11%	7%	13%
60+	10%	8%	9%	9%	8%	20%
12–17	14%	16%	14%	17%	17%	10%
18+	86%	84%	86%	83%	83%	90%

Table 5.2   Movie Admission by Age Group, 1996–1999

Source: Motion Picture Association of America, 1999

twelve, but this group accounts for the lion's share (over 80 percent) of all movie admissions. Although detailed dates on the social characteristics of moviegoers are not easily obtained, research that is available indicates the following: Single people continue to be more frequent moviegoers than those who are married. In fact, about twice as many single people compared to those who are married *frequently* go to the movies. At the other end of the attendance scale, at least a third of married people say they *never* go to the movies, somewhat more than the number of single people. More males than females describe themselves as frequent moviegoers. Finally, movie attendance tends to increase with higher educational levels among adults, suggesting that the moviegoing audience tends to be better educated than those who do not go.

The movie multiplex can draw large audiences to multiscreen theater complexes with lobbies filled with video games, refreshment stands, and other attractions. Popular in the 1990s, some of these theaters fell on hard times in 2001 and were closed and converted for use as health clubs and other businesses.

CLEANING UP THE MOVIES

As the movie industry grew massively early in the twentieth century, much of the public feared that films were having both powerful and harmful effects. A number of people believed that the new medium was negatively influencing children and teaching them unwholesome ideas. Many civic and religious leaders concluded that the movies would bring a general deterioration of moral norms and harmful political changes to American life. These concerns pressured the industry to "clean up" its product, and efforts to suppress certain kinds of content in the movies have continued. Most of the criticism now centers on films with "mature" themes—by which people usually mean those that deal with sex.

SEX AND THE MOVIES

During the 1920s, when the first strong pressures arose to censor films, the industry responded by cleaning up its own house. The Motion Picture Producers and Distributors Association appointed a former Postmaster General, Will H. Hays, to head their organization. Part of Hays's charge was to develop a system of self-regulation and to create a better public image for the movies. Hays and his group cooperated with religious, civic, and women's groups who had set up motion picture councils. During this early period, Hays's office was a buffer between the film industry and the public. Hays finally developed a tough self-censorship code, which all producers in the association had to follow. Without code approval, a film could not be shown in American theaters. Film producers who tried to defy this dictum were subjected to costly legal battles. The code restricted depictions of sex in particular. From the mid-1930s until the rise of television threatened the industry, movies avoided direct treatment of sexual themes and sexual behavior.

Meanwhile, a number of local governments screened and censored films. Even through the 1960s, Chicago gave this assignment to its police department, which called on a group of citizens to screen controversial films. Among the private groups most active in efforts to censor films was the Catholic Legion of Decency, which was established in 1934. It developed a list of recommended and nonrecommended films, and it promoted the list to both Catholics and the general public. The ratings carried a special moral force and occasionally were reinforced by bishops who warned Catholics to stay away from certain films.

Eventually, the Legion of Decency was replaced by the Catholic Church's Office for Film and Broadcasting, which published regular newsletters and film guides. A group within the U.S. Catholic Conference continues to promote this system, publishing ratings in Catholic diocesan newspapers as advisories for Catholic parents. The ratings and their assessments are as follows:

A-1: Morally unobjectionable for general patronage

A-2: Morally unobjectionable for adults and adolescents

A-3: Morally unobjectionable for adults

A-4: For adults with reservations

A-5: Morally objectionable in part for all

C: Condemned

Efforts like those of the Legion of Decency and other critical groups stimulated creation of a set of guidelines that Hays developed for the industry, the Motion Picture

Production Code. Although the code was not tough enough for groups such as the Legion of Decency, others regarded it as harsh, repressive, and too legalistic. Some film historians think the code hindered the development of American motion pictures.

By the late 1960s, the production code had been modified greatly. Numerous legal actions had broken efforts to apply rigid censorship. The industry entered a

---

insights from
MEDIA LEADERS

David Brown, Film Producer
New York, New York

David Brown is an active and honored motion picture producer who has produced more than twenty motion pictures (many in partnership with Richard D. Zanuck) including such memorable films as *Jaws, The Sting, A Few Good Men, Angela's Ashes, Chocolat,* and others between the 1970s and 2001. He has been a journalist, an author, and a magazine editor. His work as a producer has also included Broadway plays and television drama. He was honored by the Motion Picture Academy of Arts and Sciences with its coveted Irving G. Thalberg Memorial Award as "a creative producer whose body of work reflects a consistently high quality of motion picture production."

Q. How did you first get actively involved in the motion picture business?

A. I wish I could say it was love of film, but in all candor it was a personal crisis, a divorce, in fact. I was a successful magazine journalist who was receptive to a change when Darryl F. Zanuck of Twentieth Century Fox put out the word that he wanted "the best editor in New York." I was lucky to have generous friends who recommended me. Before I knew it, I was en route to Hollywood where I became head of the story department for Fox Worldwide. This was at a time when "the story" was everything.

Q. What factors have sustained your continued interest and involvement, now over several decades?

A. Bonding with Darryl F. Zanuck was a critical factor. We worked well together and I virtually became his number two executive. Today, the head of the story department wouldn't stand a chance against the marketing people and others involved in the business of filmmaking. You have to understand that I was really never young or thought of myself as such. I had been

a professional journalist as a young man, had experienced the war, and must have been sustained by fear of death, fear of poverty, and a love of the word.

Q. Your love of "the word" and of stories has taken you across a multimedia landscape embracing print and broadcast media, motion pictures, and even Broadway. Do you see this kind of participation in a converged media world becoming more commonplace?

A. For me that was really accidental. When I returned from military service at the end of World War II, I was entitled to have my old job back, that of nonfiction editor at *Liberty Magazine,* then a popular periodical. But, not wanting to displace the person who had taken my place, I was offered the job of fiction editor, which I accepted. That took me from the world of journalism and news to contacts with authors, editors, and agents. Of course, that was enormously valuable when I went to Hollywood. In my day, journalism was an avenue to motion pictures, at least for screenwriters, but most of my contemporaries thought film was a cop-out, something you did till you could write the great American novel or play. After a turbulent time in the sixties when the film *Cleopatra* shut down Twentieth Century Fox (because of massive cost overruns), I returned to New York and got a job in book publishing as head of the hardcover division of the New American Library. There I was back in a kind of journalism once again and published such books as the James Bond series and *The Founding Father,* the story of Joseph P. Kennedy and the family of JFK. What was unusual in the past—that is, working on magazines, movies, books as well as TV and Broadway—will be easier to accomplish in the future.

Q. Reflecting on a lifetime observing the motion picture industry, how do you assess its current state and probable future?

new era of self-regulation by establishing a movie classification system. Instead of barring certain films from theaters, the new system required that the public be warned of what to expect in a film. The result, which has been modified four times since it was adopted in 1968, is on the following page:

A. I've said for a long time that motion pictures are an endangered species; that they are doomed, but will never die. It is the story that will sustain motion pictures no matter what technology is involved. Some of my recent films such as *Angela's Ashes* and *Chocolat* are great stories set to film. Without a story as without a song, you have nothing.

Q. **What do you think are the best prospects—and pathways for achieving them—for young people eager to enter the motion picture field?**

A. When people ask me about getting into the business, I tell them that they need talent, and that's something no school can give you, but also drive and persistence. If you want to write, direct, act, do music, or engage in any of the major disciplines of the motion pictures, go do them, locally or wherever there is a chance. You can write a script, study the business by observing movies at the theater, mine the public library for information, and eventually get connected with an agent.

Q. **Do you recommend film school, journalism school, or other communications studies as preparation for a career in the motion picture industry?**

A. Yes, I do. Once the film and journalism schools were reviled, but now they are respected and should be. Film schools can provide the grammar and syntax of movies and journalism schools teach you how to write and edit as well as other things. My support for these schools is more than talk. I serve on the board at the Columbia Graduate School of Journalism from which I graduated and helped start the American Film Institute School.

Q. **People sometimes worry that a new technology will swallow an old one, yet motion pictures have survived television, cable, and the digital age to date. Are the movies really "here to stay" and are they**
"getting better than ever" as the industry claims, or is this just hype?

A. I've seen motion pictures pass through several periods when they feared television, cable, the VCR, and the like. Of course, rather than undercut motion pictures the new technologies have provided new avenues for storytelling and for distributing movies. TV became our greatest ally, not a threat. The same was true with cable and now pay-per-view and other new distribution methods. I don't worry much about technology putting us out of business. The challenge is always to be versatile and use technology to your advantage. In the end, this business really is not about technology. It is about storytelling. It is amazing to see how far film travels. I was in Tahiti with my wife [legendary *Cosmopolitan* editor Helen Gurley Brown] when we saw a crowd of half-naked people. As we pushed into the crowd expecting a demonstration or even a riot, we saw that they were watching a movie projected against a tin shack. They were watching *Titanic*.

Q. **What has been the most satisfying aspect of your involvement in the motion picture field? The least?**

A. The most satisfying aspect of filmmaking is being on the set with actors and directors, being in the midst of production. This is when I really "see" the film, certainly not at premieres when I'm likely to slip out and have dinner since I've seen it all as it was being created and I have no desire to sit in a theater and watch the defects. The least satisfying? Dealing with executives and other studio functionaries who are not filmmakers and who don't read much more than a précis of the film. Still there are some people who are moles in the organization who end up making creative judgments about movies. At times, they can be more powerful than studio heads.

G: All ages admitted, general audiences

PG: Parental guidance suggested, for mature audiences

PG-13: Parents are strongly cautioned to give special guidance to children under thirteen

R: Restricted, children under seventeen must be accompanied by a parent or other adult

NC-17: No one under seventeen admitted

The classification does not indicate quality; it is only a guide for parents considering what motion pictures their children should be permitted to see. The industry, through the Motion Picture Association of America, in effect puts its seal of approval on the first four categories of films and denies it to the fifth. This system won public support and stilled some criticism, but some film producers feel that the system is too restrictive. There has been no active move to overturn it, however. Interestingly, there are less than half as many G- and PG-rated films as there are films with PG-13, R, or NC-17 ratings.

Efforts to suppress a particular motion picture can backfire. Perhaps no film in recent times has aroused such an outcry as *The Last Temptation of Christ* (1988), a low-budget movie that became something of a financial success at the box office largely as a result of the furor. Various church groups and other critical people threatened and carried out boycotts and protest demonstrations. These efforts were thoroughly covered by both national and local television news, and of course, by newspapers. The publicity brought crowds of curious viewers to the theaters to see what all the fuss was about. Some observers have speculated that if the film had been ignored, it would quickly have died as a dud.

VIOLENCE AND VULGARITY

As television became a highly competitive medium for motion pictures, the industry turned away from the earlier production and review code developed by Hays. The problem was rapidly declining ticket sales at the box office. The box in the living room was displacing the silver screen downtown, in the neighborhood, and at the drive-in theater (which declined from 3,500 in 1980 to a mere 717 by 2000). Even before VCRs and cable television, people increasingly preferred to watch free entertainment on their TV sets rather than travel to a theater and pay to get in.

To meet this competition from network television, the movies began to alter their content. Once again, as they had done during the 1920s, they turned to depictions that went beyond the more conservative norms of the traditional segment of the public. Aside from the sexual portrayals previously discussed, which were always the most controversial, the producers also began to incorporate an increasing level of violence and vulgarity into their films.

In some ways, this was successful and in some ways it was not. It clearly altered the composition of the audience but it also may have reduced its size. There was limited success in that after about the mid-1960s, when the rate of decline in box office ticket sales slowed down. Fast-action drama, packed with violence and with the actors using vulgar language, was a clear change from the older, sanitized movies that had been governed by the Hays code. Increasingly, the industry began producing fast-paced films in which macho heroes shot it out, had brutal fistfights, and raced through the streets in spectacular crash-filled car chases. New genres, such as horror, surf and beach epics, and more sophisticated special effects monsters also proved to be popular. However, with these changes in content, a transformation of the audience was underway in which the movies changed from a form of family entertainment that mom, pop, and the kids all attended together into one made up of younger, single people. In particular, themes of violence and vulgarity were just right for younger audiences, but they were not appealing to older, married people and were unsuitable for their children. Thus, while the loss of ticket sales slowed, the movies effectively shut out the more conservative majority of older, married people.

Margaret DeFleur has described a very interesting pattern that can be seen when looking back at the history of the relationship between audiences, their moral norms, and the content of the movies. During the period just before and after World War I, the content of the films did not transgress general norms concerning sexual depictions, violence, or vulgarity. As the country entered the changing period of the 1920s, as noted earlier, movies increasingly challenged those norms. The Hays code temporarily halted that and reversed the trend. Challenged by television, however, movies once again began to cross the line in terms of what many people wanted to see on the screen. In recent years, further competition came to the industry from cable TV and from videocassette rental. Again, seeking increased audiences and profits, movies seemed to many to transgress traditional norms regarding sex, violence, and vulgarity. The result was a pattern of pressing forward to the limits of such norms, then drawing back when public outcries became too shrill, and waiting until people adapted to the new standards being set. When outcries became fewer, the industry would once again press on until it encountered resistance. Because of this cycle, the public gradually became *desensitized* to content of the movies that at one time would have caused a serious problem for the industry.

What DeFleur has called the "creeping cycle of desensitization" is not unique to motion pictures and can apply to other media as well. What it explains is that when movies get sexier, more vulgar, and increasingly violent, one need not assume that these changes are simply due to immoral decisions made by bad and greedy people who are in charge of the movie industry. Such people may not be saints or leaders in a movement to purify the popular culture of America, but their decisions are largely products of the economic system in which our media are embedded. Their choice can be stark—make money for their investors (highly approved) or go bankrupt (highly disapproved)! With no political system of censorship to restrain them, they supply the public with what it appears to want, and back off only temporarily when critics raise a significant fuss.

Violence in motion pictures has been a topic of concern for decades, but shoot 'em up films continue to be popular as this scene from the film *Reservoir Dogs* demonstrates.

CENSORSHIP AND POLITICS

Sex, violence, and vulgarity have not been the only categories of content at the center of outcries against movies over the years. Politics too has been the basis for censorship efforts. Many films with political themes were widely criticized during the 1930s. Battles to organize unions, fights between unions and producers, charges that some unions were tools of Communists, and accusations that some films were Communist propaganda split Hollywood in the years before World War II. During the war, political differences were submerged as the industry united behind the war effort. However, when fear of communism ignited again in the late 1940s and into the 1950s,

The Creeping Cycle of Desensitization Theory

explaining
MEDIA EFFECTS

The movie industry has survived, even in the face of competition from other media. It has found alternative markets for its products and increasingly incorporated more sexual themes, violence, and vulgar language.

The public also changed. In the movie The Outlaw (1948), Jane Russell's display of much of the upper part of her large bosom brought howls of protest from a large segment of the public. Swearing was also an early issue. The word "damn" uttered by Clark Gable in the 1936 film, Gone with the Wind, raised many eyebrows.

Today, total frontal female nudity and open sexual coupling are routinely depicted. Movies currently show savage beatings, deadly car bombings, rape, torture, and wholesale shootings with brains and blood spewing. Moreover, actors now routinely use four-letter words that would have shocked movie audiences little more than a generation back.

While politicians sometimes decry this situation, and claim at election time that they will bring the entertainment industry to heel, the outcry from the general public has largely been more muted.

Why have the movies changed so much? Also, why has public acceptance of the new standards become so tolerant?

A theory that can explain these changes has been called the "creeping cycle of desensitization." Developed by Margaret DeFleur, the theory refers to the increasing failure of traditional moral norms of society to hold back the depiction of ever-increasing levels of violence, explicit sexual behavior, and vulgar language in our movies (as well as in other entertainment media).

Contributing factors to these changes, DeFleur maintains, are the lack of control over content due to the protections of the First Amendment and the failure of critics to crack down effectively. The cycle of desensitization started in the 1920s. Movies became increasingly explicit, showing women in undergarments, young people using alcohol, and brutal

killings by gangsters. These transgressions of moral norms brought the movie production codes of the 1930s and 1940s. By the 1950s, however—especially with the decline of attendance at the box office—movies abandoned the code and began to incorporate increasing violence, explicit sex, and dirty language. As the public gradually became accustomed to this type of content, the industry pressed farther, using these themes to increase profits. Stated as systematic theoretical propositions, the theory goes like this:

1. Our movie industry operates in a system of economic capitalism, in which making profits is a major and highly approved goal.

2. Making profit with a movie requires keeping costs down and also maximizing the audiences who pay in one form or another to see the film. Sex, violence, and vulgarity attract audiences.

3. The First Amendment offers few restraints on what any medium can present to the public. This is largely left to audience tastes that define what people will or will not tolerate and pay to see.

4. The young—a large proportion of the movie audience—care little for conservative tastes. They seek pleasure and excitement via exposure to sexual depictions, vulgarities, and violence. The number of opposing critics is small.

5. **Therefore,** moviemakers, seeking maximum profits, constantly increase their depictions of sex, violence, and vulgarity. They stop only if criticism is strong, and resume after the public becomes accustomed to the new standard.

political censorship came to Hollywood as never before. The House Un-American Activities Committee, an official group of the U.S. Congress that had been active since the 1930s, held hearings and charged scores of people, including many in the film industry, with Communist activity. The hearings were followed by some prison sentences and **blacklisting** of people in the film, broadcast, and print industries.

Blacklisting was the work not of government but of private groups and it was decidedly not a democratic activity. Various lobbying groups put together lists of people they suspected of being Communists, circulated the lists privately and threatened to boycott advertisers who sponsored shows, newspapers, or magazines that hired anyone on the list, as well as producers who gave listed people work. Most of those blacklisted were not publicly accused, so they had no chance to defend themselves. Some actors, producers, writers, and others did not even know they were on such a list until no one wanted to hire them and their careers crashed. For a time performers had to be "cleared" by one of the anti-Communist groups before they would be hired. This period, when unsupported charges were frequent, is one of the darkest in media history. Postwar fear of communism was the culprit and the film industry was hard hit by the informal censorship that resulted.

Many groups outside the movie industry have exerted influence on the content of films. Congress has summoned actors and directors to public hearings, the Supreme Court has tried to define what is and is not obscene, and church groups and local officials have tried various strategies to shape, suppress, or ban American movies. The result is a constraint on the artistic freedom of filmmakers, but little if any useful feedback for them. The groups pressuring the filmmakers are too small and their interests too narrow for their efforts to constitute effective feedback for a medium intended for a mass audience. Nevertheless, their efforts can seriously distort communication between filmmakers and their audiences. Still, consumers of films have the same First Amendment rights that filmmakers do and this includes the right to protest against content they do not like.

The Bravo Television series "Inside the Actors Studio" features leading stars, such as Faye Dunaway pictured here, who are interviewed by the thorough and scholarly James Lipton, dean of the Actors Studio drama program at the New School University in New York City, where the show is filmed in front of students and guests.

EVALUATING FILMS: CRITICISM AND AWARDS

Film ratings or public protests are only part of the many assessments that filmmakers receive. The writings of critics, the selections made for film festivals, and awards and surveys of public opinions of films provide other evaluations. These assessments might suggest that there are uniform standards of excellence in films, but that is not the case. Although occasionally there may be widespread agreement on which film was the best of a year or decade, there are about as many standards for criticism as there are critics and awards.

THE CRITICS

Some people distinguish between **reviewers,** who make assessments for a general audience, and **critics,** who judge a film by more artistic and theoretical criteria and try to ascertain its social importance. The terms are used interchangeably by most people, but they can connote significant differences. Reviewers see films and discuss their content, popularity, and merits in newspaper columns or other media and make recommendations to the public. Critics do much the same. However, they are not interested in a film's popularity. Critics have their own standards against which they judge a film, although they vary from one individual to another. Because film has gained status as an art form, some critics judge a film on the basis of artistic potential and compare it with other films and theatrical productions. They consider factors such as the film's originality and its ability to project universal themes. A critic might be interested in any number of things about a film: the technical aspects such as photography, sound, the use of close-ups, and color; the quality of the screenplay as a piece of writing; the performance of the actors; and the unity and cohesiveness of the production. Some critics discuss the film in terms of the way it fits into a particular actor's or director's career. For example, a critic might discuss whether the direction and acting in the latest Woody Allen film are as good as in his previous films.

Film criticism appears in many places. Specialized industry magazines speak mainly to the movie community and to film scholars. Many general magazines and newspapers have movie reviews and criticism. *Time* and the *New York Times,* as well as others, publish annual "ten best movies" lists. NBC's popular "Today" show offers regular movie reviews. PBS has a half-hour show devoted to movie reviews called "At the Movies," which is a sort of "consumers' guide" for what is worth seeing. Local television and radio stations review films on the air. Various Internet services also list, critique, and rate films. Sometimes it seems like more energy is devoted to reviewing and criticizing films than to making them. There are even annual awards for the best film criticism.

THE AWARDS

Most organized human endeavors offer various kinds of symbolic rewards to individuals or groups that perform well. It may be a medal for wartime bravery, a diploma for completing a degree program, a plaque for selling the most insurance, or a cup for catching the biggest fish. Individuals who organize and control such awards understand their importance. As long as people take them seriously, awards satisfy needs for status recognition and give both prestige and publicity to that particular arena of competition.

Moviemaking is no exception. It has its own system for recognizing high-caliber performances and for publicizing those accomplish-

The Academy Awards and other honors invented by media industries confer status on popular culture fare. In an ironic mix of different cultural styles and standards, actress Marcia Gay Harden accepts an Oscar in 2001 for her supporting role in *Pollock,* a film about abstract artist Jackson Pollock, whose work hangs in leading fine arts museums.

ments. The granddaddy of all the movie awards is the Oscar—the gold-plated statue about a foot high awarded each year in a nationally televised spectacle by the Academy of Motion Picture Arts and Sciences. The Oscars are prizes from the industry itself to its honored few, and even though the little statues themselves are rather tacky and cheaply produced, they are the most coveted of all the movie awards. Receiving the awards has real economic value because films that win them are usually rereleased with attendant publicity and draw thousands more viewers and box office receipts.

The Academy makes awards in many categories and the list is almost endless: it includes best picture, best director, best actor, best actress, best supporting actor, best supporting actress, best screenplay adaptation, best original screenplay, best cinematography, and best foreign-language film. There are also awards for art direction, sound, short subjects, music, film editing, and costume design, as well as honorary awards, scientific and technical awards, and various awards for service to the industry.

The Academy Awards have not been without their critics. Some charge that those giving the awards concentrate on the most popular films rather than on the best or most socially significant. There is some truth to this argument. For example, one of the best films of all time—Orson Welles's brilliant *Citizen Kane* (1941)—got only one award, for best screenplay. Still, the list of Oscar winners is a kind of "who's who" of well-known films and filmmakers.

Other honors and prizes are less well known. Both the Writers Guild and the Directors Guild give awards and there are a number of awards by groups independent of the industry. The National Board of Review Awards are given for films that are recommended for children. Both the National Society of Film Critics and the New York Film Critics give annual awards for exemplary films and the foreign press corps covering Hollywood gives annual Golden Globe Awards.

Chapter Review

- Motion pictures have a technological history that includes inventions in optics, photography, and electronics and discoveries in the psychology of the perception of motion. By 1886, short, primitive pictures showing motion were being exhibited in America.

- The movie theater as we know it began after the turn of the nineteenth century with the nickelodeons. Within a few years, movies were being made for the middle class and the industry expanded to become a popular mode of family entertainment.

- As society changed rapidly after World War I, movies mirrored the new ways of life. Conservative people were alarmed at portrayals of alcohol use, easy money, fast cars, and loose morals. Extensive efforts to control movies arose and research on their effects began.

- Between 1930 and 1960, the great golden age of movies dawned and then declined. The American film industry has gone through many changes in its short history. For the most part, it has been a medium for entertainment.

- Every film is a product of technology, artistry, managerial skill, and showmanship. Making a film involves a wide range of professionals and craft workers. At various times different members of the filmmaking team have tended to dominate the shaping of films.

- The content of a film is influenced by conflicting forces: the desire for efficiency, a view of what the audience wants, and an individual's desire to shape the film. The result of this conflict has been a wide range of genres and styles in American films.

- Traditional film (shown in theaters) was once a more important medium of entertainment than it is today, but the industry has responded to the demands of new competition, changing technology, and changing audiences. Because it has adapted so well, the moving picture show, in one form or another, will remain a large, lively, and significant medium.

Notes References

1. Martin Quigley, Jr., *Magic Shadows: The Story of the Origin of Motion Pictures* (Washington, D.C.: Georgetown University Press, 1948), pp. 9–10.
2. Josef M. Eder, *History of Photography* (New York: Columbia Press, 1948), pp. 209–45, 263–64, 316–21. For a contemporary look at a motion picture technology see Steve Barclay, *The Motion Picture Image—From Film to Digital* (New York: Focal Press, 1999).
3. There were several claimants to the invention of celluloid roll film in the late 1880s. Eventually the courts decided a case on the matter in favor of the Reverend Hannibal Goodwin. However, George Eastman produced the film in his factory and marketed it to the public. See Frederick A. Talbot, *Moving Pictures: How They Are Made and Work* (London: Heinemann, 1923).
4. Talbot, *Moving Pictures,* p. 2. Also see Gail Resnik and Scott Trost, *All You Need To Know About the Movie and TV Business* (New York: Fireside, 1996).
5. Tino Balio, ed., *The American Film Industry* (Madison: University of Wisconsin Press, 1976), p. 63.
6. In 1988, the work of Theodore Case of Auburn, New York, came to light. Very early sound films (1923) were discovered in a coal bin in his home, along with documents and equipment. It now appears that Case, rather than Lee DeForest, may have first developed the critical elements in the sound movie. At this point, however, it remains an open question.
7. Adam Liptak, "Is Litigation the Best Way to Tame New Technology," *New York Times,* Sept. 2, 2000, p. B9.
8. Edgar Dale, *The Content of Motion Pictures* (New York: Macmillan, 1935).
9. Dale, *The Content of Motion Pictures,* p. 208. See also an excellent summary history of the major studios in Cobbett Feinberg, *Reel Facts: The Movie Book of Records* (New York: Vintage, 1978), pp. 376–389.
10. Motion Picture Association of America, 1999.
11. James Monaco, *How to Read A Film,* rev. ed. (New York: Oxford University Press, 1977), p. 246.
12. Feinberg, *Reel Facts,* p. xiii.
13. For an excellent abbreviated analysis of the movies, see Garth Jowett and James M. Linton, *Movies as Mass Communication* (Beverly Hills, Calif.: Sage, 1990).
14. Douglas Gomery, "The Hollywood Film Industry: Theatrical Exhibition, Pay TV and Home Video," in Benjamin Compaine and Douglas Gomery, *Who Owns the Media,* 3rd ed. (Mahwah, N.J.: Lawrence Erlbahm, 2000).
15. Schuyler M. Moore, *The Biz—The Basics, Legal and Financial Aspects of the Film Industry* (Los Angeles: Silman James Press, 2000), p. 12.
16. Peter Bart, *The Gross: The Hits, The Flops, The Summer That Ate Hollywood* (New York: St. Martins Griffin, 1999), p. 3.

17. Bill Daniels, David Leedy, and Steven D. Sills, *Movie Money—Understanding Hollywood's (Creative) Accounting Practices* (Los Angeles: Silman-James, 1998), p. xxi.

18. Gail Resnik and Scott Trost, *All You Need To Know About the Movie and TV Business* (New York: Fireside, 1996), pp. 33, 35–36, and 57–78 for an excellent discussion of "above the line" and "below the line" people in the motion picture industry.

19. Daniels, Leedy, and Sills, *Movie Money,* pp. xxi–xxii.

20. John L. Fell, *An Introduction to Film* (New York: Praeger, 1975), p. 127.

21. These estimates were obtained by one of the authors from an interview with the National Association of Theater Owners.

22. All data come from the Motion Picture Association of America, Inc., "Incidence of Motion Picture Attendance, March 7, 2000," a study conducted by Opinion Research Corporation, Princeton, N.J.

Chapter 6

RADIO: THE FIRST BROADCAST MEDIUM

WITH ALL OF THE LATEST DEVELOP-MENTS OF COMPUTERS, THE INTERNET, AND THE WORLD WIDE WEB CAPTURING headlines these days, it would be easy to assume that radio—our oldest broadcast medium—seems to be left over in the media mix. The fact is that it remains our most attended-to medium, and in addition, radio stations are profitable. While at one time it faced significant problems of competition from television, radio has adapted and found a viable niche among our current media. It is now a source for music entertainment, a means by which many people receive the latest news, a forum where ideas—both important and unimportant—are debated on talk shows, and above all, an effective advertising medium for local services and products. Radio, in short, has found a successful place among our current media and it seems likely to remain viable.

The control room, a fixture of radio broadcasting from the 1920s forward, allows a technician to sit at a control panel while a CBS Radio Network commentator speaks (pictured here about 1940). Today, control rooms exist in virtually all electronic media from local stations to global networks.

THE NEED FOR RAPID, LONG-DISTANCE COMMUNICATION

Until a little over a century ago, the lack of rapid, long-distance communication technology was a severe handicap in coordinating complex human activities, and it had been since the dawn of human history. In fact, the inability to communicate quickly over distance had more than once altered the fate of the entire world. For example, in 1588, Philip II of Spain sent the Armada, a great fleet of 130 warships under the command of the Duke of Medina-Sidonia, to crush the English. The Spanish King was angry because the English were raiding Spain's treasure ships from the New World and helping Spain's enemies. The plan was for the Spanish ships to pick up the army of Alessandro Farnese, the Duke of Parma, on the shores of Flanders and take it across the channel to invade and conquer England.

Up to that time, this was the greatest planned naval and military venture in the history of the world. It should have succeeded since the English had no effective standing army. However, as it turned out, the venture was a miserable failure. Basically, the problem was a lack of adequate communication. The Armada and Parma's army never found each other. English ships sailed out to harry the Armada in the channel, doing only minor damage, but forcing the Spanish ships northward. Problems of coordination quickly mounted. Unable to contact the nearby army that he was supposed to meet and, indeed, uncertain that it was even there, Medina-Sidonia had to abandon the invasion plan.

Bad storms arose as the ships tried to return to Spain by way of the Atlantic to the west of Ireland. Dozens of vessels foundered with great loss of life, and the whole effort ended in disaster. If the commanders of the Armada and the shore-bound army had possessed just one little CB radio each, they could have coordinated their efforts effectively. The entire history of the world would have changed, and we would probably all be speaking, reading, and writing Spanish today!

Communication devices that could conquer distance at high speed were a dream extending back many centuries. Giovanni della Porta, a scientist in the 1500s, described in his book, *Natural Magik,* a "sympathetic telegraph" for which learned men had long been searching.[1] It was a device that would be able to "write at a distance" (in Greek, *tele,* far off, and *graphos,* to write). In the imagination of those searching for a way to do this, the instrument would be prepared using a special *lodestone* (a natural magnet) that would sensitize two needles so they would act "in sympathy." That is, the needles were to be mounted on separate dials, something like compasses, but with the letters of the alphabet around the edge. If one needle were to be moved to a given position on its dial, such as to point to the letter A, the other would move to a similar position immediately, even though the devices were far from each other and not connected with wires.

It was a great idea. Unfortunately the special lodestone was never found. However, during the next three centuries there was a slow accumulation of science that eventually made such long-distance and instantaneous communication possible. Indeed, devices were developed during the 1900s that would have astounded della Porta.

Starting in the 1840s, swift, long-distance communication technologies came quickly, one after the other, within a span of about fifty years. The first was the electric dot-and-dash telegraph (1844). It was followed by the telephone (1876), the wireless telegraph (1896), and finally the radiotelephone (1906). Then, with adaptations of radiotelephone technology in the early 1920s, radio became a mass medium for household use. We saw earlier that the movies also came into existence during the last decade of the nineteenth century. By the mid-1920s, even the principles needed for television were understood and the first scheduled broadcasts took place in the 1930s.

To appreciate how rapidly all of this took place, imagine a person born in 1843—a day or so before Samuel F. B. Morse transmitted his first telegraph message. At that point in time, a message could move only as fast as a galloping horse—about twenty-five miles per hour—or a flying pigeon—around forty-five miles per hour. Other than the early trains of the late 1840s—that could travel at speeds up to about thirty-five to forty miles an hour—few increases in speed had been made since prehistoric times. Then suddenly remarkable changes came. When a person born in 1843 was only ten years old, the telegraph was regularly sending messages at a mind-boggling *186,000 miles per second* between distant points in a large network! By the time that individual was about forty, he or she could have telephoned friends at distant locations. By age eighty-five, he or she could have listened on a home receiver to regularly scheduled radio programs transmitted over a nationwide network. If that same individual had survived to an unusual 105 years, he or she could have watched news, sports, and soap operas on a home television set.

This chapter focuses on only part of that set of swift changes—the development of radio. As will be clearly explained, radio and television share a common background of technological development. They also share a common economic base and a system of societal control. For that reason, the events of history common to both media will be reviewed in the present chapter, but what is unique to TV will be presented in Chapter 7.

THE DEVELOPMENT OF THE BASIC TECHNOLOGY

To understand the ways in which the development of broadcasting was a part of more general trends taking place, we need to review very briefly what was happening more broadly in Western society at different times during the nineteenth century. Few citizens at the beginning of the 1800s could have imagined the changes in lifestyle that would soon take place in the United States. During the first decade of that century, people still traveled between towns on foot, on horseback, or on vehicles pulled by animals. Trips to distant places often took months. Goods to be purchased were handcrafted rather than factory made. Food was either grown at home or produced on nearby farms. Only a limited selection of items came to a community from distant places. Long-distance communication was by sailing ship, or by postal and courier services that used horses. The pace of society was slow indeed, and most people lived a simple rural or small-town existence.

The century was not even half over before travel time had been drastically reduced. Awesome machines, belching smoke and steam and pulling long strings of wagons, were rolling across the countryside on iron rails at what were then considered incredible speeds. Powerful ships, thrust forward by steam-driven paddle wheels, were plying the nation's waterways. Power-driven factories spewed forth standardized goods. The scope and pace of commercial activities had increased greatly. Thus, even before the Civil War, the Industrial Revolution had transformed much of the nation.

After the war ended, railroads soon connected most major American cities with scheduled service, and steam-driven ships regularly crossed the great oceans. In addition, hundreds of factories were producing shoes, farm implements, clocks, guns, cooking pots, woven cloth, tools, and a great variety of other manufactured goods. Small towns had become cities, and large metropolitan centers thrived. Food came not just from local farms but by rail and ship from more distant sources. Thus, the process of industrialization had generated a parallel revolution in the production, distribution, and consumption of goods and services of many kinds.

The development of radio was a part of these great changes. As we have already suggested, it was by applying principles discovered in the basic sciences that practical devices were developed to communicate rapidly over long distances. For example, unraveling the mysteries of electricity was a first step toward broadcasting. The Greeks had marveled at static electricity but had not understood its nature. By the 1700s, Europeans were generating gigantic static charges, but they still did not understand the nature of electricity. Then, researchers succeeded in revealing how electricity works, and how it could be stored in batteries, transmitted via wires, and used in practical applications. Discoveries of scientists such as Alessandro Volta, André Ampère, Michael Faraday, and James Clerk Maxwell laid the scientific foundations for applications such as the telegraph, the electric motor, and later, radio and television.

COMMUNICATING OVER A WIRE

The great dream of the sympathetic telegraph seemed increasingly achievable as the nature of electricity and ways to control it began to be understood. At the end of the 1700s, devices were developed by which electrical impulses could be used to send a message over wires. They were very cumbersome and limited to short distances (such as between two rooms). The system relied on static electricity and a number of separate wires, each connected to a hinged card—one for each letter of the alphabet. On a special desklike console, a charge applied at one end of a specific wire caused a spark at the other end. This, in turn, caused its hinged letter card to flop down. With great patience, and constant resetting of the letters, a message could be sent. Actually, it was a lot faster and easier just to shout from one room to the other. Nevertheless, this fascinating toy showed what problems needed to be solved to develop an electric telegraph—electricity traveling along wires, and some means to identify individual letters at the receiving end.

The first important discovery came in 1819 in England when Hans Oerstead found that a pulse of electrical current traveling a considerable distance could deflect a magnetic needle in a sort of dial at the end of the wire. He also noted that reversing the direction of the current in the circuit would reverse the deflection of the needle. With ways of patterning and interpreting the right and left deflections of the needle, the device served as a crude telegraph. This led a number of scientists, including André Ampère and Karl Gauss, to study and improve the process. By 1837, Wilhelm Cooke and Charles Wheatstone developed a working telegraph system based on this needle-deflection principle. It was actually used by railroads in England.

THE CONTRIBUTION OF SAMUEL F. B. MORSE

A much more efficient system, based on the *electromagnet,* was developed by Samuel F. B. Morse in 1844. The electromagnet itself was discovered by William Sturgeon in 1825 and then refined by Michael Faraday and Joseph Henry. It was a rather simple device. A bar of soft iron, about the size of a common wiener, is tightly wrapped in copper wire. If a steady flow of electricity from a battery is passed through the wire, the bar becomes a fairly strong magnet; stop the electricity and the bar loses most of its magnetic property. By starting and stopping the flow of electricity, an operator can make the electromagnet attract and release another piece of iron. Using this principle, Morse constructed a telegraph machine and devised a code for each letter by using long and short pulses of electricity. He was also able to attach a pencil to the piece of metal that his electromagnet attracted so as to leave a record of the transmission on a moving strip of paper.

By today's standards Morse's was a crude system. But by comparison with what was available at the time, it was a fantastic practical advance in communication technology. After the device proved reliable, Morse was able to obtain a grant from the U.S. government to field-test the system. He had a copper wire strung on poles between Baltimore, Maryland and Washington, D.C.—a distance of about forty miles. From Baltimore, on the morning of May 25, 1844, he sent the dramatic message, "What hath God wrought?" It was received in Washington with wild cheering and awe. No longer was the movement of a message limited to the speed of travel of a horse, a carrier pigeon, or a locomotive. Information could be flashed to a distant location at the speed of lightning. It did indeed seem to many observers like something that God had personally wrought.

Within a few years, with wires on poles along the railroad lines, most of the major cities of the United States were connected by telegraph. Business, the military, and—as we saw in Chapter 3—newspapers began to depend on the system for rapid communication. Undersea cables were laid even before the Civil War. Regular telegraph service between the United States and Europe was available by 1866. Yet the telegraph obviously was not a medium for the general public to use at home. It would be more than half a century before ordinary people would have a device in their homes for instantaneous mass communication without wires.

The telegraph not only initiated the era of instantaneous communication; it also set the model for the *structure of ownership* that would eventually characterize the electronic media in the United States. Even though the federal government had paid for Morse's experimental line between Baltimore and Washington, it declined to exercise control over the telegraph. The medium became the property of a private corporation to be operated for profit. This was a critical decision because it set the pattern for the telephone, radio, and television as they developed later.

COMMUNICATING WITH RADIO WAVES

Meanwhile, a German scientist, Heinrich Hertz, had been experimenting with some curious electromagnetic phenomena that he had produced using a device in his laboratory. By 1887, he had constructed a simple transmitter and receiver and had demonstrated the existence of what we know today as radio waves. The accomplishment electrified the scientific world, and experimentation with these mysterious new waves, which traveled at the speed of light, began in laboratories in many countries. This basic scientific discovery was to become the foundation of radio broadcasting.

Marconi's wireless telegraph. A few years later, Guglielmo Marconi, a twenty-year-old Italian youth from a wealthy family, who had read everything he could find about the Hertzian waves, bought the necessary parts and built his own devices to produce and detect them. He experimented with different wavelengths, types of antennae, and other features of the system. His idea was that by systematically interrupting the wave as it was being generated, he could send and receive messages in Morse code—without wires.

In 1895, Guglielmo Marconi found a way to transmit a message via radio over a distance. He synthesized Heinrich Hertz's discoveries of electromagnetic waves that traveled instantaneously without wires and the concept of transmitting messages encoded into dots and dashes via the electric telegraph. The result: a telegraph that worked without wires, one of the most important inventions of all time.

By 1895, Marconi had succeeded in sending coded messages over a modest distance across his father's estate. Thinking that his invention probably could have important uses, he offered it to the Italian government and tried to persuade them to help finance his work. But his government, deciding the device was only a novelty without practical importance, was not interested. Undaunted, and at the urging of his English mother, Marconi took his ideas to London, where in 1897 he was able to obtain a patent as well as financial backing to develop further his "wireless telegraph." Soon after, by 1901, he had built a much more powerful transmitter and succeeded in sending a simple message (a sequence of eighteen repetitions of the coded letter S) across the Atlantic. It was a startling achievement.

Radio, in this dot-and-dash form, had enormous practical advantages over the land-based telegraph that required wires. Ships at sea could communicate with each other and with stations on land. A number of stations in remote areas could hear and reply to the broadcasts of a central station. For England, with numerous colonies, a large navy, a huge merchant marine, and far-flung commercial enterprises, the wireless telegraph was a godsend.

The principal drawback of the earliest sets was that they used large, heavy equipment to achieve long-range transmission. Such a set could barely fit into a room. Not being a scientist, Marconi had chosen the wrong end of the frequency band. He reasoned that long radio waves would go farther than short ones. But it took great electrical energy to transmit them over long distances. Thus, his system required powerful electric currents, heavy wiring and switches, and massive antennae. If he had used the very short waves, he could have developed a much smaller, more portable machine. However, within a few years that became evident.

Marconi was not only an inventor but also a shrewd businessman. He successfully fought patent challenges to protect his ownership and established profit-oriented corporations to exploit wireless communication. He founded the American Marconi Company in 1899, and by 1913 it had a virtual monopoly on the use of the wireless telegraph in the United States. By that time dot-and-dash radio had come into worldwide use, and Marconi became a rich man indeed. As earlier, with telegraph by wire, the principle of private ownership and profit in broadcasting was established from the outset.

Marconi also invented a device for generating and detecting a particular wavelength for the more precise transmission of signals. He patented it in 1904. This device was important because it allowed the transmitter to broadcast on a specific wavelength or "frequency." With the receiving instrument "tuned" to a similar wavelength, signals on other frequencies could not interfere. We still tune radios to specific frequencies in this manner for transmission and reception.

The radiotelephone. During the first decade of the twentieth century, radio quickly became more than a wireless telegraph. On Christmas Eve in 1906, radio operators along the lonely Atlantic sea-lanes could not believe it when suddenly they heard a human voice coming from their earphones. A man read from the Bible, then played a phonograph record and a violin. Up to that time, only dots and dashes had ever come out of their sets. It was Reginald A. Fessenden broadcasting from an experimental station near Boston. He was able to transmit such sounds by using a telephone mouthpiece as a "microphone" and a special alternator to generate his radio waves. The dot-and-dash receivers then in use were able to detect his complex signals.

Another American inventor, Lee De Forest brought radio into its own in that same year by inventing what he called the *audion,* a three-element vacuum tube, which allowed much more sophisticated circuits and applications. De Forest's tube made amplification of radio signals possible. This, in turn, permitted the development of small reliable receivers. As a result, portable radio transmitters and receivers about the size of a breadbox became possible. They played an important role in World War I. By 1918, radio communication had advanced sufficiently for a pilot to receive and transmit signals from an airplane to people on the ground. Even by this time, however, radio was either the older dot-and-dash wireless system introduced by Marconi, or essentially an experimental device. It was by no means something that people used at home to listen to scheduled broadcasts. In other words, it was a private rather than a public medium.

Nevertheless, radio captured the imagination of the public in the early days. It seemed like a scientific marvel at the cutting edge of a new technology. People had the same fascination with it that later generations would have with early space vehicles and the Internet. For example, when ships got into trouble it was possible to summon aid by radio. One of the first examples occurred in 1898, when radio signals were used to bring aid to a vessel in difficulty. But a really dramatic rescue at sea took place in 1909, when the *SS Republic* began to sink off the coast of New York after being struck by another ship. Jack Binns, the ship's wireless operator, stayed at his post in the freezing weather for hours, sending out a distress signal. Other ships detected it and came as quickly as possible to the position indicated. All fifteen hundred passengers were rescued. It made great newspaper headlines, and the public was enthralled. Binns was regarded as a hero and was given a ticker-tape parade in New York City. Chorus girls, it was said, threw themselves at him. His employers were so pleased with him that they were going to promote him to a better post—as wireless operator on their new superliner, the *SS Titanic,* when it went into service. Binns, however, could not accept that honor as he was to be married the same day that the *Titanic* was to set sail.

On its maiden voyage, in 1912 (without Binns), the "unsinkable" *Titanic* struck an iceberg in the North Atlantic. The wireless operator tried to alert nearby ships, but their radio crews had gone to bed for the night. However, contact was made with a shore station (in Wanamaker's department store in New York City), whose stronger signal could reach more distant points. The young store operator, David

Sarnoff, stayed at his post for many hours, making contact with other vessels. Unfortunately, by the time those ships arrived the next morning, the great passenger liner had sunk to the bottom of the ocean. Some fifteen hundred people drowned, including the *Titanic's* heroic wireless operator who had tried all night to summon aid until he went down with the ship.

RADIO BECOMES A MASS MEDIUM

In increasing numbers, amateur radio fans were attracted to the medium after World War I. Although assembled sets could be purchased, they were expensive— so thousands bought parts and put together their own receivers. Plans for "crystal set" radio receivers appeared in popular magazines aimed at the home hobbyist and tinkerer. Companies marketed kits through the mail for crystal sets that even a bright child could put together. With a length of copper wire wrapped around a Quaker Oats box, a device to slide along the resulting coil to "tune" the device, and the right kinds of crystal, battery, earphones, and antenna, the home listener could pick up audible signals. Radio was the scientific wonder of the age, and the public expressed a broad interest in the medium even before regular broadcasting began.

THE PERIOD OF TRANSITION

Before radio broadcasting could be a mass medium, it had to make a critical transition. It had to be transformed from a long-range, rather cumbersome device for maritime, commercial, governmental, and hobby communication to an easy-to-use system that would bring suitable program content to people in their homes.[2]

First, radio sets had to be *small enough* for use in the home. In part, the home-built set helped to fulfill that need, but those who were not tinkerers wanted to purchase their sets ready-made. Second, their *price* had to be brought within the means of large numbers of families. Third, there had to be *regularly scheduled programs* to which people would want to listen. This was a real barrier, because there simply were no stations providing content that would interest most potential listeners. Fourth, *reception had to be reasonably clear*—that is, without annoying static and overlap between stations. This meant that there had to be a means of *regulating the use of the airwaves*, either by voluntary agreements or through some government licensing scheme. Not everyone who wanted to broadcast would be able to do so without interfering with others on the same wavelength. Fifth, and perhaps most important of all, there had to be a means of *paying for the broadcasts*.

While by today's standards the transmission equipment itself was not all that expensive, there were other costs involved. Space had to be provided to house the station, with its attendant costs of heat, light, rent, and so forth. Salaries had to be paid to engineers, to people who said things over the air, and even to janitors who cleaned up.

Within a few years all of these barriers would be overcome, and the transition to a true mass medium would take place very quickly. Enthusiasts were pointing out that need. For example, in 1916, David Sarnoff (who had played a part in trying to summon aid for the *Titanic*), had gone to work for the American Marconi Company. He wrote a now-famous memorandum to his boss that outlined the way that radio could become a medium for home use:

I have in mind a plan of development which would make radio a "household utility" in the same sense as a piano or phonograph. The idea is to bring music into the house by wireless . . . The receiver can be designed in the form of a simple "Radio Music Box" and arranged for several different wave lengths, which should be changeable with the throwing of a single switch or pressing of a single button.

The "Radio Music Box" can be supplied with amplifying tubes and a loudspeaking telephone, all of which can be neatly mounted in one box. The box can be placed on a table in the parlor or living room, the switch set accordingly and the transmitted music received.[3]

Sarnoff went on in his memo to suggest that people listening at home could receive news, sports scores, lectures, weather reports, and concerts. He also suggested that such machines could be manufactured and sold by the thousands. All his scheme needed was the addition of advertising as a source of financial support for regularly scheduled broadcasts, plus government control over frequency allocation, and it would have been a very accurate description of the future of radio as a mass medium. Sarnoff's proposal was rejected by his superiors as impractical and too visionary. However, by 1919 he had become the manager of a new company called the Radio Corporation of America (RCA), and he played a major role in bringing radio to the public as a mass medium.

Scheduled programs begin. The broadcasting of regularly scheduled programs over the airwaves did not begin in all parts of the country at once. A sort of amateur version of such broadcasts started in Pittsburgh in April 1920. An engineer, Dr. Frank Conrad, was developing transmitting systems for the Westinghouse Corporation. He needed to test his equipment after hours, so he built a transmitter over his garage at home; it was licensed as station 8XK. With the help of his family, Conrad began making regular broadcasts, using recorded music, two evenings a week. He invited people to send him postcards. Many did so or called on the telephone requesting particular victrola records. This feedback from the audience enabled Conrad to understand the reach of his station's signal.

The directors of Westinghouse, seeing the growing public interest in home radio in 1920, and intrigued by Conrad's example, decided to establish a radio station to produce regularly scheduled broadcasts in the Pittsburgh area. The idea was to provide programming for people who bought the home receivers that Westinghouse was manufacturing and selling. The firm built a transmitter in a tin "radio shack" on top of its building in Pittsburgh and licensed it as radio station KDKA. To dramatize the establishment of the station, they announced that for their first broadcast they would transmit the returns of the 1920 presidential election (Warren G. Harding versus James M. Cox).

Actually, the station received its election information from a local newspaper by phone. Nevertheless, several hundred people with sets in the Pittsburgh area learned, from signals sent over the evening sky, that Harding had won. The event was a dramatic success, greatly stimulating the sale of receivers. The station continued to broadcast regularly, presenting music, religious services, sports information, political talks, and even market reports. Its signal carried over a long distance, and people in other parts of the country tuned in. Radio station KDKA is still on the air and is recognized as the oldest radio station in continuous operation in the nation.

Chaos on the airwaves. Within months, dozens of other stations went on the air in various cities. Soon there were hundreds, and the infant mass medium became a chaotic mess. Transmitters were paid for and operated by just about anyone who wanted to transmit messages. This included department stores, wealthy individuals, automobile dealers, corporations, churches, schools, and of course, manufacturers of radio equipment. By the end of 1922, some 254 federal licenses had been issued for transmitters that complied with the provisions of the Radio Act of 1912. By 1923, dozens were going on the air every month, and about 600 were broadcasting by the end of the year. There simply were not enough locations on the frequency spectrum to accommodate everyone. Each position had at least one and sometimes several stations. Furthermore, the amplitude modulation (AM) broadcasting system in use could carry over very long distances, especially at night. People trying to listen to a local station would at the same time hear a jumble of broadcasts from other parts of the country.

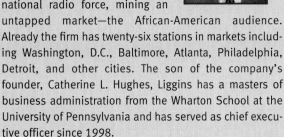

Alfred C. Liggins III
Chief Executive Officer
Radio One, Inc.
Lanham, Maryland

insights from
MEDIA LEADERS

Alfred C. Liggins III heads a much-heralded group of radio stations that is aimed at becoming a national radio force, mining an untapped market—the African-American audience. Already the firm has twenty-six stations in markets including Washington, D.C., Baltimore, Atlanta, Philadelphia, Detroit, and other cities. The son of the company's founder, Catherine L. Hughes, Liggins has a masters of business administration from the Wharton School at the University of Pennsylvania and has served as chief executive officer since 1998.

Q. You literally grew up in the offices of a family-owned radio station, but just when did you decide radio would be your career choice, rather than something else?

A. Yes, I did grow up in my mom's radio station, but after high school I went to Los Angeles to work in the record business. After a couple of years, I came back to the station and started selling airtime. I made $35,000 the first year out—this was in 1985. The next year, I made $60,000, then $100,000 and I decided, hey, at age twenty-three this is a pretty good career!

Q. What factors besides money inspire your continued interest in and dedication to this field?

A. I love the business. I love urban radio and interacting with the African-American community. It is great to be

the CEO of a company that reflects and projects the values of this community to markets in urban areas. I also like the fact that this is a platform to influence politics, culture, and other issues. Of course, it is the best way to stay connected with the rest of the media—cable, the Internet, and recorded music.

Q. Your mother, Catherine Hughes, was an experienced broadcaster, but not really an entrepreneur, at least in the sense that you are. How have you approached the challenge of being both broadcaster and entrepreneur?

A. My mom taught me the radio business including sales, programming, and community involvement—the nuts and bolts of how a radio station works. I brought an entrepreneurial spirit to the business with a dream of building an urban entertainment company. Someday I'd like for us to be the Time Warner of our field. My mother, as chairman of the board, is still the soul of the company, so our interests and abilities mesh well.

Q. What is your take on the current state and probable future of radio, including serving the African-American audience?

A. Radio is amazing. It is the medium that would not die. TV, cable, and the Internet were all predicted to be death blows for radio, but that never happened. It took cable thirty years to make a dent in broadcast television, but radio lives on and thrives. Of course,

Regulating broadcasting. Because radio transmissions respect no national boundaries, it was clear from the beginning that international agreements of some sort were needed to maintain order on the airwaves. An international structure designed to regulate telecommunications already existed, long before radio was even developed. It was the International Telegraphic Convention, organized in 1865 by twenty-five European countries to work out agreements on telegraphic and cable operations. It was quite successful, and it provided a model that by extension could be used to forge agreements on radio broadcasting.

The first conference devoted specifically to radio was held in Berlin in 1903, and important rules were agreed upon. For one thing, it was decided that humanitarian and emergency uses of the medium would get the highest priority. Thus, when ships needed aid or during other emergencies, commercial interests were to be set aside. In 1906, a second Berlin convention set forth further restrictions and rules on

radio has enormous diversity to offer. When you think that there are fifty radio stations in Washington, D.C., and one hundred in L.A., that's a healthy sign that radio will be a viable business for a long time to come. In radio you can have a good cash flow and low capital expenditures. That allows us to catch the next technological wave, to be there if and when another medium appears and takes off.

Q. Then do you see radio continuing as a separate industry, which it pretty much is today, or becoming part of digital Internet communication or some other emerging technology?

A. Well, as I said, I want to be ready for the next wave, whatever and whenever that is, but yes, I think radio will be strong for a long time, but at the same time it will converge with other media technologies. After all, the big companies want multiple distribution systems and radio is one of them—and a cost-effective one at that.

Q. What are the prospects for people entering the field of radio broadcasting?

A. They are quite good.

Q. What do you think is the best pathway for a successful and satisfying career?

A. I tell people that sales—selling airtime—is the best way to learn the business. You can make good money there and get to know what audiences and markets are all about. Of course, I realize that everyone wants to be on the air, but only a handful of radio personalities

or other on-air people make any money. Some of the morning jocks, yes, but not many. For people who want to try that I tell them to be a jock [disc jockey or on-air announcer] for a while, but then to transition to a program director slot where they can be immensely more valuable to the company. From there they can become a general manager at a station or a group vice president in a big company.

Q. What about education?

A. I didn't go to college. I later did an executive MBA at the Wharton School, but that was when I had already been in the business for a while. Business school gave me a broader perspective and taught me things that have been helpful, as the company has evolved.

Q. What is the most satisfying aspect of work in the radio field for you? The least?

A. I most like being the CEO of a public company. I like setting goals and achieving them—and I like doing that for people other than myself. I really enjoy it when we make money for the shareholders. Less satisfying? I'd say that is the intricacies and complexities of dealing with people, as the company gets larger. Remember we've gone from a "mom and son" operation to a company with seventeen hundred employees or more. Everyone has an ego and everyone has a goal. Keeping people productive and satisfied is one of the biggest and most difficult issues we deal with. This is something they really don't teach in business school or anywhere else as far as I know.

international and maritime broadcasting.[4] However, all of this had nothing to do with home radio.

The U.S. Congress confirmed these international rules in the Radio Act of 1912, which replaced a number of earlier attempts to develop laws suitable for radio. One feature of the 1912 Act was that it provided for *licensing of transmitters.* However, as it turned out, that feature failed to solve enormous problems in the development of a home radio industry because they had not been anticipated. While it required citizens to obtain a license to operate a transmitter, it provided no real way that the government could turn anyone down. Furthermore, it established no criteria for approving the operations of a new transmitter, such as a broadcasting frequency, its power, or time on the air. In fact, it really gave the Secretary of Commerce (head of the licensing agency) no way to refuse anyone who wanted to transmit!

Because the 1912 legislation did not prescribe a frequency for a new station, its owner could choose the one that he or she preferred. If several operators decided to use the same frequency, as often happened, interference and overlap increased. Some stations solved the problem by agreeing informally to broadcast only on certain days or hours. Others, less cooperative, simply increased their power sharply to blast competing stations off the air. There was some experimentation with networks, with several stations sending signals on the same frequency. However, none of these solutions were effective.

As more and more stations began transmitting, the overlapping of frequencies and broadcast hours finally made it virtually impossible to tune in to any clear signal. The chaos first brought the establishment of new stations to a halt, then sharply reversed the growth trend. Hundreds of stations simply went off the air and never returned.[5] They had no way of recovering their costs and their signals were lost in a chaos of noise.

Obviously, some sort of tight government control was needed to make the system work. However, the federal government was very reluctant to try to control the new medium. It was still a time when Americans looked on government regulation of anything as unwanted interference. Decades earlier, Congress had shied away from taking over the telegraph, and it was not about to step in and be charged with trying to limit free speech through control of the airwaves.

The Secretary of Commerce at the time was Herbert Hoover. He tried to assign frequencies to new stations on an informal basis as licenses were granted, and it did seem to help for a while. However, the courts decided in 1926 that his agency lacked the legal power to do even that. The chaos that had prevailed earlier started to return and again threatened to ruin the fledgling industry.

Finally, Congress stepped in, held lengthy conferences and hearings, and provided new legislation—the Radio Act of 1927. The Act established a very important principle: the *airwaves belong to the people.* This gave the government the right to regulate their use in the public interest. Thus, the Act of 1927 temporarily gave the government new authority to control virtually all technical aspects of broadcasting. The Act provided for a Federal Radio Commission (FRC) with broad new powers. In particular, the rules for licensing became very demanding, and those who wanted to transmit had to agree to do so only on assigned frequencies, at specified power levels, and at scheduled times. Even though the 1927 Act brought strong and effective controls to the medium, it was applauded by the industry, which had been totally unable to regulate itself.

This interim Radio Act of 1927 prevailed during the new mass medium's early years of growth and development. Within a few years, it would be replaced by the Federal Communications Act of 1934, with complex legislation administered by a permanent Federal Communication Commission (FCC) that could oversee licensing and issue rules as needed. The 1934 Act, with numerous revisions, remains the legislative foundation governing the broadcast industries, as well as all other forms of radio transmission in the United States.

ESTABLISHING THE ECONOMIC BASE OF THE NEW MEDIUM

Radio was so new that no one was sure how to pay for the costs of transmitting or, in particular, how to make a profit from the broadcasts. At first, there seemed to be a number of alternatives. After all, each of the other media available at the time— newspapers, magazines, the movies, and even the telegraph system—paid their way and made money.

Paying for the broadcasts. At first, the costs of acquiring and operating a transmitter were modest. For about $3,000 one could set up a station and start broadcasting. Operating expenses ran about $2,000 a year. Almost immediately, however, expensive, technically trained personnel and greater transmitter power were needed. Costs began to escalate. How to recoup those costs was an important question.

Clearly, *operation by the government* was one possible answer. That was the solution settled on by many societies in different parts of the world. In such a system, radio and television are operated by government bureaucrats and the content of the media is rigidly controlled. In the United States, however, few citizens wanted that kind of arrangement. The basic values of democracy conflict with government intervention in the flow of information. Therefore such a government operated and controlled system was never seriously considered.

Some visionaries thought it would be best to use a *subscription system,* where each owner of a radio receiver would have to get an annual license to operate it and pay a fee that would support the programming. Although that system was adopted in Great Britain, it was never seriously tried in the United States.

One system that was actually tried (by AT&T) was the *common carrier approach.* The principle here was similar to providing a truck or train line to carry whatever goods people might want transported and delivered. Applied to broadcasting, the transmitter was to be leased to whoever wanted to go on the air to broadcast whatever content they prepared. There were not enough takers and the idea was abandoned.

Another possibility was the *endowment* idea. Rich philanthropists would be invited to endow the stations with large money gifts, and then the station could use the earnings on investments to pay the costs of broadcasting. That system had worked well in funding universities, museums, and libraries. However, no rich philanthropists stepped forward.

Advertising as the source of profit. The challenge, then, was how to make a profit by broadcasting programs to a general public who could tune in and listen for free. About the only obvious possibility was to transmit advertising messages over the air and charge the advertiser for the time, just as newspapers and magazines made a profit by presenting such messages in print. However, there was great resistance to the use of the airwaves for advertising, at least at first. Radio seemed to most people to be a wonderful new medium at the forefront of human accomplishment and destined for nobler purposes. To use it crassly for advertising seemed a disgusting idea. Herbert Hoover strongly opposed it, saying, "It is inconceivable that we should allow so great a possibility for service, for news, for entertainment, and for vital commercial purposes to be drowned in advertising chatter."[6]

In spite of these early airwave "environmentalists," advertising once again won over good taste. There simply did not seem to be any alternative solution that could make the medium financially viable. Although scattered uses of advertising over the airwaves had been tried earlier, the system as we know it was initiated by station WEAF in New York, which made the decision to lease time to present commercial promotions. There was no particular limit on the amount of time (the idea of brief "commercials" sandwiched in between segments of a program would come later). In the summer of 1922, a real-estate firm leased a ten-minute segment to extol the virtues of some apartments in New York. It cost the firm $50.

After the idea caught on, advertisers warmed to the idea of becoming regular *sponsors* of weekly programs. These might be dance music, readings of the news, ball scores, and so on. With the number of home-owned receivers growing astronomically (see Figure 6.1) it soon became clear that radio was a very important medium by which advertising messages could reach consumers.

Early radio advertising was very polite and restrained. The initial model was *institutional* advertising; that is, the corporation sponsoring a particular presentation or program would be identified by name—but no information was provided about a specific product that it produced. To illustrate, advertising in the early days of radio would have consisted of a dignified voice saying, "This program is sponsored by the XYZ Pharmaceutical Corporation and we are pleased to present the following program." That was it!

Today, advertising messages openly identify a specific product. Some become truly tacky, such as when a brand of laxative goes into grim details about such matters as "constipation," the "softening effects" of the product, the time it takes to "gain relief," and the feelings of comfort and joy that result from elimination. Other current ads openly address such indelicate issues as diapers for incontinence among the

trends in media use

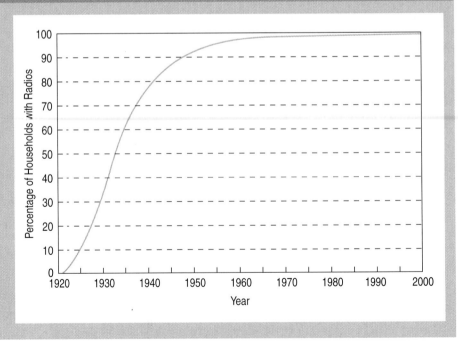

FIGURE 6.1

The Curve of Adoption of Household Radio, 1920–2000

The acquisition of radio sets by American families followed a classic adoption curve after the beginning of regular broadcasts in the 1920s. Virtual saturation of households was reached after about mid-twentieth century.

elderly, preparations for itchy anal hemorrhoids, and products to combat "erectile dysfunction." The public in radio's early days would have been truly horrified by the mention of such matters over the air, and the resulting outcry would have caused the station's license to be instantly withdrawn. Obviously, times and standards of taste have changed. (To understand how such a change can take place, see the "creeping cycle of desensitization" theory, page 154 in Chapter 5.)

Acquiring receivers for home use. Throughout the early 1920s, manufacturers marketed various kinds of sets and the public eagerly bought as many as could be produced. For several years, demand often outstripped supply. By 1922, an estimated half-million sets were in use. In 1925, that number escalated to about 5 million. By the end of the decade, some 14 million radio receivers were in American homes. (They no longer required batteries and were operated on house current.) In 1926, the National Broadcasting Corporation (NBC), led by David Sarnoff, initiated network broadcasting. The Columbia Broadcasting System (CBS) and others soon followed, and near the end of the decade, people all over the country could simultaneously hear a broadcast of the same radio program. Today, radio ownership is universal in the United States.

Thus, in the brief span of a single decade (the 1920s), radio was transformed from a long-distance signaling device serving limited interests into a medium that served an entire nation with broadcasts to home receivers. A great industry had come into existence. It was privately owned, dedicated to making a profit, and linked firmly to the world of commercial advertising. It retains those features today. However, unlike other media, it was regulated to a considerable degree by the government, especially in terms of the mechanics of broadcasting. Listening to the radio was rapidly becoming one of everyone's most important leisure-time activities. Marconi's device had truly become a mass medium.

THE GOLDEN AGE OF RADIO

During the years between 1930 and America's entry into World War II in December 1941, radio continued to develop into a medium of increasing national and worldwide importance. Following the war, radio would enjoy only five additional years, from 1945 to about 1950, of unchallenged dominance as the major broadcast medium in the United States. It would then have to meet the challenge of television. Thus, we can identify the approximate, fifteen-year period between the mid-1930s and about 1950 as the *golden age of radio.*

The programs and diversity that we see on television today are contemporary versions of much of what was on radio during its golden age. It offered an enormous variety of content. Its comedians became household names and made the entire nation laugh. Its broadcasts promoted popular dance bands and singers who gained national followings. Radio presented sports events to which millions of fans listened. The medium was used by politicians to get elected and to persuade the public to support new programs. News broadcasts were an immediate source of important information for huge audiences. Radio brought a constant flow of fads. Broadcasts promoted ever-changing dance styles and new forms of popular music. Millions of housewives listened eagerly to "soap operas" during the day. Above all, it sold the nation's goods. Radio's advertising revenues soared to stupendous levels. It was, in short, a great medium that became a significant part of almost everyone's life.

Franklin Delano Roosevelt used radio effectively, both to get his campaign messages across to voters and to assure the American people during times of national crisis. His calming voice during the Great Depression and after the Japanese attack on Pearl Harbor reassured the nation and marshalled public support for his programs.

RADIO DURING THE GREAT DEPRESSION

If ever there was a population in need of free entertainment, it was the people of the United States during the 1930s. At the depths of the Great Depression, fifteen million workers were unemployed in a population of about half of what we have today. That calculates to about 20 percent of the labor force. Today people feel that times are bad if the rate exceeds about 6 percent. It is currently about 3 percent.

As the Great Depression began, there was no national system of public welfare, no unemployment compensation, no social security or medicare for older people, no medicaid for the poor, and no government programs of public works to absorb the unemployed (all would come later in the 1930s). Farmers could not sell their crops; factories could not sell their goods. Many businesses simply shut down and locked out their employees. Mortgages went unpaid and families were evicted from homes and farms. People went without meals, without medical treatment, and even without shoes. Hundreds of thousands of children wandered without adult supervision. Hungry people foraged in the streets. Anyone who had a steady job was among society's fortunate, no matter how mean the work.

But people did have radio. It was free in the sense that all one needed to do was plug a receiver into a socket. It brought them comedy broadcasts by such former vaudeville stars as Fred Allen, Jack Benny, Eddie Cantor, and Ed Wynn. Listeners laughed at the antics of "Amos n' Andy" (a show with two white actors working in blackface in the old minstrel tradition). They thrilled to the heroism of the Lone Ranger, who brought simple justice to the old West. They were kept in suspense by The Shadow, a mysterious figure who vanquished the forces of evil. Children were excited by the airborne adventures of the Sky King and the incredible space exploits of Buck Rogers. For those with more rural tastes, there were regular programs of country music. Urbanites probably preferred the dance music of the "big bands," which transmitted live "swing" music from various hotels and ballrooms. News programs reported the latest policies of the Roosevelt administration and called attention to disturbing events overseas, such as the military buildup of Adolf Hitler in Germany, Benito Mussolini in Italy, and the Japanese conquest of Manchuria. All that did not seem very important to most listeners; few Americans were interested in the political problems of places like Europe or China.

Although one might think that the Great Depression should have held back the development of radio, that was not the case. An increasing number of stations came on the air and an ever-growing number of homes purchased radio sets. Advertising revenues grew sharply, from about $40 million per year in 1930, just as the Depression began, to over $112 million in 1935, as it reached bottom. Programming became more and more diversified and sophisticated, attracting a growing number of listeners. The networks continued to expand and dominate broadcasting.

In the mid-1930s, two things happened that were very important to the future of broadcasting. One was the establishment of the federal legislation we noted earlier (the Federal Communications Act of 1934), with a new government agency (the FCC) to supervise broadcasting in the United States. The other was the development of an entirely different technology for broadcasting called *frequency modulation* (FM).

Frequency modulation broadcasting. In 1933, a relatively obscure inventor, Edwin Armstrong, developed and patented a new kind of radio signal based on frequency modulation (FM) rather than amplitude modulation (AM). The world took little note because Armstrong did nothing to publicize his innovation. The advantages of the new system were that it was static free and that it could carry much higher and lower audio frequencies, making it an ideal carrier for music. At first, it seemed that its disadvantage was that at most parts of the frequency spectrum, FM reaches out only to the horizon. In contrast, AM signals travel from the transmitter in all directions. They rise up to the ionosphere where they are then reflected back to earth, and they can bounce back and forth between the two far beyond the horizon. Thus, AM can carry signals over very long distances (such as across the Atlantic). The FM signal is different. At very high and ultrahigh frequencies (VHF and UHF), it simply travels in a straight line in all directions and does not bounce up and down. Since the earth is not flat, such broadcasts cannot be effectively detected beyond the horizon. Furthermore, a big building or mountain that gets in the way of FM signals can garble or even stop them.

These might sound like serious limitations, and for some purposes they were (and still are). However, FM turned out to be exactly what was needed as a basic carrier of the audio signals for the new system of television, with which RCA and other corporations were experimenting. The FM audio carrier was ideal for television because it could confine a signal to a local area and not interfere with other transmitters some distance away, meaning that TV channels could be kept from interfering with each other. The same was true for radio stations that wanted to confine their broadcasts to a local area.

Unfortunately, Armstrong had to fight RCA in the courts when they started using his system for TV broadcasts. While his case was ultimately won, his bitterness and frustration led him to commit suicide some years before the settlement.

Radio and the news. Another great battle fought during the period was over who had proprietary rights to the news. In 1930, Lowell Thomas, who was to become a well-known radio news personality, began a trend by reading the news

Radio reached its zenith as a news medium during World War II—prior to the spread of television. One of the most notable and effective commentators of that period, who later made a transition to TV, was American Edward R. Murrow, who made nightly broadcasts of the German bombing of London. Murrow later became an icon of U.S. media.

over the air. Frightened by the competition radio was giving them, newspapers tried to stop local stations from using the early editions of papers as the source for their news, claiming that the radio stations were violating copyright laws. But the courts ruled that although the particular expression of a writer can be copyrighted, the factual content of news is in the "public domain"—thus, no one "owns" the news. The radio stations could broadcast news shows even if they could not afford to hire their own reporters. As it turned out, radio coverage actually *stimulated* rather than deterred interest in newspaper reading. The brief news broadcasts and bulletins provided by radio caused people to follow up to get more detailed accounts in print. Before long, the major networks had developed their own separate news-gathering operations—a system that still brings us the broadcast news today.

RADIO DURING WORLD WAR II

Radio became a global news medium as the world was plunging into war. Even before the U.S. entry into World War II, reporters around the world were able to transmit live "eyewitness" reports on major events by short wave to New York. From there they were picked up by the major networks and relayed over standard frequencies to listeners at home. Americans heard dramatic firsthand accounts from Edward R. Murrow, reporting from London in 1940 during the bombardment by the German Luftwaffe. Later, such news personalities as Robert Trout, H. V. Kaltenborn, and Elmer Davis used the medium to bring reports and interpretations of the war in Europe.

On Sunday, December 7, 1941, American families could scarcely believe their ears when they learned by home radio that the Japanese had attacked Pearl Harbor. More than two hundred Japanese carrier-based bombers devastated the U.S. Pacific Fleet and killed over two thousand American servicemen and a number of civilians. Radio played a key part in mobilizing the nation. As the war progressed, firsthand news reports came from battlefields in strange places people had never heard of— Guadalcanal, Attu, Anzio, and Iwo Jima. Throughout the war, President Roosevelt calmed the American public with frequent radio talks, reassuring the nation of ultimate victory and setting the goal of "unconditional surrender." Finally, the Allies defeated Germany and atomic bombs developed by the United States forced the Japanese to surrender. The dreadful conflict came to an end. By this time, radio was the unchallenged news medium of America.

The importance of the expansion of radio news to worldwide coverage is that it built the foundation of audience expectations for which contemporary broadcasters provide news on a global basis. For example, when CNN Headline News presents summaries of what is happening "Around the World in Thirty Minutes" on a twenty-four–hour basis, it is following a tradition that was pioneered by radio broadcasters during the late 1930s and the dark days of World War II.

THE CHALLENGE OF TELEVISION

After World War II, radio lived on in its glory for roughly five years. But, starting in 1948, television stations began to go on the air with regular broadcasts. Early in that first year, only seventeen were in operation. Before the end of 1948, however, the number more than doubled (to forty-eight). Sales of television sets increased 500 percent, and the audience for TV broadcasts grew at an astounding 4,000 percent rate in only two years! Coaxial cables began to connect communities, and the same networks that had fostered radio enthusiastically developed the new medium. No one in radio knew quite what to do. Many radio executives announced that television was only a fad and that audiences would remain loyal to the original broadcast medium that had served them so well.

As television continued to take over audiences, radio was in deep trouble. In fact, it was in danger of disappearing altogether as a mass medium. Profits plummeted and radio audiences melted away as both talent and audience interest switched to television.

RADIO ADAPTS

Radio might have died completely had it not been for its resourceful response to the challenge of television. At first, the medium tightened its belt and took on advertising accounts that could not afford costly television commercials. Then it made changes across the board that permitted it to survive on a more permanent basis.

The major form of adaptation was that the *content* of radio broadcasts changed sharply. Out went the well-developed radio drama, the soap opera, the quiz show, and other amusement fare that had been the mainstay of radio entertainment. All of that type of programming could now be found on television. In came the disc jockey, continuous music, frequent spot news, weather reports, and call-in talk shows. For the most part, radio ceased to be a national medium. Network-type programming decreased sharply, and radio became a medium mainly providing services to local rather than national audiences. In effect, then, radio *drastically changed its functions*. It gave more emphasis to music, news summaries, and call-in talk shows, and less attention to its earlier forms of drama and similar entertainment. In this way, radio survived as an intimate and community-oriented medium.

Public broadcasting. One additional set of changes that influenced radio (as well as television) was the development of *public broadcasting*. As early as 1941, the FCC had reserved a number of FM channels for "noncommercial" use. In effect this meant "educational" broadcasting. However, Congress provided no funding for such programming. A number of small radio stations eked out an existence with support from churches, colleges, and universities. Some lived on public funds, some from donations or from foundation support. In 1967, however, Congress passed the Public Broadcasting Act, creating the Corporation for Public Broadcasting (CPB), serving both radio and television. It was not actually a corporation in the sense of a profit-oriented business, and it was not exactly an arm of government. It was set up as an independent, nonprofit organization that received federal funds and allocated them to local stations within networks.

The radio part of the CPB package was National Public Radio (NPR). This division not only links radio stations into a network, but also produces various kinds of noncommercial programming for broadcasts. Today, there are about two hundred FM

radio stations in the NPR system. They all produce some programs and make at least some use of the nationally produced material. Such stations also solicit local donations and sponsors. For the many people who tire of regular AM or FM stations—with their continuous broadcasts of rock 'n' roll, country and western, or classical music and frequent commercial advertising—NPR is a pleasant relief. The nationally produced content is heavy on news, public affairs analyses, interactive talk shows, and information about music, theater, and the arts. There is even some attention to sports.

The growth of FM broadcasting. In its various formats radio is surviving the challenge of television. FM broadcasting has now become the dominant system with the majority of the radio audience in the United States.[7] AM stations tend to present a mix of news, talk, sports, and low-key, background-type music. In contrast, FM radio tends to be more focused on musical formats. NPR survives on FM with a small but dedicated following.

RADIO AS A CONTEMPORARY MEDIUM

Radio continues at the start of the twenty-first century to be America's most widely attended to medium of communication. A total of more than eleven thousand radio stations stretch across the country, with numerous signals reaching every community and neighborhood.[8] Studies show that 96 percent of the population over age twelve listens to the radio during an average week. This compares favorably to television viewing (90 percent) and newspaper reading (76 percent). Among the reasons so many people listen is that radio is the most portable of the broadcast media, being accessible at home, in the office, in the car, on the street or beach, on the Internet, virtually everywhere at any time.

Because radio listening is so widespread, it has prospered as an advertising medium. Radio stations reach local rather than national audiences, and are thus very useful for merchants who want to advertise their wares and services to people in their community. Furthermore, radio serves small, highly targeted audiences, which makes it an excellent advertising medium for many kinds of specialized products and services. As we explained in the case of magazines, this feature appeals to advertisers, who realize it would be inefficient and prohibitively expensive to tout a special-interest product to heterogeneous audiences drawn to nationally popular television entertainment programs.

Radio personalities, commentators, and talk show hosts give radio programs a humanistic, personal touch as with National Public Radio's jovial brothers, Ray and Tom Magliozzi, who call themselves "standup auto advisers" on the call-in show "Car Talk." Talk radio is a popular and identifiable radio format alongside various musical formats.

RADIO'S ROLE IN THE MEDIA MIX

Between 10 and 11 percent of all money spent on media advertising in the United States goes to radio. This percentage has remained quite stable for more than a decade, which has meant substantial growth in actual dollars brought in by radio. In 1977, for example, total radio advertising amounted to about $2.6 billion per year. By 1996, it was over $10 billion—almost a fivefold increase.[9] According to the Veronis, Suhler & Associates' *Industry Forecast,* this growth has exceeded that of the overall economy, reflecting the radio industry's robust progress.[10] Surveys show that radio gets more than 75 percent of its revenues from local advertising, about 22 percent from national advertising, and a tiny sliver (around 1 percent) from network compensation.

What is accounting for radio's renewed economic success? Experts say it is the high cost of commercial television time, which is still prohibitive for many local advertisers who can afford radio's more reasonable ad rates. Another key factor may be the emergence of remote-control devices and VCRs, which allow viewers to avoid watching TV commercials and are cutting the effectiveness of television advertising. The radio audience, on the other hand, is more captive, not able to tune out commercials quite so easily. In addition, the advertising sales forces for radio stations offer a good deal of assistance to local advertisers in preparing their spots for broadcasting. It is thought that radio's ability to attract local advertisers hurts mainly newspapers, since television is less attractive to the small, local advertiser.

Like movies and television, radio can at times be quite controversial. In Chapter 5 we discussed the "creeping cycle of desensitization." A counterpart can be found not only in some radio ads but also in certain kinds of radio programming. For example, some talk show hosts, like Howard Stern, have adopted a style in which vulgar language is frequently used. Others, like G. Gordon Liddy, are accused of being "hatemongers" in that they cater to callers who express very negative views about politicians, members of minorities, or other kinds of people and issues.

Like other media, radio exists in a very competitive economic environment. Stations in every community compete vigorously for audience share. This can lead them to present content that may cross the lines of good taste or acceptable topics that might offend more conservative members of the community. The explanation of such changes lies in the same factors that influence content in other media—such as film and television. In some cases, at least, a "creeping cycle of desensitization" can be observed as stations driven by competition for survival press the boundaries of good taste and moral norms.

An example of radio programming that some claim did push those boundaries was found in the late 1990s on a Boston radio station.[11] It provided racy morning programming aimed at a teenage audience. It was highly successful in that it attracted an astonishing 37 percent of the twelve-to-seventeen-year-old listeners in its market (a total of some 150,000 teenagers). Many listeners were even younger. A problem for many parents was with the lyrics of some of the songs. One such song advocated, "Go do it. Then find someone else and do it again." Another, delivered by female vocalists, asked, "Do you mind if I stroke you up? Do you mind if I stroke you down? Get it up; ooh that's what I want to do."[12] The singing was accompanied by moaning, which puzzled some of the younger listeners who really did not understand the meaning of the lyrics. On the other hand, radio stations have universally banned pornography star Robin Byrd's song, "Bang Your Box." She says that it is about a piano, but many disc jockeys doubt that.

On a more positive note, radio provides much for ethnic communities. There are Spanish-language, Native-American, and African-American radio stations (and even a national African-American network) as well as stations that feature programming in Greek, Irish, Scandinavian, Chinese, Japanese, and other languages. (Cable television, too, serves widely as a medium for ethnic programming, but radio is cheaper to produce than cable.)

Radio disc jockeys no longer spin "platters," as records were once called, but preside over digital music programs and are important in drawing audiences. One of the nation's best known DJs is Rick Dees of KISS-FM in Los Angeles, who won the Air Personality of the Year Award in 2000.

Public radio, especially NPR (mentioned earlier) and other forms of noncommercial broadcasting, provide important services and typically reach a large, upscale market, especially in university communities. Many noncommercial stations are owned by educational institutions, religious organizations, cities and towns, and other groups. However, most U.S. radio, like U.S. television, consists of commercial stations that rely on advertising sales to stay on the air.

THE FUTURE OF RADIO

Today, radio is a mature medium with a clear niche in the media spectrum. In its present form it is prospering, and that is not likely to change in any drastic way. As we have noted, it still commands the largest cumulative audiences in America, and it is gaining strength. As cable and satellite TV, the Internet, and VCR usage intrude on the ability of television to capture the attention of large audiences, local advertisers are returning to radio. As revenues from local advertising increase, the worth of radio stations increases, and this helps their prospects for future profitability. This trend will probably extend into the foreseeable future.

The shift to FM. A significant trend in radio has been the decline in listening to AM stations and the steady increase in those tuning in to FM stations. This has been a clear pattern of change for over the last two decades. Before about 1977, more people listened to AM stations. After that year, the pattern switched and FM listenership grew increasingly dominant. Today, nearly 70 percent of radio listeners are tuned into an FM station. That switch is unlikely to be reversed. The future of the older, more static-prone, AM band is less and less clear.

Private, low power FM stations. In the fall of 1999, the FCC began studying ways to allow private citizens and groups to license low powered (one hundred- and one thousand-watt) FM stations that would serve restricted local areas. They would not be commercial stations supported by advertising, but would be kept in operation by donations or other means. They would be able to broadcast music, local news, public service messages, or whatever content they wanted, and in any language. Thousands of such licenses would have been made available under the proposal. Predictably, the National Association of Broadcasters announced that the plan would harm the existing radio industry.[13]

Satellite broadcasting. Another new form of broadcasting in an early stage is *satellite radio*.[14] Companies marketing this system began broadcasts in 2000. The customer pays an initial fee (around $200). There is also a monthly subscription (of about $9.95). For that outlay, the customer receives one hundred channels of classical music, jazz, and other forms of content as well as talk without any commercial interruptions. Also eliminated will be the annoying fund drives that are common

trends in media use

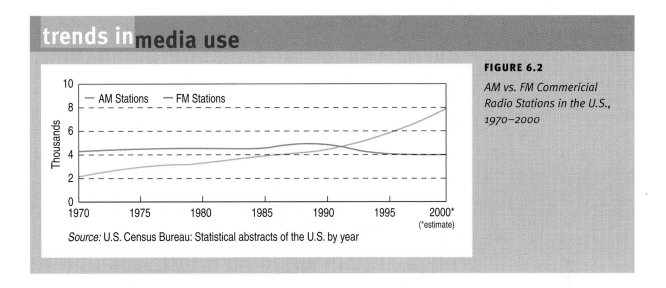

FIGURE 6.2

AM vs. FM Commericial Radio Stations in the U.S., 1970–2000

Source: U.S. Census Bureau: Statistical abstracts of the U.S. by year

on National Public Radio. One such service is XM Satellite Radio based in Washington, D.C. This firm offers one hundred channels of music, news, talk, sports, comedy, and children's programming.

The main audience being sought consists of people who drive their cars to work and elsewhere. Many currently listen to their radios while en route. The tiny (two-inch) satellite dish receiving the signal will be mounted on the vehicle and it will have a wire to a device allowing it to be plugged into a cassette or CD player on the dashboard. The idea, according to those promoting it, is to give customers many choices twenty-four hours a day, beyond what they can get from the standard commercial stations. At present, there are only two such systems licensed in the United States by the FCC (one in New York City and one in Washington, D.C.).

Satellite technology now plays a significant role in media industries as in the case of radio host Art Bell. Here, Bell poses in front of a satellite dish on top of the roof of his home where he broadcasts his popular "Coast-to-Coast" show.

Nearly all media outlets now have their own Web sites, whether they are book, magazine, and newspaper publishers; TV and radio stations (as seen here); or Web sites for Internet services.

If this system is successful, and especially if it spreads to other cities, it may eventually have an influence on commercial broadcast stations—just as cable TV and the VCR caused many problems for over-the-air network television broadcasting. Standard stations may find their share of the radio audience declining—which would hurt their profits from advertising. However, all of that remains to be seen. It may well be that commercial stations will alter what they do to meet such a challenge. Radio has adapted effectively before.

Monitoring your listening. A breadbox-sized device called MOBILTRAK has been developed to detect the radio station that your receiver is tuned to in your car as you arrive at a shopping center, concert parking lot, or mall. It does not record your conversations or any other automobile or personal information—just the station that you have tuned in. Such monitoring systems are already in use in a number of major cities. The information provided is a kind of "ratings" system by which stations in the area can tell which has the largest audience at a particular time, and what kinds of music or programs people are listening to at any particular moment. Such information is valuable to broadcasters who want to convince advertisers that they have a large market share and are providing the content that people desire. Critics such as John Roberts, director of the American Civil Liberties Union in Massachusetts, have denounced the technology as an invasion of privacy.[15]

Squeezing in more ads. Another interesting new technology, used in both radio and television, reviews taped material moment by moment. The purpose is to find small places on the tape that can be deleted, without altering the content of what people are saying. This reduces the time devoted to on-air program content by squeezing out a second here and a second there. These seconds can add up to minutes over the length of an entire program. The time saved is then devoted to more commercials! Radio stations and advertisers love it. The public may not appreciate it, but chances are they will never detect it.

Overall, then, radio has proved itself a versatile and adaptive medium, one that supplies a good deal of information and entertainment, some opinion, and relatively inexpensive local advertising. It has effectively met challenges to its place in the media mix, and it will continue to readjust and recalibrate itself as audience tastes, interests, and technology change. Like all media today, radio is sometimes owned by medium-specific companies (that have mostly radio properties). Increasingly, however, stations are being purchased by large media companies that are likely to own newspapers, magazines, television stations, databases, and other communication enterprises. Radio continues to have a market niche both in its command of audiences and its ability to sell advertising and generate other revenues.

Chapter Review

- Radio developed as a logical extension of the electric telegraph, which became a reality in the 1840s. Reliable electric telegraphy was not possible until after the invention of the electromagnet, which was at the heart of the system developed by Samuel F. B. Morse.

- When Morse sent his famous message, "What hath God wrought?" over forty miles of wire between Baltimore and Washington, D.C., the speed with which information could move changed from that of a train or a flying pigeon to that of lightning. It was a truly startling advance.

- Radio shares its early history with the telegraph. The wireless represented the achievement of an ancient dream of conquering both time and long distance to communicate quickly without wires. The first wireless patent went to Guglielmo Marconi, who spanned the English Channel with a wireless telegraph message in 1897, and then the Atlantic in 1901.

- The new form of telegraphy was an enormously useful device for communicating with ships at sea and with far-flung business, military, and diplomatic enterprises around the globe. Radio took on an aura of glamour very early when it played a critical role in rescue efforts at sea. While it would be many years before it would even start to become a household communications medium, it quickly gained a large and enthusiastic following in the population.

- During the early 1920s, under existing legislation, virtually anyone could obtain a license, build a relatively inexpensive transmitter, and go on the air. Hundreds did just that. Soon, the airways were cluttered with conflicting signals. With considerable reluctance, Congress first passed the Radio Act of 1927 and finally the Federal Communications Act of 1934, which brought radio broadcasting under the technical control of the federal government.

- An important problem that had to be solved before radio could become a household medium was how to pay for the broadcasts. After several alternatives were considered, the answer came in the form of selling airtime to advertisers—a close parallel to selling space to advertisers in the print media. This permitted the development of sponsored shows, regularly scheduled broadcasts, and a star system.

■ The golden age of radio was between the 1930s, after the medium had matured, up until it was almost displaced by television during the early 1950s. Many important features developed during the period, including worldwide radio news, FM broadcasting, and the ultimate adjustment of radio to its current format and style.

■ As a contemporary medium, radio is surviving well, largely as a local medium. Listening is widespread and radio captures about 10 percent of the nation's expenditures for media advertising. Its formats and content range from various kinds of music through talk shows, news, and sports. The majority of listeners today tune into FM stations.

■ Radio's future seems secure. It has worked out its own niche in our system of mass communications. It is a flexible medium capable of responding to changes that may come in the future. At present, in financial terms, radio is enjoying a period of relative prosperity.

■ New technologies based on satellite transmission and reception may bring subscription service to radio and change the kinds of programs to which people listen, especially in their cars.

Notes and References

1. John Baptista Porta (or Giovanni Battista della Porta), *Natural Magik* (New York: Smithsonian Institute for Basic Books, 1957). This is a modern reprint of a book first printed in the late 1500s, just after the invention of the press.
2. The details of the history of radio presented in these sections are a summary of a more extended treatment of the subject in Melvin L. DeFleur, *Theories of Mass Communication,* 1st ed. (New York: McKay, 1966), pp. 44–69.
3. Gleason L. Archer, *History of Radio to 1926* (New York: American Historical Society, 1938), pp. 112–113.
4. For an excellent discussion of these early developments (from which the authors have drawn many insights, see Sydney W. Head and Christopher H. Sterling, *Broadcasting in America,* 5th ed. (Boston: Houghton Mifflin, 1987), pp. 62–65, 435–99.
5. For the most thorough and contemporary discussion currently available of the entire broadcasting industry and the details of its development, see Sydney W. Head and Christopher H. Sterling, *Broadcasting in America,* 8th ed. (Boston: Houghton Mifflin, 1998). The present chapter incorporates many insights from this classic work. Another treatment of contemporary radio is found in Edward C. Pease and Everette E. Dennis, *Radio—The Forgotten Medium* (New Brunswick, N. J.: Transaction Press, 1997).
6. Alfred G. Goldsmith and Austin C. Lescarboura, *This Thing Called Broadcasting* (New York: Holt, 1930), p. 279.
7. Radio Advertising Bureau (www.rab.com) and Veronis Suhler Media Merchant Bank *Communications Industry Forecast 2000.*
8. Provided by the Federal Communications Commission, Washington, D.C., this number is for December 31, 1992.
9. *Broadcasting Table Yearbook,* 1996, p. xxi.
10. *Five-Year Communications Industry Forecast* (New York: Veronis, Suhler & Associates, July 2000).

11. This account is based on a report in the *Boston Globe* by David Arnold, "Racy Radio Jolts Parents," November 12, 1996, pp. A and A12.

12. The lyrics are from "Stroke You Up," by Changing Faces, Big Beat Records, Inc.

13. Allyson Lieberman, "An FM Station on Every Block?" *The New York Post,* October 18, 1999, p. 41.

14. This discussion is based on a report by Clea Simon, "Coming to Your Car, Satellite Radio," *The Boston Globe,* October 22, 1998, p. C20.

15. Erica Noonan, "Stadiums Listen in on Concert-Goers' Radio Choices," *The Associated Press State and Local Wire,* January 11, 2000.

Chapter 7

TELEVISION: THE MOST INFLUENTIAL MEDIUM

TELEVISION IS A MEDIUM OF ENORMOUS IMPOR-TANCE, POWER, AND INFLUENCE. ALTHOUGH RADIO STILL HAS LARGER AUDIENCES AND greater reach worldwide, no one doubts the preeminent role of television as a medium of communication. Television is a technology and a communication platform. It is also a communication system and an industry. It is a major force in the media economy as a connection between audiences and advertisers as well as a system of content. That content includes news and information, entertainment and sports, opinion programming, and, of course, advertising and other commercial content. Television thus delivers all the major functions of communication, but is most often seen as a medium of entertainment. As we will see in this chapter, the technology of television has been of critical importance from its early beginning as a mechanical invention, later as an electronic medium, and most recently as a digital medium.

Invention and technology have always played a critical role in television's development and in its ability to challenge, keep pace, and eventually overcome other means of communication from radio and motion pictures to newspapers and magazines, among others. Its greatest challenge at the dawn of the twenty-first century was the Internet, with its interactive capacity, extensive reach, and ability to narrowcast

Early experimental television screens were tiny—about the size of a business card or a man's wallet—and sometimes round or oval shaped. Controls were used to adjust sound and picture quality—both quite poor by contemporary standards—and only one channel was received. Though invented in the 1920s, TV did not make its debut in most homes until the early 1950s (as above), delayed in large part by World War II.

programs and messages. But even in the midst of an appliance "war" between the TV and the PC, television was making inroads as content on the World Wide Web and hoped to do even more so as a fully digital television system is implemented in the United States and in other countries.

In this and other chapters we have also referred to the enormous impact and influence of television on people's thinking as well as on their attitudes and behavior. That influence continues to be a matter of discussion and debate usually focused on television's role in the lives of children and in showcasing violence and antisocial behavior. Social scientists have studied these issues for years as have cultural critics who believe there is a link between the content of television and the images in society of women, minorities, and others.

As with other media in the new century, television hardly stands alone. It is closely linked to Hollywood and the video production studio. Its owners often have other media and communication properties and interests. Television is to some an old medium, well established in the media family, but it is also associated with new media, including cable and the World Wide Web. Cable was once a simple distribution system for existing television network stations and programs. Eventually, though, it took on a life of its own as a separable industry that used both existing TV content and generated its own original programming. Cable networks soon existed alongside over-the-air television broadcast networks. Once cable was thought to be a great medium of the future with interactive capacity and various service functions, but by the late 1990s, one critic lamented that "cable is just more TV." The satellite television industry also competes with and lives alongside over-the-air broadcast television. It can bring programming anywhere on earth and can also add its own pay-per-view services. Television is also a heavy user of Web sites and a source for them. There is truly a synergy between TV and the Internet as people follow their favorite programs online, including game shows, reality television, and others. Of course, TV networks, stations, and individual programs all have their own interactive Web sites.

In any consideration of television, technology is vitally important, and today the television, cable, satellite, and digital media industries compete, collaborate, and interact as part of what analysts simply call "the television industries."

Television was born in controversy and remains controversial today. Some claim that it is the most important medium ever developed. Others believe that it is harmful and say it is the cause of many undesirable conditions in our society. Debates about TV began early in its history with claims as to who actually invented it. Following World War I, scientists in various parts of the world—England, Japan, Russia, and the United States—began experimenting with the idea of sending visual signals over the air using radio waves. Although the earliest television technology may not have been exclusively American, there is little doubt that in the United States it was developed swiftly as an enormously popular mass medium. Transmissions began as experiments in laboratories in the 1920s. By the late 1930s, it was a fledgling broadcast medium whose signals were being transmitted a few times a week in the New York City area to several hundred people using amateur-built receivers in their homes. Although its development was temporarily halted during World War II, by the end of the 1940s it was poised to sweep through society as a mass medium for home use. During the 1950s it did just that.[1]

During its brief history, television has been a remarkably volatile medium. Its technology has steadily changed; its content has constantly evolved; its audiences have grown hugely; and large numbers of critics have continued a flow of condemnation because of its presumed effects. In spite of all that, TV quickly became and remains America's favorite, and arguably most influential, medium.

At first, the typical factory-built receiver offered small black-and-white pictures about the size of a man's wallet. They were of poor quality by today's standards, but people were fascinated with the idea that moving pictures could be broadcast over the air and received in the home. Even the commercials seemed interesting because they *moved*. Before long, however, the novelty wore off and audiences became more selective and demanding. They wanted larger screens, clearer pictures, more channels, and color. Then they wanted greater control over what they viewed, something that digital television now offers.

As new technologies arrived to satisfy these wishes, Americans gleefully adopted them. Screens grew much bigger than the early versions. Better transmitters and receivers made the picture more stable. Cable brought more channels with greater choices of programs. Color made TV more pleasurable to watch. VCRs transformed the TV set into a little movie screen in the living room. Handheld remote controls, routinely supplied with new sets, enabled audiences to exorcise ruthlessly the bothersome commercials sandwiched between segments of programs. As we will see, that upset advertisers, who started to turn to alternative media—which reduced the earnings of the networks, eroded the income of advertising agencies, and generally threw the whole television industry into turmoil. Finally, direct signals from satellites and a transformation to digital technology brought further change.

THE BIRTH OF TELEVISION

The history of television goes back a lot further than many people might suppose. In fact, in 1884, a German experimenter, Paul Nipkow, developed a rotating disk with small holes arranged in a spiral pattern that had unusual properties. It would be the basis of the earliest experiments with television. If a strong light was aimed at a picture or scene, it reflected patterns of light and dark back toward the disk. Those patterns of light passed through the holes in the rotating disk to be registered in light-sensitive electric devices. This produced a very rapid scanning effect that was somewhat like the movements a human eye makes while scanning across a page. It was realized quite early that the perforated whirling disk could produce patterns of electrical impulses that could be sent along a wire in order to transmit pictures. Later, the same patterns would be transmitted by radio. The **Nipkow disk** became the central technology for further experimentation on the transmission of images, both by wire and later by radio waves. This scanning concept is at the heart of television, even today, although it is accomplished by electronic means rather than by a mechanical disk.[2]

Although the scanning disk was unique to early TV experiments, the entire histories of radio and television are closely intertwined. All the inventions and technologies that made radio broadcasting possible are also part of the history of television. In addition, the social and economic organization of the industry was already set before TV became a reality. The medium is supported by advertising. That was never an issue. It is governed by the Federal Communications Commission (FCC). That, too, was never an issue. Its content is an extension of that developed in radio. The three major television networks that dominated early television were radio networks first. They were the same companies that pioneered commercial radio broadcasting.

Early in the 1920s, such corporations as General Electric and RCA allocated budgets for experiments with television, and other corporations soon followed. The idea seemed far-fetched and futuristic to many in the industry, but television research was authorized in the hope that it would result in an eventual payoff. General Electric employed an inventor, Ernst Alexanderson, to work exclusively on the problem, and within a short time he had developed a crude but workable system based on the Nipkow disk. However, it was not to be the system that the industry finally adopted.

DEVELOPING AN ELECTRONIC SYSTEM

Perhaps the most remarkable of the inventors who played a key role in developing the needed electronic technology was a skinny high school boy in an isolated part of the United States. Philo T. Farnsworth was a poor youngster from a large family in Rigby, Idaho, a small farm community. As a child he had started reading about electricity, and in 1922, he astounded his high school science teacher by showing him diagrams for electronic circuits that would make it possible to transmit and receive moving pictures over the air.

Farnsworth had studied reports of television experiments based on the Nipkow disk. He correctly reasoned that such a system was primitive and clumsy. He had reached the conclusion that electronic devices were needed to sweep across a scene or picture rapidly in a series of horizontal lines, and transform those variations into signals that could be broadcast over the air. Parallel electronic devices for reception and viewing were also needed. He had come up with designs of circuits for each apparatus and calculations as to how they could function. Farnsworth's teacher enthusiastically encouraged him to try to perfect and patent the system.

During the same period, just after World War I, a talented Russian, Vladimir K. Zworykin, had come to the United States to work on radio research at Westinghouse. He had been a communication specialist in the army of Tsar Nicholas, where he had worked on early television experiments before the Russian Revolution. He asked for permission to continue development at Westinghouse. Directors of the huge corporation thought it was a long shot but decided to finance the work. Zworykin, like Farnsworth, was unimpressed with the mechanical disk approach and believed that electronic systems were needed for practical television transmission and reception. He set out to work on them with the full facilities of the great Westinghouse laboratories.

Meanwhile, as Zworykin was closing in on the problem, a friend of Farnsworth's took him to California and provided him with a place to work and funding for his experiments. There, on a shoestring budget, he transformed his circuits and drawings into a working apparatus, which he built in an apartment where he kept his blinds drawn. (The neighbors thought he was a bootlegger running a still, and he was raided by the police.) Then, in 1927, the young man was able to make actual transmissions. He showed his friend how his apparatus could broadcast and receive both fixed images and small scenes from motion pictures. It was a remarkable achievement.

Having created a working system, Farnsworth took his drawings to federal authorities and applied for the first electronic television patent. His application created an uproar. The great radio corporations, taken completely by surprise, were shocked and outraged that an obscure nobody had invented, built, and asked to patent a system that Westinghouse, RCA, and others had spent fortunes trying to develop and were themselves about to patent. They immediately contested the application.

After a great deal of controversy and legal maneuvering, Farnsworth won. To regain control, RCA haggled with the young inventor who held out for a very profitable royalty settlement. Although Farnsworth reached his solution before Zworykin, the latter invented some of the most critical components of television technology: the iconoscope (electronic picture tube) and the image orthicon camera. Also in the 1920s, Scottish engineer John Logie Baird invented a television system that was adopted by the BBC. There is little agreement about who invented television as claims were made by early engineer-inventors from several nations.

Philo Farnsworth was a high school student in Rigby, Idaho, in 1922 when he showed his science teacher drawings for circuits that would make it possible to broadcast TV pictures based on electronic technology. This was a significant advance over the mechanical systems used in experiments at the time. With financial backing from friends, Farnsworth constructed the apparatus and filed a patent application just before similar steps were taken by a major corporation. This led to a great uproar and a legal battle that lasted for years. Farnsworth eventually prevailed in the courts.

THE EARLY BROADCASTS

The earliest experimental television receivers used tiny screens based on cathode ray tubes about four inches in diameter. Cameras were crude and required intense lighting. People who appeared on the screen had to wear bizarre purple and green makeup to provide contrast for the picture. Nevertheless, in 1927, a picture of Herbert Hoover, then Secretary of Commerce, appeared on experimental broadcast.

By 1932, RCA had built a TV station, complete with a studio and transmitting facilities, in New York City's Empire State Building. RCA had set aside a million dollars to develop and demonstrate the new broadcast medium. In 1936, it began testing the system, broadcasting two programs a week. By that time a few hundred enthusiasts in the New York area had constructed or obtained TV receivers and were able to pick up the transmissions in their homes. Meanwhile, the federal government had developed procedures for awarding licenses to transmitters and had granted a limited number. Thus, by early 1941, the medium was set to take off.

Suddenly, the whole world changed. After the Japanese attack on Pearl Harbor in December 1941, the war effort completely monopolized the attention of the country. Along with almost every aspect of American life, the manufacture of television receivers was temporarily delayed. All the electronics manufacturers turned to producing equipment for the armed forces, and not until 1945 did these companies return to making products for the civilian market. In the immediate postwar years, however, television stations were quickly established in a number of major cities, and the public was ready to buy sets. The television was finally ready for home use.

THE PERIOD OF RAPID ADOPTION

By 1946, the FCC had issued twenty-four new licenses for television transmitters. The networks and the advertising industry eagerly waited for the new medium to enter American homes. It seemed clear to all concerned that television might become a truly important broadcast medium. There was a great scramble to take part.

The manufacture and sale of home receivers began that same year. As sets became available, Americans rushed to buy them. However, they were quite expensive. In 1947, a set with a picture about six by seven inches cost around $400. That was more than a month's wages for many blue-collar families, and the set did not include the special antenna that had to be installed on the roof. A truly deluxe set, with a fancy wood cabinet and a mirror system for making the picture seem larger, sold for about half as much as a modest car. Obviously, only the affluent families could afford such a luxury, and so a TV set became a new kind of status symbol. Families who had receivers often invited their envious neighbors in to watch the transmissions (and to see visible evidence of their affluence). Stories circulated of people who erected an antenna to make their neighbors think they had a television, when all they really had was an antenna—with no set hooked up below. In fact, TV was regarded as such a luxury that if a family receiving welfare was found to have a television set, it was regarded as a moral outrage.

One establishment that could afford a set was the local tavern. By 1948, a television set was a central feature in almost every tavern in the country. Sports programs were the favorite, and big crowds would gather to watch the games. It is probably no exaggeration to say that the local tavern was a significant element in demonstrating and popularizing the new medium. Even today, people watch sports programming in bars and taverns, where they enjoy a communal medium as they watch a game and discuss it with fellow patrons.

THE BIG FREEZE

By the beginning of 1948, the FCC had issued approximately one hundred licenses. Some cities had two or even three stations, although most still had none. Soon, however, problems developed like those that had troubled radio in the early years. The signals of one station sometimes interfered with those of another. This led the FCC to conclude that drastic action was needed to avoid upcoming difficulties. Beginning in 1948 and extending through 1952, the commission ordered a *freeze* on the issuance of new licenses and construction permits (previously licensed stations were allowed to start up). As a result, TV transmitters could not be built in many American communities until after the freeze was lifted. The FCC wanted to study thoroughly the technical aspects of television and related broadcasting so that it could allocate frequencies to TV, FM radio, and other kinds of transmissions appropriately.

During the freeze, the FCC developed a master plan that still governs TV over-the-air broadcasting today. The system prevents the signals of one television station from interfering with those of another, thus avoiding the chaos that characterized early radio broadcasting. When the freeze was lifted in 1952, television spread quickly throughout the United States. Within a remarkably short time, it became so ubiquitous that most American families had a set. Social commentators began to speak of the "television generation" of Americans born after World War II who never knew a world without TV. The medium is presumed to have shaped their lives in significant ways.

BECOMING A NATION OF TELEVISION VIEWERS

Figure 7.1 shows how rapidly the American public adopted television. In 1950, less than 10 percent of American homes had a set. In 1960, only ten years later, nearly 90 percent had a receiver. By 1980, ownership of sets had virtually reached saturation level in American households. Today, it is very unusual to find a family without a television set, and most have more than one.

Another index of the popularity of television can be seen in terms of viewing time. The TV set has been in use during an ever-growing number of hours per day for almost four decades. In 1950, those who owned sets had them on four-and-a-half-hours daily on average. That number rose sharply year after year to more than seven hours per day in recent years (see Figure 7.2). Today, it is becoming increasingly difficult to

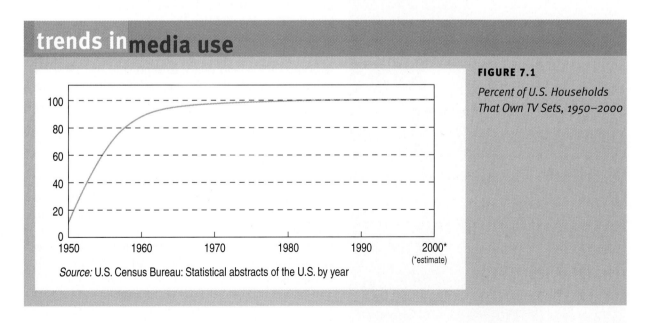

trends in media use

FIGURE 7.1

Percent of U.S. Households That Own TV Sets, 1950–2000

Source: U.S. Census Bureau: Statistical abstracts of the U.S. by year

trends in media use

FIGURE 7.2

*Daily Hours of Use of TV
Sets in U.S. Households,
1950–2000*

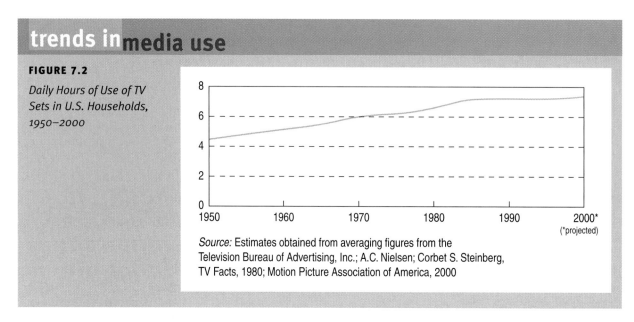

Source: Estimates obtained from averaging figures from the
Television Bureau of Advertising, Inc.; A.C. Nielsen; Corbet S. Steinberg,
TV Facts, 1980; Motion Picture Association of America, 2000

Among the great innovators of electronic media with footprints in both radio and television were Guglielmo Marconi, the Italian inventor and engineer (left), and David Sarnoff, founder of the NBC networks (right), standing together at a transmitting center on Long Island in 1933.

determine patterns of television viewing because TV sets can be used in so many ways. One can watch regular broadcasting, signals from satellites, cable channels, and videocassettes; play video games; or be connected to the Internet.

THE COMING OF COLOR

Color television got off to a slow start. Experiments had been performed with color test pictures as early as 1929, and there was much talk about commercial broadcasts in color as early as 1940. There were problems, however, in settling on the best technology. By 1946, CBS had developed a system based on a rotating disk that actually gave very good results. However, it had one major problem: the FCC insisted that the system for color transmission be such that existing black-and-white television sets could still receive a picture (though not in color), and with the CBS system that was impossible. A new set was required. In 1953, the FCC approved a different system, which had been developed by RCA in 1946. Although it produced less-refined colors, it did allow existing black-and-white sets to receive color-transmitted programs.

For a variety of reasons, the networks exercised a great deal of caution in delivering color broadcasts. At first they transmitted only a few programs in color. By 1967, though, most network programs were in color, and even local stations began to produce programs in this mode. As a result, all of the black-and-white cameras had to be phased out and new technicians needed to be trained. However, the industry made the transition to the new technology smoothly. By the mid-1990s, almost all American homes had color television receivers.

TELEVISION'S GOLDEN AGES

Two rather different periods can both be called the golden age of television. The first is the time when the medium was experiencing its most rapid period of growth—roughly from 1952 to around 1960. The second is a longer period, from about 1960 to around 1980, when network television had few competitors.

Those who identify the earlier period do so not only because of the rapid growth of the medium but also on the basis of some of the programming. Some point to it as a golden era by noting dramatic programs of high quality that were broadcast, such as "Playhouse 90." This kind of programming appealed to more sophisticated viewers. Others noted that it was a time when family situation comedies, sports, and variety-vaudeville were new features of home viewing that had very wide appeal. Among the latter, Milton Berle's "Texaco Star Theater" and Ed Sullivan's "Toast of the Town" are often cited as examples of how great television programs were in those "good old days."

Many younger people who view these programs today are at a loss to understand the glowing classifications. To them, the early shows can seem naive and even dull. Whether the programming of the period should be regarded as art, simple slapstick, or mindless and trivial pop culture of a particular era could be debated endlessly.

On other grounds, the two decades between 1960 and 1980 also can be regarded as a kind of *economic* golden age of television. It may not have been in some ideal sense of audience satisfaction or in terms of classic programming. On the contrary, at the time the public showed many signs of frustration and dissatisfaction with the medium. The period was one of turmoil in American society, beset by such issues as civil rights, the Vietnam War, and increasing crime and violence. Many blamed TV for social ills, believing it to be a powerful medium that was eroding the moral standards and the stability of the nation. As we will see later, such charges generated a great deal of interest in the effects of television.

During these decades, the medium was dominated by three major networks (ABC, CBS, and NBC) with virtually no competition. Their profit margins were very high from advertising revenue, and they commanded the attention of virtually the entire viewing audience during prime time. Cable had yet to spread to more than a small proportion of American households, and there were no VCRs for home use. The networks competed with each other, and the three of them almost totally dominated the medium. If one wanted to watch TV during the period, there were very few alternatives to viewing network programming. A small proportion of Americans did view programs on educational stations and the Public Broadcasting Service (PBS). Network television was widely criticized for broadcasting too much violence and for keeping the intellectual level of its programs low. Programs presented during the period were often designed with the tastes of the lower middle class in mind. Violence and fantasy were persistent themes. The lower-middle-class viewers in America were the ones who purchased the most beer, soap, detergent, soft drinks, and other nationally distributed products that could be advertised so effectively on television. The cumulative purchasing power of this vast majority was mind-boggling, and programming was directed (and still is) toward that aggregate monetary bonanza. That translated into simple tastes and material at a relatively undemanding intellectual level. The majority of Americans loved that kind of TV content. At the same time, more sophisticated viewers understood that, in the words of Newton Minow (then Chairman of the FCC), network television was a "vast wasteland" of mindless comedy, unrealistic soap operas, staged wrestling, cartoons, spectator sports, quiz shows, and shallow portrayals of family situations.

Somehow, though, for both of the periods mentioned above, time has transformed what many critics of the past regarded as "trash" into the present view of the "good old days" of TV. That assessment may arise in large part from the fact that the content of the period was carefully designed to fit the limited tastes and intellectual preferences of the majority. Those same people are now older, but their tastes have not become noticeably elevated. Moreover, their children have similar tastes. It is little wonder, then, that as they look back to the programs of the earlier periods they see classics, and the people who starred in those presentations as "significant performers." This makes us wonder whether some of the reality programming of the present will have nostalgic reruns twenty or thirty years from now. Much-criticized programs like "The Jerry Springer Show," which are regarded as vulgar, or others like "Survivor" and "Big Brother," in which contestants' values are in play, might return long after they go off the air. Indeed, with modern storage capacity, almost any image can be brought back or recycled.

ALTERNATIVES TO BROADCAST TELEVISION

Three technological advances played a critical role in the reshaping of the American television industry. The first was the growth of cable television. The second was the widespread adoption of the videocassette recorder. The third was the entry of direct satellite and digital broadcasting into the mix. All three are relatively recent events.

THE SPREAD OF CABLE SYSTEMS

Cable television began innocently enough. It was needed in certain locations because of the line-of-sight nature of the TV signal. For example, a community that is blocked by a large hill that stands between it and the nearest television transmit-

Reality programming has become a staple of entertainment television in the United States, Europe, and elsewhere. The shows that depict ordinary people in extraordinary situations include "Survivor," some of whose contestants/participants are shown here in August 2000.

ter cannot receive the signal. The same is true for people who live in a valley or in an area with a lot of tall buildings that block the transmission.

In the 1950s, a number of local and very small systems were set up to overcome such obstacles. The solution was to put a large community antenna in a favorable location, and to wire people's homes via coaxial cable to this central facility. Usually, the signal was amplified to make reception very clear. It worked fine, and was especially attractive to people in rural areas and other hard-to-reach locations.

At first, the number of households that were "wired" in this way was very small (less than 2 percent of homes with TV in 1960). It was actually a kind of "mom and pop" industry, with some 640 small systems each serving only several hundred or a few thousand clients. Then, the whole concept began to expand, largely because cable brought better pictures and more selection. This development angered the broadcast companies, who saw the cable operator as a "parasite" who was pirating their programs off the air and selling them for a profit. Then, as the cable companies developed better technology, they began to offer their clients television signals that had originated in cities a great distance away—effectively diminishing attention to local broadcast companies. Even worse, some of the cable companies started originating their own programming!

Lawsuits were filed by almost everyone against almost everyone else in the industry. Finally, it was resolved that the FCC had the right to regulate the cable companies, just as though they were broadcasting over the air. The broadcast companies persuaded the FCC to impose stiff, complex regulations that effectively stopped the growth of cable systems. By 1979, however, many of those restrictions were relaxed and local governments were given the right to grant franchises to private cable companies to provide service in the local community. Out of that came a great surge of development. In 1980, less than 20 percent of American homes were wired for cable. By 2000, according to Nielsen Media Research, 68.1 percent of U.S. TV households were receiving their TV programs via cable. The adoption curve continued to rise (see Figure 7.3).

The increasing adoption of cable by American households has significantly altered the entire television industry. First, it has reduced the **market share** (proportion of the total television viewing audience) that watches regular network

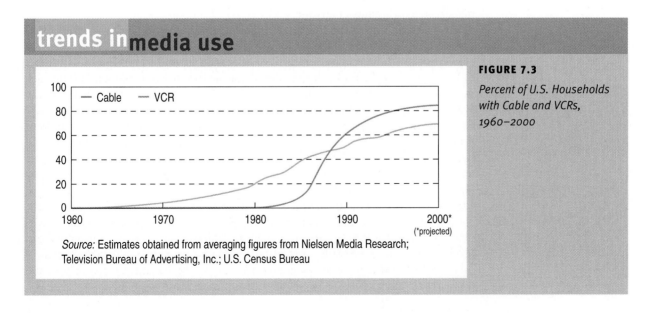

trends in media use

FIGURE 7.3

Percent of U.S. Households with Cable and VCRs, 1960–2000

Source: Estimates obtained from averaging figures from Nielsen Media Research; Television Bureau of Advertising, Inc.; U.S. Census Bureau

television. Indeed, the networks have suffered a slow but steady decline in market share for a number of years. Second, it has begun to segment the viewing public along the lines of its tastes and interests. With dozens of channels to choose from in a typical cable system, one no longer needs to view whatever the networks happen to be broadcasting at the moment. It is possible to find on most cable television, at any given time, some form of program content that will fit almost anyone's interests. Thus, a pattern is developing much like the one that developed in the magazine industry when the large, general circulation periodicals gave way to the more focused, specialized magazines. Advertisers are following these developments with keen interest. If one has a special product to advertise, it is more likely that a program interesting potential customers can be found in the cable TV lineup.

Currently there is considerable discontent with cable channels like HBO, USA, Lifetime, and MTV. The programming is often repetitive. Monthly fees are said to be too expensive, and cable channels now incorporate about as much advertising as traditional over-the-air broadcasts did earlier. Furthermore, critics complain, there has been no noticeable elevation of aesthetic tastes or intellectual standards. One used to find such content as wrestling, bowling matches, and soap operas only on broadcast television channels. Now they are most often found on cable television along with new contenders, such as direct marketing, real-estate ads, and music videos. Criticisms appear to be valid; however, cable systems in the United States still serve the same public with the same tastes that broadcast TV always has served.

THE VCR AND DVD

Like so many electronic devices, the VCR is an American invention and a Japanese success story. The Ampex Corporation in New York developed the original machine. In 1952, Charles Ginsberg, along with several other Ampex engineers, set out to develop a device that could be used to record television programs on a magnetic tape. Four years later they succeeded. The first videotape recorder was about the size of an upright piano and used large reels of two-inch-wide tape. It was quickly adopted by the TV industry as a means to record material for later broadcasting. Used in this way it was very practical. No longer did everyone have to perform live. Programming errors could be edited or changes spliced in, allowing for mistake-free programs at airtime.

At the beginning of the 1970s, a number of American companies saw the potential uses for the device and set out to manufacture and market a small home version. However, they did not agree on the size and standards of the tape and other aspects of the system. By the middle of the decade, some five different standards were used in machines on the market. All were very expensive, and the prerecorded material available might or might not fit the machine purchased.

Then the Japanese stepped in. They standardized the systems and technology, brought prices down, and sold millions of the machines, so that today more than two-thirds of American households with TVs have a VCR. Figure 7.4 shows the pattern of adoption of the VCR for home use in just over two decades. The device gave birth to a whole new industry. Today, one can rent a movie for a very modest fee at a rental agency specializing in videocassette tapes, or in some cases at supermarkets, convenience stores, or even gas stations. To feed this market, the movie industry regularly produces films in this form. A movie on videocassette can generate enormous profits long after the film has exhausted its market at regular theaters. A host of other kinds of videocassettes—ranging from exercise programs to bass fishing and home repair instruction—have made the VCR even more popular.

VCRs, once thought to be too expensive for ordinary people to buy and use, got a great boost when thousands of "mom and pop" video rental stores emerged in the 1980s. Many of these were eventually bought out and morphed into large chains such as Blockbuster Video, now omnipresent in almost every community and neighborhood worldwide.

The proliferation of home VCRs was seen first as a threat by moviemakers and broadcast companies who feared that people would record movies and programs off broadcast or cable TV, thus reducing the effectiveness of TV advertising. That fear turned out to be unfounded. For the most part VCRs are used to play rented or purchased videocassettes. Studies show that the majority of VCR users do not even know how to program their machines to record material off the air.

The tape technology at the heart of the VCR may be heading for obsolescence. With more sophisticated systems under development, it will very likely be replaced with more efficient and reliable alternatives. Movies are now becoming available on CD-ROMs. Digital storage techniques have made it possible to squeeze an entire movie onto a compact disk. With even a small CD or DVD player, a movie can be seen on a TV screen. The pictures produced have a higher quality than those seen using cassette tapes. Other, even more efficient, digital-storage systems are under development. Thus, the VCR that everyone now has may become as much a curiosity in the future as the wind-up Victrola of the early part of the twentieth century.

DIRECT BROADCAST SATELLITE

It has been possible to receive television signals from satellites for many years. Such reception first required a large satellite "dish"—about the size of a barn door—stationed near the house. It had to be capable of being lined up and realigned on demand to point directly to the satellites from which the signals were being transmitted. The system was complex and awkward. Because of the complexity, appearance, size, and cost, few American families made use of this technology, although it did serve people in rural areas who were far from both regular television stations and cable systems.

In more recent years, a number of corporations have been marketing hardware and services that bring television signals from satellites directly into the home with the use of a dish about the size of a small pizza. In some cases, the equipment is purchased; in others it is leased. In either case, the dish is permanently fixed on the roof where it is pointed at the satellite and does not have to be moved or repositioned.

Unlike the older network broadcasts, these signals are not free. The system for making a profit for the services provided is essentially like that used by cable operators. The user pays a monthly subscription fee. A variety of "packages" is available. A "basic" package offers a bare-bones number of channels that are essentially similar to what a basic subscription to a cable system provides. The user can pay additional fees to add a number of movie, sports, or other special channels that contain programming of interest to the subscriber.

Direct broadcast satellite (DBS) systems are beginning to experience a strong pattern of increased adoption. They generally offer more viewing options—that is, a greater number of channels—and their signals produce a sharper picture on the typical TV set than is often the case with cable television. At present, it is difficult to predict what the outcome will be for the cable systems, or even for the local television stations. If programming can be originated in major cities on each of the coasts and then distributed via satellite to the entire country, there may be less and less need for local **affiliates** (local television stations that distribute network and other programming to people in a given market). After years of DBS experimentation— and a failure to attract more than small numbers of rural customers—DBS seemed to take a new turn in the late 1990s as smaller dishes and new financing for the industry brought additional sports feeds and pay-per-view movies. By 2000, the industry had nearly 10 million subscribers. One respected assessment thought DBS might eventually achieve its earlier promise.[3]

Clearly, the VCR, cable TV, and the handheld remote control, which can mute television sound or change channels, have made serious inroads into traditional

trends in media use

FIGURE 7.4

Percent of U.S. Households with a Satellite Service, 1985–2000

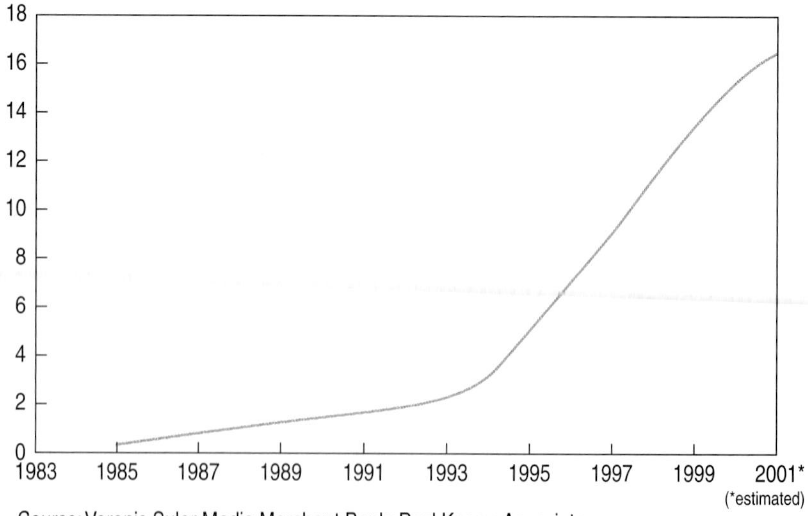

Source: Veronis Suler Media Merchant Bank; Paul Kagan Associates; Nielsen Media Research, 2000

Note: Figures include totals for SMATV (Satellite Masters Television), C-band satellite dishes, and DBS (Direct Broadcast Satellite) service.

broadcast television. The growing use of direct broadcast satellite systems and the shift to CD-delivered movies will bring further inroads. We have seen the impact of new technology on existing media in previous chapters. Alternate sources for news brought a significant decline in newspaper subscriptions. The large-circulation general magazine was a victim of the shift to TV advertising. Television viewing almost destroyed radio, and it seriously displaced moviegoing. Today, it is network TV that is in trouble—or more precisely, broadcast television of all kinds—undercut by technologies that give viewers more of what they want. The numbers of viewers are down, and consequently advertising revenues are declining. Many who in the past advertised their products almost exclusively on broadcast TV are now turning to direct mail, cable television, specialty magazines, the World Wide Web, and any other medium with which they can still reach their potential customers.

DIGITAL TELEVISION ARRIVES

For several years, using the Internet to download video was slow and inefficient because of limited bandwidth and a lack of capacity to transmit moving images rapidly. All that is changing with the advent of broadband—the so-called "Big Pipe"—which is the largest communications conduit ever imagined. Five separate industries are engaged in advanced broadband technology, something that will allow the consumer to combine video, phone, and data services with speedier access to the Internet. As communication expert Les Brown has written:

> Scarcely recognized is the effect of such great bandwidth on content and what impact that is likely to have on business and lifestyles. Content will differ markedly from what we have experienced . . . because digital broadband is interactive and can involve full motion video, multimedia, 3-D images and virtual reality.[4]

Although the five industries (cable, telephone, satellite, fixed wireless services, and cellular) are not all interested in the TV marketplace, several are, and the implications are enormous. Indeed broadband has been called "the third wiring of America," the first two being the telegraph and the telephone.

As we mention elsewhere in this book, the migration from analog to digital is a key element in understanding the new digital television.[5] Digital is a method of signal representation with specific numerical values (ones and zeros) while analog has continuously fluctuating current or voltage. For television this technology is truly revolutionary. For the consumer it means not only high-definition television (better pictures) and CD-quality audio (better sound), but also interactive capacity (feedback and talkback). Much like the incremental development of color in earlier decades, digital TV had its beginnings in the 1980s, but was not available to the public until 1998 when some TV stations in the United States started free transmission of over-the-air digital pictures and sound. In 1999, TV stations affiliated with four major networks were allowed to begin digital transmissions. While some quite expensive digital TV sets are on the market, other consumers are using conversion boxes and special antennae as the country moves slowly to a fully digitized television system, which is scheduled to occur in 2006. In addition to the presumed benefits for consumers, digital television also has important implications for production, distribution, and transmission. New and more sophisticated cameras, switchers, disc recorders, and other devices are involved.[6]

If early television meant only a few channels, and cable expanded the universe to one hundred or more, the coming digital age will bring hundreds, maybe even thousands, of new outlets and programming services. For broadcasters (TV stations and networks) it means more channel capacity, with each existing TV station getting up to six new twenty-four–hour channels. There is much debate and a myriad of unanswered questions about the changes heralded by digital television. Just what services the public will want—and support—what kind of new programming is going to be developed, costs for consumers, advertisers, and others—these are all factors that

Mark Walton
Managing Director
Onyx Media Group
New York, New York

insights from MEDIA LEADERS

Mark Walton heads a major TV programming and advertising sales distribution firm, the Onyx Media Group, whose clients include the Post-Newsweek Stations Group, Black Entertainment Television (BET), CBS New Media, and other firms. With a background in sales, marketing, and advertising, including more than a decade spent at the CBS TV network, he is a leader in organizations involved in TV distribution and programming, both in the U.S. and internationally. He is widely known and respected for his innovative advocacy of "convergence between television and the Internet."

Q. When did you first get involved with the television industry?

A. I got the TV bug when I was interviewing for jobs in graduate school. I was at the Yale Graduate School of Management after getting a journalism degree from Boston University. I was a print journalist who discovered radio during college. Along the way, I spent a summer with a big ad agency and started thinking about ad agencies and media advertising departments. I applied to both and ended up at CBS. From then on, it was television for me.

Q. What factors have inspired your continued interest and inspiration?

A. Mainly, it is the excitement of the field. With a business background, I could have worked in a traditional business such as package goods or some other industry, but I would find that too static for me. In TV, the "product line," that is, the content or programming, changes every year and at the same time, technology evolves. There is always room for new ideas. That's exciting.

Q. What have been the main influences—personal and professional—that led you to your current position of leadership in television programming and sales?

A. I'd say it was mainly an exposure to the whole field of television through different departments during my first year at CBS, when I was absolutely catapulted by the experience. Another important factor was working with the legendary Sam Maxwell who was the first network TV salesman at CBS. He was part of the "old guard" and I was privileged to be there when the old guard was looking to a "new guard" to lead the way, especially as new technologies were developing.

Q. What is your take on the current state and probable future of television?

A. To understand the current state of the business, you have to recognize that we are in an age of consolidation, which is wreaking havoc with those who are rigid and say, "I work only for a TV station that is only in competition with other TV stations!" That's not true anymore. The old walls in the field are moving all the time, and, for example, cable companies work with TV stations or the Internet, but they are all under the roof of one large holding company. It is a world with many players and all of them have a mandate to produce revenues. So, it is a very good time for the industry and people in it—if they are versatile and fluid. The future is also bright and involves the "repurposing of content" for various media, not just television.

Q. Since you have championed connections between the Internet and television, do you think that will lead to a new medium, or will we still be talking about television a decade or so from now?

A. Television will still be a major force, but it will continue to redefine itself—to expand its reach and connections to other media. As the industry takes on new dimensions, people working in TV will need new skills and a mindset for the future.

Q. We have noticed in the trade journals that you often talk about convergence and strategic alliances

will help to determine the future of this enhanced medium. Naturally, there are also political, regulatory, and private sector concerns, not to mention international issues that all need to be worked out in the next few years. Whatever the outcome of these complicated and overlapping matters, change is once again coming for television. Former NBC News President Lawrence Grossman, who co-chairs a Carnegie

between and among different parts of the television industry, which used to be dominated by a few players, like the networks. To what extent is that really happening?

A. Convergence really is happening in a kicking and screaming fashion! You see this in the way that traditional TV people are working with their Web masters. At the moment, the Web masters are undervalued and not getting enough attention. But while they are working hard to drive people to the Web site, people will also watch television. There is still something of a standoff between the old, one-dimensional types—unyielding die-hards—and those who can think "outside the box" in less conventional ways. The future belongs to those who can work more fluidly and harmoniously—connecting the traditional elements of television with new interactive approaches, mainly on the Web.

Q. What is the best pathway to a satisfying and successful career in television?

A. Well, the pathways are different for the different functions of the field. It depends on whether you are talking about creative people or business people. On the creative side, writers, editors, and designers are blessed if they have a real knowledge set, that is, knowing a lot about a given field whether that is history, political science, economics, or whatever. What I mean is a very solid liberal arts background. Communications education can be important too, but in more of a finishing sense, offering professional background or focus. It is important to really *know* something—to have a body of knowledge. On the business side of television, I believe that experience in sales is the best route. Anyone who can generate revenues is valuable and is unlikely to be moved out or downsized. Sales and selling puts you close to revenues and provides a real understanding of that aspect of the business.

Q. Based on job satisfaction, compensation, and future prospects, how would you rate the television industry and its various component parts as a career choice?

A. It is unquestionably an excellent career choice with this caveat: production and creative people are sometimes undervalued. The TV industry rewards a few people very well. Sometimes the creative people don't get the kinds of recognition—psychological and financial—they deserve fast enough and they leave the field. Television is highly competitive and frequently weeds people out. I wish it were more egalitarian, but the fact that it isn't means this is not an easy field without its hurdles. Still, it is rewarding in many ways for those who are tough enough to master the business. With some real exceptions, television is better to those on the business side, though.

Q. What is the most satisfying aspect of work in this field? The least?

A. There is nothing more satisfying than being part of an industry that touches almost every life on the planet. It is a business that has real impact and influence, not just in delivering the TV product, but connecting to other fields and human needs. For example, I just came from a breakfast where ABC announced that it was working with the surgeon general on a major health initiative to end health gaps between and among people by the year 2010. It is wonderful to be part of a field that can help make that happen. That makes me (and others in television) feel good. Much less attractive—the least satisfying aspect of television—is being on the receiving end of constant criticism. Many people have negative feelings about TV and what it does. They generalize and blame the entire medium for a few of its faults. It is important that the public not regard television as a waste of time when it is such a powerful and often beneficial medium.

Corporation initiative on digital television, sees the promise of more social interests being served by the medium, from concerns of ethnic and racial minorities to the older population, as well as many other topics.

TELEVISION AS A CONTEMPORARY MEDIUM

Like radio, from which it was derived, television is both a technology and a complex medium of communication. As its history amply demonstrates, it is also an economic system made up of communicators, advertisers, programs, content, and a large and diverse audience. It has become an omnipresent medium—the major form of mass communication preferred by the American public. As indicated earlier, the television set is on for more than seven hours per day in an average American household. At the same time, it is a medium that is little understood by its public. The majority of viewers know little about the behind-the-scenes dramas involving technology, ownership, or conflict among the individuals and groups that make up television systems.

THE ECONOMICS OF COMPETING SYSTEMS

Television signals are received from local stations over the air (or by cable). These local stations are still the backbone of the system. In 2000, there were only 1,248 commercial and 354 public television stations broadcasting in the nation. The five major networks are ABC, CBS, NBC, Fox, WB, and UPN. The Fox system is owned by Rupert Murdoch, whose holdings (as noted in Chapter 3) also include a newspaper empire. In addition, there are programming services like CNN, now owned by Time Warner, and regional systems—formed by local stations that band together and share programming and promote advertising. The U.S. government operates a large television network overseas. Ostensibly for members of the armed forces, AFRTS (Armed Forces Radio and Television Service), as it is called, reaches into seventy countries and is seen not only by people in the armed forces but also by millions of American and foreign civilians.

Once large in size and confined to broadcast studios, the hardware for video recording has gotten smaller, cheaper, and more compact as with other technologies. This continuing innovation and development is seen in this DIRECTV receiver with TiVo.

	Nielsen Media Research Night By Nights Thursday - 3/29/01								
Network	Programs	Days	Reported Duration	Start Time	End Time	Household US Rating %	Household US Share	Household (000)	Persons 2+ (000)
ABC	WHOSE LINE IS IT ANYWAY?	...T...	30	8:00PM	8:30PM	4.3	7	4428	6959
ABC	WHOSE LINE ANYWAY-8:30PM	...T...	30	8:30PM	9:00PM	5.4	8	5480	8390
ABC	MILLIONAIRE-THU	...T...	60	9:00PM	10:00PM	11.3	17	11569	16620
ABC	PRIMETIME THURSDAY	...T...	60	10:00PM	11:00PM	8.7	15	8916	12003
CBS	SURVIVOR II	...T...	60	8:00PM	9:00PM	16.6	26	16992	28121
CBS	CSI	...T...	60	9:00PM	10:00PM	13.8	21	14096	21570
CBS	BIG APPLE	...T...	60	10:00PM	11:00PM	5.5	9	5620	7513
FOX	FOX THURSDAY NIGHT MOVIE	...T...	120	8:00PM	10:00PM	3.1	5	3184	4287
NBC	FRIENDS	...T...	30	8:00PM	8:30PM	12.1	19	12362	17814
NBC	WEBER SHOW	...T...	30	8:30PM	9:00PM	9.3	14	9472	13600
NBC	WILL & GRACE	...T...	30	9:00PM	9:30PM	10.9	16	11095	16660
NBC	JUST SHOOT ME	...T...	30	9:30PM	10:00PM	10.1	15	10318	14847
NBC	E.R.	...T...	60	10:00PM	11:00PM	16.3	27	16626	24489
PAX	IT'S A MIRACLE	...T...	60	8:00PM	9:00PM	1.2	2	1261	1780
PAX	TOUCHED BY AN ANGEL-THU	...T...	60	9:00PM	10:00PM	0.9	1	924	1366
PAX	DIAGNOSIS MURDER-THU	...T...	60	10:00PM	11:00PM	1.3	2	1333	1934
UPN	WWF SMACKDOWN!	...T...	120	8:00PM	10:00PM	4.9	7	5020	8105
WB	GILMORE GIRLS - WB	...T...	60	8:00PM	9:00PM	1.9	3	1985	2711
WB	CHARMED - WB	...T...	60	9:00PM	10:00PM	2.2	3	2244	3066

Aspects of TV viewership can be measured, as with this Nielsen rating for the evening of Thursday, March 29, 2001.

Over the years, the number of independent (nonnetwork-affiliated) stations has increased. This has given rise to **barter syndication.** (The idea of syndicates for newspapers was discussed in Chapter 3. The same structure exists for broadcast companies.) Thus, a local station can get taped content from program syndicators who sell their wares to independent, nonaffiliated stations, creating what amounts to a series of small networks. Syndicated programming competes directly with network offerings. Much of the content of such syndicated programming consists of older reruns.

From the standpoint of a family viewing their TV set at home, the sources that deliver television programs can be a confusing jumble. What they see on their screen at any given time may originate from one of several networks, from an independent local station, from PBS, from basic cable service (perhaps with an add-on subscription fee), via satellite, or from their videocassette recorder.

This variety in sources really makes little difference to viewers. A given movie provides the same viewing experience regardless of who delivers it. The same is true of a ball game, a cartoon, or a nature documentary. Viewers do not care how programming comes to them, because it looks the same on the screen, regardless of what delivery system is being used. Most families do not attach a great deal of importance to the various vendors and systems from which they get their entertainment, sports programs, or even news. The main thing for them is that the programming they want to view is available to them.

However, for the players involved, the source that viewers use is of *paramount* importance. It is the basis of all-consuming battles for profit as well as economic survival within the system. Thus, *competition* among the sources that deliver programming to audiences is the central factor in understanding the economics of contemporary television.

Competition has always existed among the various networks. Every year they vie for dominance in terms of commanding the largest audiences. And in recent years competition arose between network television and its alternatives (cable TV and videocassettes) as these systems came into common use. That competition resulted in significant changes.

From the early days of TV up until the mid-1980s, regular broadcast television was very popular because of the relationship among networks, advertisers, those who produced TV content, and the audience. Advertising revenues brought high earnings to the major networks, permitting them to produce expensive programs that were well received by audiences. Thus, a kind of reciprocal system was in place. Television advertising was very costly. However, because the commercial messages shown on the popular programs reached huge audiences, advertisers were willing to pay enormous fees for tiny segments of airtime (fifteen or thirty seconds). And because of this great income, the networks were able to produce still more expensive programs with even greater appeal to the public. Thus, advertising revenues spiraled up and up, along with the size of the audience.

At the heart of this mutually profitable system is *audience attention.* The worst nightmare for both the advertiser and the television network executive is that people will not view the programs on which their wares are advertised. Various kinds of survey and polling techniques have been used to determine what kinds of people were viewing what kinds of television programs during what periods of time. For many years, the techniques used were rather simple; some were based on diaries kept at home by panels of carefully selected people, or on verbal reports of audiences contacted by phone or mail about what they had been watching.

Those ratings, whatever their limitations, became *institutionalized*—that is, deeply established—as the ultimate measure of whether a given program would be kept on the air. They remain so today. Thus, what can be called the *law of large numbers* was the prevailing principle in determining the television agenda presented by the major networks. The more eyes and ears a program attracts, the more valuable it is to an advertiser whose message is displayed during the transmission and to the broadcaster who profits from the sale of the airtime. If a program's ratings fell, even by a few points, it was in jeopardy. Many programs were simply dropped from the air if the ratings did not seem to justify what it cost to produce and broadcast them, and especially if they did not draw enough advertisers to generate sufficient profits.

The use of such ratings as the ultimate criterion by which the networks assessed the worth of a particular program was just fine with the advertisers who supported the system. It ensured that the programs on the air, and so the advertising commercials, commanded the attention of the largest possible number of potential customers. For several decades, this was how the system worked. Thus, in spite of competition among networks, the system as a whole remained rather stable for many years and the networks continued to dominate television. The law of large numbers continues to prevail today.

THE CONTENT PRODUCERS

Television networks produce much of the content that appears on television, and they have created the program genres from such entertainment fare as cop shows and lawyer shows to daytime drama (the soaps), sports, news, and other forms. The ownership of these large corporations illustrates their natural alliances. For example, ABC is now owned by Disney, which provides its own fledgling cable division and is now a giant owner of broadcasting, cable television, and other enterprises; NBC is owned by the General Electric Company. WB is owned by AOL-Time Warner and takes its name from Warner Brothers, the film studio, while Murdoch's News Corporation owns Fox. UPN (United Paramount Network) was owned by Viacom, but its future was up in the air when News Corp. acquired Chris-Craft (a broadcast company whose outlets used UPN) in August 2000.

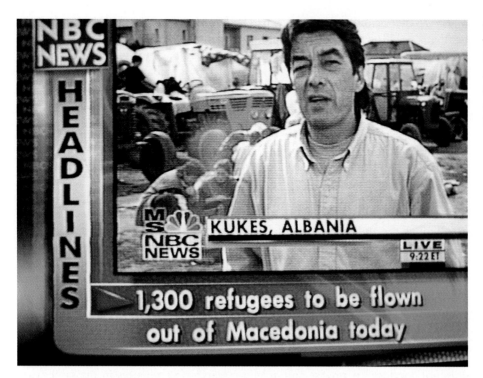

Computer graphics play a vital role in communicating information on the TV screen, as indicated here in an MSNBC news broadcast during the Kosovo crisis in 2000.

Networks have extensive business (sales, marketing, and affiliate relations) and programming (news, sports, and entertainment) divisions. As economic entities, networks sell advertisers access to an audience. The news and sports divisions produce specific kinds of programming while entertainment has a broad mandate that includes the daytime schedule (soaps and game and talk shows), Saturday A.M. children's shows, late-night programming, and prime-time programming.

People often wonder how a fall or spring schedule of a network actually evolves. It comes about through a development cycle that begins with a concept, which moves to script development, then to pilot production, audience testing, and finally an initial thirteen-week commitment as network executives breathlessly await the ratings. "The system is bizarre and makes absolutely no sense,"[7] says David Poltrack, Executive Vice President of CBS, Inc. Poltrack notes that major investments and important decisions are made before there is any serious market research of systematic audience feedback. Much of TV programming is an intuitive process.

Perhaps for that reason, a few programs often bring unexpected financial rewards at the networks. The comedy show "Seinfeld," for example, was the top earner for its network, NBC, for years before its star, Jerry Seinfeld, decided to terminate the show. A surprisingly successful show, "Who Wants to Be a Millionaire?" starring Regis Philbin, gained top ratings and had major earnings in 1999 and 2000, as did the CBS reality program, "Survivor," in 2000 and "Survivor II" in 2001. No one can predict just what program and program format will catch the public's interest and garner high ratings—leading to a long life on the air.

THE TELEVISION INDUSTRY IN TRANSITION

It is difficult to separate television as a signal transmitting business from media as an economic institution generally. Television is becoming a global industry with programming that moves across international borders. As we have pointed out, many U.S. television stations are owned by large corporations, although the number that a single owner can have is limited by law to twelve stations that do not cover more than 30 percent of the entire population of the country. Media ownership, along with that of many other business enterprises, is global. Although FCC regulations place limits on foreign ownership of broadcast properties, complex patterns of conglomerate ownership are common.

Television profits are a function of the total revenues of the whole industry—advertising sales, annual volume of advertising, network and station television billing, market ratings, and other indicators. The major players are networks, local stations, and barter syndicators who provide independent sources of programming. As mentioned earlier, the competition—cable television, videocassettes, satellite dishes, and syndication services—has brought a downturn in the economic fortunes of TV networks. Nevertheless, the networks, can still deliver impressive audiences, even though the audiences' share of total time spent with the medium is down.

In spite of the fact that a great deal is known about the social, cultural, and economic structure of the American population (as we will see in Chapter 8), one of the most poorly charted aspects of television audiences is their actual composition. For example, TV industry market researchers pay only superficial attention to the demographic characteristics of network television viewers. Cable services and public television sometimes claim to deliver "quality" or upscale audiences of viewers who are relatively well educated and affluent in comparison with the general population. However, those claims are not backed with data, and television as a whole does not conduct the precise and careful research on audiences in the same ways that marketers of many other products and services do.

An important concept of television stations is the *market* as an area. A **market** in this sense consists of a community and a contiguous area where a substantial number of people live who can be reached by a station's signal. In practical terms, this translates into a metropolitan area that includes a city. Some markets are relatively small, like the one in which Little Rock, Arkansas, is located. Others are huge, such as those of Los Angeles or Philadelphia.

THE FUTURE OF TELEVISION

The future of television will be one of somewhat unpredictable change coupled with constant debate. New technologies include a device that can be built into newly manufactured sets to enable parents to control the programs that their children will view. Entirely new systems for delivering signals to the home are under development. These systems include not only direct satellite broadcasts, which are already coming into increasing use, but they may also include fiber-optic and even microwave systems operated by telephone companies (although the telephone companies may back out). Other changes that will occur in television is the shape and clarity of the picture on the screen.

One change that began in 1997 was the institution of a system of ratings that could be used in connection with the "v-chip," now required in all newly manufactured receivers. With such a set, parents can presumably control what comes into their home. A major problem in developing this system was that parents could not tell whether a program they were about to receive contained content they did not want their children to view. To provide a solution to this dilemma, the television industry devised a system of ratings to be shown at the beginning of each program.

However, a great controversy began in 1996 over the nature of the rating system. The basic idea was that the ratings should identify how much violence, vulgar language, and sexual content was contained in each TV show. Then, the parents could control their set so that their children did not see the show, or, if they had the necessary equipment, they could use the v-chip to prevent it from appearing on their screen.

To provide for this screening, the industry opted for a system very similar to that used in the movie industry. It is a very simple system with only six categories:

- TV-Y: Children of all ages
- TV-Y7: Children seven and over
- TV-G: All audiences
- TV-PG: Parental guidance suggested
- TV-14: Parents strongly cautioned
- TV-M: Mature audiences only

Many spokespersons for parents and other groups objected to this age-based system on the grounds that it provided no real information about how much, if any, violence, vulgar language, or sexual content was actually contained within a show. A number of critics wanted a content-based system, like the one used in Canada—a system often cited as an ideal model.

At first glance, the Canadian model seems simple and effective. It is based on the same basic categories of violence, bad language, and sexual depictions. However, the system also provides points for each category, ranging from 0 to 5. For example, a program rated V-0, L-4, and S-2 would have no violence, a lot of vulgar language, and a limited amount of sexual content. On closer examination, however, the Canadian system has not worked well. Its problems came about through difficulties in identifying exactly what constitutes depictions of violence and sex. For example, "The Lion King," a popular animated feature designed for children, had violent episodes among some of the characters and was rated high on that dimension. It would probably have been screened out by a v-chip system. Similarly, "The Nanny" (which contains a great deal of sexual innuendo) was rated in the Canadian system the same as "Sesame Street." Moreover, with some sixty thousand programs produced by the TV and movie industries every year, the sheer task of analyzing them within the Canadian system proved to be an awesome one. For these and other reasons, Canadians are now abandoning their complex approach and are testing various simpler alternatives. Thus, the ultimate outcome of the debate over the nature of TV ratings remains to be seen.

One thing about the future of television is entirely clear. The tastes and preferences of the American audience will undoubtedly remain *precisely where they are* whether the signals come from satellites, phone wires, optic-cable networks, computer systems, or high-definition television (HDTV). Therefore, we will not undergo a revolution in program content that will parallel the new technological developments. Thus, whatever spectacular home TV sets are in store for us, perhaps wall-sized pictures as clear as the real world and with hundreds of choices of channels, we will still see the usual array of soap operas, sit-coms, infotainment, news, quiz shows, sports, home-shopping opportunities, religious evangelists, and political campaigns. Mixed in will be a scattering of offerings for the more serious viewer, but the great number who support the industry through their consumer purchases of breakfast foods, laxatives, and other commonly advertised products will want more of the same. Thus, the law of large numbers will prevail in the future to indicate the nature of much of the programming, as it has in the past.

Chapter Review

- Pioneering experiments on sending pictures by radio began in several countries just after World War I. The earliest attempts made use of a revolving "Nipkow disk," a mechanical system that created a scanning effect when used with a beam of light. It was not until electronic scanning was developed that television became practical.

- The first patent for an electronic television system was awarded to Philo T. Farnsworth, an obscure inventor who had worked out the basic design while still a high school student. With minimal funding he built a working model in a small apartment in Los Angeles. Vladimir Zworykin, of Westinghouse laboratories, also invented an electronic system. Court battles resulted but Farnsworth won his case and received a cash settlement.

- By 1932, a transmitter was installed in the Empire State Building in New York City. Regular transmissions began on a limited basis in 1936, with two broadcasts per week. A few hundred amateur enthusiasts who had built or purchased sets could receive the signals in the New York area. By 1940, television was capable of becoming a mass medium for home use. However, when World War II began in 1941, the need for war production temporarily halted the development of the new medium.

- The period of rapid adoption of home receivers began just after the war. Between 1950 and 1960, nearly 90 percent of American households acquired a TV set. This rapid adoption happened in spite of a freeze on the licensing and construction of new TV stations imposed by the FCC between 1948 and 1952.

- Television quickly became a part of family behavior patterns across the nation. The number of hours that sets were in use in homes climbed from about four and a half per day in 1950 to over seven in recent years. During the 1970s, color sets all but completely replaced black and white.

- Two periods can be identified that might both, for different reasons, be called television's golden age. One period, based on the popularity of certain programming and television personalities, was roughly from the early 1950s to about 1960. The second, defined more in terms of the predominance and profitability of the television networks, was from about 1960 to around 1980.

- Alternative ways to use the TV set at home have now become a significant part of the total picture. Cable systems were not a major factor in the industry until the 1980s. During that decade, the proportion of American homes receiving cable transmissions increased sharply. The VCR was developed in the 1950s, but did not gain real popularity until the 1980s. Since the mid-1980s the Japanese have sold millions of the machines.

- As an industry, television broadcasting is undergoing a number of changes. New patterns of ownership are emerging. Large corporations and conglomerates are increasingly making TV stations and even networks part of their holdings, resulting in changing patterns of competition within the industry. Also, the original networks have lost a large share of the market in terms of advertising dollars. Both cable television and VCRs are more widely used than ever before.

■ Technological changes, convergences, and trends are in store for the medium in the near future. Digitally based HDTV will be widely available within a short number of years. It will change the format and clarity of the picture seen on the screen. Cable TV will be challenged by systems of delivery via phone wires, microwaves, and satellites. These changes will offer more channels but are unlikely to create a content revolution.

Notes and References

1. See "The Development of the Television Industry," Melvin L. DeFleur and Sandra Ball Rokeach, *Theories of Mass Communication,* 5th ed. (White Plains, N.Y.: Longman, 1989), pp. 110–122.
2. For a thorough history of television up to the mid-1970s, see Eric Barnouw, *Tube of Plenty: The Evolution of American Television* (New York: Oxford University Press, 1975).
3. Benjamin M. Compaine and Douglas Gomery, *Who Owns the Media?,* 3rd ed. (Mahwah, N.J.: Lawrence Erlbaum, 2000), pp. 266–270.
4. Les Brown, "The Nascent Age of Broadband," Fordham Center for Communications and the Broadband Forum, 1999, updated edition in Lawrence K. Grossman and Newton N. Minow, *A Digital Gift to the Nation* (New York: Century Foundation Press, 2001), pp. 55–72.
5. Tony Feldman, *An Introduction to Digital Media* (London: Routledge, 1997), pp. 1–3. For some useful definitional material see Wilson Dizard, Jr., *Old Media/New Media, Mass Communications in the Information Age* (New York: Longman, 2000).
6. Charles M. Firestone and Amy Korzick Garmer, eds., *Digital Broadcasting and the Public Interest* (Washington, D.C.: The Aspen Institute, 1998), pp. vii, xi.
7. David Poltrack, executive vice president of CBS, Inc., in lecture February 7, 2000, Fordham Graduate School of Business, Lincoln Center, New York.

Chapter 8

THE NEW MEDIA: COMMUNICATION FOR THE DIGITAL AGE

FROM THE BEGINNING, THE NEW MEDIA HAVE BEEN ASSOCIATED WITH A REVOLUTION IN INFORMATION TECHNOLOGY AND THE RISE OF the computer. At first, new media included only online information services, cable television, and satellite dishes, but with the rise of the Internet and the World Wide Web as "platforms" of choice, new media have taken on a larger and fuller meaning. New media are distinguished from "old media," which are sometimes called "traditional," "conventional," or "vintage" media, such as those means of communication covered in earlier chapters of this book, namely newspapers, magazines, broadcasting, and motion pictures. New media are the product of "convergence," the coming together of all forms of communication into a unified, electronically based, computer-driven system. New media are *digital* and *interactive*. They are at present largely associated with the Internet or with various digital storage devices from CD-ROMs to DVDs and others. But the new media also include cable, satellite, and various broadband technologies. New media involve digital *storage* of information, its *retrieval* and *dissemination*. And they are ever changing.

Watching television and using the Internet at the same time in the same room is increasingly common, as media researcher John Carey learned in ethnographic studies of TV and Internet audiences. Rather than compete with each other, the two media devices actually interact and work together.

For our purposes here, we will distinguish "new media," those with a mix of editorial service and advertising, from the broader world of "e-commerce" or "e-business," which is primarily concerned with product promotion, sales, and retailing or with financial services and information technology. New media are part of the world of e-commerce (or the so-called new economy) just as the old media are part of the market economy and commercial development. But they are a distinct aspect of the new economy, one mostly concerned with communicating information, opinion, and entertainment. Of course new media have their commercial aspects, such as the accumulation of audiences, advertising, and messaging services. Obviously, it is difficult to track, sort out, and fully define the new media, given the rapid changes they are experiencing.

DIMENSIONS OF NEW MEDIA

In January 2000, the old media giant Time Warner (itself a fusion of Time, Inc., a multimedia publishing firm, and Warner Communication, a motion picture and electronic media firm) was acquired by America Online (AOL), a giant of the new media. This acquisition created shock waves in the media industries. For the first time ever a new media entrepreneur took over a traditional media company, causing a writer in the *Wall Street Journal* to declare that the transaction "marked the beginning of the end of old mass media." And while it was easy to see what Time Warner was—a mix of "old analog content" including CNN, Time, Warner Brothers studios, WB network, and HBO—many people were not quite sure just what AOL was. It was an Internet search engine or portal for content and information, of course, but just how it had managed to merge with one of the world's biggest media companies was puzzling to many. A product of the overheated new economy of the 1990s, AOL had grown rapidly in just over a decade to be worth $164 billion on the stock market. One commentator asked, "What is it anyway?" and enumerated these possibilities:

> Digital post office? Private club? Bulletin board? Newspaper? Music distributor? Radio broadcaster? Wannabe television network? All of the above? Or if you prefer, none of them. AOL is, at its core, an architecture, a set of digital protocols, rules, and structures, some of them proprietary, some of them Internet-based, imbedded in software, running on servers and linked up to networks.[1]

Digital communication and face-to-face conversation, as well as food and drink, came together in cyber cafés equipped with PCs and Web access.

In the studios of MSNBC in New York City, then-presidential candidate George W. Bush listens to anchor Brian Williams in September 2000 a few weeks before the contested 2000 election.

New media are themselves in search of a satisfying definition. The New York Media Association, an industry group, says, "The new media industry combines elements of computing technology, telecommunications and content to create products and services which can be used interactively by consumers and business users."[2] If *media* are, in the words of the *Encarta World Dictionary* (1999), the "various means of mass communications thought of as a whole . . . together with the people involved on their production,"[3] then the *new media* are best summed up in the term "interactivity," which *Encarta* says is "the exchange of information between a person and a machine, such as a computer or a television."[4]

When the Chief Executive Officers of new media companies were asked to say what terms by which they preferred to identify new media, they chose *interactivity, digitization, convergence,* and *addressability,* in that order. They also mentioned terms like *real time.* One executive said, " We're talking about digitally transformed experience extending the walls of [media] organizations beyond traditional boundaries," while another said that the new media are "simply interactive and plastic."[5] Unlike television or motion pictures that are "communal media," in the words of media economist Bruce Owen, the Internet is an "isolating, individual medium that is really quite solitary,"[6] as individuals surf the Web and connect with specific sites alone in front of a computer screen. Other commentators would disagree, saying that the new media create communities of interest with specific content and messages for those interested while at the same time inviting feedback and interaction.

The results of a study at Fordham University's Graduate School of Business in 2001 identified eight terms to specify new media, including: *digital, convergent, interactive, renewable, customized, adaptable, intuitive,* and *pull-oriented.* That study defined new media as "media and communication activities made possible by the digital revolution and distinguished from traditional mass media. They are both the technical means of acquiring information, storing and retrieving it, as well as the content delivered to the consumers and users in this system. New media can be used for traditional media functions such as information gathering, distribution, access and display."

As the twenty-first century began, the most prominent "appliance" for new media communication and activity was the *personal computer*. The PC enables easy access to the Internet and the World Wide Web, and allows users convenient connections through search engines and portals to a wealth of information available in cyberspace along what has been termed "the information superhighway." New media technologies also include such "broadband" industries as cable, wireless, lightwave, and digital broadcast satellite (DBS).

The story of media, as earlier chapters in this book indicate, has always been one of new technologies or platforms challenging those popular at the moment. The print media industries—newspapers and magazines—once worried that they would be overtaken by the telegraph, but in fact they used it to their own benefit. Motion pictures have survived several waves of challengers, as have radio, network and cable television, and satellite communication. The famed 1947 Hutchins Commission on a free and responsible press worried about obstacles to new media technologies.[7] It was specifically concerned with FM radio, television, and fax newspapers. Other early users of new media referred to cable television and videotext systems that used the lower strip of the TV screen (the vertical blanking interval) to transmit messages and information. In the 1970s and 1980s, various electronic information services appeared, mostly for the purpose of providing financial information at banks, as well as data for libraries, universities, and scientific institutions. When college students first became familiar with online searches, they used the medium in libraries and considered it useful for researching term papers, rather than as a form of information or entertainment.

In the early 1990s, the Internet, a network of networks, known previously to the military, scientists, and academics, gained public acceptance thanks to the invention of the easily accessible World Wide Web (www).

FACTORS INFLUENCING NEW MEDIA

The new media are the result of a major shift from a society that mostly depended on agriculture and manufacturing to one that is based on what sociologist Daniel Bell calls the "manipulation of information." This shift makes us now an **information society** in which more people are employed in various information and communications industries, including the media, than in all other sectors of the economy. The new media, which would have been possible only in science fiction as recently as three decades ago, were made possible by the merger of television and computer technologies, or what is called **convergence**—the coming together of all forms of human communication in an electronic-based, computer-driven system.[8] Some commentators say this happened when television sets began to "talk" to computers, or when the merger of communications and computers—what Harvard University's Anthony Oettinger calls "compunications"—occurred. The communications revolution, or the change to an information society, evolved over a thirty-year period as electronic systems designed to retrieve, process, and store information and data were developed and integrated with each other. The equipment that once only collected statistical data was then able to bring together text, data, sound, and image. One of the authors of this book called this "the united state of media" that was made possible by more portable, cheaper, and more user-friendly technology. Thus, "the digitalization of almost everything," can be explained by Nicholas Negroponte of the Massachusetts Institute of Technology Media Lab as a situation in which "formerly mass media evolve into a personalized two-way street of communication. Information is no longer *pushed* at consumers; instead people or their digital agents *pull* or help create the information they need."[9]

NEW MEDIA AND THE COMING OF CONVERGENCE

Communication, thanks to the new media, is interactive (or interacting with and instantly "talking" back to an information source) and can be stored and retrieved in electronic form. However, not all new media technologies result in public communication. Some, like e-mail, are mostly person-to-person communication, while others, like online chat groups, are mostly simply electronic bull sessions for groups of people who want to talk to each other and share information about a common interest, ranging from sexual problems to Middle Eastern cooking. What are currently called new media are made possible by the convergence or coming together of various media industries that previously maintained quite separate identities and relationships with citizens and consumers. For example, cooperative ventures between and among broadcasting companies, telephone companies, cable firms, and computer software companies, unimagined in the past, are creating new media. An early example was MSNBC, a joint venture of Bill Gates's giant, Microsoft Corp. and NBC. This firm publishes on four "platforms"—two twenty-four–hour cable television networks, CNBC and MSNBC, a cyberspace news and information service, and a traditional broadcasting network, NBC.

Without convergence, the new media would not be possible. That convergence, as we will explain later, has required revolutionary changes in the economics—structure and operation—of the media industries, that is, they must work together for new media to occur. A newspaper company might, for example, work with a telephone company, cable provider, and a broadcasting company to produce an electronic newspaper. Similarly, the hardware and software must also be able to interconnect and work together. Finally, the laws and rules under which communication industries operate must also approve. Separate laws and privileges for print media and broadcast media do not work in the new media environment. An electronic database offering news and information as well as video games is a new medium, not an old style magazine or a conventional broadcaster.

WHAT IS THE INTERNET?

To Martin Irvine of Georgetown University the typical answer to the question, What is the Internet? (answer: the global network of computer networks), is not enough. To Irvine, who heads a culture, communication, and technology program, the Internet has three components:

- a *worldwide computer system* using a common means of linking hardware and transmitting digital information
- *a community of people* using a common communication technology
- a globally distributed *system of information*

He quickly adds that the Internet, or "Net," in practical and functional terms is:

- a *twenty-four-hour nonstop global forum and communication system*
- an *online library and international information system*
- a *business* and *corporate* communications medium
- a *distance* and *remote education system*
- a *commercial transactions medium*
- a *multimedia delivery system for news and entertainment*
- a *government information service*
- *all of the above simultaneously*[10]

But as we have mentioned earlier, not everything on the Internet is new media as we define them. Originally organized in the 1960s by the U.S. Department of Defense, the Internet was at first used by scientists and university professors as various technical problems were worked out. Until the early 1990s, few ordinary people had ever heard of the Internet or the World Wide Web, which is a system for delivering hypertext and multimedia files over the Internet. Hypertext is a type of document that has links to other documents. Especially important to Internet development worldwide was the introduction of Mosaic, a Web browser, in 1993.[11] To technology expert Wilson Dizard, "The Internet is a major factor in redefining the meaning of mass media," but he admits that the distinctions between old and new media are rapidly blurring as people grapple for terms to describe what the new digital information services can and might do in the future.[12] Hundreds of millions of people worldwide are using the Internet and the World Wide Web for individual messaging and for communication to outside audiences large and small, as well as within institutions and organizations. There are, of course, various closed systems and proprietary online services that are not technically a part of the Internet. In fact, the major services like America Online and CompuServe existed long before they provided an Internet gateway for their clients. By the late 1990s, when demand for the Internet exploded, most commercial online services and private networks owned by AT&T and Microsoft converted to the Internet proprietary online. Al Sikes of Hearst New Media and a former Chairman of the Federal Communications Commission, calls the Internet "today's new media conundrum." He says, "The Internet is expensive to access, artistically primitive, painfully slow, and overpopulated with garbage. And it is wonderful. It gives voice to those who don't have a radio or TV frequency or a printing press. It transcends boundaries; while some contend that it is a source of disunity, if you are thinking globally it is a source of unity."[13]

Almost all media firms are *dot-coms*, although there are some new media that use other domains such as .edu for university newspapers and .net for some information providers.

While there are many books and manuals about the Internet, its protocols and uses, it is important to remember that every e-mail address, which uses the "network of networks," has three aspects: a *user* name, a *host* name, and a *domain* name. The user and the host are always separated by the @ sign, and usually distinguish individual users such as people from the organization of which they are a part, such as a university, a company, or another organization. The domain name indicates the kind of institution to which the user belongs. The domains currently in use are listed below:

- .edu: Educational and research organizations
- .com: Commercial (business) organizations
- .gov: Government nonmilitary organizations
- .mil: U.S. military branches
- .org: Nonprofit organizations
- .net: Network organizations and access providers[14]

figure8.1

Confusion Among TV Networks Due to Expansion of Digital TV Licenses

CONVERGENCE IN THREE DIMENSIONS

There are three kinds of convergence: *economic convergence,* which blurs and merges the once-clear lines between print and electronic media and allows mergers and new economic arrangements; *technological convergence,* in which the new machines talk to each other through an intelligent network; and *regulatory convergence,* which removes legal roadblocks.

Without the advent of communication satellites that link messages all over the globe, personal computers, various computer networks, and software, the new media would not exist. But the New media are more than new technical inventions, they also are a process in which several social forces have combined to create a powerful new communications capacity with, as mentioned earlier, technological, economic, and regulatory applications.

Technological Invention and Applications. The invention of compact, high-speed computers, software on which to run them, and a worldwide network of networks—the Internet—were key to new media development. This meant that complex information storage and retrieval efforts, once found only in massive university and industry computer labs, were available to ordinary individuals at a relatively low cost. Software programs called search engines allowed for instant retrieval of information, and thus made it possible for people to navigate the complex, interactive digital world called cyberspace. In the modern system, various computer systems and networks were linked to others, not just in a localized geographic area, but worldwide.

Economic Demand and Consumer Need. At the same time, all the computer inventions and new tools or games in the world would have little meaning if the economic system was not friendly and if consumers did not want the products that were produced. "The media wars" in the 1990s, when various media industries like newspapers fought telephone companies and others to hold onto their special relationship (or franchise) with readers (or news consumers), gave way to the current decade in which mergers and acquisitions connect once quite separate industries with each other. For example in the 1980s, the ABC television network merged with Capital Cities Communication, a newspaper and broadcast company. In the 1990s, the combined company became part of the entertainment giant, Disney, known mostly for its movies and amusement parks. CBS first acquired Westinghouse in the 1990s and later was acquired by Viacom, the global media giant that had once, decades earlier, been a small CBS division. As a result of these combinations it was said that consumers were able to get various communication "products" from the same firm, and the firms welcomed the new media ventures that would draw on their various resources to create information and entertainment content. This was called *synergy*. For the communications companies that run the mass (as well as specialized) media, this meant *economies of scale*, and for the consumer, *cost savings*. Critics, however, warned of the dangers to democracy if too much media power was placed in too few hands.

Regulation and Law. Many of the new media would have been blocked if it had not been for the "deregulation" of communication industries, which happened through various government rulings and legislation, mainly the important Communications Act of 1996. The Act relaxed many rules that had in the past made it illegal for various media industries (for example, cable and telephone companies) to work together. Because much of broadcasting and other forms of electronic communication are regulated by the government in the United States and in other countries, greater freedom—and less regulation—has been friendly to the coming of new media. In the past, many of the new agreements between computer software makers, broadcast companies, newspapers, and media industries would have been prohibited by laws that were meant to prevent monopolies and too much control by any one media company. Previously, the government was regulating the "scarcity" of communication, such as a limited number of TV channels; but in the new media age there is an abundance of communication, with scores of new cable channels and an unlimited access to the Internet.

A major convergence of old and new media (and old and new economies) occurred with the acquisition of Time Warner by America Online in January 2000. The deal between the two companies and their leaders Steve Case (left) of AOL and Gerald Levin (right) of Time Warner created the world's largest communication company in 2001 when regulatory hurdles were cleared.

Still, in 2000, the courts came down hard on the software giant Microsoft and warned that antitrust remedies still existed as a means of stopping monopoly control. The case was still on appeal in 2001. The courts also took on the digital music distributor Napster for violating intellectual property laws. For all its benefits, the digital world also has its shady side. Hackers have induced viruses that have nearly created panic, and the sex trade uses the Internet as do various unsavory characters engaged in Internet crime. There are also issues involving the invasion of personal privacy in e-commerce and the theft of intellectual property. The Internet has much to celebrate, but is also full of mischief, from easily transmitted rumor, gossip, and misinformation to outright crime. For these reasons, even in the face of a general deregulation of communications industries, misuse of the Internet and other problems have led lawmakers to take a closer look at this, the freest medium of all.

UNDERSTANDING DIFFERENCES—THREE DOMAINS

In his book, *Mediamorphosis,* Roger Fidler says that all communication and media can be seen in three domains—interpersonal, broadcast, and document. As he puts it, they are:

- *Interpersonal domain:* one-to-one forms of oral/expressive communication with content that is not structured or influenced by external mediators. This also includes communication between humans and computers and might involve specific online information searches. Examples of communication in this domain include online chat, e-mail, and computer games;
- *Broadcast domain:* mediated, few-to-many forms of aural/visual communication with content that is highly structured and directed to audiences sequentially from beginning to end, in relatively fixed locations, and in scheduled, predetermined periods of time. Examples of communication in this domain include cable TV, FM radio, music videos, and some informational Web sites.
- *Document domain:* mediated, few-to-many forms of textual/visual communication whose content is packaged and presented to individuals primarily through portable media. Examples of communication in this domain include the World Wide Web and hypertext documents.[15]

UNDERSTANDING NEW MEDIA

As a former newspaper editor and graphic artist, Fidler helped to pioneer electronic online services for newspapers and eventually wrote a book that allowed him to think more deeply about media and technology—why some things work and others do not. He called the process "mediamorphosis," which he defines as "the transformation of communication media, usually brought about by the complex interplay of perceived needs, competitive and political pressures and social and technological innovations." Thus, the process by which new media come about is, as we explained earlier, the interaction of three interrelated forces involving various forms of invention, money, and politics.

To Bill Gates, founder of Microsoft, the new media wonders of the present will evolve into a virtual world where all TV sets and computers are linked to a global, intelligent network that can carry out transactions for people who are drawing, for example, on the three domains mentioned above. Eventually, says Gates, in his book *The*

Road Ahead, communication and human behavior will merge and become invisible, with the so-called media simply being tools of no more interest to most of us than are the component parts of automobile engines.[16] This suggests a high degree of reliance on new media technologies, something that the novelist E. M. Forster anticipated in a short story written before 1914 entitled "The Machine Stops." In Forster's story, people lived under the earth in compartments and relied completely on a massive, global communication system called "the machine."[17] As he put it in his imaginary tale:

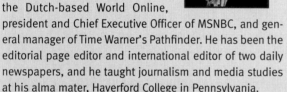

James Kinsella, Member of the Board of Directors, Former Chief Executive Officer *Tiscali*, Milan, Italy

insights from **MEDIA LEADERS**

One of the most widely watched leaders of the new media, James Kinsella has served as chairman of the Dutch-based World Online, president and Chief Executive Officer of MSNBC, and general manager of Time Warner's Pathfinder. He has been the editorial page editor and international editor of two daily newspapers, and he taught journalism and media studies at his alma mater, Haverford College in Pennsylvania.

Q. When did you first get interested in new media?

A. Fresh out of Haverford College in 1982, I was an editor for a weekly paper in California when a friend gave me my first modem and introduced me to the world of BBS (bulletin board services). This was the precursor of today's online media. Actually, I took some early computer courses in high school in St. Louis and later in college, but decided that my career should be in communications, not computers. As it happens, I didn't have to make that choice after all.

Q. When did you first understand that?

A. Shortly after I started playing with BBSs, one of my friends started one of the first online magazines. It was slow and painful to download, but it convinced me this was the future of the media.

Q. How so?

A. The possibilities were there from the beginning if you looked for them. True, the eighties variety modem was crude—essentially two rubber cups that fit awkwardly over the transmitter and receiver of a conventional telephone. To connect to a BBS, you communicated computer to computer through a series of codes. The setup was dodgy, at best, and when you finally connected, you could communicate at speeds no more than 300 baud—or about 1/100 of the speed of the

average connection today. Still, the experience for me was like Saul's on the road to Damascus. About that time, I met some friends who were equally fired up by this new communications tool.

Q. Did you do anything about it?

A. Yes, I asked my boss to let me start a business "online" and he very wisely said "no." So I relegated my passion for computers and got a job in journalism as an executive at what was then a major metropolitan daily in Los Angeles. For me, a turning point was taking a sabbatical leave to write a book about the AIDS epidemic and how the media covered it. That was revealing and forced me to look carefully at the whole media landscape. I thought its future was not bright. I went back to the *Los Angeles Herald Examiner,* only to learn that the paper was being shuttered. The future of newspapers looked pretty bleak. I shed some tears along with everyone else in the newsroom that day, but the next day I felt liberated. With a bunch of used computers, a copy machine, and a printer, I decided to start my own business. That led to the launch of a company that eventually became one of the world's first commercial Web sites.

Q. What factors inspired your continued interest and inspiration?

A. At one level it was being part of change, great change. The conventional wisdom was that the Internet changes everything—competition itself, the economics of the industry, and attitudes of people who lead media businesses. This is true, but it also the case that "speed kills," that is, those who are fixated only on daily decisions miss the larger landscape, which is all about delivering information and entertainment services to customers. Principles like qual-

"'The machine,' they exclaimed, 'feeds us and clothes us and houses us; through it we speak to one another; through it we see one another, in it we have our being. The machine is the friend of ideas and the enemy of superstition; the machine is omnipotent, eternal; blessed is the Machine.'" But, added Forster, "The machine was still the creation and implement of man, but in practice all but a few retrogrades worshipped it as divine." Eventually, the machine gets out of hand and "year by year it was served with increased efficiency and decreased intelligence. The better a man

ity and reliability drive me in developing new businesses for people.

Q. What have been the main influences, personal and professional, that have led you to your current role with a global online firm?

A. Drive and the desire to compete and win. I guess I inherited that as the youngest of five brothers. My earliest memories are of competing against my brothers (and a sister) in sports and other family adventures. I was often frustrated and had to try harder. I also learned to take risks, some foolhardy, some smart. Professionally, I've witnessed the winning instinct in companies where I've worked and among their top executives, including Bill Gates at Microsoft and Gerry Levin at Time Warner. The will to win drives them and defines how they work. That influenced me too, but I give the main credit to my siblings.

Q. What is your take on the current state and probable future of new media?

A. First, I think new media really are not such a dramatic departure from the past, but part of a long trend in technology that allowed immediate delivery of signals over long distances. The "network" of the Internet really isn't new either, but the protocol that allows it to work with content is. It is the development of the language, not just the network that has changed everything. I think the term "new media" will disappear and so might the word "Internet." Instead we'll talk about the "network" by which a family will receive most of its content as well as home information applications. And it might be that the appliance for this home communication system or internal "network" will be the television set.

Q. What is the best pathway for a satisfying career in digital media or e-business?

A. There is no perfect way to build a career, but the work life you craft depends on your own creativity and curiosity. If I had to give advice about this, I'd say learn three things:

(1) The language of technology—learn as much as you can about technological changes and how they shape our future. Programming courses, yes, but reading, reflecting, and thinking is more important;

(2) The language of business—understand how market forces work, how they rearrange the media landscape in Internet time, how fortunes are made and lost;

(3) Languages, generally. It is trite to say it, but the world has gone global and while English may be the *lingua franca,* knowing other languages is fundamental to living and working abroad.

Of course, it is critical to learn how to "exploit" the technical delivery system with desirable content and to fashion effective business strategies.

Q. What is the most satisfying aspect of work in this field? The least?

A. When you work in this field you can actually change the world, and that is both the most and least satisfying aspect of what I do. It is a great thrill to launch a new media product or develop a new way of doing things—twenty four hours a day, seven days a week. You see radical improvements for consumers—and there is nothing that can match that excitement. By contrast, though, it is profoundly disappointing and discouraging when something you thought would change the world wasn't bought by "that world." What I do has made me happy and wealthier than I ever thought I would be and confirms my hunch that communications and computers are certainly compatible.

knew his own duties upon it, the less he understood the duties of his neighbor and in all the world there was not one who understood the monster as a whole." Eventually, this proves disastrous as the Machine slows and stops, leaving the world and humanity to perish.[18]

On August 17, 1996, some people wondered if their "machine," or access to the Internet, had stopped. That was the day when America Online crashed. News and information services, business travel, and other functions of everyday life were massively disrupted and this major impact led to serious concerns about the extent to which people depended on new communication systems, which can break down. In 2000, the love bug virus and other similar computer viruses demonstrated how vulnerable the world of cyberspace can be.

WINNERS AND LOSERS

Futurists often forecast new media developments decades ahead of their actual appearance and some new technologies turn out to be disappointing. Some analysts of media say that one should not take a new media technology seriously until it has the capacity to reach 50 percent of the population. Others say that the 50 percent mark is too severe as a test and does not account for smaller, segmented audiences that can give a new medium a start before it becomes popular. Technology scholar John Carey reminds us that it took one hundred years for the newspaper to reach the magic 50 percent figure; the telephone, seventy years; radio, only about ten years; and television less than a decade. By contrast, cable television was invented in the 1950s and took nearly forty years to reach a majority of American households. It will likely take the Internet about six years to reach 50 percent of all U.S. households and institutions, while the rest of the world lags far behind.

Consumer online services such as America Online, Prodigy, and Lycos, which offer information on demand as well as e-mail, succeeded in a field where other new media efforts failed. Online services trace their origins from early experiments in the United States and Great Britain. They were called either *teletext* or *videotext,* both of which used the lower lines of the television screen (the vertical blanking interval), rather than computers. The Knight-Ridder Company set up Viewtron, the first videotext service in the United States, and operated it between 1979 and 1986 as a bold new media experiment before calling it quits due to lack of consumer demand and advertising support. The Viewtron failure, according to Roger Fidler, was due to a failure to understand consumers and other considerations, which he lists as:

- Consumers did not want more information.
- It was not a newspaper.
- The cost was too high.
- The medium was not compelling.[19]

A decade later Fidler himself led an effort to develop the flat-panel technology, also for Knight-Ridder, only to have that effort quashed by the company in favor of PC-based Internet solutions. Undaunted, he now runs the digital media center at Kent State University.

ONLINE INTERNET SERVICE

An even earlier experiment was Warner Amex's QUBE system in Columbus, Ohio—an interactive television trial that allowed viewers to make programming choices and engage in "electronic democracy" through electronic town meetings and regular polls. This service was in operation between 1977 and 1985, and was eventually abandoned after failing to make money for its owners, due to limited, crude technology that made consumers worry about their privacy. The two failed experiments, like that of "facsimile," which was used for so-called "radio newspapers" in the 1930s and 1940s and delivered to "dumb" terminals in the home, may have died because their owners lacked patience. Technologist Paul Saffo, like John Carey, says that a successful new technology often takes as long as thirty years to move from the laboratory to widespread consumer use.[20]

THE INFORMATION SUPERHIGHWAY

Beginning in the early 1990s, the federal government promoted the concept of an "information superhighway" in which all persons would be part of an interactive communications process with instant access to global information. The term "information highway" goes back at least to 1909 when an ad for AT&T described the Bell System as "a highway of communication."[21] In its current use, it is mainly a visionary notion that all people everywhere should be able to connect with all information everywhere. Such an idea assumes that computers have the capacity to gather, process, and retrieve all information, entertainment fare, and other human communication. The technology of computer systems would presumably make this possible, and the result would be accessible to people through computers or advanced (sometimes called "smart") television sets. By 2001, the term has come to mean connecting with all of the content on the Internet and the World Wide Web as well as that which comes over the television set, mainly on cable channels. Thus, the information superhighway is the system or infrastructure that lets communication companies offer services on television or on the computer screen. It is also the content produced, whether by TV programs, online services, electronic newspapers, or other media forms. It is also the interactive trafficking of people using the system. Computer scientist Michael Dertouzos of MIT says that the information superhighway is not a "highway" or a two-way road system at all, instead it is a communications marketplace where all kinds of media companies and other interests bargain both with and for information.[22] Of course, the global superhighway can reach people everywhere as long as they have access to computers with the capacity (and memory) to handle all of the information.

THE ECONOMICS OF NEW MEDIA

While the precise definition of "new media" is still in play, in that they do allow people to talk back directly to those who bring news and information, entertainment, opinion, and advertising—and can even initiate the communication process themselves. There are, of course, differences between the home pages and web sites of giant media entrepreneurs—which are backed by thousands of workers in developing content, the capacity to promote and advertise their wares, and other advantages of size and resources—and those produced by students or other individuals as a means to communicate with friends and acquaintances.

From early writings about the benefits of new media technologies, commentators have argued that one of the eventual results would be a more accessible communication system, allowing opportunities for people to communicate with and through media to get information, debate issues, solve problems, and forecast the future. Former NBC News President Lawrence K. Grossman sees the new media and the new telecommunication systems as potentially "redistributing political power" and fostering an electronic republic.[23] Others argue that the new media will instead foster fragmentation and move us away from the more unified world of mass communication, where a few large entities, mainly broadcasters, would command massive audiences and therefore "speak" to the nation, if not the world. The new media and their complex networks allow for greater access and greater reach than ever before, but not necessarily larger audiences, due to the competition of thousands upon thousands of news services, home pages, and other services.

As we indicated at the outset of this chapter, there have always been "new" media. In the last two centuries these have included the telegraph, which brought us wire services; the modern telephone (telecommunication), radio and TV (over-the-air broadcast communication), cable (broadband communication), and others. Some new media inventions begin subtly and then have a larger impact than is expected. For example, the invention of a software package called Aldus Pagemaker in the 1970s allowed news organizations and individuals to design and lay out pages electronically with greater ease than had previously been the case. The system was developed by a newspaper and computer company executive, Paul Brainerd, who was once the editor of the student *Minnesota Daily* at the University of Minnesota. Although he worked for an old medium—newspapers—Brainerd created software that made him "the father of desktop publishing." As a result of his invention along with cheap offset printing processes, many individuals and organizations developed their own highly professional newspapers, newsletters, and magazines, something that previously would have required costly investments in printing equipment and typesetting. This enhanced access to communication for many people who were then able to use tools of design and production that had previously been beyond their reach. Pagemaker, which Brainerd eventually sold to Adobe, expanded access to information and the communication process in the same way as the personal computer and the Internet. Brainerd now runs a charitable foundation in Seattle, Washington.

By 2000, some 50 percent of U.S. households had computers and on an average day, 56 percent of adult Americans go online. Others were connected in schools and offices. While celebrating the Internet's dramatic growth and the explosion of electronic commerce, as well as institutional and individual Web sites, there was a concern for a growing "digital divide," especially affecting people in rural areas, African Americans, and Hispanics, the elderly, and low-income people generally. Public officials like Larry Irving, then assistant secretary of commerce, worried about closing "the gap between information haves and have nots." The commerce department even issued a report called "Falling Through the Net."

Like radio and television in earlier eras, new media have been scrambling for a suitable means of measurement. While television and cable can identify the size and demographics of their audiences, Internet-based new media services have had more difficulty in doing so. Although the Nielsen ratings now survey online and digital audiences, which is especially useful to news and entertainment Web sites, there is little agreement about just what the term "visitors" to a Web site means as compared with loyal subscribers to newspapers and magazines or even to those who pay cable fees. Still mostly a free service that makes its profits on advertising and e-commerce, new media have some difficulties comparing their audiences to those of the old media. This was very much at issue when AOL acquired Time Warner, although the Internet giant did have documentation on those who use the site as a portal or search engine.

FINANCING NEW MEDIA

While it quickly became evident that almost anyone could establish a Web site, some are little more than ego trips for their creators, including those devoted to promoting films or rock stars, narrowly gauged chat rooms, and others. Still a few individuals like Matt Drudge used the Internet for fame and fortune, offering up a new and snarky journalism that violated the rules of traditional media, such as the verification of facts and the search for reliable evidence. Drudge, who became famous for leaking revelations about President Clinton's personal behavior (actually gathered by an old medium, *Newsweek*) demonstrated the speed and power of Internet news. More seasoned entrepreneurs joined forces to create the larger and more reputable sites.

As new media emerged, they did so in two different but overlapping environments. Some were developed by creative *entrepreneurs,* private individuals who organized small new media firms. Others were part of *large media empires* looking for new audiences and revenues. Those who initiated new media ventures without the benefit (or deep pockets) of an established media company ranged from tiny start-ups with a few employees to others with several hundred. Many of the new ventures were self-funded by those who started them. Others got their funds from private investors, corporate investors, venture capital firms, or even grants. At the same time, large media firms set up new media divisions or departments, sometimes as a hedge against the future at their individual print and electronic properties. Remembering that only a few horse-and-buggy firms survived into the automobile era, the traditional media firms and outlets began to explore the Internet. At some newspapers, for example, a limited online edition was established that simply redistributed the content already being gathered for the ink-on-paper edition. In other instances, the online edition hired a separate staff and began to gather and disseminate its own information. At a giant media firm like Time Warner, the new media operations began with an effort to "turn magazines into television," an effort that had little success. About the same time, the firm created an online information service, drawing on its magazines (*Time, Fortune, People,* and *Sports Illustrated)* to offer an electronic edition, through a pioneering service called Pathfinder that used the Internet. In Raleigh, North Carolina, the respected *News & Observer* created Nandonet, an early and successful Internet newspaper. Some of the Internet products, as they were called, were little more than promotional devices for a skeptical traditional medium, while others thought new media had real potential of its own, not simply as an extension of old media.

A study of new media executives published in spring 2001 gathered information about revenue sources for new media. Those responding cited product sales as their main source of revenue, followed by advertising and subscriber fees. Also

Shawn Fanning (pictured) and Sean Parker, cofounders of Napster, an online music distribution service, were at the center of an explosive court battle with the music industry in 2000 and 2001. At issue was the intellectual property and the rights of artists, music firms, and other creative people. Other college music sites continued as the courts blocked Napster, which eventually worked out a licensing deal with recording companies.

important were licensing fees—allowing others to use the information or products on a given site—and consulting fees in which the new media managers helped others for a fee[24] or for free. Media like the *Wall Street Journal* and Microsoft's *Salon.com* were early promoters of paid subscriptions, while media like the *New York Times* invite their Web visitors to register for a free service. Others simply welcome everyone—hoping to build a loyal following to sell to advertisers. Earlier new media also went through this debate. In the 1960s and 1970s, cable companies charged for a monthly hookup but offered their programming or content free of charge. Cable promoters bragged that they took "no advertising" and one could watch movies and sports events without interruption. Before long, the cable began to charge for its different "tiers" of service, offering some material "free," but charging for various "premium" channels as well as pay-per-view programming. The new media are in their earliest stages of economic development as they try to attract and aggregate audiences, link their own original content with that gathered and provided by others, test out various advertising and promotional strategies, and affiliate with other, complementary media.

THE NEW MEDIA AND THE NEW ECONOMY

The new media, while in the works for decades, were clearly integral to and benefited from the new economy of the 1990s and the first years of the twenty-first century. The arrival of the information revolution came when people were engaged in messaging and selling information, the manufacturing and extracting of the old economy. As America became more of a service economy that was linked by computing technologies, new services and products emerged. Computer and software firms triumphed and their stocks exploded on Wall Street. Concurrently, the *dot-com* firms emerged as content providers who offered information, e-business, and entertainment for their audiences. The value of these firms accelerated rapidly and soon nearly every possible product had a site of its own. Old and new media firms were themselves part of this dot-com explosion, often creating multiple sites in the same organization to capitalize on the new interest in Internet communication and e-business.

As indicated earlier, the World Wide Web has advanced new media in both the private business and the public communication sectors. Public media, such as National Public Radio and the Public Broadcasting Service and their member stations, virtually all have Web sites and new media operations. These get some of their funding through public subscription, government funding, foundation grants, and product sales. So new media need not always be commercial.

At the dawn of the new century, the new media are plentiful and growing. They represent large media firms and well-known media names as nearly every old medium has a new media Web site or service. Many analysts predict that the expansive number of new media firms will merge and combine and others will simply go out of business. Studies suggest that there is a limited amount of time and money that consumers will be willing to devote to information and entertainment media. Whether old media firms will give way to those of the digital age is subject to much speculation and no one has definitive answers. However, on April 14, 2000, the stock market crashed for many dot-coms and new-media firms. The crash was likened to the famous crash of 1929 for these new segments of the economy. Subsequently, other stock values continued to slide—well into spring 2001—but most analysts believe that this is simply a market correction for a new technology that will ultimately triumph.

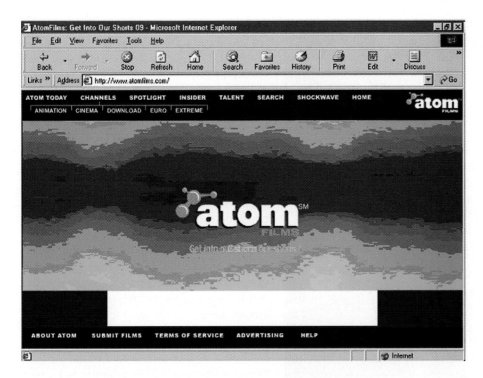

The motion picture industry, like other media businesses, promotes its wares and communicates with businesses and consumers on its own Web sites. The Internet presence for the movie industry includes sites for studios, actors, and other interests.

THE GLOBAL VILLAGE OR THE ADDRESSABLE AUDIENCE?

The Canadian media guru Marshall McLuhan published his influential book, *Understanding Media,* in 1964 and predicted a "global village" that would be made possible by new technologies. That seemed to happen in 1980 with the coming of CNN, the cable news service that connected viewers across the globe. McLuhan imagined a media-sculpted society with people communicating personally across continents and around the world. By 2000, it was clear that the technical means for McLuhan's vision was available thanks to the Internet and the World Wide Web as well as to satellite communications.

As mentioned earlier, much of the debate about universal communication is linked to technology, economic resources, and content that satisfies. Regarding technology, the current debate between the benefits of the *television set* versus the *personal computer* or even a liquid crystal *"flat panel" touch screen* will no doubt lead to new appliances and methods of delivering new media messages. Some say that the technology is already ahead of the content of programming, arguing that there is not enough content available. Years ago, Bruce Springsteen wrote "Thirty-seven channels and nothing on." Cable television and many Web sites have the same refrain. In the 1990s, when cable industry people predicted that Americans would soon have 500 channels and that new digital television would make even more possible, no one seriously argued that there was enough content to fill up that much time. Media critic Jonathan Alter was asked to make a list of 500 possible channels, but he gave up at 350. The consumer and audience needs of the twenty-first century will likely produce creative programming, including the idea of *repurposing* of information, a hallmark of the Internet age wherein old material is reformatted and presented again and again to audiences. MSNBC's popular "Time and Again" program with Jane Pauley is an example of the "repurposing" of old TV news footage to tell new stories. The SCI FI channel's shadow

The concept of a "global village" and instantaneous digital communication was advanced in the theories of the Canadian media scholar and analyst Marshall McLuhan, famous for his book, *Understanding Media*, and for his aphorism, "the medium is the message."

characters who comment on the absurdity of old movies is another example. And even E!'s "Talk Soup" repurposes clips from talk show episodes.

As for Internet content, there are tens of thousands of Web sites. A useful glimpse into the best of them is provided each year at the annual Webby Awards in San Francisco, sponsored by the Academy of Digital Arts and Sciences. In a zany and glitzy ceremony, the Academy honors the best sites on the Web in some twenty-seven categories ranging from news and sports to activism and education. At this event the Web's content providers, as they call themselves, mimic the tradition of the motion picture Oscars, but true to web culture, limit their acceptance speeches to five words. Some of those utterances at the 2000 awards were:

"They said I could only. . ." (*The Onion*; humor)

"I'm not Paul Smith." (Paul Smith; fashion)

"Screwing with your mind." (Nerve.com; print/zines)

"Is this thing edible?" (Epicurious; food)

"Thanks, come talk to us." (Café Utne; community)

The Webbys, which support and encourage the progress of new media, are given for sites that have their own content, are independently produced, or repurpose other people's material.

TRACKING NEW MEDIA

Anything written about new media is subject to continuous change and thus a book that treats this topic runs the risk of being outdated long before it is published. For example, some much-heralded journalistic Web sites in 1999 were on the verge of financial collapse by spring 2001, as the expectations of the founders were quashed by a lack of customers to pay for the service. One such enterprise, ABPNews.com, that included in its staff the eminent Pulitzer Prize–winning reporter Sydney Schamberg, was said to provide the best crime and criminal justice coverage anywhere, but failed to attract advertising dollars or other revenues. It is clear that like other expansive financial booms in the past, when new enterprises sprouted like grass seeds, the new media will be subject to enormous spurts of growth, followed by mergers, joint ventures and concentration of ownership. Where there were dozens of specialized news sites in 2000 and 2001, they could possibly converge into a few by 2003 or sooner. Thus, the best way to stay current with new media is to:

- *Watch new media associations, industry groups, and publications:* There are already scores of these and they all have Web sites to promote their identities and hawk their wares.

Table 8.1 Favorite Portals or Search Engines (top at-home portals in March 2000, according to Nielsen Net Ratings)	
Online Usage Survey	
yahoo.com	21.1%
aol.com	19.0%
msn.com	15.8%
go.com	9.1%
netscape.com	8.5%
lycos.com	7.5%
excite.com	6.1%
altavista.com	5.7%
snap.com	3.8%
looksmart.com	3.3%

Table 8.2 New media Content Categories (Webby Awards, 2000)	
Activism	Kids
Arts	Living
Broadband	Music
Commerce	News
Community	Personal Web Site
Education	Politics and Law
Fashion	Print and Zines
Film	Radio
Finance	Science
Games	Services
Health	Sports
Humor	Television
Travel	Weird

Note: Awards are also given for technical achievement and excellence in online art.

- *Be conscious of the "appliance wars:"* Just how new media are delivered, whether by PC, TV, liquid crystal flat panel, or some other means, will provide useful insights about what the consumers prefer.
- *Compare old media content:* What do new media offer in the way of what business people call "value-added" information or services? No electronic newspaper will outdistance a cheap printed newspaper filled with predictable information until it provides something more in an equally portable fashion.
- *Consider audience yardsticks:* The people and institutions that use media, from advertisers to politicians and various other business interests, understand the idea of subscriptions and user fees in exchange for numbers of readers and viewers. "Visits" to Web sites and "hits" are not yet well understood or measured very precisely. Eventually they will be, and those new yardsticks will also include interactive feedback.
- *Look at business strategies:* Beyond selling their audience numbers, what business strategies will the new media use to finance themselves and to encourage revenues from several sources to pay bills?
- *Remember that the new media are more than the Internet:* The fast-paced world of broadband communication is offering new outlets for communication, some which will succeed.

- *Do not forget yesterday's losers:* Just because a technology or content strategy does not work immediately, do not count it out. The fax process was invented in the nineteenth century, got some use in the 1930s and 1940s, only to be declared a loser by 1950. In the 1980s, the technology of facsimile got new converts and it was suddenly important again.
- *Not everything changes:* As critics and commentators obsess on changes in the world of communication, it is always wise to see what is not changing and to understand why. Trendy new media activities aimed at a youthful audience may disappear while media aimed at older people in a world of increased longevity might prosper.

TRANSFORMING OLD MEDIA

Separating and distinguishing the new media from the old media is difficult since one important impact of new media has been the transformation and extension of old media. For example, the book publishing industry, still very much wedded to traditional paper books, is also producing e-books, available online or in electronic storage formats. Book publishing also relies heavily on electronic commerce to sell and distribute books, as evident on sites like Amazon.com and barnes&noble.com. Most newspapers have Web sites or digital editions and the print editions direct their readers to the digital product for more information. The same is true with magazines and some magazines only exist as digital editions, forsaking the older paper form altogether. Radio stations and networks make heavy use of the World Wide Web to deliver Web broadcasts and growing numbers of consumers are getting their radio service online. Television interfaces with the Internet in a variety of ways—through programming, advertising, and online sales. Television and cable are becoming digital services that are less reliant on over-the-air broadcasting or actual cable and fiber optic connections. The fields of advertising and public relations are awash with digital connections and proudly use the platform of the Internet, not only to extend their traditional business, but also to create virtual services.

Just when the new media will evolve (or some say dissolve) into a distinct medium of their own, perhaps embracing and building upon old media forms, depends less on technical capacity and invention than on consumer habits and preferences. To what extent people will give up old print and turn to electronic forms for reading and viewing on the screen will be determined by the ease of hardware and software operation, cost, convenience, and habit. On these matters, the jury is still out and is likely to be out for some time to come. Thus, new media will likely interact with and coexist with old media in terms of individual media products. At the same time, converging ownerships are already combining what we call old and new under the same corporate roof. One early indicator of the popularity of the new media with traditional media employees has been the exodus of people from old media companies to the new dot-com firms. Although in terms of total employees and total revenues, the traditional media still dominate the communications landscape.

THE FUTURE OF NEW MEDIA

As we have indicated, the nature and definition of new media keep changing, but the digital revolution is quite different from anything that human beings have pre-

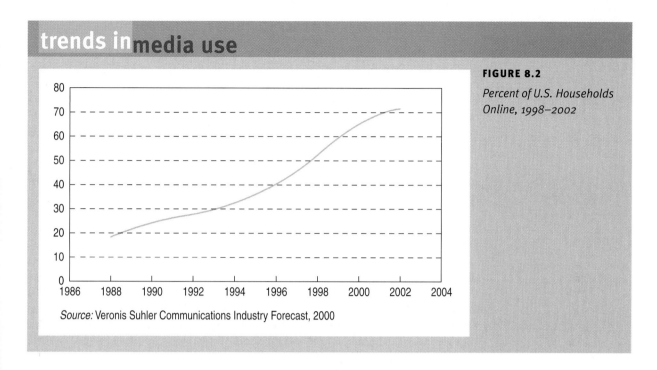

trends in media use

FIGURE 8.2

Percent of U.S. Households Online, 1998–2002

Source: Veronis Suhler Communications Industry Forecast, 2000

viously experienced, with communication messages crossing borders and returning from all points on the planet. The new media of the present engage in instantaneous and interactive communication. They merge text and data with sound and pictures. They mostly use personal computers, but can also be linked to the television set. In fact, some critics say that there is a burning appliance war between the television set and the personal computer with some doubt about who will win. Some think that both will win and attract certain followings and interfaces while others think that a new device or appliance will emerge and render both obsolete. It is important to remember that new media refer to the technology of delivery (the machine used), the software or systems that allow the communication process to occur, as well as the actual content that is communicated.

Whether a new medium is largely concerned with information (online services); entertainment (video games and pay-per-view movies); opinion (bulletin boards, chat groups, and cybersalons); or advertising (home shopping services, on the TV and on the PC screen); in the end it will compete with other existing media. Some will supersede old media, taking over their functions. For example, the newspaper industry for years blocked telephone company entry into the online news world because they feared that electronic classified ads would eventually kill newspapers, which depend on these important revenues. Most new media live alongside old media and the most successful of them integrate with the older media enterprise and eventually the public does not know the difference. At one time cable television was seen as the mortal enemy of over-the-air television broadcasting. After all, cable was a scavenger taking its content from over-the-air TV and redistributing it to viewers. Now cable is both a delivery system on which traditional television relies as well as a programming service with its own distinctive networks like CNN, Arts and Entertainment, ESPN, the History Channel, and many others.

IMPACT OF NEW MEDIA ON OLD

Just what the impact of the new media is on the old media is still uncertain, or "in play" as Wall Street analysts say. There are two immediately evident impacts. First, old media firms, notably newspapers and television networks, have developed Internet strategies to capitalize on the benefits of the Internet in delivering news, entertainment, and information and in expanding their business-as-usual presence beyond print and electronic media. By early 2001, these efforts had proved less than stellar with newspapers, magazines, and television networks reporting marginal to poor returns from such activities compared with their regular operations. Still, many argued that their digital divisions were investments in the future rather than immediate short-term gains.

In some instances, new media operations were simply folded into traditional media companies and outlets, but for the most part new media activities that were part of the old media landscape did less well in accumulating profits than did free-standing Internet companies. For other media industries such as cable TV, motion pictures, and recorded music, the Internet has proved to be a blessing and a curse. Cable channels have extended their presence by creating up-to-the-minute Web sites and by establishing links to specific content sites such as those representing sports, pay-per-view movies, and others. Motion picture companies have established Web sites for individual films, actors, and directors, thus stirring up more interest in their products and also selling various items associated with films, such as toys. The recorded music industry, whose profits depend on the sale of CDs and DVDs were hit hard by "free music" that could be downloaded from such online services as Napster, which faced court challenges and prohibitions in 2000. Protection of copyright is vital to music and movie industries and the Internet has provided a difficult challenge since Internet users expect all the content to be free, an idea very much under siege at the dawn of the new century.

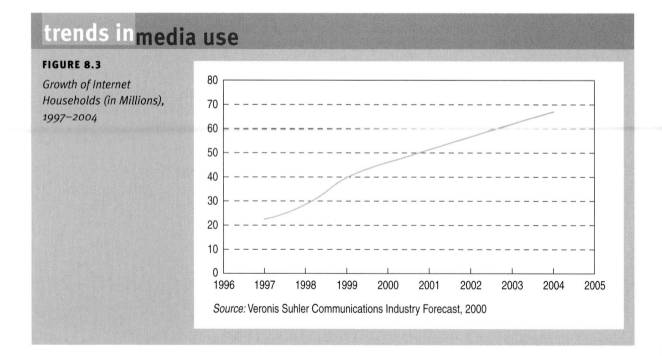

trends in media use

FIGURE 8.3

Growth of Internet Households (in Millions), 1997–2004

Source: Veronis Suhler Communications Industry Forecast, 2000

For advertisers, the Internet has proved to be a new channel of distribution and one that can target advertising to a very specific demographic audience, thanks to the precision of digital marketing information. To some extent, the issue of measuring the impact of the new media on the old is rendered meaningless by deals like the Time Warner AOL transaction, wherein the old and the new will be integrated together into a single large corporation with different technologies and channels collaborating with each other.

Chapter Review

- New media historically have evolved from old media, but the introduction of the information age, or the communication revolution, with the link between computers and communication, represents a major breakthrough if not a new era.

- New media platforms such as online services and interactive television allow for the delivery of content much faster than was previously the case and also allow for consumers to order up their communication fare, rather than relying on that which is selected for them by others.

- The Internet or the "network of networks" and the World Wide Web have paved the way for global developments in communication.

- New media enterprises are typically the products of the interplay between economics or the market, new technologies themselves, and politics or the legal-regulatory arenas.

- Convergence is the result of the innovations in technology and related developments which involve a "united state of media" and the coming together of all forms of communication into a single electronically-based, computer-driven system.

- Some of the new media are mainly interpersonal and individual messaging media, while others seek audiences and try to influence the media marketplace.

- New media typically merge with old media and eventually are not noticed as anything new at all.

Notes and References

1. Peter Huber, "The Death of Old Media," *Wall Street Journal,* January 12, 2000, p. A22, also see Michael J. Wolf, *The Entertainment Economy: How Mega Media Forces Are Transforming Our Lives* (New York: Random House, 1999).
2. PriceWaterhouseCoopers and New York New Media Association, Third New York New Media Industry Survey, New York, 2000, p. 6.
3. *Encarta World English Dictionary* (New York: St. Martin's Press, 1999).
4. *Encarta World English Dictionary,* p. 934.
5. Everette E. Dennis and James Ash, "Tracking the New Media-Management Views and Evolving Industry," *International Journal of Media Management,* spring 2001.
6. Bruce Owen, *The Internet Challenge to Television* (Cambridge, Mass.: Harvard University Press, 1999). Information was also drawn from a lecture by Bruce Owen at the Fordham Graduate School of Business, March 23, 2000.

7. *A Free and Responsible Press, Report of the Hutchins Commission* (Chicago: University of Chicago Press, 1974 reprint of 1947 edition), p. 32.

8. Everette E. Dennis and John V. Pavlik, "The Coming of Convergence and its Consequences," in Pavlik and Dennis, *Demystifying Media Technology* (Mountain View, Calif.: Mayfield,1993), p. 14; also see Pavlik, *New Media Technology, Cultural and Commercial Perspectives* (Boston: Allyn & Bacon, 1997), and Dan Lacy, *From Grunts to Gigabytes, Communications and Society* (Urbana, Ill.: University of Illinois Press, 1996).

9. Nicholas Negroponte, *Being Digital* (New York: Alfred A. Knopf, 1995). See also John Seeley Brown and Paul Duigid, *The Social Life of Information* (Cambridge, Mass.: Harvard University Press, 2000).

10. Martin Irvine, *Web Works* (New York: W. W. Norton, 1997), pp. 1–6.

11. Bruce L. Egan, *Information Superhighway Revisited, The Economics of Multimedia* (Boston: Artech, 1996), pp. 40–46.

12. Wilson Dizard, Jr., *Old Media New Media, Mass Communications in the Information Age,* 2nd ed. (New York: Longman, 1997) p. 5.

13. Alfred C. Sikes in Roger Fidler, *Mediamorphosis, Understanding New Media* (Thousand Oaks, Calif.: Pine Forge Press, 1997), p. xiii.

14. Irvine, *Web Works,* pp. 1–6.

15. Fidler, *Mediamorphosis,* pp. 31–44.

16. Bill Gates, *The Road Ahead* (New York: Viking, 1995), pp. 225–227.

17. E. M. Forster, "The Machine Stops," *The Eternal Moment and Other Stories* (New York: Harcourt, Brace & Company, 1928).

18. Forster, "The Machine Stops," p. 78.

19. Fidler, *Mediamorphosis,* pp. 151–158.

20. "Paul Saffo and the 30-Year Rule," *Design World,* 24 (1992), p. 18; and John Carey, "Looking Back Into the Future: How Communication Technologies Enter American Households," in Pavlik and Dennis, *Demystifying,* pp. 32–39; Margaret H. DeFleur, "The Development and Adoption of Computers in American Society," forthcoming; and Everette E. Dennis, *Of Media and People* (Newbury Park, Calif.: Sage Publications, 1992) pp. 113–118 for a discussion of convergence and communication education and John Carey quotations.

21. A. Michael Noll, *Highway of Dreams—A Critical View Along the Information Superhighway* (Mahwah, N.J: Erhlbaum Press, 1997), p. 17. See also Joseph Turow, *Advertisers and the New Media World* (Chicago: University of Chicago Press, 1997).

22. Michael Dertouzos, "El Mercado de la Informacion," in E. Dennis, M. Dertouzos, B. Nosty, R. Nozick, and A. Smith, *La Sociedad de la Informacion, Amenazas y Opportunidades* (Madrid: Editorial Complutense, 1996), pp. 31–43.

23. Lawrence K. Grossman, *The Electronic Republic, Reshaping Democracy in the Information Age* (New York: Viking, 1995). See also Lawrence K. Grossman and Newton N. Minow, *A Digital Gift to the Nation* (New York: Century Foundation Press, 2001).

24. Dennis and Ash, "Tracking the New Media-Management Views and Evolving Industry."

Part Three

MEDIA AUDIENCES, SERVICES, AND SUPPORT

Chapter 9

INTERNATIONAL COMMUNICATION AND GLOBAL MEDIA

FOUR DECADES AGO, THE CANADIAN MEDIA GURU MARSHALL MCLUHAN ENVISIONED A "GLOBAL VILLAGE" OF INSTANTANEOUS COMMUNICATION linking all peoples of the world. With the help of satellites and computers, he thought, it would be possible for individuals and institutions, including the mass media, to move messages across borders to any point on the globe.[1] At a time when most media organizations had quite limited reach—many, like national newspapers and broadcast systems, staying mostly within their own countries—this seemed a fanciful idea, more like science fiction than cold reality.

An expansion of press freedom and independent media occurred in the 1990s with the rise of self-styled democracies and market economies in many countries heretofore under totalitarian governmental controls. Cambodian soldiers examine an English-language paper, published in Phnom Penh.

Today, the international, or global, media scene is more complex than ever and reviewing it is vital to understanding U.S. media fully. The coming of the Internet and the World Wide Web provides the wherewithal for truly global communication. At the same time, there are global media companies reaching out to distribute their products to people in as many locations as possible. These companies and other media industry firms are creating international ownership of former U.S.-owned media companies and organizations. And overseas, U.S. media firms are establishing a footprint and are buying up media. Making sense of international communication and the global media scene is difficult because it is ever-changing. All of this activity, whether regarded as a good thing or a potential danger to freedom of expression (something we will deal with later), is made possible by three factors:

1. *Media technologies*—from satellite communication to the Internet and other digital means of creating products and transmitting them easily to distant places, something impossible in earlier times.

2. *Governmental changes* and the loosening of regulation—including the collapse of communism, emerging democratic states with market economies, and the worldwide trend toward deregulation of media, once tightly controlled or monitored by individual countries.

3. *Economic incentives* and new markets—including the new economy, where technology and media industries play a larger and larger role creating new markets, as a true information evolution comes to the national and world scene.

Still, in the midst of such an optimistic view, there is concern that giant, global media companies can have a negative effect on diversity of communication and free expression. The digital divide, discussed in Chapter 8, between the haves and the have-nots of the digital age is especially true on the international scene where rich countries, mostly in the industrialized West, have great advantages over the often poor, developing nations. That problem has been greatly underscored in recent years, but the idea of Western dominance of communication is a longstanding issue.[2]

THE RISE OF GLOBAL MEDIA

Large media corporations and conglomerates are a fact of life at the beginning of the twenty-first century. Critics on the left, such as Robert McChesney and Edward Herman, see global media—big companies seeking global audiences—as "missionaries of global capitalism"[3] that are menacing to diverse, locally-owned media that reflect local culture and ideas of specific nations and regions. There is a greater concentration of ownership than ever before and it can be argued persuasively that there is a cheapening of content and a dumbing down of media fare to reach larger and larger audiences around the world. Another media scholar, David Demers bluntly asks whether global media are "a menace or a messiah?" He also questions whose interests global media serve and whether they lead to social control.[4]

To some extent, global media companies, especially those based in the United States—like Disney ABC, AOL Time Warner, and Viacom—are greatly interested in selling Western media content abroad. They accelerate the influence of U.S. TV programs and Hollywood movies overseas as they drown out international films in the United States. Some media companies, like Sony, disagree with this assessment, noting that their music divisions make international films from India, Australia, and other countries available to audiences in the United States, through digital downloading. This, they say, would not have happened in earlier times when communication mostly stayed behind national borders.

Of course, the international or global media economy is part of worldwide economic changes, wherein business seeks worldwide demographic markets to sell goods and services. Naturally, they use the media as tools. All this has been enhanced and hastened by the Internet, which has underscored and extended the advantage that Western media companies already had around the world.

On the positive side of global media are the boundless opportunities for individuals to get news, information, and entertainment from every corner of the globe quickly and cheaply. Worldwide media consolidation and growth also has allowed for greater specialization and for service to interests of all kinds. For Americans, ideas that began in other countries such as reality TV programming led to shows such as "Survivor," "Who Wants to Be a Millionaire," and "Big Brother." One example of such global reach is the "Millionaire" game show that began in Britain in 1998, then turned into a global subculture. "Sesame Street," however, is an example of a program with a better reputation that is also widely exported abroad. The effect of global programs on local programming is widely debated.

Once it was possible for government regulation and licensing to control—for the most part—the communication within its borders. Now, with technologies that easily cross borders, whether via Internet, satellite, fax, or other methods, it is difficult for governments to stop such a flow. Not that they have not tried. The Chinese regularly have retaliated, though not always effectively, against people and foreign governments who tried to hawk their media wares in that country. In Germany and France, laws that prohibit swastikas and other politically objectionable material have been used against U.S. Web portals and media companies. In both instances, and many others, such action against outside media and popular culture promoters is unlikely to be effective in the long haul, so pervasive is the new media technology. At one time, border guards could search people's bags for contraband books and magazines, or the government could jam broadcast signals. Now, for better or worse, borders are porous and communication is free to go most anywhere it wishes.

In the midst of communication of plenty, fostered by global media—admittedly for their own benefit and profit—there is still a great gap between communication-rich and communication-poor countries and people. The global media companies are businesses, not charities, and they have had neither interest in "wiring" the developing world, nor can they easily reach the billions who are not yet online—using the Internet as part of the global village that McLuhan envisioned so long ago.

International communication has been part of the American scene since the first colonists brought newspapers, books, and broadsides with them and waited patiently for news to come by ship. It was the invention of the telegraph that separated transportation and communication and allowed information to travel across time and space without benefit of horse, rail, or water travel. For years, international communication meant wire services like Reuters of Great Britain or the Associated Press of the United States. Most major countries—France, Germany, and Italy, for example—also had their news services that crossed borders and oceans by wire and cable, though most of their business was in their own country.

DIMENSIONS OF INTERNATIONAL COMMUNICATION

To understand how the world communicated and what impact that activity had, diplomats, journalists, and scholars thought of international communication mainly in three broad topics. One is *international news coverage*—how we and the rest of the world cover international news and the planet generally. A second broad topic focuses on *comparative international journalism and world press systems*. The concern here is how the media of the world are organized and how they operate. The third is referred to as *mass media and national development*. The main topic here is how media play a role in what were then called "underdeveloped" countries of the third world, which usually meant parts of Africa, Asia, and Latin America. The term "undeveloped" gave way to "developing," just as "foreign" has been replaced by "international," which refers to anything involving two or more nations or nationalities, such as an "international incident." More recently, people concerned with communication across borders talk about "globalism" and the global media, which means just what McLuhan talked about—communication that can reach anybody, anywhere, anytime (or almost).

As we indicated earlier, one of the most visible examples of global communication is the Cable News Network (CNN), which, while based in Atlanta, Georgia, brings news and information from every continent—even from such closed societies as Myanmar (formerly called Burma) and North Korea. Delivered in the United States over cable television systems, CNN employs communication satellites to move news, information, and pictures from nearly two hundred countries and maintains an army of correspondents around the world. In most countries of the world, in business offices and hotels as well as in rural villages, CNN can be seen. In Asia, Star TV, owned by the media mogul Rupert Murdoch, has a huge footprint and several channels of programming across the most populous countries in the world—China, India, and Indonesia. Of course, the various news services, like the Associated Press and Bloomberg, both old and new, also have worldwide connections and cover the globe, but principally provide news for U.S. media outlets. At the moment, CNN is one of the most visible examples of global communication, with the instantaneous ability to bring news from the scene of the latest coup or natural disaster virtually anywhere in the world.[2]

HOW WORLD MEDIA ARE ORGANIZED

Before considering the various global and international media, it is important to understand how different press and media systems are organized in various regions and countries of the world. Until the early 1990s, most of the world's media could be divided between those that were part of the Western or capitalist world and those that belonged to the Socialist or Communist world. During the Cold War between East and West from 1945 to 1991 or so, Western-style media were largely independent of government and professed press freedom. Media in the countries of the former Soviet Union, China, and elsewhere were part of the machinery of government in totalitarian states. This is still true in China, North Korea and Cuba at the time of this writing.[3] Western media-watch groups, such as Freedom House, then and now, referred to the news media of the world as "free, partly free, or not free," based on whether or not the press was independent of direct governmental control. Most of what was called the "free press" got its funding from advertising or reader-viewer subscriptions from the private sector. Exceptions were state broadcasters in Europe, like the BBC, which was sanctioned by the government, but got its revenues from a license fee paid by all taxpayers. In the United States, public broadcasting—radio and television—began with government funding, but eventually got support from the private sector, especially from charitable foundations and businesses.

Media scholar Robert L. Stevenson of the University of North Carolina distinguished among five different media systems or models in his book *Global Communication in the Twenty-First Century* including:

- **Western mass media**—mostly privately owned media firms, large and small, in North America, Europe and Japan with broad constitutional guarantees of media freedom.

- **Authoritarian media**—those in autocratic states, past and present, that are subject to government or religious authority and controls, as in some parts of the Islamic world, military dictatorships in Asia, and some countries in Latin America.
- **Communist media**—this system of state or party controlled media still exists in China, North Korea, and Cuba, and to a lesser degree in a few places where elements of the old Soviet system still survive.
- **Development media**—these include the mixed public-private media arrangements in some developing countries in Africa, Asia, and Latin America.
- **Revolutionary media**—media that are part of a revolutionary or liberation movement aimed at displacing the existing order either in earlier history like the American and French revolutions or more recently in various developing countries that threw out their colonial masters.

As with other media systems, these sometimes overlap and evolve, as with revolutionary media such as the Polish Solidarity movement press of the 1980s and 1990s, which were soon more like media of Western Europe and the United States.[7] What Westerners called the "free and independent media" usually had free press guarantees from government and could appeal to an independent judiciary in times of conflict. In the socialist states, not only were newspapers, magazines, and broadcasting part of the government, but different bureaucracies supervised different aspects of their operations. For example, the Russian newspapers *Pravda* and *Izvestia* had a government or party-supervised editorial staff, but did not own their own presses or distribution system. Printing was done by another government bureau and distribution by yet another. This was very different from the Western model where a newspaper would produce its own editorial content, operate its own presses, and hire its own carriers to put papers on doorsteps or at newsstands.

THE END OF THE COLD WAR

With the collapse of communism across Eastern Europe—the former U.S.S.R. in the Balkans and elsewhere—the role of the media in former socialist societies changed greatly. About the same time, many military dictatorships in Latin America and Asia also collapsed and media that were once controlled by the government in those countries also made changes, often looking to the West for examples. In Eastern Europe, for example, the role of media in society changed radically. Instead of being party or government monopolies, new independent media sprang up and some old party papers proclaimed both their independence and their new links with the market economy

On an informed hunch, NBC's Tom Brokaw went to the Berlin Wall in November 1989 and was the only network anchor on the scene when the famed Wall fell, thus scoring an important exclusive report.

and capitalism. The changes for the media of the former "second world," as the communist states had been called, meant such important changes as redefining:

- *the role of media and government;*
- *the basis of financial support*—from government subsidies to free-market advertising, subscriptions, etc.;
- *the role of the journalist*—from government employee to private sector professional;
- *the definition of journalistic content*—from official news sanctioned by government, to more diverse news, often critical of government; and
- *the role of the audience*—moving from guaranteed "captured" audiences to competition for news consumers.[6]

U.S. VERSUS EUROPEAN NEWS MODELS

As the press of the newly independent states of the former Soviet Union and Eastern Europe grew from onetime underground sheets, called the *samizdat* press, to mainstream news organizations, many Western observers and consultants arrived on the scene. The fledgling press was besieged by Western media companies, mostly from Germany, France, Great Britain, and Scandinavia, who wanted to "invest" in the new enterprises. German media giants like Bertelsmann and Axel Springer quickly bought up many newspapers. In Hungary, for example, within two years, there were no locally-owned daily papers.

When it came to editorial content, many of the papers followed the European model of interpretative news, which blends fact and opinion with analysis. Others were enthusiastic about American-style journalism, sometimes called "the journalism of fact," which tries to distinguish news stories from the opinion and advocacy material on editorial pages. A battle over which style of journalism should prevail ensued as some papers in Poland and the Czech Republic, for example, preferred the U.S. style of journalism while others sought more politically oriented material with a definite point of view or editorial slant.

THE DEVELOPED MEDIA OF WESTERN EUROPE

Much like the complex media of the United States, the media of Europe are highly developed products of an industrialized and information society. Of course, European media predate the media of the United States by hundreds of years and American newspapers were modeled on those of England, France, and other countries.

While newspapers and magazines have remained strong in Europe, with a mix of national and provincial sheets, many of them are closely associated with or connected to political parties (much like the U.S. press in an earlier period). Europe's electronic media, such as Britain's BBC or Italy's RAI, have also been powerhouses, but were usually formed as public service enterprises with either partial or full government support. While the U.S. broadcasting system—radio and television—lived in the commercial market and depended on advertising most European media did not. In fact, advertising on the air came quite late in several European countries.

The structure of European broadcasting also limited its growth, and in several countries a single network or two dominated the airways for most of the twentieth century. Now, with privatization and the lifting of some government controls, Europe's television operations are blossoming, though they still lag behind the United States in multichannel and cable growth and development. In fact, one

British observer, Jeremy Tunstall, says "the media are American,"[8] meaning that the U.S. style of media, especially television, dominates much of the world these days and sets a standard for the European and other regional media.

One fact of European media that should not be overlooked, however, is its growing ownership concentration by moguls who often have holdings in the United States and elsewhere in the world. British firms are strong in book publishing, for example, while the Germans have vast newspaper, electronic media, and magazine interests, as do French and Italian companies. Names like Berlesoni (Italy), Bertelsmann (Germany), Hachette (France), and Murdoch (Great Britain/Australia) are dominant powers in world media.

In 1995, Tunstall was asked to revisit his thesis in an article, "Are the Media Still American?" He offered a qualified "yes," suggesting that American dominance might not last. "Two of America's oldest media offerings—the news services and Hollywood—still retain a remarkable strength on the world scene," he said. Still, with the emergence of the information superhighway and digital communication, he predicted that a joint venture between the United States, Europe, and Japan would play a larger and larger role. And he concluded, "The position of American media industries resembles the general position of America on the world scene: the United States is the only media superpower, but it is a media superpower in gradual decline against the world as a whole."[9] The reason for this is the rise of global media companies in Canada, Great Britain, France, Italy, Japan, and other places that are giving American media a run for their money. At the same time, reliance on

figure9.1
The Building Blocks of Bertelsmann

The New Strategy
Bertelsmann wants to turn Napster into a platform for downloading and selling all its media products, including books and films as well as music.

Authors & Books
Toni Morrison, John Grisham, Danielle Steele, John Irving, Pat Conroy

Random House, Bantam Dell, Doubleday, Book-of-the-Month Club

Music & Artists
Arista Records, RCA, Windham Hill

Whitney Houston, Annie Lennox, Barry White, Eros Ramazzotti, Santana, Puff Daddy

Magazines & Newspapers
Nearly 100 worldwide including Stern, Geo, Family Circle, Fitness, McCall's, Parents

Internet
bol.com, bn.com (joint venture) for online books and music

CDNow, Lycos Europe, Pixelpark

Television
RTL Group, Europe's biggest broadcaster (joint venture with Pearson PLC, Audiofina)

U.S.-originated information is diminished as people everywhere generate their own media content and dispatch it digitally around the globe. In the world of entertainment, Hollywood itself is partly owned by foreign firms, such as Sony, and entertainment industries are evolving in many other places.

ASIA'S DYNAMIC AND DISTINCTIVE MEDIA SCENE

Even before the collapse of communism in Europe, profound economic and social changes came to Asia. That part of the world, once regarded as underdeveloped and poor, soon had some of the richest nations in the world. Except for China and North Korea, which are still Communist states with monopoly media, most other Asian countries follow a democratic model in their governments and have independent media. Examples are Japan, Korea, Taiwan, Singapore, Malaysia, Thailand, and Hong Kong (governed by the British until midyear 1997, when it was handed over to the People's Republic of China), which pledged to allow a traditional press freedom for fifty years.

Ironically, Asia is where much of communication began—paper was invented there and the first newspaper appeared hundreds of years ago. That legacy, however, was lost to history and has little to do with the modern Asian media. The emerging media of East Asia, like their counterparts in the West, deliver information and news, convey opinion, offer entertainment, and provide a marketplace for goods and services through advertising, but their editorial voices and other content differs greatly. These differences are philosophical. While media in the United States and elsewhere in the West are the product of Western enlightenment with an emphasis on freedom and individual rights, the media of much of Asia are influenced by Confucian philosophy, which stresses consensus and cooperation. As one study puts it, "Thus what may look the same is actually quite different in function."[10] The consensus model of Asian media has meant more cooperation with government than is the case in the West, where conflict and adversarial disputes are more often the case. That means, in many countries, the kind of investigative reporting that embarrasses government or business, which is so common in the West, is not welcomed. In some instances, in Singapore, for example, the restrictive media system has little formal censorship, though journalists often engage in self-censorship. Malaysia's Mohammed Mahatir and Singapore's long-time leader Lee Kwan Yew (now a senior minister in the government) oppose Western-style freedoms and any absolute notion of freedom of the press. They argue that Western values have led to a breakup of families and a disruption of government. Singapore and some other countries keep a tight leash on their press in an otherwise free-market economy and sometimes penalize foreign media who "abuse their welcome." For example, both *Time* and the *Wall Street Journal* have been banned and fined in Singapore for reporting on the government and military in unflattering articles.

Outsiders in several Asian countries cover international news at their own peril and sometimes are expelled for angering local authorities. Asia's media scene, like that of Western Europe and

Reflecting the great changes that have affected world media even in Communist countries, reporters from Hong Kong media interview a regional Chinese official outside the Great Hall of the People in Beijing, China.

North America, is highly diverse and complex, ranging from national dailies in Japan, with millions of readers, to a vast array of magazines, television programming, a movie industry, advertising and public relations enterprises, and various new media cyberspace ventures. At the same time, rural Asia relies on community radio and small, often poor vernacular newspapers and broadsheets. As in other parts of the world, there are vast differences between urban and rural communication in Asia.

DEVELOPMENTAL JOURNALISM AND INFORMATION IMBALANCES

In Asia and in some parts of Latin America and sub-Saharan Africa, developmental journalism is advocated by the government and leaders of society who argue that their countries are fragile, fledgling democracies with many internal and external threats. They believe that a pesky, Western-style press can undermine and destabilize the government. They urge the practice of developmental journalism where the press will transmit values in support of the government's vision for development. In such a system, teaching the language and helping foster new agricultural methods is more important than covering the news or criticizing the government.

Striving for national cohesion, rather than diversity or disruption, is strongly urged by the leaders in countries like Malaysia and some West African states as well. Developmental journalism in the media, print, and broadcast, is part of a larger notion of using mass media as tools for national development. The important role of the media in promoting health, nutrition, agricultural production, and safety cannot be denied. Developmental journalism has also been used in many countries that gained their independence from Western colonial powers like Great Britain, France, and The Netherlands and wanted to bolster their economies and improve their standards of living.

Arguments over the role of the press and media in the development process have ensued for decades. For more than twenty years, a debate over the New World Information and Communication Order (NWICO) raged in the United Nations, where developing nation leaders lined up against those from the more-developed West. The NWICO was viewed as a threat to press freedom since one plan called for the licensing of journalists—not uncommon in some countries—which was loudly denounced in the West. This debate was connected to concern over an "information imbalance," which argued with considerable evidence that most news and information is "manufactured" in the West and imposed on developing societies. The United States and other western nations, it is argued, have a disproportionate amount of the world's information resources and technology. Because people in the West write and control the news, they determine the images of much of the rest of the world, the critics argue. This has been called "global communication dominance"[11] and in this discussion the United States is an information superpower with enormous influence because of its great wealth and the presence of global media, such as the AP and CNN. This is an old argument and although the once fiery United Nations debate has abated, there is still considerable support for breaking the "imbalance," especially in Latin America and Asia. All this is linked to news coverage of the whole world, with the United States and the West getting most of that coverage in most countries, while less developed, but still highly populous, countries like India, Indonesia, and Nigeria, for example, get relatively little attention,

Latin America's media scene—like that of Eastern Europe and East Asia—has experienced considerable democratization and change in the last two decades following in the model footsteps of democratic Costa Rica, known for its effective government and independent media as well as being the only country in the region without an army. Here, San Jose, Costa Rica's channel 7 broadcasts the nightly news.

which hurts their economic development and political influence in the world. Here again, we see the great importance of communication, globally and at home. If the NWICO debate had any impact, it was to heighten awareness of news imbalances in the West while sensitizing the developing world to Western press freedom values.

MEDIA DEMOCRATIZATION

Though often mentioned in the same breath by critics, the media of Asia and Latin America could not be more different. Latin American media have benefited by a robust economy for most of the 1990s as well as increasing democratization. Thus, the rise of media conglomerates such as Globo, one of the largest television networks in the world, in Brazil, and the Cisneros Group in Venezuela are becoming players on the world stage. Latin America has large, sophisticated newspapers in major and provincial cities, well-developed radio for both news and entertainment, a growing television industry and various new media and online services. With the growth of democracy and the rise of a robust middle class, Latin America has seen a massive growth of magazines and cable. Much of the Latin American press, itself part of an old media system, dating back to the late 1700s, looks to North America for role models. For example, the *Wall Street Journal* has a Latin American service that is heavily used by the major papers in most countries. Latin America is known for its *telenovellas,* or soap operas, which are not only used in Latin America (including Central America and Mexico), but also in the United States—which has an increasing number of Spanish-language cable channels, and even in Europe and Southeast Asia. One Caracas, Venezuela-based company, Phelps-Granier, exports its *telenovellas* to several countries where they are either played in Spanish or dubbed into other languages. Only Communist Cuba stands apart from the rest of Latin America in the rise of democracy, market economies, and independent media.[12]

THE ELITE PRESS, INFLUENCING THE INFLUENTIAL

Virtually every major country of the world—and some smaller ones too—have important and highly visible newspapers, variously called, "quality, class, prestige, and elite journals," according to John Merrill, an authority on international media. Says Merrill, "In the vast global wasteland of crass and mass journalistic mediocrity is a small coterie of serious and thoughtful internationally oriented newspapers that offers a select group of readers an in-depth rational alternative."[13] Merrill says that these papers are mostly found in the "information societies"—countries with highly educated populations, technological sophistication, and well-developed media systems.

explaining MEDIA EFFECTS

Cultural Imperialism Theory

A theory associated with international communication is often termed *cultural imperialism*. The basic idea is that the mass media, along with other industries in Western societies, follow a deliberate policy designed by powerful economic and political interests to *transform* and *dominate* the cultures of other people. This process is focused in particular, say those who oppose it, on countries that during the Cold War came to be called the "third world."

This transformation is said to be displacing traditional values, beliefs, and other important features of the way of life in the receiving societies. It takes place, say those who subscribe to this theory, in spite of efforts on the part of the non-Western societies to resist such change.

At the heart of this process of domination are the Western mass media, which convey news and entertainment to people in many parts of the world. The content of these media, say the critics, emphasizes contemporary events in Western societies, secular beliefs and values, plus the material culture of both Europe and the United States.

The foundation for this theory came from three areas of scholarly concern about the role of the media in international communication. The first was a body of research and analysis from the 1950s and 1960s that led to the conclusion that mass media were a very important factor in *national development*. The media were found to be useful in bringing about rapid social change in those societies that valued this goal. The second was an often-heated debate within UNESCO during the 1970s and 1980s protesting the domination by Western organizations of the *flow of news* all over the world, emphasizing the developed societies. Many third world leaders resented this and fought for significant changes. The third is the current predominance in foreign markets of the products of American and European industries, in particular, their *films* and *television programs*.

These processes of international communication have come to be interpreted by critics as *imperialistic*. That is, American and European powers deliberately use the media to impose Western material culture, and the many kinds of freedoms embodied in democracies on people who prefer to retain their traditional values, beliefs, political structures, and ways of life.

Stated formally, the theory assumes that:

1. The content of print and broadcast news, plus movies and television programming, produced by organizations in the United States and Europe is *widely distributed throughout the globe* to non-Western and so-called "developing" countries.

2. Citizens who live in such societies have only *limited choices* for media-provided information and entertainment outside those brought to them by Western global distribution systems. (Local systems lack the necessary resources to compete.)

3. Those in less-developed societies who receive the content distributed by Western global systems are exposed to what many in the audience perceive as *attractive alternatives* to their own material culture, values, and traditional ways of life.

4. Such audiences are led *to adopt, or want to adopt,* goods, services, values, and lifestyles that they see portrayed in the Western media, which creates both political unrest and markets for goods that can be exploited by Western powers.

5. **Therefore,** the developed societies *deliberately engage in cultural imperialism* by distributing media content that systematically undermines and replaces traditional beliefs, values, and lifestyles—leading people to prefer Western political systems, material goods, and perspectives.

Elite international papers are typically defined as international in scope; serious in general tone; and wide-ranging in coverage of politics, economics, the arts, and other matters of significant concern. They also have an "institutional identity," which involves good writing, high quality journalism, and a strong and distinctive editorial voice, all produced by a high-caliber staff. The elite press is not sensational, tabloid fare. One recent roster of elite papers—a top twenty world list (including some high-caliber American entries) was:

Asahi Shimbun (Japan)

Berlingske Tidende (Denmark)

Corriere della Sera (Italy)

Daily Telegraph (Great Britain)

El Pais (Spain)

Frankfurter Allgemeine Zeitung (Germany)

Globe and Mail (Canada)

Le Monde (France)

Los Angeles Times (United States)

Melbourne Age (Australia)

Miami Herald (United States)

Neue Zürcher Zeitung (Switzerland)

New York Times (United States)

NRC Handelsblad (The Netherlands)

O Estado de S. Paulo (Brazil)

Suddeutsche Zeitung (Germany)

Svenska Dagbladet (Sweden)

Sydney Morning Herald (Australia)

Wall Street Journal (United States)

Washington Post (United States)

NEWSPAPERS AND MAGAZINES WITH INTERNATIONAL REACH

While most newspapers in the United States serve a single city, state, or region, several U.S. media organizations have exceptional international outreach, even if their circulations are modest. Such papers include the venerable *International Herald Tribune,* published in Paris and jointly owned by the *New York Times* and *Washington Post. USA Today,* owned by Gannett, has international editions in Europe and Asia. Dow Jones publishes the *Asian Wall Street Journal* and the *European Wall Street Journal* as well as an insert service for Latin American newspapers. The *Christian Science Monitor,* funded by the Church of Christ, Scientist, bills itself as "an international newspaper" and is distributed worldwide. Two American newsmagazines—*Time* and *Newsweek*—both have international editions as do such business magazines as *Business Week.* International publications with considerable presence in the United States include two from Great Britain, the *Economist,* a weekly newsmagazine which has a larger circulation in the United States than in the United Kingdom; and the *Financial Times,* a worldly competitor to the *Wall Street Journal* with strong European economic coverage. The *European,* originally founded by the controversial late press baron Robert Maxwell, also reaches an audience in the United States. For people near the U.S.-Canada border, Toronto's prestigious national newspaper, the *Globe and Mail,* also has a following.

COVERING THE GLOBAL VILLAGE

For many, international communication is world news coverage in U.S. media. Making sense of the rest of the world is a major challenge for newspapers with a "shrinking news hole," and for television news programs with a limited twenty-two minutes of content in a half-hour period. Typically these factors have guided editors in selecting international news for U.S. audiences:

1. Political importance
2. Economic importance
3. Security relationships
4. Breaking news, such as natural disasters

Countries that play a vital role in the world, such as major powers like Russia, China, Germany, and Japan, usually get high news priority. Similarly, countries and regions with strong economic ties to the United States such as Japan, Canada, and Mexico get covered. Those who either threaten our security or contribute to it get high priority for news coverage, which accounts for coverage of Iraq during the Gulf War and former U.S.S.R. during the Cold War. For many editors, the Cold War—the clear division between East and West politically and economically—capitalism versus communism—was a strong organizing principle for news. Since the end of the Cold War, no new organizing principle has been found, and the media face what *Foreign Affairs* editor James F. Hoge, Jr., calls "the end of predictability."[14] Hoge says that the end of the Cold War both added confusion to our understanding of "what is important" and also encouraged a kind of journalistic isolationism with more emphasis on the domestic scene. The Associated Press's Louis D. Boccardi says that his journalistic "army" has been redeployed and that news coverage now includes both major world events and happenings, and also such global themes as the economy, the environment, international security, world health, and others. This takes news coverage of international events and issues beyond what author and correspondent Mort Rosenblum describes in his book *Coups and Earthquakes: Reporting the World for America.*[15] One of the authors of this book, in a speech at Tufts University, called for a systematic approach to "covering the whole world" by making sure that major topics and countries do not get left out.

Visitors to the United States and virtually every international student who has ever spent time at an American university complains about the lack of coverage of their country in U.S. media. There has been a steady decline of international news in major newspapers and on network television in recent years, but there is considerable coverage in many specialized magazines and online services. Still, some critics rightly complain that whole sections of the globe, notably the Islamic world and the Middle East generally, are virtually invisible. One study showed that nonadvertising content of newspapers devoted to international news over a ten-year period ranged from a low of 2.8 percent to a high of 9 percent.[16] At the same time, one editor who listened patiently while a French professor lambasted him for lack of coverage of France in a large Midwest daily responded coolly, "We don't edit this newspaper for visiting Frenchmen!" Another take on that comes from Alabama editor H. Brandt Ayers who has urged more coverage of international affairs in the "heartland press because virtually every local community has businesses which are either owned by foreign interests or whose major competition is overseas." Journalism school dean John Maxwell Hamilton, in a book entitled *Main Street America and the Third World*[17] also argued for more coverage of developing countries because of their growing connection to the United States.

NEW MEDIA WORLDWIDE

The development of new media made possible by the convergence of communication, advanced technology, the Internet, and the World Wide Web has great potential, but it is still largely unknown. While this is a global information and retrieval system, which gives individuals access to increasingly international sources, the success of online services, cybersalons, electronic newspapers, and other new media products is still undetermined. Key issues will be the reform of telecommunication industries and state-owned telecommunication authorities to allow more public access to electronic communication. Many companies, including the global media giants, have invested in new media operations and experiments and hope for growing consumer interest and adoption.

INTERNATIONAL MEDIA ORGANIZATIONS

Several groups and organizations monitor international communication, including such industry-oriented groups as the International Press Institute, based in Vienna, Austria, which tracks issues like freedom of the press. This effort is also undertaken by the New York-based Freedom House.

The Committee to Protect Journalists monitors threats and violence against journalists internationally, calls attention to their plight, and even petitions governments on their behalf. The International Institute of Communications in London takes a special interest in international broadcasting and telecommunications developments. For educators, the International Communications Association encourages research as does the International Association for Mass Communication Research. Virtually all media industries have international associations, hold conventions, and produce publications. The same is true with such media and media-related interests as publishers, public relations practitioners, advertising industry personnel, television executives, and others. Clearly, globalism—communicating with others with shared or common interests elsewhere in the world—is now commonplace in the media industries.

Chapter Review

- International communication involves media with an international reach as well as the media industries of other countries and regions. It also includes news coverage of the world in U.S. media and the use of media in national development. Increasingly, media enterprises are global—being connected to a global economy.

- Trends worldwide include more independent, free-market media in the wake of the Cold War. International news coverage in the U.S. has declined in mainstream media, but is still found in specialized publications and services.

- Different parts of the world have different approaches to news gathering and dissemination. For example, the European model, seen in Western Europe and increasingly in the former socialist states of Eastern Europe, is interpretative and analytical and usually linked to a political party of philosophy. Unbiased or objective reporting is not claimed nor advocated.

- European media are contentious, however, and like those of the United States, are derived from ideas first introduced during the Enlightenment—individual rights and critical press freedom. By contrast, the Asian model is not one that promotes conflict, but instead cooperation and harmony. This comes from

Confucian philosophy and is dramatically different from ideas of press freedom and independence common in North America.

■ In sum, international communication is understanding foreign press systems, watching how the U.S. media cover international or foreign affairs; and realizing that in some countries "developmental journalism" is the norm and urges the media to assist with national development and nation-building, rather than being an independent and critical—often adversarial—force of their own.

Notes and References

1. Matie Molinaro, Corinne McLuhan and William Toye, eds.; *Letters of Marshall McLuhan* (Toronto: Oxford University Press, 1987), pp. 253–254. For a link between McLuhan's theories and the informational millennium see Paul Levinson, *Digital McLuhan* (London and New York: Routledge, 1999).
2. Everette E. Dennis and John C. Merrill, *Media Debates: Communication in a Digital Age* (Belmont, Calif.: Wadsworth, 2001).
3. Robert W. McChesney and Edward S. Herman, *Global Media: Missionaries of Global Capitalism* (New York: Continuum International Publishing Group, Inc., 1997).
4. David Demers and Lee Becker, eds., *Global Media: Menace or Messiah?* (Cresskill, N.J., Hampton Press, 1999).
5. "Around the World, What It Takes To Be a Millionaire," *New York Times,* August 20, 2000, p. 7.
6. Jon Vanden Heuvel and Everette E. Dennis, *The Unfolding Lotus, East Asia's Changing Media* (New York: Media Studies Center, 1993), pp. 1–3; 134–135). Dennis, George Gerbner, and Yassen Zassoursky, ed., *Beyond the Cold War* (Newbury Park, Calif.: Sage Publications, 1991) pp. 1–18; also see Dennis and Vanden Heuvel, *Emerging Voices, East European Media in Transition* (New York: Gannett Foundation, 1990).
7. Robert L. Stevenson, *Global Communication in the Twenty-First Century* (New York: Longman Publishing, 1994); also see Everette E. Dennis and Robert Snyder, eds., *Media & Democracy* (New Brunswick, N.J.: Transaction, 1998).
8. Jeremy Tunstall, *The Media Are American: Anglo-American Media in the World* (London: Constable, 1977); also see Tunstall, "Are the Media Still American?" *Media Studies Journal,* fall 1995, pp. 7–16.
9. Tunstall, "Are the Media Still American?" p. 7, 11.
10. Vanden Heuvel and Dennis, *Unfolding Lotus,* p. 23.
11. Dennis and Merrill, *Media Debates,* Chapter 19 on "Globalism and the Media."
12. Michael Salwin and Bruce Garrison, *Latin American Journalism* (Hillsdale, N.J.: Lawrence Erlbaum Associates, 1991), and Jon Vanden Heuvel and Everette E. Dennis, *Changing Patterns—Latin America's Vital Media* (New York: Media Studies Center, 1995). See zonalatina.com for current news of Latin American media industries.
13. John C. Merrill, "Global Media: A Newspaper Community of Reason," *Media Studies Journal,* fall 1990, pp. 91–102.
14. James F. Hoge, Jr., "The End of Predictability," *Media Studies Journal,* fall 1990, pp. 1–11.
15. Mort Rosenblum, *Coups and Earthquakes: Reporting the World for America* (New York: Harper, 1979); also see Rosenblum, *Who Stole the News* (New York: Wiley, 1993) and Everette E. Dennis, "Watching the Whole World," Charles Francis Adams Lecture, Tufts University, March 5, 1992.
16. Michael Emery, "An Endangered Species, The International Newshole," *Media Studies Journal,* fall 1989, pp. 151–64. The best recent study is in Stephen Hess, *International News and Foreign Correspondents* (Washington, D.C.: Brookings Institution, 1996).
17. John Maxwell Hamilton, *Main Street America and the Third World,* 2nd ed. (Cabin John, Md., and Washington, D.C.: Seven Locks Press, 1987).

Chapter 10

POPULAR CULTURE: ENTERTAINMENT, SPORTS, AND MUSIC

chapter outline

One of the longest and lasting cultural struggles has pitted the educated practitioners of high culture against most of the rest of society, rich and poor, which prefers the mass or popular culture provided by the mass media and the consumer goods industries.

Herbert Gans, *Popular Culture and High Culture,* 1999[1]

A ONCE-FAMOUS PHOTOGRAPH OF TWO BOYS CARRYING A GARBAGE CAN HAD THIS CAPTION: "WHAT ARE YOU THROWING AWAY that will be valuable tomorrow?" A visit to any antique or collectibles shop will quickly tell you which throwaway items of the past are now regarded as valuable. Items such as old signs and post cards, medicine bottles, calendars, medals, buttons, and comic books are part of that inventory. These and other "artifacts" or objects are clues to popular culture— what ordinary people enjoy, use, and consume. The totality of popular social and artistic expression is usually referred to as **popular culture,** distinguishing it from elite (or high) culture, which is discussed later in this chapter.

Not all popular culture is part and parcel of the mass media. For example, printed legends on T-shirts, messages on milk cartons or beer cans, folk songs, and new dance steps, not to mention fashion and hairstyles, which are perpetually changing indicators of the popular culture, all tend to evolve with or without media attention. However, much of media, from videocassettes and comic books to advertising symbols and icons and many other examples, are clearly integral to media industries.

Today, popular female vocalists are icons of popular culture and transmission agents for popular tastes and values. The music industry is replete with awards and honors for top-selling albums and their producers as evidenced in singer Britney Spears performing at the American Music Awards in 2001.

At the beginning of the twenty-first century, a millennial mania occurred as television and movie producers, futurists, scholars, and businesspeople began to speculate about the meaning of the new century. Souvenirs of all kinds began to appear, as did new books, articles, TV programs, and other media fare designed to celebrate the millennium. Although some historians regarded this flurry of activity as fundamentally silly fanfare, they also allowed that the end of every century, since the 1400s, has stimulated such activity.[2] In the late nineteenth century, people flocked to futurist writings such as *Looking Backward,* a Utopian work by Edward Bellamy, which predicted the future of communication, architecture, travel, and other aspects of life.

When the Industrial Revolution of the nineteenth century introduced factories with regular workdays, it also defined, and eventually expanded, people's leisure time. With larger blocks of free time available, the demand for amusement and entertainment expanded, and with it came *popular culture,* which we now associate closely with our contemporary mass media. Before popular culture arrived, the rich and otherwise well-off had their cultural amusements and sports, and people who worked in factories and their families also had their own distinctive brand of entertainment. As historian Richard Maltby writes, "The city amusements of the late 19th century were prototypes for ephemeral consumption: saloons, dance halls, pool rooms, and roller-skating rinks; dime novels and illustrated papers, circuses, amusement parks, burlesque shows, and professional sports; melodrama and cheap seats in the theaters and concert halls."[3]

Meanwhile, the burgeoning industrial production in the United States and Europe needed more consumers to buy products—a development that led to organized promotion and advertising. The means of promoting consumption went hand in hand with the rise of popular entertainment and mass media, which aided in the process of consumption. Eventually, Maltby writes, popular culture became "something you buy" as opposed to traditional folk culture (games, songs, crafts, etc.), which was "something you make."[4]

Although they worried about the "year 2000" problem of predicted computer failure (one that failed to materialize), people at the turn of the new century speculated about the future and imagined a host of changes, all reflected in popular culture from tacky Web sites for TV shows to the latest toys, games, and posters.

THE NATURE AND IMPORTANCE OF POPULAR CULTURE

The mass media, as they began and evolved, have been players in the creation and promotion of popular culture. Some "media products," like dime novels, provided entertainment, while others, like billboards, newspapers, and magazines, were vehicles for advertisements that helped sell goods and services that were being produced. Eventually, much of the entertainment that was once offered to only small audiences expanded its reach through the use of the media. Thus, cheap novels were also serialized in newspapers and magazines, while live drama eventually made its way onto radio and television. Likewise, sports that began on the playing field quickly became fodder for newspaper stories and electronic media broadcasts.

THE MEDIA AND POPULAR CULTURE

The content of popular culture was, by definition, aimed at large audiences of mainly middle and lower classes of varied education and income. Thus, there was an attempt to reach the *largest audience possible* with pleasurable, easily understood fare. Critics constantly complained that the popular culture offerings of the media were debasing and driving out so-called high culture or art.

Early in the debate between the defenders and critics of popular culture, the terms "lowbrow" and "highbrow" were coined. They were first used by the journalist and critic Will Irwin in a series of articles in the *New York Sun* in 1902 and 1903. The inevitable "middlebrow" came later. A lowbrow described a person who had vulgar or uncultivated tastes, while a highbrow was said to aspire (or pretend to) to

One of the most popular entertainers of all time—and in his day, the most famous man in the world—was actor Charlie Chaplin, as seen here in his celebrated film, *Modern Times*. Produced as popular culture to make money, this film (as was the case with all Chaplin's work) has passed into the more rarified world of "high culture," and is now valued as a classic for its artistic merit.

"a high level of cultivation and learning." A "middlebrow" simply accepted and sometimes celebrated mediocre fare somewhere between the other two."[5]

Scholars, critics, journalists, and others have continued to debate and discuss these terms as they have assessed and examined both the content and effects of popular culture. All these concepts are explained later in the section of the chapter that includes a discussion of the entertainment function of the media. It focuses on media content in the forms of soap operas, comic strips, television sitcoms, advertising art, and play-by-play spectator sports. While considering both the content and supposed impact of such examples of popular culture, the material mentioned above, this chapter also considers the "money connection," because popular culture is *big business* when it is presented through the mass media.

Much of the content of the mass media is popular culture that is being sold for a profit, and that profit based on popular culture is integral to the economics of the media. Audiences are courted to consume popular culture, ranging from popular entertainment to sports and even pornography. People will probably argue forever about whether a given image or presentation is popular culture or not. So, too, will they debate the probable impact of such material: whether or not it is harmful, and whether it drives out better-quality performance, more high-caliber design, or more elegant writing.

DEFINING POPULAR CULTURE

But just what is popular culture? Like many other topics of debate, it has been defined in many different ways. Critic Ray Browne, who has written several books on the subject, broadly defines popular culture as "all those elements of life which are not narrowly intellectual or creatively elitist, and which are generally though not necessarily disseminated through the mass media."[6] Additional features are provided by scholar David Madden, who has written, "It is anything produced or disseminated by the mass media or mass production or transportation, either directly or indirectly and that reaches a majority of people."[7]

Even more inclusive definitions can be found. British historian Lord Asa Briggs wrote a book titled *Victorian Things,* treating such objects as tools, medals, hats, and other artifacts of popular culture.[8] In fact, buttons, as in campaign buttons and items such as T-shirts, are themselves expressions of popular culture. Sociologist Herbert Gans has written musingly about T-shirts and the slogans and legends on them, indicating even that the messages and advertisements displayed on the ones worn by women tend to be different from those on the ones worn by men.[9]

Some students of popular culture study virtually anything that people use in everyday life—the lettering on cigar boxes, beer cans and wine labels, advertising in both print and electronic media, billboards, and other messages that communicate effectively. The American Museum of Advertising in Portland, Oregon, has exhibits dating from ancient Greece that show how advertising signs and other symbols have communicated with everyday people throughout history. There is even a set of long-forgotten "Burma Shave" signs from the 1930s, recalling a time in America when successive phrases on humorous roadside advertisements provided amusement for motorists. For example, a "Burma Shave" series advertising a now-discontinued shaving cream proclaims "Free, free, a trip to Mars for 500 empty jars!"

While all of these phenomena of everyday life hold their own fascination, in this chapter we will not discuss in detail elements of popular culture that are not specifically part of the mass media—although some of them, such as fast food and clothing styles, do rely on the media for popularization. Somewhat arbitrarily, then, we can formulate a definition of popular culture as it will be discussed in the present text. Simply put: It can be defined as mass-communicated messages that make limited intellectual and aesthetic demand—content that is designed to amuse and entertain media audiences. Popular culture, in this sense, is disseminated by all of the print, film, and broadcast mass media. Indeed, the term covers most of what they disseminate. Our focus then, is on *media* popular culture—namely, media presentations such as reality programming, game shows, soap operas, spectator sports, crime drama, movies, and popular music, the content of which can be classified as entertaining.

THE IMPORTANCE OF POPULAR CULTURE STUDY

Debates over the value of the popular arts and the supposed superiority of high culture have gone on for decades, with the idea that much that is popular is unworthy junk. Thus, each generation seems to decry the reading habits, musical tastes, and other popular addictions of the young. One reason for all educated people to observe and understand popular culture is simply to try to *keep up with what is happening in society.* As musician Bob Dylan wrote in his "Ballad of a Thin Man," a response to attacks on popular culture: "You've been through all of F. Scott Fitzgerald's books/You're very well read, it's well known/But something is happening, and you don't know what it is, do you, Mr. Jones?"

In the 1980s and 1990s, public funding of popular arts led to considerable controversy. Photographer Robert Mapplethorpe received support for exhibits of his work from federal funding. Many people who came to see the exhibit were surprised, and not a few were shocked, to find that some of his photographs showed nude males and homoerotic themes. The fact that federal funds were used for the exhibits ignited a national controversy. Conservative senators demanded that funding be withdrawn from the National Endowment for the Arts, or at least that strong rules be imposed on the agency. This, of course, raised questions about popular culture and freedom of expression. The debate over the issue has never been fully resolved and it has implications for the entire issue of what is acceptable in popular art. The Mapplethorpe photographs were widely published, especially by fringe media such as zines and on sexually explicit Web sites, but were also the topic of heavy media coverage.

Japanese sociologist Hidetoshi Kato maintains that "the mass media can be seen as one of the most decisive factors shaping the populace of a society." Kato continues: "the belief systems and behavior patterns of the younger generation in many societies today are strongly affected by the messages they prefer to receive (or are forced to receive) either directly or indirectly through mass media."[10]

This kind of influence on audiences is what communications scholar Michael Real calls "mass-mediated culture." Read argues that though it may be distasteful to some, there are good reasons for studying popular (or mass-mediated) culture.[11]

1. It offers delight for everyone.
2. It reflects and influences human life.
3. It spreads specific ideas and ideology internationally.
4. It raises far-reaching policy questions, challenging education and research.
5. It is us.

Although these reasons may seem self-evident to today's students, many universities have been reluctant in the recent past to allow the serious study of popular culture. At the University of Minnesota, for example, Arthur Asa Berger, had a difficult

Nostalgia, or a lure of the past, plays a large role in popular culture products, as people collect souvenirs of earlier times. There is a market for cultural artifacts, such as campaign buttons, posters, old newspapers, and other reminders of familiar past experiences.

time getting the approval of his Ph.D. committee in order to write his dissertation on Al Capp's comic-strip character "L'il Abner." Few English departments in American universities are interested in having their students study pulp fiction or Gothic romances, although these books command far greater audiences than the most respected literary classics. Art history courses are not much interested in advertising art, although it is produced by an impressively large labor force and consumed by millions. American history classes do not take note of the meteoric rise of the fast food industries, although firms like McDonald's have delivered enough sandwiches to their customers to form a line from the earth to the outer reaches of the solar system. In other words, the study of popular culture seems "tainted" to many snobbish intellectuals, even though it influences people in many powerful ways.

In the present chapter, we reject such positions that imply that popular culture can be dismissed with a wave of the hand. Some reasons for taking popular culture seriously in the study of communication are that (1) it reaches almost all of the public in one form or another; (2) whether we like it or not, it influences the way we think, act, dress, and relate to others; (3) it has a tremendous economic impact on the media; and (4) it strongly influences almost all mass-communication content.

Furthermore, what is today's popular culture might become tomorrow's high culture. For example, editor Tad Friend, writing in the *New Republic,* maintains that "Popular entertainment that outlasts its era gets re-examined by new critics, represented to a new audience, elevated and enshrined."[12] Some well-known examples include Matthew Brady's Civil War photographs, the movies of Charlie Chaplin and Buster Keaton, and the music of Patsy Cline and Jim Morrison. Also, even though many deplore it, historians today often study an era through its popular culture because it tells a great deal about what people liked and enjoyed. This accounts for the popularity of reruns of old TV shows, decades after they were introduced. People nostalgically seek familiar themes and territory.

Closely associated with popular culture studies are two kinds of media research. One is the study of *heroes* and the other focuses on *images*. The popular heroes of any period—athletes, rock stars, film sex goddesses, and even some of our military leaders and major politicians—are "products" of mass media portrayals. Similarly, one learns a great deal about a given culture, for example, by its media portrayals of the images of women in advertising or the images of minority groups like African Americans, Latinos, and Native Americans in news photographs. The frequency with which people appear and the way they are depicted says a great deal about the values of a society and the decisions that media people make. In the early 1940s, for example, the *New York Times* and other newspapers mentioned African Americans mostly under the grisly topic of "lynching," rather than covering their achievements. Even earlier, many media stereotyped various ethnic groups in denigrating ways, again indicating the current social values of their popular culture. By the year 2000, two New York City museums sponsored exhibitions of photos of lynching scenes—not as popular and grisly news this time, but as historical and cultural artifacts.

CRITIQUES OF POPULAR CULTURE

As we indicated, the subject of popular culture has often erupted into a debate over its benefits and potential harm. That debate usually centers on the commercial nature of popular culture ("filthy lucre") and the tendency of low-rolling material to crowd out high-quality forms of literature, plays, and art. This is said to endanger high culture given the fact that the audience for information, entertainment, and cultural material is only so large, and that the person who buys comic books, might be buying them instead of serious literature. It also is said that too much consumption of popular culture, such as watching poor-quality television, has a negative effect on the viewers, creating a nation of couch potatoes. In other words, an argument that begins with the negative effects of popular culture on individuals is quickly extended to society. Some critics say that too much popular culture and kitsch dulls an individual's sensibilities and by extension demeans society as a whole. This is the "dumbing down" argument, wherein people will have lower and lower standards. For example, movies aimed at preteens can drown out more sophisticated films that do not have the same audience appeal. Sometimes, concerns about the negative effects of popular culture cross borders. For example, the nation of Canada has long been concerned about the cultural imperialism, wherein U.S. media fare drowns out Canadian cultural products. The same view has been made globally in what has been called media imperialism, where too much Western media and cultural content overwhelms the local fare in such locations as Africa, Latin America, and some parts of Asia.

POPULAR CULTURE AS ENTERTAINMENT

Virtually all popular culture has an entertainment function. It is typically designed to amuse and serve as a pastime. However, it can also be argued that some popular culture content, such as advertising, is deadly serious about promoting a product or a point of view. Not all entertainment is associated with the media. An example is the circus, which is promoted and advertised in the media but stems from a circus tradition dating back to the Roman Empire. Today, however, the media are the important delivery systems for most kinds of popular culture, which in many cases would not exist at all in the absence of mass communications.

Of the media we discuss in this book, it is the content of television and film that is most concerned with entertainment. Newspapers, once a major source of entertainment, now provide utilitarian information. However, they still also carry a considerable amount of entertainment. They rely heavily on *feature syndicates* that bring in entertainment fare. Radio, once an important news medium, is now mainly devoted to entertainment, with its emphasis on music, talk shows, and sports broadcasts. Cable is both an entertainment and an information medium, but clearly entertainment is its dominant concern. Books, our oldest medium, also deliver both serious information and entertainment. The Internet has plenty of popular culture fare, but at present is more information than entertainment driven.

MEDIA INFLUENCES ON CONSUMER ART

One of the most controversial—and most fascinating—social and cultural effects of the media is the constant invention and spread of popular songs, cheap paperback novels, formula TV drama, low-grade film thrillers, comic-strip characters, and other material of unsophisticated content. Such material reaches enormous proportions of our population. People hum the latest popular tunes, suffer the latest problem of a soap-opera heroine, exchange analyses of the latest big game (based on news reports), and organize their activities around the weekly television schedule. In short, media output is at the heart of American popular culture. The development of well-articulated theories concerning both sources and influences of popular culture represents a frontier of theory development that has been widely, but not systematically, explored. In the present section, we look at this area of mass communications and offer a tentative theory to explain why this type of content has become such a preoccupation of our media.

People have debated the artistic merits of media-produced culture and its impact on society for generations.[13] Media critics and defenders have disagreed hotly about whether deliberately manufactured mass "art" is blasphemy or a blessing. These analyses of mass communication and its products as art forms take place *outside the framework of science.* Media criticism is an arena of debate where conclusions are reached on the basis of personal opinions and values, rather than from analysis of carefully assembled data. Nevertheless, those who praise or condemn the content of mass communication perform an important service. They offer us contrasting sets of standards for judging the merits of media content. We may choose to accept or reject those standards, but by exercising some set of criteria we can reach our own conclusions about the merits of popular music, soap operas, or spectator sports.

CULTURAL CONTENT AND TASTE LEVELS

In the sections that follow we review a tentative theory of mass-communicated popular culture induced from discussions of two issues: (1) the merits of various forms of popular culture manufactured and disseminated by the media, and (2) the levels of cultural taste that characterize segments of the American population that are served by these media. These discussions are based on the *strong opinions, clear biases, and personal sets of values* of a number of critics. You may find these admittedly biased opinions consistent with your own views, or you may violently disagree. In either case, they illustrate the types of analyses found in debates about popular culture. (Hopefully, they will clarify your own thinking about popular culture.)

To understand how popular culture has become (and why it is) so ubiquitous as the prevailing content of the American media, we need to place it into a more general context of artistic products. Prior to the development of the mass media, critics tell us there were essentially two broad categories of art. These were **folk art** and **elite art**.[14] Today, neither is believed to be of more value than the other. However, there is an important relationship between the two according to the popular culture theory.

Folk art. This category of artistic products is developed out of the spontaneous effort of anonymous people. Such art is unsophisticated, localized, and natural. Its makers may be talented and creative and yet never receive recognition for their works. It is a grassroots type of art, created by its consumers and tied directly to the values and daily experiences of the maker. Thus, villages, regions, and nations develop characteristic furniture styles, music, dances, architectural forms, and decorative motifs for articles of everyday use. Folk art never takes guidelines from the elite of society but emerges as part of the traditions of ordinary people.

Elite art. Products of elite art represent "high culture." They are deliberately produced by talented and creative individuals who often gain great personal recognition for their achievements. Elite art is technically and thematically complex. It is also

"Kitsch" or schmaltzy artifacts and images of popular culture are commonplace in America and elsewhere. The late rock singer Elvis Presley has inspired a cult following and the production of considerable kitsch such as these commemorative plates displayed by souvenir dealer Sid Shaw.

highly individualistic, as its creators aim at discovering new ways of interpreting or representing their experience. Elite art includes the music, sculpture, dance, opera, and paintings that originated mainly in Europe and were given acclaim by sophisticates from all parts of the world. Although it has its great classics, it is marked by continuous innovation and is now produced in many countries. Novelists, composers, painters, and other creative artists constantly experiment with new forms and concepts.

Kitsch. In modern times, many critics maintain that both folk art and elite art are threatened by a tragically inferior category. The rise of privately owned, profit-oriented media linked to low-cost manufacturing have brought radical change and created a completely new kind of popular art—cheap newspapers, magazines, paperback books, radio, movies, and television. The products of this new art form began catering to massive, relatively uneducated audiences with undeveloped aesthetic tastes.

The content of this new art form, say its critics, is unsophisticated, simplistic, and trivial. Its typical literary forms are the "whodunit" detective story and the sex magazine; its typical musical composition is the latest rock hit; its typical dramatic forms are the soap opera, the game show, the comic strip, and the sexually explicit or violent movie. The term widely used to label such mass-mediated product is the German word *kitsch*. Similar in meaning to the English word "junk," referring to trashy and garish items that are in bad taste and have no artistic merit. Popular culture theory posits that it is the result of people's unrelenting demands on the media to provide entertainment content that produces the current deluge of kitsch.

A Theory of the Negative Effects of Kitsch

explaining
MEDIA EFFECTS

In a capitalistic economic system, profits are applauded and business success is given a high value. The American mass media operate in just such an economic and cultural system.

In order to make a profit, each of the media must present a constant flow of popular entertainment that critics agree has little or no artistic merit.

"Winners" among the media are those that attract attention—with high ratings, large circulations, massive sales at the box office, or large numbers of "hits" on their Web site. Those who attract only limited audiences can be considered to be "losers."

The majority of the people reached by these media have limited interest in "high" or "elite" culture as entertainment. Elite culture consists of such content as classical music, modern and traditional folk art, and dance forms such as ballet and contemporary theater. Such forms are appreciated by a limited number of sophisticates who tend to be affluent and well-educated.

In contrast, the majority who attend movies, watch TV, or read newspapers prefer *kitsch*—low-level cultural content. Typically, this consists of sexy and violent films, fast-moving cop and robber shows on TV, comic books for the young, rock and western music, professional football, or other live sports broadcasts.

The majority of citizens who consume these media products have limited levels of discretionary income, less educational attainment, and relatively simple lifestyles. However, it is these very people that purchase the products most commonly advertised by the media. It is their collective (rather than individual) purchasing power that attracts advertisers to use the media.

A rich family may purchase a fancy car or an expensive boat, and bring a profit to their producers. However, *millions* of families purchase toothpaste, paper towels, and soft drinks. Collectively, these purchases far outstrip the profits that can be made from luxury items or products. For that reason, a medium such as TV or any other that is dependent on advertising revenue must have content that appeals to the vast

majority of citizens. This *reduces the stature* of both elite art and of genuine heroes.

The theory of the negative consequences of kitsch, therefore, can be summarized in the following propositions:

1. The advertising-supported American mass media must produce and distribute a constant flow of *popular culture* in order to maximize their profits via circulations, ratings, box-office receipts, or other indices of audience size.

2. Much of the popular entertainment produced and presented by these media has been judged by critics to be of deplorable quality—that is they classify it as "kitsch" (banal and shallow content without artistic merit).

3. Those who produce popular culture as media content often "mine" elite culture for story plots, tunes, characters, or themes—"dumbing down" what they incorporate from more sophisticated music, plays, literature, and art.

4. Media-presented popular culture portrays celebrity sports figures, singers, talk-show hosts, and other entertainment personalities as "heroes" while all but ignoring individuals who genuinely deserve that label.

5. **Therefore,** popular culture threatens the existence of genuine artistic cultural products by mining elite and folk art for commercial purposes and by reducing the importance of genuine heroes whose deeds and ideas have made significant contributions to our society and culture.

Criticisms of kitsch. Critics charge that in manufacturing kitsch, those who produce it for the media often "mine" both folk and elite art for crass commercial purposes. They do so "the way improvident frontiersmen mine the soil, extracting its riches and putting back nothing."[15] As Clement Greenburg wrote:

> The precondition of kitsch . . . is the availability close at hand of a fully matured cultural tradition, whose discoveries, acquisitions and perfected self-conscious kitsch can take advantage of for its own ends.[16]

Why do critics see kitsch as such a problem? They maintain that the older separation between elite art and folk art once corresponded to the distinction between aristocracy and common people. Although they do not necessarily approve of the aristocracy, they believe that it was critical to the existence of the most developed forms of art. Prior to the emergence of mass communication, according to the critics' claim, folk art and elite art could coexist because they had clearly defined constituencies.

Then came the dramatic spread of the media to all classes of society, geared to the largest numbers of consumers with purchasing power. The tastes of these consumers were not linked to either folk art or elite art—they were best satisfied with content characterized by low intellectual demand. The result was a deluge of inconsequential kitsch.

Kitsch affects all levels of society and art, because it competes for the attention of everyone. Its constant presence and attention-grabbing qualities are the source of its popular appeal. Thus, critics conclude, people who earlier would have read Tolstoy now turn to one of a few dozen formula writers of mysteries and romances. Those who might have found entertainment at the symphony, ballet, or theater now tune in to Madonna or wrestling; those who would have gained political wisdom from modern versions of Lord Bryce and Alexis de Tocqueville now watch the latest "analyses" of Geraldo Rivera or Chris Matthews.

In other words, popular culture theory states that products that are low in artistic taste drive out elite art and higher culture, just as bad money drives out good money. In assessing the principal characteristics of popular culture, the critic Dwight MacDonald maintained that: "It is a debased, trivial culture that voids both the deep realities (sex, death, failure, tragedy) and the simple, spontaneous pleasures. The masses, debauched by several generations of this sort of thing, in turn come to demand trivial and comfortable cultural products."[17] Furthermore, the theory maintains, kitsch represents a double-barreled form of exploitation. Those who control the media not only rob citizens of a chance to acquire higher tastes by engulfing them with less-demanding media products, they also reap high profits from those whom they are depriving.

If it is true, this theory of popular culture leads to three major predictions: First, kitsch presumably diminishes both folk art and elite art because it simplifies their content, and in using them, it exhausts the sources of these arts. Second, it deprives its audiences of interest in developing tastes for more genuine art forms. Third, it is mainly a tool for economic exploitation of the masses.

These predictions represent serious charges. To try to evaluate the merit of this theory we can attempt to determine if at least one of the above conclusions is true. To do this, we can look at one aspect of popular culture—the heroes created by the media. Does the presence of media-created idols of kitsch tend to diminish the stature of genuine heroes as the theory predicts? Moreover, does a fascination with such media-created heroes lessen interest in meritorious accomplishments in real life? Furthermore, is economic exploitation a real factor?

Heroes of the media as kitsch. As is suggested above, one way of inferring whether our theory of popular culture has merit is to look at the kinds of heroes that our mass media have created. In early America, critics say, heroes and heroines were extraordinary individuals with rare personal qualities who performed admirable deeds. The list of heroes admired by the eighteenth- and nineteenth-century Americans included such notables as George Washington, Robert E. Lee, Sacajawea, Daniel Boone, Harriet Tubman, Geronimo, Davy Crockett, and Harriet Beecher Stowe. These men and women were real people who performed deeds that truly had a significant impact on history. They did not win acclaim because they were pretty or entertaining, but because they had powerful determination to succeed in situations requiring courage, dedication, and self-sacrifice.

Even as the media arose in the twentieth century, the tradition of heroes lingered. Soldier Alvin York and pilot Eddie Rickenbacker emerged as the great heroes of World War I. But after that (following the rise of the new media), the number of real heroes known by their actual deeds began to thin out noticeably. Perhaps the last great hero, and one of the most adulated of all time, was Charles A. Lindbergh. His solitary 1927 flight across the vast Atlantic in a single-engine aircraft required steel nerves and an iron will. It was a feat that manifested all of the qualities that Americans admired and made him the most acclaimed hero of the twentieth century—at least until the media of film and broadcasting came into their own.

The change in our heroes that came with the full development of these media is the subject of a famous classic study. The sociologist Leo Lowenthal examined biographies in popular magazines, believing that ordinary people best understand history and contemporary affairs in terms of famous people. Looking at political, business-professional, and entertainment heroes, Lowenthal concluded that heroes are a product of the values and tastes of the time. For example, in the early years of the twentieth century, *idols of production* in fields like business, politics, and industry dominated magazine biography, but more recently the *idols of consumption,* persons from entertainment, sports, and the arts have moved ahead in popular appeal.[18]

Hero study traces its origins back even earlier to an essay by the historian Thomas Carlyle published in 1885, which demonstrated how forceful personalities have shaped history. Although the "great man" or "great woman" theory of history is now on the wane, scholars and media critics still find the study of heroes useful in examining people's attitudes and values. In effect, heroes become symbols for public hopes and aspirations, and according to cultural critics, thus serve a positive social function.

Are the days of true or real-life heroes gone? Some people feel that they are. As the media assumed a greater presence, many critics maintain, a new *hero of kitsch* began to replace the *hero and heroine of the deed.* These new objects of public adulation are not individuals with extraordinary personal qualities. Instead, they are media-created idols known for their sex appeal, their alluring voices, or their athletic or other performance abilities.

It is greatly to the advantage of the media and those who create and supply popular culture to convince their audiences that the products they provide are *truly important.* One way that this is done is through highly publicized "competitions" in which a multitude of awards (Oscars, Tonys, Emmys, MTV awards, Heisman trophies) are presented to the creators of kitsch, ever more frequently in highly publicized, televised ceremonies. These events powerfully reinforce the illusion that these are the people in our society that really "count." Yet, critics ask, are they simply modern versions of "The Lone Ranger," who was, as sociologist Richard Quinney noted "nothing more than a creation of commercial enterprise"—a creature who had no real existence aside from images on film?

Thus, the view posed by popular culture theory is that most contemporary heroes are media creations of kitsch, whose fame derives, not from extraordinary acts that can inspire and benefit society, but from images on the screen, sounds from CDs and cassette tapes, or their ability to sell their words on paper. While some gain fame for their performances, others become notable as pure inventions—imaginary characters who have no real existence outside a movie, soap opera, or prime-time sit-com. There is ample reason to believe, say the critics, that in treating these illusions as though they are important, our society has merged fantasy with reality in a final commitment to kitsch.

There are several identifiable categories of such media-created heroes. First, there is the *hero of the ball and stick.* Babe Ruth and Red Grange are among those that lead the long list of athletes that became celebrities through media attention, followed by today's Michael Jordan and Tiger Woods. Clearly, these individuals are superb athletes and have received extraordinary financial rewards. Yet critics find it difficult to account for their immense popularity on grounds other than the status conferred on them by the media.[19] Striking a ball skillfully with a bat, racket, or club contributes little to the national destiny. Athletic skill is scarcely the stuff by which advances in civilization are made.

Another significant category is the *hero of the titillating tune*—the singer instantly recognized by millions of fans. Few members of the older generation in the United States would fail to identify the voices of Bing Crosby or Frank Sinatra. Today, the sounds of Madonna and Ricky Martin command instant recognition. The musicians and songs made famous through the media constitute an important part of today's kitsch. Here, popular culture shows its roots in folk art and elite art, since many songs that have made it to the top of the popularity lists are based on music from classical and American folk traditions, such as grassroots American ballads and the earliest jazz.

Of even greater interest are the *heroes of superhuman power.* Characters of the imagination have long intrigued people. One could easily speculate, for example, that the various "supermen" of today's media are the counterparts of ancient mythological deities with fantastic powers who appeared in human form. There is a timeless attraction to fantasies of power and success that allows the entertainment of millions through the unusual deeds of a long list of fictional characters with superhuman capacities. Generations of readers have admired and coveted the powers of Superman, the Shadow, Wonder Woman, and Batman. Characters with superhuman strength, the ability to predict the future, or hear peoples' cries for help are often featured in TV shows and videos.

Musical styles and celebrity come together in popular music choices, as seen here in the gyrating song and dance of Latin singer Ricky Martin, truly a celebrity of popular culture linked to ethnic interests and trends. Here, the singer, a contemporary sex symbol, performs at a concert in Miami, Florida.

Other contemporary media characters have human limitations, but are remarkably capable of combating the forces of evil. Here can be included the police *heroes of screeching tires,* the cloak-and-dagger *heroes of international spydom,* and the steely-eyed "private eye." The list would not be complete without the *heroes of legal ploy* and the venerable *heroes of suture and scalpel.* What hard-working private eye measures up to Buffy the Vampire Slayer? Who can defeat James Bond or Dirty Harry? The capacities of real people in the real world are pale in comparison.

How, then, can we evaluate this theory? The charge that popular culture draws from elite culture can be clearly substantiated in many cases. However, whether popular culture should be *condemned* for doing so is an open question. The conclusion that the public is forced to pay for popular culture also seems correct, for the public ultimately pays the high salaries of media heroes and heroines that become part of the costs of advertising and marketing the products of the sponsors. On the surface, this does look like the "economic exploitation of the masses," but the final assessment must be based on one's personal values.

Finally, the charge that media heroes diminish interest in accomplishments in real life can be considered valid, when one considers that the significant achievements of "ordinary" people are often moved into the back pages of the paper. The accomplishments of scientists, artists, and others who make significant contributions to our culture seldom receive much recognition, while gossip about celebrities often makes front-page headlines. Overall, then, the theory of popular culture makes important arguments. However, the degree to which these aspects of popular culture actually represents a *threat* to the public as a whole remains a matter of personal judgment.

"TASTE PUBLICS" AS MARKETS FOR MEDIA PRESENTATIONS

The theory of popular culture makes important assumptions about taste levels among the public. Just what are the different levels of taste among those that the media serve, and how are these tastes linked to the production of kitsch? We can take a brief look at these issues in the present section. The analysis of "taste publics," like debates about the merits of popular culture, is outside the framework of science and it proceeds from individual opinions and standards. Judgments must be made about whether enjoying a particular artistic product represents "high" or "low" taste, or something in between, and judgments about "good" and "bad" taste depend on subjective values, not scientific criteria. Here, the aim is only to focus our attention on significant factors in the basic support system of American media.

Because the task is difficult and the risk that others will disagree strongly is great, not many scholars have analyzed—in the United States —what have come to be known as "taste publics." Sociologist Herbert Gans has used the method of qualitative observation to identify five major levels of taste in American society.[20] In the sections that follow, we describe these taste publics and the content that they tend to prefer. Our description is based largely, but not exclusively, on Gans' analysis. Education may be the most important element in defining taste levels, but many other factors such as class, age, gender, and race are also involved.

The **high-culture taste public** likes the products of the "serious" writers, artists, and composers. High culture is found in "little" magazines, in off-Broadway productions, in a few art-film theaters, and on rare occasions on public television. It values innovation and experimentation with form, substance, method, overt content, and covert symbolism. Styles tend to change often. Painting, art, and sculpture, for example, have been dominated at one time or another by expressionism, impressionism, abstraction, conceptual art, and so forth. In literary fiction, high culture has emphasized complex character development over plot. Modern high culture explores psychological and philosophical themes, among them alienation and conflict.

Clearly, this form of culture would have little appeal to the majority of the usual audience of most of the media. For this reason, it is seldom found in mass communication. Members of the small segment of the public that prefers high culture consider themselves elite and their culture exclusive.

The **upper-middle taste public** is concentrated in the upper-middle, socioeconomic class—which is composed mainly of professionals, executives, managers, and their families. These people are well educated and relatively affluent, but they are neither creators nor critics. For the most part they are consumers of literature, music, theater, and other art that is accepted as "good."

To characterize the upper-middle-class public, one might generalize that they prefer fiction that stresses plot over characters or issues and favor stories about people like themselves who have successful careers and play important parts in significant affairs. They tend to like films and programs about likable upper-middle-class people in upper-middle-class settings. They read *Time* or *Newsweek* and enjoy the kind of new media fare that appears in *Wired.* They might well be familiar with classical music and opera but dislike contemporary or experimental compositions. They purchase hardcover trade books, support their local symphony orchestra, and occasionally attend the ballet. They subscribe to magazines like the *New Yorker, National Geographic,* and *Vanity Fair.*

Although this group is fairly large, its influence on media content is actually quite limited. Some television dramas, public affairs programs, and FM radio represent the upper-middle level, but most media content is at the level below it. The reason is that, as a group, while the upper-middle-class is relatively affluent, it is simply not large enough for aggregate purchasing power to add up to an impressive part of the total of the nation.

The **lower-middle taste public** is the dominant influence in mass communication, for two reasons. First, the lower-middle taste public includes the largest number of Americans; second, it has sufficient income to purchase most media-advertised products. The people of this level tend to be white-collar workers (for example, public school teachers, lower-level managers, computer programmers, government bureaucrats, druggists, and higher-paid clerical workers). A substantial number are college educated, many with degrees in technical subjects. This public often consciously rejects the culture preferred by the taste levels above it, but occasionally it appreciates and pursues some of their forms, especially once they have been transformed into popular culture.

The lower-middle-class public continues to support religion and its moral values. It tends to like books, films, and television drama in which old-fashioned virtues are rewarded and happy endings still occur. Thus, it tends to disapprove of positive portrayals of homosexuality, promiscuity, or other "deviant" lifestyles. The lower-middle-taste public likes unambiguous plots and heroes. They loved the late actor John Wayne, for instance, who espoused traditional virtues. They seek neither complexity of personality nor philosophical conflicts as dominant themes. People of lower-middle tastes commonly read romance novels; buy magazines like *Us;* and enjoy television programs such as "Bay Watch," family and situation comedies, cop-and-crook dramas, musical extravaganzas, soap operas, and quiz shows. In music, country-western, easy listening, and golden oldies radio stations are favored. Such music makes few intellectual demands on its listeners.

The **low-culture taste public** consists mainly of skilled and semiskilled, blue-collar workers in manufacturing and hands-on service occupations (factory line, auto repair, furnace servicing, and routine plumbing). Their education level tends to be at the vocational school level or lower. Younger members of this category attend vocationally oriented community colleges. Although still numerically large, this taste public is shrinking. More blue-collar families are now sending their children to four-year colleges, and many manufacturing industries are rapidly being replaced.

The taste public for low culture dominated media fifty years ago and still plays a part in 2001. But because its purchasing power is currently somewhat less than that of the lower-middle level, it is being replaced by that category as the dominant influence on the media. However, the media continue to produce a substantial amount of unsophisticated content for this audience.

The taste public for low culture likes action—often violent action—in film and television drama. It is to please this public that the media resists efforts to censor the portrayal of violence. This group enjoys simple police dramas, comedy shows, and Western adventures. Programs with a lot of slapstick, shows like "Wheel of Fortune," wrestling, and country-western music are popular with this group. They like to read the *National Enquirer,* confession magazines (for women), and *Wrestling* (for men).

The **quasi-folk taste public** is at the bottom of the socioeconomic ladder. It is composed mainly of people who are poor and have little education and few occupational skills. Many are on welfare or hold uncertain or unskilled jobs. A large portion are nonwhite and of rural or foreign origin. Although this group is numerous, it plays only a minor role in shaping media content, primarily because its aggregate purchasing power is so low.

The art appreciated at this bottom level of taste resembles that of the low-culture level. These people tend to like simpler television shows, and in many urban areas foreign-language media cater to their needs. These people also preserve elements of their folk culture. For example, they may hold religious and ethnic festivals and social gatherings and display religious or ethnic artifacts and prints on the walls of their homes. Colorful murals adorn the streets of some urban ethnic neighborhoods.

In a 1999 revision of his classic book, *Popular Culture and High Culture,* sociologist Herbert Gans points out the connection between culture and class, noting that poor and undereducated people often cannot afford tickets to the opera and might not feel comfortable in art museums surrounded by affluent people. Of course, age, gender, and race also play a key role in popular cultural selections. Other scholars have introduced the term *omnivores* to account for people who make their taste choices from many menus—cutting across popular and high culture. Of course, taste publics encompass a kind of shorthand for analyzing popular culture. Many people are *omnivores,* with interests and tastes that run the gamut from dumbed down and nearly mindless TV fare to complicated computer games to music and art of all kinds. The conflict between popular and high culture is very real in society, however, and often accounts for what we watch on TV or have access to in other media.

IMPLICATIONS OF POPULAR CULTURE THEORY

As the previous sections have made clear, popular culture as media content must be understood in terms of both the aggregate purchasing power and taste preferences of various segments of the public. Regardless of the protests, claims, and counter-claims of the critics, the media *must* continue to produce content that appeals to the largest taste publics, because it attracts attention that they sell to sponsors in order to stay in business. There is little likelihood, given these dependent relationships, that the media on their own will bring about a cultural revolution by emphasizing high- or even low-upper-middle culture. The obvious prediction for the future is that lower-middle and lower tastes will continue to dominate American mass communication. Thus, no matter what the future holds in bigger screens, clearer pictures, more channels, or alternative modes of delivery, the taste of the lower-middle category will continue to dominate and define the nature of the majority of mass media content.

ENTERTAINMENT MEDIA AND POPULAR CULTURE

As mentioned in Chapter 1, entertainment is one of the central functions of the media and it is also a form of media content. Entertainment is defined variously as "an activity to occupy one's time and attention agreeably, especially a public performance." In the debate over popular culture, as just reviewed, entertainment is commonly regarded as "frivolous, superfluous, and unimportant," and is distinguished from the arts, which are supposed to challenge and enlighten the mind, as "deeply moving the human spirit and permanently changing one's perspective on life." Of course, that is a somewhat overblown and idealized view, though it is often thought that in media content, information is more important and more worthy than entertainment. This is probably true if one is comparing television coverage of a presidential election or of a war with, for example, a light, situation comedy. There are those who will argue that entertainment fare often has a deeper meaning and makes a statement about our culture. This is the notion that we are what we watch and read—or at least that it reflects our practices and values as individuals and as a society. Thus, the city of Baltimore, Maryland, proudly proclaims itself "the city that reads," while no U.S. city brags that its residents watch or play more videos than any other.

If there are some forms of entertainment media that can be considered "pure," they are motion pictures, recorded music, video games, and perhaps a few others. Television, as we discussed in Chapter 7, if one totals the amount of time devoted to purely entertainment and sports programming as opposed to news and public affairs is largely an entertainment medium. The same is true of cable programming, which to many is simply regarded as more television, though technically it is not. Fiction books are entertainment media, they also have feature material, puzzles, comic strips, and other content that is pure entertainment.

Entertainment media are probably the best expression of popular culture. Indeed they are usually devoted to popular culture content, although some high culture (concerts, operas, and ballets, for example) is also found there. However, contrary to the view expressed above, entertainment media are not trivial or unimportant. They generate the lion share of media revenues, though it is difficult to separate purely entertainment media from those devoted to information and opinion, since there is so much overlap and blurring. It is estimated, however, that entertainment media account for well over 60 percent of all media revenues and that is probably a conservative figure.

explaining MEDIA EFFECTS

Critical Cultural Theory

Critical cultural theory is derived from an ideological rather than from a research basis. It can be used for interpreting the processes and effects of mass communication in the American society. Essentially, it is a perspective for setting forth a *priori*—without the need for proof—the nature and consequences of mass communications. It is less a theory and more a framework of conclusions consistent with and derived from the ideas and political teachings of Karl Marx as well as various post-modernist critics and commentators.

The interpretations of history advanced by Marx in the middle of the nineteenth century had a profound influence on political and economic thinking around the world. The program of revolutionary change that he prescribed, and twentieth-century conceptions of communism, which were derived from his analyses, became foundations of the political structures of the Soviet Union, China, Cuba, North Korea, and a number of other countries. The lives of billions of people were influenced by the ideas of Marx.

While most of the Communist governments that were founded on the ideas of Marx have either collapsed, merged into other forms, or been greatly modified, his concepts continue to shape some scholars' beliefs and interpretations.

Media research and theoretical analyses in the United States has mainly been developed within a framework that has been derived from the *physical sciences* via the *social sciences*. The goal has been to examine the content of mass communication empirically to disclose undesirable influences of media content (violence and sex) that may have harmful influences on behavior. That goal, say critical cultural scholars, is not acceptable. What researchers should be doing, is studying the exploitation of audiences within a framework of *power relationships* that explain how those who own and control the media use them to preserve their power.

The media, say these critics, are used by those in control. They deliberately encode messages into popular entertainment and news, maintaining people's beliefs that the society is just, admirable, and the most natural form of social order. This is false, the cultural critics state. In fact, most people receive meager rewards for their work. Only a few become wealthy or have great power in the capitalist system. However, those in control use the media to keep people believing it is the best of all systems. That is:

1. The Western industrial nations have a power structure based on *capitalism,* which includes both an economic and a political system.

2. The mass communication industries, which are designed to yield *profits* for their owners and are protected by a complex of laws, are a central part of that power structure.

3. The content of mass communications provided to audiences is designed deliberately to support the values of that capitalist system and to *maintain the existing structure of power.*

4. Media audiences constantly receive lessons encoded into the messages they receive that make capitalism seem *attractive, proper,* and *fair.*

5. In fact, the capitalist system is *improper* and *unfair* because the majority of the people in the system receive relatively meager benefits compared to their contributions. Only a few, in positions of power, receive great benefits.

6. **Therefore,** those who control the media are deliberately or unwittingly *exploiting* audiences for their own benefit by using the media to reinforce the capitalist ideology—thereby keeping their audiences bound to the system and avoiding challenges to their power.

THE FEATURE SYNDICATES AS SOURCES FOR POPULAR CULTURE

Among the media industry activities that help us better understand popular culture are feature syndicates (among the earliest of these vehicles), sports media (and content), as well as the recording industry.

Some of the most durable of the delivery systems that bring entertainment content to the print media are the feature syndicates. We discussed these earlier in terms of newspapers. However, they have also become the model for television syndication.

As we noted in the chapter, the earliest syndicate was organized just after the Civil War. Others quickly followed suit, and by the late nineteenth century Irving Batchelor and S. S. McClure (who later became famous as magazine publishers) and others organized feature syndicates—which indicates a formal system for distributing a particular "feature," such as a regular political analysis, a comic strip, or a gardening column to newspapers that subscribe to the service. William Randolph Hearst organized his King Features Syndicate in 1914. By the early 1900s, syndicates were offering opinion pieces, political cartoons, and comic strips as well as columns on fashion, personal problems, politics, and other topics, and there was considerable competition among them. Almost from the beginning, the syndicates played an important role in making the work of particular writers and artists popular among millions of readers.

Unlike today's wire services, which supply both print and broadcast media, the syndicates at first aimed almost exclusively at the print media. Now, the major broadcast networks (ABC, CBS, NBC, Fox, UPN, WB, and PBS), as well as some independent companies, distribute material that is to local television and radio stations what syndicated material is to newspapers and magazines. Local radio and television news and evening magazine programs often include material that comes from a network source acting as a kind of electronic syndicate.

What the syndicates provide. To understand the source of much popular culture that winds up in the media, it is necessary to understand the role of syndicates. In particular, the print syndicates supply a great deal of the entertainment and opinion material for newspapers, including serializations of popular books, columns by noted political commentators, comic strips, and editorial cartoons. Other syndicates serve the television industry. In addition, some syndicates sell design services, graphics, and even newsstand racks. To the print media, they promise that their product will bring circulation gains, something every newspaper covets, and readership studies indicate that the syndicates are sometimes right.

The King Features Syndicate claims to have the greatest array of comic strips for the Sunday papers. This syndicate has feature columnists who cover everything from astronomy to zoos. The syndicate has many old favorites that go back a couple of generations, but it also carries material from the rock magazine *Rolling Stone*. In addition, subscribers have access to puzzles and game columns.

Tribune Media Services (formerly the New York Daily News–Chicago Tribune Syndicate) offers "Dear Abby," the nation's most widely read advice column, and a variety of other columnists and comic-strip writers. Along with crossword puzzles and other amusements, the syndicate carries the editorial cartoonist Wayne Stayskal as well as "Youthpoll," which keeps track of young people's opinions. Tribune Media Services gets about 60 percent of its revenue from its comics; the rest comes from the text features, puzzles, and a graphics service. The Washington Post Writers Group claims to offer "bylines that build readership." Among its services are political commentary by George F. Will and David S. Broder, economic analysis by Hobart Rowen and Jane Bryant Quinn, and media criticism from Sander Vanocur and E. J. Dionne. It also provides columns by Ellen Goodman, illustrations by Geoffrey Moss, editorial cartoons by Tony Auth, and the Book World Service.

How the syndicates work. A former syndicate editor, W. H. Thomas, wrote, "Of all the outlets available as a market for creative talent, none is so little understood or so ill defined as the newspaper syndicate, that insular and elusive shadow-organization which exercises so much power within the various communications media."[21] Little is written about syndicate organizations, probably because even the largest of them are modest in size and complexity. In spite of this lack of publicity and the variations among the syndicates, we can make some generalizations about how they work.

Syndicates coordinate many people and tasks, including contracts between the creators of syndicated material and the syndicate itself and contracts between the syndicate and subscribing newspapers. They handle the flow of money from the newspaper to the syndicate and also the payment of royalties to the writers and artists. Their production staffs prepare material for distribution to various media outlets, and they promote and market their products through personal contact, advertising, and other means.

Acquiring material. First, the syndicates must acquire the content that they want to distribute. To do so they maintain regular contacts with writers, artists, designers, and others. Acquisition can be complicated and secretive, as in the negotiations for a president's memoirs. Or it may result from simply opening the morning mail. Freelance writers and artists frequently send material to syndicates. The syndicates often serve as representatives for their writers and artists, much as literary agents represent authors. Contracts must be negotiated; the new "property" (comic strip or column, for example) must be prepared for marketing; then the material can be sold to clients.

The syndicate usually offers a newspaper a contract for a variety of materials, supplied for a specified time at a specified cost. Like the wire services, the syndicates have a sliding scale of fees; papers with small circulations pay less. Some syndicates make it financially attractive for a newspaper to take several of their offerings, but most often, newspapers buy material from several syndicates. Sometimes there is vigorous competition for a feature.

Managing and marketing. Syndicates must manage and market their wares like any business that produces a product. New items are added constantly; unsuccessful columns and cartoons are dropped. Robert Reed, former president of the Tribune syndicate, said that syndicates are always on the lookout for new talent but are cautious in signing new artists and writers. A property succeeds or fails on the basis of the numbers of papers.

Sometimes syndicate personnel must coordinate many talents. In 1917, John F. Dille was a creative businessman with experience in advertising when he founded the National Newspaper Syndicate. Although Dille was neither an artist nor a writer, he is credited with originating adventure comic strips. The most notable accomplishment of his syndicate was the science-fiction strip "Buck Rogers." Dille got the idea for "Buck Rogers" from a science-fiction article in a magazine. He talked the author into writing for a comic strip that was based loosely on the story. Then he hired an artist to work with the writer, and "Buck Rogers" was born. But Dille's involvement with the strip did not end there. He knew scientists at the University of Chicago and often relayed their ideas about the future to his artist and writer. Perhaps more important, Dille convinced newspapers to buy the new strip. It prospered, appearing in some 287 newspapers at the height of its popularity.

Thus syndicates are multifaceted organizations that link a wide variety of creative energies to potential outlets. Syndication can be carried out by large organizations or by the self-syndication efforts of a single writer or artist. Syndicates are essentially brokers, but they can also be quite creative, as was John Dille. Today, some syndicates are responding to the communication revolution by making substantial changes. Tribune Media Services, for example, became an information service with a broader mandate than it had previously had, and ceased calling itself a syndicate.

The importance of syndicates. From their beginnings, feature syndicates and other kinds of syndication arrangements for the work of writers, artists, television producers, and the like have provided content for media unable to produce material of this kind and quality on their own. This began when daily newspapers could not afford their own resident editorial cartoonist or comic-strip artist and reached out for popular names and fare from other cities for a fraction of the cost. The same is true with columnists, puzzle makers, and authors of daily horoscopes. Syndicates were cost effective, and also allowed local media of all kinds to get famous names and popular material from other places in front of their readers, viewers, and users and thus raise their ratings and readership rates. Syndicates have been important in the spread of popular culture—images and ideas. They have also added diversity to the content of individual media that would otherwise be stuck with the limitations of a local, resident staff. However, they have also made the media more homogenous, so that the options available to the audience can look pretty much the same from one geographic area to another. At the dawn of the twenty-first century, syndicates and other forms of distributed content have found new demographic audiences whose interests cross national borders, thus allowing for global distribution of material once confined to more limited locales.

SPORTS MEDIA: CONTENT AND CULTURE

Sport is a form of popular culture that is deeply rooted in modern society. From neighborhood games to school, college, and professional sports, it is so pervasive in our society that even presidential debates have to step aside rather than compete for public attention and approval. In the 2000 presidential campaign, for example, the timing of the Olympics was key to the scheduling of presidential debates, and no political party would have dared to suggest preempting a game for a debate to pick the next President of the United States. In the midst of an important tennis playoff a few years ago, the CBS Evening News was delayed for several minutes, resulting in a famous incident when Dan Rather stomped off the set. Tennis taking precedence over the news points out the apparent economic and psychological value that sports has for television.

Sports, as presented in the media, has considerable international clout. Several years ago, when the United States had no diplomatic relations with China, it was media coverage of table tennis matches between Chinese and American teams that

The great stars or heroes of sports are notable for their winning and record-setting achievements, such as pro golfer Tiger Woods, the winner of golf's Grand Slam of four professional tournaments who also won the prestigious Master's tournament twice. The popular and photogenic Woods serves as a spokesman for Nike and is one of the most visible sports figures in the world. He is sometimes called the Babe Ruth of golf, recalling another great sports figure.

Lia Vollack, Executive Vice President, Music, *Columbia Pictures,* Los Angeles, California

insights from MEDIA LEADERS

As Executive Vice President of music at Columbia Pictures, Lia Vollack oversees all aspects of the creation and marketing of music for soundtracks for all Columbia, Screen Gems, and Revolution pictures. Vollack has been at Columbia since 1997; she successively served as Vice President and Senior Vice President of music before beginning her current position in June 2000. Her projects have included soundtrack music for such films as *Charlie's Angels, Godzilla, Can't Hardly Wait,* and *Cruel Intentions.* These soundtracks led to albums that garnered triple-platinum, platinum, and gold label sales. Before joining Columbia, she was a freelance music supervisor and editor on such films as *Longtime Companion, The Usual Suspects* (an Oscar winner), and *Austin Powers: International Man of Mystery.* Before that, Vollack was an executive at MGM and a sound designer on Broadway.

Q. How did you initially get involved in the music business?

A. In a pretty unconventional way, without much planning. I graduated early from high school, at age sixteen, and had thought about going to music school in Boston, and later ended up at the University of Colorado for a couple of years. I decided that was not quite suitable for me, so I hooked up with rock bands including The Ramones. At first, I volunteered to work as an engineer and learned the business along the way.

Q. How did you get to your current position as a high-ranking executive in charge of music for one of the world's most important studios?

A. Well, after working as a recording engineer for bands, I pretty much learned the music business on my own.

I got my first studio job at MGM after various freelance assignments that exposed me to all aspects of working with the music business—balancing creative activities with artists as well as the management side. My career has been marked by a continuing series of relationships with creative people, and the most exciting thing is creative collaboration. In my job, I try to bring a lot of creative ideas and people together, such as connecting a director with a passion for a particular kind of music with a composer and artist—and having it work. This business is all about complementary creative visions. It is always collaborative.

Q. From your perspective, how do you see the current state and probable future of the music business, whether in the movies or elsewhere?

A. Well, of course, all aspects of the business are all connected—from the composers and artists whose creative energies must mesh with the business side to be successful. There is enormous synergy in this business that involves record labels, television, radio, motion pictures, and so on. Having said that, I think the future of the business is strong and increasingly so, though it can be cyclical. For example, in 1997, eleven of the top twenty records on the *Billboard* chart were soundtrack albums from movies. Suddenly, everyone wanted to get involved and expectations were too high. The market got glutted and there were too many soundtracks. This was not good for artists or for the business. But the demand for soundtracks will come back—as always. What we really want is to produce compelling music for the movies so that a person will leave the theater and head for the record store to buy the album.

brought a breakthrough. Sadly, the Olympics has also been used as a tragic staging ground for international politics, for example, during the 1972 Munich Olympics when Israeli athletes were attacked and killed by terrorists. In 1980, then President Jimmy Carter blocked U.S. participation in the Moscow Olympics to protest the Soviet downing of a Korean aircraft in violation of international law.

There is also a whole sports-culture industry, ranging from toys and games to cards, calendars, magazines, books, T-shirts, and other clothing items. The demand for such items is promoted by media coverage of sports and by advertising that fea-

Q. What impact is the consolidation of media industries, especially the various music labels, having on the music business?

A. It has reduced competition. There are fewer and fewer options for artists [within the mainstream movie and record companies] and there are fewer people to talk to—both for me and for individual artists. Purchasing music for use in motion pictures is obviously increasingly noncompetitive. It is harder for the young artist to break out of the box and into the movies.

Q. How has technology and the digital revolution affected the business?

A. Of course, Napster comes to mind and I am anti-Napster because I believe that people who create and produce music deserve to be paid for it, not to have their work appropriated. I am optimistic about a solution to this problem, though, and feel that the benefits of the Internet for everyone can be reconciled with the needs of the music business.

Q. What are the prospects for people entering the music business, broadly defined?

A. If you are really motivated and passionate about it, opportunities are there. In my own case, I had no connections, no family ties, or experience in New York or Los Angeles. I didn't ever graduate from college and learned that there are always jobs in the music business, if you are willing to make a modest start—as someone's assistant or in any humble aspect of the business, whether on the creative side with bands, or in the publicity or marketing department of a studio. One of the top people in the business I can think of started off in the publicity department.

Q. What about education? Is there any "sure-fire" route?

A. Not really. Some people in the business studied music, others have law degrees, some went to film school or somewhere else. Most people serve a kind of apprenticeship arranged by themselves that is pretty varied, depending on their particular interest. There are, of course, music programs in business and film schools and courses in engineering schools. More important than any specific education is becoming part of the film community, really getting to know how it works, who does what, and so on. And let's face it, that usually means living in New York, Los Angeles, or Nashville—where the music business is centered.

Q. What is the most satisfying aspect of work in the music field for you? The least?

A. Most satisfying? That's easy—when you find the right artists and sign them, get a hit, and have the marketing and promotion—[it] all works and clicks. That's when it is perfect for the movie being cast and perfect for everyone involved. The least satisfying? That's when you have a great creative idea that everyone agrees about, but for one reason or another it won't work because of business restrictions or timing issues, say with artists whose management want them on the road when you need them in Hollywood. Sometimes things are just out of sync—the artist loves the movie, but the director doesn't like the song. Of course, satisfying moments far outweigh those that are not or I wouldn't be here.

tures sports and sports figures. Sports have also been a major source for America's heroes. In baseball, figures like Babe Ruth, Lou Gehrig, Joe DiMaggio, and Mickey Mantle made a lasting impact in sport and American life. In virtually every sport there have been great "heroes," such as Joe Louis and Muhammad Ali from the world of boxing. Whether it is hockey, tennis, golf, basketball, football, or baseball, each sport has its great figures, known by their athletic feats and by their personalities. Americans, in general, know sports heroes far better than they know their national leaders or powerful figures from other fields.

If the amount of attention given to an aspect of popular culture is any indication of its importance, then sports heads the list of popular culture fare. Sports coverage in the media, whether in newspapers or on network, cable television, and pay-per-view television, is dominant in terms of the time and space it occupies and the revenues it brings to media. Sports coverage occupies 20 percent of all newspaper space and 25 percent of television's weekend and special-event coverage. Roughly 19 percent of all newspaper reporters cover sports, and 21 percent of all consumer magazines include sports reports. No other subject gets as much media attention.

Sports is a vital form of popular culture and has wide appeal. Images of winners and losers, success and failure, pain and pleasure are drawn from sports. Without muscular sports metaphors in the language, American businesses would probably not communicate at all. The most valuable and expensive advertising times on television are during the Super Bowl, the World Cup, and the Olympics.

The earliest sports journalism in the United States and elsewhere emphasized the pastimes of the wealthy, such as hunting and horseracing. Pastimes of the poor or common people received less attention. Though this has changed greatly over time, sports journalism today has a middle-class bias and covers mainly baseball, football, hockey, and a few other major sports. Upscale sports like skiing, golf, and tennis also get considerable coverage, while the down-home pastimes of less affluent people such as bass fishing, professional wrestling, and stock car racing are rarely covered in the sports pages.

In a very real sense, both media industries and sports date from the Industrial Revolution, when people began to have more leisure time. Newspapers at first paid little attention to sports, and some leading editors such as the legendary Horace Greeley of the *New York Tribune* seemed ambivalent about sports and its coverage. As historian John D. Stevens points out, Greeley once devoted six columns of coverage to a prizefight and a one-column editorial denouncing the brutality of the sport in the same issue. Still, sports and newspapers grew up together, and as the penny press of the 1830s developed, sports coverage helped draw ordinary people to these inexpensive, highly popular papers.

Henry Chadwick, an Englishman who came to America in 1824 at the age of thirteen, became America's first important sports writer and was especially influential in popularizing baseball. He wrote for the *New York Times,* Greeley's *New York Tribune,* the *Brooklyn Eagle,* and the *New York Clipper,* where he covered, promoted, criticized, and helped to standardize the rules of baseball.

Although Chadwick did not invent baseball, he was known in his lifetime as the "Father of the Game." According to Stevens, until the advent of baseball there was no uniformity to the games played across America. Baseball was at first an entirely amateur affair, but by the late 1860s, players were being paid—sometimes under the table. The Cincinnati Red Stockings was the first team to admit that it had professional players—this admission came after a season of fifty-seven wins, no losses, and one tie.

Chadwick played an important role in covering and commenting on baseball during this period, and he also published the first annual baseball guides. He noted that there was little agreement about the number of players on a team and the specific rules of the game. In his compilations, he summarized rules and helped to institutionalize baseball. People in distant places who had never seen the game played learned it from Chadwick's writings. This remarkable man urged the use of gloves and chest protectors for catchers, criticized team owners, and helped organize the first professional sportswriters organization. Chadwick is credited with helping to make baseball the national pastime, and was one of the first nonplayers elected to the Baseball Hall of Fame in Cooperstown, New York.

Tennis, like golf, once an elite sport of the well to do, has gained popular appeal through televised tournaments and professional play beginning with great players like Arthur Ashe, John McEnroe and Billie Jean King. The Williams sisters—Venus and Serena—here at the U.S. Open, are great players and champions in that tradition.

Sports columns, like those written by Chadwick, became sports pages and eventually sports sections of newspapers. They were also the forerunners of sports magazines. Sports coverage spread over time, with other artifacts of popular culture such as sports books, baseball cards, and other materials appearing along the way. With the advent of radio, actual coverage, including play-by-play action, was possible, and the dominant role of sports in the press, while still important, was never the same again. Television ushered in a new era of sports media fare and also a new era of media economics, wherein the rights to broadcast games of popular teams, the Olympics, and the Super Bowl generated huge revenues.

Sports broadcasting was largely invented and defined by two important events: David Sarnoff's coverage of the Jack Dempsey–Georges Carpentier championship boxing match in 1921, and the 1958 National Football League championship game between the Baltimore Colts and the New York Giants. Author Huntington Williams says that the first event launched prizefighter Dempsey, one of the most popular and mythic sports figures of all time, as a hero of popular culture, and established Sarnoff and his fledging National Broadcasting Company (NBC) as the leader of post–World War I radio (and eventually television). The National Football League game coverage established professional football as the first money sport of the television era.

The narrators of sports programs on radio and television became legends in their own time as well. In the 1920s Graham McNamee, who first covered the 1923 World Series, understood the game and communicated it well to the public with a rich, baritone voice and colorful play-by-play announcing. He was such a popular figure that he once received fifty-thousand letters during a World Series. And, of course, he and others who joined him in the broadcasting booths in stadiums all over America brought their listeners the heroic exploits of great teams and players, which themselves became legends of sport.

In the television era, ABC Sports, an independent company owned by the ABC network, did not treat sports as mere entertainment or as a subset of news, but as a subject of its own. With live productions of sporting events, the network staged extravaganzas and harnessed new technology, dazzling the public with instant replays and other marvels of the electronic age. Under the leadership of Roone Arledge, one of the greatest programmers in modern broadcast history, and with the collaboration of engineer-technologist Julius Barnathan, ABC Sports harnessed satellites, employed minicams, and developed computer graphics long before they were used by other networks for sports, news, or entertainment. Most visible to the public, through three decades of television's championing of sports, was announcer Howard Cosell, sportscaster for "Monday Night Football." With a distinctive style and personality, Cosell became the most famous figure in television sports. He dominated the screen with his opinionated interviews, analyses, and play-by-play action. He even appeared in movies playing himself.

Television revenues took professional sports from mostly local, modest enterprises to billion-dollar enterprises. By the 1990s, the television networks fell behind cable as a competitor for the best sports fare, the sports industry itself was again in charge, and television was more of a vehicle for its distribution. The ESPN networks, twenty-four–hour, all-sports services on cable, became a regular feature of most fans' TV diet.

There is no doubt that sports programming will remain as one of the most popular forms of popular culture. While there are significant segments of the population who have little interest in, or even detest, spectator sports, the ability of such content to attract attention makes it an advertiser's dream, for selling many kinds of products.

Sports and their significance.   In this chapter, we have considered sports as media content, specific sports media, and the role of sports in our culture. We have not specifically looked at the economic impact of sports on the media or as a part of the media industries, which is considerable. To do that requires considering the sports marketplace in the United States and globally. In the United States alone, that includes national network programming, over-the-air advertising, national and regional cable networks, multichannel video growth, and the increasing role of digital content on the Internet. The links between such U.S.–based companies as Rupert Murdoch's News Corp., which also owns Fox Sports, has an impact across Europe and Asia.

As media content, sports play a significant role, as previously mentioned. It consumes large shares of time and space in print and electronic media, and it accounts for large revenues. There is great audience appeal for the major sports like professional baseball, football, and basketball, for example, as well as golf, tennis, and increasingly, soccer. There are studies examining this content, which is largely entertainment and promotional in nature. It will likely be a staple in media fare for some time to come. Indeed, Internet entrepreneurs often refer to sports as one of the "killer apps" of the new media, meaning that this content application is seen as a hot source of revenue. Other killer aps include sex and business information.

The specific sports media—TV, cable television, radio, pay-per-view, and magazines—are a part of larger media industries and live by their rules. For example, TV networks have sports divisions along with their entertainment and news divisions.

At the time of this writing, although there are hundreds of sports on the Internet, many are extensions of larger sports media enterprises such as ESPN, *Sports Illustrated,* and others. This could change and a distinctive digital sports media industry might evolve, both related to and independent of the sports media that exist today.[22]

Much has been written about the impact of sports on popular culture. The various taste publics favor different sports, for example, and the kinds of sports that people engage in are reflective of cultural values and interests. Baseball was once called "the national pastime" in America, while the British favor cricket and soccer, and Canadians champion hockey. Increasingly, however, as media become more global, sports also take on a global presence, which is nowhere more evident than at the Olympic Games, when the prowess of the athletes of different countries is celebrated and marketed through sports media, mainly television.

MUSIC MEDIA: CONTENT AND CULTURE

As previously discussed, music has always been one of the most distinct aspects of popular culture. Our images—visual and aural—of people and societies from the ancients to the present include music, whether the ballads and songs of old, or the continuing role of classical music and the coming of ragtime, jazz, rhythm and blues, doo-wop, rock 'n' roll, hip hop, and other forms that reflect current tastes and preferences. Every generation of the modern era has had its own music, often scorned and discouraged by an older generation when compared with memories of their own music from an earlier time.

Like sports, music is entertainment; it is also content for music in its own right (as in video concerts and records) or as part of other media fare (such as the soundtracks of movies or themes for TV programs). Music in the media began in print with music publishers producing sheet music for sale, which they still do. But very

Popular music is a major source of celebrity performers, as witnessed by celebrated singer/songwriter Elton John (left) and rap musician Eminem, both controversial in their time, in a much ballyhooed joint appearance at the 2001 Grammy Awards. The appearance on stage brought together the flamboyant and gay John with the rap artist who has bashed gays and promoted violence in his songs.

Table 10.1 Top Ten Selling Albums in 2000		
Album/Artist	**Units Sold (Millions)**	**Recording Company**
No Strings Attached/'N Sync	9.9	Jive
The Marshall Mathers LP/Eminem	7.9	Web/Aftermath/Interscope
Oops! . . . I Did It Again/Britney Spears	7.9	Jive
Human Clay/Creed	6.6	Wind-Up
Supernatural/Santana	5.9	Arista
1/The Beatles	5.1	Apple/Capitol
Country Grammar/Nelly	5.1	Fo'Reel/Universal
Black & Blue/Backstreet Boys	4.3	Jive
Dr. Dre—2001/Dr. Dre	4.0	Aftermath/Interscope
The Writing's On the Wall/Destiny's Child	3.8	Columbia/CRG

Source: Billboard

early on, music had a link with electrical media, from early cylinders and discs to records, magnetic tape, and videodiscs. These technical inventions were employed by the music and recorded music industries and also used the medium of radio, television, and the Internet to reach masses and individual taste publics.

As a distinct industry that obviously works with other media industries and media platforms (notably the Internet, radio, television, and motion pictures), recorded music is "a producer of cultural goods, working in what may be the most uncertain, most volatile of media businesses," as professors Eric Rothenbuhler and John Strick of the University of Iowa have written. They continue: "Consumer taste in recorded music is more ephemeral than consumer taste in newspapers, magazines, popular novels, TV shows, or movies and they also have more options for expressing that taste . . . Yet the industry has succeeded, attracting consumer dollars and time at equivalent levels."[23] Another scholar, Geoffrey P. Hull explains succinctly:

> In order to produce income, a record company usually referred to as a "label" gains control over a master recording of a performance by an artist to sign an exclusive recording for producing a recording for purchase by consumers. The label therefore has two basic functions that it must perform: acquire masters and market (them).[24]

For years, the recorded music industry did just that, often acquiring and developing artists along the way, artists whose music and words reflected the interests and values of various taste publics. The rules included the copyright and ownership of music and the payment of royalties and other fees to the labels, artists, and other professionals in the creative pipeline. This arrangement was dramatically challenged in the 1990s when the record industry found itself struggling against rampant unauthorized downloading of its music on the Internet. Court decisions in 2000 and 2001 involving Napster, the Internet music service, brought the conflict of media to a head. While these decisions in federal courts will probably prove to be diversions involving infringement of intellectual property, they do signal the changing nature of the recorded music industry and how people get their music.[25]

Of course the Internet is a useful marketing tool for CDs and DVDs as well as other music products. New technologies are revolutionizing music distribution. Music lovers can download the latest album by their favorite artists. Truly, the Internet has conquered the music industry in the same way that radio, television, and the movies did in earlier times.

figure 10.1

Multimedia Recycle High and Popular Culture

Music as popular culture. In assessing the recorded music industry, communication scholar Simon Frith wrote that "the history of the record industry is an aspect of the general history of the electrical goods industry, and has to be related to the development of radio, the cinema, and television. The new medium had a profound effect on the social and economic organization of entertainment so that, for example, the rise of record companies meant the decline of music publishing. And piano-making empires, shifting roles for concert hall owners and live-music promoters."[26]

The importance of music. Volumes have been written on the impact and influence of music on the temper and tone of society and culture. Nowhere is the debate between high and popular culture more prevalent and pointed. Indeed, the kind of music offered by a medium largely signals the audience it seeks. Nowhere is this more true than with radio, wherein the programming formats use musical

Although Napster, the music-distribution site, stirred controversy in 2000 and 2001, the music industry itself has been a heavy user of the Internet—from major labels to individual bands and artists. Here, the Dave Matthews Band promotes its records, tapes, and videos, as well as concert dates.

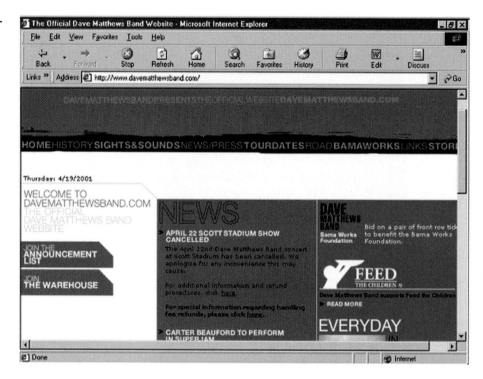

styles and preferences. Thus, we have easy listening, hard rock, country and western, Latino, and other station formats. As stated earlier, music is a media industry of its own (recording labels and their parent companies, music publishers), but is dependant on various old and new media outlets for distribution. Music can convey and influence people's attitudes and feelings as it both speaks to particular generations and crosses generational lines. Music is another area where the omnivores are rampant—omnivores are people whose tastes embrace different forms of music and other popular culture. Obviously one can enjoy the classical music of the high culture taste public and any other musical styles that predominantly appeal to people in different class, racial, and ethnic groups.

Chapter Review

- A great need for popular culture was created by the Industrial Revolution of the nineteenth century. Factories with regular workdays defined and expanded people's leisure time. With larger blocks of free time available, the demand for amusement and entertainment expanded in the form of mass communicated diversions, amusements, and entertainment.

- Much of the content of the mass media today is popular culture that is sold for a profit and integral to the economics of the media. Audiences are courted to consume popular culture, ranging from various forms of entertainment to sports and even pornography. People will probably argue forever about whether a given image or presentation is popular culture or not.

- Somewhat arbitrarily, for purposes of the present text, we can formulate a definition of popular culture. Simply put: It is mass communicated messages that make limited intellectual and aesthetic demands—content that is designed to amuse and entertain media audiences.

- Some reasons for taking popular culture seriously in the study of communication are: (1) It reaches almost all of the public in one form or another. (2) Whether we like it or not, it influences the way we think, act, dress, or relate to others. (3) It has a tremendous economic impact on the media and strongly influences almost all mass communication content.

- People have debated the artistic merits of media-produced culture and its impact on society for generations. Media critics and defenders have disagreed hotly about whether deliberately manufactured mass "art" is blasphemy or a blessing. These analyses take place *outside the framework of science.* Media criticism is an arena of debate where conclusions are reached on the basis of personal opinions and values, rather than carefully assembled data.

- Folk art consists of products that are developed spontaneously by anonymous people. It is unsophisticated, localized, and natural. It is produced by many unknown artists who are talented and creative but who receive no recognition for their contributions. It is a grassroots type of art created by its consumers and tied directly to their values and daily experiences.

- Elite art is deliberately produced by talented and creative individuals who often gain great personal recognition for their achievements. It is technically and thematically complex and often highly individualistic, as its creators aim at discovering new ways of interpreting or representing their experiences.

- In modern times, many critics maintain that both folk and elite art are threatened by kitsch—a tragically inferior category. With the advent of cheap newspapers, magazines, paperback books, radio, movies, and television, this new form of art made its debut, catering to massive, relatively uneducated audiences with undeveloped aesthetic tastes.

- To assess the theory of popular culture, one form of mass communication provides evidence—the heroes created by the media. The presence of media-created idols of kitsch tends to diminish the stature of genuine heroes as the theory predicts. Moreover, a fascination with such media-created heroes lessens interest in meritorious accomplishments in real life.

- The theory of popular culture makes important assumptions about taste levels among the public. Several different levels of taste exist among those that the media serve. These are high culture, upper middle, lower middle, low, and quasi-folk taste levels. The largest is the lower-middle level, which has the greatest aggregate purchasing power and therefore its preferences dominate the production of media content.

- One of the most durable of the delivery systems bringing entertainment content to the print media is represented by the feature syndicates. A syndicate coordinates many people and tasks, including contracts between the creators of material, the syndicate itself, and contracts between the syndicate and subscribing newspapers. It also handles the flow of money from the newspaper to the syndicate and the payment of royalties to the writers and artists.

■ Sports is a form of popular culture that is deeply rooted in modern society. From neighborhood games to school, college, and professional sports, it is so pervasive in society that even presidential debates step aside rather than compete for public attention and approval.

■ Music is a critical indicator of popular culture—expressing the values and references of different generations.

■ If the amount of attention given to an aspect of popular culture is any indication of its importance, then sports heads the list of popular culture fare. Sports coverage occupies 20 percent of all newspaper space and 25 percent of television's weekend and special-event coverage. Roughly 19 percent of all newspaper reporters cover sports, as do 21 percent of all consumer magazines. No other subject gets as much media attention.

Notes and References

1. Herbert J. Gans, *Popular Culture and High Culture,* rev. ed. (New York: Basic Books, 1999), p. 3.
2. Asa Briggs and Daniel Snowman, *Fins de Siècle: How Centuries End, 1400–2000* (New Haven, Conn.: Yale University Press, 1997).
3. Richard Maltby, *Passing Parade: A History of Popular Culture in the Twentieth Century* (New York: Oxford, 1989), p. 8. See also David Nasaw, *Going Out: The Rise of Public Amusements* (Cambridge, Mass.: Harvard University Press, 1999).
4. Maltby, *Passing Parade,* p. 8.
5. William Morris, *Morris Dictionary of Word and Phrase Origins* (New York: Harper & Row, 1977), p. 101.
6. Ray B. Browne, "Popular Culture: Notes Toward a Definition," in Browne and David Madden, eds., *The Popular Culture Explosion* (Dubuque, Iowa: William C. Brown, 1973), p. 207.
7. David Madden, "Why Study Popular Culture?", in Ray B. Browne and Madden, eds., *The Popular Culture Explosion* (Dubuque, Iowa: William C. Brown, 1973), p. 4.
8. Asa Briggs, *Victorian Things* (Chicago: University of Chicago Press, 1988).
9. Herbert J. Gans, "Bodies as Billboards," *New York Times,* November 11, 1985, p. 29.
10. Hidetoshi Kato, *Essays in Comparative Popular Culture, Coffee, Comics and Communication,* No. 13 (Honolulu, Hawaii: Papers of the East-West Communication Institute, 1976).
11. See Michael R. Real, "The Significance of Mass-Mediated Culture," in Real, *Mass-Mediated Culture* (Englewood Cliffs, N.J.: Prentice-Hall, 1977).
12. Tad Friend, "The Case for Middlebrow," *The New Republic,* March 2, 1992, p. 24.
13. The term "culture" is being used here in an aesthetic sense rather than in the way anthropologists and sociologists use the term (and as it is used elsewhere in the present book). The reason is that in the literature on popular culture, the term is used consistently to refer to art, music, drama, and other aesthetic products.
14. Michael R. Real, *Mass-Mediated Culture* (Englewood Cliffs, N.J.: Prentice-Hall, 1977), pp. 6–7.
15. Dwight MacDonald, "The Theory of Mass Culture," *Diogenes,* summer 1953, p. 2.
16. Clement Greenberg, "Avant Garde and Kitsch," *Partisan Review* (fall, 1939), p. 23.
17. MacDonald, "The Theory of Mass Culture," p. 14.
18. Leo Lowenthal, "Biographies in Popular Magazines," in Paul F. Lazarsfeld and Frank N. Stanton, *Radio Research,* 1942–1943 (New York: Duell, Sloan and Pearce, 1944), pp. 507–548.

19. Paul F. Lazarsfeld and Robert K. Merton, "Mass Communication, Popular Taste, and Organized Social Action," in Wilbur Schramm, ed., *Mass Communications* (Urbana, Ill.: University of Illinois Press, 1974), pp. 69–94.

20. Gans, *Popular Culture and High Culture,* revised ed. (New York: Basic Books, 1999), pp. 100–120.

21. W. H. Thomas, ed., *The Road to Syndication* (New York: Fleet, 1967), p. 12.

22. Linda K. Fuller and Haworth Press, *Media-Mediated Relationships: Straight and Gay, Mainstream and Alternative Perspectives* (Binghampton, N.Y.: Haworth Press, 1995).

23. Erik W. Rothenbuhler and John M. Streck, "The Economics of the Music Industry," in *Media Economics, Theory and Practice,* Alison Alexander et al., eds. (Mahwah, N.J.: Lawrence Erlbaum Associates, 1998), p. 219.

24. Geoffrey P. Hull, "The Structure of the Recorded Music Industry," in *The Media & Entertainment Industries,* Albert N. Greco, ed. (Boston: Ally & Bacon, 2000), p. 76.

25. "Copyright in the Age of Napster," *New York Times,* July 29, 2000, p. A26 and Allen Weiss, "The New Jukebox, How the Internet Conquered the Music Industry," in *Marshall* (USC Business School), summer 1999.

26. Simon Frith, "Copyright and the Music Business," *Popular Music,* vol. 7, 1987, pp. 57–75. Also see Simon Frith, *Performing Rites: On the Value of Popular Music* (Cambridge, Mass.: Harvard University Press, 1998).

Chapter 11

ADVERTISING: USING MEDIA IN THE MARKETPLACE

RUNNERS, YEAH, WE'RE DIFFERENT.

The Supernova is different too, with great support and cushioning for an amazingly smooth ride.

In this print magazine ad for Adidas America, the athletic shoe manufacturer declares, "Runners, yeah, we're different"—the slogan used by the company to accentuate its distinctiveness as well as the individualism of the lone runner.

BECAUSE OF THE WAY THE ECONOMIC AND POLITICAL INSTITUTIONS OF THE UNITED STATES DEVELOPED OVER THE LAST FOUR centuries, it has become impossible to imagine American business and industry and the mass media without also thinking of advertising. The American way of life today has—as one of its truly necessary features—a robust advertising industry, which can persuade consumers to buy the products and services that producers provide. Although many people deplore ads on TV, highway billboards, the Internet, or elsewhere, advertising is an engine that keeps the economic system going. Its persuasive effects result in *jobs* at each point along the complex process of production and distribution, which begins with raw materials and ends with finished consumer products from which profits are made. Add to that mix a host of services that are advertised, and one has spanned virtually the entire American economy.

Within a media perspective, advertising is a critical part of the financial foundation on which rests our system of mass communication. It is one of two great streams of revenue that support American media industries. That is, advertisers pay communications media well to present messages designed to market products and services. The second stream of revenue comes from individuals and families who buy magazines, subscribe to newspapers and cable services, and consume records, videocassettes, and related media products.

In some societies advertising plays no such role. Historically, this was the case in the former Soviet Union and the nations of central and eastern Europe, which were all under the Soviet Union's control up to the late 1980s and early 1990s. Under the command economies of these formerly totalitarian countries, the media were both funded and controlled by the state. There simply was no advertising to bring income. This changed after the collapse of communism, and local and international advertising appeared almost overnight. Only in a few places today, such as North Korea, is commercial advertising unknown. Nonetheless, even there, "ads" praising the country's leader are prevalent. From these considerations, an important principle can be derived: *Advertising is essential to any modern market economy.* There are no known instances in which there is a free market *and* an advertising-free society.

This chapter briefly looks at advertising's history, and then reviews the organization of the advertising industry and the way its professional communicators develop their messages. This includes the advertising industry's attention to its strategies of persuasion, the types of media that are used, and the kinds of research that play an important role in the process. The chapter also discusses both criticisms of the industry and controls that are exercised over advertising.

ADVERTISING IN AMERICA: A BRIEF HISTORY

The American Museum of Advertising in Portland, Oregon, has examples of advertising going back to the Greeks and Romans. Such notices called attention to the products of artisans who hand-produced products ranging from weapons to clothing. Although historians often date modern advertising in the United States to the last decades of the 1800s, some forms of advertising are actually much older than that. The earliest advertising messages were communicated even during the Middle Ages and were those of criers or simple signs above shops. Another origin of modern advertising was the trademarks used by craftworkers and early merchants to distinguish their wares from those of others. The watermarks of printers were also distinctive forms of advertising.

In colonial America, advertisers used many media. Coffee, chocolate, and tea, to name a few items, were hawked in messages on printed broadsides (pamphlets), announced in simple ads in almanacs as well as in the early newspapers and other periodicals. Early communications media thus were already factors in the marketplace for goods and services even before modern newspapers arrived. But advertising was not much of a source of revenue for colonial newspapers. They depended on subscriptions paid by readers and in some cases on government printing contracts for public announcements. Advertising in colonial times was very subdued—even primitive—by modern standards and rarely overshadowed the editorial content of the papers.

According to Daniel J. Boorstin, until recently social historians have all but ignored both early and contemporary advertising. Even most journalism histories seldom deal with advertising's role in creating the modern mass media. One historical factor that does stand out to help explain why modern advertising took hold and developed quickly in the United States is *abundance*. It seems clear that where resources are scarce, there is little or no need for manufacturers or producers to promote their wares. As economic historian David Potter wrote:

> It is when potential supply outstrips demand—that is when abundance prevails—that advertising begins to fulfill a really essential function. In this situation the producer knows that the limitation upon his operations and upon his growth no longer lies, as it lay historically, in his productive capacity, for he can always produce as much as the market will absorb; the limitation has shifted to the market, and it is selling capacity which controls his growth.[1]

THE INDUSTRIAL REVOLUTION

During the 1800s, advertising changed from primitive messages on simple printed handbills and crude outdoor announcements—such as signs painted on barns—to complex messages published in newspapers and magazines.

A number of colorful individuals stood out in the 1800s who understood the power of advertising. One was P. T. Barnum, whose circus (modestly characterized as "The Greatest Show on Earth!") became enormously popular. He grasped the principle that constant overblown claims, garish messages on posters or handbills, along with colorful parades through towns prior to the performance, brought in the public and its money.

Patent medicines. Starting even before the Civil War, a number of hucksters—the proverbial "snake-oil salesmen"—began to sell various products that were (it was claimed) guaranteed to cure a long list of human ailments. Although not strictly a product of the Industrial Revolution, in many ways these patent medicines led the way in demonstrating the huge financial benefits that could be achieved by advertising.

One of the most remarkable advertising successes of all times was achieved by a Quaker woman from Lynn, Massachusetts. On her kitchen stove she would occasionally cook up a mixture of herbs, seeds, and roots and give bottles of the stuff—well laced with alcohol—to her female friends. They reported that the mixture seemed to relieve what were delicately termed at the time "female complaints" (e.g, menstrual cramps, kidney discomfort, and others). In retrospect, it is little wonder that the women felt better. The strong alcohol base of the product could make almost anyone feel a bit better. In 1875, her two sons had the idea of promoting the mixture for sale by using pamphlets, and eventually through an ad in the *Boston Herald*. They called it "Lydia Pinkham's Vegetable Compound." Almost immediately, they received a large number of orders from patent medicine wholesalers.

When that happened they began a systematic and nationwide advertising campaign, based in part on newspapers but also by using huge signs painted on barns, houses, and even large rocks. One of the most effective features of their ads was a picture of Lydia Pinkham herself: a dignified and rather elegant lady who had such a look of sincerity and honesty that few could doubt her claims.

But it was both expanding world trade and the Industrial Revolution, with its huge increase in the production of factory-made goods, that would make advertising so essential to the growing economy. All during the 1800s the need for advertising grew naturally as manufacturers, importers, and retailers wanted to market their expanding arrays of goods. As was noted in Chapter 3, as the nineteenth century progressed, advertising in newspapers accounted for an increasing proportion of their content and earnings. Newspapers were the ideal medium. The commercial announcements and notices of the time were mainly for locally marketed goods and services.

The development of brands.   Up until about the time of the Civil War, most of what was for sale at local stores was purchased in bulk. There were few "brands" as we know them today. The development of brands for packaged, bottled, and canned goods, as well as other products, was one of the most important developments in the history of advertising. A brand did two things: (1) It standardized the product, bringing "predictability" as to its characteristics for the consumer. If the purchaser was familiar with the brand, he or she knew just what it would be like when the package was opened. In fact, brands often ensured that the consumer would develop a kind of "loyalty" to the product, based on repeated satisfaction. (2) Brands also worked well for advertisers. They provided a clear identity for a product—the merits of which could be promoted in advertisements. Slogans were produced to reinforce these consistency and merit ideas. With advertising, a bar of soap could be portrayed as being associated with a phrase such as "it floats." Or, a brand of coffee could be promoted as "good to the last drop," or that it was "mountain grown." These two ideas helped reinforce recognition of the brand name. Before brands, for example, crackers came in barrels and were sold by weight. The same was true of flour, beans, and rice. Household liquids, such as vinegar or syrup, were stored in tanks and were dispensed to customers in jugs or other containers that many brought with them. Buying foods like cheese followed a similar pattern: chunks were cut from a large, round cheese and wrapped in cloth or even newspaper. There were no brand-labeled packages, boxes, or bottles of such products displayed on shelves from which the consumer could choose. A woman who wanted to buy soap would indicate to the store owner the number of pounds she needed, and then that would be cut from a large slab. She would use that product not only to wash her family's laundry, but also for her family's bath. The problem with such bulk-purchased goods was that there was no way to predict consistency of quality, taste, ingredients, or effectiveness.

Other changes came in the promotion of products through advertising. As early as 1851, a soap manufacturer named B. T. Babbitt introduced the preformed *bar* of soap, wrapped in its own paper cover. When the public was initially unresponsive to the product, Babbitt introduced a history-making innovation. He offered a *premium.* For every twenty-five empty soap wrappers a buyer presented, Babbitt promised a handsome colored picture in return. The lure attracted buyers by the thousands, and the idea of premiums took hold. We have been living with them ever since. For example, a major cigarette manufacturer currently offers one million prizes for coupons obtained by purchasing packs. These premiums range from a free package of cigarettes to cool T-shirts and even a free trip to an exotic place for two. Many public health authorities believe that this practice has been a factor in recent increases in teen smoking.[2]

By the end of the 1800s, the shift to brands was to open a whole new world of advertising. It took a while for the innovation to catch on. Surpassing the successes of even the patent medicines was the creation of three major name-brand items—which were new in 1900. One was Royal Baking Powder—a simple mixture of bicarbonate of soda and a dry acid substance. When mixed with wet ingredients, the powder could be substituted for yeast—a rather considerable convenience for the housewife. Another successful brand was a soap made from vegetable oils (rather than the usual animal fats). This made it lighter than water, so a bar would float. It was said to be 99 and 44/100 percent pure (whatever that meant). The Procter family of Cincinnati marketed it as Ivory Soap. Still another was an inexpensive brand of footwear (Douglass Shoes) that were nationally marketed. Soon there were many manufacturers competing to produce and market a lengthy variety of commonly used household and personal items under brand names, which would be packaged in convenient cans, bottles, and boxes.[3] This competition made advertising even more essential.

Nationally circulated general magazines. In the late nineteenth century, a combination of improved transportation, cheap new postal rates favorable to regularly issued publications, and the desire of business for national markets stimulated the growth of national magazines. At first the magazines were little interested in advertising and restricted it to a single page at the end of the periodical. Gradually, however, they began to follow the lead of Benjamin Day and his remarkably successful penny newspaper—that is, to depend significantly on advertising revenues to recover their costs and increase their profits. Soon, the idea caught on that the reader should be able to buy the magazine for a fraction of its actual production cost, and that advertising should pay handsomely for advertising space. This turned out to be a very successful formula, and by the 1890s, magazines were inexpensive to buy and contained large amounts of advertisements. Some had hundreds of thousands of subscribers and were a truly effective way of presenting products to consumers.

The nationally circulated magazines appealed greatly to women. As was explained in Chapter 4, many offered special sections of interest to women, such as child-rearing, recipes, advice on fashions, plus serialized fiction. For the housewife, the profusion of goods advertised in these magazines offered a wondrous display of the abundant life. They also taught women their place in society as both consumers and homemakers.

> As advertisers increasingly defined women as their target audience, advertising-dependent magazines presented their women readers with fiction that encouraged them in their role as consumers. This encouragement took different forms depending on the class of women addressed. Magazines addressed to cash-poor women presented ways to earn money to buy advertised goods and helped to justify their purchase, while suggesting that such consumption could be consistent with their values of thrift and moral responsibility. Magazines addressed to middle-class women, on the other hand, discouraged autonomous work and encouraged them to seek fulfillment in shopping and the emotional caretaking of their families.[4]

Department stores. Another consequence of the Industrial Revolution and the expansion of world trade in the late 1800s was the department store. One of the earliest and most successful was Wannamaker's in Philadelphia. By 1880, it had established itself as a shopper's paradise. Establishments such as these displayed a dazzling array of goods never before assembled in such a way for the examination and shopping convenience of consumers. Just walking through their floors and aisles, and ogling the things that one might purchase, was an adventure. Such shopping came to be a regular part of the weekly routines of many urban, middle-class women. However, to get women into the store and encourage them to purchase, it was necessary to advertise the goods and services that they would encounter when they arrived. Newspapers were the advertising medium of choice. Department stores were local, as were the newspapers themselves. Thus, before the age of the automobile, which currently accounts for a huge part of the revenues of newspaper advertisers, the department stores were steady and profitable purchasers of advertising space.

A second event contributing to the development of consumerism, and also based on the Industrial Revolution, was the establishment of mail-order department stores. Montgomery Ward and Sears, Roebuck & Co. began to retail an abundance of wares through their catalogue. Mail-order catalogue sales were made possible when Rural Free Delivery began, a new feature of the U.S. Postal Service that had come into being shortly after the Civil War. This was a blessing for rural Americans, who made up the majority of the population. Farm families, previously isolated from seeing the great abundance of goods available, because of their dispersion on farms, could now examine a dazzling array of goods in the catalogues and order them through the mail to be delivered by parcel post. Advertising such products under the brand names of the mail-order houses was a major development in retailing and a landmark in the history of advertising.

Establishing the advertising agency. As the advertising industry grew, newspapers and magazines developed their own internal advertising departments catering to those commercial interests that wanted to buy their advertising space. Publications began to compete aggressively for the advertiser's business, especially in towns where there were competing media. Large retail organizations that purchased large amounts of advertising also began to established their own advertising departments to plan and place their ads.

What was to come was an independent *agency* that worked neither for the media directly nor under the control of businesses that needed to advertise their wares. What emerged was an organization that coordinated the activities of both—and derived a profit from each. The idea was slow in catching on. The very first advertising agent using this strategy to open shop in the United States was Volney Parker. In Philadelphia in 1848, he began soliciting orders for advertising for newspapers. His customers produced their own copy that touted their wares. What Volney did was to buy large blocks of newspaper space cheaply, and then sell it at a profit to those who wanted to advertise their products in the paper. Within a few years, others launched similar firms in Boston and New York City.[5]

During later decades in the 1800s, various kinds of intermediaries were facilitating the relationship between commercial enterprises and media organizations. As was the case with Volney, at first these intermediaries were merely space brokers who arranged for the placement of ads. Later, they expanded their operations to provide other kinds of services and became the world's first *advertising agencies*—organizations that specifically provided advertising copy, creative assistance, and management of advertising strategies to large numbers of clients. By 1910, a number of such agencies had been established in New York City, Boston, and other large cities. They

Members of the staff of an advertising agency present and review proposed commercials and a print campaign for a new product in a process that is repeated daily in the industry.

had begun to provide their customers with full services in creating advertising messages and campaigns, as well as in buying media space in newspapers and magazines, which were likely to be read by audiences who would be interested in their products.

ADVERTISING-SUPPORTED MODERN MEDIA

In the twentieth century, as new mass media were developed, the importance of advertising in promoting products accelerated greatly. Radio and television were ideal media to carry both national and local advertising, and they were especially effective. As we have seen in earlier chapters, the broadcast media soon became dependent on advertising revenues. One reason why they were effective was that their audiences paid nothing; a newspaper or magazine required the receiver to purchase a subscription or a copy of the publication. Broadcast messages were not only free but were also difficult to avoid. Thus, broadcasting for both local and national advertising was added to print as a major transmitter of persuasive messages.

Generally, then, as the industrial society developed and matured during the nineteenth and twentieth centuries, a *symbiotic relationship* developed to provide the financial foundation of the American system of mass communication. Many would agree with David Potter, who in 1969 said that "Marconi may have invented the wireless and Henry Luce may have invented the news magazine, but it is advertising that has made both wireless and news magazines what they are in America today."[6]

Thus, the main features of the modern advertising industry were already in place by the time of World War II. Its development both depended on and stimulated the growth of both the old and the new mass media. It could not have flowered without businesses eager to make profits, without the media eager to earn revenue by carrying their advertising messages, and without consumers ready to spend money—

income earned from jobs in the great industrial growth that was taking place in the United States. Thus, advertising became a deeply established social institution linking our nation's productivity, our mass media, and our consuming public.

THE STRUCTURE OF THE CONTEMPORARY ADVERTISING INDUSTRY

The advertising industry exists for the purpose of putting businesses who want to market and distribute goods and services in touch with consumers who want to buy and use them. Viewed in this way, the advertising industry today is a kind of facilitator between the advertiser and the public. Components of the industry include: (1) *advertising agencies* of various kinds, (2) *media service organizations,* (3) *suppliers of supporting services* ranging from research to commercial art, and (4) *advertising media.* The last category includes print, electronic, digital, outdoor, specialty, direct-mail, and a number of highly specialized or even exotic types of advertising. These are only the bare bones of the industry, and everything on the list comes in several versions, variations, and sizes. For example, there are massive national advertising agencies with offices in scores of cities in the United States and abroad, and there are small, local agencies with only a handful of employees and a few accounts.

Although the advertising industry is made up of a broad spectrum of independent business interests, and is by no means a tightly controlled national entity, it is held together by various voluntary organizations and associations. There are, for example, associations of advertisers and advertising agencies. These include the important American Association of Advertising Agencies (or four As) and the Association of National Advertisers (the clients of agencies), as well as regional and state groups. There are also media associations concerned with advertising, including the Newspaper Advertising Bureau, the Outdoor Advertising Institute, the Television Bureau of Advertising, and the Cable Television Advertising Bureau, to name only a few.

figure11.1

The Structure of a Typical Advertising Agency

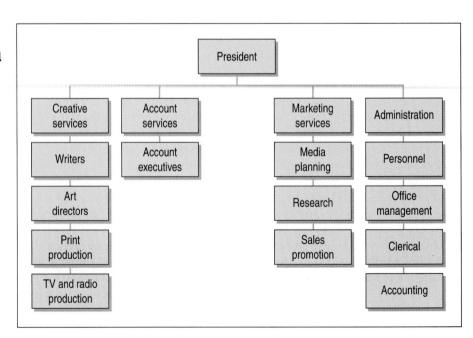

Table 11.1 Rankings of Advertising Agencies by Income (in millions)		
A. Top Ten U.S. Agencies by Worldwide Gross Income	**(in millions)**	**Percentage Change**
1 Dentsu, Inc., Tokyo	$2,108.8	14.5
2 McCann-Erickson Worldwide, New York	$1,864.7	14.3
3 BBDO Worldwide, New York	$1,414.9	11.5
4 J. Walter Thompson Co., New York	$1,270.4	10.5
5 Euro RSCG Worldwide, New York	$1,269.0	15.5
6 Grey Advertising, New York	$1,193.4	12.9
7 DDB Worldwide Communications, New York	$1,078.0	10.5
8 Publicis Groupe, S.A., Paris	$1,009.2	16.9
9 Leo Burnett Co., Chicago	$957.7	14.3
10 Ogilvy & Mather Worldwide, New York	$937.9	9.4
B. Top Ten U.S. Agencies by U.S. Gross Income	**(in millions)**	**Percentage Change**
1 Grey Advertising, New York	$535.8	12.2
2 J. Walter Thompson Co., New York	$496.2	19.5
3 McCann-Erickson Worldwide, New York	$466.9	18.7
4 FCB Worldwide, New York	$452.8	12.2
5 Leo Burnett Co., Chicago	$396.8	6.7
6 Euro RSCG Worldwide, New York	$378.4	20.6
7 Y & R Advertising, New York	$365.1	7.6
8 BBDO Worldwide, New York	$361.1	7.3
9 DDB Worldwide Communications, New York	$342.8	8.3
10 Ogilvy & Mather Worldwide, New York	$327.7	13.0
C. Top Ten U.S. Cities for Advertising by Billing	**(in millions)**	**Percentage Change**
1 New York	$54,851.0	16.6
2 Chicago	$15,373.5	13.7
3 Los Angeles	$11,581.4	9.7
4 Detroit	$9,909.7	21.0
5 San Francisco	$6,651.6	19.7
6 Boston	$4,853.8	28.4
7 Minneapolis	$ 4,438.1	9.6
8 Dallas	$3,364.5	12.2
9 New Jersey	$2,791.3	7.2
10 Atlanta	$2,153.4	13.9

Source: Reprinted with permission from the April 24, 2000 issue of *Advertising Age.* Copyright, Crain Communications, Inc., 2000.

These organizations and others produce regular publications that carry news of the advertising industry. Some are general-interest periodicals for advertising (like *Advertising Age*), whereas others are very specific (like *Folio,* which deals with magazine marketing). Each category of advertising (direct mail, outdoor signs, packaging, and so on) has its own publications.

All this adds up to a huge industry with a substantial economic impact. In the late 1990s, American businesses spent more than $126 billion per year on advertising, including that conveyed by the media and such other approaches as direct-mail marketing. Industry analysts predict that this number will approach $200 billion by the early 2000s.

Of the total amount of advertising spending as the 1990s came to a close, media were getting about 60 percent, with the rest going to such activities as sales promotion, direct marketing, package design, and other activities. It was estimated that the top one hundred advertising agencies—the principal "middlemen" between advertisers, the media, and the public—were getting about 36 percent of this amount, which represented a slight but noticeable decline from earlier decades. It has also been estimated that well over a quarter million people are currently employed in advertising. More than half of them work in advertising agencies in the United States. The U.S. Bureau of the Census currently estimates that there are nearly fifteen thousand establishments engaged in the advertising business, including nearly ten thousand advertising agencies.

The trend toward concentration of ownership that we have seen elsewhere in the communication industry has also characterized advertising. The top grossing agencies, which make up only a tiny fraction of the total number of such firms, handle about one third of all of the nation's advertising business! For example, Young & Rubicam, the largest agency in the United States, now has worldwide billings over $8 billion annually, with forty U.S. offices and over two hundred offices in other countries.

The various elements of the advertising industry noted above are interrelated parts of a dynamic system that is very competitive. The image of the harried advertising account executive often presented in movies and television may be an overstatement, but advertising is a field marked by intense energy and fervent competition as agencies and firms do battle for accounts.

TYPES OF ADVERTISING AGENCIES

At one time, most major advertising agencies and the preponderance of the advertising business were based in New York City—mainly in and around Madison Avenue. While there were strong regional centers like Chicago, Boston, Los Angeles, and a few others, serious national advertisers usually looked to New York for big-time agencies. In the 1980s and 1990s, with the advance of Internet technologies, many local and regional agencies in smaller cities like Atlanta, Minneapolis, Seattle, Portland, and Kansas City began to pick up major national accounts outside of their own regions. The industry is still firmly planted in New York, which remains the capital of virtually all of the mass communications industries. But observers are closely watching these regional developments.

Advertising agencies have come a long way since the nineteenth century, when they were essentially space brokers. Today, there are several different types. One is the *full-service agency,* which performs virtually every aspect of the advertising process for its clients. Another is the *creative boutique,* which is much smaller and is focused on providing creative ideas for ads and on execution of those ideas. Still another is the *specialist agency,* which focuses on particular products or services, such as foods, women's products, or financial services. A fourth is the *in-house agency* or *department,* which serves a single industry, chain of stores, large manufacturer, or other business. The role played by each is reviewed briefly.

Full-service agency. The full-service agency employs writers, artists, media experts, researchers, television producers, account executives, and others as part of the organization. Advertising scholar William Arens has identified three main functions of the full-service advertising agency:[7]

1. *Planning.* The agency must know its client, its product, the competition, and the market well enough to recommend plans for advertising.

2. *Creation and execution.* The agency creates the advertisements and contacts the media that will present them to the intended audience.
3. *Coordination.* The agency works with salespeople, distributors, researchers, and retailers to see that the advertising works.[8]

Within the full-service agency are several major functions and groups that work as a team to accomplish their overall goals. These can be summarized in the following terms:

1. *Account management.* The account executive and his or her staff provide services to a firm or product. An account management director is responsible for relations between the agency and the client.
2. *The creative department.* The creative director supervises writers, directors, artists, and producers who write and design the ads, including video production and Internet applications.
3. *Media selection.* A media director heads a department in which the specific media to be used for particular ads are chosen.
4. *The research department.* Advertising messages are pretested and data are gathered to help the creative staff fashion a specific design and message. The research director supervises in-house research and hires outside research firms for more extensive national and regional studies.
5. *Internal control.* The administrative operations of the agency, including public relations, are concentrated in one department.

An administrative director runs the agency. Of course, large agencies have a board of directors and the usual trappings of any big business.

An advertising agency offers *service,* and it is confidence in that service that brings the client to pay a significant percentage of their total billings (costs of their advertising efforts) to the ad agency. The exact amounts can differ but 15 percent would be typical. Just what happens from the time of the initial contact between an agency and a client to the finished advertising campaign varies considerably, depending on the size of the agency and the nature of the account. But essentially, this is how it works.

To establish a relationship with a client, the *account management director* either contacts a business—say, a local company that manufactures solar heating devices—or someone from the business contacts the advertising agency. Indeed, the company may contact several agencies and ask all of them for ad proposals—with the understanding that only one will receive the account. The account management director then selects an *account executive* from within the agency, who arranges a meeting between *company executives* from the solar heating firm, his or her boss (the account management director), and other appropriate people from the agency. They discuss potential advertising objectives, the budget, and the timetable. In many ways, the strategy can be compared to that used to plan a military operation or campaign. The first step is *intelligence-gathering.* In a process called "situation analysis," every conceivable set of facts about the product, its consumers, as well as the expectations of the client is reviewed before any attempt is undertaken to design ads or a campaign. Such questions are asked as: Exactly what does this device do? What kinds of people use it and for what purpose? How is it better than its competitors? Who are likely future customers for the device? What advertising has been done in the past with what media, what appeals, and what results? What medium will best reach the likely customers? What persuasive strategies and appeals are likely to be effective in a new ad campaign?

Once the full set of background information and facts about the product are understood, the account executive goes to work inside the agency. The *research department* conducts studies or assembles information to answer some of the questions about potential consumers. The agency's *creative department* holds brainstorming sessions, discussing ideas for a potential campaign. *Artists* and *writers*, who have been informed of all background facts and research results, create sample ads. These may be rough sketches of newspaper or magazine advertisements, broadcast storyboards for television (which are a series of drawings on a panel indicating each step of a commercial), or other preliminary versions of ads being prepared for other media. Depending on how complex and detailed the campaign will be, a variety of other specialists may be involved, such as sound engineers, graphic artists, lighting experts, and actors.

The results of all this creative activity are the *preliminary versions of ads* from which the final versions will be chosen. These ad candidates are then *pretested* on

Leo Burnett USA, the advertising agency, produced this emotion-evoking television commercial for Hallmark Cards, Inc., which featured a surprise 100th birthday party for an African-American woman. The universal appeal of this commercial led to its designation by *Advertising Age* as one of the 50 Best Commercials of the 1990s.

potential consumers. The agency's research department conducts or supervises this pretesting and suggests which of several approaches would probably work best for the client. In recent years, copy-testing research has grown in importance, wherein all elements of a print ad or broadcast commercial are tested carefully for consumer reactions. This process removes some of the financial risks of advertising and generally pleases the client. Research also guides the agency and client in deciding what media to use. Various options are print, broadcast, the Internet, outdoor advertising, on matchbook covers and subways, and so on.

The account executive then gathers this information and, along with other agency personnel, conducts a *presentation* for the client company. Potential costs are clearly laid out so that the company can evaluate the proposal. This type of presentation is often elaborate, with slide and videocassette presentations and sample ads. Research and creative personnel discuss various features of the ads, and members from the media department discuss the advantages and disadvantages of using particular media for the campaign. Now the ball is in the client company's court: The client executives either accept or reject the agency's proposal. Their acceptance may, of course, be conditional on various modifications they prefer.

Once the go-ahead is given, the account executive coordinates activity within the agency to produce the actual ads. He or she works with the *media department* to contact the appropriate media and arrange for the advertising campaign to reach the public. The research department prepares its strategy to *evaluate* the campaign so that the agency can present evidence about whom the campaign has actually reached and with what results. Hopefully, these will ensure that the account will be renewed in the future.

Finally, the advertisement reaches the *consumer* as he or she reads a newspaper or magazine, watches TV, listens to the radio, surfs the Internet, or uses some other medium. This is, of course, the "bottom line," where "the rubber hits the road." Brand building is a critical goal, but the ultimate test of the effectiveness of any advertisement or campaign is not whether the client likes the ads, but whether they bring about an increase in the sales of the product or service. The goal, after all, is to motivate an ample number of consumers to head toward a local store to buy the product or use the service. Some ads fail this test; others succeed.

Creative boutique. A boutique agency, unlike its full-service counterpart, has more limited goals and offers fewer services. It is essentially a *creative department* and may hire other agencies and independent groups to provide other kinds of advertising services for particular clients and products or services. Often boutiques work closely with in-house agencies—that is, a small ad group or department formed by a business to handle its own products. Most boutiques are small agencies established by people who once worked for full-service agencies.

Specialist agency. Obviously, to reach just the right target audience, advertisements must be placed in appropriate media. Space or time has to be arranged so that the ad can appear in those media. Specialist agencies, which are sometimes called *media service organizations,* exist to provide an important service for advertisers. They buy space in the media at reasonable rates. They then negotiate with advertising agencies who need to use that space or time. Many people in these media service organizations also once worked for advertising agencies.

One type of media service organization is the national advertising representative, who has special expertise in network television rates and knows the ideal times to display particular kinds of products. Often national advertising representatives buy blocks of television time in advance and then sell the time to various advertising agencies for particular accounts. They get involved with an account late in the game, usually after a lot of planning has been done. Other kinds of media service organizations include independent design firms and television production companies. Usually they work with the advertising agency and not directly with the advertiser.

In-house agency or department. Whole industries, as well as large department stores or other businesses, sometimes have their own internal agencies or advertising departments. Unlike advertising agencies, which are independent "middlemen" serving several accounts or businesses, the advertising department of a business works exclusively with that firm's products or services and is part of its staff. This department has an intimate knowledge of the business or industry and makes proposals for advertising plans and strategies. Its main concern is the final outcome—increasing sales or heightening the awareness of a particular product or service. Advertising departments work closely with independent advertising agencies,

Advertisements can appear almost anywhere, even on the body of a bus as this appeal to tourists to "Experience Downtown Orlando" in Florida. This is a moving form of outdoor advertising. Ads are found on billboards, in cabs, in skywriting, in print and electronic media, and increasingly on the Internet.

which compete for their business, and present alternative proposals for an advertising campaign. Some retail advertising departments are organized and function just like a small advertising agency, and place advertising directly with local media. For more complicated transactions that involve research and other specialties, however, they are likely to look to independent agencies for assistance.

ADVERTISING MEDIA

All of the standard mass media are, of course, advertising vehicles. Newspapers, magazines, television and radio stations, cable companies, the Internet, and other media are all involved. Some have advertising departments. At both the national and the local level, the media compete vigorously for advertising dollars. Each of the major media has some kind of national advertising association that gathers data and tries to show that its medium is the "best buy" for reaching particular audiences. At the local level, advertising salespeople who work for media organizations—such as newspapers or radio or TV stations—sell space or time, either directly to a business or to a business through an advertising agency or media service organization.

In selecting a medium, the business or advertising agency considers what target audience is to be reached, the cost of advertising, and the effectiveness of a medium for reaching the desired consumers. While various sources report slightly different data, it is clear that newspapers get the largest share of the advertising dollar among the traditional mass media—currently about one fourth. This is followed by television, with about one fifth. Other media are direct mail (just under one fifth), the yellow pages (less than 10 percent), radio (only about 6 percent), magazines (around 5 percent), and all other types (about 15 percent).

Since the late nineteenth century, media that carried advertising dominated the communications industry and produced the lion's share of advertising-derived media revenues. During the 1990s, however, that began to change. Such segments of the media industry as the World Wide Web, videocassettes, premium and pay-per-view cable channels, television shopping networks, business information services, and others became increasingly important factors in the media mix. Some segments carry advertisements but others do not. Increasingly, audiences are being asked to pay more of "the freight" for their media fare. For example, newspapers and magazines have steadily raised their prices in recent years, and pay-per-view events such as prizefights and wrestling matches may charge as much as $50 for a single evening's event. Internet newspapers and various specialized digital newsletters are used instead of the traditional forms. Advertising is not central to such media. In such a climate, it is probable that advertising will play a slightly less significant role than in the past, and certainly the idea that people pay little or nothing for their media because of advertising will no longer be true.[9]

The "other types" of advertising media include *retail signs* and *displays* in stores; *specialty advertising,* as on pens, calendars, and similar items; *outdoor advertising* on billboards and other large surfaces; *transit advertising* in the form of placards on buses and other vehicles; and *business-site advertising* in such settings as trade shows. There are even rather exotic forms, such as an *electronic headline advertising* in taxicabs, and even commercial messages posted in public restrooms. But this list gives only a hint of the diverse media for advertising. There are even firms that specialize in skywriting and towing of banners by aircraft, or messages on blimps.

Not to be overlooked as a major advertising medium is *direct mail* and *telemarketing* (via the telephone). Both are growing very rapidly. Direct mail began with low rates offered by the post office for deliveries of catalogues, brochures, broadsides, and other materials. Advanced technologies are now being used to call potential customers on the telephone (automated dialing, etc.). As further advances are made in communications technologies it is virtually certain that they will be added to the list of "advertising media."

figure11.2 **Advertising Spending by Medium**

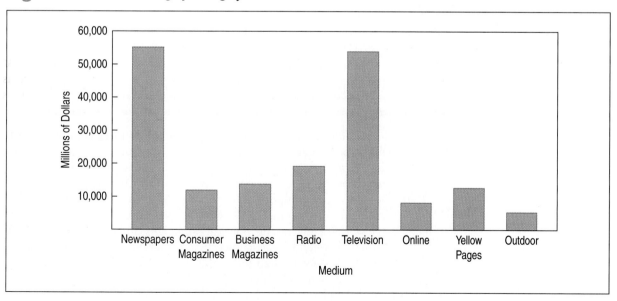

Table 11.2	Top Ten National Advertisers		
Rank	**Advertiser**	**Ad Spending in 1998 (in millions)**	**Percentage Change**
1	General Motors Corp.	$2,940.4	−4.8
2	Procter & Gamble Co.	$2,650.3	−3.4
3	Philip Morris Cos.	$2,049.3	−4.1
4	DaimlerChrysler	$1,646.7	−0.4
5	Sears, Roebuck & Co.	$1,578.3	7.5
6	Ford Motor Co.	$1,520.7	11.3
7	AT & T Corp.	$1,428.0	12.1
8	Walt Disney Co.	$1,358.7	7.9
9	Pepsi Co.	$1,263.4	1.2
10	Diageo	$1,205.7	−1.9

Source: Reprinted with permission from the September 27, 1999 issue of *Advertising Age*. Copyright, Crain Communications, Inc., 1999.

Table 11.3	Prime-Time Media Buys

These were the most expensive prime-time advertising buys for commercials during the 2000–2001 television season based on thirty-second units.

	$ per :30
ER (NBC)	$620,000
Friends (NBC)	540,000
Will & Grace (NBC)	480,000
Just Shoot Me (NBC)	465,000
Everybody Loves Raymond (CBS)	460,000
Cursed (NBC)	410,000
Becker (CBS)	365,000
Drew Carey (ABC)	360,000
Monday Night Football (ABC)	360,000
Ally McBeal (Fox)	335,000
The Simpsons (Fox)	335,000

Source: Reprinted with permission from the October 2, 2000 issue of *Advertising Age*. Copyright, Crain Communications, Inc., 2000.

ADVERTISING AS PERSUASIVE COMMUNICATION

The idea of *persuasion* has ancient roots. Centuries before mass communication became available, when the human voice was the only medium that could be used, *rhetoric* was used as a strategy for influencing the beliefs and actions of people. It was a time when the words used in a speech, the ways in which arguments were presented, and the elegance of composition of messages were the only means available to sway the judgments and conduct of listeners. In that sense, rhetoric is as important today in the world of advertising, political campaigns, and fundraising as it was when Mark Antony delivered his classic speech honoring the death of Julius Caesar. In any promotional message devised today, the message must be constructed with exquisite care if it is to achieve its goal. Words have to be carefully selected; arguments explaining why people should take the recommended actions must be skillfully organized; and the overall composition of the message must fit easily into the cultural habits of the target audience.

In more modern times, social scientists have studied various strategies that have been used to persuade populations to believe or behave in a host of different ways.[10] The process of persuasion lies at the heart of such widely studied activities as *propaganda*—using media to sway peoples' commitments to such matters as loyalty to a particular leader, acceptance of a specific political system, willingness to make personal sacrifices in times of war, and so on. Persuasion also is the basic process of the *political campaign* in countries within which ordinary citizens can play a role in selecting their leaders as they compete in elections. It is also fundamental to shaping or changing *public opinion* as legislators need to seek popular support for particular social programs or economic policies.

In such contexts, a very large body of research and theory has accumulated revealing the *persuasive strategies* that communicators have used in seeking to accomplish their goals. Such strategies are based on underlying psychological and sociological assumptions about how human beings can be motivated to adopt particular beliefs or to take actions that are desired by the communicator.

Not all advertising focuses on a specific product, such as diapers, oatmeal, or soap. Such ads are the mainstay of the industry and the goal is to motivate purchases. Another form of advertising, called *institutional advertising,* is much less direct. For example, a company that makes paper and other forest-related products presents a television commercial or full-page magazine picture in color about the virtues of a beautiful, well-managed forest showing cute animals, but saying nothing about its specific product, providing only the corporation's name. The goal is, of course, to get the public to associate the corporation with the "selfless" ad and lovely images—fostering beliefs that here is a company that "really cares."

One of the basic issues in designing any form of persuasive message, regardless of the strategy employed, is to define exactly what the message is expected to accomplish. There are at least two ways to define success in terms of persuasion. One would be that some *personal orientation* has been changed—as in the institutional example above—in which some opinion, belief, feeling, or attitude of members of a target audience have been altered in ways desired by the communicator. A more demanding definition would be that a particular form of *overt behavior* on the part of audience members has been triggered. This means that a person actually buys the product, votes for the candidate, gives a donation, or engages in some other form of action that the message is intended to motivate. Both of these outcomes can be important, often for different types of clients, but the underlying strategies on which they are based may have much in common.

BASIC STRATEGIES FOR CONSTRUCTING PERSUASIVE MESSAGES

What basic strategies are available for the persuasive communicator who wants either to alter personal orientations or to motivate an audience to engage in a specific overt action? While there are many strategies that can be used, there are two that are basic. One that is very widely used in advertising is based on the assumption that both personal orientations and overt actions are based on *individual psychological factors*—either emotional or rational—that determine how a person will behave in a particular context. Persuasive communicators who develop their messages based on this idea are using a *psychodynamic* strategy. Another approach is to assume that peoples' beliefs and their overt actions are shaped by the context of social rules and shared cultural expectations of people around them. Here, messages are designed to convince the receiver that a particular form of belief or action is required by that context. Communicators using this set of assumptions make use of a *sociocultural* strategy for constructing their persuasive messages.[11]

The psychodynamic strategy. Modern advertising messages often use either emotional appeals or those based on reason (a cognitive approach) to persuade members of a target audience to purchase a particular product. An example of the use of reason would be an ad for an automobile that stresses economy of purchase and operation—claiming that "the [brand of car] is the choice of those who want the lowest initial price, the best gas mileage available, the highest trade-in value, the best record of repair costs, etc." Not all products lend themselves to this approach. Far more common is the use of *appeals,* which are more likely to be based on emotional needs, desires, and wants than on reason or rationality. Here, ads are based on such inducements as appeals to status—suggesting that "purchasing this product will cause others to see you as a more important person." Also common are sexual themes—indicating that "using this product will make you more attractive to members of the opposite sex, and that purchasing it will bring you more opportunities for engaging the behavior that you desire." Other commonly used appeals are based on greed, humor, fear, pride, envy, or other psychological states that presumably can be aroused by the message.

A simple interpretation of how such advertisements work is that the persuasive message arouses some sort of *feeling* or emotional state within the individual's psychological functioning, and this increases the receiver's motivation to behave in the manner desired by the advertiser. It is an old idea, but it does illustrate the psychodynamic strategy. As advertising scholar John Jones explains this rather elementary theory:

> To understand how advertising works, we need to know the order of events. . . .
> The earliest theory was based on a simple chain of causality described by Charles Raymond as *"learn, feel, do."* In this theory, people receive factual knowledge about a brand. As a result, their [feelings] toward the brand change and they develop a preference for it. Then they buy it. (italics added)[12]

The sociocultural strategy. It is obvious that the culture within which an individual makes decisions about action is profoundly important in shaping his or her behavior. Simply put, cultures shape actions, even though to someone looking on from outside some actions may seem bizarre or even insane. In traditional India, for example, the culturally approved practice of *suttee* dictated that when a woman's husband died it was the duty of a faithful wife to kill herself by throwing herself on his funeral pyre. Another example is during World War II, Japanese aviators deliberately dove their bomb-filled aircraft onto U.S. naval vessels. Other Japanese military personnel killed or sacrificed themselves in a parallel manner. Many Americans thought these actions were barbaric, but they were dictated by the requirements of the Japanese Bushido code—a set of cultural rules defining the proper norms and role definitions expected of a warrior.

In the United States, culture also dictates action. Strong cultural norms, role definitions, requirements of social ranking, and the existence of many forms of social controls (rewards and punishments) are deeply understood by the majority—and compliance is routine. Advertisements that call attention to these cultural requirements and urge the purchase of particular products or try to persuade people to engage in other kinds of actions to conform are based on a sociocultural strategy. This was precisely the strategy used in a recent Massachusetts antismoking campaign in which a series of ads was aimed at youths. As researchers Michael Siegal of Boston University and Lois Biener of the University of Massachusetts reported, ". . . the advertisements aimed to denormalize tobacco use by showing youths that smoking by their peers was not the *norm.*"[13] In the commercial world, an example would be an ad that urges the use of a particular mouthwash or a brand of deodorant. In such cases, the risk of offending accepted norms about bad breath or body smells provides a motivation for purchasing the product. Other ads may be based on *role definitions,* such as a mother's duty to provide certain nostrums to her child suffering from a cold or flu. *Ranking* is used in ads that show some high-ranking celebrity endorsing a product—assuming that the consumer wants to be like that prestigious person. In the case of *social controls,* advertisements for greeting cards are based on the culturally accepted concept that sending such missives is a sort of moral requirement on birthdays, anniversaries, Valentine's Day, and so on. Violate these norms and you risk criticism or even rejection (social control).

Thus, the basic approach used in the sociocultural strategy is straightforward: A persuasive message defines a cultural requirement. It indicates the consequences of failing to conform. It shows that use of the product will allow the consumer to avoid those negative consequences. In contrast to the simple *learn-feel-do* formula of the psychodynamic strategy, it is based on a *conform-or-be-punished* approach.

There are obviously many other ways in which persuasive messages can be designed. Advertisers are quite possibly the most creative professionals in the American labor force today. They constantly invent new ways to advertise and promote the wares of their clients. Some of them work enormously well and become a part of the popular culture. Others are less effective, and some are simply duds. But whatever strategy is being used, advertisers are following in the steps of ancient orators like Cicero, Socrates, Aristotle, and others who couched their arguments in persuasive rhetoric to try to get people to adopt their ideas.

CUTTING THROUGH THE CLUTTER: THE PROBLEM OF GAINING ATTENTION

If an advertisement is not seen and understood by members of the target audience, it is just so much wasted effort. Therefore, one of the most precious commodities for the advertiser is *attention.* For that reason, those who create the content of ads strive for compositions of words, colors, images, and sounds that capture and focus the attention of the TV viewer, the magazine or newspaper reader, the Internet surfer, or the radio listener. A major problem is the sheer volume of media content that exists today. Quite obviously there are limitations on the time that people can spend during any twenty-four hours attending to the media. Therefore, it is essential that advertisers understand in depth the exact nature of their target audience, the kinds of media to which they attend, and the pattern of interests and tastes that will bring such people to attend to a particular advertisement positioned among dozens, even hundreds, of competitors. An ad's ability to break through the clutter (of competing messages) and gain the attention of the right consumers, then, is a critical matter that can spell success or failure for any particular ad.

Creating ads that can do this, and at the same time retain the persuasive appeals that will sell the product or service, is one of the most creative challenges that exists in the contemporary communications world. If an agency does not have the kinds of individuals who can visualize ways in which their advertisements can capture the right attention of the right people, it will soon go out of business.

There has been a constant flow of advertising styles and content over the years in efforts to attract attention. In the 1890s, advertising styles included ornate and highly decorated soap and cosmetic ads. By the 1920s, these were gone and were replaced by the clean lines of the art deco designs. These gave way to psychedelic posterlike ads of the 1960s and early 1970s. More recently, during the 1990s, the clean and orderly Swiss Gothic look yielded to the more traditional and formal design we see today. It is, say design experts, all a matter of coordinating art and typography with content. Advertising that works is therefore an index of popular culture. That was recognized as far back as 1917, when writer Norman Douglas claimed, "You can tell the ideals of a nation by its advertisements."[14] Thus, changes in advertising over the years have been closely tied to changes in American society as a whole.

THE ROLE OF ADVERTISING RESEARCH

The advertising industry is a great generator of research. The reason is that those who pay for advertising are increasingly demanding *accountability*. They are not content with airy assurances from the advertising agency that "of course our ads for you are working—they are so clever that there can be no other conclusion." Clients are demanding hard evidence that the ads will be effective even before they get released to the media. After they have been presented to the public clients want data that show whether or not the ads are achieving their goals. Therefore, each of the advertising media hires research firms, rating services, and other groups to gather data showing the pulling power of that medium. To meet the goal of accountability, then, agencies conduct or contract for research on potential ad designs and actual effectiveness of the ads they prepare in terms of people's awareness of their clients' products and responses to them. In addition, academics—including sociologists, psychologists, and anthropologists—conduct research on the industry and its effects. Various types of researchers study topics such as marketing strategies, persuasive appeals, the psychology of consumer decisions, the effectiveness of different media, and every aspect of consumer behavior.

The results of certain kinds of research can be found in trade publications and academic periodicals, such as the *Journal of Advertising* and the *Journal of Advertising Research*. Some associations and groups will provide copies of research reports (for example, on the ability of magazines to sell a particular product such as whiskey) to anyone who asks for them. Much of the research on the effectiveness of advertising, however, is *proprietary*. That is, the results are the intellectual property of those who produce or pay for them for their own use, and then they hide the results from the public. Some proprietary results are gathered by research firms and then sold to the highest bidder. Such research may be conducted by a specific company for its own use or by agencies for particular clients. Much proprietary research is self-serving, designed to demonstrate that a consumer or advertising agency or business has been wise to take a certain action. As a result, there are always questions as to its objectivity. Businesses sometimes hire consultants to help them sort out the various claims of these kinds of researchers.

STUDYING THE EFFECTS OF ADVERTISING

If conducted within the rules of sound science, research can reveal whether a particular ad or campaign actually has the effects hoped for by those who have designed it. Mentioned above was an example of persuasive advertising based on a sociocultural strategy—urging youths to refrain from smoking. It was a $54 million television campaign sponsored the Massachusetts Department of Public Health. The goal of the campaign was to reduce the number of teenagers in the state who took up smoking. Funded by the state agency, the investigators followed a sample of six hundred of the state's teenagers for four years. None were smokers at the beginning of the study (although a few had experimented with cigarettes). The research focused on the effects on those who had been systematically exposed to a series of antismoking TV messages aired over several years in the state. The question was whether the ads were effective in preventing teenagers from becoming habitual smokers. Each of the ads showed a devastating health effect on a habitual smoker. Typical was a very ill-looking woman shown laying on a hospital bed breathing through an oxygen tube. In the ad she explained that she had been a heavy smoker for many years and that her resulting emphysema was now so advanced that it was probably going to be fatal. These were moving messages showing real people with real health problems. The ads stressed that smoking was not normative among young people. The results indicated that among children twelve to fourteen years old who had attended to the ads, taking up smoking had been cut in half (compared to similar youths who did not see the ads). This was a dramatic and very clear effect. However, among somewhat older children, whose orientations to smoking had already been formed before exposure, the normative strategy used in the ads had little effect.[15]

Advertising researchers may use surveys, panel studies, or experiments. Briefly, in panel studies (such as the smoking study discussed above), researchers may take a group of subjects and analyze their beliefs or behavior over time. In experiments, they may set up "treatment" and "control" groups to determine the effect of advertising messages. But whatever the method used, Russell Colley claims, good research on advertising effectiveness must make "a systematic evaluation of the degree to which the advertising succeeded in accomplishing predetermined goals."[16]

What are these goals? If advertising is successful, says Colley, it results in a sale, and to do that it must carry consumers through four levels of understanding: (1) *awareness* of a brand or company, (2) *comprehension* of the product and what it will do for them, (3) a *conviction* that they should buy the product, and (4) *action*—that is, buying the product.[17] Colley urges advertisers to use precise research, including the following types, to evaluate whether an advertisement has succeeded: (1) *Audience research.* This involves gathering basic data on the audience to be reached, including the number of people in various groups (based on age, sex, religion, and so on) who see and respond to advertising. (2) *Media research.* Media research involves studying the particular characteristics of each medium and what it can do, including comparisons of the pulling power and persuasiveness of various media. (3) *Copy research.* This means making comparisons of reactions of typical target audience members to particular advertisements. For example, researchers might compare the effectiveness of ads using a sexual appeal with those that arouse fear, humor, or some other reaction.

CONSUMER AND LIFESTYLE RESEARCH

A more general type of research focuses on *consumer behavior*. Much of this is also privately funded, proprietary, and hidden from public view. From their studies of consumers, researchers help businesses and ad agencies learn who their most likely consumers are and what kinds of advertising are most likely to reach them. They might study how needs, drives, and motives affect consumers' buying, how perception of an advertisement might vary among different categories of consumers, and what opinions, attitudes, beliefs, and prejudices should be taken into account in fashioning a particular message.[18] Some researchers focus on a clearly defined

John Zweig, Chief Executive Officer Branding & Identity, Health-care, and Specialist Communications, *WPP Group plc,* New York, New York

insights from
MEDIA LEADERS

John Zweig, a recognized leader in the fields of advertising and marketing, heads a major division of one of the world's leading communications firms with national, multinational, and global clients that offer advertising, media investment management, specialist communication, and other services. The group's companies include J. Walter Thompson, Ogilvy & Mather Worldwide, and others. WPP has some seventy-five companies with thirteen hundred offices in ninety-two countries with fifty-five thousand employees.

Q.   What first inspired your interest in the advertising and marketing communications field?

A. My father was in the advertising business in the fifties and sixties, so I was introduced at an early age. At first, I was probably most impressed that he ran a live television program and could tell you when sixty seconds were up without looking at his watch. But by the time I was a teenager I came to appreciate the range of skills advertising calls upon, the colorful and creative characters who populate the business, and the opportunities it offers to learn about and experience so many different industries. Today, I realize that my father was a pioneer in terms of his ability to relate specific product marketing problems to deeper human needs and aspirations. In this sense you could say that I was inspired by what the business could be—rather than what it often is.

Q.   How did you get from these interests to a position of leadership in a complex global firm that aspires to be "the preferred provider of multinational marketing services?"

A. Along with the natural curiosity and affinity for communication, which are the first requirements, I had the good fortune to experience the field from a number of perspectives—as a musician performing on beer and dog food jingles, as a writer of print and broadcast advertising copy, and as a brand manager at Procter & Gamble which, at least at that time, was recognized as a premier training ground among pack-

aged goods marketers. From P&G, I went to a small healthcare agency which I later ran and eventually sold to the WPP Group; and, through WPP's depth of resources and global reach, we were able to build the company into the largest marketing resource of its type in the world. Sir Martin Sorrell, who founded WPP, recruited me to the parent company in hopes that I could lead similarly successful initiatives across other disciplines and geographies. While it hasn't been a linear or completely logical progression, I have always found opportunities arising more as a consequence of the drive for growth and contribution, rather than from any prescribed education or background.

Q.   You have seen this field move from individual ad agencies to a business environment that is highly integrated and global in operations and ownership. What unanticipated challenges has that presented for you and your colleagues?

A. The challenge of consolidation and growth on a global scale is preserving the creative spark that started the whole thing in the first place. Advertising and marketing are ideas-based businesses and the impact of ideas determines whether our clients and their customers are enchanted, enthralled, and delighted. This has little to do with size. In fact, size can mitigate against it.

In a similar sense, becoming "highly integrated" can block individual autonomy and initiative, which are essential to creativity. There are many other challenges that relate to the management of imagination as opposed to manufacturing a product, but the key thought is that it cannot be engineered. It is a dynamic growth process which, only if you can tolerate the ambiguity and unpredictability, can you unlock the higher forms of collaboration and global, if not universal, potential.

Q.   What is your take on the current state and probable future of the advertising field?

A. Responding to the question exactly as phrased, I would say that both the current state and probable future of "advertising" are very limited. It is widely recognized that conventional television, radio, and print media have become fractionated; consumers are increasingly cynical and apathetic; and clients are changing their advertising agencies faster than they are changing their own CEOs and VPs of marketing. Everyone everywhere is demanding more for less.

Despite all of this, marketing communications is coming off a banner year and attracting both new talent and investors from sources that wouldn't have taken the industry seriously a few years ago. Marketing strategy has become synonymous with the overall business strategy, and "the brand" pervades everything. If we rise to this opportunity, in terms of our openness to its evolving character and values, and demonstrate our willingness to employ new ways of reaching people on their terms rather than ours, the prospects are fantastic—beyond anything we have seen or even imagined.

Q. **To what extent has the organization and structure of advertising been altered by the digital revolution, especially with regard to identifying and reaching businesses and consumers?**

A. Despite all the talk about speed and flexibility, the advertising business has been remarkably wed to the status quo. If you were to look at an organization chart of any of the big agencies from decades ago, the titles and structure have changed relatively little. The digital revolution has largely occurred outside of the mainstream, and the start-ups, roll-ups, and spinoffs have thus far resulted in very few sustainable businesses.

Ironically, one of the biggest boons to conventional advertising last year was plus $200 million worth of dot-com branding work (which has all but disappeared today). Where interactive media have had a transforming impact is in customer relationship marketing. This has not historically been the purview of advertising agencies, but rather of sales and distribution support, market research, and direct marketing.

Increasingly, capabilities in these areas are becoming part of our integrated offering, and we have acquired or made investments in at least fifty different businesses in order to both learn from and assimilate these skills. Of course, eventually all marketing will be relationship marketing, and digital media will predominate. But value-creating information and service will always come first, and without this being the primary emphasis, all that new technology offers is garbage at the speed of light.

Q. **What are the prospects for people entering this field today?**

A. Today, marketing and advertising present more career opportunities than does management consulting, investment banking, or dot-com start-ups. It is the only field that fuses the psychological, sociological, emotional, and aesthetic—with the commercial. Businesses are arguably the most powerful social institutions, and marketing is how a business communicates its values. It has become the rhythm of civilized life.

[That sense of involvement with humanity] is the most important basis for entering the field, rather than the money, which is also very good. However, while money is one important source of motivation, it really only touches the mind and moves the body.

Q. **In your experience what is the most satisfying aspect of working in this field? The least?**

A. To be adding value and producing an extraordinary impact for our clients through our imagination is intrinsically satisfying. Many people underestimate imagination by thinking of it as a tool to aid our physical experience. It is much more than that—it is the very essence of our being, our link with the infinite. What could be more fascinating? At its worst, the business suffers from the superstition of materialism—that everything can be fixed, that it shouldn't require any risk, and that the only true rewards are money and celebrity.

category, such as children. These specialists might examine children at different stages of their development, and then predict what kinds of things kids tend to like at certain ages and how they may influence their parents' purchases of toys, food, and so on. Advertising agencies may then use this information to prepare particular kinds of commercials, such as those for Saturday morning cartoon shows.

Another area of study is *lifestyle research,* which grew out of surveys studying trends in American living patterns and buying behavior. These studies inform advertisers about the changing attitudes and lifestyles that characterize potential consumers at different ages and stages—information that can be immensely helpful in fashioning an advertising campaign. For example, research shows that many older people today are moving out of larger houses where they raised families, into smaller new condos and apartments where they live alone. If they are interested in simplifying their domestic tasks so that they can have more free time, then they are new potential consumers for several specific types of goods. These would include such as items as single-serving frozen food dishes, microwave ovens, and airline tickets.[19] It would be worthwhile, then, for companies producing these items to use ads and media that are likely to reach that target audience.

Generally, then, advertising research has *applied* objectives. Its purpose is not to uncover basic concepts and theories that explain human behavior. Rather, it is to help stimulate sales of specific products or services to specific categories of consumers. Not surprisingly, this use of research, aimed at discovering how to manipulate people, has aroused considerable criticism. Although the research tries to demonstrate the effectiveness of particular advertisements and campaigns, critics claim that no scientific cause-and-effect relationship can be established between a given ad and the product or service it seeks to sell. Many social scientists believe that there are just too many uncontrollable variables in almost any situation to prove that particular ads actually work. In spite of these criticisms, however, those preparing or funding ads *believe* that advertising works—and they are the ones making decisions to spend millions of dollars to promote products and services.

ASSESSING TARGET AUDIENCES IN AN AGE OF MARKET SEGMENTATION

Although advertisers would like to sell their wares to everyone, they know that is not possible or perhaps even desirable, and so after careful research they go after a particular *segment* of the market. That segment may be defined by age, income, gender, education, race, and so on. At one time, most advertising was *product-oriented;* that is, the content was mainly concerned with a persuasive message about the attributes of the product. Now most advertising is *user-oriented,* with messages aimed at the specific needs, interests, and desires of particular consumers. As historian Daniel Pope puts it:

> Segmentation campaigns are user-focused and concentrate on consumer benefits rather than product attributes. They show people with whom the target audience can identify; people who represent a credible source of authority for them or who express their latent desires and dreams. Marketers hone in on consumers whose lifestyles and personalities have been carefully profiled.[20]

This new emphasis also suggests problems for the ethical presentation of advertising. It is much easier to apply a "truth in advertising" standard to statements about the qualities of a product than to apply indirect appeals to the desires of a segment of the audience. The trend toward market segmentation has also led to some specialization in advertising agencies and promoted the growth of media that appeal to a specific rather than a general audience.

Increasingly, a considerable yield of research evidence is emerging from what John Phelan of Fordham University calls "noble hype," that is, information campaigns aimed at good causes, such as the prevention of AIDS, heart disease, and other problems that affect society. A considerable amount of money has been poured into information campaign studies that use direct advertising strategies and messages to achieve such goals. The dramatic success of AIDS advertising—which is credited, in part, for the decrease in sexual activity likely to spread the disease—seems in a preliminary way to bode well for advertising effectiveness. At the same time, other researchers and critics say that AIDS is a special case that does not apply generally.

CRITICISM AND CONTROL OF ADVERTISING

Few people doubt that advertising has a significant impact or that it plays an important role in America. Most would agree that it reflects the culture and ideals of America—although many people also find that idea disturbing. Noting its importance, however, is very different from granting approval, and advertising has been criticized on many grounds. Some disparage advertising in general for its economic and social effects. Others criticize the content of some ads or their effects on some groups. These criticisms, as we shall see, have led to attempts to *regulate* advertising.

ECONOMIC AND SOCIAL CRITICISMS

A favorable view of advertising claims that it stimulates competition, which is good for the economy, and that it encourages the development of new products, which is good for consumers. Proof of the pudding, defenders say, is that people choose to buy the new products. And consumers are happier because they can choose from a greater variety of goods—a diversity stimulated by advertising. Advertising helps keep the economy and the number of jobs growing by encouraging people to buy more. And, by giving consumers information, advertising also helps them buy wisely. Advertising, then, is a key cog in the economic machine that can give us the good life and the fruits of capitalism—the "American dream."

However, critics have many answers to these comments. First, a great deal of advertising has nothing at all to do with objective information and does not help consumers make wise choices. Yet, even though they do not benefit, people must pay for advertising because its cost raises the price of the goods they buy. Therefore, say such critics, advertising is wasteful.

What is more, faultfinders say, rather than stimulating competition, advertising contributes to monopoly. Large firms can easily afford to invest in expensive national advertising, whereas smaller firms cannot. Larger firms can then perpetuate and even expand their hold on the market. For example, there are few local brands of cola that effectively compete in the marketplace alongside Coca-Cola and Pepsi. Even in the absence of an actual monopoly, some economists see advertising as hindering the development of perfect competition and leading to the condition known as imperfect competition. Several consequences may follow, including, according to critic Neil Borden, "improper allocation of capital investment," "underutilization of productive capacity and underemployment," "relatively rigid prices," and increasingly severe cyclical fluctuations in business, from inflation to recession and back again.[21]

According to Borden, even the diversity of goods stimulated by advertising is not beneficial. Anyone who has visited the breakfast cereal aisle of a large supermarket will understand that comment. Consumers, writes Borden, "are confused by the large number of meaningless product differentiations and consequently do not make wise choices."[22] Other critics point to more general supposed effects of advertising on individuals and society. Advertising is often believed to be manipulative and deceptive—indirectly teaching us that people are objects to be manipulated and deceived. By creating new wants and desires, advertising is also said to distance people from their "true" selves, contributing to their alienation and dissatisfaction, and making life an unending and hopeless quest for trivial goods or for the perfect image.

We certainly cannot evaluate point by point either the economic or social analyses advanced by advertising's critics, and we have stated their complaints rather briefly. But note that advertising is a form of mass communication, and the principles we will review in Chapter 15, regarding the media's influence on individuals and society, apply in general to advertising as well. That is, we should not think of advertising messages as "magic bullets" that cause uniform effects among all who receive them. Moreover, we would be ill-advised to consider the people seeing or hearing the messages as passive dolts receiving them helplessly, whether they want to or not. Nor should we think of advertising as a single, isolated cause of behavior, such as a decision to purchase a product. Reaction to advertising messages are locked into complex causes and influences that prevail among media audiences. Only a great deal of careful research will reveal the answers to whether the long list of criticisms of advertising are valid.

Discerning students who have taken a course in economics may recall how textbooks in that field devote little attention to advertising. The distinguished Harvard economist John Kenneth Galbraith said there is a good reason why such texts downplay its importance. Economists like to believe that consumer wants are held deeply within the human psyche. They subscribe to the idea of consumer sovereignty. But Galbraith writes:

> So long as wants are original with the consumer, their satisfaction serves the highest of human purposes. Specifically, an original, inherent need is being satisfied. And economics as a subject matter or science thus becomes basic to the highest human service. But [this] holds only if wants cannot be created, cultivated, shaped, deepened, or otherwise induced. Heaven forbid that wants should have their source in the producer of the product or service as aided and guided by his advertising agency.[23]

Thus, it would downgrade some of the most basic principles of economics if it were true that consumer wants were actually generated by advertising and not by human nature itself.

THE ISSUE OF CHILDREN AND ADVERTISING

Few aspects of advertising have generated more concern or research than advertising directed at children, specifically television commercials. Critics fear that children's advertising creates wants that cannot be fulfilled and that it prompts them to ask their parents for innumerable things that they cannot afford. Thus, children's advertising may generate tension and conflict in the family and teach many lessons that are simply wrong because children mistake advertisements for realistic portrayals of the world. In defense of such advertising, supporters maintain that it helps children learn to be consumers, a role that is vital to our economy.

Any evaluation of advertising's effect on children requires answers to several questions, including: (1) To what extent do children pay attention to commercials? (2) What, if any, effects do commercials have on children's thinking processes? (3) Can they, for example, distinguish between fact and fantasy in a commercial? (4) What, if any, influence do children exert on their parents' buying as a result of commercials?

Government, foundations, ad agencies, and other businesses have spent a lot of money to answer these and similar questions. Research by advertisers and ad agencies, however, is devoted understandably to one purpose: to determine how to make better and more persuasive messages. Although their results are usually kept secret, we are beginning to get some answers to these questions from outside researchers.

To date, the findings suggest that the younger the child, the fuller the attention he or she pays to commercials. However, their trust in commercials declines with age.[24] Very young children do not know the difference between TV commercials and programs. They pay a good deal of attention even to commercials that would seem to be irrelevant to them, such as ads for beer or household cleaning products. Perhaps they are simply using the commercial to learn about what is unfamiliar to them. As they get older, children pay less and less attention to commercials, and by the time they are adolescents they usually scorn them. The evidence so far indicates that children do pressure their parents to buy the products they have seen advertised. Overall, however, we do not yet know enough about advertising's effects on children, and many questions have yet to be explored in depth.

Meanwhile, critics such as parent groups are taking their concerns to the government and seeking controls on advertising. In the controversy over advertising appeals to children, particular media (such as television) have debated with consumer groups and government. The *Wall Street Journal* has noted that while network television had high standards for children's advertising, independent stations usually did not. While the networks barred the over-glamorization of a product or the use of exhortative language such as "Ask Mom to buy . . .," independent stations were quite lax on these and other points. As criticism mounted, the Better Business Bureau continued to urge local TV stations to be more vigilant, and eventually the board of the Association of Independent Television Stations endorsed guidelines for children's advertising. Finally, the U.S. Senate passed legislation to limit the number of commercials aired during children's programs.[25]

SOURCES OF CONTROL

Whatever the general effects of advertising, the content of many advertisements has often been attacked for being in poor taste, making exaggerated claims, and using annoying hucksterisms. As a result of these specific sins, some controls on American advertising have developed. Shabby practices led to a gradual erosion of the ancient principle of *caveat emptor* ("let the buyer beware") toward one of *caveat venditor* ("let the seller beware")—that is, toward regulation. Advertisers today live with certain constraints, some imposed by the government and some by the industry itself.

Regulation by government. As early as 1911, *Printer's Ink,* an industry magazine, called for greater attention to ethics in advertising and proposed a model statute that made fraudulent and misleading advertising a misdemeanor. Before long, with

Flashing banner ads are a hallmark of the Internet age and digital advertising, as used here by the major bookseller Barnes & Noble to promote the popular Harry Potter series. These ads have had a seismic effect on book publishing, linking publishers to other media such as television and motion pictures.

a strong push from the Better Business Bureau, most states enacted it as law. Although there is doubt about its effectiveness, the statute was a statement on advertising ethics as well as being a standard-setter. A few years later, in 1914, the Federal Trade Commission (FTC) also set up some ground rules for advertising. In administrative rulings over the years, the FTC has written rules related to puffery, taste, and guarantees in advertisements, and generally has taken a considerable interest in the substantiation of advertising claims. At times the FTC has demanded "effective relief" for those wronged by misleading advertising and has levied fines against companies engaging in unfair, misleading, and otherwise deceptive advertising.

The Federal Communications Commission also scrutinizes advertising. In addition, several other federal agencies, including the Food and Drug Administration, the Post Office Department, the Securities and Exchange Commission, and the Alcohol and Tobacco Tax Division of the Internal Revenue Service influence advertising. State and local governments have passed laws on advertising for lotteries, obscenity in ads, occupational advertising, and other matters. Government controls over advertising relaxed considerably in the era of industry deregulation from the 1980s to the present.

Industry codes of ethics. In the private sector, various advertising organizations and individual industries have developed codes of ethics to govern advertising. The broadcasting industry, for example, has codes that set standards for the total amount of nonprogram material and commercial interruptions per time period. (However, a long-standing limit controlling the amount of time commercials could air for each hour of programming for adults was relaxed considerably during the deregulation of broadcasting that began in the 1980s. In fact, say some critics, today some programs are, in fact, hour-long paid advertisements. Most of these air late at night and promote business-success schemes, real-estate deals, "classic" record collections, and other products and schemes.) In many states, local industry organizations such as advertising review committees and fair-advertising groups promote truth in advertising. The National Advertising Review Council promotes ethical advertising and fights deception, and the Better Business Bureau prepares reports on particular firms and their advertising.

Court rulings. In recent years, both the public and private sectors have followed closely various court decisions regarding whether or to what degree the First Amendment's guarantee of freedom of speech and the press extends to advertising. To date, the courts have distinguished between advertising that promotes one's views, which is *protected* by the First Amendment, and advertising that is designed only for commercial gain, which is *not*—although at times it is difficult to separate the two. This is being modified, however, as a doctrine of commercial speech has developed in the courts—which has defined the rights of businesses to communicate their views. Typically, courts have stoutly defended what they call "political speech," or expression that promotes public discussion of public affairs. The courts have until recently been less kind to "commercial speech," which is aimed at selling products. Now, all that is changing as commentators recognize that separating public and private speech is difficult at best.

Consumer groups. In addition, many consumer groups monitor advertising and protest when they object to particular content. These groups range from the Action for Children's Television, which opposes much of TV advertising aimed at children, to religious groups that object to newspaper ads soliciting sex.

Advertisers have in the past responded to public criticism, and advertising itself has undergone constant change. For example, for many years radio and television commercials included very few African Americans or other minorities. When they did appear, they were often shown in trivial or demeaning roles. But by the late 1960s, advertisements began to portray minorities more frequently and more realistically. Today, minorities are frequently seen in all forms of advertising. Similar changes have begun to take place in the portrayals of women, who have typically been shown behaving either idiotically in domestic situations or as passive sexual objects. The same is true of elderly people, who have often appeared as doddering simpletons or as cranky and growling consumers.

While there have been modest improvements, advertising still often deals with stereotypes. In the 1960s, feminist writer Betty Friedan in her classic book, *The Feminine Mystique,* drew attention to sex-role stereotypes in advertising. Many years later, researchers Thomas Whipple and Alice E. Courtney wrote that there have been only relatively cosmetic changes. In fact, they found that the use of women as sex objects in advertising is on the rise, which would be consistent with the "creeping cycle of desensitization" theory:

> Nudity, seminudity, innuendo, double-entendre and exploitive sex are being used with increasing frequency and intensity. Advertising continues to exploit women's sexuality, to demean them, to objectify them, and show violence and aggression against them.[26]

Many advertising professionals would take issue with these critiques, saying that advertising reflects public tastes and that feminism has had a definite impact on advertising content. Other advertisers are likely to say, "Gee, I'd really like to avoid these stereotypes, but I've got to use them to survive."[27] However, others argue that research shows that avoiding stereotypes can be effective, and they urge a re-education of advertisers.[28] If a large part of the public becomes unwilling to accept demeaning stereotypes, advertising will probably soon follow the public's lead. After all, advertisers are not trying to mold society or public opinion—though they may in fact influence both. They are trying to sell goods, and will change their message if need be to appeal to the public. If critics can arouse the people to complain enough or can convince advertisers that the public is annoyed, they have a good chance of changing specific aspects of advertising messages. Critics argue that they want to raise the standards of ad content, not censor communication.

It is likely that the debate over sexual stereotyping in advertising will continue for a long time. Many advertisers appeal blatantly to sexual desire, and much of what they put before the public is clearly sexist. Occasionally various groups representing women, religion, and other social forces protest and even urge the boycott of particular products. Since advertisers almost always want to avoid controversy—after all, they want to sell products, not enrage consumers—some of these protests have worked.

Formerly, sex appeal in advertising was largely aimed at men and exploited women in the process; yet this has changed in recent years as suggestive poses of men are now commonly featured, displaying males as sex objects in an explicit manner heretofore unknown in advertising. Thus far, few men have objected. It is possible, of course, that advertising does not influence people as much as its critics claim. Sociologist Michael Schudson argues that advertising is not nearly as important, effective, or scientifically targeted as either advocates or critics imagine. Advertisers are often quite cautious in deciding on their advertising outlays and take few chances. In the end, says Schudson, advertising rarely has a chance to create consumer wants, but instead reinforces what already exists. In assessing the role of advertising in American society, Schudson makes the following observations:

1. Advertising serves a useful informational function that will not and should not be abandoned.
2. Advertising probably has a socially democratizing influence, but one with an ultimate egalitarian outcome.
3. The most offensive advertising tends to have the least informational content.
4. Some advertising promotes dangerous products or promotes potentially dangerous products to groups unlikely to be able to use them wisely.
5. Non-price advertising often promotes bad values, whether it effectively sells products or not.
6. Advertising could survive and sell goods without promoting values as bad as those it favors now.
7. Advertising is but one factor among many in shaping consumer choice and human values.[29]

Critics who object not to specific aspects of some advertisements but to advertising's broader effects on individuals, society, and the economy will not see the changes they desire any time soon. Government is unlikely to impose stringent controls. Advertisers are likely to continue to appeal to our desires to be attractive, liked, and somehow better than our neighbors—in short, to have more or better of just about anything, whatever may be the psychological, cultural, or economic effects of these appeals so long as they think the messages work. Furthermore, advertisers are likely to continue to engulf us with their messages unless there are monumental changes in the economy and society.

All of the above considerations lead to a reaffirmation of our central thesis: The media, the economy, advertising, and the population as consumers are inextricably linked in a deeply institutionalized way. Thus, advertising is a central social institution in our society.

Chapter Review

- Advertising is a form of controlled communication about a particular product (or service), which attempts to persuade an appropriate audience, through the use of a variety of appeals and strategies, to adopt a belief or to make a decision to perform an action, such as to buy or use a product or service.

- Advertising is essential to both the nation's economy and to its mass media, for which it is their principal source of revenue. Without that revenue, Americans would not have their current great variety of mass communication content from which to choose.

- Advertising began long ago, but it expanded greatly as the Industrial Revolution came with its expansion of consumer goods. Advertising for such products as patent medicines led the way and proved how successful it could be. Advertising product brands gave it an even larger place in the economy. The development of department stores and nationally circulated magazines were important milestones in the field's history.

- As the need for advertising grew, agencies were developed to provide services to both the media of the time and to those who wanted to market their products. Today, there are three major types of such groups: large and small "creative boutique" advertising agencies, media service organizations (also called specialist agencies), and in-house advertising departments.

- Today, advertising agencies are comprised of managers, writers, artists, researchers, and other specialists. Boutique agencies and various media service organizations offer more limited, specialized services.

- Advertising researchers study various categories of consumers, focusing on their lifestyles and the characteristics that can lead them to purchase specific products. They also investigate the influences of specific advertising campaigns and test which ads might be most effective.

- Virtually any medium via which a persuasive message can be brought to the attention of some segment of the public can be used to transmit advertising messages. These include the usual mass media as well as many kinds of specialized forms—such as matchbook covers, billboards, blimps, subway posters, and many others.

- Advertising today is a $126 billion industry that employs nearly a quarter million people in America. However, concentration of advertising into large firms is a trend that can be found throughout the media and other industries.

- Advertisers use both psychodynamic strategies, with both rational and emotional appeals, and sociocultural strategies, based on conforming to cultural requirements to develop persuasive messages. Cutting through the clutter and gaining attention is one of advertisers' most difficult tasks.

- The advertising industry has many critics. Some economists claim that it is economically wasteful because it decreases competition, increases consumers' costs, and channels investment away from more productive uses. Other economists claim that advertising promotes competition, diversity, and wise buying decisions. There are no clear answers to such charges.

- Some critics maintain that advertising debases both individuals and their shared culture. Still others claim that advertising that makes exaggerated claims, is in poor taste, is used to exploit children, and sometimes presents negative stereotypes of particular groups.

- Those who recognize the importance of advertising, but want it to be carried on with higher standards, have set up guidelines to prevent misleading, offensive, and excessive advertising.

- Although advertising can be criticized on many grounds, it will be with us for the foreseeable future. It plays a critical role in promoting our nation's goods and services and in funding our media. Simply put, it is a deeply established social institution in our society.

Notes and References

1. David M. Potter, *People of Plenty,* 2nd ed. (Chicago: University of Chicago Press, 1969), p. 172.
2. Richard Knox, "On Teen Smoking, Ads Work Both Ways," *The Boston Globe,* March 1999, p. B-1.
3. Stephen Fox, *The Mirror Makers: A History of American Advertising and Its Creators* (New York: Morrow, 1984), pp. 13–39.
4. Ellen Gruber Garvey, *The Adman in the Parlor: Magazines and the Gendering of Consumer Culture, 1880s to 1910* (New York: Oxford University Press, 1996), p. 8.
5. The historical examples discussed in these sections are drawn from Fox, *The Mirror Makers,* pp. 13–39.
6. Potter, *People of Plenty,* p. 168.
7. William F. Arens, *Advertising,* 6th ed. (Chicago: Irwin, 1996), pp. 76–80.
8. John S. Wright et al., *Advertising,* 5th ed. (New York: McGraw-Hill, 1982) pp. 161–162.
9. *Media Private Market Value Estimates,* Paul Kagan Associates, Inc., 1992.
10. Gerald R. Miller, "Persuasion," in Charles R. Berger and Steven H. Chafee, *Handbook of Communication Science* (Newbury Park, Calif.: Sage Publications, 1987), pp. 446–483.
11. Melvin L. DeFleur and Sandra Ball Rokeach, "Theoretical Strategies for Persuasion," *Theories of Mass Communication,* 5th ed. (White Plains, N.Y.: Longman, 1989), pp. 272–293.
12. John Phillip Jones, *What's in a Name: Advertising and the Concept of Brands* (Lexington, Mass.: Lexington Books, 1986), p. 141.
13. Michael Siegal and Lois Biener, "The Impact of an Anti-Smoking Media Campaign on Progression to Established Smoking: A Longitudinal Study," *The American Journal of Public Health,* 90, 2000, p. 384.
14. Norman Douglas, *South Wind* (1917), in *Bartlett's Familiar Quotations,* 13th ed. (Boston: Little, Brown and Company, 1968), p. 840.
15. Siegal and Biener, "The Impact of an Anti-Smoking Media Campaign," pp. 47–48.
16. Russell H. Colley, *Defining Advertising Goals for Measured Advertising Results* (New York: Association of National Manufacturers, 1961), p. 35.
17. Colley, *Defining Advertising Goals,* p. 38.

18. Wright et al., *Advertising,* p. 392.

19. Otto Kleppner, *Advertising Procedure,* 7th ed. (Englewood Cliffs, N.J.: Prentice-Hall, 1985), pp. 301–302.

20. Daniel Pope, *The Making of Advertising* (New York: Basic Books, 1983), pp. 289–290. See also Kim B. Rotzoll and James E. Haefner, *Advertising in Contemporary Society* (Cincinnati: South-Western, 1986).

21. John S. Wright and John E. Mertes, *Advertising's Role in Society* (St. Paul, Minn.: West, 1974), pp. vii–viii.

22. Wright and Mertes, *Advertising's Role,* pp. vii–viii.

23. John Kenneth Galbraith, "Economics and Advertising: Exercise in Denial," *Advertising Age,* November 9, 1988, p. 81.

24. For an extended discussion of research evidence on television advertising and children, see Robert M. Liebert, Joyce N. Sprafkin and Emily S. Davidson, *The Early Window: Effects of Television on Children and Youth,* 2nd ed. (New York: Pergamon Press, 1982) pp. 142–159.

25. Joanne Lipman, "Double Standard for Kids' TV Ads," *Wall Street Journal,* June 10, 1988, sec. 2, p. 1. See also "Congress Approves Limiting TV Ads Aimed at Children," *Wall Street Journal,* October 20, 1988, sec. 2, p.6.

26. Thomas Whipple and Alice E. Courtney, *Sex Stereotyping in Advertising* (Lexington, Mass.: Lexington Books, 1983).

27. Kitty Chism, "Advertising Stereotypes," *Washington Post,* December 13, 1983, p. 135.

28. Whipple and Courtney, *Sex Stereotyping.*

29. Michael Schudson, *Advertising, The Uneasy Persuasion: Its Dubious Impact on American Society* (New York: Basic Books, 1984), pp. 239–241.

Chapter 12

PUBLIC RELATIONS: INFLUENCING BELIEFS, ATTITUDES, AND ACTIONS

FOR CENTURIES THOSE IN POWER HAVE SOUGHT WAYS TO INFLUENCE THE BELIEFS, ATTITUDES, and actions of their followers by using a variety of communication strategies. Almost universally, their goal was to inspire awe and respect on the part of their supporters and fear on the part of their enemies. To accomplish those purposes they had their scribes record on stone, papyrus, parchment, and other media glowing accounts of their accomplishments. Some claimed divine status. For example, almost four thousand years ago, the Babylonian King Hammurabi had his scholars develop a set of 283 laws to govern his empire. He had the laws inscribed on huge square blocks of stone that were placed in the center of each city in his domain. On each side, he had carved a representation of himself receiving those laws from the sun god. This communication was designed to convince his people of his special status and the lofty origin of his laws. Given the limitations of the time, this strategy was as modern and successful as any professional communicator could devise today to enhance a leader's public image.

Demonstrating damage control in public relations, the Ford Motor Co. chief executive officer, James Nasser (foreground), listens to congressional testimony on auto safety in Washington, D.C., against the backdrop of a wrecked Ford Explorer.

As the above example suggests, even though they did not call it by that name, powerful people have been engaging in public relations communication for a very long time. Even today, the purposes behind many public pronouncements and displays of power are for reasons of *publicity*—expanding the number of people who are aware of some person, policy, or program. Public relations is also often associated with *propaganda,* that is persuasive communications designed to gain people's approval—or as we might say today, "to capture their hearts and minds"—concerning some action taken or planned, some individual, or some decision that has been made. (The term "propaganda" originally referred to the Roman Catholic Church's efforts to "propagate the faith" through the communication efforts of missionaries, which in many respects was a kind of public relations campaign.)

Publicity and propaganda are time-honored objectives. Certainly both played major roles in the American colonies before the Revolution, when committees of correspondence (patriots advocating separation from England) sought to win the support of the public. Also, many American presidents have had a need to sway public opinion in a direction favorable for their policies. Abraham Lincoln, for example, had a definite "public relations problem" with his Emancipation Proclamation of 1862. It freed all slaves in states and territories at war with the Union—but not in those fighting on the northern side. Several states not in the Confederacy were reluctant to give up the idea of slavery, and Lincoln had a "hard sell." If he had been able to use public opinion polls at the time, (they did not exist) he might never have issued his Proclamation until he prepared the population for it with public relations efforts. Similarly, in 1939 President Franklin D. Roosevelt began (unsuccessfully at first) to persuade the American people that it was in the country's best interests to come to the aid of the British in their fight against Adolf Hitler. By 1941, he had begun to turn the situation around with his speeches and policies. However, the need was eliminated after the Japanese bombed the Pacific fleet at Pearl Harbor. During the twentieth century, other national leaders such as Gandhi and Martin Luther King, Jr., became masters of communications designed to promote approval of their social and political goals. Thus, throughout both ancient and recent times, efforts to change public beliefs, attitudes, and behaviors through the use of effective communication strategies have been a part of human society.

THE DEVELOPMENT OF PUBLIC RELATIONS

As a professional field, public relations (using that actual term) has a much briefer history. It grew out of reactions to the "public be damned" attitude that characterized American big business at the turn of the nineteenth century. As the 1900s began, the "captains of industry" who ran the nation's corporations did as they pleased regardless of what people thought. Eventually, however, the public became aroused over their excesses—especially after many of their practices were exposed by the "muckraker" journalists of the time. To counter this negative trend, many of the large corporations began to use public relations in one form or another to head off confrontations.

BIRTH OF THE PUBLIC RELATIONS AGENCY

A forerunner of the modern public relations *agency* was the Publicity Bureau of Boston, founded in 1900 by three former newspapermen. They established an important pattern in the way that public relations services were provided for clients. For a fee they would promote a company's causes and business interests by getting favorable stories placed in newspapers and by other forms of *managed communication*. The bureau's early clients included AT&T, Harvard University, Fore River Shipyard, and Boston Elevated (trolley lines.)

By 1911, the bureau had died, but other public relations and press agencies had quickly been formed. For example, publicist and former journalist Ivy Lee, after working for political candidates and the Pennsylvania Railroad, recognized the value for businesses of a positive public image and the possibilities of creating such an image systematically through favorable publicity. He set up a firm providing services that we would now call public relations activities to help businesses communicate with the public. His clients eventually included what was perhaps the most famous of all "captains of industry," John D. Rockefeller, Jr., and his infamous Standard Oil Company. Another early publicist was Pendleton Dudley, who at Lee's urging opened an office on Wall Street. According to Scott Cutlip, a scholar who studies public relations, Dudley denied that early public relations efforts were in direct response to the muckraking journalists.

During these early days, public relations specialists were called "publicity men," or sometimes "press agents." In 1919, the newspapers of New York took a census of the number who worked regularly in that capacity in the city and found that there were about twelve hundred actively employed.[1] Furthermore, their functions were well understood by that time. Journalism scholar Walter Lippmann noted that it was their task to use the media (mainly newspapers at the time) to provide the public with "interpretations" of events related to their clients:

> The development of the publicity man is a clear sign that the facts of modern life do not spontaneously take a shape in which they can be known. They must be given a shape by somebody, and since in the daily routine reporters cannot give a shape to facts, and since there is little disinterested organization of intelligence, the need for some formulation is being met by [press agents and publicity men].[2]

Thus, there was a thriving public relations industry by the time of World War I. Its professional communicators performed the same services as their modern counterparts. However, these communicators had only the print media with which to work as they attempted to create favorable meanings and images among the public for those they represented.

Today, the field of public relations has grown into a sophisticated and complex occupational field, with a large part of the work carried on either by relatively large agencies or by public relations departments in many kinds of corporations, government agencies, and nonprofit groups. However, some old-fashioned publicity agents (still using that name) continue to work, especially in New York City, serving the needs of people and groups in such high-visibility fields as the entertainment and fashion industries.

DEFINING PUBLIC RELATIONS TODAY

Although it is a complex field, it is not difficult to define the basic nature of public relations in terms of what its practitioners actually do. Public relations is an organized communication process, conducted by people who make a living as professional communicators. It can be defined in terms of conducting the following activities:

> *Paid professional practitioners design and transmit messages, on behalf of a client, via a variety of media to relevant and targeted audiences in an attempt to influence their beliefs, attitudes, or actions regarding some person, organization, policy, situation, or event.*

While this is a complex definition, it sets forth the basics of what practitioners actually do. However, it does not provide enough details so that nonspecialists can actually understand the field in greater depth. Taking each of the ideas in the definition and explaining them more fully will help.

Practitioners. Professional public relations practitioners are usually people whose education, and perhaps prior employment, has been in a field in which writing and producing other forms of messages has been a major focus. Such practitioners serve many types of clients. They may work in an agency that contracts for services, as discussed earlier, or they may be salaried employees of a corporation, government agency, or nonprofit group, such as a charity, museum, or university. They may have a title such as "information specialist," "public affairs officer," or "press secretary," but their activities are similar regardless of the setting in which they work or the clients they serve.

Messages. Public relations specialists develop communication strategies and prepare many kinds of messages, using many kinds of media—including news releases and information campaigns. Most messages are of a routine nature. Examples are brochures that provide information about a corporation, government agency, or nonprofit group. Other examples are newsletters distributed to various "stakeholders," such as alumni, employees, stockholders, and so forth. Annual reports on the status, activities, and accomplishments of an organization is still another example. Public relations specialists also assist in preparing news stories and other information to be released to the press with the hope that this information will appear in the paper or news broadcast.

Clients. There are almost as many kinds of clients served by public relations practitioners as there are individuals and groups in the United States that produce materials and services for the public. These include corporations and industries that manufacture goods, local, state, and federal government agencies, the military, institutions that provide for health-care services, investment firms, banks, schools, colleges and universities, organized charities, religious groups, and so on. To this comprehensive list could be added public personalities, such as prominent actors, singers, politicians, preachers, and musicians, who need a constant flow of publicity in order to foster beliefs about their importance on the part of the public.

Media. Virtually every kind of medium used for communication today plays some part in the activities of public relations specialists. Information is prepared and transmitted using newspapers, magazines, radio, and television. Increasingly, information about their client or employer is prepared for distribution via the Internet or in the form of a CD-ROM. In addition, practitioners design special events, such as trade-show displays and formal presentations of new products. They write speeches and magazine articles for their employers or clients. They provide briefings, talking points, and hold practice interviews. They help prepare clients and employers for formal speeches, public appearances, and meetings with the press. In addition, their clients or employers may sponsor sports events—ranging from golf competitions to bass fishing contests—which are designed for public relations purposes.

In some cases, public relations specialists have to prepare messages intended to achieve *damage control.* If an airplane crashes, a train derails, or a tanker spills oil, public relations practitioners help to design messages aimed at limiting the negative consequences for their client. That does not mean that the public relations specialists either avoid responsibility or misrepresent the situation (which can happen in some cases). More often, they help design information releases or help management focus on steps that the public sees as meeting their responsibilities. Serious mistakes are made by those who try to cover up, deny, or lie about a bad situation.

Audiences. The messages developed and transmitted by public relations specialists are prepared for many different categories of people. Obviously, some are broadly defined and are intended to be read or viewed by the public at large—as in a news release prepared for the readers of a local newspaper, or an interview designed as a local TV news story. Beyond that are more narrowly defined groups, such as the constituents of an office holder, the employees of a large company, or the personnel of a major military organization. Another group might be the investors who hold stock in a large corporation. Sometimes the intended audience is very narrowly defined. For example, information may be prepared specifically for the surviving family members of an air crash or a military accident. In any of these cases, the public relations practitioner must understand the nature of that audience and the impression that will be made on them after receiving the specific information that is being prepared.

Influences. The bottom line in public relations is to have the messages that are transmitted accomplish the purposes for which they were designed. There are many such purposes and each depends on the complexities of the situation. For example, a long-range public relations campaign may be designed to alter the behavior of the public regarding some form of action that has national significance. An example is the Smokey Bear public service campaign conducted by the U.S. Forest Service. Starting in 1949, the cartoonlike bear, wearing the wide-brimmed hat, has for more than fifty years been saying, *"Only YOU can stop forest fires!"* Smokey and his message is

Increasingly media convergence is seen in Internet ads placed in print and electronic media, drawing viewers and readers to the Web.

known by almost every person in the United States. The campaign was so effective that the public reacted very negatively when in 1992 the Forest Service wanted to set some fires deliberately to burn accumulated dry branches and other materials on forest floors to reduce the danger of fires caused by lightening.

Many public relations messages have less dramatic goals. Many are designed to turn the public around regarding some person, issue, or event that has taken a negative turn. For example, film star Rob Lowe became the object of a well-publicized scandal in which he was videotaped in a sexual encounter with two teenaged girls. Lowe sought to redeem his reputation, express remorse for his earlier behavior, and build an audience for his upcoming movie titled, *Bad Influence*. He enlisted the help of public relations specialists and followed an orchestrated strategy to restore his public image as a credible, if sometimes wild, young actor. In a carefully planned media tour, Lowe made the rounds of television talk shows to promote his film. The guest spots were the actor's first public appearances after the scandal. Much of the credit for Lowe's successful "comeback" was due to the help of public relations professionals, who understand the tools needed to engineer a favorable image for celebrities and other public figures.

The majority of messages are much more mundane than either of these examples. Indeed, many are prepared to *inform* rather than persuade. They may consist of a news story about a new CEO taking over the reins of a corporation, the release of a new model of a product, an explanation of a new policy by a government agency, or a briefing about a campaign by a military spokesperson.

PUBLIC RELATIONS VERSUS ADVERTISING

The above discussion may make public relations and advertising seem somewhat alike. Like advertising, public relations is a controlled communication process in the sense that it is planned and organized and depends in large part on the mass media to convey its messages. But unlike advertising, which makes use of *purchased slots of media space and time,* public relations does not have such easy access to mass communications. Some critics call advertising space "captive media," since an advertiser buys and uses it according to his or her own discretion. Public relations messages, on the other hand, do not use space or time purchased so that messages will appear in the media. Instead, the messages are offered persuasively to editors, news directors, and others who then determine whether or not that information is worth including in their agenda.

Although some public relations campaigns may involve advertisements, such as those that promote tourism, or the general integrity of a corporation like Dow Chemical, public relations specialists often use more indirect, persuasive means to build a favorable climate of opinion or achieve other goals. Moreover, public relations efforts are not always identifiable. We know an advertisement when we see it on television or in a magazine, but we do not always know the source of a news article, or who is actually staging a golf tournament, bowling contest, or other public event—even though these events may be part of a carefully planned public relations campaign. Rarely do public relations people announce exactly what they are doing or for what purposes. Thus, while public relations personnel may use advertising as part of their overall activities, they are much more involved than advertisers in the total process of communication, from initiating the message to getting feedback from the public.

In summary, public relations is a complex activity and a professional field in which paid communicators design and distribute messages for a great variety of purposes. Overall, it is a field representing a very broad spectrum of communication activities. Some activities are clearly essential for the adequate functioning of the society. Others are less significant, except to the people involved. In either case, public relations is deeply dependent on the mass media. Through the activities of its practitioners, much of what is learned by the public about people, activities, and organizations in their society is generated to accomplish one or more of its goals. In the final analysis, then, public relations is a set of strategies for *deliberately manipulating meanings* in ways that are not always apparent to the target audience, so as to influence the audience's interpretations of a person, group, or policy represented by the communicator. This does not necessarily mean, however, that such manipulation is necessarily deceptive or unethical.

PUBLIC RELATIONS SETTINGS AND ACTIVITIES

Public relations practitioners today go by many names, among them public relations counselors, account executives, information officers, publicity directors, and house organ editors. They are found virtually everywhere—in the private sector in business, industry, charities, churches, labor unions, and so on. In the public sector they are in all levels of government from the White House to the local school or fire station. The number of people employed in public relations is impressive. The U.S. Department of Labor estimated in 1950 that there were 19,000 people engaged in public relations and publicity work. By 1970, this had grown to 76,000. Today, there are more than 170,000 working in jobs with those words in their title. This is a very low estimate because the figures include only the rather narrow category who use the label "public relations and publicity writers." In contrast, the U.S. Bureau of the Census reports that nearly half a million persons are currently engaged in various forms of public relations work. Of this number, about 45,000 work for public relations or management firms.

Public relations activities are conducted in a variety of organized ways. Most are carried on as team efforts by various kinds of groups: Perhaps most common is the *independent public relations counselor,* or *agency.* This person or organization operates much like an advertising agency or law firm, taking on clients and representing them by conducting public relations activities on their behalf. The client may be an individual who wants better understanding from the public, or a large company that wants an experienced firm that can provide special services. These services may include conducting research and designing publications to help the company's own in-house public relations staff. Agencies represent only a relatively small part of this labor force.

Somewhat related is the *public relations department* within a particular business, industry, or other setting. These departments act as part of the overall management team and attempt to interpret the firm to the public and internal constituents. A public relations department will also provide channels for feedback from the public to management. In industry, these departments are expected to contribute to the firm's profits by helping it achieve its overall business goals. The public relations department of General Motors, for example, sets communication goals to support and enhance the corporation's economic achievements. Public relations departments of a similar nature also exist within nonprofit and educational institutions. Publicity for organizations such as colleges and labor unions usually involves a range of internal and external activities, from publications to fund drives.

Public relations departments also provide services within governmental agencies, which can be at the federal, state, or even local level. In government, the terms "public information" and "public affairs" refer to any activity that communicates the purposes and work of an agency to the general public or to users of the agency's services. For example, welfare recipients need to know about the policies of the state social services department, and taxpayers need to know how their money is being spent. Similarly, a metropolitan police department typically has a "public affairs" department to provide information about its services and accomplishments to citizens.

Other individuals who carry out organized public relations activities are *specialized consultants.* These people range from political advisers who work exclusively on public relations problems during election campaigns to information specialists who are experts in communications in a specific field such as health, transportation, or insurance.

A related form of organized public relations activity is provided by *policy consultants.* These specialists suggest and design courses of action to public and private institutions that want to develop a policy for the use of information resources. These types of institutions may want to influence the policies of Congress or the Federal Communications Commission, or develop an early warning system to assess and trace the influences of a particular issue or program on corporate clients. This is a new area of public relations that expanded considerably during the 1990s.

Finally, the field also includes communication specialists in *technical areas.* For example, in Chapter 6 we discussed consultants who try to improve the ratings of a radio station's news programs. Others include specialized firms that work with corporate clients to help them better understand and work with television, training programs for company presidents who serve as spokespersons, and placement services that get corporate clients on the air in various cities. Technical specialists also include graphics practitioners who provide full-service publication assistance, producing publicity messages that fit into an organization's overall public relations plan.

As in any dynamic industry, new ways of accomplishing goals constantly emerge. For example, a number of advertising agencies have recently acquired many established public relations firms or have set up new ones within their own organizations. Many public relations practitioners and media critics fear that public relations, if it becomes a branch of advertising, will become a servant of product promotion and not maintain ethical practices. They assert that the credibility of an independent public relations agency is greater than that of a public relations program under an advertising agency.

Recent changes in the communication industry have complicated the world of public relations. Independent public relations agencies are becoming less common as advertising agencies acquire and subject them to the corporate requirements of the parent company. It is too early to predict whether this trend within the industry will continue or what it will mean for public relations practice.

TYPICAL TASKS AND WORK ASSIGNMENTS

As the above discussion suggests, the actual tasks and work assignments of public relations practitioners vary widely from one professional setting to another. Much depends, of course, on the position of the practitioner within the power hierarchy of the agency. In some businesses, the vice president for public relations is a high-ranking person who is involved in all major corporate decisions and a part of the policy-making team. In other firms, the public relations officer has less power and is brought in only to provide "damage control" through publicity. Still others are the drones of public relations—entry level or low-ranking employees who do the many day-to-day tasks that are necessary in a public relations campaign. Thus, at the top end of the organization are those who engage in tactical and strategic planning while those at lower levels perform more routine tasks involved in implementing such plans.

Top-level policy makers set long-term objectives and usually agree on some realistic expectations for results. This somewhat abstract agreement is then channeled into specific approaches, using publicity tools ranging from sponsored events to television presentations and press conferences to Web sites and information pamphlets. Thus, the complete public relations process involves planning and implementation—both in the overall thinking and in the precise technical work that make achievement of the goals possible.

Lone practitioners, or people in small firms, usually do everything—ranging from designing both strategy and tactics to writing copy for press releases. In any case, there are a number of specific tasks that must be accomplished in implementing a campaign. In larger firms with a significant division of labor, the work assignments may be highly specialized. For example, a particular specialist may spend most of his or her time writing news releases for a political candidate. Another may specialize in communicating new, high-tech information to nurses or engineers. In smaller firms, personnel will handle a wider range of duties. However, regardless of the size of a public relations agency or department, certain categories of work assignments are common. One leading text lists common tasks and specific forms of work:

1. *Writing:* producing news releases aimed at the general media and drafting copy for specialized publications, brochures, posters, catalogues, and other pieces intended for distribution to the public
2. *Editing:* revising and checking texts of speeches, company magazines, newsletters, and electronic bulletin boards
3. *Media relations and placement:* getting clients in the newspaper and on the air, and coordinating media coverage of events

4. *Special events:* organizing media events such as anniversaries of organizations, openings of new programs, sponsored performances, donations of money, and dedications of new facilities and similar ceremonies
5. *Speaking:* writing and delivering speeches to various groups on behalf of the client organization
6. *Production:* working with designers, typesetters, editors, and producers to present material in printed or visual form
7. *Research:* evaluating programs, developing questionnaires for surveys, and analyzing media coverage of an event or issue
8. *Programming and counseling:* developing a plan for the client or department and giving advice about how to handle a particular event or limit negative publicity
9. *Training and management:* providing training services to employees, advising them on how to set a proper climate in a firm, and coordinating employees of varied skills and backgrounds to ensure the success of a program[3]

In addition to being able to perform the above kinds of work, effective public relations practitioners usually must have certain personal qualities. Publicists usually have excellent written and oral communication skills; are at ease socially; have a thorough knowledge of the media, management, and business; and have the ability to function both as problem solvers and decision makers. Other common qualities are stability, common sense, intellectual curiosity, and a tolerance for frustration.

PUBLIC RELATIONS CAMPAIGNS

Public relations practitioners or agencies work in systematic ways. Typical of their activities on behalf of clients is the *public relations campaign.* This is an organized way of communicating carefully designed messages with specific meanings to targeted audiences that are important to the client. In contrast to a single news release, speech, or television interview, a campaign orchestrates many kinds of messages that are presented in many different ways making use of a number of media to achieve its goals.

Public relations campaigns become necessary for businesses and other organizations under many kinds of circumstances. Some have positive goals in mind; others may not. For example: (1) A business has been causing industrial pollution and is gaining a bad reputation. The business now wants to convince the public that it is dedicated to protection of the environment. (2) A health maintenance organization (HMO) wants to erase the stigma of being too profit-oriented to the detriment of the quality of health care provided. (3) An educational institution has experienced a bad sports scandal with consequent negative publicity. Enrollments have dropped, and it now wants to attract students and get alumni donations to resume. (3) A government agency promoting prenatal child care for the poor wants women to make better use of its services. All these groups achieve their goals with public relations campaigns.

The first and most obvious task of the specialist designing a public relations campaign is to meet with the client at length and go over exactly what goals are being sought. Those goals must be clearly understood and agreed upon by all parties. These sessions must include full disclosure of what efforts have been made in the past, by whom, and using what strategies; and what worked and what did not. Another obvious problem is money. What, precisely, is the budget that is being allocated by the client to the campaign? A timetable needs to be established, and decisions must be made as to the specific indicators that will be used to decide whether the goal of the campaign was accomplished or not.

According to public relations scholars Cutlip and Center and Glenn Broom, any effective public relations campaign must be designed around four basic stages or steps:

1. *Fact-finding and feedback.* This stage involves background research on the desired audience. This can be research in the scientific tradition as well as impressionistic observations by knowledgeable observers and careful studies of public opinion. The public relations practitioner uses this information to define the problem and to identify the psychological and demographic characteristics of the audience to be reached.

2. *Planning and programming.* The publicist uses the information from the fact-finding stage and plans a broad strategy for the entire public relations program. As noted above, this strategy includes a timetable, media, budgets, and possible targets for the message.

3. *Action and communication.* In this stage the publicist initiates the actual communication process using the media and the appropriate publicity tools. Pamphlets are distributed, speeches are given, events are sponsored, and news releases are sent to media organizations, etc.

4. *Evaluation.* After the program is initiated and carried out, it is assessed in several ways: by measuring changes in beliefs, attitudes, and opinions among particular publics; by counting the number of news clippings or reports on radio and television in order to evaluate the effectiveness of contacts with the news media; or by interviewing key opinion leaders. If carried to its logical conclusion, the evaluation should affect future public relations activities, depending on what worked and what did not.[4]

To illustrate how these steps would be implemented in actual practice, a typical public relations campaign can be reviewed. As indicated, it begins with the recognition of a problem or the perceived need for an image change of some sort. As an example,

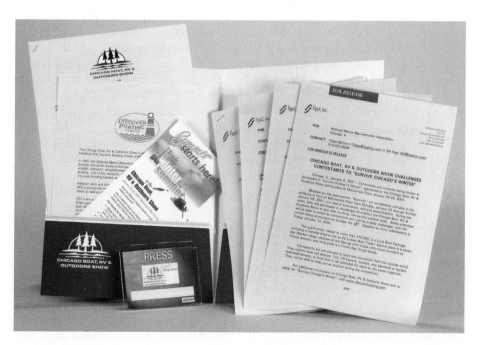

Press kits prepared by public relations agencies brief reporters and other media personnel on events, activities, and issues, as with this press kit for the Chicago Boat, RV, and Outdoor show.

assume that the tourism board of the state of New York is unhappy with the state's revenues from visitors and thinks it might be due to a poor public image. The board decides to investigate further and hires a public relations firm. The firm conducts research among selected publics such as regular vacationers, travel agents, and travel writers for newspapers and magazines. Surveys assess what these people know about vacation possibilities in New York State. The results indicate a lack of public awareness or misconceptions, and reveal concerns that keep tourists from vacationing in the state.

Next, the public relations firm prepares a campaign proposal suggesting a variety of measures likely to increase tourism in the state. Suppose that because all Americans obviously cannot be reached through a limited campaign, the firm decides to direct its efforts at travel writers, hoping that they will say something positive in their articles about New York State as a vacation area. To influence the writers, the firm will distribute news releases, hold press briefings, and even organize tours. In addition, it will send special mailings to travel agents to encourage them to direct their clients to select New York State as a vacation site. If they decide to try to reach the general public with the campaign, the firm proposes to place a series of advertisements on national television and in newsmagazines. Based on advice from advertising agencies and on research on the demonstrated effectiveness of particular media, the firm selects the best combination of media in which to place these messages.

As a next step, the firm presents the campaign proposal to the client—the leaders of the tourism board. Assuming that the board accepts the proposal with a few modifications—and the budget, timetable, etc., are agreed upon—it then commissions the public relations firm to carry out the campaign. At the end of the campaign, the firm conducts an *evaluation* surveying the same groups of people who provided the initial evaluation of attitudes and opinions to see if their thoughts have changed. In addition, the firm looks at subsequent tourism figures and attempts to ascertain whether the campaign actually had any effect on them.

This example reveals one of the real problems with public relations. That is, the people who carry out information campaigns are not disinterested social scientists seeking to advance knowledge, rather they are *profit-making entrepreneurs* (or perhaps government employees eager to advance in their jobs). Thus, they may look selectively for "proof" that their information campaign has worked. If it clearly has not, publicists may try to convince their clients that uncontrollable factors, such as a poor economy, too many crime reports in the media, or pre-existing negative stereotypes about New York, caused the public relations program to fail, despite their best efforts. Naturally, clients who hire the firm are free to make their own judgments about what works and what does not. Scholarly evidence about such public relations campaigns—and there is far too little of it—suggests that many such efforts are simply unsuccessful. It is difficult to change embedded beliefs and attitudes; and even if they are changed, much research shows that patterns of behavior will remain unchanged, even if attitudes are modified. The reason for this is that decisions to take specific actions (e.g., to go to a particular site for a vacation) are embedded in a host of variables and factors other than beliefs and attitudes about a particular location for a vacation. So changing attitudes very often does not change behavior. However, practitioners dispute this evidence with practical and often compelling (but selected) examples.

Leaders in public relations are quick to point out that their work involves much more than mass communication. Sometimes they distinguish *internal* from *external* communication. Internal communication is communication within an organization directed to its members. For example, a labor union communicates to its members through newsletters, meetings, bulletin boards, and other internal media. This kind of communication is aimed at a discrete group of people, not at the general public through mass media. In contrast, external communication transmits messages via the mass media to a large, diverse audience or to particular segments of the population outside the organization.

MANAGING ELECTIONS

A kind of organized public relations work that has expanded greatly in recent years is managing election campaigns. Today, public relations consultants often serve as the strategists and managers of such campaigns during elections. In particular, they key their efforts to opinion polls and the results of focus groups. Although they usually stay out of the public eye, such consultants occasionally appear on CNN and various network talk shows to speak on behalf of their clients. Typically, however, they avoid the limelight and engage in a kind of guerrilla warfare, by plotting strategy, designing modes of attack, and coaching defensive responses for their clients when they are under fire.

This kind of organized activity brings together public opinion research, strategic planning, and more traditional public relations. According to Jerry Hagstrom of the *National Journal,* who is an expert on this new form of public relations, there is an elite corps of about forty Washington, D.C.–based polling and media firms that play a profound role in national presidential campaigns and other races. Similar firms exist across the country and typically serve the Republican and Democratic parties. And, although national campaigns are the most prestigious races, Hagstrom observes that the most elite consultants usually center their efforts on statewide campaigns because they are more financially lucrative.

Hagstrom states that this new cadre of consultants has virtually replaced state and local political bosses and party chairpersons as behind-the-scenes power brokers. What was once done intuitively by political operatives is now in the task of consultants. In dealing with the media, public relations campaign managers often engage in what has come to be called "spin control" (a term from billiards, where a left or right spin can be put on a ball, making it curve to one side or the other as it moves across the table). They do so with carefully controlled use of language. For example, if an opposing political figure has unintentionally made an error in reporting the use of campaign funds, a political *spinmeister* may advise his or her client to attack the opponent by characterizing the situation as a "disgraceful scandal" and claim that "people who violate decent standards of behavior should never be allowed to hold public office." Spin control from the other side, aimed at minimizing damage, may have his or her client claim that "unintentional mistakes are being escalated out of control by my opponent using wild claims in a political vendetta."

Carefully orchestrated spin-control measures during election campaigns truly can make a difference. For example, during the 2000 presidential and congressional elections, advisers to the Democrats persuaded them to characterize Republicans—who proposed sizeable federal income tax cuts in order to return a portion of the large budget surplus to citizens—in a very negative way. They claimed, in candidates' speeches, TV ads, as well as other media, that these were efforts to "benefit the rich," to "allow Social Security and Medicare to fail financially." These tax cuts, the Democrats claimed, would "slash aid to the poor and reduce income for senior citizens, while denying them access to medical care." These themes were repeated endlessly during the campaign and were intended to convince voters that the Republicans were tight-fisted fiscal Neanderthals who wanted to protect the "fat cats," and had little concern for those with limited incomes or for older people, whose Social Security benefits and access to health care would be at risk.

The press conference, or media briefing, is a standard means for communication by business, political, governmental, nonprofit, and other groups concerned with promoting their interests—or doing damage control. Karen Hughes, director of communications for George W. Bush in his run for the White House and now counselor to the President, is shown here answering questions from the press.

Republican spin-control advisers, on the other hand, were successful in attaching the meaning of "irresponsible big spenders" to Democrats. They claimed that expensive new federal programs planned by their opponents would make it impossible to reduce the federal debt and to fund Social Security and Medicare to protect citizens from financial failure in the future. The intention was to scare taxpayers that fiscally irresponsible new measures to aid the poor, planned by Democrats, would eat into middle-class family incomes. Thus, language providing interpretations of situations that arise in connection with candidates is couched in ways intended to reflect either favorable or damaging meanings and images. What usually spins out of control in such situations is the facts.

Political campaigning, then, has become a battleground of public relations managers who are experts of assessing public opinion and desires, and who can design messages that resonate with voters. Many critics complain that this has shifted the democratic process of election campaigning from a more traditional one in which candidates make their principles and plans clear, to one in which they shift from one position to another as advisers use polls to manage their messages.

PUBLIC RELATIONS AND THE MEDIA

We noted that there is an important difference between advertising messages and most of the messages that are prepared by public relations practitioners. Advertisers simply purchase the time or space in print or broadcast media and place their messages where they want. Public relations practitioners can do this, of course, but they are far more likely to try to get the media to accept (without cost) news releases, interviews, and other messages favorable to their clients (but which are not easily seen as public relations efforts).

Individuals or interests that want to achieve a positive public image by using the mass media in this way face at least two barriers: First, the media are independent entities with their own goals—which may *conflict* with those of the publicity seekers. For example, a politician's desire for positive coverage on the evening news obviously would conflict with the local television station's intention to disclose the same politician's alleged wrongdoing. Second, there is great *competition* for limited space and time in the media and other public forums, and many worthy individuals and causes simply cannot receive the media attention and public exposure they desire.

THE GATEKEEPING PROCESS

An important theory explaining how the media select only a limited number of news stories to print or air in a particular edition or broadcast is the *gatekeeping theory* (see Chapter 3, page 78). This theory is important in understanding the complex relationship between public relations and the media. It states that those who select the content for the daily newspaper, news broadcast, or online news site do so by using a number of criteria to decide what is "newsworthy." They realize full well that there is only a limited amount of time or space that they have available. Only those stories judged to be most important, or in which their audience will be most interested, will be given priority. Those that meet these criteria will be selected from the abundance of stories that are available to them from reporters, wire services, and the like. The latest news release from a public relations agency, press secretary, or political consultant may not survive this test. Indeed, unless it has some special quality that the editors and news directors feel is important, it is likely to get ignored.

On the other hand, public relations practitioners know this full well. They have no illusions that editors will eagerly accept and make public any kind of news release or other information hand-out that they prepare. To help in opening the channels, a public relations practitioner will try to become acquainted with those who make news decisions. An effective public relations specialist will establish *good personal relationships*—intended to generate and maintain confidence and credibility—with reporters, editors, and news directors. However, journalists often remain wary and are not likely to trust just any public relations person who approaches them with information.

A RELATIONSHIP OF MUTUAL DEPENDENCY

Adding to this complex relationship between public relations and journalism is the fact that these two groups *need* each other. They live in a *state of mutual dependency*. A careful examination of any daily newspaper or television news broadcast will reveal that a very large proportion of what appears in the news has its origin in someone's news conference, news release, or other form of material originally prepared by a public relations or public affairs specialist and then released to the press. This does not mean that the press blindly makes public whatever practitioners provide. Reporters follow up, interview people with other points of view, and so on. Nevertheless, much of the agenda in the daily press has its start with public relations specialists.

To illustrate, if a plane crashes, public money is misappropriated, or a corporation is caught harassing women or mistreating minorities, some spokesperson for the relevant organization (airline, government agency, corporation) will hold a news conference. Their purpose in appearing before reporters is not just to provide information. It is to put the best possible interpretation (spin) on what happened, how the situation could not have been foreseen, what the corporation, for example, is doing about it, and so on. Such press conferences are not casual appearances. Most such presentations are *carefully rehearsed* ahead of time with the aid of public relations specialists—who warn of damaging questions that are likely to be asked and who develop ways of deflecting ones that are likely to create harm to the agency or authorities.

The reporters, on the other hand, *need news.* On a typical day there may be little going on that is actually newsworthy. While some minor events might be made interesting by clever writing (a pie-eating contest, a dog that falls through the ice on the pond, or another service-station robbery), it is often the case that these do not provide enough copy to fill out the day's news agenda. In such cases, journalists have to make use of what public relations people supply because *something* has to appear in the paper for subscribers to read or on the newscast for viewers to see. The reporters must meet deadlines and have very little time to generate alternatives to what the practitioners are providing. About all they can do is to flesh out the provided story with a few quotes from experts or from individuals who represent contrary points of view and with some background information.

Another example of the dependent relationship between public relations and journalism, is the video news release (VNR)—a self-serving promotion of a person or organization presented on videotape provided by practitioners. These are especially important for television news broadcasts. Originally used by companies to promote their general image or to respond to a crisis, VNRs are now increasingly used by political candidates as well. More than 10 percent of television stations were using VNR material from the major presidential candidates in the most recent primaries and general election.

For television stations, VNRs conveniently provide much needed visual material for the news. For one thing, they reduce filming costs. Moreover, in some instances, the only way a local station can get direct access to major candidates is through VNRs or satellite news conferences, both of which are paid for by the candidates. Thus, the stations get the material cheaply and do not have to spend time and resources digging it up independently. The practitioners get their message on the air for their clients with the spins that they want.

The VNR is a very flexible medium that can effectively represent virtually any point of view. For example, they have been used by various industries to dispute environmental claims, and similarly, by environmental groups to make negative claims with equal fervor. When a firm is in the midst of a major labor dispute, the VNR allows the company spokesperson or CEO to put the firm's position forward to employees without press intervention. In any crisis, the client's interpretation can be presented without troublesome reporters asking awkward questions. Supporters of corporate VNRs say that this is an appropriate use of corporate communications in an era when it is difficult for a firm to get its message across without constraints or disruption from the press. Sometimes VNRs are used to save time and money when a firm or special interest group wants to get its message across in several markets without extensive travel or personal appearances from its executives. In effect, then, the VNR is an advisory from an organization making a plea for publicity and understanding. Media organizations are then free to use the material verbatim, edit it heavily, or identify it as a statement from those appearing therein.

An ethical problem associated with this kind of communication concerns identification of the source. When television stations do not identify the VNR as such, they do their viewers a disservice. Yet stations do not always give the public due warning that self-serving VNR material is produced by the candidate or company represented and was not subject to usual journalistic checks for accuracy.

Thus, in spite of their basic distrust of each other, public relations practitioners and journalists continue to live in a state of uneasy mutual dependency. Even a casual examination of the agenda produced by a daily paper or newscast will reveal that many stories—often the majority—are products of routine happenings in business, government, entertainment industries, education, politics, and so on. Here, reporters clearly rely on those who speak for politicians, personalities, corporations, and other special interests in the society. Thus, it is out of such complex interactions and exchanges that much of the daily news is generated and shaped.

LOBBYING AS PUBLIC RELATIONS

A special form of public relations is *lobbying,* although some experts would not see it as part of the field. Notwithstanding, lobbying has many similarities to the kinds of activities we have described as constituting public relations. Lobbyists are persons employed "to influence legislators to introduce or vote for measures favorable to the interests they represent."[5]

To achieve their influence on behalf of their clients, lobbyists rely mainly on *interpersonal communication* and *informal contacts* with those whom they try to influence. Nevertheless, lobbyists are persons or groups paid to engage in efforts to influence the beliefs, attitudes, and actions of specifically defined target individuals through the use of deliberately designed messages. Defined in this way, they fit quite well within the broad definition of public relations provided earlier. The main differences are that lobbyists seldom use the mass media and they focus their influence attempts narrowly on legislators.

Where did the name come from? When they were first identified in the nineteenth century as a distinct group of influence peddlers in Washington, D.C., they stood in the lobby of the venerable Willard Hotel in that city. The hotel still stands only a short walk from the White House and a few blocks from the Capitol building.

The convention is a major public relations and promotional tool wherein people come together to advance their cause and meet other people in the same industry as well as clients and customers. Conventions are an important source of revenue, a vehicle for high-level targeted communication, and a boon to public relations, as seen in the exhibit hall of the National Association for Cable Television Convention in Los Angeles. There are international, national, and regional conventions held for almost every interest (or group) known to humankind.

Many politicians of the time walked to the hotel to have lunch or an evening meal. When office holders came through the long, narrow lobby, those wanting to influence them would clutch at their sleeves and try to get their attention (much as had influence-seekers at centers of power since organized government began). In time, they came to be called "lobbyists." Even today, the Willard Hotel proudly tells its guests that the name was born right there.

Lobbyists represent a great variety of groups and interests. These include trade associations, veteran's groups, labor unions, political action committees, consumer advocates, professional associations, churches, foreign governments, and many more. There are literally tens of thousands of organizations and individuals who want to influence the legislative process. A lobbyist might be a lawyer, public relations practitioner, or policy expert who has been hired to influence the work of Congress. Not all work at the federal level; some represent clients at state and even local centers of government.

Federal law requires that lobbyists register with the Records and Registration Division of the Capitol Hill Lobbying Office. There are over 6,000 registered individual and group lobbyists in Washington, D.C., alone. They represent more than 11,000 active and about 28,000 inactive clients (those who have not been represented on Capitol Hill for the last three months). Some of the groups identify themselves as lobbying specialists. Others are public relations agencies, law firms, and "think tanks" (various mission-oriented institutes and centers).

Lobbying and lobbyists have always been a subject of controversy. Some critics regard them with deep suspicion. For example, in 1993 in a classic case, lobbying got on the news agenda very quickly when the late Ron Brown—former Chairman of the Democratic National Committee—was appointed Secretary of Commerce by President Bill Clinton. Brown had been a member of a well-known and very influential lobbying firm, Patten, Boggs and Blow, which had represented many special interests in Washington, D.C., over the years. Questions were raised as to whether Brown would favor those whom his firm had represented in the past. His untimely accidental death took this concern off the agenda, but the issue remains even today regarding others who make similar moves from a lobbying firm to government office.[6]

A move by any person between lobbying and government, or the reverse, illustrates a continuing focus of criticism. There is a constant rotation of individuals between government service and private influence-seeking roles. The problem that many people see is that former government officials or employees, when they return to or take jobs in lobbying, will use their inside knowledge and contacts to give the special interests that they represent an unfair advantage. There are now laws that prevent them from doing so, at least for several years after they leave office.

For a number of years, the two largest lobbying and public relations firms in Washington, D.C., have been Hill, Knowlton, Inc., and Burson-Marstellar, Inc., each of which has ties to advertising and public relations groups on a worldwide basis. Clients pay huge fees to be represented by such groups, and their annual billings are in the millions of dollars. Such firms use every conceivable tool and process to promote, change, or impede legislation pending before Congress that can have an effect on their clients. Sometimes even getting a single word changed in a bill (e.g., from "shall" to "may" or from "never" to "seldom") can mean millions to a client. Similar to the work of more traditional public relations firms, these types of lobbying and public relations firms organize events, perform research, develop communication strategies, or sometimes shape news, on behalf of their clients. Lobbyists at both federal and state levels write articles, make speeches, design campaigns, buy advertising, influence journalists, and try to guide public officials.

While many critics deplore all lobbying and lobbyists, others point out that they have a legitimate role in the process of government. They do bring a great deal of information to the attention of office-holders, which should be taken into account as laws are formed or modified. They bring together those who have legitimate interests with those who can have powerful influences on those interests. Often, legislators need to know who will be affected by the outcome of bills under consideration. The downside comes when special interests gain an advantage over the public good and scandals arise. Fortunately, consumer groups, the press, and our government constantly monitor lobbyists for ethical and other kinds of violations.

PUBLIC RELATIONS AS AN EMERGING PROFESSION

The term "professional" is an ancient one, going back to the Middle Ages, when there were only three basic "learned professions"—divinity, law, and medicine. What set them apart from other vocational pursuits were these major criteria: (1) Each had an extensive *body of sophisticated knowledge* requiring long periods of formal study to learn and master. (2) Their practitioners used that body of knowledge on behalf of the public *within a set of ethical norms.* And (3) their practitioners *monitored each other* to insure compliance with the norms, rejecting from their ranks those who engaged in unethical practices. To some extent, that prestigious interpretation of "profession" has survived, and many people want their particular type of vocational activity to be regarded as such. Among those are public relations practitioners. Today, there is a strong movement in public relations to develop the field as a profession.

Earlier, when the field was being established, no particular credentials were required to become a public relations specialist. Indeed, many of the earliest practitioners were simply ex-journalists who had an understanding of the workings of the press and who knew how to get stories about their clients into the pages of the newspapers. Moreover, it was all done by the "seat of the pants." That is, there was no body of concepts and principles that had been developed by systematic research. It was a field in which intuition, creativity, insights, and lore held sway. Often the guesses and inspirations of practitioners led to success; just as often they did not.

The label "professional" is now widely applied by the public to designate virtually any specialized occupational group. Thus, we hear of "professional" hairdressers, prizefighters, bartenders, and even dog groomers. However, it is the traditional meaning of the term, and its prestige, to which public relations practitioners and educators aspire, and there is evidence that at least some progress is being made. Today, two major factors are playing a central role in the evolution of public relations as a professional field. One is the increasing establishment and acceptance of *courses and degree programs in higher education*—meeting the criterion of formal study. The other is *systematic research and scholarly inquiry*—aimed directly at the second criterion, developing a complex body of knowledge. This body of knowledge consists of a growing accumulation of concepts, principles, theories, and practical solutions that are used in the practice of public relations.

A very important question concerns the third criterion of what constitutes a profession in the classical sense. This is whether or not the field's practitioners use that knowledge for the benefit of the public within an ethical framework. Furthermore, do they effectively monitor each other and reject those who transgress the ethical norms? That certainly is the case in the law, in medicine, and (perhaps less clearly) in the clergy. In the section that follows, we focus on public relations within the framework of these three formal criteria of a true profession.

Richard D. Jernstedt
Chief Executive Officer
Golin/Harris, **Chicago, Illinois**

insights from
MEDIA LEADERS

Richard D. Jernstedt is one of the most widely respected and professionally active leaders in the public relations field. He is the chief executive officer of a large, globally oriented public relations firm, which also owns other firms. Previously, he was executive vice president and president of Golin/Harris, where he has spent much of his career. Before joining the firm, he worked for the Container Corporation of America. Jernstedt has won a Silver Anvil Award from the Public Relations Society of America and serves as a director of both the International Public Relations Association and the Arthur W. Page Society.

Q. How did you initially get involved in the public relations field?

A. I became interested in some form of "journalism" very early, when I became editor of a mimeographed newspaper in the eighth grade. That led to an active role on my high school newspaper and yearbook staffs. At the same time, I got involved in a whole variety of event-planning activities in high school and college. Then, I majored in journalism at the University of Oregon and thought of a career in advertising and public relations. After college and with some generous letters of recommendation, I became a public affairs officer in the U.S. Navy. For almost three years, I served on board aircraft carriers (one at a time), which took me around the world. I was the ship's "PR man," which involved internal communications to the crew; managing the ship's TV and radio stations; publishing a daily newsletter, a monthly magazine, and a "cruise book." I also took care of media relations and served as the captain's ghost writer.

Q. That sounds like more than a full plate of activities that could have taken you in different directions.

A. Yes, it was, but looking back those assignments brought together my interest in writing and communicating to and for others—all linked to constant challenges in the field of communications and public relations, which I chose to follow.

Q. What factors have sustained your interest in and commitment to public relations over the years?

A. It is what I said before and the fact that public relations work is managing, explaining, preventing, promoting, and defending change. The variety and stimulation of the work makes it terrific career for someone who likes to be a part of the news, dealing with what's happening, and relaying information. Of course, there is variety. No two days are ever the same. And it is important work as we help clients communicate effectively to key constituencies. Best of all, you always meet and work with interesting people.

Q. What have been the main influences that have led you to your current position as Chief Executive Officer of a global communications and management firm?

A. First, it was being in the right place at the right time. When I arrived at Golin/Harris twenty-three years ago, we were a small firm with one large client—McDonald's. After several exciting years on the McDonald's account with increasing responsibility, I worked to build up the "other side" of the office, bringing in new business and recruiting excellent talent. And we grew. We moved from thirty people to thirteen hundred people. Of course, the public relations industry

PUBLIC RELATIONS EDUCATION

Public relations has been taught in universities since 1923, when Edward Bernays organized the first course at New York University. Early on, it was taught mostly in journalism schools that were largely newspaper-oriented and not always hospitable to the inclusion of public relations in the curriculum. This prejudice toward public relations has faded over the years, although a few journalism schools still bar it from the curriculum. The first formal undergraduate degree program in public relations was established at Boston University in 1947. In more recent times, speech-communication departments also have added public relations programs, as have many

has grown as it offers the right services to the right clients. We've been fortunate to have resources from our parent company that allowed us to acquire other firms. Always, there is a chance to learn and grow in this company.

Q. **What is your take on the current state and probable future of public relations? To what extent is the success of Golin/Harris indicative of the field in general?**

A. Well, it is a very exciting time for public relations generally—and for us at Golin/Harris. The profession itself—and yes, I regard it as a profession—is being understood and valued by more people all the time. It is no longer an afterthought of crumbs from the table, using money left over from the all-important advertising budget. Its importance is now, more than ever, recognized and valued. Why? Because, public relations is essential to the success of all kinds of enterprises—businesses, associations, not-for-profits, individuals. To be sure, public relations people are more important than ever as advisers to senior management. That's because we are in a period of information overflow that is characterized by information interaction. Experts are necessary to help manage, process, target, and respond to this flow. And it will be better (or worse) depending on your point of view as we go forward. More resources will be applied to the public relations function. That means public relations will constantly be redefined and broadened. Yes, I am bullish about the future of this field.

Q. **What is the best pathway to a satisfying career in this field for people beginning today?**

A. The main thing is to keep learning. Stay on top of trends, technology, audiences, and attitudes. Learn what your client needs to be successful and deliver it. For the person entering the field today, it is important to be bold, to challenge yourself and your management. There is no limit to the role you can play if you are prepared, motivated, and anxious to serve. It is also awfully important to be global, to think globally. Realize that the world is getting smaller. That means understanding the differences between cultures in the markets important to your clients, products, services, people, and communications.

Q. **Based on job satisfaction, compensation, and long-term prospects, how would you rate public relations as a career choice?**

A. Very high. For those interested in communications careers, this is a hot category. It is growing in size and importance. In fact, some studies say it is the third fastest growing profession in the country. The compensation is good and getting better.

Q. **What is the most satisfying aspect of work in this field? The least?**

A. Most satisfying: the creative, ever-changing nature of the work and the people in it. And the realization that the work is important while being challenging and fun.

Most frustrating: the people who don't understand this yet. Clients who don't recognize the value of your counsel (sometimes until it's too late). And staff who don't recognize the potential of the contribution that can be made to clients.

comprehensive communication schools and colleges. In addition, there are individual courses in public relations at community colleges and industry trade schools.

Today, public relations has not only developed into a rapidly growing field of study in higher education, but also it has taken other important steps to try to establish itself as a profession. For example, the organization that periodically examines and approves of journalism and mass communication curricula in the United States also reviews public relations course work in specific institutions to determine if it qualifies as an "accredited" sequence. (Other regularly reviewed areas of study are news-editorial, magazine, and radio-television news.)

There are several hundred professors of public relations offering courses in schools or departments of journalism and communications and in speech-communication programs in the United States, and every year thousands of students major in the field. Student internships are available with public relations firms, businesses, government agencies, and professional associations. Dozens of textbooks and a number of technical journals reporting research results are devoted to the field. Public relations practitioners also have their own national organization, the Public Relations Society of America (PRSA), with student chapters on many campuses as well.

A formal curriculum in public relations at the undergraduate level usually includes substantial work in the liberal arts and sciences. Typically, a public relations major includes an overview course on public relations as a communication field, an advanced course in public relations methods, and other specific courses of instruction in various aspects of the field—depending on the size and sophistication of the program. Public relations curricula at the graduate level usually involve formal communication theory courses and (science-based) research training as well as instruction in the field's areas of specialization. Over the last three decades, public relations has become one of the most popular communication majors as students in the information age realized the importance of the field and of other media-consulting activities. The fact that the field pays more than most other media-related industries is an added attraction.

The purpose of public relations education is to promote the field as a professional communications activity, to produce a well-educated work force, and to foster research. However, this does not mean that people who aspire to work in public relations must major in public relations at a university or college. Although there is a great and growing demand for people formally educated in public relations, many still get into the field by working for newspapers or other media. Some people come into public relations as specialists—for example, they may have a background in public health and take up a public relations assignment in that area. Thus, there are many pathways to a public relations career. At the same time, most university-based public relations programs have the advantage of having close links with the industry and are better positioned to help their students get jobs in the field.

PUBLIC RELATIONS RESEARCH

A second significant area of development in public relations is research. This, too, represents an effort to gain full professional status by fulfilling the first criterion of having an extensive body of specialized knowledge. However, as will be clear, in many ways that body remains to be developed.

Much of the research done in the field by practitioners stems from practical rather than theoretical considerations. Clients want to see what kind of "bang" they have received for their "buck." This means that "research" consists mainly of assessing the results of a particular campaign or determining the needs of a client in order to develop an appropriate strategy. Although public relations was once carried out with little formal evaluation, businesses and governmental departments increasingly require that public relations practitioners document expenditures and provide reliable evidence that some kinds of benefits flow from those costs.

Much of the body of more sophisticated knowledge relevant to the impact and influence of public relations continues to be derived from basic media and communication research conducted by social scientists and academic media scholars.

Thus, research has been accumulating on such general topics as the process of persuasion; how media agenda setting takes place; the nature of attitudes and their links to behavior; and how public opinion is formed, influenced, and translated into policy shifts or the behavior of some category of citizens.

At the same time, a growing field of applied research—more specifically focused on problems and practices in public relations—has also emerged. Some public relations agencies and departments conduct in-house assessment studies simply to take stock of their activities. Other applied research is done in universities by public relations professors. This type of academic research is broader in scope and less parochial than that typically done by public relations practitioners. University research usually aims at establishing general concepts, patterned relationships, and theories that help explain processes and effects in the field. Thus, this research makes important contributions to the growing body of knowledge that is developing for the field.

Public relations scholar John V. Pavlik has identified at least three general reasons for conducting basic public relations research: One is understanding public relations *as communication,* which involves building communication theory and studying the effects of public relations activity on the individual, group, and society. A second is *solving practical problems* in the field, including monitoring the public relations environment, measuring social performance, and auditing communication and public relations. A third stems from the need to *monitor the profession,* by taking stock of how public relations practitioners, individually and collectively, are performing technically and ethically.[7]

At the practitioner level, much of the in-house public relations research done by agencies gives clients feedback and helps them improve communication with their constituencies. Some critics say that such research is manipulative, but defenders say it is simply intelligent, systematic information that can make the client more sensitive to the desired audience. How public relations people use such information is up to them—hopefully most will use it ethically.

The state of *proprietary* public relations research (yielding results that are kept secret by an agency or practitioner) and its actual use by people in the field is difficult to ascertain. The largest and most powerful public relations firms and government departments spend a considerable amount of time and money testing their messages and monitoring campaigns for evidence that they are having some effect. At the same time, many small public relations firms and individual practitioners make limited use of research in their work. Some publicists do not use research at all, preferring an intuitive "seat of the pants" approach. General usage on a day-to-day basis of the kinds of public relations research typically reported in academic journals is limited. Yet such research contributes to that much-needed body of knowledge that can help imaginative and thoughtful practitioners and planners move toward professional status.

ETHICAL ISSUES AND CRITICISMS

As public relations continues its struggle to be recognized as a profession, one of its major problems lies in the *public image* of the field and in developing and enforcing a meaningful *code of ethics.* As we noted earlier, almost from its beginnings public relations has had its detractors. Critics charge that public relations activity is manipulative, self-serving, and often unethical. They maintain that it distorts and blurs issues in its attempts to persuade the public, and that publicists will use just about any means to assure a favorable image for their clients.

Such charges are not without foundation. There are unscrupulous people in public relations. The same is true of physicians, lawyers, or any other profession. However, in public relations, questionable or unethical practices can become especially visible because of the nature of what these practitioners do. Unlike the botched surgery or the ineptly handled legal case that the public does not learn about, the products or outcomes of public relations practitioners are usually open to scrutiny. Public-spirited groups and the news media make special efforts to try ferret out deceptive activities. As a result, public relations practitioners who transgress norms almost immediately receive unfavorable press coverage. In addition, even if not detected immediately, unethical practices sometimes backfire and at a later time harm the image that public relations is meant to polish.

To its credit, the field makes extensive efforts to reduce poor practices. To be *accredited* by the Public Relations Society of America, a practitioner working professionally in the field must pass tests of communication skills and agree to abide by a code of good practice. In addition, many college and university programs include courses on public relations ethics. Hopefully, these conditions taken together will eventually limit flagrant deceptions of the public.

In spite of these efforts, those who criticize the basic task of public relations focus on a more fundamental problem: They raise the question as to whether there is something less than honorable in a business devoted to enhancing the image of a corporation or individual by selectively suppressing truths that would bring criticism if known, and emphasizing only favorable meanings. To the critics, this is a serious charge and it is this aspect of the basic mission of many public relations campaigns that is most troublesome. Defenders say that a corporation or individual has every right to put on the best face possible before the public. Moreover, public relations practitioners do provide useful information to people in an increasingly complex and bureaucratic world—although most would agree that in an ideal world such information should be balanced with information from more objective sources.

As efforts toward professionalization of the field continue, such negative views of the field may change. One reason they may change is that during the past twenty years, the important concept of "public accountability" has found increasing favor among public relations specialists. This idea has received much attention and has been integrated into public relations education, thinking, and practice. The accountability concept is tied to the idea of "corporate social responsibility," which stipulates that a business ought to contribute as much to the common good as to its own economic success.

According to this idea, a responsible corporation should make a *positive contribution* to local communities or to the nation as a whole in which it is allowed to function. Indeed, many corporations and local firms have done this. As a profit-oriented industry, however, public relations still has a long way to go in this respect, and it often appears to lack accountability. For example, after Hurricane Hugo hit the Caribbean islands in the 1990s, promoters of tourism quickly organized information about which islands and resorts were still open for business—even though they had been hit by widespread destruction and were in the midst of relief efforts. While some criticized this seemingly insensitive campaign, others argued that the future employment and prosperity of the islanders depended on sustaining the tourist trade. In such a case, critics of public relations may charge that no one represents the consumer. On the other hand, publicists may counter that their own ethical standards prevent them from deliberately misleading the public, and that the promoters were doing a service by providing accurate information in the midst of rumor and misinformation. There are no easy answers, and there will be none until the canons of ethics for such complex public relations situations are further developed, clarified, and universally adopted by the field.

Today, one of the major ethical sore points among critics of the industry lies in the area of public relations during elections. Political campaign consultants often approach and sometimes cross the ethical borderline. Negative or "attack" ads provide a case in point. These can be both deceptive and unfair. A classic example in modern times, often cited, was developed by Roger Ailes, who worked for George Bush in his successful presidential campaign against Michael Dukakis. The campaign Ailes designed ran negative television ads that many critics said appealed to racial fears among white voters. The most criticized was the so-called "Willy Horton" ad that showed convicts going through a revolving door—to represent a prison furlough policy approved by Dukakis as a liberal Governor of Massachusetts. The meaning conveyed was that candidate Dukakis was so liberal that he was insensitive to the fact that a convicted African-American murderer (Horton) was knowingly let out on furlough only to commit another terrible crime. In addition, Ailes admitted that he planted other doubts in reporters' minds about Dukakis, knowing full well that the imputations were false. Ailes and other political consultants who "play hardball" in their public relations efforts are often criticized by the press and their colleagues. However, as long as they successfully accomplish their goals in getting people elected, it is doubtful that they will change their tactics.

Attack ads played a significant role in the Bill Clinton versus Bob Dole presidential campaign. Democrats targeted Newt Gingrich (Republican Congressman from Georgia and Speaker of the House) in particular, with negative ads that many citizens felt crossed the line. On the other hand, candidate Dole's consultants focused forcefully on President Clinton's personal troubles with women toward the end of the campaign with very negative ads. In the 2000 presidential election, campaign ads, paid for by the National Association for the Advancement of Colored People, tried to associate George W. Bush with a brutal, racially inspired murder in Texas while Al Gore was accused of being hostile to gun owners by the National Rifle Association.

Research shows that even though many voters say that they deplore attempts to influence their votes with negative advertising, such attack ads really do work. Michel Elasmar, Philip Napoli, and Melvin DeFleur reviewed the accumulated research on the issue and studied their influence.[8] It is clear that such ads can bring about changes in vote intentions among the electorate. Given such findings, it is likely that public relations consultants advising candidates and helping design their communications will continue in this practice.

THE FUTURE OF THE FIELD

While many efforts are being made by public relations to be identified as a "profession" in the traditional sense, it is clear that the field has a way to go. The current status of the field can be assessed against the three criteria discussed above: Progress is clearly being made on the first criterion. That is, through research and scholarship the field is assembling a *body of complex knowledge*. Moreover, that accumulated knowledge is now being taught in formal courses and degree sequences in

Public relations firms were early users of the Internet, recognizing the value of its interactive capacity. Most of these sites are primarily aimed at business-to-business communication, rather than individual consumers or audience members, although the site is open to all.

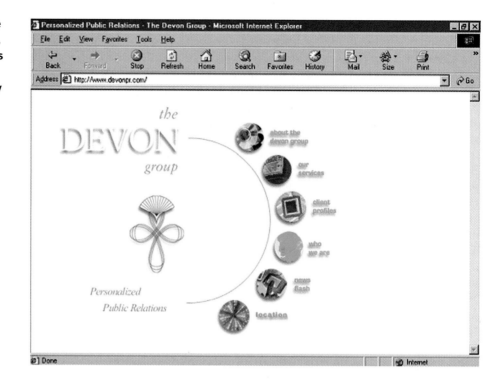

colleges and universities. There is less certainty as to how well the second criterion is being met. That is, it could be hotly debated whether public relations practitioners *serve the public* with their knowledge. In some ways they do, but there are grounds for concluding that for the most part they serve only those well-heeled clients who can afford their fees. Indeed, many critics believe that public relations campaigns often deliberately fool the public by suppressing damaging information and emphasizing only positive messages about their clients. Finally, there is as of yet no codified set of ethical norms to which public relations practitioners universally subscribe, and there certainly is no way in which those who cross the line on ethical standards can be drummed out of the profession—as clearly is the case in both medicine and the law. Therefore, it will be interesting to see, in the years ahead, if the field can resolve these problems and gain the public trust that has largely failed to develop over the years thus far.

One way in which public relations will continue to change in the future is through the development of new strategies to reach relevant publics. That is not to say "serve" the public—the benefits go to clients who pay the bills. In any case, practitioners seek ways to make use of technological advances in communication systems within the United States and all over the world. With new media available, public relations specialists have been able to design new formats, such as home pages and sites on the World Wide Web, CD-ROMs that present information to clients and the public, video news releases, and other ways of presenting messages about their clients to relevant receivers.

Today, public relations messages compete with other kinds of information for public attention in an environment that includes many kinds of media and a great variety of sources. Increasingly important are personal computers connected to the Internet and its World Wide Web. Many millions of people worldwide access a vast array of specialized information via this medium. E-mail enables people, both within and between groups, to transmit and receive information of many kinds. Computer-based teleconferencing brings small groups together for discussions, even though they may be at sites remote from each other. Public relations agencies, consultants, and individual practitioners make use of all of these media for a variety of purposes. For example, Web sites and home pages have become very common. Many are sophisticated and "interactive" in that a person contacting them can access various kinds of information by clicking on "buttons" designed in the system. Often, an agency will post important information for potential clients or journalists on such a system. This makes it easier for them to receive it, as opposed to making telephone calls to get the same information, with their inevitable recorded voices and requests to press different numbers to reach specific people.

This continuously evolving world of privatized communication does not rely on mass media in the traditional sense at all. It is targeted to specific individuals, within both established groups and new constituencies. The digital medium offers a more precise way of reaching a desired audience than, say, the special-interest magazine. In fact, the most specialized publication probably has a more diverse readership than the audiences currently being targeted by new data services. There is also a considerable online news industry that has been undergoing a pattern of increasingly rapid use. Special-interest newsletters, often transmitted electronically, reach every conceivable category of the public, from chocolate lovers to travelers of exotic countries to fans of professional wrestling. Thus, many "publics" that desire highly specific information can be reached with new media.

In a basic sense, the future of public relations is not difficult to predict. It is a field that has developed rapidly over the last century, and regardless of its critics, there is no doubt whatever that it will continue to be an essential part of our complex society in the future. Organizations that produce goods and services that are important to the public need public relations to maintain goodwill and favorable attitudes on the part of those that consume their products. The public, on the other hand, benefits when such organizations continue to function—employing people, providing products and services, and conducting activities that the society requires.

As explained, there is a relationship of dependency between public relations and journalism. Reporters, editors, and news directors need information that public relations supply because it makes up a large part of what journalists report to the public. In turn, public relations practitioners are dependent on the news media to transmit many of their announcements, campaigns, and releases to their audiences. Thus, public relations will remain a field intricately interwoven into the major media, activities, and affairs of the society. It is completely unrealistic to assume that its importance will diminish in the years ahead.

Chapter Review

- Public relations can be defined as the work and outcomes of paid professional practitioners who design and transmit messages, on behalf of a client, via a variety of media to relevant and targeted audiences in an attempt to influence audience's beliefs, attitudes, or even actions regarding some person, organization, policy, situation, or event.

- Many of the communication strategies used today in public relations have ancient origins. An example is the sun-god strategy used by Hammurabi to characterize his laws. That dates back four thousand years. However, the field's more modern origins lie in the "publicity men," "press agents," and agencies that developed in New York City early in the twentieth century. Their task was, much as it is today, to improve the image of clients.

- Most, but not all, public relations efforts make extensive use of the mass communications. Practitioners constantly try to draw attention to their clients by information transmitted by the media in news reports, talk shows, or in any form of print or broadcast content that can show their client in a favorable light.

- An uneasy relationship exists between the field of public relations and the media—more specifically, journalism. However, each is dependent upon the other. Much of what appears in the news has origins in events or information released by public relations practitioners. At the same time, such practitioners are deeply dependent on the media as a means of transmitting their messages to their desired audiences.

- Lobbying can be considered as a special, if controversial, form of public relations. Lobbyists use a variety of interpersonal and other communication techniques to try to influence legislators as they initiate, modify, and pass laws that can have an influence on their clients.

- Today, there is a strong movement among its practitioners and educators to try to transform public relations into a *profession*. Whether this will be successful or not depends on how well the field meets three major criteria: (1) developing a body of sophisticated knowledge, (2) using that knowledge for the public good within a system of ethical norms, and (3) ensuring compliance to those norms by monitoring practitioners.

- The accomplishment of the field in both education and research would appear to satisfy the first criterion. There is considerable doubt of whether the field's practitioners always try to use that knowledge for the benefit of the public within an ethical framework. Furthermore, efforts to monitor each other and reject those who transgress the ethical norms have not been impressive, to say the least.

- Therefore, the field has a number of problems to solve before it can gain professional status in the classic meaning of that term. It will be interesting to see, in the years ahead, if the field can resolve these problems and gain the public trust that has thus far failed to develop over the years.

Notes and References

1. Frank Cobb, *The New Republic,* December 31, 1919, p. 44. For a critical assessment of PR history, see Larry Tye, *The Father of Spin: Edward L. Bernays and the Birth of Public Relations* (New York: Crown, 1998) and Stewart Ewan, *PR—A Social History of Spin* (New York: Basic Books, 1998).

2. Walter Lippmann, *Public Opinion* (New York: Harcourt, Brace and Company, 1922), p. 345.

3. Lippmann, *Public Opinion,* p. 64. See also James E. Grunig and Todd Hunt, *Managing Public Relations* (New York: Holt, 1984), Chapter 5. A useful text is Dennis L. Wilcox, Philip Ault, Warren K. Asee, and Glen T. Cameron, *Public Relations: Strategies and Tactics,* 6th ed. (New York: Longman, 2000). See also Scott M. Cutlip, Allen H. Center, and Glenn M. Broom, *Effective Public Relations,* 8th ed. (Englewood Cliffs, N.J.: Prentice-Hall, 1999).

4. Scott M. Cutlip, Allen H. Center, and Glenn M. Broom, *Effective Public Relations,* 6th ed. (Englewood Cliffs, N.J.: Prentice-Hall, 1985), pp. 138–230. See also Cutlip, Center, and Broom, *Effective Public Relations,* 8th ed.

5. *American Heritage Dictionary of the English Language* (Boston: Houghton Mifflin, 1970). See also Clarke L. Caywood, ed., *The Handbook of Strategic Public Relations and Integrated Communications* (New York: McGraw-Hill, 1996).

6. The nation was saddened when Ron Brown was killed in an airplane crash in 1996.

7. John V. Pavlik, *Public Relations: What Research Tells Us* (Beverly Hills: Sage Publications, 1987).

8. Michel Elasmar, Philip Napoli, and Melvin DeFleur, "The Effect of Television Advertising on Voting Intentions During the 1996 New Hampshire Primaries," paper presented at the Broadcast Education Association, Las Vegas, Nevada, 1997.

Chapter 13

THE AUDIENCE: CHARACTERISTICS OF USERS OF THE MEDIA

Suburban neighborhoods continue to grow and reflect changing audiences for American media.

IN 1854, IN HIS LITERARY CLAS-SIC *WALDEN,* **THE RENOWNED AMERICAN AUTHOR HENRY DAVID** Thoreau observed that each human being was different from others, and that the diversity among us should be respected. He wrote:

> If a man does not keep pace with his companions, perhaps it is because he hears a different drummer. Let him step to the music which he hears, however measured or far away.[1]

Like Thoreau's marcher, we all step to a different drummer when it comes to attending to mass communications. We do so because, psychologically, each of us is a unique individual with distinct interests, tastes, and preferences in what we want to read, hear, view, and communicate to others.

Each person's priorities are a consequence of what he or she has been taught or has learned on his or her own. One may love spectator sports, detective mysteries, quiz shows, professional wrestling, and soap operas, while another shuns such popular culture and prefers classical music, poetry, serious drama, political commentators, and documentary films.

The development of each person's pattern of preferences is heavily influenced not only by inherited factors, such as age and gender, but also by the social environment in which the person has lived. That social environment includes the individual's family, friends, neighborhood, community, and society—plus all of the specific groups that have been a part of that person's life at home, school, work, and play. It also includes the social categories into which each member of an audience can be classified—income level, educational attainment, religion, race, or ethnicity. In various ways, each of these factors plays a part in determining the media content that a particular person will attend to or ignore, find interesting or dull, be influenced by, or remain unmoved. It is for that reason that the *personal and social characteristics* of the American population—the audience for each of our media—is of profound interest to mass communicators. Those who understand that audience, its patterns of preferences and their sources, have a better chance of succeeding than those who are unaware of its variations. The great diversity of the American population, including its past and current directions of change, then, are key aspects of the mass communication process.

Because these aspects are so important, this chapter begins by focusing on the basic factors that underlie audience individuality. It examines the distinctions that can be found among us in terms of age, gender, income, education, race, and ethnicity. It also examines how these factors continue to change in the American population. Then, the chapter discusses ongoing trends in audience-related social processes, such as urbanization, migration, and family composition—all of which can modify peoples' communications behavior.

The final issue addressed in the chapter is how these various differences, preferences, and priorities among the audience are *assessed* so that professional communicators can obtain an understanding of who selects and attends to what. Various kinds of rating systems and other ways of measuring audience attention to media presentations reveal its size, composition, and patterns of usage.

Within the perspective of theories that aid in understanding mass communication, by examining the American population as media audience, this chapter looks at the *receiving end of the linear model* of mass communication. In the six stages of that model, we noted that the process begins with *professional communicators* who decide on *the nature and goals of the message;* additional steps are *encoding the intended meanings* and *transmitting the message* via the specialized technologies of print, film, broadcasting, and computer-based systems to a *heterogeneous audience* that *attends and responds selectively.* In chapters 2 through 8, we discussed those technologies and indicated how each medium develops and transmits its messages. Various types of content were also discussed in chapters 9 through 12. It is the final stage of the linear model in which members of the large and diverse audience selectively attend to, perceive, and assign meanings to what they read, view, or hear—to be influenced in their feelings, thoughts, or action—that are the subject of this chapter.

As we have made clear, our system of mass communication rests solidly on private ownership, free enterprise, and competition in the marketplace. While there are exceptions, the bottom line in the system is that it is designed to earn money from its audiences, either directly or indirectly, in order to produce *profit*. That is, content is prepared for the media that the audiences will buy directly, or that will attract their attention to advertising designed to motivate them to purchase goods and services. Thus, an understanding of the tastes and interests of the audience and their sources that bring them to make selections from the media are the *sine qua non*—the absolute necessity—for anyone who attempts to be successful in the mass communication business.

The sections that follow do not try to sort out details about which specific media reach exactly how many people with particular kinds of content. Instead, the discussions focus on the nature of audiences, some of their preferences, and the techniques used by the major media to assess them. Similarly, these sections also do not try to identify the kinds of influences mass communications have on audiences, which will come later (in Chapter 15). Instead, this chapter focuses on the historical and contemporary sources of diversity in the American audience. It discusses the sources of that diversity and how it is undergoing changes that have implications for contemporary mass communications. This will help make clear the reasons for which we indicated in our discussion of the linear model that the "multitude of receivers will have a multitude of ways in which to select and assign meanings to a multitude of incoming mass communicated messages."

Essentially, the first section of our discussion of the American population as "audience" reviews two major issues: One is the *size* of the population and how that continues to change. A second is its complex *composition*. By composition we refer to such factors as age, gender, education, income, race, and ethnicity. All of these factors lead to multicultural and personal diversity in our media audiences, providing the basis for modern counterparts of what Thoreau had in mind when he posed his metaphor. Because each of us is different in our personal combinations of social identities, we do indeed hear different drummers as we select and respond to content from the media. This leads each of us to step to music that may not be perceived in the same way, or even heard at all, by other kinds of people, as we think about or act upon these selections.

THE CHANGING AMERICAN POPULATION

The sheer number of people in a population can be critical to the success or failure of particular kinds of media at particular times. We saw earlier that one of the reasons why magazines failed in colonial American was because when they were introduced the population was too small and too scattered to provide a viable market. In addition, we saw that it was the growth of population in such urban centers as New York City, and generally along the more populated eastern seaboard, that provided the initial audiences for the penny press—the forerunners of modern newspapers.

Today, with our population exceeding 283 million, there is little danger that there will be too few people in the nation as a whole to support any major medium. Indeed, the U.S. population is forecast to double in size during the twenty-first century. On the other hand, that population has never been, and is not now, evenly distributed among the states and within local regions. Population can influence decisions such as to where to have a TV cable system, where to establish home delivery of a newspaper, or whether it is economically feasible to build a movie theater in a local mall. Furthermore, the size of any population—local or national—*changes* over time, which can have significant influences on the viability of particular media. This is particularly true at the local level: If a town or city is losing population, its newspapers, radio stations, and even its movie theaters may fall upon hard times as the numbers they serve decline. The opposite is obviously true if the community is growing. We need to understand, therefore, what factors determine *population size* and *change,* both at a national level and in particular areas or communities.

FACTORS PRODUCING POPULATION GROWTH OR DECLINE

The size of any population in any particular area at any particular time is a product of three specific factors: the number of *births* that increase the population during a particular period, the number of *deaths* that occur during that period and remove people from the population, and the pattern of *migration* into or out of the area that results in a gain or loss of residents. If one knows the trends in these three factors, one can anticipate their nature in the years ahead. Predictions of population size are not difficult, at least on a short-term basis. These are important data, then, in management decisions for whether or not to provide various kinds of media services.

A problem in predicting population size is that all three of the above factors can change rapidly and rather sharply. The birth rate in a particular area can rise or fall as people make decisions about starting, expanding, delaying, or stabilizing the size of their families, which happens as the economy waxes and wanes. The death rate generally rises or falls depending on the availability of medical treatment and as public health measures (clean water, inoculation programs, effective waste disposal, and food inspections) deteriorate or improve. Migration is not as easy to predict as people move into or out of an area due to the availability of work, welfare benefits, housing, protection from crime, religious or racial intolerance, and so forth. In fact, among the American population, where people chose to live changed greatly during the twentieth century as a product of births, deaths, and migration.

To gain an appreciation of how population size—and numbers of people available for media audiences—can change as a result of the above three factors, we can review our pattern of population change at the *national* level during the twentieth century. It was during this period that our mass media saw their major patterns of

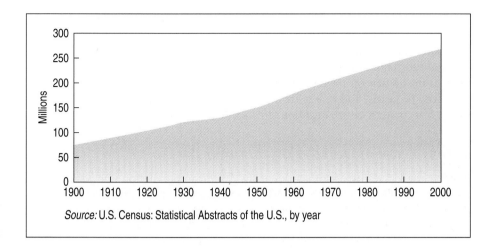

figure13.1
Growth of the American Population, 1900–2000

Source: U.S. Census: Statistical Abstracts of the U.S., by year

growth. While the print media were already well established as the century began, radio, motion pictures, and television in all its forms developed after 1900.

As Figure 13.1 shows, there was long-term expansion of the American population throughout the previous century. Actually, that expansion started earlier, as soon as the 1800s began; by 1840, large numbers of immigrants were already pouring into the United States. At the end of the 1800s, the population had reached 76 million—up sharply from its mere 5.3 million at the century's beginning—that is an astonishing 1,335.7 percent increase in essentially three generations (of about thirty years each). This increase was mainly due to one of the largest human migrations in the history of the world as millions of immigrants poured into the United States.

All during the nineteenth century, attracting immigrants was a deliberate national policy. Shortly after the United States was established, it acquired vast new territories. The undeveloped land was an open invitation to external aggressors. Settlers were needed to farm and secure millions of square miles when the nation's geographic boundaries expanded as a result of two huge land acquisitions. The first acquisition was the Louisiana Purchase of 1803, which—for a mere $15 million—added what are now the states of Arkansas, Iowa, Kansas, Missouri, Nebraska, North Dakota, South Dakota, and most of Minnesota, Montana, Oklahoma, Louisiana, and Wyoming. The second acquisition, following a war with Mexico, was the result of the 1848 treaty of Guadaloupe-Hidalgo. It permitted the United States to acquire, for another $15 million, what is now California, New Mexico, and Utah, plus major parts of Arizona, Texas, Colorado, and smaller sections of other states.

These monumental real estate bargains (about three cents per acre) opened enormous territories to settlement. In 1862, during the Civil War, the federal government established the Homestead Act, which allowed any citizen—even any non-legal resident who had filed a declaration to become a citizen—to acquire ownership of up to one hundred eighty acres of public land free of cost by promising to reside and farm on the site for five years. Entire regions were populated by immigrants taking advantage of this extraordinary offer.[2] No one in the history of the world had simply given away such large amounts of land.

To develop the nation's agriculture more rapidly, Congress, through the Morrill Act of 1862, granted large tracts of land to the states to establish colleges, where off-spring of the settlers could study the "agricultural and mechanical arts." These educational sites have become our great land-grant colleges and universities.

Institutions with the term "State" in their titles were established in this way (e.g., Ohio State, Michigan State, and Washington State universities.) The result of all these land transactions and population movements during the nineteenth century was that the majority of the American population lived on farms. The United States reached the 50 percent urban/rural point in the 1920s in which half of the population lived in farms. Today, less than 2 percent of Americans continue to live ON farms. This pattern of urbanization (town and city growth) was a major change.

IMMIGRATION AS A BASIS OF CULTURAL DIVERSITY

In 2000, the U.S. Census estimated that the American population was just over 280 million—up 204 million from the 76 million at beginning of the 1900s. Although this is a growth of 259 percent—which is enormous—it is far less than the rate of expansion in the previous century. One of the important features of our current rate of population growth is that it is largely a result of *immigration,* through which the population continues to increase. In fact, according to the Bureau of the Census estimates, the United States added another 25.4 million during the 1990s alone.[3] While the birth rate is declining in the United States, large numbers of immigrants (legal and illegal) still continue to pour in. Many come from Mexico; others arrive from Asian countries, South America, and the Caribbean.

Because of the legality of slavery prior to the Civil War, millions of Africans arrived in the United States over a span of more than two hundred years. Today, their offspring remain our largest distinct minority category, contributing to diversity in the American population. (That is changing as the Hispanic population continues to grow.) In addition, millions of Europeans came as part of the earliest large-scale immigrations in the 1800s to settle in the northeastern and midwestern states. These vast parts of the country were virtually empty of farms and settlements at the time, and federal authorities wanted immigrants from Europe to settle and farm the land. The fact that Native Americans were already there did not trouble the young nation. They were either killed or forced onto reservations. The immigrants who replaced them during the early and mid-1800s were mainly from England, Ireland, Scotland, France, Scandinavia, and Germany.

Toward the end of the 1800s, the origins of the immigrants shifted to southern and eastern Europe as millions of Italians, Poles, Russians, Czechs, and Hungarians arrived through the great port of entry at Ellis Island in New York City's harbor. Many remained in cities on the eastern seaboard, but others went on to the upper Midwest and found work in mines, mills, and factories.

The importance of these immigration patterns is that they produced a nation of great ethnic, racial, and cultural diversity. In this sense, the emerging United States was a different kind of nation than those in Europe and Asia, where even today the racial and ethnic composition of populations remains more or less stable.

As Table 13.1 shows, by the 1990s the population of the United States was one made up largely of the offspring of immigrants. The grandparents, or even parents, of many contemporary American families arrived in this country in the late nineteenth or early twentieth century. The cultural values and lifestyles that they brought are still to some degree alive and well in the United States. We can see that in our ethnic neighborhoods, foods, folk festivals, and diverse religious groups.

During the period of the great immigrations, the national policy was that of a "melting pot," in which all immigrants were expected to drop their foreign ways and merge into a single American culture. It was an important policy at the time, and one that had been deliberately adopted. The melting-pot concept was intended to

Table 13.1	U.S. Population by Ethnic Group, Census of 1990		
Ethnic Group	**Population (thousands)**	**Ethnic Group**	**Population (thousands)**
European		**Hispanic**	
English	49,596	Mexican	7,693
German	49,224	Puerto Rican	1,444
Irish	40,166	Cuban	598
French	12,892	Dominican	171
Italian	12,184	Spanish/Hispanic	2,687
Scottish	10,049	Colombian	156
Polish	8,228	Spanish	95
Dutch	6,304	Ecuadoran	88
Swedish	4,345	Salvadoran	85
Norwegian	3,454	Total	13,017
Russian	2,781		
Czech	1,892	**Asian**	
Hungarian	1,777	Chinese	894
Welsh	1,665	Fillipino	795
Danish	1,518	Japanese	791
Portuguese	1,024	Korean	377
Total	207,099	Asian Indian	312
		Vietnamese	125
Middle-Eastern		Total	3,294
Lebanese	295		
Armenian	213	**Other**	
Iranian	123	Jamaican	253
Syrian	107	Haitian	90
Total	738	Hawaiian	202
		Native American	6,716
African		French-Canadian	780
Afro-American	20,965	Canadian	456
African	204	Total	8,497
Total	21,169	Grand Total	253,814

Source: U.S. Census: Statistical Abstract of the U.S., 111th ed. (Washington D.C., 1991); these data were not published by the 2000 Census when population totals rose to 283 million overall.

unify the nation politically and reduce the risk that age-old blood hatreds and ethnic animosities would create destructive political conflict in the United States. (Currently, one can see the result of such problems in Canada, where French descendants have tried to divide the nation. The same is true of the former Soviet Union with its problems in Chechnya, the ethnic conflict in the Balkan countries that made up the former Yugoslavia, and the stressful tribal upheavals in Africa.)

In retrospect, the melting-pot policy worked very well at the time. Today, on the whole, we are able to function relatively smoothly within our secular democratic institutions that separate church and state, which are not organized along distinctions based on language or nationality of origin. The United States did not form a checkerboard of separate cultural, religious, or political identities. We also share a common language—even though others are also spoken. Moreover, although there are people in this country with almost every conceivable ethnic and religious background, there is a widely shared *general American culture* that is overwhelmingly visible in the content of our mass media. There is minority and foreign-language media content readily available, but it represents only a fraction of what is offered overall.

At the same time, the melting pot now is seen by at least some Americans as "politically incorrect." In retrospect, it is not difficult to understand that point of view. The melting-pot policy brought disrespect to other people's cultures. In many cases it produced prejudice, discrimination based on ethnicity, and conflicts between parents and children. Because of these consequences, some feel that with our general culture well institutionalized, and the secular government unchallenged, the nation can now adopt a policy of *cultural pluralism.*

INTERNAL MIGRATIONS

A factor that works in the other direction, to reduce certain kinds of differences between people in audiences is *internal migration*—the movement of people within the nation's borders.

A number of distinct major shifts in population within the United States took place in the twentieth century. These shifts resulted in redistributions of the population into various regions. The most visible of these internal migrations have been the following four:

1. The great *westward* movement—which to some extent still continues. This caused high rates of growth in most of the western and southwestern states during recent decades.
2. The *farm-to-city* movement that attracted millions of rural people to cities and factory towns as job opportunities arose through the growth of industry. This has now virtually stopped, but it greatly accelerated the growth of the urban centers.
3. A large *south-to-north* movement of population that took place as African Americans left the harsh conditions of the South to seek work in the industrial North. The majority of the urban black communities that exist in

Shoppers in a busy Hispanic neighborhood in New York City affirm the importance of ethnic identity in the audience for media, advertising, and various commercial products and interests.

northern cities today grew sharply as a result of this trend. It was accelerated greatly during the two world wars when factory workers were badly needed in war industries.

4. A continuous *exodus to the suburbs* as the white middle class escaped from what they perceived as crime, racial tensions, and other stressful conditions of the city. This led to vast expansions of suburban communities in all parts of the nation. This movement continues in full force.

During the past two decades, other internal migrations have been identified. For example, increasing numbers of people from northeastern and other states have moved to the *sun belt*—the warmer regions of the United States. Some sought economic opportunities as these southern states changed from agriculture to other types of industries. Many older Americans sought more favorable weather conditions and lower living costs for their retirement. In many parts of the country, there has also been an *expansion of small towns* that are within commuting distance of large cities. Finally, as many younger, upwardly mobile middle-class families seek to avoid commuting and desire the benefits of city life, they have moved back to more urban areas. This has resulted in the *gentrification* of formerly rundown areas in some cities in which older homes and neighborhoods are upgraded. This has the consequence of forcing out poorer residents who can no longer afford to live there.

IMPLICATIONS FOR MASS COMMUNICATION

Both the massive immigration and internal migrations of people that have characterized the American population have had significant implications for mass communication. Adding millions of people from a long list of foreign countries to the population of the United States left a legacy of cultural diversity, resulting from the racial and ethnic subcultures, which in many respects, continue to exist. This is a factor that can create barriers for communication, which can increase conflict and animosity. For example, African Americans, Native Americans, Hispanics, and indeed all other racial and ethnic groups are sensitive to their treatment in the media. This has become abundantly clear over the years. To be "politically correct," encoding of media messages must be done with a clear understanding of the beliefs, attitudes, and values of people from diverse backgrounds. Professional communicators ignore this principle at their own risk.

The cultural diversity existing in the population has produced media aimed at specific populations. In Chapter 3, we noted the existence of substantial ethnic press. In a similar way, a number of magazines, radio programs, movies, and television shows are produced mainly for persons who identify with one racial, religious, or ethnic group. These media serve not only as a means to preserve cultural differences, but as vehicles for advertising, political debate, and entertainment for the groups involved.

While, as we have shown, immigration from abroad and other sources of cultural differences have been significant factors in creating diversity, other factors have had a reverse effect—leading toward cultural similarities. For example, as noted, the American population is also one that has constantly been on the move, migrating and relocating within the nation's expanding borders. Over the generations, this has mixed diverse people in ways that have reduced their differences, producing a strong and unifying general American culture. For example, as a result of population movements from the North to the sun-belt states, the older, deep-seated southern culture is being challenged—right down to regional attitudes and accents.

Thus, internal population shifts have to some extent resulted in a kind of "homogenization effect" in national tastes for certain kinds of media content. Because of the relatively predictable nature of the general American culture, the media have been able to present entertainment—soap operas, evening crime drama, game shows, films, and other kinds of content—that is not bound to particular regional or other kinds of subcultures. Each major socioeconomic level has media products that appeal to their tastes and interests in all parts of the country, creating a true *national* audience for our print and broadcast media.

DEMOGRAPHIC COMPOSITION AS A SOURCE OF AUDIENCE DIFFERENTIATION

We have reviewed a number of changing characteristics of the American population, which have resulted from various kinds of migrations. However, additional contemporary sources of social differentiation in media audiences can be seen in their *contemporary demographic composition*. Important among them are *age, gender, education, ethnicity,* and *income*. There are others as well, but these three have a particularly strong influence on what people select from the mass media.

AGE AS AN AUDIENCE CHARACTERISTIC

No factor is more important in the process of mass communication than age. Significant trends have taken place in the American population with respect to this demographic factor. The most pronounced among them is that we are now living much longer on average than we were a century ago. And there is every likelihood that the aging trend will continue. As Figure 13.2 shows, in 1900, the average life expectancy at birth was 47.3 years.[4] By 1995, it had risen steadily to 76.3. This continued to rise, reaching 76.7 in the year 2000. It will be even higher in the decades to follow. This trend has truly significant implications for media audience interests, tastes, and preferences. For example, the number of people over age 65 who consistently view MTV can probably be counted on the fingers of one hand! The same can be said of the number of young adults who regularly listen to "golden oldies" on the radio.

The causes behind this extension of the average human life expectancy are not as obvious as they may seem. It is clear that advances in sophisticated medical treatment have made a contribution. However, the trend is less associated with heroic surgical interventions that replace organs or miracle drugs that cure dread diseases, than it is with much more mundane measures. For the most part, the extension in life expectancy is a result of rather simple public health practices and basic preventative measures that have reduced the influence of infectious diseases as our leading causes of death. To illustrate, at the beginnings of the 1900s, such diseases regularly struck large numbers of people. In the year 1900, for example, 200 people for every 100,000 in the population died of influenza and pneumonia. In fact, during the influenza epidemic of the winter of 1918–19 alone, more than half a million Americans died of the dreaded disease within a span of a few months.[5] By 1960, just over half way through the century, the rate of deaths due to influenza was down to a mere 0.2 fatalities per 100,000—a 1,000 percent drop in the rate! The number of deaths from small pox, tuberculosis, diphtheria, typhoid fever, dysentery, whooping cough, scarlet fever, and malaria showed similar declines.

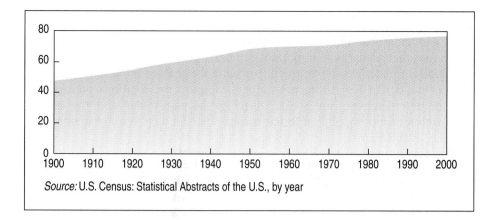

figure 13.2
**Life Expectancy:
Average Age at Death of
Individuals in the U.S.,
1900–2000**

Source: U.S. Census: Statistical Abstracts of the U.S., by year

Older people were particularly vulnerable in earlier years, and mortality from these diseases kept the average age of the population low—as it had been for centuries. The benefits of preventative measures that now seem simple and obvious to us were not understood in the past. However, medical experts increasingly discovered the microorganisms that caused these diseases and took steps to control them, which included sanitary sewage disposal, purification of water, quarantining those who were already infected, and the use of effective vaccines.

These public health measures, coupled with more attention to the prevention of industrial accidents—a major cause of deaths among males in particular—began to extend the average life expectancy of our population. Today, this trend continues. The effects of smoking have been uncovered, and we are moving rapidly toward a smokeless society. The relationship between diet, exercise, and health is now clearer to many Americans, and they are taking steps that will extend their lives.

Even more subtle factors adding to life expectancy are related to the number of years one spends in the labor force and the age at which one retires. To illustrate, the age at which a worker entered the labor force in 1870 was 13 years on average. That increased steadily in the 1900s. By 1950 it was over 17 years. The trend continued and now the average age is just over 19 years old. Age at retirement also contributes to life expectancy. In 1870 there was no expectation of "retirement." Workers continued on the job as long as they were physically able to do so—usually until they died. (So much for the "good old days!") The idea of a "normal retirement age" at age 65 was not recognized as part of our culture until the years of President Franklin D. Roosevelt, during the 1930s. Today, the average age at retirement is 63.6. Thus, workers are spending fewer years on the job and are therefore subject to less stress and possible occupational accidents. Even hours working at home on such chores as washing, ironing, mowing the lawn, shoveling snow, and the like have declined (from 1,825 hours annually in 1870 to 1,278 in 1990). Thus, older people today have much more leisure time, fewer risks from work, and (as we will see later) more secure incomes. All of these factors permit them to live longer than they did in earlier years.

Finally, because of a sudden rise in the birth rate during the two decades following World War II (the so-called "baby boom"), the sheer number of older people in the population will increase sharply, starting in about 2010. All of these factors, trends, and events are important in understanding age as an important demographic category related to the composition of media audiences. Simply put, older people attend to very different patterns of media content than do the young, and the population of older people will continue to increase in the future.

GENDER AS AN AUDIENCE FACTOR

Males and females do not select identical kinds of content from the mass media. This means that gender is an important demographic factor in trying to determine what kinds of material will work well to achieve the goals of professional communicators that design advertising, news programs, sports presentations, popular culture for entertainment, and so on. A review of past trends and the current composition of our population in terms of gender can help in understanding the influence of this factor.

For reasons that are not entirely clear, there are more males than females born in all human populations! The number of males per 100 females in a population is called the *sex ratio.* Worldwide, about 106 girl babies arrive every year for each 100 boys. This sex ratio of 106 is perhaps nature's way—based on a long evolution—of ensuring the survival of the species. In prehistoric times, many males were killed in the hunt, and as human societies became more complex and competitive, more men died in battle. Consequently, the male death rate was always higher than that of women. In fact, it still is. Today, females outnumber males in our population. As Figure 13.3 shows, for every 100 females in 2000 there were only 96 males. The sex ratio dropped steadily during the past century until the early 1980s. Since that time there has been a modest reversal of the trend.

One reason for the changing sex ratio in the American society is that the number of males at the beginning of the twentieth century was greater because of the typical pattern of immigration. That is, males came in larger numbers than females. Some—but not all—later sent for their families. Then, as the factor of immigration declined in importance, the higher risks for males in the labor force and wars altered the ratio.

Today, many women survive their husbands and continue to live on into old age. Thus, the sex ratio is closer to 100 among younger adults than is the case for seniors. Among the elderly, women continue to outnumber men to a considerable degree. This is an important feature in understanding the older audience and in developing programming specifically for those individuals.

THE INFLUENCE OF EDUCATION

Educational attainment in the American population has been rising for many decades. This has truly significant implications for the content people want in mass communication. The overall trend is clear: Educational attainment has increased greatly since World War II. For example, in 1940, the average years of formal edu-

figure13.3

Ratio of Males per 100 Females in the U.S. Population, 1900–2000

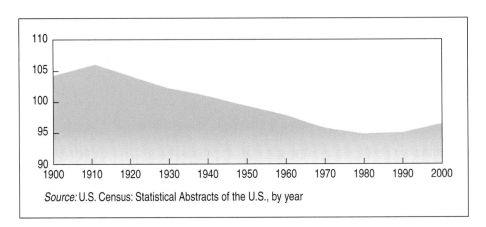

Source: U.S. Census: Statistical Abstracts of the U.S., by year

cation among the American population was 8.4. Clearly, the majority had less than a high school education. Since that time, the number of high school graduates has increased steadily. In addition, the percentage of the population with a college degree has risen sharply. Among adults 25 years and older, just over 24 percent have a bachelor's degree (males are at 26.2 percent and females 21.7 percent). That is a four-fold increase from 1950. Therefore, we have, as a nation, become far more educated than was the case at the middle of the twentieth century. That trend is expected to continue as more and more young people pursue their education through college and beyond.

This great advance in education is a product of several factors. One is the history-making concept of free (tax-supported) and mandatory education for all children under the age of 18, which was introduced by Horace Mann in Massachusetts in 1834. Before that, it was mainly the children of the well-to-do who became educated. At the time Mann proposed his policy, it seemed to conservative citizens a wild and radical idea, and they opposed it bitterly. However, it spread to all the states, and as a result, we have a population deeply devoted to education today. Our system of state-supported education extends beyond secondary school to community colleges, four-year institutions, and great public research universities that are all funded mainly by tax revenues. We also enjoy the largest number of private schools, colleges, and universities in the world. These, along with government-supported programs, such as the GI Bill, Pell grants, and student loans, have opened educational doors to almost all individuals who have the motivation and intellectual capacity to earn degrees.

A second factor in raising educational levels has been the nation's high level of support for college-level education. The United States is unique in the world on this issue. Not only do the majority of parents want their children to go to college, but also new programs have been developed in Congress making it financially possible for large numbers of children to do so. As will be seen in the section below, education is a critical factor in the lives of citizens as well as in the functioning of the media.

INCOME AS AN AUDIENCE FACTOR

Income is a critical demographic factor in understanding media audiences. It is a central factor in making decisions about media content at various taste levels. Obviously, the higher one's family income, the more big-ticket items one can afford, and this plays a part in advertising certain kinds of luxury goods. Actually, however, those who design and produce media content are not deeply concerned with the truly affluent. There simply are not enough of them! What drives media decision-makers in designing content is the *number of families who will be able to purchase* different kinds of products. For example, there are only a limited number who can buy a luxury yacht or a diamond ring worth thousands of dollars. However, there is a huge number of families with enough income to purchase such mundane items as toothpaste, breakfast cereal, soft drinks, and paper towels. Since there are millions of them, their collective purchases represent a huge source of income for those who manufacture and market such products. Influencing purchasing decisions of large numbers with at least some income by attracting attention to advertisements that appear on television, radio, or in other media, then, is a factor that drives the majority of decisions about the nature and taste level of media content.

As Table 13.2 shows, income is not distributed equally among the various kinds of people we have discussed thus far. For example, as in earlier decades, *age* is an important factor. Large numbers of older citizens remain near the bottom of the

Table 13.2 Monthly Income by Education and Gender					
	Not a High School Graduate	**High School Graduate**	**Some College**	**Bachelor's Degree**	**Master's Degree**
Males	$1,211	$1,812	$2,045	$3,430	$4,298
Females	621	1,008	1,139	1,809	2,505
Total	906	1,380	1,579	2,625	3,411

Source: U.S. Census: Statistical Abstract of the U.S., 1996

Table 13.3 Monthly Income by Education and Ethnicity					
	Not a High School Graduate	**High School Graduate**	**Some College**	**Bachelor's Degree**	**Master's Degree**
Whites	$951	$1,422	$1,649	$2,682	$3,478
Blacks	713	1,071	1,222	2,333	2,834
Hispanics	786	1,106	1,239	2,186	2,605
Total	906	1,380	1,579	2,625	3,411

Source: U.S. Census: Statistical Abstract of the U.S., 1996

income distribution. Since World War II, the incomes of seniors has improved somewhat. While they remain at the bottom, increased numbers of companies and other organizations have provided their retired workers with pensions. Seniors who worked also have Social Security income. Thus, their incomes are more reliable. However, about 50 percent of those 65 or older—particularly women—live on Social Security as their sole source of income. The more affluent have investments and own their own homes, having paid off their mortgages. Nevertheless, seniors as a whole remain the poorest age group—other than teenagers just entering the labor force with limited education.

Another truly significant factor in determining income is *education*. Simply put, for all categories in the population, the more education one has attained, the higher one's income (on average). As Table 13.2 shows, those who have the most advanced educational attainment earn more than four times the income of those who did not complete high school.

Income differs considerably by *gender*. Again simply put, men make more money than women (on average), whether they are single mothers or fathers, or live alone. This shows up in Table 13.2, where females who are the main breadwinners earn significantly less than their male counterparts. Another important condition related to income is *race* or *ethnicity*, as can be seen in Table 13.2. On average in 1999, African Americans had the lowest annual incomes of any of the categories listed. Similarly, those of Hispanic origin had lower monthly incomes than their white and Asian counterparts. The critical factor in this comparison is their level of education.

IMPLICATIONS FOR MASS COMMUNICATION

Age, gender, education, and ethnicity, then, are basic demographic factors that have a truly significant influence on income levels and consequently the media habits and content selections of the American audience. Different tastes and preferences exist among these categories. Those who make decisions about what type of content will characterize our media understand this very well. For example, it has been very well established that older people follow the news avidly (both in print and broadcasting). However, fewer seniors have sufficient income to purchase many products. Seniors also have lower levels of use of the Internet; they attend fewer movies and select ones that are different from those that appeal to youths and young adults. Seniors do watch more television, especially during the day. Obviously, they have more time. Young and old have very different preferences in music, and therefore their radio listening tends to be very different among these social categories.

Gender is not as powerful a factor in determining selections from media as age and education. However, women do have different preferences in content than men in many ways. As a category, they have less interest in sports and they tend to dislike violent films. They are more likely to read romance novels than adventure or war stories. For understandable reasons they attend more closely to presentations about child-rearing, fashions, and beauty products. Since significant numbers are not in the labor force, women attend far more often to the daily soap operas than men. At the same time, women are similar to men within specific age and educational categories. They have about the same interest in public affairs and political news.

No conditions of the audience play a greater role than the *combination* of education and income in determining what selections people make from available media content. Those that are well-off and well-educated, as compared to those who are poor with limited schooling, select different books, read different parts of newspapers, use the Internet in different numbers and ways, attend different films, prefer different types of TV programming, and listen to different radio programs.

THE CHANGING AMERICAN FAMILY

Media messages are received and interpreted not by isolated individuals but normally within the context of people's families. Our families influence not only what we attend to but also how we understand and act upon what we receive. It is within the decision-making context of this important human group that most people decide what products or services they will purchase, for what candidates they will vote, what pundits they will believe, whether they will contribute to a particular charity, or what they will consume in the way of popular entertainment. Since the family is such a significant influence on media behavior, its characteristics need to be discussed briefly.

Our families changed significantly during the twentieth century—and especially after World War II—roughly marking mid-century. Families changed in terms of size, the percentage of women working outside the home, the process of family decision-making, and in terms of aggregate family purchasing power. Each of these trends has had important consequences for mass communications.

TRENDS IN FAMILY SIZE

At the beginning of the twentieth century, when Americans were mainly farmers, the *extended family* was common and households included a larger number of people. That is, the grandparents, parents, and their children—three generations—often lived in the same farmhouse. Other relatives, such as a widowed aunt or aging father-in-law, might have also lived in the same home. In addition, families included on average a larger number of children than they do today. For example, in 1940, the average size of a family in the United States was 3.76. By the end of the twentieth century, this had fallen to 2.61, which is a decline of over 30 percent. Today, more than ever before, there are far more single-parent families, persons living alone, and couples with no children. Obviously, such smaller families will attend to and use of almost all forms of mass communications in ways that differ from those that have more members.

CHANGING RELATIONSHIPS BETWEEN HUSBANDS AND WIVES

Slowly during the 1900s, the American family changed from one that was male dominated to our current more egalitarian pattern. As that century began, few husbands wanted their wives to work. Men were supposed to be the "breadwinners," supporting the family by their earnings alone. Men of the time fully accepted that obligation. Those who could not accomplish that were regarded as "weak." But, since men were the economic "providers," they felt entitled to make the major decisions in the family concerning monetary matters.

For the most part, the husband's views and preferences prevailed over those of wives and children. For example, as the 1900s began, women were supposed to be submissive to their husbands in all matters. Their role in the family was to serve as child-bearers and homemakers. They had little power, no right to vote, and until relatively recently, were not even allowed to own property. Women could not initiate a divorce, take out a mortgage in their own name, or obtain credit at a store. In general, then, the traditional family was almost completely *male-centered*. It had a clearcut division of labor—one in which neither wives nor children had much of a voice in their own destiny.

Because of these characteristics, the American family at the beginning of the twentieth century was a very different economic and consuming unit than it is today. Because few women had control of the family purse strings, they played only a minor role in purchasing decisions. Typically, their husbands doled out an allowance for them to purchase their clothing and the family food. As the 1900s started, fewer than one in five women of working age were in the labor force. Most of these worked as teachers, domestic servants, or factory hands. There were almost no professionals, such as doctors, lawyers, or professors.

Today, drastic changes have taken place. The movement for equal rights for women began when (in 1848) the first Women's Rights Convention was held at Seneca Falls, a small community in upstate New York. In the twentieth century, the movement's greatest achievement was *women's suffrage*. Women gained the vote when the nineteenth Amendment to the Constitution was ratified in 1920. While the movement waned for several decades, women's roles began to change during World War II, when many entered the labor force temporarily. Those who worked at war jobs earned high wages and learned to enjoy financial independence. During the decades that followed, a new *feminism* evolved, and it has drastically altered the status and freedoms of women in our contemporary society.

Although patterns of sexual harassment and limitations on women's economic opportunities remain, the American family is now very different than it was even a few decades ago. Power tends to be shared, and husbands increasingly take responsibility for household chores, including shopping for domestic products. Women have a much greater voice in decisions about major purchases. For example, automakers have found out that women constitute a large market. Consequently many have changed their designs, products, and advertising accordingly. Even children have

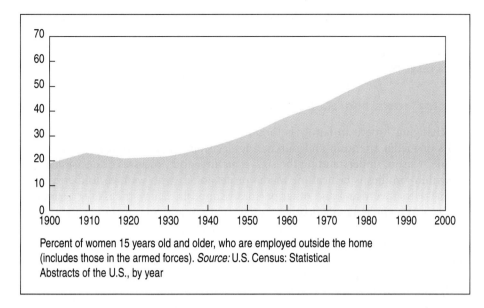

figure 13.4
Women in the Labor Force, 1900–2000

Percent of women 15 years old and older, who are employed outside the home (includes those in the armed forces). *Source:* U.S. Census: Statistical Abstracts of the U.S., by year

money to spend and freedom to make choices—a fact not lost on those who advertise such items as fast foods, toys, clothing, athletic shoes, popular music, and films.

FEMALE PARTICPATION IN THE LABOR FORCE

No feature of family life has undergone more drastic change than the movement of women into the world of work. We noted that few women worked at the beginning of the 1900s. But as the twentieth century moved on, the proportion of females of working age who held jobs outside the home increased steadily. While many women entered the labor force to work in factories during World War II, the trend started long before and it has continued well into the present.

This trend toward two-income families had a heavy impact on the mass media industries. For one thing, it considerably increased the aggregate purchasing power of American families. Perhaps it is more accurate to say that, during times of inflation, it kept disposable income from eroding. Clearly, families with both the husband and wife employed continue to have more discretionary income than was the case in times of the single breadwinner.

The down side of women in the labor force is that many women who work today are single, largely as a result of divorce. The proportion of our society who are divorced has risen sharply in recent years. For those who married in 2000, about half (50 percent) will divorce later. The percentage of people in the society who have already divorced has risen sharply. For example, in 1970, only 3.2 percent of the population had been divorced. By 2000, that had risen to 8.4, an increase of over 160 percent in just thirty years!

This pattern places many single women at an economic disadvantage. There are more divorced women in the society than men—largely because divorced men tend to remarry rather quickly, returning to the two-income pattern. Another economic burden for such women is that if children are involved, the courts tend to follow tradition and award their custody to the ex-wife. This has created a significant number of families in our society in which a working mother provides the sole or major support for her children. These are largely low-income families, because women lose the purchasing power of the husband as the marriage is dissolved, even if child support is paid. There are other single-parent families, with some made up of never-married women and others of divorced men. In all of these families, patterns of media usage tend to differ from those of intact families.

IMPLICATIONS FOR MASS COMMUNICATION

The changing American family is the foundation for understanding many of the habits of media attention and purchasing decisions of contemporary Americans. For that reason, understanding the size, structure, and processes of decision-making within families is critical for media professionals who want to influence purchasing with advertising and other persuasive appeals. Today, the family is smaller, less likely to include members other than the parents and their children, and it is far more democratic in its decision-making. The majority of women of appropriate age are employed outside the home, and they are now much more important as consumers of a variety of products than they were just a few decades ago. Even children have money to spend which adds up to a considerable aggregate.

In summary then, the trend toward two-income families has increased family purchasing power, or at least kept it from serious erosion during inflationary periods. At the same time, other family-related trends have had a negative impact on women's aggregate purchasing power. In particular, the increase in the number of single or divorced mothers raising their children alone has created a growing number of consumer households with little discretionary income.

Overall, these changes in the American family, along with all of the demographic factors of population growth, race, ethnicity, age, gender, and education, have created a complex and constantly changing audience. Professional mass communicators must constantly understand these changes as they try to discover and chart who will attend to their messages with what effects. Because all of the trends we have described will continue in various ways, the audience of the future will be *unlike* that of today. But whatever its size and composition at a given point in time, the social categories discussed above will continue to play a significant part in shaping the beliefs, attitudes, and behavior of every individual who turns to the mass media for news or entertainment, and who receives information about products to buy.

ASSESSING AUDIENCE COMPOSITION AND ATTENTION

Each of the media faces the task of discovering and continuously *assessing* the size and composition of its audience. If professional communicators did not know the nature of their receivers and how they were responding, they would soon be out of business. But as the present section will show, the assessment of audience size and composition is carried on in a variety of ways.

In principle, there could be three kinds of feedback information flowing to professional communicators from their receivers: *simultaneous feedback, delayed feedback,* and *systematic audience research.* Having effective feedback makes it easier for professional communicators to reach the largest number of people, tailor the nature of their messages to the capacities and interests of their audience in attempts to prompt them to take some form of desired action (buy, vote, believe, donate, etc.).

Simultaneous feedback takes place in face-to-face or interpersonal communication. However, *only in a very limited sense is it a part of the mass communication process.* As we pointed out in our discussion of the linear model of mass communication, there are very few occasions when receivers are actually visible to a professional communicator while he or she is delivering a message. It can happen, as in the case of a news report where a reporter is among a crowd of people, or in a call-in type of program on radio or television, where at least some members of the audience can be in direct touch with the communicator. For the most part, however, simultaneous feedback messages from the audience are not available as the message is being formulated or transmitted.

Delayed feedback is another matter. Indicators of approval or disapproval of media content come from many sources. For example, there is often a considerable amount of commentary and criticism that flows from individual members of the audience back to the communicator. Newspapers regularly print at least some of their "letters to the editor," in which individuals denounce or applaud news stories or other material that has been printed. Large metropolitan papers get several thousand of these a year (but print only a small selection). Most other newspapers receive from one hundred to about five hundred a year, depending on their size. Similarly, people write to or call in to radio or television stations to air their views about particular broadcasts. Even filmmakers receive mail with comments on their products. The limitation of such material is that it is scarcely representative of the views of the majority of the audience. Such delayed feedback tends to come mainly from disgruntled people with an axe to grind and who are sufficiently motivated to write or call to take issue with the communicator.

Sometimes such delayed feedback takes a more organized form. From time to time, various groups take strongly critical positions on the content of mass communication. A religious group may object to the way in which sacred ideas or events are depicted in a film and organize demonstrations at theaters where they are being exhibited. An organization representing a minority group may through threats of boycotts put pressure on local or national media concerning the way their people are portrayed. An organization of educators, mothers, or even physicians may deplore the content of television and seek the assistance of Congress to bring about change.

Data garnered from surveys are part of public life and public policy in America, frequently serving as the centerpiece for news conferences, as in this one discussing Asian-American voting patterns in California.

Many professional groups, such as police organizations, seek change in the content of television, the movies, and even the recording industry. Some mount nationwide petition drives to put pressure on professional communicators for change.

Are the media sensitive to such pressures from their audience to a point where they actually alter the nature of their messages? The answer is "sometimes." We saw in Chapter 5 that, in its early years, the film industry became very concerned about public criticism and adopted a strong production code that completely cleaned up the movies—for a while. However, during the 1950s and '60s, the code became ineffective when television reduced movie attendance sharply. Films then turned to violence, sex, "dirty" words, special effects and gore, or whatever would result in boosting paid admissions without creating too much of an uproar. At one time or another, codes and conventions pertaining to virtually all of the media have been formulated by various groups. The problem with almost all such agreements is that they are voluntary and lack effective enforcement provisions. The result is that when financial pressures arise, they become ineffective or are simply forgotten.

Awards and prizes are still another form of delayed feedback. Each industry has its contests at which its products are judged for various (largely symbolic) recognitions. The movies have their Academy Awards; the newspapers have Pulitzer Prizes; the advertising industry awards Clios for ads judged by various professional criteria; and so it goes.

The ultimate form of delayed feedback to the media is *profit.* If a particular kind of film fails to bring in the dollars at the box office (or video rental store), it is unlikely that others will be produced within the genre. If a television series fails to attract the advertisers that the network needs, it will not be on the air very long. If a newspaper's or a magazine's circulation falls below a certain level, it will be out of business. Thus, *audience approval* in the form of paid admissions, rentals, subscriptions, purchase of products, and so forth, in the final analysis, is the only truly effective form of delayed feedback.

Media managers understand very well the need to assess their audiences in terms of size, composition, interests, tastes, and purchasing power. In order to do that, a number of organizations providing such services have been developed over the years to measure the numbers of people who attend and to determine their demographic characteristics. This is critical information for each of the media. They use this form of delayed feedback continuously to design and redesign their presentations in order to gain the attention of their audiences, to satisfy their interests and needs, and to elicit from them behavior they deem desirable. In the sections that follow, we outline briefly the major forms that such audience assessment takes for print and broadcast media.

MEASURING CIRCULATIONS OF PRINT MEDIA

The basic assessment of audience size for a newspaper or a magazine is its *circulation,* which means paid subscriptions plus other sales by mail or single copies. Obviously, large numbers of readers attract advertisers who want their message seen by as large a number of people as possible—and they will pay for the process. Early newspapers and magazines were often guilty of exaggerating the numbers of their readers and subscribers. To end this practice and promote reliable, impartial reports, a group of advertisers, advertising agencies, and publishers formed the Audit Bureau of Circulations (ABC) in 1914. It is essentially a combination research organization and auditing firm that makes periodic checks on circulations reported by newspapers and magazines that make use of its services. Today, most newspapers and magazines in the United States are ABC members. The data provided by the ABC provide an important form of delayed feedback to the medium, and critical data to advertisers and advertising agencies who want precise numbers before deciding whether to place their ads. Market penetration, as represented by circulation, is an important indicator of audience composition and the apparent value of the medium to the advertiser.

The ABC sets standards for circulation (such as solicitation methods and subscriptions) and requires a publisher's statement of circulation and other data every six months. The statements are checked, processed, printed, and distributed by the ABC. Once a year an ABC auditor goes to the offices of the newspaper or magazine and examines all records and materials necessary to verify the claims of the publisher's statement of circulation. Information provided by the ABC in its semiannual reports includes audited, paid-circulation figures for the six-month period, with breakdowns for such things as subscriptions versus newsstand sales and data on regional, metropolitan, and special-edition circulation. The report also includes an analysis of a single issue of the publication in terms of the market area it reaches and much more.

Several other organizations and groups provide basic circulation data for the print media as well as audience figures for broadcast stations. Among them are Standard Rate and Data Service, which reports audited audience/circulation figures and lists advertising rates, policies, and practices. Still more audience data are available from the Association of National Advertisers, the American Newspaper Publishers Association, the Magazine Publishers Association, and others.

EVALUATING MOVIE AUDIENCES

As we suggested earlier, the most significant means of gauging the response of any audience to any message transmitted by any medium is by determining the amount of *profit* that it eventually derives for its owners. For films, measuring profit and thereby the response of the audience is relatively straightforward. The total number of dollars derived from paid admissions to movie theaters—box office receipts—is the major form of delayed feedback. Other income from TV, VCR, and DVD releases, plus foreign sales, is also important.

A daily trade newspaper, *Variety,* keeps track of the box office earnings of each film released and shown in the United States. Every week, a report is prepared showing the earnings of, and several other kinds of information about, the fifty films that lead the list. Each is followed week by week until its earnings are low enough that it falls out of the top fifty. The necessary data for *Variety's* Weekly Box Office Report are derived from a systematic survey, by an independent research firm, of some sixteen hundred theaters that are located in approximately twenty cities. It is a simple and reliable system, and the results are closely followed by the entire industry. They provide a clear-cut means of assessing whether Americans like what has been produced well enough to pay for a ticket. However, it is not the only form of delayed feedback indicating a measure of a film's success. Once a movie has been shown in most theaters around the country, it is released in video form for purchase and rental or released for television viewing. In addition, many American films are shown in large foreign markets. A movie may not be a top box office success at home but do well in the home video market or in other countries.

A number of other approaches to analyzing audience response to films are used—both before release and after. Some studios make use of *focus groups.* These are composed of about a dozen to twenty carefully selected people who see the movie before it is finally edited. If they dislike certain parts of it, it may be edited.

**Humphrey Taylor, Chairman,
*Harris Poll (Harris
Interactive)* New York,
New York**

insights from MEDIA LEADERS

One of the world's top pollsters and a leader in survey research, Humphrey Taylor was both president and chief executive officer of Louis Harris and Associates and founder of his own market research and polling firm in Great Britain before moving to the United States in the 1970s. His election polls are known for their uncanny accuracy.

Q. How did you first get interested in polling and survey research?

A. It was purely accidental, possibly going back to a fascination with numbers and people. As a college student, I once found myself in Place Pigalle in Paris among prostitutes. To kill time I started counting and categorizing till the sun came up. I used my training in math, had a good time talking to the women, and stayed out of trouble.

Q. Did you have any inkling then that you might someday be a pollster?

A. No, not at all. After boarding school in Scotland and college at Cambridge and service in the British army, I was a colonial administrator in Tanzania where I was immersed in local politics and issues like economic development, hospitals, elections, and even taxes. We were always trying to figure out what kind of policy

solution would work with different tribes and religions. When I returned to England, I needed a job and wondered what I could do with this experience and a degree in mathematics and social anthropology.

Q. And what did you do?

A. I got a job in market research and eventually started doing opinion polling, which is the most visible part of the marketing and survey research industry. I did all kinds of research for business, media companies, and political parties. Eventually I started my own company.

Q. What inspired or influenced your career in this field— and your present place in it?

A. I read an important book, Teddy White's *The Making of the President,* and realized how important a pollster could be in politics and public life. I first learned about Louis Harris, who was Kennedy's pollster, in the book and was inspired by the idea that polling was an exciting field with real impact on people's lives.

Q. That apparently led you to America and a job in the Louis Harris organization, eventually moving to the top job in a major survey research organization. So what has that involved?

A. Quite a lot. In brief—some eight thousand surveys in eighty countries for governments, corporations, foun-

Some consultants analyze film scripts even before they are produced in an attempt to forecast whether it will have audience appeal and why. Still other analysts interview people or persuade "sneak preview" audiences to fill out a questionnaire right after they have seen a film. All of these techniques can provide useful information.

RATINGS AND THE BROADCAST AUDIENCE

The paid circulation of a magazine or newspaper and the amount of money people pay to see a movie can be audited rather easily. But getting reliable information about the audience for a broadcasting station or a network is more difficult. Here, no physical object, like a ticket, newspaper, or magazine passes from one hand to another. Moreover, broadcast messages can occupy long periods of time and reach their audiences in different ways and at varying levels of intensity. Consequently, wrote broadcast historian Sydney Head, "No single universally accepted way of measuring broadcast consumption has evolved. Instead, several research companies using rival methods compete in the audience measurement field."[6] They use differ-

dations, and others on subjects ranging from transportation and insurance to housing, welfare planning, education, and—my favorite subject—health care. Understand that modern pollsters first accumulate data, and then interpret it.

Q. And has this work proved exciting, useful, and important?

A. Yes. I believe that some of our research has even changed the world. And, of course, a pollster can make a good living too.

Q. You once spoke of "ten polls that shook the world." What did you mean by that?

A. Well, specifically, we did a poll that found 10 percent of British people over 65 were so cold in the winter that they were close to hypothermia, and this became a major public policy issue. A survey we did in the United States on "The Myths and Realities of Aging" led to the abolition of mandatory retirement at sixty-five while another survey was credited with adding $3 billion to federal programs for the education of children with disabilities. The worldwide privatization movement was spurred by survey research. Pollsters can influence policy—and sometimes that influence is profound.

Q. Any disappointments?

A. Yes, often we find that public opinion and survey data clearly offers intelligence and answers public policy problems, but politicians and government officials choose to ignore them anyway. Of course, not all polls are beneficial to society by any means. They provide information and sometimes they show that the public likes a draconian security measure or serious violations of human rights, for example.

Q. What is your overall view of the value of opinion polls and this endeavor for a career?

A. They can have enormous importance in strengthening democracy and guiding leaders, but because the best polling data are value-neutral, they can be used for either desirable or undesirable ends. But, yes, it is an exciting and satisfying career. And survey research in this digital age is a real growth industry thanks to the Internet.

Q. What is the best route to a career in your field?

A. A solid education, broad interests, a journalist's sense of what's important or potentially important. And, of course, writing skills, oral presentation skills, an ability to synthesize and produce under tight deadlines. Study in fields like sociology, statistics, and survey research is also useful. This is more than a measurement job; it is a place for creative, smart people to connect practical research questions with social change.

ent procedures to chart audience size, characteristics, and behavior. Over the last twenty or thirty years they have frequently changed these methods to keep pace with new techniques for using surveys and statistics.

Broadcast audience assessment, in one form or another, has been around a long time because radio, from its early days, and later television, have had to justify their worth to advertisers who agreed to sponsor certain programs.[7] In addition, *ratings,* which involve audience as well as program and advertising analyses, have played a central role in determining the shape of broadcast content in America since the 1930s. The first ratings were done by advertising agencies, but before long the networks organized their own research departments. Later, independent research rating services joined in. Today, each of the major networks has a large research department that investigates such topics as the influence of television on children as well as trying to determine which programs will succeed with the audience.

In the world of television, the influence of ratings has gotten more intense in recent years, as cable, satellite, the Internet, and other new technologies have attempted to capture the traditional broadcast audience. For decades, the various techniques of assessment were quite crude. They were based on telephone interviews and a number of other procedures, such as diaries people kept on their viewing habits. Essentially, these efforts measured simple factors, such as when TV sets were turned on, not who actually watched and with what degree of attention. (As we will note, that limitation has now been reduced somewhat with the use of new devices and techniques.)

At one level, broadcast ratings have generated increasingly complex quantitative assessments of who is watching, when, for how long, and with what intensity. At another, these "number crunching" ratings have inspired the ire of critics, who have called for new assessments. Their objections may be justified as dense numerical ratings are quite limited in what they tell us about the *quality* of television and its overall effect. The issue of critical examination of the social and cultural consequences of television raised in industry circles is echoed in universities, where scholars argue that quantification can lead to self-fulfilling results and does not necessarily yield much new knowledge about either the medium or its audience.

Types of ratings. One way to measure the audience in an area is to relate the number of receivers in working order to the total number of households. The result is the relative saturation, or *penetration*, of the broadcast medium in a particular area.[8] Obviously this figure is not much of a measure of the viewing audience, because it says nothing about the behavior of people, who may or may not be using their TV sets regularly. Penetration (or saturation) measures reveal the *potential* audience. Today, however, virtually all homes have TV sets.

The search for more precision in calculating the broadcast audience led to systems in which the *relative audience size* for a particular time slot or program is calculated. Various measures are used in this approach. One kind are *instantaneous rating reports* that indicate the audience size at a particular moment; another are *cumulative reports* that give figures for a period of time, thirty minutes, for example.

More specifically, three measures frequently provided by audience measuring services are: (1) the "rating" of a particular program, (2) the "share" of the total audience that is tuned to a particular station (among those available) at a given time, and (3) an index of "households using television" (again at a given time). These provide a set of comparative indices that tell within a specified market area how well a particular station is attracting viewers as well as how well the programs that they offer are competing for the audience that is viewing at a particular time. The differences among these forms are important. They can be expressed as follows:

A program's *rating* is defined as the number of households receiving the program, divided by total TV households in the market area (multiplied by 100). Or, in terms of a calculating formula:

$$Rating = \frac{\text{Households watching a particular program}}{\text{Total households in area with TV sets}} \times 100$$

Thus, in general terms, the rating is the *percentage of the potential audience* made up of TV-set-owning households in an area that could be watching or listening to a particular program aired in a particular time slot. It is a critical measure of program popularity.

Another important index is *HUT*, which stands for *households using television*. This does not tell much in itself, but this percentage is needed in order to calculate the share of the active or viewing audience at any time that a particular station or program is attracting. HUT is defined as the number of households in the area *with their TV sets turned on,* divided by the total number of households that own sets (again, multiplied by 100). In terms of calculation:

$$HUT = \frac{\text{Households in the area with the TV set on}}{\text{Total households with TV sets}} \times 100$$

Still, a third index is a program's or a station's *share.* This can be defined as the percentage of the audience presumed to be viewing *programming offered by a particular station at a particular time.* This is often used as a measure of the success of the station (rather than the program) in competing for its slice of the available audience pie in its market. This index can be calculated by the following:

$$Share = \frac{\text{Households tuned to a particular station}}{\text{Households in area with TV sets on}} \times 100$$

These measures may seem complex, or at least a bit confusing, but each provides somewhat different information that is helpful to both broadcasters and advertisers in sorting out how many people are attending to a station or a program at any given time. Rating services also provide estimates of the composition of the audience, with some demographic data about age, gender, education, and so on.

Research on the broadcast audience has undergone many changes over the years. Today the audience is examined in terms of its overall size potential, its actual size, its stability over time, how much actual time it spends with particular programs, and the degree of viewer loyalty, which is called *tuning inertia.* In addition to national television and radio ratings, there are also local station and market ratings for broadcasting, as well as relatively new services that measure the cable audience.

Cable television ratings have proved difficult. They involve measures of *cable penetration* (the percentage of overall viewers actually on the cable) and *audience viewing patterns* across many more channels than is the case with conventional broadcasting. Radio research typically measures a much smaller audience than television, because there are so many radio stations, and they aim at limited segments of the audience with their specific formats (rock, country-western, news).

Obtaining ratings. Radio and television ratings are obtained in rather similar ways. In all audience research, after the area or "market" has been designated, some more or less representative set of people—a sample—must be selected. The people are contacted; data obtained from them are recorded in some way so that it can be analyzed; and reports are prepared for users. More than fifty companies conduct research on a national level, and scores of others do local and regional research that leads to ratings of some kind. Their first step is to define the local population or area of interest. Two major broadcast rating services, *Arbitron Company* and *Nielsen Media Research,* provide national and local ratings. Arbitron developed one method for defining the areas of interest in the television industry. They divide the United States into over 260 market areas called "areas of dominant influence," or ADIs. Nielsen uses another term, "designated market areas." Each of the nation's 3,141 counties is assigned to one of the areas and the markets are ranked according to the number of television households.

The ADIs range from New York City, with more than 7 million television households, to Pembina, North Dakota, with just over 6,500. The information is used by media advertising buyers to try to capture specified audiences.[9]

Researchers use various techniques: telephone interviews, in-person interviews, listener/viewer diaries, or receiver meters. Arbitron, which conducts research for both radio and television, asks a sample of about four thousands listeners or viewers to keep a daily diary each week of their viewing/listening behavior. Radio listeners, for example, are asked to indicate the amount of time they listen and the stations they are listening to, including the specific program and the place in which they are listening (for example, at home or away from home, including in a car). Samples are drawn from each market area and are weighted to provide a picture of the viewing or listening habits of the people who are asked to keep diaries. Needless to say, the system has many limitations. People forget to fill out the diaries. Some put in data to make it seem like they listened, even if they really did not. Less than half of the diaries distributed to the sample come back to Arbitron with usable data.

For years, the Nielsen ratings, from which the television network programs were ranked, were based on data accumulated from a device called an *audiometer*. It was attached to television sets in a sample of about seventeen hundred American homes. All it recorded was how long the set was on and to what channel it was tuned. It provided no information as to whether someone other than the family dog was actually viewing. However, the device delivered the information to a central computer through a telephone-linked network. This allowed rapid daily processing of data, which were analyzed for the national prime-time ratings. For ratings of local programs, Nielsen also used diaries. In addition to diaries and audiometers, a considerable amount of telephone sampling added to what the electronic media knew about their audiences.

The people-meter controversy.   In the late 1980s, as computer-driven audience research became more precise, a new technique for audience assessment was introduced by Nielsen, Arbitron, and other firms. The *people meter* consists of a small box

The portable "people meters" have become an important part of television, cable, and other audience research for the media. Here, a meter is inserted into its docking station.

that sits on top of the TV set and a hand-held gadget (like a remote channel changer) by which people can record what they say they are viewing. Nielsen used about four thousand such systems in a supposedly random sample of households. Each provided information on various demographic factors for the rating company. While viewing, members of the family pressed buttons that recorded times and stations. As viewers turned on their people meters and recorded their viewing, the information went instantly over phone lines to a central computer, yielding almost instantaneous rating analyses. Originally tested on an experimental basis, people meters proved so popular that they replaced the diary system. They seemed to work well, with about 90 percent of the households providing usable data.

Problems remain with all approaches to obtaining ratings. Some critics are concerned because any system of sampling has its flaws. For example, they maintain that young, urban viewers with a "high-tech" orientation would be more likely to let Nielsen come into their houses and wire them for a monitoring device. It was also thought that people who would cooperate with systems for automatic data recording would be more likely to be cable television viewers. Finding a reasonably accurate assessment of the viewing audience from which generalizations can be drawn remains difficult, making assessment of audience size for any station, cable channel, satellite system, or program educated guesswork at best.

Recently, some television stations have had cause to distrust ratings provided by Nielsen. For example in October 1999, the CBS drama *Judging Amy* disappeared from screens in Boston due to a failure of the Bell Atlantic fiber-optic cable used to deliver the program to homes. The scenes were blank for twenty minutes. However, the next day when the Nielsen ratings for the program arrived, they showed that the blank screen had seventy-two thousand viewers![10]

Audiences for the news. News programs have not been immune to the probes of researchers and rating services, and their audiences are regularly measured in the same way as other programming. But in addition to the rating information, news broadcasters frequently make use of *consultants*. These are individuals and firms who, for substantial fees, analyze a station's news operation and advise it as to how its ratings and share can be improved. Thus, such companies as Frank N. Magid Associates and McHugh and Hoffman are really marketing experts concerned mainly with "packaging" the news to achieve the greatest possible audience. Their recommendations often have much less to do with journalism, as such, than they do with theater and nonverbal communication. As two educators have written:

> Few [of the consultants' suggestions] deal with the complexities of news writing, best uses of resources, lines of communication, controversial reporting, or other journalistic topics. They have traditionally convinced station managers that the anchorwoman needs to convey more warmth on the air, the sportscaster needs to have silver teeth fillings replaced with more telegenic porcelain fillings, the weathercaster needs to practice getting rid of his lisp.[11]

Outrageous and superficial as these examples seem, they do reflect the kinds of recommendations that the consultants make. They may urge the station to build new and better sets, suggest more elaborate weather-forecasting equipment, and tell the anchorman to get a new hairpiece or wear a sweater vest. For years, the most visible sign of the news consultants' work for local stations has been "happy talk" news, in which anchor people deliver the news in chatty fashion with frequent friendly comments to sidekicks who are on camera. Other evidence of the consultants' advice is the "action news" format, which includes more stories of shorter length. This format is the result of the consultants' conviction that the majority of viewers are not too bright and have short attention spans.

Station managers take these recommendations seriously, although many news directors have resisted them. In some places the consultant's recommendations have virtually dictated major changes; in others the information is used advisedly in reshaping the format of a program. Many consultants do have an undeniable talent for boosting ratings. In any event, the use of these consultants shows clearly that news programming on radio and television, like entertainment programming, competes vigorously for an audience. Better ratings mean a bigger share of the market and thus greater profits.

Generally, whether measuring audiences for radio or TV, for entertainment or news, all rating services have problems gaining acceptance in homes. Some people simply refuse to cooperate; others do so halfheartedly or provide flawed data. These forms of resistance distort the results, although the rating services say they try to correct for these problems. No one outside these very secretive and competitive organizations really knows for sure how severe these distortions are, because the services do not readily share information about their methods and procedures. (An exception is Arbitron, which has published a book explaining its methodology.) But regardless of the actual quality of the ratings, they are taken very seriously by the broadcasting industry. Indeed, these ratings sometimes cause major losses in advertising revenues, people's jobs, and careers.

RATINGS AND AUDIENCE DIVERSITY

Finally, all of the ratings services try to break down the broadcast audience in terms of the categories we discussed earlier—age, gender, education, income, ethnic background, and so forth. As we indicated, it is these indicators of diversity that are the matrix within which tastes and preferences are formed and consumer decisions are made. Precise knowledge of such characteristics has become increasingly important as broadcasters try to attract specific kinds of audiences.

In addition to rating information organized around such categories, various kinds of commercial researchers probe the size and stability of the audience, seasonal variations, the hours spent viewing, and other factors. A number of market research firms look at audiences as potential consumers. The Axiom Market Research Bureau, for example, uses a large national sample of consumers (25,000) and collects information from them to learn how people use products and the media and how different categories of people make their buying decisions. This research offers its subscribers information about some 450 products and services, 120 magazines, 6 newspaper supplements, the nation's major newspapers, network television, and television usage as well as radio usage by type of program. The resulting data can help an advertiser decide which medium to use to sell laxatives, perfume, beer, or some other product to specific types of people.

Readership or viewership and product data are also correlated by W. R. Simmons & Associates Research, which studies the composition of audiences of magazines, newspaper supplements, national newspapers, and network television programs in terms of selective markets. Other firms, like Opinion Research Corporation, provide selective market information about the reading patterns of categories such as executives and teenagers. Still another firm, Lee Slurzberg Research, focuses on the African-American consumer and black-oriented media.

Other market research firms collect and disseminate information about advertising rates and mechanical specifications, advertising volume, and advertising effectiveness. One such firm, Daniel Starch & Staff, Inc., studies different categories of readers of consumer magazines, general business and trade periodicals, daily newspapers, and other publications. It also notes reading intensities or the reactions of readers to particular typographical devices and approaches.

Individual newspapers or broadcasters sometimes hire firms to probe the composition of their audiences in more detail. The circulation losses of American newspapers over the last two decades led to a good many of these studies. One study, commissioned by a large metropolitan newspaper, examined what was in the paper and what various categories of people read. The confidential report described the study's recommendations in the following terms:

> The prescription outlined here is: It points out what kinds of things might be cut out of the paper to improve readership, and also what kinds of things readers seem to want more of. It points out how differences in readership are related to such things as the subject of a story, its orientation, where it takes place, where it appears in the paper, the writing approach used in the story, the length of the story, the size and quality of its headline, the size of the newshole and the number of items on the page where the story appears, and the size of any photographs used to illustrate the story.[12]

Clearly, specially commissioned studies of this kind offer recommendations that, if followed, would alter the newspaper in the hope of gaining a larger and more dedicated audience. Thus, the various rating services and market researchers do not provide static indicators of audience preferences but information that can be used to change the content or format of a program or publication.

Most of the information we have been discussing is gathered for internal use by advertisers and media organizations. Sometimes, as in the case of the Nielsen ratings, the information is published widely in the press, but still its main use is internal. The public sometimes sees the consequences of the ratings but rarely knows much about how the ratings were determined or why decisions were made. On rare occasions, a disgruntled Nielsen employee has revealed anecdotes about the internal operations of the firm. Beyond this kind of insider's view, however, little is known about these audience-assessment organizations, which have so much influence on the media.

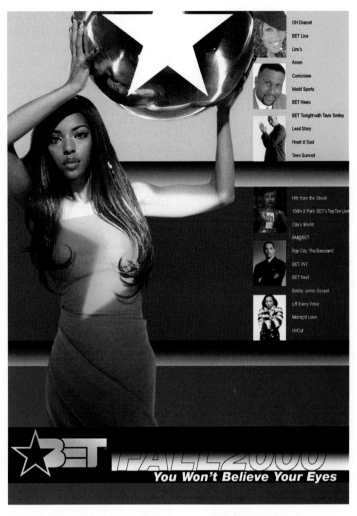

BET (Black Entertainment Television) makes a pitch for its fall 2000 season in this insertion in *Advertising Age* magazine.

Chapter Review

- Each of us attends to and acts upon mass communications because of our individual differences in tastes, interests, beliefs, attitudes, and values. These are shaped by our experiences in the different social groups and categories (age, gender, education, income, etc.) into which we can be classified.

- The American society is rich in ethnic and cultural diversity. That diversity is based in large part on the history of the nation, during which a huge and constantly growing population was brought together from virtually all parts of the globe in the largest migration in human history.

- The American population has always been characterized by various internal migrations within its borders. These have included flows of population westward, from South to North, farm to city, city to suburbs, and to sun-belt states from those farther north. These migrations tended to mix people, reducing their differences, and eventually producing a general American culture.

- Most of our citizens are of European origin. Immigrants from northern Europe came first, followed by others from southern and eastern Europe. In addition, many came from Africa. In more recent times, the greatest numbers of immigrants have come from Mexico, Latin America, and Asian countries.

- The family is the most significant consuming unit, and its trends and current status are important for professional communicators. American families are now smaller and organized differently than in earlier times. Relationships have changed between husbands and wives, with the latter gaining power and economic influence. Divorce rates are increasing.

- The women's movement of the previous century and its more contemporary phase completely altered the role of women in the American society. Women now exercise considerable economic power as consumers. This was particularly true after the majority of women entered the labor force.

- The media depend mainly on delayed feedback in one form or another to judge how well their messages are being received by the complex audience and if their goals are being achieved. A variety of groups have developed ways to assess the size and composition of the audiences for each of the media. The media also depend upon audience research conducted prior to designing content.

- Newspapers and magazines depend on the Audit Bureau of Circulation to monitor their claims about readers and subscribers. These figures are used by advertisers who must judge where their print advertising will attract the attention they seek.

- The movie industry depends on box office receipts to judge how well audiences like their products. These data are systematically gathered and reported by *Variety,* an industry periodical. Data on movie releases to videocassette, DVD, and TV, plus foreign sales, are also important.

- Various approaches have been taken for measuring audiences for the broadcast media. They have changed in various ways through the years. These approaches have included passive devices that merely recorded when the sets were on, diaries completed by samples of people, phone surveys, and the people meter.

- For the media, billions of dollars are at stake from advertising and other sources. Therefore, the assessments of audience size, interest, and behavior are of critical importance to mass communicators. Therefore, any technology is likely to be criticized by one group or another. Indeed, all of them have flaws and none provides completely reliable and valid data.

Notes and References

1. Henry David Thoreau, *Walden, or Life in the Woods* (New York: Vintage Books, 1991), p. 261

2. The first Homestead Act was signed by President Abraham Lincoln in 1862. In 1909, the amount of free land was increased to 320 acres. Then, in 1916, it was expanded again to 640 acres (reflecting the fact that only less desirable land remained to be awarded). By the end of the nineteenth century, over a quarter billion acres of land had been distributed under the Homestead Act. See also Craig L. LaMay, "Justin Smith Morrill and the Politics and Legacy of the Colleges Act," in Lawerence K. Grossman and Newton N. Minow, *A Digital Gift to the Nation* (New York: Century Foundation Press, 2001).

3. U.S. Bureau of the Census, *Population Projections of the United States by Age, Sex, Race and Hispanic Origin, 1992–2050.* (Washington, D.C.: Government Printing Office, 1992).

4. This means that if one were born in 1900, one could expect to live 47.3 years on average, providing that the death rates prevailing that year remained constant throughout one's lifetime. Of course, they do not, and the older one becomes, the greater the chance of living on for additional years. This is a reflection of the improvements in public health measures and medicine that constantly take place.

5. U.S. Bureau of the Census, *Vital Statistic Rates in the United States, 1900–1940* (Washington, D.C.: Government Printing Office, 1943).

6. Sydney Head and Christopher Sterling, *Broadcasting in America,* 5th ed. (Boston: Houghton Mifflin, 1986), p. 227.

7. For a detailed discussion of the history of broadcast audience measurement, see Hugh Malcolm Beville, Jr., *Audience Ratings: Radio Television and Cable* (Hillsdale, N.J.: Lawrence Erlbaum Associates, Publishers, 1988).

8. Head and Sterling, *Broadcasting in America,* pp. 373–403.

9. Head and Sterling, *Broadcasting in America,* p. 228. See, generally, Head and Sterling's excellent discussion of audience measurement, pp. 373–403.

10. Don Aucoin, "Local TV Stations Giving Nielson Low Ratings, *The Boston Globe,* November 18, 1999, p. A-1.

11. Julius K. Hunter and Lynn S. Gross, *Broadcast News: The Inside Out* (St. Louis: Mosby, 1980), p. 280.

12. From a confidential report prepared by a market research firm for a large metropolitan daily newspaper.

Part Four
MEDIA ISSUES AND INFLUENCES

Chapter 14
CONTROLS: POLITICS, POLICIES, AND ECONOMICS

Chapter 15
MEDIA EFFECTS: EXPLAINING THE PROCESSES AND INFLUENCES OF MASS COMMUNICATION

Chapter 16
ETHICS: ASSESSING MEDIA BEHAVIOR AND CONTENT

Chapter 14

CONTROLS: POLITICS, POLICIES, AND ECONOMICS

Courts, the stage for the drama of law and order in society, are covered closely by the media, especially in celebrated cases like this one in the murder trial of Baltimore Raven linebacker Ray Lewis. Here, Lewis's attorney cross-examines witness Chester Anderson.

Politics and media are inseparable. It is only the politicians and the media that are incompatible.

Walter Cronkite, former CBS anchor

When they say it's not about the money, it's about the money.

Fred W. Friendly, former CBS News president and

Columbia University professor

THE MASS MEDIA MUST EXIST WITHIN A PARTICULAR ECONOMIC SYSTEM WITH ALL ITS REALITIES, HARSH AS WELL AS HAPPY, AND THEY ALSO MUST COPE WITH THE IDEOLOGY OF A PARTICULAR GOVERNMENT. LIKE OTHER SOCIAL INSTITUTIONS, THE MEDIA WIND THEIR way through the economic and political systems. As we have noted in previous chapters, a new technology is often the driving force that ignites the factors (or controls) that influence what media do and how they do it. In this particular chapter, we deal with *communication policy,* mainly in the realm of law and regulation, that affects media industries and eventually media audiences. But communication policy also includes the powerful role of the media economy in what is largely a *commercial* communication system in the United States. We look first at political protections and constraints in the context of the role of government, then touch on economic factors. We have dealt repeatedly with the media economy in chapters on individual media and in our discussions of the historical development of communication industries as well as the role of advertising within all of the media. Here, we treat media economics briefly to tie together some of the considerations introduced earlier.

In the United States, even as media are becoming more global (see Chapter 13), they are beset with apparent confusions and contradictions. For example, the media in the United States enjoy extensive freedoms that are envied around the globe and embodied in the First Amendment to the Constitution of the United States, which prohibits government interference with freedom of speech and press, and which has generally been applied to the modern media system. "No law means no law," the great First Amendment absolutist Justice Hugo Black used to thunder—meaning that freedom of the press meant that government, including all of its branches, should keep "hands off" the free media. However, there are libraries full of court decisions, statutes, and other evidence of communication law in the United States, some of it promulgated by the very Congress that was and still is prohibited from doing so in the First Amendment.

It is also curious that the government still to some degree regulates a media system that is mostly commercial, living within a market economy. This is especially true for broadcasting and some other electronic media. In such a system there is a continuous debate about just what the *public interest* is and how it is to be expressed and accounted for—something required and mandated by government in various communications acts. The assumption made here, and also found in much of the literature of communication law and history, is that media get enormous freedoms on behalf of the public as part of a democratic system. What they give back to the public—their public duty—is presumably information, entertainment, opinion, and a platform for selling goods and services. But just how they do this and whether the public has any say in the matter is often a source of discussion and sometimes even government action.

SEARCHING FOR THE PUBLIC INTEREST

Over the years, media people, scholars, and jurists have raised the question, "freedom of the press for whom?" One Supreme Court Justice asked whether freedom of the press was an "individual right" to be exercised by any criteria or an "institutional right" assigned to the media. With another First Amendment right, that concerning *religion,* this question is rarely raised because any individual can exercise freedom of religion, and at the same time, organized religion claims rights as an institution guaranteeing religious freedom. Until the Internet came along, it was difficult to argue that individuals could easily exercise freedom of the press except as members of the audience. This led some critics to say that freedom of the press belongs only to those who own a press or broadcast station. Not unreasonably, then, the conflict that exists between government and the media has involved the free flow of information, the content of communication, the ownership of the media, and other matters.

As noted earlier, the print media have long had fairly unconstrained freedom, because theoretically there is no limit on the number of publications that can be produced. Electronic media have had to live with a limited broadcast spectrum that led to government regulation of radio, television, telecommunications, and some aspects of cable television. In these instances, government has been both a traffic cop and an evaluator of the performance of the broadcast system. Unlike many European countries, broadcasting in the United States opted for a commercial approach, which was mainly supported by advertising instead of a public service system. This distinction is less important today, however, as electronic media around the world are moving closer to the market model and away from public support and government or partial government direction and control.

The issue of diversity of voices in the marketplace of ideas—the objective of the laws under which U.S. broadcasting have traditionally operated—is less relevant in the era of the Internet, when almost anyone can have a Web site and attempt to communicate with the world. How effectively, and with what impact, is another issue. But technically, what was once impossible in a broadcast system with limited spectrum space is now a reality—at least to the extent that people are wired to the Internet or a cable system.

For years, defining *the public interest* was mostly conceived in economic terms. Anything the public was interested in was deemed to be *of* public interest. Whether it met a more subtle test that separated matters *of public interest* from those truly *in the public interest* is another consideration that requires much study and analysis. However, for decades broadcast regulation in the United States tried to enforce a *public interest standard* by requiring public affairs programs, minority hiring, and equal time for political candidates.

We treat media economics in this chapter as a factor influencing the nature and shape of communications, closely linked to the legal and regulatory framework in what we regard as a capitalistic or free-market economy. There are plenty of media critics, mentioned in earlier chapters, who decry this system, or at least its current practices, as they worry about the concentration of ownership, biased cultural and political content, the dumbing down of entertainment, and other factors. And while the system does change, even if this change is incremental, it is the reality of today, rather than someone's theoretical ideas about an ideal system.

As noted above, in a society that regards its media system as independent with guarantees of press freedom enshrined in the Constitution, a discussion of "controls" on the media may seem curious. Control, after all, is at the other end of the continuum from freedom. Where there is complete and authoritarian control, there can be little, if any, freedom. In the American context, however, controls are in fact constraints that allow the balancing of various individual and social interests with those of the media. Such controls include *communication policies* that set standards and allow for resolution of disputes as well as the *political activity* that shaped those policies in the first place.

In colonial America, people worried about royal charters that licensed the media of the day, giving permission to publish and disseminate information, which we discuss later in this chapter. Today, Americans and citizens of other countries are concerned about potential controls or constraints on cyberspace and the free flow of information. While censorship may be technically impossible on the Internet, there have been efforts to block pornography and political material in the United States and Germany, and to stop political dissidents in China. Also high on the agenda is the ownership of information or intellectual property as well as matters of privacy and publicity.

Not all controls involve government. While censorship is an official act of a government to block communication, merchants can refuse to stock certain objectionable CDs and videos, books, or magazines. Media owners can decide whether or not to carry a cable channel or pay-per-view offering. Influence on advertisers from economic, religious, educational, and other interests can also play a role in the communications process. Thus, there are very real influences of policy and politics that shape the operations and content of our media system.

This chapter describes the political conditions that confront the mass media in America. We make a distinction between the media as "the press" or news media—which includes both print and broadcasting components—and "mass communications," whose efforts are mainly directed toward entertainment or advertising. We will discuss both because, as will be made clear, it is often difficult to separate the news media and mass communications sharply within a discussion of political controls. All are part of an integrated system and all are affected by the entire complex of political factors that relate media and government to the American society.

Against a worldwide standard, American media, whether delivering news or entertainment, are separate from government; they operate independently and are not reliant on government funds or supervision. At the same time, it should be said that media systems in Latin America, Asia, and Russia, once tightly controlled by government, are moving toward full democratization. That is, they are liberalizing, and the once stark contrasts with the United States no longer exist. However, exceptions remain in totalitarian states such as Cuba, North Korea, and China.

As we point out in Chapter 13, looking at media in a country by country comparison is no longer very useful. There is now a global media system with global media companies that must live within the laws of various nations in an internationally acceptable manner. The rather liberal media laws and traditions of the

As immigrants poured into the United States around the turn of the nineteenth century, Ellis Island, sometimes called the "Golden Door," was the first stop before they settled in the New World adding great ethnic, cultural, racial, and religious diversity to America. Immigrants have often been at the center of free-speech and press debates as they tested the limits of prejudice and tolerance.

United States do not always apply abroad and naturally this reality is shaping what media companies can do. In a world of cross-border communication, there are some international agreements about the Internet, intellectual property (copyright), and satellite transmissions, but there is also much that is yet undefined.

By deeply established tradition, the news media in the United States have an obligation to deliver information, debate, and opinion to the public, and are often described collectively as a "trustee" or "representative" of the people. They have been variously labeled the "watchdogs of the public interest," and even as the "fourth estate," implying that they are almost a branch of government. Quite often, this role puts the press in conflict with the government, as it did, for example, during the Watergate scandal in the mid-1970s, the Iran-Contra scandal in the late 1980s, or Whitewater and the impeachment process in the late 1990s. Additionally, as we will discuss later, the press and government often are at odds during wartime. This has been true in the United States from the American Revolution through the short-lived naval and military operations of the Persian Gulf War and subsequent "wars" and peace keeping missions in Bosnia, Kosovo, and sub-Saharan Africa. In most conflicts, the government not only controlled the conduct of troops, it also attempted to *control* information about the war, especially information related to national security. Leaders of the news media, in their desire to deliver information and form opinion on this important public concern, naturally resisted and even resented that control.

Sometimes, conflict between the press and the government centers on particular individuals or events. For example, the press may focus on the alleged sexual or financial misconduct of members of Congress or the executive branch. Another area of conflict between government and the press is the coverage of elections, especially presidential elections. In presidential campaigns, the candidates and their campaigns are often sharply critical of the press, charging bias and unfair portrayals.[1] One recent candidate decried what he called "the dangerously liberal press," while his opponent also smarted at media criticism but for different reasons. In other countries, disputes with the press during elections have often led to censorship of a harsh nature. That has not been the case in the United States. While politicians who are elected to office sometimes retaliate by withholding information or making life difficult for the press, they have only rarely attempted censorship and punitive action. Still, media people are almost always wary of potential problems of this kind, knowing that the general public holds a generally negative view of the media. In fact, one recent survey suggested that if the public could reconsider the Bill of Rights in the U.S. Constitution, it would not grant so much latitude and freedom to the press.

Freedom of the press, as guaranteed by the First Amendment of the Constitution, is a basic tenet of American government. The Amendment guarantees the rights of assembly and speech, not only to private individuals, but to all who operate our media as well. This principle has frequently been tested and interpreted by the courts so as to prevent censorship of the movies, to extend free expression rights to the electronic media, and even to allow advertisers and public relations practitioners to speak their minds—within certain limits that we will discuss. Thus, direct government control over our media is very limited indeed. But as we indicated earlier, communication in the United States (and elsewhere in the world) is largely influenced by *economic competition,* which exerts its own marketplace controls.

The political regime under which the mass media exist in the United States is complex and subtle, and the government and the press frequently clash for a variety of reasons. One is the conflict over *rights,* described later in this chapter. Another is the desire of private and public interests within the country to *communicate directly* to the people through the press without any editorial interference. Although much of the content of the media is routine and noncontroversial, some material creates friction and, as we mentioned earlier, supports the idea of an adversarial press attempting to check and balance the power of government. Of course, the government is not without means to fight back. It is this competition that best characterizes the true nature of the way the media navigate in our political environment.

To survive in our system, the mass media perform two major functions. First, they provide a forum of communication for the nation, a *commonality of interest.* The daily agenda for public discussion is set by the press and this provides a priority list of topics and issues to talk about. That agenda allows public opinion to form and emerge as people discuss topics within the context of the information provided by the press. Second, the media serve both as an *advocate* and an *intermediary* for the citizenry as they debate the topics on the news agenda from the standpoint of various social, economic, and political institutions.

The first function leads to consensus and cooperation, whereas the latter may lead to conflict. Service as a *forum of communication* allows the media to be a central nervous system for the nation, while service as an advocate or an intermediary is a correcting device that represents the people when institutions need an independent evaluation. For example, a government agency that is performing poorly will not announce its shortcomings to the public, which deserves to know them. It is the responsibility of the press as watchdog of the public interest to report them.

Thus, our news media exist in an atmosphere of both consensus and conflict. The balance between the two is closely related to the ability of the press to adjust to the political and governmental climate at any specific time. The news media both report on the activities of government and occasionally participate in it as petitioners in court or as supporters (or opposers) of candidates for public office.

To understand our press fully, it is vital to realize that for the most part, they see themselves as nonideological entities, or as instruments of fairness and impartiality in a world of self-serving politicians and government officials. Some citizens, especially those who are criticized by the news media, obviously have a different view. But in comparison with news systems that openly declare partisan political allegiances, such as those in Great Britain and France, our press is to a large extent politically independent and generally nonpartisan. Occasionally the press may endorse political candidates, but the media are not part of any political party or funded directly by the government—the hallmarks of media in other countries.

POLITICAL PROTECTIONS: THE CONSTITUTIONAL FRAMEWORK

Political as well as economic considerations place limitations on media in all democratic systems. In Great Britain, for example, although newspapers are privately owned it is a crime to publish anything from public documents unless prior authorization is obtained. Reporters are allowed to report only what is said at a trial, nothing more. Pretrial publicity is not permitted.

Although we have the First Amendment, the government frequently does prohibit the press from printing whatever it wishes. For example, in the 1990s, the Minnesota Supreme Court ruled in a lawsuit against a newspaper that printed certain information. The case centered on whether an agreement between a reporter and a source (who had been assured of confidentiality) was a legally binding contract. In *Cohen* v. *The Minneapolis Star Tribune,* a reporter promised a Minnesota publicist that his role in leaking information would be kept confidential. The reporter's editors disregarded the promise and revealed the source's name—making him very angry. He sued, and after several appeals he finally won. The newspaper had claimed a First Amendment privilege to do what it wished with the information he had supplied. On appeal, the Court ruled that a verbal promise of confidentiality is a contract that must be honored and ignored the newspaper's First Amendment claim. The court awarded $200,000 in punitive damages to the plantiff.[2]

As can be seen in the above legal case, the political environment of the American media has two fundamental elements. First, a guarantee of freedom of the press is *clearly embodied* in the U.S. Constitution. Second, that freedom is *not absolute.* As it has come into conflict with other rights and freedoms, legal limitations on freedom of the press have been established. We begin an examination of these limitations by looking at the constitutional guarantee of a free press that arose from America's colonial experience.

THE HISTORICAL LEGACY

As we discussed in Chapter 1, prior to the Revolution, the American colonies were ruled by England. Governors representing the Crown were appointed for each colony to ensure that English laws and English policies prevailed. With English law came a specific set of legal relationships between the press and the government. One principle embedded in those laws was that of *prior restraint;* that is, the government could not only punish those responsible for illegal publications but it could also prevent the publication of material it did not like. The government, in short, could censor publication.

In England, the Crown had not enforced its prior restraint laws for many decades before the American Revolution. Although as noted in chapters 3 and 4, it had jailed or fined some individuals whose publications it did not like. English pamphleteers and newspaper writers in the eighteenth century often criticized the government without reprisal. But in the colonies, where rebellions were an ever present possibility, the Crown's governors sometimes required that any comment on the government's activities be reviewed and approved before publication. As detailed in our history of the newspaper, the governors would occasionally decide to crack down, as in the case of Ben Franklin's brother James, who was jailed and later forced to give up his paper for criticizing the government, and the celebrated case of John Peter Zenger, publisher of the *New York Weekly Journal.*

As was explained in Chapter 3, Zenger was charged with seditious libel—for defaming the Crown and its governor. At his lawyer's urging, the jury found him not guilty, because what he had published—although critical of government—was true. The jury's verdict thus asserted the right of citizens to speak out against the government. The Zenger case did not change the existing British laws regarding seditious libel, but it did put public opinion firmly behind the idea that newspapers should be allowed to print the truth, even if it was contrary to the wishes of the government. All during the remaining time of English rule, the principle of prior restraint remained a part of the legal system, but it was seldom enforced.

THE FIRST AMENDMENT

Curiously enough, despite the key role played by newspapers, pamphlets, and broadsides (one-page flyers) in mobilizing support for the American Revolution, the framers of the U.S. Constitution did not mention freedom of the press in the original document. For one thing, they could neither agree on what the concept meant in practical terms, nor see how such a provision could be enforced. In addition, some of the members of the constitutional convention argued that there was no need to guarantee such freedoms.

Before the Constitution was finally ratified, however, several states insisted on a list of amendments that guaranteed a number of freedoms. These were accepted and we have come to know them as the Bill of Rights. Prominent among these is the First Amendment, which states, "Congress shall make no law . . . abridging the freedom of speech, or of the press." These words are known as the free speech and free press *clause* of the First Amendment. (The First Amendment also includes guarantees of freedom of religion and freedom of assembly.) At first glance, the clause seems clear and unambiguous. Yet through the years, as additional media have come into being, the press and the government have become enmeshed in a tangle of issues that have confused the public, perplexed the most able jurists, and placed a variety of constraints on those who operate the mass media.

How could such confusion occur? At the outset, we should recognize that even in the first days of the Republic, many of the founders had mixed feelings about the merits of a "free press" and the extent to which it should be unfettered. Some had qualms because it seemed obvious that newspapers were instruments of political power. For example, newspaper enthusiasts today are fond of quoting Thomas Jefferson, who wrote, "Were it left to me to decide whether we should have a government without newspapers, or newspapers without government, I should not hesitate a moment to prefer the latter." Less frequently quoted is the qualifying sentence that followed: "But I should mean that *every man should receive those papers and be capable of reading them*" (italics added). And almost never quoted are the disillusioned remarks of Jefferson after being opposed frequently by the press. He bitterly noted, "The man who never looks into a newspaper is better informed than he who reads them, inasmuch as he who knows nothing is nearer to the truth than he whose mind is filled with falsehoods and errors."

Almost all Americans will nod vigorously in agreement if asked whether they believe in freedom of the press. It ranks with motherhood, the family, and the American flag as a source of national esteem. But when pressed on some specific case—such as pornography, criticism of their favorite public figure, or unfavorable stories about themselves—their assent to a free press is likely to vanish. Generally, then, support for freedom of the press is often based, not on the idea that the government simply has no right to control the press, but on the belief that a free press is the best method for insuring a well-informed public and a stable democracy. When the press appears to be doing a poor job of informing the public, support for its freedom is likely to diminish.

The issue of freedom of the press (media in general) is complicated by issues related to libel, offensive material (e.g., sacrilegious films and pornography), technical needs to control the airwaves, secrets during wartime, and many other issues. It is further complicated by jurisdictional boundaries between various courts. For example, over the years, most libel cases were fought in the state courts under state statutes. Federal courts rarely intervened to broaden press freedom until well into the twentieth century. By then, the debate over freedom of the press had become more complicated with the appearance of film and the broadcast media.

Are movies, soap operas, and radio programs forms of "speech" and are their creators "the press," and therefore protected by the First Amendment? In 1915, the Supreme Court ruled in *Mutual Film Company* v. *Ohio* that cinema was a "business, pure and simple, originated and conducted for profit." Therefore, the Court continued, it was not protected by constitutional guarantees of free speech and a free press. But in 1952, the Supreme Court reversed this decision, after the state of New York forbade the screening of an Italian film, "The Miracle" in the state because it was "sacrilegious." When the case was appealed in the Supreme Court, it ruled that the state had no power to censor films on religious grounds.[3] The effect was that films gained the protection of the First Amendment.

Radio and television present a more complicated situation. Whereas, in principle, there are no limits to the number of newspapers that can be published or films produced, the number of frequencies that can be used for broadcasting has been severely restricted, although liberalized in recent years. This historical difference between broadcasting and print has provided the basis for a host of government regulations regarding broadcasting. In other words, broadcast regulation has been justified by the scarcity of channels. Therefore, government regulates the owners of broadcast stations by granting and renewing broadcast licenses, as well as by regulating content to some extent. As we shall see later in this chapter, regulations regarding broadcasting are generally compromised between the principle that "the public owns the airwaves" and the Constitution's guarantee of freedom of speech.

As the media developed, especially with multiple cable channels, digital television, and Internet broadcasts, the idea of a scarcity of channels became obsolete. New technologies have greatly expanded the means by which messages can be transmitted to audiences. For example, with the advent of cable television, direct broadcast satellite transmission, as well as such emerging technologies as broadband, we are entering a period, not of broadcast scarcity, but of *abundance*. While this has led to a certain amount of deregulation, some of the old regulatory regime still reigns. Perhaps the greatest source of conflict over the right to a free press comes from the fact that it is only one among many other important rights. The right to a free press sometimes conflicts with society's right to maintain order and security. For example, the press's exercise of its freedom may conflict with the ability of the police and judges to do their jobs, or with the government's ability to maintain the secrets it deems necessary for national security. Freedom of the press may also conflict with the rights of individuals, such as the right to privacy and the right to a fair trial. As a result of these conflicts, the courts have frequently ruled against the press's right to publish anything it pleases. The most important limitations on the press imposed by the courts concern *libel, coverage of trials, obscene material,* and *government secrets.*

As we noted in Chapter 7, television is in the midst of yet another revolution—that of a conversion from conventional *analog* to *digital* transmission. This means an expansion of the number of channels a given station can offer, which may create a new wireless cable television system that enables customized messages to be targeted to individuals, something not available today. All this is supposed to happen by the year 2006—though it may be delayed—and has ignited an important debate among policymakers, businesses, and the public. Much of the debate centers on how the *public interest* can best be served in a digital era when technology has pushed aside many of the guidelines that have protected the public in the past. And while there will be more and more abundance of TV and other wireless and electronic options for people, there are still many aspects of the communication system that are regulated by the government. Thus, President George W. Bush, Congress, and various regulatory agencies and private sector groups have their work cut out for them. As Charles Firestone and Amy Korzick Garmer of the Aspen Institute have written, "quite simply, the move to digital broadcasting will likely change the very nature of the most powerful and important medium of communication in the world."[4]

TECHNOLOGY'S ROLE—FROM PRINTING PRESSES TO CYBERSPACE

Government controls have often focused on technology as a way of encouraging access to information or blocking it. From early printing presses, which were licensed, to cyberspace, which is currently the subject of official law in the United States and other countries, governments acting as agents for citizens (or for leaders or both) have always played a role. Without a royal license in many European and Asian societies, printers were not allowed to make copies of their works for distribution. Because absolute monarchs believed that they should control all communication—and thus have a clear sense of what was being said and by whom—they guarded this authority jealously. The right to print freely and distribute news, information, and opinions was central to revolutions in the United States, France, and other nations, and often still is as undemocratic regimes are replaced. In the 1980s and 1990s, as communism fell in the former U.S.S.R. and its satellites, military regimes were toppling in Latin America, and Asia was charged by new economic prowess. All three conditions led to much more freedom of communication, either guaranteed by law or encouraged by more democratic regimes. Still, even in the freest of societies, government agencies act as traffic cops to assign broadcast frequencies, register copyrights, prevent harmful advertising practices, and oversee other social or citizen functions.

Much of the activity of the government and other institutions trying to monitor, administer, or influence communication has been *driven by technology*. To prevent a kind of broadcast anarchy, it was necessary to assign frequencies and channels for radio and television. Later, cable systems were "franchised" in local communities, that is, given to a cable operator to develop, since it was believed that only a monopoly system would be economically feasible. Telecommunication or telephone systems also benefited from the same kind of monopoly, much of which was subsequently broken. Federal agencies evolved to administer communications, trade, and other arenas where monitoring and adjudicating disputes was believed to be essential.

In the 1990s, as various media industries (telephone, cable television, broadcast, motion pictures, and newspapers) vied for control of new media enterprises (see Chapter 8), old regulatory schemes were scrapped for a new one. The Telecommunications Reform Act of 1996 was passed by the U.S. Congress and signed into law. It permitted various business connections between media industries that previously would have been in restraint of trade and subject to antitrust laws, which exist to break up monopolies. The legislation also relaxed the rules for media ownership and content. For most observers the new act was profoundly important. To many in the media industry, it deregulated a once highly regulated industry and allowed for more competition. To critics, the new law was the handiwork of big media companies and was a "license to make money" that was unconnected to the public interest. The Clinton administration (and its predecessors from Jimmy Carter to George Bush) said that the new law was a tradeoff that freed broadcasters and other media industries from regulation in return for business growth and new jobs. And there was also the hope that the law would spur the growth of the Internet and make it more widely available to school children in the classroom and all citizens at home within a few years.

One part of the Telecommunications Reform Act that drew considerable controversy was the Communications Decency Act, which banned indecent or patently offensive speech. The Act imposed criminal sanctions for content transmitted over the Internet that was deemed obscene or indecent. The Act made it a crime to use an "interactive computer service" to send minors "any comment, request, suggestion, proposal, image or other communication that, in context, depicts or describes, in terms patently offensive as measured by contemporary community standards, sexual or excretory activities or organs."[5] Although signed into law by President Bill Clinton, many civil liberties and cyberspace groups objected, saying that any control over the Internet would "criminalize" speech and curtail the free and open system for which the Internet is known. The case was reviewed in the courts and struck down by a federal court in Philadelphia. The Internet and other forms of digital communication may have increased access to communication, but they have not ended the government's interest in monitoring and controlling content. It is inevitable that every new technology will arouse legal and other government control interests. Sometimes these reflect citizen interests, for example, parents in the case of the Internet, or specific industries that are trying to block new competition. In all disputes over technology, both sides cite the *public interest* rationale for their actions. Even the highly favorable exemption of e-commerce and the new media from sales taxes is a *government control,* although a positive one.

PROTECTION FROM LIBEL

Injunctions against making false, defamatory statements about others have ancient origins. The Ten Commandments include the injunction, "Thou shalt not bear false witness against thy neighbor." In ancient Norman law it was written that "a man who falsely called another a thief or manslayer must pay damages, and holding his nose with his fingers, must publicly confess himself a liar."[6] The idea that a person whose reputation had been damaged by another's untrue public statements is entitled to compensation was passed on to the American colonies through English law and from there found its way into our contemporary legal system. Today, libel laws not only protect the reputations of individuals, but also those of corporations and businesses. With the development of media with huge audiences, it became possible to "bear false witness" and damage reputations on a very large scale, with very serious economic consequences.

LIBEL LAWS AND THE MEDIA

Every year, libel suits are brought against newspapers, magazines, book publishers, and broadcast stations. They constantly test the principle of freedom of the press. The courts must weigh the right of the press to publish freely against the right of people to preserve their privacy, reputation, and peace of mind. The situation is complicated in the absence of any federal statutes concerning libel. It is a matter of state law, and each state has its own statutes.

State laws usually give news reporters and the news media some protection against libel suits. They usually allow publication of public records and "fair comment and criticism" of both public figures and public officials. Unfortunately, it is not entirely clear who qualifies as either under the laws of the various states. However, various court cases have defined *public figures* essentially as persons who are well-known. Examples are prominent sports stars, entertainment personalities, widely read novelists, and even well-known scientists and professors.

In recent years, reporters and the media have also received constitutional protection from libel suits. In a 1964 case, the *New York Times* v. *Sullivan,* the Supreme Court considered for the first time whether state laws regarding libel might be overturned on the grounds that they violate the First Amendment to the Constitution. During the height of the civil rights conflict in the South, the *Times* had published an advertisement that indirectly attacked the Birmingham, Alabama, Commissioner of Public Safety. An Alabama jury ruled that the *Times* had to pay $500,000 in damages because the advertisement included some misstatements of fact. But the Supreme Court overruled the Alabama jury, holding that its decision violated freedom of the press. Essentially, the Supreme Court held that a full and robust discussion of public issues, including criticism of public officials, was too important to allow the states to restrain the press through their libel laws.

After 1964, it became very difficult for public officials to claim libel damages. According to the Supreme Court, only when public officials could prove that the press had shown "malice," "reckless disregard of the truth," or "knowing falsehood" could they sue for libel.

By no means was the libel issue decided once and for all in *Times* v. *Sullivan.* Since that time, courts have repeatedly redefined who is and who is not a public official or a public figure. And in a 1979 case, *Herbert* v. *Lando,* the Supreme Court ruled that courts could inquire into the state of mind of a reporter to determine whether there was malice present as a story was written. Furthermore, there have been many large libel judgments against the media.

MULTIMILLION DOLLAR LIBEL SUITS

While the Supreme Court did not radically rewrite the law of libel in the 1980s, other conditions—mainly economic ones—called attention to the importance of libel as a constraint on freedom of the press. A number of dramatic libel suits captured headlines during the decade. General William Westmoreland, who led American forces during the war in Vietnam, sued CBS for his depiction in a documentary about the conflict, but dropped his suit in the last days of the trial; a gubernatorial candidate unsuccessfully sued the *Boston Globe;* and Mobil Oil President William Tavoulareas successfully sued the *Washington Post.* Entertainer Wayne Newton sued NBC and won in a case involving charges that the singer had consorted with members of organized crime. In 1990, the *Philadelphia Inquirer* lost a multimillion dollar libel suit to a local official. All of these cases had one thing in common: large amounts of money were involved, in what have been called "megabuck libel verdicts," or substantial legal fees. Whatever their outcome, libel suits of this kind are extremely expensive and sometimes take years to litigate. The rising cost of libel trials involves not only those judgments of the courts that penalize the media, but also legal fees and increasing libel insurance premiums.

Some critics cite an increasingly conservative judiciary as one of the reasons for mounting libel costs, although David Anderson, a law professor at the University of

Texas, argues that the media win nearly as many cases as they lose in the courts.[7] Still, win or lose, the legal costs are substantial. Some observers say that increasing costs have been responsible for diminishing investigative reporting (the so-called "chilling effect"), while others say that the costs check the growing power of the media in necessary ways. It should be noted that many large libel judgments are greatly reduced by judges or as the result of a decision on appeal. Almost all knowledgeable observers agree, however, that the cost of libel is having a significant effect.[8]

Libel law and libel cases always bear watching because the law in that area is complex, and it is relatively easy to bring a suit. Communication law scholar Donald M. Gillmor of the University of Minnesota points out, in a widely cited book, that although the media often win libel cases or have them thrown out of court, there is still a great cost due to legal fees that can be especially harmful to small publications and broadcasters. Gillmor sees public officials and celebrities as the culprits in many libel suits, and he proposes to deny protection to those with "high visibility and the resources to communicate with broad sections of the public," saving the tougher provisions of libel law for ordinary citizens who are genuinely damaged by the media and who have little ability to fight back.[9]

A libel reform movement gained some publicity in 1989 when the Annenberg Washington Program mounted a proposal for libel reform and urged its adoption at the state level. However, it got few takers. Interest in libel reform typically comes from the media after major cases are lost, but to date such reform has had little public support. More importantly, the legal profession has little enthusiasm for reform, perhaps because lawyers would stand to lose huge fees under any such plan.

Other proposals have been made to circumvent libel and other media-public confrontations. One such proposal was advanced by Robert Chandler, an Oregon publisher, who called for community complaint councils that would have less authority than press councils as discussed in Chapter 3, but would still offer a safety valve for public feedback.[10] The durable Minnesota News Council has also taken up cases on a trial basis in other states and has proposed a modest "nationalization" of their efforts. In Washington State, a journalism complaints council was developed in the 1990s. In 1997, on the fiftieth anniversary of the Hutchins Commission, which first introduced the idea of press councils to America, a new push for news councils began. This time the leader was TV journalist Mike Wallace of CBS's *60 Minutes* who saw hope in the Minnesota News Council and wanted to see it tried on a national basis.[11] Various public interest groups and foundations have supported press councils and media assessment projects, but few have taken hold in any legal sense.

Lawyers rightly argue that libel and other press law issues have become increasingly complex in recent years as defendants from other countries have sued American media in foreign courts. For example, the former prime minister of the Bahamas, Lyndon Pindling, once sued *Time* magazine in Canada, where the libel laws are more restrictive than those in the United States. There are similar suits against U.S. media in Britain. Since the media are increasingly global and have a legal presence internationally, they are often susceptible to the laws of all of the countries where they operate, many of which run counter to press rights under the U.S. Constitution. This is likely to be a growing area of libel litigation.

Legislative branch oversight of a wide range of public activities and concerns are often scrutinized on television in controversial congressional hearings. Here, Lt. Col. Oliver North testifies in 1987, some years before he transformed his celebrity status into a hosting job for his own radio and cable TV talk shows.

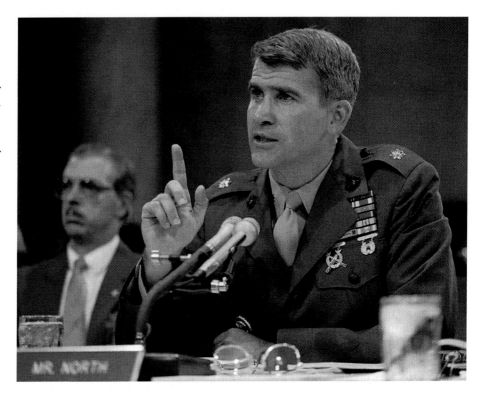

LIBEL AND CONGRESS

Members of Congress are virtually immune from libel suits. Statements made on the floor of Congress or in congressional committees are regarded as related to their responsibilities as public officials. Therefore, they can and often do make irresponsible public statements about issues and people, and they are protected by the knowledge that they will not wind up in court. The late Senator Joseph McCarthy provides a classic example of the abuse of this protection.

In the 1950s, McCarthy gained national and even worldwide attention by claiming that the United States was in the grip of powerful but hidden Communist infiltration. Using the media to whip up public fear of a "vast Communist conspiracy," he accused prominent individuals in government, business, education, military, the film industry, and even the clergy of being "subversive," "fellow travelers" or "card-carrying members of the Communist Party." The media gave his outrageous claims worldwide coverage.

McCarthy's accusations helped to create a climate of fear that wrecked reputations and ruined careers all over the nation. Finally, however, the media that had helped McCarthy's rise assisted in his downfall. As a result of his accusations, Congress held formal hearings on Communist influence in the U.S. Army, which were televised daily to a national audience. McCarthy's tactics were so outrageous that, after seeing him in action, the public concluded that he was an irresponsible demagogue. He lost credibility and his bid for power came to an end. Since then, McCarthy's name has become synonymous with unfair attacks without evidence. In political campaigns the term "McCarthyism" often reemerges, and is well established in the language as meaning guilt by association and innuendo.

TRIAL BY MEDIA

The Constitution guarantees freedom of the press, but in the Sixth Amendment it also guarantees a fair and speedy trial to defendants. Sometimes publicity about a crime and the suspected criminal seems to make a fair trial impossible. The classic example of how the press can turn a case into a sensational and disruptive event and thereby deny the defendant's right to a fair trial occurred in the prosecution of Dr. Sam Sheppard in the 1950s. Trial by publicity has been played out many times in high profile court cases, especially that of O. J. Simpson. Indeed, Court TV owes its existence to the public's fascination with sensational trials involving celebrities and others.

Sheppard was a well-to-do osteopathic surgeon in Ohio. One night his wife was brutally beaten and stabbed to death under mysterious circumstances in their suburban home. The police were baffled because there were no witnesses and few clues. Long before the police investigation had been completed, the local newspapers decided that Sheppard was guilty. One headline read "Quit Stalling—Bring Him In;" another asked, "Why Isn't Sam Sheppard in Jail?" Numerous editorials and cartoons proclaimed him guilty. Later, Sheppard was arrested and charged. The trial itself was overrun with reporters and photographers, and the jury was not adequately shielded from negative publicity about Sheppard. One newspaper even printed a photograph of Mrs. Sheppard's bloodstained pillow, retouched so as to "show more clearly" the alleged imprint of a "surgical instrument."

The prosecutor found no witnesses to the murder, and the only evidence he presented was circumstantial (for example, Sheppard was having an affair with another woman). Yet, Sheppard was convicted and spent many years in prison before the Supreme Court finally reviewed his case. It declared his trial invalid, largely because of the publicity and improper legal procedures. Ohio tried Sheppard again and he was acquitted, but by this time, of course, his life was shattered. He died in 1970, still a relatively young man. As late as 2001, his son was still trying to clear his name with DNA evidence.

The American Bar Association (ABA) took action to protect defendants against unnecessary publicity before trial. Because of the Sheppard case, along with the publicity surrounding accusations against Lee Harvey Oswald (the alleged assassin of President Kennedy), they convened a national commission to establish better rules for the protection of defendants. Led by Justice Paul Reardon of the Massachusetts Supreme Judicial Court, the ABA Commission, in the late 1960s, suggested rules to restrict the release of prejudicial information. For judges, court officers, attorneys, juries, prosecutors, and the police, these rules carried the weight of law once they were adopted by federal and state courts.

For the press, the Reardon guidelines were voluntary. Nevertheless, in more than thirty states, beginning in the late 1960s, "fair trial-free press" committees charged with promoting recommended "codes of conduct" were set up. The guidelines were even issued on little cards for reporters, and for the most part they worked well. Then, in a Washington State case in the late 1970s, a judge used the voluntary guidelines as the basis to restrict press coverage of a murder trial. The fear that this could happen elsewhere quickly unraveled many, though not all, of the codes of the state committees.

Today, few reporters use the Reardon guidelines as such, and there is renewed discussion of the need for some voluntary curbs in a period when television, more often than newspapers, has become increasingly sensational—a phenomenon journalism historian John D. Stevens has called "wretched excess."[12] However, screaming newspaper headlines that might be considered prejudicial are not a thing of the past. In covering many celebrated trials in recent years, supermarket tabloids like the *National Enquirer* or the *Star,* as well as big-city tabloids such as the *New York Post* or *Boston Herald,* have featured accusatory headlines about such highly visible defendants. Few examples of "wretched excess" outdistanced the massive and continuous coverage given the case of former football hero O. J. Simpson who was tried and acquitted in a double murder case in 1995 and in a civil case in 1996. This case inspired highly sensational coverage and nightly debates on cable talk shows like "Rivera Live" with Geraldo Rivera, Charles Grodin, Larry King, and others. Issues of violence and sex were merged with race and social justice. The case consumed a major portion of news coverage during the first trial—one newspaper, the *Atlanta Journal and Constitution,* devoted nearly one-fifth of its entire national and international news content to the subject, and the major networks were not far behind. Another sensational case that got massive coverage was the bombing of Atlanta's Olympic village in 1996 and the accusations against a security guard, Richard Jewell, who was subsequently cleared. (See Chapter 16 for a more detailed treatment of this case.)

The intense publicity surrounding celebrated cases makes it common for defense attorneys to seek a variety of remedies to help their clients get a fair trial. One such remedy used by the courts, in addition to challenging potential jurors and sequestering the jury, is *change of venue,* such as occurred in 2000 when the trial of the New York police officers in the Amadu Dialo death case was moved to Albany in upstate New York. The assumption is that in another location jurors would not be influenced by prejudicial publicity.

In a famous scene from one of the most publicized murder trials ever seen on television, O. J. Simpson holds up his hands to display a new pair of gloves like the ones that figured in the famed double-murder case.

Celebrated trials in recent years doubtless have received considerable prejudicial publicity. Just what can be done about this kind of media attention, which informs the public, but also trammels individual rights, is uncertain. Some commentators have called for new rules for news gathering and a return to the Reardon Commission guidelines.

MORAL VALUES: OBSCENITY AND PORNOGRAPHY

Do parents have the right to protect their children from seeing advertisements on the street for pornographic movies, or from seeing pornographic magazines displayed at the local drugstore? Many Americans would answer *yes,* but the Supreme Court's answers have been ambiguous. The most emotional issue in recent times has been *child pornography*—magazines and films depicting young children engaged in explicit sexual acts with adults and with each other. Public pressure prompts Congress to hold hearings on the subject with some regularity, usually resulting in various laws to curtail the distribution of such material. As a result, the media are virtually forbidden to produce, distribute, or sell child pornography. This issue has accelerated in the age of the Internet.

Two very different conceptions of the role of the government underlie debates about the regulation of obscene material. Some First Amendment absolutists deplore censorship of such material, arguing that the government should not attempt in any way to regulate the moral behavior of its citizens as long as the people involved are consenting adults. On the other hand, others are more conservative and see censorship of obscenity as the proper duty of local or even national government. They tend to feel that a safe society can be maintained only through government regulation of personal behavior, such as sexual activity or the use of alcohol and drugs.

Over the years, the media have received strange and convoluted signals concerning pornography and obscenity. The Supreme Court seemed to side with the conservatives in 1957 when it announced, "Obscenity is not within the area of constitutionally protected speech or press" *(Roth* v. *United States).* That may seem clear enough, but it has not been easy to determine what is or is not obscene. In the 1960s, material could not be declared obscene if it had "any redeeming social value" whatsoever. Then, in 1973, the Court made it easier to ban materials by relaxing this standard. Moreover, it stated that material should be judged by local authorities according to standards that "prevail in a given community" *(Miller* v. *California).* Thus, what is considered obscene in one community may not be obscene in another. But since this decision, the Supreme Court has overturned some efforts by local governments to ban materials. What can and cannot be censored on obscenity grounds remains far from clear.

In the face of public pressure, the media have censored themselves to some extent. Various industry associations have drawn up codes limiting the treatment of material related to sex. A classic example is the self-regulation of the movie industry in the 1930s, when the self-imposed Motion Picture Producers and Distributors Code became so puritanical that at one point not even butterflies could be shown mating. Later, in the 1950s, the comic book industry voluntarily (if grumpily) curtailed production of horror comics in response to a public outcry. (Congressional hearings were held to determine whether such comic books were harmful to children.)

Today, the National Association of Broadcasters forbids (rather unsuccessfully) the use of "dirty" words and explicit sexual content. The relative purity of broadcasting, however, is also a result of the Federal Communications Commission's enforcement of the Federal Communication Act's strict rules against obscenity. For example, in the 1990s, the FCC fined a Los Angeles radio station for airing allegedly obscene and off-color commentary by the controversial radio-TV host Howard Stern, who has frequently run afoul of regulators and writers of his explicit, highly charged broadcasts.[13] More recently, conflict has flared between feminists and producers of lurid, sexually explicit material. Here, the old liberal-conservative split over censorship of pornography has come unglued, because many politically liberal feminists believe that pornography is so offensive and damaging to women that censorship is warranted.

Although we have been dealing here with moral values as they are embodied in the law, the role of the media as a moral teacher and "enforcer" of values, too, has come up repeatedly in recent years. Arguing that the media are not taking on the role once filled by the family, church, or school, critics urge more care and accountability among media professionals. However, this is strictly a voluntary matter, not something that can be enforced by the courts or other authorities.[14]

THE GOVERNMENT'S SECRETS DURING NATIONAL CRISES

In times of national crises, such as during wars, reporting some kinds of information can give the enemy a clear advantage. Recognizing the security risks, Americans have generally accepted some form of censorship during wars and politically sensitive periods including Communist scares in the 1950s, the Cold War, and others. Espionage is frequently an issue whether there is a war or not. Even many fervent civil libertarians agree that the government deserves and requires protection during wartime. But such censorship obviously contradicts the guarantee of a free press and limits the public's right to know.

In times of both peace and war, government secrecy has led to many controversies. For example, in October 1983, when the United States invaded the small Caribbean nation of Grenada, military commanders barred the press from the island, and thus the war zone. Journalists and broadcasters vigorously protested the government policy as unprecedented and unwarranted censorship; the White House replied that it was trying to protect the lives of the media people. After Grenada, a commission involving military officers, government officials, and representatives of the press was set up. It recommended guidelines for the coverage of military actions and suggested the formation of a press-broadcast pool for future operations.

In the next decade, when Iraq invaded Kuwait, causing the United States to send troops to Saudi Arabia, press access again became an issue in various foreign capitals and on the front lines with the troops. The 1991 Persian Gulf War against Iraq revisited the conflict between press and government. From the beginning of what was a very popular conflict, in contrast to Vietnam—which was not only unpopular, but also the subject of massive demonstrations and other protest activity—the press complained that the rules of access to information from the front were too restrictive and prevented effective coverage. A pool system representing the entire press corps was in effect, and military "handlers" who followed reporters to their interviews were heavily used. The Pentagon argued that it was simply trying to prevent the release of information that would undermine military operations or endanger the lives of troops. The result was tightly controlled information, released at formal press briefings, and little opportunity for reporters to pursue stories independently, especially if they required access to the battlefield area. At the war's end, there was an almost universal agreement that the media had been kept at bay, and, in effect, the media lost the information war. So strong was media dissatisfaction with the restrictions that, after the war, a unified committee representative of U.S. print and broadcast media petitioned the Pentagon and the White House to consider a set of rules and procedures for future wars.

DIRECT CENSORSHIP IN WARTIME

In past wars, the government has been able to use various indirect methods to protect its secrets. One of the earliest indirect ways used to control information was to deny access to telegraph, cable, and similar facilities. Reporters then either had to let military censors screen their copy or try to transmit it in some other way. For example, when the battleship *Maine* blew up in the harbor of Havana, Cuba, in 1898, the U.S. government immediately closed the Havana cable to reporters. Similarly, at the outbreak of World War I, the British immediately severed the cables between Germany and the United States. American reporters had to use the English-controlled cables between Europe and the United States and submit their copy to rigid British censorship.

The government also has imposed censorship through codes, regulations, and guidelines. During World War I, the Espionage Act of 1917 stipulated fines and prison terms for anyone interfering with the war effort in any way. For example, criticism of arms manufacturers was said to be unpatriotic. This enraged newspaper publishers, and legal battles over the issue went all the way to the Supreme Court. Such censorship was later declared unconstitutional, but Congress passed new, even stricter laws to control information. The Sedition Act of 1918 made it a crime to publish anything that abused, scorned, or showed contempt for the government of the United States, its flag, or even the uniforms of its armed forces. As a way to enforce the law, such publications could be banned from the mails.

On December 19, 1941, only a few days after Japanese forces attacked Pearl Harbor, President Roosevelt created the U.S. Office of Censorship and charged it with reviewing all communications entering or leaving the United States for the duration of the war. At the peak of its activity, the office employed more than ten thousand people. Its main objective was to review all mail, cables, and radiograms. A Code of Wartime Practices for the American Press was also issued to newspapers requesting voluntary cooperation from the nation's editors and publishers. Its purpose was to deny the Axis powers any information concerning military matters, production, supplies, armaments, weather, and so on. For the most part, those responsible for the content of the print media cooperated very well, and often exceeded the guidelines set by government. A related code was issued for broadcasters, and their cooperation was also excellent. The system of codes, regulations, and guidelines in practice during World War II worked because the media cooperated voluntarily. The United States attempted to find a way to deny vital information to the enemy without using official censors, and by and large it succeeded.

Even during peacetime, the press has often censored itself to protect the national interest. In 1960, for example, the Soviet Union shot down an American U2 spy plane. The incident temporarily ended attempts to improve Soviet-American relations. For a year before the plane was shot down, however, James Reston of the *New York Times* had known that American spy planes were flying over the Soviet Union, but "The *New York Times* did not publish this fact until one of the planes was shot down in 1960."[15] Later, as a favor to President John F. Kennedy, Reston withheld information about the planned U.S. invasion of Cuba at the Bay of Pigs.

CHALLENGES TO GOVERNMENT SECRECY

Although the press often engages in voluntary censorship, there are many examples when the media and the government have been locked in conflict, disputing the government's right to censor the news. Because our shared belief in the need for freedom of the press became such a tradition very early in the life of the nation, any effort by the government to limit that freedom has always met with hostility.

During the Civil War, for example, the fifty-seventh Article of War stipulated a court martial and possible death sentence for anyone, civilian and military alike, who gave military information to the enemy. However, newspapers were an indirect source of military information, and Confederate leaders went to great lengths to obtain copies of major Northern papers because they often revealed the whereabouts of military units and naval vessels. As a result, the U.S. War Department tried to prevent newspapers from publishing any stories that described the movements of troops or ships. Editors generally ignored these orders. Even after the war, General William Sherman refused to shake hands with Horace Greeley, publisher of the *New York Tribune,* maintaining that Greeley's paper had caused a heavy loss of life by revealing troop movements to the enemy.[16]

Thus, even in wartime, Americans have questioned censorship, asking what kind of controls should be imposed and by whom. Clearly, the government has the need to protect itself and a duty to protect the nation. But the press claims a right to inform the public of what the government is doing, and the news media maintain that the public has the *right to know.* Therefore, an inherent conflict exists between the right to a free press and the need to control information that would be damaging to the government.[17]

During the Johnson administration, the Defense Department put together a forty-seven–volume history of American involvement in Vietnam from 1945 to 1967, including secret cables, memos, and other documents. The history, which came to be known as the Pentagon Papers, was classified as *top secret.* In 1971, Daniel Ellsberg, who had worked on the papers, but later opposed the war, leaked them to the *New York Times,* hoping that their release would turn public opinion against the war and help bring about its end. Although the papers were both stolen and classified, the *Times* began publishing a series of articles summarizing the contents and some of the documents themselves.

The Nixon administration went to court to stop the *Times* (and later other newspapers) from printing additional articles on the papers, arguing that their publication would endanger national security. In response, the courts issued a temporary restraining order, stopping the *Times* from continuing its planned series on the papers. In effect, the courts imposed prior restraint.

Eventually, the case went to the Supreme Court, which ruled against the government. The government had failed to convince the Court that publication of the Pentagon Papers constituted a danger severe enough to warrant suspending freedom of the press. Relieved and triumphant, the newspapers resumed their articles. (Ellsberg was later tried for stealing the documents.) Yet the Supreme Court's decision in the Pentagon Papers case is still regarded as controversial and it resolved little of the debate between government and the press. Conflict continues over the press's right to publish, the public's right to know, and the government's need to protect the secrecy of some activities.

During the 1980s, the Reagan administration engaged in a contentious tug of war with the press over access to government information. President Ronald Reagan proposed sweeping changes in the Freedom of Information Act, which provides public access to the various departments and agencies of government, and issued executive orders making access to information about agencies like the FBI and CIA more difficult. Professional groups such as the Society of Professional Journalists and the American Society of Newspaper Editors campaigned vigorously against these restrictions. In this instance, there was profound disagreement between the government, which claimed that it acted in the best interest of the people by limiting access, and the press, which said that the public was better served by the free flow of information.

POLITICAL CONSTRAINTS: THE AGENTS OF CONTROL

We have discussed several specific areas in which freedom of the press, as guaranteed by the Constitution, is limited, not absolute. But in practice, freedom of the press depends not only on this abstract constitutional framework but also on the daily decisions of courts, bureaucrats, and politicians.[18] The constitutional framework itself continues to evolve as specific problems and conflicts arise. Moreover, in particular cases the actual freedom of the press may differ from its theoretical freedom. Therefore, we look next at the various agents of political control of the media, including the courts, legislatures, the White House, bureaucrats, and even private citizens. These groups may exert both formal controls on the media and informal influence on the flow of information.

THE COURTS

We have seen that the courts often act as referees in conflicts between the rights of the press, the rights of individuals, and the rights of the government at large. This role is nothing new—as early as 1835, the French writer Alexis de Tocqueville observed, "Scarcely any political question arises in the United States that is not resolved sooner or later into a judicial question." Today, we are even more litigious, and conflicts involving the media often lead to lawsuits in local courts. Some of the resulting verdicts are appealed and occasionally wind up in the Supreme Court.

Often, the Supreme Court's interpretations of either prevailing laws, or the Constitution itself, have broken new ground and established new policies. In recent years, the Court has ruled on a long list of issues affecting the media, including newsroom searches, libel, confidentiality of journalists' sources, regulation of advertising, and laws regarding copyright and cable television. These rulings have often been the center of immense controversy. The prevailing view in the press is that, for many years, the Supreme Court under Chief Justice Warren E. Burger was generally, though not always, hostile to the press and its claims. Dan Rather of CBS News went so far as to claim that the Supreme Court had been "repealing the First Amendment" by its decisions. Many legal scholars, however, disagree.

What we see in the courts when the press is on trial is a legal battle involving private citizens, the media, and the government. It is all a matter of "rights in conflict." As journalist Anthony Lewis once wrote:

> We have libel suits because we think a civilized society should take account of an interest besides freedom to criticize. In other words, individuals have rights too; sometimes they conflict with the rights of the press. It is not uncommon to find rights in conflict; that's why we have judges. But sometimes the press sounds as though the Constitution considers only its interests. If a network or a newspaper loses a case, "That's it, the Constitution is gone; Big Brother has taken over." Well, I don't think life is so simple. The interest of the press may not be the only one of constitutional dimension when there are conflicts.[19]

As a social institution, the media pay more than passing attention to personnel changes at the Supreme Court. Since every presidential election reminds us that presidents do make Supreme Court and other judicial appointments (subject to Senate confirmation), people speculate about how a liberal, a moderate, or a conservative justice might vote on matters involving press freedom or communication policy. At one level, some commentators, among them Eli Noam of Columbia Business School, believe that there is little difference between Democrats and Republicans on basic communication policy issues. However, those that do exist are often differences on matters of dissent and the rights of the press to gather information, process, and disseminate it freely. Sometimes fears about the court on First Amendment matters are unfounded. However, such fears may be justified.

In a 1987 case, involving evangelist Jerry Falwell and *Screw* magazine publisher Larry Flynt, the court found for Flynt, who had written scurrilously about Falwell. Chief Justice William Rehnquist himself wrote the majority opinion, proving that it is often difficult to predict what the Supreme Court will do. According to media scholar David Anderson, however, press defendants appearing before the Court, from its beginning two hundred years ago to the present, have generally fared worse than other defendants.[20]

THE LEGISLATURES

While the Supreme Court is the final staging ground for many media battles, the first rounds of these battles are fought in state legislatures. These bodies promulgate laws that have considerable impact on the mass media. They may amend or rewrite statutes dealing with libel, misrepresentation, business taxation, newspaper advertising, cable television, and many other subjects. Most major lobbying groups for the media, such as state broadcast and newspaper associations, have representatives at their state capitals continuously looking out for their interests.

Congress's influence on the media is greater than that of the state legislatures. Postal rates for books and magazines, for example, loom large on publishers' balance sheets. Like other businesses, the media can be hurt or helped by congressional decisions regarding taxes, antitrust policy, protection of copyrights or affirmative action; in addition, both houses of Congress have subcommittees that deal specifically with communications issues and policies. In the past, Congress has investigated the financial structure of the communications industry, tried to determine whether television networks pressured producers not to release films to pay-cable systems, written new copyright laws, passed laws on campaign spending in the media, and considered regulation of television advertising and a federal shield law.

In its regulation of broadcasting, Congress sometimes is accused of meddling with freedom of the press. On occasion, congressional committees call upon network heads, other media executives, and journalists to testify. Some refuse to do so, arguing that having to "report" to the government on their internal operations is an intrusion on freedom of the press. But to date, Congress has taken no draconian measures to force compliance.

THE EXECUTIVE BRANCH

The web of government influence gets more tangled when we consider the executive branch, which includes the White House and a host of government departments and agencies. Many bureaucrats in federal departments and agencies exercise formal control over information through the government's classification system. Others exercise informal controls over the flow of information to the press and the public. Both federal and state governments are composed mainly of large bureaucracies that manage their own public relations, anxiously trying to maintain a favorable public image. At the federal level, agencies such as the FBI, the Department of Agriculture, and the Pentagon spend millions each year on domestic public relations. In fact, every division of government has its own information officers and staff, and reporters depend heavily on these official spokespersons for information about the daily workings of the government. Reporters often have no way of assessing the validity of this information. Much of the news that is reported about the government is, therefore, what public relations people hand out to the press. Thus, through press releases, news conferences, and interviews, the bureaucrats control most of the news that appears about their agency or group. Obviously, this kind of control limits the ability of the press to gain access to factual information they need to inform the public.

The White House also exercises informal influence on the flow of information. For example, it is a tradition for the president's press secretary to select a limited number of reporters from the pool of more than two hundred assigned to the White House beat to cover an important political briefing or social event. The remainder of the pool must then obtain information from those selected. Whether the White House regards a member of the pool favorably or not has a significant influence on that reporter's prospects for firsthand access as he or she attempts to provide coverage.

The executive branch also has more formal sources of influence on the media. The president appoints members to the two agencies that have power to regulate parts of the media, the Federal Trade Commission and the Federal Communications Commission. More importantly, the White House can propose new legislation to Congress, as well as lobby for or against any proposals that Congress considers. As previously mentioned, during the early 1980s, the Reagan administration, in an effort to tighten security, proposed changes in the federal Freedom of Information Act. It also issued a series of *executive orders*—which do not require the approval of Congress—intended to prevent leaks and curtail other activities by government employees. In one order alone, more than one hundred thousand former and current government employees were required to submit all articles, speeches, and even letters to the editor of their agencies for prepublication review. Although some commentators defended this practice for "national security" reasons, the American Society of Newspaper Editors called the new policy "peacetime censorship of a scope unparalleled in this country since the adoption of the Bill of Rights in 1791."[21]

REGULATION AND OTHER CONTROLS

The Federal Communications Commission (FCC) makes and enforces rules and policies that govern all kinds of communication industries, from telephone companies to television networks. The FCC's rulings have the status of law and can be overturned only by the federal courts or by congressional action. Its rules govern advertising, ownership of broadcasting stations, obscenity, and a number of special circumstances. For example, the FCC and the courts legislated a personal attack law, which gives individuals who are attacked by a broadcast station airtime to respond. The FCC also enforces the equal time rule for political candidates, which states: "If a licensee shall permit any person who is a legally qualified candidate for any public office to use a broadcasting station, he shall afford equal opportunities to all other such candidates for that office in the use of such broadcasting station." Based on the equal time rule, the commission later formed the fairness doctrine, which grants equal time to people representing issues and causes. Subsequently in the 1980s, the FCC dropped the fairness doctrine ruling, stating that it penalized the media and had outlived its usefulness in an era when abundance replaced scarcity of broadcast signals. Some members of Congress maintained that the fairness doctrine inhibited speech on the part of the media and the public, whereas most disagreed and reinstated the doctrine, only to have it vetoed by then President Ronald Reagan. This convoluted series of changes, and other aspects of broadcast regulation, are frequently debated by media people, legal scholars, and legislators.

Much of the FCC's attention is given to interpreting its own rules as it resolves disputes between various interests. In some instances, these rules are very specific, as is the equal time rule. But in other instances they are vague, and the commission frequently wrangles over terms like "the public interest," trying to determine just what it is in each circumstance.

The FCC plays a large role in the regulation of the electronic media in the United States. In 2001, William Kennard (pictured), an architect of deregulation and the triumph of the new economy, turned over the reigns to his successor Michael Powell.

The FCC also handles the issuance and renewal of broadcast licenses granted to radio and television stations. It has the power to revoke licenses, but it rarely does so. In recent years, the government has greatly simplified procedures for license renewal and diminished its demands for detailed information from broadcasters. Still, the FCC is charged with seeing whether and how well a broadcast station is serving the public's interest, convenience, and needs. Although broadcasters often complain of the heavy hand of government, the FCC has been remarkably lenient in renewing licenses. In fact, one critic compared the relationship between the FCC and the industry to a wrestling match wherein "the grunts and groans resound through the land, but no permanent injury seems to result."[22]

A case in point is the FCC's handling of obscenity. The Federal Communications Act of 1934 gives the commission the power to revoke the licenses of stations that broadcast obscene or indecent material over the airways. Although there have been numerous instances of stations running pornographic films and comedy routines in the past, the maximum penalty usually imposed by the FCC is a small fine.

The deregulation of broadcasting, discussed in earlier chapters, has altered the role of the FCC in recent years. Although the commission has had a major economic impact, its rules on media content, children's programming, advertising, and even obscenity have relaxed considerably. Still, the very existence of a government agency regulating the entire communications industry is widely viewed as a constraint on broadcasting. Even with much less rigorous rules today, compared to earlier years, many broadcasters still grumble about the FCC, which they regard as a bureaucratic nuisance. However, the notion that broadcasters are obliged to fulfill the public trust by accepting a government license makes them markedly different from the print media. Former Chief Justice Warren Burger as a federal appeals court judge once stated:

> A broadcaster seeks and is granted the free and exclusive use of a limited and valued part of the public domain; when he accepts that franchise it is burdened by enforceable public obligations. A newspaper can be operated by the whim or caprice of its owners; a broadcast station cannot.[23]

CONTROLS BY THE FEDERAL TRADE COMMISSION

Over the years, the Federal Trade Commission (FTC) has conducted hearings to determine whether the growing concentration of ownership in the media influenced the flow of information. Although the hearings generated no definitive answers, media owners denounced the FTC for its potential interference. Those hearings reflect only a small part of the FTC's interest in mass communication and other industries. Like the FCC, the FTC is an independent regulatory agency of the federal government that exists for the purpose of preventing unfair competition. In relation to the media, this task generally translates into the regulation of advertising.

Since its inception in 1914, the FTC has viewed deceptive advertising as unfair competition. Both the FTC and the FCC have brought suits against manufacturers and the media for false claims or misrepresentations. A classic illustration is the Rapid Shave case. Rapid Shave aired a television commercial in which a voice-over claimed that shaving with Rapid Shave was especially easy because it had a "deep wetting" ingredient. A demonstration showed a piece of sandpaper being shaved clean with Rapid Shave. Yet the commercial failed to mention that the sandpaper had been soaked in water for nearly an hour and a half prior to the demonstration. And in another version, a Plexiglas surface sprinkled with sand was used in lieu of real sandpaper. The case was in the courts for six years while the commercial continued to be shown. Finally, the Supreme Court banned such trickery.

Another example of deceptive advertising banned by the FTC promoted Profile Bread. Its makers claimed that Profile Bread contained special ingredients that were helpful to dieters and that each slice had one-third fewer calories than other brands. Actually, the manufacturer was simply slicing the bread one-third thinner than a standard slice.

The most famous consumer protection case, however, came not from the FCC or the FTC but from Congress, which banned cigarette advertising from television and required manufacturers to label each package with a warning to users that cigarette smoking could endanger their health.

Although the FTC directs its actions mainly against individual advertisers, it has a strong indirect effect on the mass media, which are the channels for advertising. For example, when the FTC ordered Profile Bread to stop implying that its product had special ingredients, it clearly influenced the content of all advertising.

In recent times, the FTC has been very active, and has cracked down on a lengthy list of food distributors that have been using such terms as "lite" and "low fat." New regulations have been issued requiring that the consumer be provided with detailed information about such claims as well as ingredients on labels on the products.

The FTC issues warnings before moving to formal orders. Some of these orders have the effect of law, and the commission can and has levied punitive fines on manufacturers, sometimes for hundreds of thousands of dollars.

Decisions by the FTC have defined the scope of deception in advertising, discussed the concept of truth in advertising, and denounced puffery, or exaggerated claims. The FTC also legislates rules, holds conferences on trade practices, issues guides for advertising and labeling practices, and hands down advisory opinions for advertisers, requesting advance comments about advertisements. In recent years, the FTC has frequently called on communications researchers to help examine issues such as the effects of television commercials aimed at children.

DEREGULATION AND OUTSIDE PRESSURES

Underlying deregulation has been the assumption that competition in the marketplace is the best way to conduct business in America, and that government rules, even if intended to protect the public, are an intrusion. Recently, both the FCC and the FTC have been more lenient in regulating the communication industry. This reflects the general trend toward deregulation of various industries, which we discussed in previous chapters with regard to newspaper and broadcast ownership.

By the early 1990s, there was again a call for more government regulation of television. In 1991, former FCC Chairman Newton Minow declared in a speech that revisited his famous "Vast Wasteland" speech thirty years earlier:

> I reject the view of an FCC chairman in the early 1980s who said that "a television set is merely a toaster with pictures." I reject this ideological view that the marketplace will regulate itself and give us perfection.[24]

The famous 1961 speech denounced television's content as being vacuous and of low quality. To Minow, thirty years later, little had changed.

Overall, regulation of the media by the FCC and FTC is a complex arena that is constantly evolving. Regulation policies and implementation are shaped by many views and the uneasy relationships between each government agency and the media will continue to generate debate.

Political influences and pressures on the media do not exist in either isolation or the narrow confines of a government agency. Private lobbyists and special interest groups attempt to influence the media for their own purposes. Congressional committees sometimes provide them with a forum and allow testimony either in favor of or against a piece of legislation affecting broadcasting and the print media. Over the past few years, lobbies and other special interest groups have tried to influence such matters as the amount of violence on television, hiring policies in the media (especially with regard to women and minorities), election coverage before the polls close, the screening of sexually explicit movies in local theaters, and a variety of other issues. These issues change, but one thing remains constant: major public concern about the media will often become a political issue, because public concerns shape government legislation and agendas.

The complexity of communication-related issues causes some scholars and critics to ponder whether the United States needs a more coherent communication policy. At present, our policy, if there is one, is spread among various governmental branches and the private sector. As new issues arise, it is difficult to know whether they should be resolved by the FCC, Congress, the executive branch, or some other body. Some even argue that many policy issues are simply resolved by the private sector because the government does not take enough interest.

At the dawning of the twenty-first century, the issue of digital television emerged. This followed earlier concerns over high definition television (HDTV). Amid global competition from Japan and Europe, U.S. manufacturers had difficulty in the race to be competitive partly because they lacked an overall policy with which to standardize their products. They sought guidance from the FCC, and outlined a technical standard that Congress could challenge in the future. Without a communication policy per se, it may be difficult for U.S. communications industries to speak with clarity in their dealings with the rest of the world. This problem is likely to persist, and perhaps there will one day be a council of communications advisers, as media lawyer Stuart Brotman has proposed, or at least a presidential commission to make recommendations about how various technical, legal, and economic disputes can be handled and resolved.

ECONOMICS OF MEDIA INDUSTRIES REVISITED

As noted earlier, virtually every chapter of this book deals with the economics of media industries, so integrally connected is mass communication with the economic system. We have already mentioned the largely commercial nature of the media economy. We say "largely" rather than exclusively because there are publicly supported media such as the Public Broadcasting Service, National Public Radio, the U.S. Government Printing Office, and other "public sector" media.

Of course, government and prevailing opinion often play a role in what might seem from afar to be largely commercial transactions. For example, in 1999 and 2000, when two massive media mergers were announced—Viacom's acquisition of CBS and AOL's of Time Warner—these transactions had to wind their way through the political and regulatory system. There were congressional hearings and action before the Federal Communications Commission since it was necessary to get approval for various aspects of these corporate marriages. In a country where monopolies are usually forbidden by federal law, these four firms had to make their case in Washington, D.C., before their Wall Street deals were fully consummated.[25]

And while it can be rightly said that we live in an era when government is usually friendly to business developments like these, there are exceptions to the rule as Microsoft learned in its protracted antitrust action brought by the federal government.

In the context of controls and driving forces that shape, influence, and guide the media, there is nothing more potent or more powerful than the economy. If in fact the media were once small players in the overall national or world economy, that is no longer true as the big media and telecommunication mergers of recent years have indicated. Indeed, as this is written, the press is full of speculation about the whole series of old media-new media combinations that could change the shape of the media economy. Similarly, the media once lived mostly behind national borders and relied on local and national economic factors to garner their audiences and produce their revenues. Today, global companies produce global media for global audiences, thus crossing national borders in more than a physical sense—in an economical sense as well.

MEDIA AND THE NEW ECONOMY

In a real sense, the media industries bridge the so-called sea changes—what some call the paradigm shift in communication and entertainment industries—in the economy. The media were a product of the industrial revolution as they produced a product (newspaper, magazines, books, and the like) that was, in fact, manufactured and sold. The media industries produced cultural objects that they sold to audiences, sometimes with middlemen involved, such as theater owners, bookshops, etc. But they were a part of manufacturing and extractive industries. Even news was a commodity for sale to readers, listeners, and viewers. To some extent, radio and television changed that equation. Their products—programs and content—were sold to stations that subsequently garnered audiences and the stations then sold their audience access to advertisers. The motion picture studios were also a manufacturing entity producing films and later videos for rental to audiences. All this was part of what people now call the old economy.

With the coming of digitally driven computer communication, the media became a part of the information revolution later renamed the "new economy," which is made up of firms that sell information, interactive relationships, and digital access to various products through e-commerce.

When America Online (AOL) announced that it was acquiring the media giant Time Warner, the news shocked the world. Highly valued shares of the Internet portal and information company AOL made that firm more valuable than Time Warner, even though Time Warner had more tangible assets—subscribers, buildings, employees, etc.—and AOL was more of a virtual company whose main assets were information storage and retrieval, and a sound rating on Wall Street, where investor confidence reigns. All this was enhanced by the fact that the media sector was one of the fastest growing segments of the U.S. and world economy on stock exchanges around the world.

The American media system and that of much of the rest of the world now takes two forms, what scholar Wilson Dizard calls "big media/little media."[26] Big media are the giant communication companies and conglomerates like Sony, AOL Time Warner, Viacom, and others. They also include major media groups such as newspaper companies, magazine publishers, book publishing groups, broadcast groups, multisystem operators (cable), and others. Some of the big media may be a single entity such as an independent broadcast station or newspaper while others represent many "media properties," as the individual units are called, and some cut across the industry lines. For example, a firm may have both print and electronic media operations.

At the same time, there are little media start-ups or entrepreneurs, sometimes begun by a single individual with a Web site and operated with little overhead to a targeted audience. These firms are found almost everywhere these days, but especially in the Silicon Valley of California, New York City's "Silicon Alley," and Boston's electronic corridor. Sometimes these start-ups are the handiwork of rugged individualists, not unlike the pioneering printers of colonial America. They and their colleagues seek financing through venture capital and other sources of funds. If they are successful in taking their privately held firms to the initial public offering (IPO) stage on the stock market, they have created a publicly held company of which people can buy shares.

Media companies and thus the media economy have two fundamental sources of revenue or income—advertising and user fees. There are some other sources such as syndication rights, but mainly they rely on their "sales" to advertisers of audiences and their revenues from subscriptions, newsstand sales, monthly cable, Internet, and other fees.[27]

CORPORATE CULTURES AND REVENUE MODELS

While the media originally based their business plans on the *law of large numbers* in which they delivered larger and larger audiences to advertisers, they are increasingly involved with the *law of right numbers*—specific demographics of audience or even psychological preferences. Newspapers, magazines, radio, and television were masters of the large numbers. They found advertisers who paid much, if not all, of the costs of production. Then they gave their audiences a bargain—a newspaper or magazine for a fraction of the amount it really cost. For example, a newspaper that might cost $3 to produce was sold for fifty cents. Television, of course, is the master of large numbers, delivering massive audiences for the Super Bowl, the Olympics, or a celebrated trial, all paid for by advertisers as the viewers paid for only the television set and the electricity needed to power it.

The "right numbers" idea includes audiences targeted by specific age, demographic factors, and geographic area. Magazines that delivered specialized fare to targeted audiences first advanced specific income brackets or educational audiences. Thus, a skier would pay a premium for a glossy specialized magazine that was only partly paid for by advertising. Cable programming followed this model and also offered programs like MTV and VH-1 for young audiences and Lifetime for female viewers. Some program fare also aimed at lifestyle or "psychographic" differences, such as people who want luxury goods and famous brand names, even though they might not be in the highest income bracket.

As for their structure, media and media firms range from the family business model (a kind of "mom and pop" operation) wherein a single individual or family owns and controls the enterprise. Some of these family operations, like the *Forbes* magazine group, can get quite large. Other media follow the corporate model with financing from various sources and executives who work for a board of directors. There are also media industry groups, such as a large publishing firm that produces scores of magazine titles, or a newspaper group (sometimes called a chain) with papers (a.k.a. "properties") in several cities and countries. Media groups might own print, broadcast, and electronic media enterprises and seek what they call "synergy"—working together and benefiting from corporate cooperation. Conglomerates most often own a variety of firms such as communication media and other enterprises like hotels, pharmaceutical companies, and the like.

FREE MARKETS AND REGULATORY CONTROLS

There is much written about the motives, corporate culture, and long-term effects of the media environment of which we are now a part.[28] The wild card will be the role of digital communication, including the Internet, where many firms have high stock values, but few are yet profitable as this is written. Some new media are part of old media companies while others are independent, online enterprises. The Internet economic model currently is unsettled. Most of the content and informational offerings of the Internet are "free" for the user and paid for by advertisers, product manufacturers, etc. A few media firms are now charging for subscriptions and encrypting their content. The Internet offers both the "right audience" of highly specialized and specific individuals as well as potentially massive cumulative audiences. It combines the best of the large circulation and narrowly oriented audience segment. It is both "broadcasting" in the sense of reaching millions or even billions and "narrowcasting" to small, segmented audiences. Of course, it also has the advantage of interactivity. At the same time, the Internet, unlike television, does not reach everyone and there is a growing "digital divide" which we have explained earlier.

In recent years, many media have refined and modified the "large numbers" model including newspapers with business plans that carefully segment their markets, seeking upscale readers instead of serving the general interest reader as they once did. This is disturbing to many critics who fear that communication for the common person, pioneered in America and transmitted to the world, may be in jeopardy. Others say that the world will soon be fully connected, and nearly universal communication will be possible.

So, it is clear that the world of old and new media traverse the old and new economies. At the moment, these operate with only modest government intervention and oversight. This could change, of course, since politics and policy are creatures of economic trends. In good times, regulation and control usually declines, but when depressions, recessions, and other downturns come, the role of regulation accelerates as the media economy lives on a continuum between optimum freedom, even near absolute freedom, and control by the government and the public sector.

Chapter Review

- Although most Americans approve of a free press and believe that we have one, the mass media in the United States operate in a complex web of limitations arising from politics and government.

- The First Amendment forbids Congress to make laws restricting the freedom of the press, but that freedom often conflicts with other rights, such as the right to privacy and the right to a fair trial.

- Libel laws are intended to protect people from false and damaging statements made about them, and libel suits today can result in awards of millions of dollars.

- The courts have sometimes placed restrictions on the press to try to limit publicity that might prejudice juries, but generally efforts in this area have centered on voluntary cooperation from the press.

- Obscene material is not clearly protected by the First Amendment. Although the courts take action to prevent the publication or broadcast of material deemed obscene, debate continues over what exactly constitutes obscenity and how far it should be controlled.

- During wartime, restrictions on the press have ranged from outright government censorship via codes and guidelines to voluntary self-regulation by the media. In peacetime, the federal government may attempt to keep information secret for national security reasons, but the media frequently disagree with the government about this policy.

- Reporters claim a right to keep their sources confidential. Some have been willing to go to jail rather than choosing to identify their sources when ordered to do so by the courts.

- The courts are frequently referees when the right to a free press and other rights conflict. Legislatures and the executive branch also influence the press, both through formal powers and informal influence over the flow of information. Both bureaucrats and politicians through informal influence can introduce bias in what is reported.

- The FCC has the power to regulate many aspects of broadcasting, but it is sometimes less than vigorous in doing so. Groups of private citizens as well as public opinion exert other pressures on the press.

- Overall, although the American media are generally free from direct government control or outright censorship, they are greatly influenced by economic and political conditions. As economic conditions, legal interpretations, and political pressures constantly change, so too will the media.

- The media are largely *commercial* enterprises and live within the rules of the larger economy.

- The new economy of the present day is partly driven by technology and communication (or media industries).

- A "law of large numbers" in media economics lives alongside a "law of right numbers," the first aiming for the biggest possible audience, the second seeking targeted, segmented portions of the audience.

- Media revenues come mainly from advertising and user fees, such as cable subscriptions, etc.

- Broadcasting and narrowcasting coexist in the modern media world, although one aims for the biggest possible audience, while the other seeks targeted, segmented portions of the audience.

- Media revenues come mainly from advertising and user fees, such as cable subscriptions, etc.

- Broadcasting and narrowcasting coexist in the modern media world, although *interactivity* and *digital* communication is changing the stakes.

Notes and References

1. Everette E. Dennis, "Liberal reporters, yes; liberal slant, no," *American Editor,* January/February 1997, pp. 4–10. An excellent source on the politics and ideology of journalists is David Weaver and G. Cleveland Wilhoit, *The American Journalist* (Bloomington, Ind.: Indiana University Press, 1996).

2. This was a complex case that was tried, reversed, and taken to the U.S. Supreme Court, which sent it back to the Minnesota court. The newspaper appealed twice, but the final verdict went to Cohen. See 479 N.W.2d 387 (1992) and 481 N.W.2d 840, 1992, Supreme Court of Minnesota. See also Matthew D. Bunker et al., "Triggering the First Amendment: Newsgathering Torts and Press Freedoms," *Communication Law and Policy,* vol. 4, 1999, p. 273.

3. John L. Hulting and Roy P. Nelson, *The Fourth Estate,* 2nd ed. (New York: Harper & Row, 1983), p. 9.

4. Charles Firestone and Amy K. Garmer, *Digital Broadcasting and the Public Interest* (Washington, D.C.: The Aspen Institute, 1998).

5. "Government Enjoined from Enforcing Indecency Law," in *The News Media and the Law,* summer 1996, p. 19.

6. William S. Holdsworth, "Defamation in the Sixteenth and Seventeenth Centuries," *Law Quarterly Review* 40, 1924, pp. 302–304.

7. David Anderson, "The Legal Model: Finding the Right Mix," in *Media Freedom and Accountability,* Everette E. Dennis, Donald M. Gillmor, and Theodore Glasser, eds. (Westport, Conn.: Greenwood Press, 1989).

8. Everette E. Dennis and Eli M. Noam, eds., *The Cost of Libel: Economic and Policy Considerations* (New York: Columbia University Press), 1989.

9. Donald M. Gillmor, *Power, Publicity, and the Abuse of Libel Law* (New York: Oxford University Press, 1992).

10. Robert W. Chandler, "Controlling Conflict: Working Proposal for Settling Disputes Between Newspapers and Those Who Feel Harmed by Them," working paper from the Gannett Center for Media Studies, New York, 1989.

11. Evan Jenkins, "News Councils: The Case for . . . and Against," *Columbia Journalism Review,* March/April 1997, pp. 38–39.

12. John D. Stevens, *Wretched Excess* (New York: Columbia University Press, 1990).

13. "A Fine for Radio's Trouble Maker," *New York Times,* October 1992.

14. John C. Merrill, *The Dialectic in Journalism: Toward a Responsible Use of Press Freedom* (Baton Rouge: Louisiana State University Press, 1989). See also Everette E. Dennis and John Merrill, *Media Debates: Communication in the Digital Age* (Belmont, Calif.: Wadsworth Publishers, 2002).

15. James Reston, *The Artillery of the Press* (New York: Harper & Row, 1966), p. 20.

16. Frank Luther Mott, *American Journalism,* 3rd ed. (New York: Macmillan, 1962), pp. 336–338.

17. Hulting and Nelson, *The Fourth Estate,* p. 9. See also Everette E. Dennis and Robert Snyder, eds. *Covering Congress* (New Brunswick, N.J.: Transaction, 1998).

18. J. Herbert Altschull, *From Milton to McLuhan: Ideas and American Journalism* (White Plains, N.Y.: Longman, 1989).

19. Anthony Lewis, "Life Isn't So Simple as the Press Would Have It," *ASNE Bulletin,* September 1983, p. 34.

20. David A. Anderson, "Media Success in the Supreme Court," working paper from the Gannett Center for Media Studies, New York, 1987.

21. Tony Mauro, "Reagan Imposes Ironclad Grip on Words by Government Employees" *1983–1984 Freedom of Information Report* (Chicago: Society of Professional Journalists, 1984).

22. R. H. Coase, "Economics of Broadcasting and Government," *American Economic Review, Papers and Proceedings,* May 1966, p. 442. See also Roger G. Noll and Monroe

E. Price, eds., *A Communications Cornucopia, Essays on Information Policy* (Washington, D.C.: Brookings Institution Press, 1998). See also Philp M. Napoli *Foundations of Communication Policy* (Cresskill, N.J.: Hampton Press, 2001).

23. *United Church of Christ v. the Federal Communications Commission,* 349 F2d 994 (D.C. Cir. 1966).

24. Newton H. Minow, "How Vast the Wasteland Now?" Gannett Foundation Media Center public lecture, New York, May 1991.

25. Peter Huber, "The Death of Old Media," and Michael J. Wolf, "And the Triumph of Broadband," *Wall Street Journal,* January 11, 2000, p. A22 and Reuven Frank, "A Slight Case of Merger," *The New Leader,* October 18, 1999, pp. 20–21. Another useful background source is Alison Alexander et al., *Media Economics, Theory and Practice* (Mahwah, N.J.: Lawrence Erlbaum Associates, 1998).

26. Wilson Dizard, *Old Media, New Media,* 3rd ed. (New York: Longman, 2000).

27. Ken Auletta, "Ten Rules of the Information Age," *At Random,* spring/summer 1997, and Albert Greco, ed., *Media and Entertainment Industries* (Boston: Allyn and Bacon, 2000).

28. Benjamin M. Compaine and Douglas Gomery, *Who Owns the Media? Competition and Concentration in the Mass Media Industries,* 3rd ed. (Mahwah, N.J.: Lawrence Erlbaum Associates, 2000). See also Susan Tifft and Alex S. Jones, *The Trust* (New York: Random House, 2000) for a textured discussion of "family" ownership at the *New York Times.*

Chapter 15

MEDIA EFFECTS: EXPLAINING THE PROCESSES AND INFLUENCES OF MASS COMMUNICATIONS

The impact and influence of television on children has been on the public agenda for decades and continues to be a matter of considerable concern to researchers, policymakers, and the public. More than fifty years of research has yielded contrasting views.

UNDERSTANDING MASS COMMUNICATION REQUIRES MORE THAN JUST A REVIEW OF THE BACKGROUND AND CONTEMPORARY status of our various media. It also requires knowledge of the efforts of media scholars and researchers, who over more than a century have developed *explanations* in the form of theories of how the process of mass communication takes place and the kinds of influences that media content has on audiences. A number of such theories have already been presented in previous chapters. It is the goal of this chapter to extend that effort by showing how our current theories of the process and effects of mass communication were developed by social scientists and media researchers over a number of decades. Seven major theories were developed as those investigators and scholars conducted a variety of research efforts now regarded as classics. The results of those studies led to a constant process of formulating, testing, and revising those theories that now permit detailed understanding of many features of the process and effects of mass communication.

EARLY VIEWS OF MEDIA INFLUENCES

Almost as soon as the penny press started producing daily newspapers for ordinary citizens, there were thoughtful observers and writers who were concerned about their influences. Some scholars of the time saw them as having great benefits for the population; others saw them doing great harm. However, there was only speculation because there were no media researchers who actively sought to assess the influences and effects of the print media available at the time using scientific methods. One respected writer believed that the cheap newspapers would *reduce individuality* and *create similarity* in the population. Alexis de Tocqueville was a French scholar who traveled widely in the United States from 1835 to 1840, when modern newspapers had recently been invented and were starting to be widely adopted. He wrote extensively about the nature of the American democracy and its people. Specifically, de Tocqueville proposed that increased communication among members of a population, such as took place via the new type of newspaper, would lead to a severe loss of individuality. He subscribed to what came to be called the *dead-level theory*. The idea of this theory is that if everyone is exposed to the same flow of ideas, then they will all be influenced in a uniform manner. This exposure and influence will lead them to be very similar to each other in what they know about, think about, and (inevitably) in the ways in which they act.

This theory was widely believed for many years by intellectuals—before research changed their understandings. For example, many decades later, writing in *Harper's Magazine* in 1904, journalist John Burroughs explained that if all the people in a society are exposed to the same topics and ideas, they become very similar in their thoughts and ideas. As he put it:

> Constant inter-communication, [as takes place when everyone reads the same newspapers] makes us all alike; we are as it were, all pebbles on the same shore, washed by the same waves.[1]

Other writers were more positive about the effects of newspapers. One of the founders of modern sociology was Charles Horton Cooley, an American scholar who wrote extensively about the influences of both interpersonal and mass communication processes on human nature and the social order. Writing in 1907, Cooley proposed that the existence of modern newspapers *expanded the awareness* of people about other parts of the world, creating a much more extended mentality. He pointed out that before they existed, with their daily editions and wire services bringing news from afar, people knew little about what went on beyond their local area:

> . . . public consciousness of any active kind was confined to small localities. Travel was slow, uncomfortable, costly [and dangerous]. The newspapers appearing weekly in the larger towns were entirely lacking in what we would call news . . . People are far more alive today to what is going on in China, if it happens to interest them, than they were to events a hundred miles away.[2]

Moreover, Cooley wrote, newspapers and the other new forms of communication he saw (such as the telegraph and telephone) were developing diversity and differences among people. He explained this beneficial influence of mass communications with a *theory of individuality*. The newspapers, he pointed out, were bringing a remarkable variety of ideas to their readers—information about almost anything one could conceive of. With such an abundance of specialized topics to choose from, a person could pursue virtually any kind of interest. Anyone, he wrote, "having a [specific interest] should be more able to find influences to nourish it. If he has a turn, say, for entomology, he can readily through journals, correspondence and meetings get in touch with a group of men similarly inclined and with a congenial tradition."[3] In other words, as people developed such specialized interests, and pursued them through modern means of communication, it had the result of making people different from one another—thus creating *diversity* and *individuality* in the population.

By the beginning of the 1900s, then, and on into the early decades of the twentieth century, there remained a variety of views as to the effects of mass communication. Some claimed that they were of great benefit to humankind, expanding awareness and understanding of events beyond the local environment. Others pronounced that they were a menace—creating a dulling uniformity in the thinking and actions of the majority. All sides of the debate, however, believed that *newspapers had great power* over individuals, and that they played a major role in shaping public opinion, moral norms, and patterns of overt behavior in modern society. Similarly, as film and broadcasting arrived in subsequent decades, people became deeply concerned about the problems for society that these even newer media were presumably creating.

Eventually, the uniform influence theory first advocated by de Tocqueville and elaborated by others seemed to dominate. A major factor supporting this view, and what came to be called the *magic bullet theory,* was the extensive and very successful use made of propaganda by both the Allied and the Central powers during World War I (1914–1918).

The stakes were enormous and governments on both sides felt justified in sending stories (even fake ones) to their press about the brutality and evil deeds of their enemy. They did so to motivate their civilian populations—to keep them working enthusiastically in factories and on farms to supply the arms, food, and fiber needed by their militaries. They also had to convince parents, who were sending their young men to the awful slaughter of trench warfare, that their cause was just, that the enemy were inhuman brutes, and that God was on their side.

It worked! Almost any story about the war was avidly read. Moreover, there was no reason to believe that the newspapers of the time would lie. The result was that entire populations were trained to hate their enemy, to work long hours for the cause, and to accept the sacrifices that military service required. The consequence was that the media (newspapers, magazines, and to a limited extent film) were seen by scholars as well as by the public as having *great power*. It seemed clear that their messages reached everyone; and that they influenced all members of their audiences equally, causing them to respond in much the same way. Essentially, then, following World War I, people in our society shared a set of assumptions that our mass media have *immediate, uniform,* and *powerful* effects. It was this set of assumptions that was fundamental to what came to be called the *magic bullet theory*. Although never formulated systematically at the time, its basic ideas were at center stage just before systematic research on mass communications got its start.

MEDIA EFFECTS RESEARCH BEGINS

A critical issue for understanding mass communications today is whether or not—as many citizens assume—the "magic bullet" assumptions *still* provide a valid perspective for assessing the influences of our media. That is, as the twenty-first century begins, do mass communications have powerful, uniform, and often negative

explaining
MEDIA EFFECTS

The Magic Bullet Theory

The earliest general theoretical perspective on the influence of mass communication was derived from the ideas of late nineteenth century social scientists, who viewed the social order as a *mass society*. While its basic assumptions were widely shared when empirical research began, it was never developed formally as a specific set of propositions. But for several decades, scholars have referred to its essential ideas as the *magic bullet theory*.

Even though we realize today that it never matched reality, it was a beginning point for considering the process and effects of mass communication.

This theory also reflects Charles Darwin's evolutionary ideas. Before he published his *Origins of Species* (in 1859), conceptions of the nature of humankind emphasized *religious* origins. Human beings were said to be unique "rational" creatures created in the image of God. After Darwin, scientific thinking began to stress the importance of *genetic* and *biological* factors as causes of human behavior.

Influenced by this genetic perspective, social and behavioral scientists rejected "rational" views of human nature and stressed its *animal* side. They assumed that people were higher animals, and like other animals they inherited a set of *uniform inherited instincts* (derived from their evolutionary history). It was assumed, therefore, that human behavior was shaped by such biologically based "instincts," causing people to react more or less similarly to whatever "stimuli" (situations confronting them) came along. Thus, under this conception of human nature, responses made to stimuli were shaped either by "instincts," over which they lacked rational control, or by other "unconscious" processes that were not guided by intellect.

This was a frightening view, and it had a strong influence on thinking about the power of mass communications. It portrayed human populations as composed of irrational creatures that could be swayed and controlled by cleverly designed mass communications "stimuli."

This theory led people, early in the century, to believe that those who controlled the media could control the public. Thus, the magic bullet theory implied that the media have direct, immediate, and powerful effects of a uniform nature on those who paid attention to their content. This theory, summarized below, represented both popular and scientific thinking. It assumed that a media message reached every eye and ear in the same way, like a symbolic "bullet," bringing about the same changes of thought and behavior in the entire audience.

1. People in "mass" society lead *socially isolated lives* with limited social controls exerted over each other because they are from diverse origins and do not share a unifying set of norms, values, and beliefs.

2. Like all animals, human beings are endowed at birth with a *uniform set of instincts* that guide their ways of responding to the world around them.

3. Because people's actions are not influenced by social ties, and are guided by uniform instincts, individuals attend to events (such as media messages) *in similar ways*.

4. People's inherited human nature and their isolated social condition lead them to *receive and interpret* media messages in a uniform way.

5. **Therefore,** media messages can be thought of as symbolic "bullets," striking every eye and ear among the members of their audience, and resulting in effects on thought and behavior that are *direct, immediate, uniform,* and *powerful*.

effects, such as *eroding our moral standards* by depicting unacceptable sexual conduct, or by *stimulating aggression* among children and adults by portraying violence? Do they *degrade our language* by an increasing use of coarse and vulgar words? Do they present and get people to believe in *misleading images* (whether positive or negative) of the character and actions of our leaders? Do their misrepresentations *limit our ability* to make intelligent political decisions? Are mass media messages used as *insidious instruments of persuasion,* shaping what we think we need and what we want to buy? More generally, do they shape *how we conduct our lives?*

A NATIONAL DILEMMA

Questions of this kind point to a potentially serious challenge to basic democratic values posed by our mass media. If the answer is "yes" to any of them, it follows logically that the broad concept of "freedom of the press" (and the right to portray social life in movies and on TV in any way producers want) may not be a very good idea. That is, allowing anyone who controls a medium to print, broadcast, or display any content that they wish, for any purpose that they wish, may not be in the best interests of our society as a whole. If some kinds of mass communications unfairly *cause unacceptable conduct* or significantly *mislead* large numbers of people, it would seem logical to conclude that the content of the media should be closely controlled. That is, it should be *censored* so as to eliminate those forms of content that create unacceptable effects.

The difficulty with such a conclusion is that the cure may be worse than the problem. Most Americans would find such controls completely unacceptable. Obviously, this issue goes to the heart of the issue of freedom of expression and our cherished constitutional guarantees. Therefore, it is little wonder that debates about effects of mass communications are conducted with such vigor.

A central problem, if such a censorship policy were to be adopted, is *how to decide* whether or not a particular medium or form of mass communication has effects that are personally or socially destructive? Some in society who speak out on this issue would use the teachings of religion, or the assumptions of a particular (liberal or conservative) political ideology to reach their decisions as to what should be allowed to be transmitted to the public. However, most scholars who study the media take the position that among the alternatives for understanding the effects of mass communication, *research conducted within the scientific perspective* provides the most trustworthy answers. No one would claim that research findings are always right. Studies can be done poorly, or they can pursue the wrong questions. However, *in the long run,* scientific investigation seems to many to be the most effective way to gain reliable information to make decisions about complex and perplexing questions, such as those that concern the influences of mass communications.

THE NATURE AND FUNCTIONS OF RESEARCH

Quantitative studies of the process and effects of mass communication make use of the research methods of the social sciences. These include using the logical designs of the *experiment,* the systematic sampling and measurement techniques of *surveys* (similar to opinion polls), and the formal procedures of *content analysis* (careful inspection and statistical analysis of existing messages in print, film or broadcast format). Each of these depends on a set of techniques, methods, and practices that have been derived from the research methodology originally developed in the physical sciences. Over decades, they have been adapted and refined for the study of communication issues and questions. Obviously, mass communication research does not use microscopes, test tubes, or other devices used in physics, chemistry, or biology, but it does make use of the same underlying logic for making decisions as to whether the results that are observed in a particular study are merely products of chance, or products of the influence of communication factors that bring about certain outcomes or consequences. Using such research methods, specific hypotheses can be tested and conclusions can be reached that help to decide the merits of various kinds of theories that have been advanced.

Other kinds of studies are done on a qualitative basis. Often these are *long-term studies* of factors that cannot easily be observed by an opinion-poll–type survey completed in a day or two, or by conducting some kind of short-term experiment. In other words, carefully observing trends and changes in a society over extended periods of time can sometimes yield important information about media influences that cannot be discovered in any other way.

Distinctive research goals.   There are many kinds of mass communication research, using many different strategies, conducted for a variety of purposes. Some studies are designed to determine in a preliminary way if a theory can be formulated that can explain a particular kind of influence or effect that can be observed in a population. Other studies can indicate whether a particular theory that has already been formulated—and which may seem to be valid—can accurately describe and explain a particular type of media process or effect. These applications of scientific methods are often called *basic* research—seeking explanations, rather than practical uses.

Another category is called *applied research.* This consists of studies undertaken for various kinds of clients who have some problem related to communication. The goal may be to compare two possible advertising messages to see which appeals most to potential consumers. Or, a goal may be to determine the best campaign strategy for a person running for political office. Still other applied projects may be conducted to assess how well a public relations campaign is working to shape or change the attitudes of some segment of the public toward a personality, a corporation, or a government's policy.

While applied research is an important part of commercial, governmental, and nonprofit enterprises in the United States, we are concerned in this chapter with more *basic scientific research* aimed at developing and assessing theory. The goal here is to try to describe and explain the processes and effects of mass communication, so that the ways in which these take place can be better understood. However, the distinction between applied and scientific research is not always clear. Often, the one contributes to the other. Findings from applied research often clarify a theory. Or, the development of a theory can provide a useful guide for the applied researcher.

Scientific research moves the cutting edge forward.   In this chapter, we will review a number of investigations completed during various periods of media history. Our reason for this approach is that these studies have become "milestones" in the search for trustworthy theories that help explain the processes of mass communication or its influences on individuals and the society as a whole. During the nearly seven decades since this type of research began, literally tens of thousands of additional studies were published—testing, expanding, and modifying our knowledge of the process and effects of mass communication. It is not possible in a single chapter to summarize such a large body of research results. It is for that reason that the focus in this chapter is on the classic studies.

The story of these research efforts is similar to what happens in all branches of scientific endeavor. That is, while some yielded conclusions that were and still are still quite *correct,* others were *inconsistent.* Still others (seen in hindsight) were just plain *wrong.* However, we will see that as the ability to conduct research on the influences of the media improved, additional understandings were provided by each new investigation. Thus, scientific research is "self-policing." As the "cutting edge" of research moves forward, incorrect conclusions are gradually eliminated, and are replaced with alternatives that more adequately describe the realities of mass communications and their influences. It is this *self-corrective* feature of science that makes it an attractive means of gaining trustworthy knowledge in the long run.

Generally, then, it is the larger picture that counts. There is little doubt that in the early studies, the research methods used were crude and often inadequate. The theories developed from them were quite simple, and some are now obviously invalid. However—and this is a major point—during the nearly seven decades represented by these studies, *there has been a slow but steady accumulation of valid knowledge* about how our media function, and what they do and do not do to individuals and our society. That kind of development is exactly what research is all about.

EARLY RESEARCH SEEMED TO SUPPORT THE MAGIC BULLET THEORY

Scientific research on the effects of mass communication lagged far behind the development of the media themselves. Large scale studies did not begin until the late 1920s. The reason for the delay was that the necessary statistical tests, research strategies, and measurement techniques required to conduct such investigations— using the logic and methods of science—were not available. By the 1920s, research procedures were sufficiently developed within the social sciences—mainly psychology and sociology—for investigation of the effects of mass communication to become possible.

As we follow the story of media research during the subsequent decades, we need to understand (1) the *basic theories* that researchers developed over the years, (2) how they used *increasingly sophisticated* research methods for studying the effects of mass communication, and (3) how new findings sometimes forced them to *change or even to abandon* some theories.

The Payne Fund studies of movies and children. Social scientists interested in large-scale research on the effects of mass communication first focused on the movies. There were clear reasons for this choice. During the first decade of the twentieth century, movies were a novelty. During the second decade, they became the principal medium for family entertainment. By the end of the 1920s, feature-length films with soundtracks had become standard, and the practice of going to the movies for entertainment at least once a week had been deeply established.

Meanwhile, the public had become uneasy about the influence of the movies on children. In 1929 alone, an estimated 40 million minors, including more than 17 million children under the age of fourteen, went to the movies weekly.[4] Critics raised alarming questions about their effects. Were the new picture shows destroying parents' control over their children? Were they teaching immorality? Films with unwholesome themes—horror, crime, immoral relationships, and the illegal use of alcohol (during Prohibition)—were especially troubling.

No government agency existed to give money to investigators who wanted to assess the impact of films on children, but a private group (the Motion Picture Research Council) decided to seek research data in order to develop a national policy concerning standards in the production of motion pictures. This council called together a group of social scientists to plan large-scale studies to probe the effects of motion pictures on youth. A private foundation called the Payne Fund was persuaded to supply the necessary money.

The overall results of the Payne Fund studies seemed to confirm the charges of the critics of the movies and the worst fears of parents. Their results indicated *widespread* and *significant influences* on childrens' ideas and behavior. When its thirteen reports were finally published in the early 1930s, the Payne Fund studies were the best available evaluation of the impact of motion pictures on children. The assumptions and prediction of the magic bullet theory seemed to have been confirmed, and parents were deeply concerned!

These researchers used approaches that included collecting and interpreting anecdotes about responses to movies, conducting experiments that measured attitudes and behavior, analyzing responses to survey questionnaires and performing systematic analyses of the content of films. By today's standards of research, many of these studies now seem quaint and naive. Indeed, in the years that immediately followed their publication, some became quite controversial. Details about the way data were collected and the conclusions reached came to be widely criticized by research specialists. On the other hand, the public did not care about these technical controversies. They saw the results as confirming their worst fears—the movies had powerful and negative effects on children. The technical criticisms of research procedures by scholars seemed to lay persons like debates over fine points of navigation conducted while the ship was sinking.

Radio reports the invasion from Mars. On October 30, 1938, horrible creatures from Mars invaded the United States and killed millions of people with death rays. At least, that was the firm belief of many of the 6 million people who were listening to the CBS show "Mercury Theater of the Air" that evening. The broadcast was only a radio play—a clever adaptation of H. G. Wells's science-fiction novel,

Actor and director Orson Welles raises his arms in front of a CBS radio microphone during a rehearsal of the "Mercury Theater of the Air" in the 1930s in New York City, paving the way for dramatic TV shows that followed.

War of the Worlds. But it was so realistically presented, in a "newscast" format, that the many listeners who tuned in late missed the information that it was only a play. They thought that Martian monsters were really taking over.

If there had been any doubt that a mass medium could have a powerful impact on its audience, that doubt was dispelled as soon as the next day. Among those who believed the show was a real news report, large numbers *panicked.* They saw the invasion as a direct threat to their values, property, and lives—and literally the end of their world. Terrified people prayed, hid, cried, or fled. A high school girl later reported:

> I was writing a history theme. The girl upstairs came and made me go up to her place. Everybody was so excited I felt as [if] I was going crazy and kept on saying, "What can we do, what difference does it make whether we die sooner or later?" We were holding each other. Everything seemed unimportant in the face of death. I was afraid to die, just kept on listening.[5]

Among those who believed that the Martians were destroying everything, and that nothing could be done to stop them, many simply abandoned all hope:

> I became terribly frightened and got in the car and started for the priest so I could make peace with God before dying. Then I began to think that perhaps it might have been a story, but discounted that because of the introduction as a special news broadcast. While en route to my destination, a curve loomed up and traveling at between seventy-five and eighty miles per hour, I knew I couldn't make it though as I recall it didn't greatly concern me either. To die one way or another, it made no difference as death was inevitable. After turning over twice the car landed upright and I got out, looked at the car, thought that it didn't matter that it wasn't my car or that it was wrecked as the owner would have no more use for it.[6]

Such accounts showed that the broadcast was accepted as real by many people who thought they were going to die.

In fact, the Mercury Theater and the actors had no intention of deceiving people. The script was written and the program was presented in the tradition of telling "spook stories" for Halloween. It was clearly identified as a play before and after the broadcast and in newspaper schedules.[7] But the newscast style, the powerful directing, and the talented performances of the actors conspired to make the presentation seem very real. The result was one of the most remarkable media events of all time.

Findings inconsistent with the magic bullet theory. Immediately after the broadcast, social psychologist Hadley Cantril hastily began a research study to uncover the causes of panic in a general sense, as well as reactions to the radio broadcast. More specifically, he sought to discover the psychological conditions and the circumstances that led people to believe that the invasion was real. Although the scope of the investigation was limited and its flaws numerous, the Cantril study became one of the milestones of mass media research.[8]

Actually, only 135 people were interviewed in depth. Most were people who had been frightened by the broadcast, and all came from the New Jersey area, where the Martians were said to have landed. Most of the subjects were located as a result of the interviewers' personal initiatives. No pretense was made that those interviewed were a representative sample. In addition, just prior to the start of the interviews, two extensive tabulations of listeners comments, commissioned by CBS, were made available to the researchers. All the mail received by the Mercury Theater, CBS station managers, and the FCC, was analyzed and 12,500 newspaper clippings related to the broadcast were systematically reviewed. The results provided a sensitive study of the feelings and reactions of people who were badly frightened by what they thought was the arrival of Martians.

The researchers concluded that "critical ability" was the most significant variable related to the response people made to the broadcast. Critical ability was defined generally as *the capacity to make intelligent decisions*. Those who were low in critical ability tended to accept the invasion as real and failed to make reliable checks on the broadcast; for example, they did not call authorities or listen to other stations.

Especially low in critical ability were those with strong religious beliefs, who thought the invasion was an act of God, and that it was the end of the world. Some thought a mad scientist was responsible. Others were disposed to believe in the broadcast because war scares in Europe (in 1938) made catastrophe seem more plausible. Those high in critical ability tended *not* to believe the broadcast was real. They were more likely to be able to sort out the situation, even if they tuned in late. These people tended to be more educated than those low in critical ability. In fact, statistical data obtained from CBS revealed that amount of *education* was the single best factor in predicting whether people would check the broadcast against other sources of information.

The conclusions derived from the Cantril study posed a *dilemma*. In some ways, the magic bullet theory was supported, but in other ways it was not. For example, it was clear that the radio broadcast brought about some very powerful effects. Yet, *they were not the same for everyone*. This was not consistent with the magic bullet theory. To be consistent, the broadcast should have had about the same effect on everyone who heard it. But the Cantril study isolated individual characteristics of listeners that strongly influenced their response: critical ability and amount of education. For the public, the War of the Worlds broadcast seemed to reinforce a belief in the great power of the media, but many researchers saw that the magic bullet theory had flaws.

BEYOND THE MAGIC BULLET: SELECTIVE AND LIMITED EFFECTS

We next review two classic studies that were milestones in *replacing* the magic bullet theory. One examined soldiers in training during World War II, and the second analyzed the presidential election of 1940. Both studies helped build new ways of understanding how and to what extent mass communications have the power to influence ideas, opinions, and behavior.

THE "WHY WE FIGHT" FILM EXPERIMENTS DURING WORLD WAR II

By the time of World War II, social scientists had developed fairly sophisticated techniques of experimentation, measurement, and statistical analysis. The military therefore felt that they could contribute to the war effort. In one project, the Army formed a special team of social psychologists to study the effectiveness of a set of films that had been designed to teach recruits about the background of the war and to influence their opinions and to motivate them.[9]

When America entered the war in 1941, many young men were ill-informed about all the reasons for America's participation. It was a society that was without television—our main source for news today—and people were both less educated and less informed. Everyone knew about Japan's attack on Pearl Harbor, but not everyone knew about the rise of fascism, Hitler's conquest of Europe, his alliance with Mussolini, or the consequences of militarism in Japan. Moreover, the United States was (and still is) a nation with diverse regions, subcultures, and ethnic groups. The newly drafted soldiers included men from such unlike categories as farmers from Tennessee; ethnic men from big-city slums; small-town, middle-class youths; and young men from the ranches of the West. All were plunged into basic training, but many understood only dimly what it was all about.

Goals and conduct of the experiments. The Chief of Staff, General George C. Marshall, had decided that the troops needed to be told *why* they had to fight, *what* their enemies had done, *who* their allies were, and *why* achieving victory would be a tough job. They had to learn that the war had to be continued until the Axis Powers agreed to unconditional surrender. Since no one (not even Marshall) knew about the atom bomb being built, which would ultimately end the war in Japan, everyone thought that the terrible conflict would drag on for several additional years after Hitler was defeated.

General Marshall believed that special orientation *films* could give the diverse and poorly informed recruits the necessary explanations of the causes of the war and would provide an understanding of why it would not end soon. He hoped that it would also result in more positive attitudes toward America's allies (Great Britian and France), and generally create higher morale.

A top Hollywood director, Frank Capra, was hired to produce seven films—a series called *Why We Fight.* The U.S. Army gave the job of studying their effectiveness to social psychologists in the Army's Research Branch of the Information and Education Division. The basic plan was to see if exposure to such a film would result in measurable influences on the understandings and orientations of the soldiers. These included a firm belief in the *right of the American cause;* a realization that *the job would be tough;* plus confidence in *our side's ability to win.* The U.S. Army officials also hoped that by presenting the facts, the films would create *resentment of Germany and Japan* for making the fight necessary. Finally, they anticipated that seeing the films would foster a belief that through military victory the political achievement of *a better world order* would be possible.

We can summarize the procedures used rather simply: Four of Capra's *Why We Fight* films were used in a series of well-conducted *experiments.* Great control over the experimental conditions was possible, because the subjects were under orders to participate in the experiments. The soldiers were under the watchful eyes of tough sergeants who saw to it that they took the research seriously and that none "goofed off." (Few experimenters today could match this!) Under such conditions, several hundred men who were undergoing training were given a "before" questionnaire that measured understanding of fact, various kinds of opinions and overall attitudes. These questionnaires were carefully pretested on at least two hundred soldiers in order to minimize ambiguities in their language. Then the men were divided (by company units of about a hundred men each) into *experimental groups* and a *control* group. Each company that was designated as an experimental group saw one of the four films from the *Why We Fight* series. The control group saw a neutral film that did not deal with the war.

After they had seen a film, all subjects answered an "after" questionnaire. It measured the same variables as the first questionnaire, but the questions were rephrased so that repeated exposure to the test could not account for changes in responses.

Thus, by comparing the amount of change in each experimental group with that of the control group, the effect of the films could be assessed.

The researchers were surprised when no dramatic results were obtained! The films produced only minor changes in their audiences. Thus the effects were *very limited.* For example, seeing the *Battle of Britain* (one of the films in the series dealing with Royal Air Force's defense of England against the bombers of the Luftwaffe) increased the recruits' factual knowledge about the air war over Great Britain in 1940. As a result of knowing those facts, it also changed specific opinions about a few of the issues treated in the film. But it produced *no broad changes,* such as increased resentment of the enemy or greater willingness to serve until the Axis Powers surrendered unconditionally. The results were much the same for the other films studied.

Implications: media have limited effects. Generally, the researchers concluded that the *Why We Fight* films—with powerful propaganda messages—were modestly successful in teaching soldiers *facts* about events leading up to the war. They were also modestly effective in altering a few *specific opinions* related to the facts covered. But they clearly had *no great power* to fire soldiers with enthusiasm for the war, to create lasting hatred of the enemy, or to establish confidence in the Allies. Moreover, the effects were different for soldiers with low, medium, and high levels of education. Generally, soldiers with more education learned more from the films, although their attitudes were little influenced. These results certainly did not confirm earlier beliefs in all-powerful media. And the finding that variations in education modified the effects flatly contradicted the old notion that communications were *magic bullets* penetrating every eye and ear in the same way, creating similar effects in every receiver. For all intents and purposes, the older theory of uniform influences and powerful effects *died* at this point. Even today, the U.S. Army film studies are seen as models of careful research. They left no room for doubt about either the precision of their methods or the validity of their conclusions.

EFFECTS OF THE MEDIA IN A PRESIDENTIAL CAMPAIGN

One major study, actually conducted in 1940 but published several years later, focused on a presidential election campaign. Sociologists Paul Lazarsfeld, Bernard Berelson, and Hazel Gaudet probed the web of influences within which voters made up their minds as a result of mass media coverage of Republican nominee Wendell Wilkie's challenge to Franklin D. Roosevelt, the Democrat incumbent. In a now-classic work called *The People's Choice,* the researchers studied the role of mass communications as influences on voters.[10]

This study is a landmark for two reasons. First, its scale was large and its methodology sophisticated. In fact, even today, few studies have rivaled it in these respects. Second, the findings revealed completely new perspectives on both the process and the effects of mass communication.

Great improvements in research methods. Lazarsfeld and his colleagues interviewed some three thousand people from both urban and rural areas of Erie County, Ohio. It was an area that had voted in presidential elections much like the entire nation for decades. Interviewing began in May 1940 and ended in November of the same year, when Roosevelt defeated Wilkie. All three thousand subjects were interviewed in May, and they agreed to give further monthly interviews as the election campaign progressed.

Media coverage of the contested 2000 presidential election in Florida focused massive attention on ballot counting in the race between George W. Bush and Al Gore. Judge Robert Rosenberg of the Broward County canvassing board uses a magnifying glass to view a dimpled chad on a punch-holed ballot in November 2000.

The research strategy used was new at the time and very clever: A random sample of six hundred was selected from the three thousand interviewed and designated as the *main panel.* The remaining twenty-four hundred were randomly divided into four additional panels of six hundred each. Those in the main panel were interviewed each month from May to November for a total of seven interviews. The other four groups served as *control* panels and each was to be interviewed only one more time. One of the four control panels was given a second interview in July, another in August, and another in October. At each point, the results of these interviews were compared with those of the main panel. This procedure allowed researchers to see how *repeated interviews* were affecting the main panel compared to each fresh panel. After three such comparisons they found that the repeated interviews were having *no measurable cumulative effect,* and they decided that using the fourth panel was not necessary. Thus, the researchers were confident that their findings were meaningful, and were not an artificial result of their multiple interviews of the main panel.

Some respondents decided early for whom to vote; some decided late. Some shifted from one candidate to another; some who had firmly decided fell back into indecision. Always the interviewers tried to find out *why* the voters made these changes. They also focused on the social categories into which the subjects could be classified. Rural and urban dwellers were compared. People at various income levels were contrasted. The same was true of people of different religious backgrounds, political party affiliations, and habits of using the media. Using complex methods, the researchers found that these category memberships could be used with fair success to *predict* voting intentions and actual voting behavior.

Media as part of a web of influences. Then, and even more now, much of a political campaign is waged in the media through both news reports and paid advertising. But Lazarsfeld and his colleagues did not find all-powerful media controlling voters' minds. Instead, the media were just *one part of a web of influences on voters.* People's personal characteristics, social category memberships, families, friends, and associates as well as the media all helped them to make up their minds. Furthermore, the media did not influence all voters in the same way. When the media did have an effect, three kinds of influences were found. The researchers called these influences *activation, reinforcement,* and *conversion.*

Activation is the process of getting people to do what they are "predisposed" to do by their social category memberships—pushing people along in ways they are headed anyway. For example, for almost fifty years in Erie County most well-to-do Protestant farmers had voted Republican. In contrast, most Catholic, blue-collar, urban workers had voted Democratic. Indeed, all across the country, many voters tend to have certain socially based predispositions for and against each of the main political parties. Yet, even though many voters in Erie County said they were undecided as the campaign progressed, the media helped activate voters *to follow their predispositions.*

Reinforcement is a different process. Fully half of the people studied already knew in May for whom they would vote in November. They made up their minds early and never wavered. Does this mean that the media had no effect on such voters? Not at all. The media were important in such cases because they strengthened the voters' intentions. Political parties can ill afford to concentrate only on attracting new followers. The intentions of the party faithful must constantly be reinforced through communications that show that they have made the right choice. The media campaign is used to provide this reassurance. Clearly, reinforcement is not a dramatic effect, but it is a critical one. It keeps people doing what they already are doing.

Finally, conversion was rare. The presidential campaign presented in the mass media did move a few voters from one party to the other in Erie County, but the number was small indeed. Most people either made up their minds in May, went with the party they were predisposed toward, or paid attention only to the campaign of their own party. Conversion took place among a very small number who had only weak party affiliation to begin with.

Perhaps the major conclusion emerging from this study is that the media had not only *selective* but *limited* influences on voters. When people talk of the media's power, the ability to convert is what they usually have in mind. But the researchers found that of their subjects, approximately 16 percent showed *no* effect of the media; 9 percent showed *mixed* effects; 14 percent were *activated;* 53 percent were *reinforced* (the largest influence); and a mere 8 percent were converted. The concept of an all-powerful media, reaching every eye and ear to influence behavior uniformly was clearly inconsistent with a growing body of research findings.

Serendipity: the two-step flow of communication. One unexpected but extremely important finding emerged from *The People's Choice.* It was a two-step process of communication, which described both the flow of *personal influence* in interpreting the campaign and the word-of-mouth *diffusion of the news.* Its discovery occurred almost by accident, in a way that scientists call "serendipitous."

About halfway through the Erie County study, the researchers began to realize that in addition to the mass media (radio, newspapers, and magazines at the time) another major source of information and influence for voters was *other people.* The researchers found that many individuals did not learn about the election from the media. Instead, they turned to family, friends, and acquaintances to obtain information about the candidates and the issues. Inevitably, those who provided the information also provided *interpretation.* Thus, the two-step flow of information

Two-Step Flow of Communication Theory

While most people get their news and other kinds of information directly from the mass media, stories are often transmitted to additional receivers by word of mouth. Thus, even in our sophisticated "information" society, with its satellites, computers, and news media with worldwide reach, word-of-mouth communication is still a part of the mass communication process.

In a now-classic study of the role of the mass media in the 1940 presidential campaign of Franklin D. Roosevelt versus Wendell Wilkie, communication researchers Paul Lazarsfeld, Bernard Berelson, and Hazel Gaudet rediscovered the importance of the diffusion of information through interpersonal communication.

To their surprise, they found that many of the people they were interviewing did not get their information about the issues and candidates directly from the media at all, but *from other people* who had read about the campaign in the newspapers, or who had listened to the broadcast speeches of the candidates on the radio.

The researchers found that such "opinion leaders" passed on information to other people who had much less contact with the media. As they did so, they had an *influence* on the way the information was interpreted. Thus, the term "opinion leaders" described not only their activity of word-of-mouth transmission but also their role in providing personal interpretations.

Out of that famous research project came a theory that has come to be called the "two-step flow of communication." It is important in understanding the word-of-mouth transmission of news to a larger audience than just those who are initially exposed. The two-step flow of communication process has been widely studied since it was first formulated in the 1940s.

Most of us can recall learning of some major news event this way, but modern research on word-of-mouth transmission of news has shown that it is not a very reliable or accurate system for moving complex information that includes many details.

explaining MEDIA EFFECTS

Such word-of-mouth diffusion of news stories works best for short messages of a dramatic nature, such as "the space shuttle blew up," "the president has been shot," or "we won the big game." But the theory has been well verified, and it can be summarized in the following set of assumptions and their prediction:

1. The mass media present a constant *flow of information* about a great variety of topics of interest and importance to people in contemporary society, but most people attend only selectively.

2. Some people, at all levels of society, *attend more fully* to the media than others and become more knowledgeable than their families, friends, or neighbors in certain areas of media content.

3. Among those who attend more fully are people who become identified by others as *opinion leaders*—persons like themselves, but who are especially knowledgeable and trustworthy as sources of information and interpretation about certain areas of media content.

4. Such opinion leaders often *pass on, by word of mouth, information about specialized topics* that they obtain from the media to others who have turned to them to obtain news and interpretations about those topics.

5. **Therefore,** Mass communications often move in *two distinct stages*—from the media to opinion leaders, who attend directly to media presentations about selected topics—and then by word of mouth to other people whom they influence with their information and interpretations.

between people also included a flow of influence. (The researchers called this *personal influence* in contrast with *media influence*.)

Those who served most often as sources of information and influence had two important characteristics: (1) they had given great *attention* to the media campaign, and (2) their socioeconomic status was *similar* to that of those whom they influenced. In other words, voters were turning for information and influence to people who were *like themselves* but whom they regarded as *knowledgeable*. Thus, in the two-step flow, content moves *from the mass media to opinion leaders,* who then *pass it on to others* whom they inevitably influence. Since *The People's Choice* was published, hundreds of other studies have tried to understand the nature and implications of the two-step flow theory and the personal influence of opinion leaders as part of mass communication.

Implications: mass communications have selective and limited influences. It was overwhelmingly clear by this time that the old magic bullet theory was completely inadequate and had to be totally abandoned. Meanwhile, as the century progressed, the social and behavioral sciences made great advances in understanding the nature of human beings, both individually and collectively. These discoveries would prove to be important in understanding the process and effects of mass communication.

By the 1940s, psychologists had discovered the importance of *learning* in human beings. The older idea of uniform inherited instincts as guides to conduct was abandoned. They developed numerous theories and explanations of how the learning process played a part in shaping the organization and functioning of the human psyche. It was clear that people varied greatly in their learned beliefs, attitudes, interests, values, and other psychological attributes. The key idea was that *individual differences* in what people learned led to *great interpersonal diversity*. It became clear that no two human beings were organized psychologically in exactly the same way. Each person, as a result of learning in his or her unique personal environment, had a different psychological organization—through which the individual perceived and interpreted the world. It was obvious that those individual psychological differences contributed to the patterns of selectivity with which people attended to the media.

Even earlier, sociologists and anthropologists, who had studied the emerging urban-industrial society intensively, also found a picture of *great social diversity*. In this case, it was based on the numerous *social categories* into which people could be classified. Societies had complex social class structures, based on such factors as income, education, and occupational prestige. People were grouped into other categories by their race, gender, ethnicity, political preference, and religion. Within each category *distinct subcultures* developed, bringing people within a given category to share many beliefs, attitudes, and forms of behavior. These also played a part in shaping the ways in which people attended to the media and were influenced by them.

Also important, social scientists found that people did not live socially isolated lives in a "lonely crowd" existence. In rural areas and even in big cities, they still maintained *social relationships* with family, friends, and acquaintances. These had truly significant influences on their interpretations and actions toward the world in which they lived. These social ties were also a significant factor influencing people to attend to mass communications in specific ways.

In summary, then, it came to be understood that these sources of diversity—individual psychological differences, social category subcultures, and patterns of social relationships—all had powerful influences on the mass communications behavior of individuals. *The People's Choice* research on the presidential election had truly been a breakthrough in revealing the foundations for a new general theory of the selective and limited effects of mass communication based on such considerations. While the authors of that study did not actually set forth that general theory, its basic ideas were widely understood, and it came to be the central way to explain the process and effects of mass communication. During the decades that followed, the theory received wide support from literally hundreds of research studies of the ways in which people attended to and were influenced by the mass media. Today, the basic assumptions of the theory that replaced the magic bullet formulation can be summarized as shown in the adjacent boxed feature.

Selective and Limited Influences Theory

Research on the effects of mass communication began during the late 1920s with the Payne Fund studies of the influence of movies on children. The results seemed to support the "magic bullet" theory indicating that motion pictures had widespread and powerful effects on their audiences. But newer research offered a different interpretation.

In 1940, a major study of a presidential election was conducted in Erie County, Ohio. The results showed that media had only three kinds of limited influences: The media *activated* some people to vote who might have stayed home and they *reinforced* the already firm views of others. Only a few, weakly tied to their initial choice, were persuaded to *change* their vote from one party's candidate to the other.

These results revealed that two kinds of factors were important as influences on what people selected from the media to read and hear. These were their *social category memberships* and their *social relationships* with friends and family. Thus, the results of the mass communicated campaign were selective and limited.

Research, done for the army during World War II, also led to a conclusion of selective and limited effects. Soldiers who were shown training films, about the reasons for the war and the nature of the enemy, learned a number of facts from their exposure. However, they underwent only minor changes in their opinions and no changes in their more general attitudes about the war or their motivation to fight. What changes did occur among these soldiers were linked to their *individual differences* in such matters as intelligence and their level of formal schooling.

Following the war, a number of additional experiments confirmed that exposure to, interpretation of, and response to a persuasive message was influenced by a host of factors. Specifically, the degree to which a person was influenced was related to both the characteristics of the message and the receiver.

explaining MEDIA EFFECTS

This accumulation of research made it necessary to abandon the earlier "magic bullet" theory that forecast powerful, uniform, and immediate effects. It was necessary to develop explanations that took into account the fact that different kinds of people selected different kinds of content from the media and interpreted it in many different ways. Thus, the new theory emphasized both selective and limited influences. It is summarized in the following propositions:

1. People in contemporary society are characterized by great psychological diversity, due to learned *individual differences* in their psychological make-up.

2. People are also members of a variety of *social categories* (income, religion, age, gender and many more). Such categories are characterized by subcultures of shared beliefs, attitudes, and values.

3. People in contemporary society are not isolated but are bound together in webs of *social relationships* based on family, neighborhood ties, and work relationships.

4. People's individual differences, social category subcultures, and patterns of social relationships lead them to be *interested in, attend to,* and *interpret* the content of mass communication in very selective ways.

5. **Therefore,** because exposure to media messages is *highly selective* and interpretation of content *varies* greatly from person to person, a mass communicated message will have only *limited* effects on the public as a whole.

AUDIENCES USE MEDIA CONTENT TO OBTAIN GRATIFICATIONS

Between 1940 and 1950, before television was widely available, a number of scholars were trying to go beyond the mere recognition that people were selective in what they turned to in the daily flood of mass communications. They wanted to understand what psychological factors motivated their choices. That is, they wanted to understand what *gratifications* resulted (what needs were fulfilled and satisfactions obtained) when audiences selected and attended to media content. Soon, studies began to provide answers and an explanation was developed. It was called the "uses

Cartoonist Donna Barstow takes on couch potatoes and the effects of television in this rendering from *Brill's Content* magazine.

and gratifications theory." In retrospect, because of the focus on satisfactions and need-fulfillment, a better name is "uses *for* gratification," and that will be the phrase used to identify this theory in the present text.

This new focus of research did not seek an explanation of the "effects" of mass communications. Instead, it sought to understand and explain a part of the "process" by which specific messages from specific media selectively reached specific segments of the audience. It sought to explain various kinds of gratifications that the content of the media provided once it had been selected by members of an audience. In that sense, it extended the factor of selectivity by addressing audience motivation underlying the selective and limited influences theory.

Eventually, a new theory was developed. It portrayed the audience as *active* in freely choosing and selectively consuming message content, rather than as *passive* and "acted upon" by the media—as had been the case with the magic bullet theory. That is, it stated that because of a variety of psychological needs, people sought out content to provide satisfactions that they desired to obtain from the available media.

GRATIFICATIONS FOUND IN MEDIA CONTENT

In one of the first studies of uses for gratification, Herta Herzog interviewed women who listened to radio's daytime serials (soap operas). In 1942, she found that they listened for a variety of reasons.[11] Some found satisfaction in *identifying* with the heroes or heroines of the dramas who suffered many problems. (The term "identifying" implies that a person *is like*, or *wants to be like*, a person that is portrayed, such as a heroine in a soap opera.) By doing this, they said, they could understand

Uses for Gratification Theory

By the 1940s, during the golden age of radio, it had become clear that mass communications had limited and selective influences on individuals who were exposed to a particular message. However, a different kind of question began to be asked by researchers of the time. Why did audiences deliberately *seek out* some kinds of media content and *completely ignore* others?

That is, *why* did people intentionally listen to particular kinds of radio broadcasts? *Why* did they buy a particular kind of magazine or book? *Why* did they turn first to a particular section of the newspaper? *Why* did they peruse the latest advertisements of movies so as to find particular kinds of films?

The researchers began to realize that these are very *goal-oriented* forms of behavior. They indicated clearly that audiences did not simply wait placidly to receive whatever content happened to come their way. Audiences were seeking content from the media that they anticipated would provide them with *certain kinds of satisfactions.* In other words, receivers wanted to use the information in some way *to obtain gratifications* for their needs.

After several massive studies of the audiences for the daytime radio serials of the late 1930s and early 1940s, media researchers formulated the *uses for gratification theory* to try to explain why audiences do not passively wait for media messages to arrive. Instead, it sought to explain why *audiences are active,* deliberately seeking out forms of content that provide them with information that *fulfills their needs.*

This theory focuses on psychological factors—each member of the audience has a structure of interests, needs, attitudes, and values that play a part in shaping selections from the media. Thus, one person, with a particular set of needs and interests, might seek satisfactions through exposure to sports, popular music, wrestling, and detective dramas. Another, with a different psychological makeup, might prefer wildlife programs, political analyses, symphonic music, and literary classics.

explaining MEDIA EFFECTS

The central propositions of the uses for gratification theory emerged from a long list of investigations that have been completed over a number of decades. It has remained as an important explanation of why people select the media content that they do. While it has not previously been stated in formal propositions, in summary its basic ideas can be expressed in the following statements:

1. Consumers of mass communications *do not passively wait* for messages to be presented to them by the media.

2. Members of audiences are *active* in that they make their own decisions in selecting and attending to specific forms of content from the available media.

3. Those choices are made on the basis of individual differences in *interests, needs, values,* and *motives* that have been shaped by the individual's learning and socialization within a web of social relationships and social category memberships.

4. Those psychological factors *predispose* the person to have an interest in particular categories of media content from which they can obtain *diversion, entertainment,* and *respite.*

5. **Therefore,** members of the audience will actively select and attend to specific forms of media content while ignoring or rejecting others in order to *fulfill their needs* and to *provide gratifications* of their interests and motives.

their own woes better. Others did so to obtain *emotional release.* For example, they could cry when tragedies befell their favorite person depicted in a drama, or could feel rewarded when something good happened to that character. Still others engaged in *wishful thinking* about the adventures of soap opera characters who had interesting experiences. In addition, many felt that the serials were a source of *valuable advice* about how to handle their own family difficulties, e.g., how to deal with ungrateful children, or a straying husband.

Another classic study of uses for gratification was completed in 1945. Sociologist Bernard Berelson conducted an exploratory survey of people's reactions to a two-week long strike by those who delivered New York City's newspapers.[12] He found that when people had been deprived of their newspapers for many days, they missed them "intensely." However, when the researcher probed more deeply into exactly what they missed, only a third said it was "serious" news presented by the paper—

most kept up with that via radio. Actually, in response to detailed probing, ". . . different people read different parts of the newspaper for different reasons at different times."[13] Some did miss information about public affairs. Others felt deprived because they could not read the comics or the sports pages daily. All of these categories of newspaper content filled needs and provided gratifications that went unfulfilled during the strike. Other gratifications were obtained by following the news so as to gain social prestige by seeming knowledgeable. Still other satisfactions came from personal advice columns, human interest stories, and vicarious participation in the lives of the rich and famous.

As television swept through the population during the decade of the 1950s this new theory would play a role in guiding research on why people viewed the programs. In fact, as we will see below, one of the largest studies of children and television ever conducted was based on the theoretical perspective of uses for gratifications.

CHILDREN AND TELEVISION

By 1960, television was reaching almost every family in every corner of the country. Just as the public grew alarmed over the movies during the 1920s, they grew concerned about television. What was this new medium doing to them? And, most of all, what was it doing to their children? A trickle of research in the early 1950s did little to quiet the public's fears. It showed that when a family acquired a TV set it changed the lives of its children in a number of ways. It reduced the time they spent playing, postponed their bedtime, and modified what they did in their free time. Children with TV spent less time attending movies, reading, and listening to the radio.[14] But no one knew whether television viewing limited or broadened children's knowledge, raised or lowered their aesthetic tastes, changed their values, created passivity, or stimulated aggression. Research was urgently needed to clarify such issues.

Today, literally thousands of research reports have accumulated on the subject of children and television, but three early investigations stand out as landmarks. The first was a comparison of television viewers and nonviewers. The second was a series of studies on the relationship between portrayals of violence and aggressive conduct by children. The third was not a single investigation but a synthesis of the findings of several hundreds of studies conducted over a ten-year period between 1979 and 1981.

In 1960, Wilbur Schramm, Jack Lyle, and Edwin Parker published the first large-scale American investigation of children's uses of television.[15] The study was concerned, not with what television does *to* children, but with what children do *with* television. In that sense, it was in the tradition of the uses for gratification theory. The researchers looked at the content of television shows, the personalities of young viewers, and the social setting of television viewing. In eleven studies, conducted in both the United States and Canada, they interviewed nearly six thousand children, along with fifteen hundred parents and a number of teachers and school officials. They used in-depth interviews and standardized questionnaires, with statistical analyses of the results. In the end, they had an impressive mass of quantitative data, plus detailed insights about children's viewing patterns and their uses of television.

Patterns of viewing. Very early in the life of the children studied, television emerged as the most-attended to mass medium (it remains so for children today). By age three, children were watching about forty-five minutes per weekday, and

Television and children got attention at the highest level of government at the 1999 White House Conference on Television and Children when President Clinton spoke about the V-chip and youth violence in a ceremony attended by Hillary Rodham Clinton, AOL Time Warner chairman Steve Case, actor Andrew Shue, and cabinet secretary Donna Shalala.

their viewing increased rapidly with each additional year. By the time children were five years old, they watched television an average of two hours per weekday, and by age eight the average viewing time had risen to three hours. In fact, it startled Americans to learn that from ages three to sixteen, in any given year, their children spent more time watching television than they spent in school! Only sleep and perhaps play took up as much or more of their time.

Children's tastes in television programs varied with their age, gender, and intelligence, but their families were the chief influence on taste. Middle-class children tended to watch realistic, self-betterment programs. Working-class children viewed more programs that provided sheer entertainment or fantasy.

Gratifications obtained from the programs. For several reasons, *fantasy* was one of the most important pleasures obtained from TV. This type of gratification was derived from being entertained, from identifying with exciting and attractive people, and from getting away from real-life pressures. In other words, television provided a pleasurable experience that was free from the constraining limitations of daily living. Thus, fantasy, provided both escape and wish fulfillment.

One important finding was that children often turned to television for *diversion,* but in fact they often received *instruction.* This teaching was neither formal nor planned, nor did the youthful viewers *intend* to learn anything. Such unplanned, unintentional education is called *incidental learning.* This is a very important concept that continues to help us understand the influence of television on children even today. What is learned is related, of course, to the child's abilities, needs, preferences, and patterns of viewing. The incidental lessons taught by television are not necessarily objective or correct. TV sometimes portrays reality realistically, sometimes falsely. But whatever their validity, such lessons are a significant source of instruction for young viewers.

Basic finding: viewing television seemed to pose few dangers. Overall, the results from this massive study did not reveal truly dramatic problems for children arising from television. Indeed, the effects of the medium on this audience were selective and limited. Although the researchers found that children were preoccupied with viewing, they did not find that they were passive receivers of evil influences from it. Instead the selective effects of television depended on factors such as the child's family, mental ability, group ties, age, gender, needs, and general personality.

Although the study had some flaws in its methods, its findings remain important. It offered further evidence of the validity of the selective and limited influences theory. It showed that TV's influences vary among children with different individual characteristics and among those of one social category of children to another. Furthermore, the research evidence supported the central thesis of the uses for gratification theory, explaining why programming choices were made. Essentially, children actively selected what they viewed and that content fulfilled many needs and provided a variety of satisfactions.

THE ISSUE OF TELEVISION CAUSING JUVENILE VIOLENCE

Fear of harmful effects resulting from viewing television was the motivation for conducting the largest single research program ever aimed at understanding the effects of mass communications in America. It has been the case in American society that as each new medium appeared, vocal critics pronounced it to be the cause of society's mounting ills. The fact that these ills are rooted in the long-term trends of migration, urbanization, industrialization, and poverty is not readily accepted by most of the public. They want simpler answers. The media are visible targets to blame. Thus, it is not surprising that many people during the late 1960s saw television as the cause of the nation's rising rates of delinquency and crime, mounting levels of juvenile violence, and deterioration of traditional moral values among the young.

THE REPORT TO THE SURGEON GENERAL

As fears of the medium grew, public concern brought pressure on Congress to "do something." In March 1969, Senator John Pastore said on the floor of Congress that he was:

> exceedingly troubled by the lack of definitive information which would help resolve the question of whether there is a causal connection between televised . . . violence and antisocial behavior by individuals, especially children.

With Pastore's urging, Congress quickly appropriated $1 million to conduct research into the effects of television. The National Institute of Mental Health (NIMH) became the agency responsible for managing the program. NIMH appointed a committee of distinguished communication researchers to design the projects and a staff to do the routine administration and to prepare a final report.

All the distinguished researchers on the committee, however, first had to be "approved" by the television networks—which is somewhat like asking the fox to designate who will watch the chickens! Some researchers who had published negative opinions about networks, were actually blacklisted from participation. Needless to say, many highly qualified investigators thought that such exclusions were unethical and simply refused to play any part in the project.

In any case, the surgeon general of the United States charged the committee with two goals: (1) to review what was already known about television's effects, and (2) to launch new studies on the subject. Eventually, in 1971, some sixty studies, plus reviews of hundreds of prior investigations, were published in five volumes and a sixth summary volume.[16] Many issues were addressed, including the influence of advertising, activities displaced by television, and the information learned from television. A major focus, however, was on *televised violence* and its *influence on children*. We can review briefly some of the main findings on this topic.

Network television's violent content. Just how violent were network television shows at the time of the study? Volume one of the research report presented some striking answers. For example, one researcher studied a full week of prime-time television in the fall of 1969. He found that eight of every ten programs contained violence. Even more striking, the hours during which children viewed most were the most violent of all. What kind of people were shown as aggressive? Violence was carried out on the screen mostly by men who were free of family responsibilities. About three-fourths of all leading characters were males who engaged in violence. They were American, middle or upper class, unmarried, and in the prime of life. Killings occurred between strangers or slight acquaintances, and few women were violent. (In real life most killings involve family members or people who know each other.) Overall, then, television's portrayals of violence were very *frequent* and very *unrealistic*.

Social learning from models for behavior. Television content clearly presents large amounts of violence. But do such portrayals provide *models* that children imitate that cause them to become more aggressive? In an attempt to answer this question, one volume of the report to the surgeon general reviewed all the research that had been published on what psychologists call *observational learning*. This kind of learning is just what the term implies. As a result of seeing the actions of someone else, the observer adopts the modeled beliefs, attitudes, or behavior.

Findings from earlier research on modeling behavior (not part of the surgeon general's project) are important to the issue of whether portrayals of violence on television can provide models that stimulate aggression among children. The most widely known studies of modeling up to that time were those done in the early 1960s by psychologist Albert Bandura and his associates.[17] Bandura had children watch a live (or sometimes a filmed) human model strike a large inflated "Bobo" doll (a large clownlike figure that always springs back upright if punched or hit). In one experimental condition children saw the model *rewarded* for this aggressive behavior (punching the doll). In a second condition, children saw the human model receive *no consequences* for such aggression. In a third experimental condition, the subjects observed the model being *punished* for punching the Bobo.

Each group of children who had received these "treatments" were then left in a room full of toys—including a Bobo doll like the one the model had beaten. The children who had seen the model rewarded, or receive no consequences for aggressive behavior, showed a great deal of *direct imitation*. They too beat up the Bobo doll. Those who had observed the model being punished for aggression were *much less likely* to be violent toward the doll. It seemed clear that children copied or did not copy the behavior of the model, depending on whether or not aggressive behavior was punished.

Media Information Utility Theory

explaining
MEDIA EFFECTS

People in societies such as ours rely on the media to provide them with many kinds of information. They read books, newspapers, and magazines. They go to the movies, watch TV, surf the Internet, rent films for their VCRs, and listen to the radio in their cars. In many cases they do this because media content is entertaining, fulfilling deep-seated needs, and providing complex psychological gratifications.

However, people in modern society also have come to rely heavily on mass communications for many other kinds of information (unrelated to entertainment) that they use for routine purposes. For example, they have to find out where they can purchase a car, clothing, food, or other things at the best price; to locate suitable housing, a job, the latest fashions; or sometimes to meet someone to date or even marry. In short, people are *dependent* on the media to provide many kinds of utilitarian information that has little to do with fulfillment of deep-seated needs or providing complex psychological gratification.

At an earlier time, when modern media did not exist, word-of-mouth communication was the source for such information. People had networks of families and friends from which they obtained the information they needed for routine matters. Populations of similar cultural backgrounds lived together in small communities generation after generation. Thus, social ties between people were both extensive and deep.

In modern life, and especially in urban areas, those networks are much more difficult to establish and maintain. People of many diverse backgrounds live in physical proximity to each other. However, they often differ from each other in terms of ethnicity, race, education, income, eligion, political affiliation, and other characteristics. Such social and cultural differences pose many *barriers* to open communication through word-of-mouth channels. This tends to inhibit contacts and the free exchange of ideas between people, leading them to turn to other channels, less personal sources, to get the information that they require.

Today, the mass media provide that information. In their news, advertisements, syndicated columns, and even in their entertainment content, they provide a great deal of practical information that people use. That is, the media provide a constant flow of advice, interpretations, information, instruction, and role models that people use as a basis for making choices. Thus, they become dependent on this kind of mass communicated information. Stated formally:

1. People in all societies need to make *decisions* about routine and practical matters, such as obtaining food, shelter, clothing, transportation, entertainment, and other aspects of daily life.

2. In traditional societies people were linked together in well-established networks of friends and family. It was through those networks that they obtained by *word of mouth* the practical information that they used for such decisions.

3. In urban-industrial societies, composed of unlike people brought together, populations are *greatly differentiated* by race, ethnicity, income, education, occupation, religion, and social class.

4. Because of such social diversity, urban industrial populations have *fewer effective word-of-mouth channels* based on deeply established social networks through which they can obtain the practical information they routinely need.

5. **Therefore,** people in urban-industrial societies become *dependent on mass media* to obtain the utilitarian information that they require to make many kinds of routine daily decisions.

Later, to check to see if the subjects had understood the actions of the human models, the children in all three groups were asked to show the experimenter what the model had done. They were able to do so without difficulty. In other words, *observational learning* had taken place regardless of whether the model had been rewarded or punished. The children knew full well that the model had beaten the doll. However, whether the children imitated that behavior depended on what experimental condition they had been in—on what they had observed to be the consequences of being aggressive.

What do such experiments mean? There is no doubt that children often imitate what they see others doing, and most psychologists believe that such modeling is an important factor in personality development. But does this mean that children

Modeling Theory

explaining
MEDIA EFFECTS

The American mass media, especially television and movies, present many depictions of people acting out patterns of behavior in various ways. These can be ways of speaking, smoking, relating to members of the opposite sex, dressing, walking, or virtually any form of meaningful action. These depictions can serve as "models" of behavior that can be imitated, and people who see such actions depicted may adopt them as part of their own behavioral repertoire.

One explanation of how and why this can take place is *modeling theory*. It was derived from a more general perspective called "social learning theory" originally formulated by psychologist Albert Bandura. Social learning theory provides explanations of the ways in which individuals acquire certain forms of behavior by seeing them performed by someone else, whether the media are involved on not. When applied to adopting forms of action portrayed by actors and depictions observed in the media, it is called "modeling theory."

The reason why modeling theory is particularly relevant to television programs and motion pictures is that they actually *show* actions performed by persons (models). That is, in the course of various kinds of dramas or other content, models can be seen acting out, in various kinds of social settings, the behavior that an observer may find attractive. Thus, the modeled behavior is depicted more realistically than if it were only described and heard in verbal terms, as in radio, or if it was read in print form.

Modeling theory does not imply any *intentions* on the part of the media, the model, or even on the part of the viewer. The adoption of a form of action after seeing it portrayed in the media may be entirely *unplanned* and *unwitting*. Certainly there is no implication that those who designed or performed the media depiction *intended* them as models for others to adopt (with the exception of behavior modeled in advertisements). Thus, viewers may imitate a behavior pattern, whether or not the people who created the portrayal intended it to serve as a guide, and the effects of viewing a model can be completely unrecognized on the part of the imitating party.

In the modeling process, the receiver first *encounters* a media presentation of the model depicting the behavior. If the person *identifies* with the model, he or she may *reproduce* the form of action portrayed by the model. But, before permanently adopting it, it must have some positive *benefit* for the observer. If so, the behavior may be tried out, and if adopting it *solves some problem* for the person, it may be used again and again in similar circumstances.

Stated more formally, modeling theory can be summarized briefly in terms of the following set of assumptions and their predictive proposition:

1. An individual *encounters a form of action* portrayed by a person (who models the behavior) in a media presentation.

2. The individual *identifies with the model;* that is, the viewer believes that he or she is like (or wants to be like) the model.

3. The individual *remembers and reproduces* (imitates) the actions of the model in some later situation.

4. Performing the reproduced activity *solves some problem* or *results in some reward* for the individual (provides positive reinforcement).

5. **Therefore,** receiving positive reinforcement increases the probability that the person will *use the reproduced activity repeatedly* as a means of responding to similar situations in the future.

blindly imitate violence portrayed on television? There are no clear answers. Modeling influences in experiments may be very different than the effects of mass communication in "real life," where family controls are in place. Nevertheless, the results of these experiments, along with an accumulation of subsequent research, led to the formulation of *modeling theory*.

Television and adolescent aggression. Other studies that were a part of the *Report to the Surgeon General* did look at attitudes and behavior in real-life settings. In the volume entitled *Television and Adolescent Aggression,* eight projects are reported that attempt to (1) measure adolescent use of television, (2) measure adolescent aggressiveness, and (3) relate use of television to violent behavior.[18]

Perhaps the most interesting of these studies is one by Monroe Lefkowitz and his associates. This ten-year *longitudinal* project covered one set of subjects over a period of a full decade—unusual in communication research. Some 436 children in Columbia County, New York, were tested while in the third grade and again ten years later. The children were asked to rate themselves and each other on such characteristics as popularity and aggression. The researchers also interviewed the parents. The ratings and interviews revealed that a child who was unpopular in the third grade tended to be unpopular ten years later. It also showed that such unpopular children tended both to watch television more and to become more aggressive as they got older. Thus, frequency of viewing violence portrayed on television was related to actual level of aggression in the group studied, and the effects of viewing television violence were greatest for those who viewed most often. This seemed to confirm the role of TV in stimulating aggression.

Overall, the studies of adolescent aggression found that specific kinds of youths were more likely to both watch televised violence and to be aggressive. The youths studied were males, younger adolescents, those of lesser intelligence, and those in lower socioeconomic levels. Thus, among youths in these social categories, viewing violence on television and aggressiveness went together. At the same time, the relationship between these behaviors was not strong enough to imply that television *flatly caused* the aggressiveness. This is an important point in interpreting such research. To show that two things tend to occur together is not the same as showing that one of those things actually causes the other.

Overall findings: viewing violence on television may cause aggression.
The final report of the advisory committee, entitled *Television and Growing Up,* contains a summary of the findings of the above and a number of additional studies. It makes recommendations concerning further research and public policy. Finally, it offers a statement about the relationship between televised violence and aggressive behavior. After reviewing the entire body of evidence, the Scientific Advisory Committee concluded that televised portrayals of violence *could be harmful to some children.* As they put it, the issue posed a potential public health problem:

> Thus the two sets of findings (laboratory and survey) converge in three respects: a preliminary and tentative indication of a causal relation between viewing violence on television and aggressive behavior; an indication that any such causal relation operates only on some children (who are predisposed to be aggressive); and an indication that it operates only in some environmental contexts. Such tentative and limited conclusions are not very satisfying [yet] they represent substantially more knowledge than we had two years ago.[19]

The Committee's conclusions from the research findings created a storm of controversy. Senate hearings were held in 1972 to explore what it all meant. The public, disregarding all the hedges, limitations, and qualifications of the scientists, focused on the idea that *television causes kids to be aggressive.* The television industry, seizing mainly on the shortcomings of the research and the tentative nature of the conclusions, declared the findings to be *of little importance.* Many media critics were outraged; a number of the researchers charged that their work had been misrepresented. Perhaps the final word went to Surgeon General J. L. Steinfield:

> These studies—and scores of similar ones—make it clear to me that the relationship between televised violence and anti-social behavior is sufficiently proved to warrant immediate remedial action. Indeed the time has come to be

blunt: we can no longer tolerate the present high level of violence that is put before children in American homes.[20]

In effect, then, the surgeon general of the United States concluded that *televised violence may be dangerous to your child's health!* However, that conclusion was still hedged with caveats that only certain kinds of children were influenced under certain kinds of conditions.

Perhaps most interesting of all is the clear contradiction between the implications of the findings from the studies of Schramm and his associates, a decade earlier, and those of the *Report to the Surgeon General.* The first suggested that television posed no dangers to children, while the second suggested that, for some, the medium could be dangerous. Here, then, is the classic situation that often confronts a scientific community. Which one is the correct interpretation? As we indicated earlier, the answer always lies in further research leading to theories that more closely portray reality.

THE SECOND REPORT TO THE SURGEON GENERAL

By 1980, the pace of research on the effects of television had increased sharply. In fact, 90 percent of *all* research ever done on the effects of viewing television on behavior (up to that time) was done between 1971 and 1980—the decade following the publication of the first *Report to the Surgeon General.* So many research findings were available that it was difficult to grasp their overall meaning. Additionally, the *Report to the Surgeon General,* on children and violence, had created many controversies and left many questions unanswered. Because of these two factors, Julius Richard, then the Surgeon General, asked the National Institute of Mental Health to undertake a *synthesis* and *evaluation* of the mass of research evidence that was then available. Thus, in 1982, a decade after the first report, a second was published.

The increased pace of research. The new *Report to the Surgeon General,* entitled, *Television and Behavior: Ten Years of Scientific Progress and Implications for the Eighties,* was not based on new research sponsored by the government.[21] Instead, it was a compilation of the main findings of more than twenty-five hundred studies of the influence of television on behavior, most of which had been published between 1979 and 1981.

Overall, this was an enormously valuable synthesis and evaluation of thousands of research studies on television, showing how the medium influenced a number of forms of behavior. Seven broad areas of influence were reviewed. These included (1) television and health, (2) violence and aggression, (3) pro-social behavior, (4) cognitive and affective aspects of viewing, (5) the family and interpersonal relations, (6) social beliefs and social behavior, and (7) television's effects on American society.

It is not possible to summarize in a few paragraphs the nature of the thousands of studies and details of findings of so massive an amount of material. We can, however, focus on that part of the report devoted to studies of violence and aggression. The report noted that television had been and remained devoted to showing violence. By the time of the publication (in the early 1980s), the portrayal of violence on television had continued unabated since the 1950s, with only a few minor fluctuations. In fact, over the decade covered in the report, there had been an *increase* in violence in children's weekend programs, which by the end of the period had become more violent than prime-time television.

Confirming findings: viewing of televised violence by children clearly does cause aggression. A major difference in conclusion between the first and second *Report to the Surgeon General* was that there was no longer any question whether or not a relationship existed between exposure to violent television programs and increased tendencies toward aggressive behavior among *some categories* of children and youths viewing such content. However, as is the case in the association between smoking and cancer, one cannot predict on an individual basis. That is, it is not clear whether violent programs will cause a particular person to become more aggressive. However, the totality of evidence for inferring that viewing violent programs raises *rates* of aggression among those children that are heavy viewers was even clearer than it was in the earlier *Report to the Surgeon General.*

The question for future research, said the report, is not whether exposure to violence raises the probability that a person will engage in aggressive behavior. That conclusion has been well established. The problem that researchers faced during the years that followed was to discover exactly *what* portrayals of violence, and *what* psychological factors, lead people with *particular personal and social characteristics* to become more aggressive after being exposed. As yet, research has not fully answered those questions.

THEORIES OF LONG-TERM INFLUENCES ON SOCIETY AND CULTURE

Those who study and evaluate the process and effects of mass communications in modern society have long been troubled by a perplexing and recurrent *contradiction.* When they try to understand the influence of mass communications in our society, two *opposite conclusions* can be reached. Both are clearly based on trustworthy sources of information. And—compounding the problem—both of those conclusions seem to be correct!

The contradiction is this: Looking at the research findings that have been produced over a number of decades leads to a clear conclusion that the media have only *selective and limited influences* on most people's beliefs, attitudes, and behavior. However, anyone who has even an elementary acquaintance with recent American history must reach the quite different conclusion that, frequently, the media have had very *powerful influences* on a number of social and cultural situations, trends, and processes within our society.

This perplexing dilemma has to be resolved. Did the research reveal a false picture of minimal effects? If so, that would contradict our earlier claim that science reveals trustworthy knowledge. Or, is our reading of recent history faulty when it seems to show that mass communications often have powerful effects on our society and culture?

To resolve that dilemma, we will show in the present chapter that *both conclusions are correct!* That is, the media do have weak effects; but they also have powerful effects. That may sound like impossible double talk. However, the key to understanding this seemingly irreconcilable puzzle lies in recognizing the difference between *short-term* effects on individuals and *long-term influences* on a population's shared beliefs, attitudes, and behavior that can change cultural norms and social institutions in the society at large.

One problem with developing such long-range theories is that they go *beyond* what can currently be confirmed by easily observable research evidence. That is, they deal with influences and effects of mass communications that cannot be readily uncovered by short-term scientific experiments or one-time surveys. Yet, these theories are more than just opinions and guesses. Powerful media effects can be revealed by careful observation of historical events and trends over long periods of time.

It is not difficult to show that mass communications can play a vital role in stimulating social and cultural change. In this section, we will look at two theories explaining ways in which the media can be instrumental in promoting long-term changes within a society. The first, the *theory of the accumulation of minimal effects* helps in understanding how changes in public opinion and other shared beliefs in a population can take place.[22] Examples of such changes are public support for and beliefs in reducing pollution, limiting access to guns by juveniles, getting drunk drivers off the road, or reducing smoking by the young. The second, *social expectations theory,* explains long-term media influences on people as they slowly acquire clearer and clearer conceptions of the organization, functions, and consequences of key groups within a society—groups in which they personally play no part, but which they understand quite well.

ACCUMULATION THEORY: THE "ADDING UP" OF MINIMAL EFFECTS

One way to understand long-term media influences is to identify the factors that must be present before minimal effects can "add up." This can show how the media often have a great deal of influence in shaping people's ideas and interpretations of a situation, even though any particular message they present to any one individual probably will have quite limited effects in a short-term sense.

There are three factors that must be present in a situation before accumulation theory can explain how significant changes occur over a long period. First, the media must focus *repeatedly* on a particular issue; second, they must be relatively *consistent* in presenting a more or less uniform interpretation; and third, the major media (newspapers, radio, television, and magazines) must *corroborate* each other with parallel content.

But what evidence is there that powerful media effects are brought about under such conditions? Clearly, no such evidence can be derived from either short-term experiments or from surveys completed at a particular point in time. However, *historical analyses* can supply examples that show the theory in action. We can identify very obvious examples of accumulative effects by looking at changing patterns of public response to certain events that have occurred in recent decades where media played a decisive role.

We begin with the sending of the our soldiers and marines to Somalia, Haiti, and Bosnia and the U.S. Air Force to bomb Kosovo and Serbia. These armed interventions in our recent history show very clearly the dramatic consequences to society that can result from *consistent, persistent,* and *corroborative* media attention to human tragedies. However, to show that these actions were not something totally unique, we will also briefly examine several additional examples.

Armed interventions. Sending military forces of the United States to invade or bomb a foreign country is a drastic step in international affairs. This has happened a number of times in recent years. In the past, when the U.S. Marines were dispatched to another country (such as Nicaragua and China earlier in the twentieth century) other nations strongly condemned the action. However, not only did the U.S. armed forces "invade" Somalia, Haiti, and Bosnia in more recent times, and then bomb Kosovo and Serbia, but also they received the approval of much of the rest of the world.

How could this happen? How did our leaders get the public to go along with such drastic action? Accumulation theory provides one answer. In 1991 and 1992, night after night on American television, viewers saw pictures of pathetic starving people in Somalia. These pictures showed little children in such a wretched state of starvation that they looked like skeletons. It was painful just to watch. The cause of their plight was shown to be the local "warlords" who were preventing humanitarian efforts to bring them food. No one claimed in any of the media that these starving people deserved their plight, that the warlords were justified, or that the United States should ignore the situation. In other words, the portrayals in all of the media were *consistent, persistent,* and *corroborative.* As a result, public sentiment built up to a point that President George Bush was able, with a high level of approval, to take the extraordinary step of invading another country. Much of the world had seen the same pictures. They raised few objections; indeed most people in other countries applauded; a number even participated. Without the accumulation of minimal effects over time, providing a strong base of public opinion, however, it is doubtful that the invasion would have occurred.

Later, during the Clinton administration, the media played much the same role by providing a constant flow of accounts and images of suffering in Haiti and in Bosnia. Similarly, dreadful television pictures, magazine stories and newspaper accounts of "ethnic cleansing" in Kosovo preceded bombing campaigns in that area, and in the case of Serbia, much the same occurred. In both of these cases, public support for military action was strong. That is not to say that mass communications *caused* these interventions, but such policies would never have been supported without accumulative changes that took place among the public as a result of repeated, consistent, and corroborative media content.

Smoking and health. A second example of the accumulation of minimal effects is the twenty-five–year campaign against smoking—waged largely in the media. The continuous, consistent, and corroborated portrayal of smoking as harmful to health in news and public service campaigns slowly but surely brought about a significant change in the thinking and actions of large segments of the public. Eventually, the public supported a variety of new laws concerning that habit.

Although old movies on TV still show everyone smoking, media messages about its dangers became increasingly present and consistent in the media. Ultimately, cigarette ads were barred from appearing on TV, and no messages were deliberately presented to persuade people that credible authorities thought that smoking was healthy and risk free.

Many additional examples could be cited, showing ways in which effects *slowly accumulate* when consistent messages about a topic are persistently presented and corroborated across media. They would include our current emphasis on avoiding fats and cholesterol in our diets, our increasing preoccupation with exercise and our shared concerns about the dangers of using drugs and alcohol. At one time, the messages from the media concerning drugs were mixed. Now, the media have placed the negative aspects of these problems high on their agenda and have brought them sharply into focus for the public. Finally, in the same general category, we can note the role of the media in helping to define the dangers of AIDS and the benefits of "safe sex."

The Theory of Accumulation of Minimal Effects

After several decades of intensive research, it became widely accepted that any particular mass communicated message (news story, movie, advertisement, television presentation, etc.) had only selective and limited effects on the media audience. Hundreds of experiments and other kinds of research, studying different kinds of persuasive messages, aimed at changing people's beliefs, attitudes, and behavior, failed to reveal any really strong influences on all of those who were exposed to such messages.

At the same time, year after year, changes could be observed taking place in society that many scholars believed were significantly influenced by the media. Thus, there was a dilemma concerning the ability of the media to influence people's ideas and behavior. Scientific research revealed a picture of a weak media having, at best, only limited influence on people. But systematic observation of ongoing events in society suggested a much more powerful role. For example, it appeared to many observers that mass communication played a significant part in bringing about such changes as Richard Nixon's resignation due to the events of Watergate, the Civil Rights Movement of the 1960s, the redefinition of the Vietnam War that took place in the United States, and many changes related to smoking and other health behavior.

Clearly, some way of resolving this apparent dilemma was needed. Both the scientific research and the careful observation of historical events seemed to lead to sound conclusions—even if they were completely opposite. Finally, it came to be understood that almost all of the scientific research was based on *short-term* studies, making use of brief experiments and one-time surveys. The historical observations of changes in society *extended over time*. The resolution of the dilemma came when it was realized that both conclusions could be correct. In a short-term sense, the media may have very selective and limited influences. But over a long period, small changes in a few people at a time can eventually add up to significant long-term influences.

explaining MEDIA EFFECTS

As it turned out, it was those issues on which the media focused *repeatedly,* and in relatively *consistent* ways, that changed people over time. If those conditions prevailed, and if the various media—print and broadcast—*corroborated,* with each other by presenting the same interpretations, truly significant changes could take place in people's beliefs, attitudes and behavior. From these considerations the theory of the accumulation of minimal effects was developed. Its basic assumptions and logical prediction are as follows:

1. The mass media begin to focus their attention on and transmit messages about a *specific topic* (some problem, situation, or issue).

2. Over an extended period, they continue to do so in a relatively *consistent* and *persistent* way and their presentations *corroborate* each other.

3. Individual members of the public increasingly become *aware* of these messages and, on a person-by-person basis, a growing *comprehension* develops of the interpretations of the topic presented by the media.

4. Increasing comprehension among the audience of the messages supplied by the media, begins to *form* or *modify* the meanings, beliefs, and attitudes that serve as guides to individual behavior regarding the topic.

5. **Therefore,** as individual-by-individual changes in beliefs and attitudes accumulate, new shared *norms* emerge, resulting in *widespread changes* in audience behavior toward the topic.

SOCIAL EXPECTATIONS THEORY: LEARNING GROUP REQUIREMENTS

Another way of looking at long-term influences on media audiences is to note how, over time, people learn the rules and requirements for acting out parts within various kinds of groups by seeing them portrayed in media content. Here, the focus is not on isolated specific acts that are acquired from mediated models, but on developing an understanding, over time, of the pattern of customs and routines of behavior expected within specific groups by seeing their portrayals in the media.

More specifically, what is it that must be learned by a particular individual for effective participation in a group, or for being accepted in any kind of social setting? In every human group there is a complex set of understandings of what behavior is expected. Those expectations must be acquired before the individual can act effectively in such circumstances.

To understand this process we can begin by noting the essential features of any human group, large or small. First, groups are made up of people who come together to accomplish a *goal* that they deem important—and which cannot effectively be accomplished by the same number of individuals acting alone. Thus, it is the *coordination* of their actions into an organized "teamlike" pattern that gives the advantage to the group over solitary action.

It is the rules of that teamlike coordinated behavior—often called the group's *social organization*—that set it apart from actions taken by individuals alone. Without such a pattern of social organization, learned and followed by each member of the group, their collective actions would be chaos. Thus, groups—from the smallest family to the largest government agency or corporation—have rules and expectations that define and govern the activities of each of their members, if their collective goal is to be accomplished.

What are the major components of such a shared pattern of social organization, and how do human beings acquire their personal knowledge of such requirements? Briefly stated, social organization can be defined as *that pattern of general group norms, specialized roles, ranking positions, and the set of social controls used by the group to ensure reasonable conformity to its requirements.* Each of these components of organized social activities is important in stabilizing a group and getting its members to work effectively for whatever goals brought its members together in the first place.[23]

Group *norms* is an easy idea to understand. Every group has a set of general rules that all members of a particular group are expected to follow. These may have to do with the way people dress, use certain specialized language, greet each other, and so on through literally hundreds of activities that make up the behavior performed in the group. They differ greatly according to the type of group. The norms of army life are very different from those of a religious order, and both are very different from the norms followed by members of a local labor union or students in a college or university. Nevertheless, all such groups have some set of general norms that all members must learn, understand, and follow to a reasonable degree. How do people who never enter such groups learn such norms?

Social *roles* is also a basic concept. These are more specialized rules that apply to persons playing particular parts or defined positions in the group. Such definitions of expected behavior must be understood, not only by the person performing a particular role, but also by those who must relate their own roles to it. For example, imagine a baseball team in which the batter, pitcher, and every other player understands only what he or she is to do in their position, but not what each of the other players are supposed to do under various circumstances. It would be chaos, and the goal of winning could never be accomplished. Thus, the key ideas regarding roles are both *specialization* and *interdependence.* That is, in most groups, the role requirements for each position in the group are not only different (specialized), but they are also interlinked with the specialized activities of other members. It is this feature of a coordinated "division of labor" that makes groups far more efficient than the same number of uncoordinated individuals. Again, how do people in a society of interdependence gain knowledge of the roles of others who they never personally contact?

A key idea in social organization is *ranking.* There are few groups, if any, in which every member has precisely the same level of authority, power, status, and rewards. Even in informal groups of friends, some members are leaders and are looked up to, while others are followers and command less prestige. In large and complex groups, many ranking layers exist. People at different levels have varying amounts of power and authority and they receive different amounts of respect and rewards. Such differences in ranking arise from many sources. Generally speaking, those at the top take the greatest responsibility; they possess scarce but critical skills; they have had extensive experience and they are not easily replaced. Those with opposite characteristics tend to remain at the bottom. However, most people can identify the basic social ranking of many categories of people. How do they acquire such knowledge?

Finally, every human group makes use of *social controls*. Maintaining the stability of a group takes place through the use of some combination of rewards and punishments. These are used by a group to prevent excessive deviation from, and to reward conformity to, its social expectations. They can range from mild sanctions, such as words or gestures of approval and disapproval, to really significant actions

explaining
MEDIA EFFECTS

Social Expectations Theory

The term "socialization" refers to the process by which individuals learn how to take part in, or at least to understand, various kinds of groups in their society. Such groups range from the family and children's playmates early in life, to increasingly complex groups as the person grows older. The individual goes on to school, then begins work and generally must understand and deal with a remarkably wide variety of groups in his or her community and in the society.

Every human group has its own set of rules that must be followed. They include all of its customs and expectations for many kinds of social behavior. If the individual does not conform to these social expectations in a group, he or she risks social criticism and even rejection. Such expectations include *norms* (general rules for all members), *roles* (specialized parts for people in specific positions), *ranks* (defining who has more or less power, authority, or rewards), and *controls* (procedures used to reward or punish people for conformity or deviance).

But what are the sources from which we acquire our knowledge about the social expectations of others? The answer is that there are many. Obviously, we learn from our family, from peers, from schools, and from the general community. But, in our modern world, there is another source from which we acquire a great deal of information about the social expectations of people who are members of various kinds of groups. That source is our mass media.

By watching television, going to a movie, or even by reading, one can learn the norms, roles, and other components of social expectations that make up the requirements of many kinds of groups. One can learn what is expected of a prisoner in a penitentiary, a father or mother, a nurse in a hospital, or a corporation president conducting a board meeting. Or, one can find out how to behave when at the horse races, in combat, gambling in a casino, or having dinner at an elegant restaurant (even if one has never been in such places).

There is, in short, an almost endless parade of groups and social activities, with their behavioral rules, specialized roles, levels of power and prestige, and ways of controlling their members portrayed in the media. There is simply no way that the ordinary individual can actually participate in most of these groups, so as to learn by trial and error the appropriate forms of conduct. The media, then, provide broad if unwitting training in such social expectations.

This influence of the mass communicated lessons transmitted about such activities can be termed the *social expectations theory*. Its essential propositions can be summarized in the following terms:

1. Various kinds of content of the mass media often portray *social activities* and *group life.*

2. These portrayals are *representations of reality* that reflect—accurately or poorly—the nature of many kinds of groups in American society.

3. Individuals who are exposed to these representations receive *lessons* in the nature of norms, roles, social ranking, and social controls that prevail within many kinds of common groups.

4. The experience of exposure to portrayals of a particular kind of group results in *learning of behavior patterns* that are expected by others when acting within such a group.

5. **Therefore,** these learned expectations concerning appropriate behavior for self and others serve as *guides to action* when individuals actually encounter or try to understand such groups in real life.

of control, ranging from awarding medals to those who perform in a significantly positive way to executing those whose deviations are too great to tolerate. Most groups allow limited deviation from norms, some personal variability in the manner in which people fulfill role requirements, or even some disregard for rank. However, there are always limits beyond which sanctions will be invoked.

People in societies without media learn these social requirements by a slow process. Older members in the society teach the young, or they acquire the needed knowledge by a process of trial and error, which can sometimes be painful. In a media society, however, an enormous variety of groups and social activities are *portrayed in mass communications*. These can serve as a rich source of learning for their viewers. Virtually every school child can explain who participates in a criminal trial, and how the police explain Miranda rights. They can sort out the basic role structure of a jail, or of a rich person's home where servants work. All can explain military ranks and the basic organization of a ship's crew at sea—even though few have ever actually participated in any such groups. They learn this information by viewing the depictions of such social groups on television, in the movies, or in other media. Thus, social expectations theory explains that extensive knowledge of norms, roles, ranks, and controls can be acquired through a process of *incidental learning*—by exposure to media portrayals of many aspects of social life and kinds of human groups.

An important caution is that the way that various groups are depicted in media—in movies, television programs, or even in print, may be misleading, inconsistent, or just plain wrong. Nevertheless, they often provide audiences with a source from which they can acquire beliefs (right or wrong) about the requirements of many kinds of groups that they may have to deal with at some point in their socially interdependent lives.

IMPLICATIONS OF LONG-TERM THEORIES

Both accumulation theory and social expectations theory aid in resolving the contradiction that we posed earlier in the present section. It remains entirely true that from a short-term perspective mass communications have very limited and very selective influences on individuals. There is every reason to be confident in that conclusion. However, repeated exposure to a consistent message can change people. It still may be less than dramatic for any particular person, but it does happen, and such changes add up. Eventually, among large populations repeatedly exposed to relatively consistent interpretations presented and corroborated across media, an accumulation of individual influences eventually results in significant change.

It must be recognized that the existence of such long-term influences has not been supported as yet by systematic research that fits the requirements of science. Methods for making clear, quantitative, and unambiguous observations of media influences on long-term changes in individuals or on society and culture have yet to be developed. Accumulation theory, and social expectations theory therefore, are relatively new and remain to be checked against reality through systematic research.

On the other hand, looking at long-term trends and changes in a society, and trying to see if they are possibly a product of the accumulation of small changes appears to be a promising strategy. Many such changes have taken place in the United States in which the mass media may indeed have played a part. Not cited in the above discussion of long-term changes is public support for the Civil Rights Movement, in which the new television medium repeatedly showed to the nation abuses of and discrimination against African Americans in education, voting, employment, housing,

A boy looks at a scantily clad woman on an Internet Web site, which reflects the continued public concern about questionable material available online and easily accessible to children. Commissions, conferences, and even laws have addressed this issue over recent years, building on earlier concerns about the impact on children of sexual material on television and in the movies.

and many other areas of daily life. No other medium had ever done that in quite the same visual way. When corrective legislation was finally passed by Congress, its remedies were not resisted by the majority of citizens. A similar case can be made about the war in Vietnam. At first, it was accepted by most Americans as a viable strategy for containing the (then) expansive Soviet Union. But as television brought dreadful scenes of the realities of that war into America's living rooms, a substantial segment of the population turned against it. Furthermore, the continuous news coverage of organized resistance to the war, including riots, college sit-ins, and other disturbances, showed that divisions over the war were seriously disrupting the country. All of this, prominently displayed on television, appeared to change the minds of many people. Over time, negative assessments accumulated to an extent that the president finally brought the war to an end.

Long-term perspectives do avoid the limitations of short-term research, but they also do not fit the model of empirical science. Much more precise methods for controlled observations need to be developed if this strategy is to pay off. But given these caveats, what has research actually accomplished in explaining the processes and effects of mass communication? One answer is that *it has shown the way to get the answers*. And furthermore, considerable progress has already been made. A major conclusion that can be drawn from what has been presented in this chapter is this: Using the logic and methods of science—suitably adapted for the study of mass communications—requires the following strategy: (1) conducting research that yields findings from which theories can be derived, (2) conducting further research that tests out in realistic settings the validity of the derived explanations, (3) modifying such explanations if new data show that they need change (or abandoning them if necessary), and (4) using such theories, when supported, as the best available explanations of how mass communications influence people.

What are the alternatives? Essentially they are: (1) reaching conclusions on the basis of preconceived political ideologies, without comparing those conclusions against facts, (2) using personal hunches or speculations to decide on the truth, or

(3) reaching conclusions based on the dictates of some religious theology or other set of *a priori* (previously accepted) conceptions of reality. For most scholars, intellectuals, and researchers who study the processes and effects of mass communication, these alternatives do not seem as attractive as the use of scientific research in seeking answers.

Chapter Review

- Before modern research methods were developed, many scholars speculated about the influence of the mass press on audiences. Lacking objectively assembled facts, and relying on hunches and opinions, each came to different, and often contradictory, views.

- The earliest research was guided by the assumptions of the magic bullet theory, explaining that the media have immediate, powerful, and universal effects. The findings of studies, such as those of influences of the movies on youth, seemed to support that idea.

- As research progressed and became more sophisticated, the assumptions of the magic bullet theory seemed less and less accurate as descriptions of reality. It was finally abandoned.

- Further research, such as that on women and the radio soap operas, revealed that audience members with different psychological and social characteristics actively select from available media content that will gratify needs or provide satisfactions.

- In a study of a presidential election campaign, it was found that media messages and influences often flow in a two-step process, first to opinion leaders who attend firsthand and then to others in the population. In election campaigns, media messages can activate voters and reinforce prior predispositions, but they seldom convert people from one party or position to another.

- Studies of televised violence do not support the idea that the medium routinely sends youths into the streets to become aggressive after attending to depictions of violence. Aggressive behavior is more closely linked to the personal and social characteristics of individuals. However, televised violence may raise the probability of aggressive acts among certain categories of youths.

- Theories, now supported by research, aid in understanding such processes as modeling of behavior that is depicted in the media, in which the actions performed by persons in media content serve as sources for adoption of particular forms of behavior.

- If a particular idea or situation is portrayed repeatedly, consistently, and uniformly by several media, it can have a long-term accumulated influence on individuals and the society as a whole.

- Another long-term influence is learning the social expectations regarding norms, roles, ranks, and controls in groups within which an individual plays no part, but to which the person is linked in a web of mutual social dependencies.

Notes and References

1. John Burroughs, "Some Natural History Doubts and Conclusions," *Harper's Monthly Magazine,* August 1904, pp. 360–364.
2. Charles Horton Cooley, *Social Organization* (New York: Charles Scribner's Sons, 1909), p. 82.
3. Cooley, *Social Organization,* p. 91.
4. Edgar Dale, *Children's Attendance at Motion Pictures* (New York: Arno Press, 1970), p. 73; originally published in 1935.
5. Hadley Cantril, *The Invasion from Mars: A Study in the Psychology of Panic* (Princeton, N.J.: Princeton University Press, 1940), p. 96.
6. Cantril, *The Invasion from Mars,* p. 98.
7. Howard Koch, *The Panic Broadcast: Portrait of an Event* (Boston: Little, Brown, 1970).
8. The full account of the study and its findings can be found in Cantril, *The Invasion from Mars.*
9. C. J. Hovland, A. A. Lumsdaine, and F. D. Sheffield, *Experiments on Mass Communication,* Vol. III of Studies of Social Psychology in World War II (New York: John Wiley and Sons, 1965).
10. Paul Lazarsfeld, Bernard Berelson, and Hazel Gaudet, *The People's Choice* (New York: Columbia University Press, 1948).
11. Herta Herzog, "What Do We Really Know About Daytime Serial Listeners," in Paul F. Lazarsfeld and Frank N. Stanton, *Radio Research, 1942–1943* (New York: Duell, Sloan and Pierce, 1944), pp. 3–33.
12. Bernard Berelson, "What Missing the Newspaper Means," in Paul F. Lazarsfeld and Frank N. Stanton, *Communications Research, 1948–1949* (New York: Harper and Brothers, 1949), pp. 111–129.
13. Berelson, "What Missing the Newspaper Means," p. 116.
14. Eleanor E. Maccoby, "Television: Its Impact on School Children," *Public Opinion Quarterly,* (1951), pp. 421–444; also Paul I. Lyness, "The Place of Mass Media in the Lives of Boys and Girls," *Journalism Quarterly,* 29 (1952), pp. 43–54.
15. Wilbur Schramm, Jack Lyle, and Edwin Parker, *Television in the Lives of Our Children* (Palo Alto, Calif.: Stanford University Press, 1961).
16. Each volume has this title with a different subtitle; the subtitles are *Media Content and Control* (Volume 1), *Television and Social Learning* (Volume 2), *Television and Adolescent Aggression* (Volume 3), *Television in Day-to-Day Life: Patterns of Use* (Volume 4), *Television's Effects: Further Explorations* (Volume 5). The various reports were prepared by George A. Comstock, John P. Murray, and Eli A. Rubenstein. They were published by the Government Printing Office, Washington, D.C., in 1971. The summary volume, *Television and Growing Up,* appeared in 1972.
17. A. Bandura and S. A. Ross, "Transmission of Aggression Through Imitation of Aggressive Models," *Journal of Abnormal and Social Psychology,* 63 (1961), pp. 575–582.
18. *Television and Growing Up,* p. 11.
19. Surgeon General's Scientific Advisory Committee on Television and Social Behavior, *Television and Growing Up: The Impact of Televised Violence.* Report to the Surgeon General, United States Public Health Service (Washington, D.C.: U.S. Government Printing Office, 1971), p. 11.
20. J. L. Steinfield, "TV Violence is Harmful," *The Reader's Digest,* April 1973, pp. 34–40.
21. *Television and Behavior: Ten Years of Scientific Progress and Implications for the Eighties* (Rockville, Md.: National Institute of Mental Health, 1982).
23. This particular theory has been developed for the purposes of this text and it does not appear by this name in the theory literature.
24. For an extended treatment of these features of social organization and how they shape behavior for the members of human groups see, "Social Organization," in Melvin L. DeFleur, et al., *Sociology: Human Society* (New York: Random House, 1984), pp. 72–104.

Chapter 16

ETHICS: ASSESSING CONTENT AND BEHAVIOR OF THE MEDIA

A friendship between reporter and source lasts only until it is profitable for one to betray the other.

Maureen Dowd, *New York Times*

AS THE QUOTATION ABOVE INDICATES, ACCU-RACY, AND THEREFORE *CREDIBILITY*, ARE VERY IMPORTANT TO JOURNALISTS AND OTHERS IN the media industries as well. Indeed, it is the single most vital factor for the survival and success of the communications industry. As our previous chapters have shown, those who present the news, public relations campaigns, advertising, and other media content want the public to believe that they are telling the truth and that they are transmitting their messages within ethical bounds. After all, professional communicators know only too well that if the information, opinion, and even entertainment they present to the public lacked believability it would quickly erode public confidence and they would lose their audience. Communications in a civilized society must not only be competent but also credible to be valuable to people. Thus, ethics is more than an arcane topic that is debated by religious authorities, do-gooders, and philosophers. It is a deeply practical concern across all of the communications industries. When ethical norms are violated, it upsets most professional communicators because it threatens their livelihood. In the interactive, modern era this continues to be important.

Media both cover and are influenced by judicial actions as in the Florida vote recounts following the 2000 presidential election. Not only did media closely attend to the post election maneuvering, but some news organizations (the *New York Times* and *Miami Herald* among them) even carried out their own recounts. Attorney William Scherer argues about the bad recount practices while he waves a local newspaper.

MEDIA-WIDE ETHICS WATCH

Much of the concern about media ethics is directed at the *content* of *communication* (the accuracy of a newspaper or magazine report, the selective editing of a television program, or whether a photograph is truly representative) or the *behavior of communicators,* especially journalists (whether they exercised professional standards or not). However, this is only a small part of the ethics dilemma for media industries. First, ethics is a vital matter for all of the communication functions—information, opinion, entertainment, and advertising/marketing. Second, all media industries confront the ethics issue, though some are noisier than others about it. This being said, most material on media ethics is associated with news, information, and journalism since they have a great importance to the functioning of society and the ability of people to communicate effectively with each other. However, unethical content and behavior in motion pictures, on Internet Web sites, or in the practice of public relations and advertising can have great impact in direct and indirect ways.[1]

Ethics is relevant to people across the media industries, not just information gatherers and purveyors. It makes a difference whether advertising salespersons represent themselves with honesty and integrity. The same is true for the heads of television networks, book publishing firms, news services, video production companies, and others. Whether the "media person" is an entry-level employee, a middle manager, or the chairman and chief executive, ethical behavior and ethical breaches can and do become matters of public concern. High profile television hosts like Jerry Springer and Jenny Jones whose "trash TV" programs can be tasteless and grotesque have found themselves in the heat of controversy when guests on their shows who felt wronged subsequently committed murder and other antisocial acts, which were said by some to be linked with the show. The media luminary Rupert Murdoch has been criticized for advancing the tabloid cause and cheapening media content. The publisher of the *Los Angeles Times* was accused of blending journalistic and advertising functions, breaking what some believe should be a "church-state" division by becoming involved in a profit sharing venture with a convention center.

Think of ways that the various media industries get involved in ethical disputes and controversies.

- **Motion pictures:** often rapped for distorting reality when treating real life and historical figures in films
- **Book publishers:** deciding to cancel a publishing contract because of outside pressures
- **Advertising:** exploiting the sexuality of children to sell products
- **Internet Web sites:** engaging in plagiarism and misuse of others' intellectual property
- **Public relations:** misrepresenting a client's background and record
- **Television:** sensationalizing and distorting events and issues

Of course, there are many more good and bad examples, and as we later note, there is a great public and professional preoccupation with ethics that has led to many ethical codes, standard setting, and professional groups eager to enhance media ethics.[2]

The issue of ethics affects not only mass communications but also everyone who is in public life. It is involved in matters of personal morality, campaign financing, and various conflicts of interest and other matters. Concern over ethics is also a lively one across American society. It is not uncommon for charges of breaches of ethics to be front-page news, whether the charge involves the government, a business, or any other institutions or individuals in our society. In the 1990s, critics worried about Internet privacy, plagiarism, Wall Street greed, government corruption, and hypocrisy in the lives of politicians, televangelists, and other public people.

Of course, scandals and other incidents that are spurred by ethics issues are rarely simple. It is not just a matter of right and wrong, but also discovery of the questionable act and public exposure. Sometimes that is the work of "whistleblowers," people inside an organization who make revelations, often at great personal risk. Sometimes, they do it for a noble cause, such as serving the public interest; other times they are angry and disgruntled employees who want to get back at their bosses. In still other instances, ethics violations are made public by political enemies of the people under fire.

While public interest in ethics varies over time, it has been exceptionally high since the 1990s, especially in the face of a Presidential impeachment. It seems, in fact, that there is no field that is exempt from ethical concerns, as various conferences and seminars have pointed out. Ethical conduct is on the docket in businesses, churches, schools, and other institutions. It is not unusual for a newsmagazine, like *Time, U.S. News & World Report,* or *Newsweek* to cover ethics as a beat and even to feature ethics as a cover story.

While public preoccupation with ethical issues across so many fields is rare, media ethics has long been a subject of public discussion. Some critics ridicule the idea that competitive and profit-driven media can operate within an ethical framework. But most knowledgeable people disagree, saying that no media system can exist very long without public confidence, and that requires accurate, honest, and believable communication. As we have explained in previous chapters, this does not mean that the media industries are always reliable or that all of them share the same values or ethical standards.[3]

DISTINGUISHING ETHICS AND LAW

Some people wonder why ethical breaches are not punishable by censure, fines, or prison sentences. The answer is that many questionable practices and apparent deceptions are not necessarily illegal. There are whole categories of criminal acts prohibited by law including murder, robbery, theft, and many others. There are also various civil offenses and torts (or hurtful acts) that are also unlawful because legislation was enacted so defining them and courts (including juries and judges) make determinations in cases involving individuals who are sued by someone claiming damages. A moral code evolves based on social custom, but does not necessarily cross the legal line where blame can be assessed. For example, it may be unpleasant if your neighbor is repeatedly shunning you and being rude and inconsiderate. This may hurt your feelings, but in most instances that's tough and you have no legal course of action to say otherwise. If, on the other hand, your neighbor posts a large sign denouncing you and accusing you of a crime you did not commit, you can sue for libel and if you win your case, collect damages.

For the media, there are some acts that are clearly illegal such as breaking into an office to steal papers, deliberate misrepresentation by claiming to be someone else, engaging in insider trading in the stock market, and other acts that are usually thought unnecessary by courts in gathering the news. Sometimes such instances

At one end of the continuum of discussions of media ethics are the sensational headlines of the supermarket tabloids, which focus on entertainers and other celebrities. These publications are in stark contrast to stricter standards of mainstream media.

also lead to ethical disputes. For example, a few years ago, the *Chicago Sun-Times* bought a bar called The Mirage and operated it to have a window on various city inspectors receiving payoffs and committing other criminal acts. The newspaper, in fact, misrepresented itself to gather news.

In another case involving unethical methods (lying on a job application and use of hidden cameras), ABC News's "Primetime Live" program exposed the food handling practices of the Food Lion grocery chain, but a North Carolina court fined ABC News a whopping $5.5 million. Even though ABC News found unhealthy and improper practices in the food stores, the jury was offended that the reporters misrepresented themselves in getting the story, pretending to be ordinary employees rather than reporters. Still others like Mike Barnacle, the former *Boston Globe* columnist, were fired for fictional portrayals, simply making up information and representing it as fact.

About the same time, a news organization in New York City considered buying a racehorse to get a window on the role of organized crime in horse racing and even presented the idea to law enforcement officials. The idea was eventually dropped.

Another perplexing case that led to spirited debates about media ethics was that of Richard Jewell, a security guard accused in the 1996 Olympic bombing in Atlanta. Jewell was a suspect fingered by the FBI and other law enforcement officials who also tipped off the press. While never formally accused of the crime, he was hounded by the media and law enforcement officials and subject to a flood of negative publicity. Eventually, charges against him were dropped and he sorrowfully asked, "How can I recover my reputation?" Constitutional lawyers doubted that Jewell had much of a case against the press, which based their reports on police and FBI tips, but nevertheless most people in various surveys believed that Jewell was wronged. Eventually, NBC News and CNN settled out of court with the suspect. Other litigation went on for years.

In the Jewell case, wide publicity was given to apparently false accusations and the issue was whether the press acted too zealously and recklessly in emphasizing the suspicion against the security guard without also balancing such claims against his rights—and consistent denials. The media, according to Lawrence Grossman, a former president of NBC News, has trouble "saying it is sorry for much of anything. Reporters just don't like to admit that they are wrong—even when they are shown to be so after the fact."[4]

The Jewell case was especially illustrative because, initially, Jewell was thought to be a hero whose bravery was trumpeted in news stories and interviews. Then, when he was suspected of the bombing, press coverage emphasized the accusation and "hounded him like an animal," in his words. Jewell and his mother couldn't leave their Atlanta home without encountering a sea of cameras and microphones and shouting reporters.

Whether the Jewell case represented a breach of ethics has been the subject of many seminars, articles, and television debates—with no clear answers.

Early Childhood   Content may be suitable for persons ages 3 and older. Contains no material that parents would find inappropriate.

 Mature   Content may be suitable for persons ages 17 and older. May contain mature sexual themes or more intense violence or language.

 Everyone   Content may be suitable for persons ages 6 and older. May contain minimal violence and some comic mischief or crude language.

 Adults Only   Content suitable only for adults. May include graphic depictions of sex and/or violence. Not intended for persons under the age of 18.

 Teen   Content may be suitable for persons ages 13 and older. May contain violent content, mild or strong language, and/or suggestive themes.

 Rating Pending   Product has been submitted to the ESRB and is awaiting final rating.

Please be advised that the ESRB rating icons, "EC", "E", "T", "M", "AO" and "RP" are copyrighted works and certification marks owned by the Interactive Digital Software Association and the Entertainment Software Rating Board and may only be used with their permission and authority. Under no circumstances may the rating icons be self-applied or used in connection with any product that has not been rated by the ESRB. For information regarding whether a product has been rated by the ESRB, please call the ESRB at 1-800-771-3772 or visit www.esrb.org. For information regarding licensing issues, please call the IDSA at (212) 223-8936.

GROWING CONCERN OVER MEDIA ETHICS

Consumer ratings offer qualitative judgments for parents and others interested in media fare of all kinds. The Entertainment Software Rating Board, for example, offers rating symbols that help parents, children, and young adults select computer games that are appropriate for their use.

As a general field, ethics is a branch of philosophy that tries to promote good values and goodwill as opposed to mean-spirited or venal behavior. Some critics feel that the issue of media ethics is too broad and illusive to have much meaning. For example, no unified field of media ethics offers rules or standards that apply to all media fields. What is taboo for a newspaper reporter may be business as usual for an advertising salesperson from the same organization. Ethics, say critics, is simply a matter of personal integrity. This ties the question of ethics for the media and media organizations to personal standards of forthright, honest, and competent behavior.

Others say that ethics is a collective concept, and that corporations, networks, and newspaper publishing chains have a responsibility to see that they are honest and competent. The value of this may seem obvious, but in a society where business is often described as "dog eat dog," the idea that the media industry should be socially responsible and a good corporate citizen to the public might be dismissed as platitudinous. Indeed, some argue that the phrase "media ethics" is an oxymoron—a contradiction in terms. The reason it is not is that media organizations and their people clearly have a self-interest in being ethical, especially in the sense of being moral and credible.

Ethical behavior in a general sense is not hard to define. It simply means that people should not lie, steal, cheat, or commit other antisocial acts. Ethics is doing what is "right," but the problem is that "right" is defined differently by different people. Thus, the need exists for serious attention to media ethics in a society that is increasingly concerned about the ethics of all occupational groups and professionals, whether they are lawyers, doctors, architects, or journalists. A commitment to basic ethical standards is what binds us together as a society, distinguishing us as socially responsible as opposed to self-serving individuals.

All of the media and their supporting systems—including the news, book publishing, movies, cable, newsletters, advertising, public relations, and other enterprises—are governed by general business ethics. Moreover, most of them also have

Controversial figures often push the frontiers of free speech, as was the case with *Hustler* publisher Larry Flynt, whose sexually provocative magazine has often had him in the courts—and even made him the subject of a movie. Whatever his views and practices, he is regarded as a hero of the First Amendment by many civil libertarians.

codes of ethics, standards of conduct, and good ethical practices for their employees. Most people who work in the media, ranging from financial writers to videographers, agree to abide by certain standards or rules that embody ethical values. Most, however, include few explicit ethical values beyond those taught generally in the family, in churches, or in schools.[5]

At one time, some areas of communication were virtually exempt from ethics. For example, people did not apply the same standards of fact and verification to advertising and public relations that they did to newspapers and magazines, arguing that advocates should have license to make the case for their clients to the point of exaggeration. Whether justified or not, people tended to discount a "public relations approach" or self-serving political or ideological appeals. Similarly, religious observers proclaiming their faith were not necessarily expected to be fair and impartial.

Now that is changing, partly because of the blurring and merging of the various functions of the media. For example, it is no longer possible to distinguish easily between informational news and entertainment, for example. News programs increasingly use entertainment devices, dramatic language, and simulations of probable events, even if they did not occur that way. A good story sometimes carries the day, even if it is not true. Thus, ethics are sometimes a casualty in the competitive struggle for a good story.

Sometimes, careless attention to ethics brings confusion as to just what constitutes news. Through the 1990s, electronic media executives and critics worried about the injection of entertainment values into the news, especially as tabloid TV shows won viewer allegiance. At the same time, a respected poll indicated that many Americans had trouble distinguishing news and entertainment fare on television. And no wonder, in 1999 there was a raft of firings—when magazine and newspaper journalists were caught plagiarizing or fabricating information.

Similarly, it is difficult to sort out when a particular article or program is news, entertainment, opinion, or even advertising. The blurring of lines between the traditional and modern functions of the media is creating an ethical dilemma. Under conventional "rules," there are clear ethical definitions of what news is supposed to be. It is clearly to be separated from opinion. Opinion has great latitude to do and say what it will, though there is typically a standard of "intellectual honesty" applied. Entertainment fare also has wide latitude and may engage in almost any kind of fiction. As these forms merge, the role and function of ethics appears to get lost in the confusion.

Comic artists and editorial cartoonists have often faced the problem of crossing the line between information and entertainment. Comic strips like "Doonesbury" have so enraged some people such as the late Frank Sinatra that lawsuits have been filed to protest humorous commentary. Such fare has increasingly been subject to libel suits, although ridicule is the basis for even offensive humor.

As new media industries evolve, ranging from business information services to pay-per-view TV fare and home shopping services, the question of what is ethical often arises. CNN financial commentator Lou Dobbs was criticized for appearing in a promotional tape for a brokerage house. Some critics believed that Dobbs violated the public trust he had as a financial commentator and newscaster on the cable network. This was the tip of the iceberg about the extent to which reporters should mix their roles. In the film, *The People vs. Larry Flynt,* Donna Hanover, a New York television anchor and commentator who was married to New York City's Mayor Rudolph Giuliani, appeared in the film, which was said by some to undermine family values by glorifying Flynt, the controversial publisher of *Hustler* magazine. Other questions about reporters' ethics and independence arose in articles in the *New Yorker* by media critic Ken Auletta and in an important book by author and editor James Fallows. At issue: celebrity reporters taking large speaking fees from businesses, trade associations, colleges and universities, and others. To Auletta and Fallows, the practice is clearly wrong and needs public exposure. Others say that as long as the reporter's employer knows, there is no problem. The question, as we will see later in this chapter, has to do with conflicts of interest. Does a reporter breach his or her credibility by taking fees on the side as a celebrity and public speaker, while still maintaining a position of independence in covering the news? Some say yes, others say no, not unless there is a clear conflict of interest. That is, say, a reporter speaking for a fee at a trade association meeting and then covering news about that same group later. Some highly compensated reporters who are on the lecture circuit maintain that they never cover the organizations they speak for, but others are not so sure, arguing that many issues these days are commingled and hard to separate out.

SPECIAL PRIVILEGES, SPECIAL RESPONSIBILITIES

Are we being unreasonable when we demand that our press be fair and act ethically? The answer to that question is less clear than many might suppose. By consulting legal authorities, one may learn a good deal about the range and scope of the *rights* of news organizations and the people who work for them. First, there is the general franchise for press freedom laid out in the Bill of Rights, specifically the First Amendment. Then, there are rights set out in state constitutions, statutes, and various court decisions. Far less common is the discussion of the *duties* and *responsibilities* of our protected press and mass media. In fact, in 1947, when the famed Hutchins Commission on Freedom of the Press suggested that the press has such obligations, the press protested strongly and denounced the commission's report.

The Hutchins Commission was a privately financed effort to look carefully at freedom of the press in America, especially in the years immediately following World War II. The Commission, made up of philosophers, legal scholars, and other intellectual and cultural leaders, wanted publicly to encourage a system of expression that was responsible to society at large, yet free to practice without constraints. It made recommendations for the government, the press, and the public, none of them binding, but all intriguing as statements of social criticism and as a plea for ethically sensitive media. Among other things, the Commission proposed *press councils* made up of responsible citizens that would monitor the press and provide feedback to the media and other mass communication agencies. Over the years, the Hutchins Commission's report has gained respect and is now regarded as one of the most important documents in the history of American media. At the same time, it has no official standing.

Robert Maynard Hutchins, the brilliant chancellor of the University of Chicago in his thirties, chaired the Commission on Freedom of the Press and released an important 1947 report, *A Free and Responsible Press,* which is a cornerstone for media ethics and responsibility even today.

Under the First Amendment to the Constitution of the United States, there is no requirement that the media be fair, responsible, or accurate. The courts have stated this quite explicitly, yet increasingly there is a higher standard of media performance evident in libel cases and other legal action against the mass and specialized media. It is not uncommon these days for those suing the press to bring expert witnesses into court to testify that a particular story or program did or did not meet "normal professional standards." Although there is no accepted norm for such standards, courts have looked to witnesses for guidance. In fact, some feel that they may write an ethical code for media institutions, perhaps without constitutional authority.

BEYOND THE FIRST AMENDMENT

If the mass media derive their legal authority from the First Amendment, they derive their moral authority from holding the public trust. From the beginning, the media have claimed to play two roles: that of the *social conscience* of society or a representative of the people in a nonlegalistic sense, and that of a *profit-making* business that needs to survive to fulfill its first obligation. Newspapers have long cultivated this kind of self-image. In contrast, because of government regulation, broadcasting and other electronic media have been regarded as less free than the print media and therefore required to serve the public "interest, convenience and necessity," as stated in the Federal Communications Act. However, just where legal requirements end and ethical ones begin is not clear.

Other media institutions, such as advertising and public relations, have also laid claim to moral authority and assert that they pursue ethical ends in their work, although this claim may rest on shaky ground and is often disputed. Media support services, like wire services and syndicates, have generally been guided by the standards of the news media. Their value is in the quality of the work they produce, whether it is accurate news reports or entertainment matter such as comics, columns, and puzzles. Some media institutions, such as newspapers and newsmagazines, regard themselves as having more elevated ethical standards and concerns than their advertising agencies or political public relations consultants.

THE LONG STRUGGLE FOR PROFESSIONALISM

Institutional media ethics have evolved considerably since the press of the nation's early years—a time sometimes called the dark ages of American journalism. In Chapter 3, we saw that the early press was often scurrilous, making unwarranted partisan attacks on political figures with little regard for truth or accuracy. Later, a sensational press played on the public's morbid curiosity to stir up the audience and attract readers. The press was known to run hoaxes and engage in deliberate deception. For example, even Benjamin Franklin, sometimes in a tongue-in-cheek manner, made up interesting characters to illuminate the columns of his newspaper. We mentioned the famous "moon hoax" of 1835, in which the *New York Sun* claimed that an astronomer in South Africa had observed lifelike creatures on the moon through his telescope.

Hoaxes continue to the present day and are sometimes transmitted on the Internet where instant communication is not always checked carefully. In 1996, journalist Pierre Salinger accused federal agents of covering up details of a major airline crash based on an Internet report that later proved to be false.

As the press became more responsible in the late nineteenth century, editors urged dedication to the public interest and proclaimed statements of noble purpose. Although some of these statements were platitudes that would have been hard to enforce, they did establish the tradition of a public-spirited rather than a self-serving press. Eventually, it was generally believed that the newspaper and magazine press had obligations of fairness and impartiality that went far beyond those of typical businesses. While there was no enforcement clause for such assumptions, they were later supported by codes of ethics and books extolling the idea of a virtuous press crusading to rectify wrongs in a world where corruption and foul play were rampant. Journalism organizations ranging from publishers' and editors' societies to education groups also proclaimed concern for ethics and public accountability.

THE RISE OF MIXED-MEDIA CULTURE

Two leading commentators, Bill Kovach and Tom Rosensteil, have argued that the examples cited above are only the beginning of a blurring and merging of media functions, thus creating a new mixed-media culture. They say that beginning with the massive coverage of O. J. Simpson's double-murder trial and continuing through the Monica Lewinsky–Bill Clinton scandal, there was a convergence of media trends involving commercial exploitation and sensationalism. As they put it in their 1999 book *Warp Speed: America in the Age of Mixed Media,* the post–O. J. media culture is:

> A newly diversified mass media in which the cultures of entertainment, infotainment, argument, and analysis in tabloid and mainstream press not only work side by side but intermingle and merge. It is a culture in which Matt Drudge sits alongside William Safire on "Meet the Press" and Ted Koppel talks about the nuances of oral sex, in which "Hard Copy" and CBS News jostle for camera position outside the federal grand jury to hear from a special prosecutor.[6]

Although these observations are hardly new, these commentators and others feel that big media with its commercial interests in promoting movies alongside books and newspapers are drivers for this effect. They and others also worry that the media are cheapened in the public mind when newscasters advertise products or one-time spin-doctors and spokesmen are subsequently employed as news analysts and commentators. For example, George Stephanopoulos, former President Clinton's one-time communications director, and Tony Blankley, who had the same duties for Newt Gingrich, landed top jobs with networks, thus crossing the line between media manipulator and media practitioner. This again, is nothing new as political figures and media people have often moved back and forth. The difference now is that the public gets cynical about matters of credibility.

The new mixed-media culture is said to have five characteristics:[7]

- A neverending news cycle makes journalism less complete: The twenty-four hour demands of cable, television, and Web sites often lead to sloppy and incomplete reporting—fragments rather than whole stories.
- Sources are gaining power over journalists: People with self-interests and axes to grind offer more information with strings attached and media rush to publicize rumors, leads, etc.
- There are no more gatekeepers: This is a bit of an exaggeration, but there is less editing, fact checking, etc., than was formerly the case and Web reports often have none.
- Argument is overwhelming reporting: An argument culture has emerged and often drowns out factual information on various cable news programs and commentaries that are more like shouting matches than reasoned presentations.
- The "blockbuster mentality": The media love big stories that dominate the news for days, even weeks and months, whether the O. J. Simpson trial, the deaths of Princess Diana or John F. Kennedy, Jr., or the Clinton scandals. This massive overcoverage again drowns out other legitimate news.

The implications of these and other factors on news and entertainment fare in the United States and globally are significant. There is a tendency to do "made for TV" fictional movies that often run head-on into public life and public affairs. One such example was a TV movie in 2000 about the Kennedy women that was actually delayed so as not to intrude on the 2000 Senate campaign of Edward Kennedy. Famous trials and controversies are quickly fictionalized and exploited, thus confusing the public and raising questions about the role of communication media in society. There are many points of view in play on these topics from critics who scold media owners for their callous exploitation to others who believe that this is just the price of freedom of expression.

John F. Kennedy, Jr., was a celebrity of popular culture from his earliest childhood as the son of the President of the United States and later a sex symbol and editor of his own *George* magazine before his untimely and heavily covered death in an airplane crash in 1999.

Ethical expectations and demands are crossing national boundaries as a result of the international concern about honesty, ethics, and accurate information. For example, although China's political news remains highly suspect, its financial information is now more accurate, for the international market expects and demands it and no market economy can function on unreliable information. This being the case, the issue of ethics is not only here to stay, but will probably play a greater role in all kinds of media—not only in conventional news media, but in new media that under earlier standards might not have been held accountable.

According to many commentators, media ethics really refers to journalistic ethics, or the moral conduct and behavior of journalists doing their work as news gatherers, editors, and disseminators of information for the larger society. Journalists are expected to produce reliable and believable information gathered under scrupulously honest conditions and checked along the way for accuracy. On occasion, an ethical breach in journalism receives publicity. For example, *TV Guide* once deliberately printed a misleading photograph of Oprah Winfrey's head on actress Ann Margaret's body. Realizing that misrepresentation and deception are almost universally regarded as unethical behavior and that the photo might jeopardize *TV Guide*'s credibility as a serious and respected publication, the magazine later recanted.

In the 1990s, at the outset of the O. J. Simpson case, *Time* magazine doctored a photo of Simpson by darkening his skin color to make him look more sinister. The result was a debate over whether this visual alteration was an act of racism, something always unethical, if not illegal. This is what journalism professor Paul Lester calls "images that injure," pictorial stereotypes in the media. In a book by the same name, Lester and several contributors decry racial, gender, age, and physical and sexual orientation stereotypes that cause psychological pain, ridicule, or embarrassment to individuals and groups.[8] Often, allegations of racism or sexism are at the root of many ethical dilemmas for the media. Here, perception is often deemed more important than the motivation of the communicator. Thoughtlessness is more often a greater culprit than recklessness or deliberate efforts to denigrate others through images—still photos, moving images, cartoons, line drawings, and others. However, this ethical concern often runs head on into satire and humor. Some depictions—visual and verbal—by cartoonists, humorists, and others are meant to be funny or ironic, but still have the potential of offending someone someday.

Closely connected to this debate is the complex and continuing controversy over what is called "political correctness," an idea that suggests there are appropriate ideas acceptable to most of society. This suggests that attacks on people for their race, gender, sexual orientation, disability, or other characteristics are out of line. Some argue that, carried to the extreme, this view thwarts free speech, however hurtful or inappropriate that speech may be. Another view suggests that political correctness carried to an extreme is counterproductive for a free society. Richard Bernstein, a *New York Times* reporter, in his book *Dictatorship of Virtue*, argues that multiculturalism often insists on adherence to one view "with truth or fairness often falling victim to the demands of ethnic or racial self-esteem."[9]

As the foregoing examples illustrate and as we have shown elsewhere in this book, certain controls influence what the media do and how they do it. These controls include economic, political, and legal factors, but they also include cultural and philosophical forces. Media ethics is one such force.[10] The manner and method that the various media of communication use to conduct their business and carry on discourse with the rest of society are often under scrutiny.

Here the media do not stand alone, but are seen in the context of social responsibility in general. Concern with ethics and ethical behavior has focused on business, government, religion, news media, and other institutions. Generally, then, some of the growing concern over media ethics has come from outside critics. However, some has also come from internal sources who want to elevate and advance the work of newspapers, magazines, radio, television and cable, databases, advertising agencies, public relations firms, and other media organizations or support services.

As our discussion has shown, media ethics is not an obscure or irrelevant topic, but something that arises daily as citizens observe the way media institutions relate to their communities as participants, observers, and critics. Ethical dilemmas also arise over the content of the media—whether it is entertainment, news, opinion, or advertising—as well as over the behavior of media people. In a simple sense, ethical choices are between right and wrong, good and bad, and matters that are genuinely in the public interest or harmful to the common good.

Complicating the problem of examining and understanding media ethics is the fact that as simple as choices may seem at first, they typically are not. Ethical decisions involve complex human relationships and often pit values cherished by the media against those preferred by other people. The media are concerned with communicating to the rest of society, whether in news stories that emphasize conflict, in opinion journals that feature debates, or on entertainment programs that often promote consensus and reinforce values. Different media obviously have different purposes, yet most want to be considered ethical. Sometimes though, public exposure involves information about a person or organization that has heretofore been protected from outside scrutiny. In such instances, a person's right to privacy conflicts with the media's interest in public disclosure. There is often no legal issue here, but an ethical issue—a matter of personal choice between doing what is good for society versus doing what is good for an individual.

MEDIA CRITICISM AND MEDIA ETHICS

If there has been a consistent thread promoting media ethics over the years, it has been media *criticism,* which dates back to the nineteenth century. Critics typically charged the press with violating common decency and obscuring the truth. Many American presidents have criticized the press for what they regarded as irresponsible reporting. For example, during the period of muckraking (Chapter 3), magazine journalists, just after the turn of the century, crusaded to clean up sweatshops and reform corrupt businesses and governments. Soon afterward, the press confronted considerable criticism led by President Theodore Roosevelt, who thought muckraking journalism was far too negative for the nation. Press critics, such as Upton Sinclair, began to censure the press for its internal inconsistencies and conflicts of interest, and even went so far as to claim that the press itself was corrupt and deliberately poisoning information. Much of this reproach concerned ethics, for rarely was it suggested that the transgressions of the press were illegal, only unethical.

Journalism schools, established in the years before World War I, often had professional practice courses that promoted ideal or ethical behavior. The public outcry over ethics also led to a variety of codes and voluntary guidelines for the media. (The "Printer's Ink" statutes aimed at deceptive advertising mentioned in Chapter 11 were one set.) The American Society of Newspaper Editors issued the "Canons of Journalism" in 1923. This was followed by similar codes promulgated by the Newspaper Association of America, the Associated Press Managing Editors, various broadcast organizations and stations, including the CBS network and public relations organizations. Over a fifty-year period from the 1920s to the 1970s, the bulk of American media developed ethical codes. Most were strictly voluntary but some were part of the work rules of media organizations. Employees who violate the codes of their organization today may be disciplined or even fired.

A DOUBLE STANDARD

Media criticism that centers on institutional, individual, or content-related ethics generally distinguishes between the editorial and business functions of the media. Editorial employees were once expected to avoid conflicts of interest, check their

Society of Professional Journalists Code of Ethics

Preamble

Members of the Society of Professional Journalists believe that public enlightenment is the forerunner of justice and the foundation of democracy. The duty of the journalist is to further those ends by seeking truth and providing a fair and comprehensive account of events and issues. Conscientious journalists from all media and specialties strive to serve the public with thoroughness and honesty. Professional integrity is the cornerstone of a journalist's credibility.

Members of the Society share a dedication to ethical behavior and adopt this code to declare the Society's principles and standards of practice.

Seek Truth and Report It

Journalists should be honest, fair and courageous in gathering, reporting and interpreting information. Journalists should:

- Test the accuracy of information from all sources and exercise care to avoid inadvertent error. Deliberate distortion is never permissible.
- Diligently seek out subjects of news stories to give them the opportunity to respond to allegations of wrongdoing.
- Identify sources whenever feasible. The public is entitled to as much information as possible on sources' reliability.
- Always question sources' motives before promising anonymity. Clarify conditions attached to any promise made in exchange for information. Keep promises.
- Make certain that headlines, news teases and promotional material, photos, video, audio, graphics, sound bites and quotations do not misrepresent. They should not oversimplify or highlight incidents out of context.
- Never distort the content of news photos or video. Image enhancement for technical clarity is always permissible. Label montages and photo illustrations.
- Avoid misleading re-enactments or staged news events. If re-enactment is necessary to tell a story, label it.
- Avoid undercover or other surreptitious methods of gathering information except when traditional open methods will not yield information vital to the public. Use of such methods should be explained as part of the story.
- Never plagiarize.
- Tell the story of the diversity and magnitude of the human experience boldly, even when it is unpopular to do so.
- Examine their own cultural values and avoid imposing those values on others.
- Avoid stereotyping by race, gender, age, religion, ethnicity, geography, sexual orientation, disability, physical appearance or social status.
- Support the open exchange of views, even views they find repugnant.
- Give voice to the voiceless; official and unofficial sources of information can be equally valid.
- Distinguish between advocacy and news reporting. Analysis and commentary should be labeled and not misrepresent fact or context.

- Distinguish news from advertising and shun hybrids that blur the lines between the two.
- Recognize a special obligation to ensure that the public's business is conducted in the open and that government records are open to inspection.

Minimize Harm

Ethical journalists treat sources, subjects and colleagues as human beings deserving of respect. Journalists should:

- Show compassion for those who may be affected adversely by news coverage. Use special sensitivity when dealing with children and inexperienced sources or subjects.
- Be sensitive when seeking or using interviews or photographs of those affected by tragedy or grief.
- Recognize that gathering and reporting information may cause harm or discomfort. Pursuit of the news is not a license for arrogance.
- Recognize that private people have a greater right to control information about themselves than do public officials and others who seek power, influence or attention. Only an overriding public need can justify intrusion into anyone's privacy.
- Show good taste. Avoid pandering to lurid curiosity.
- Be cautious about identifying juvenile suspects or victims of sex crimes.
- Be judicious about naming criminal suspects before the formal filing of charges.
- Balance a criminal suspect's fair trial rights with the public's right to be informed.

Act Independently

Journalists should be free of obligation to any interest other than the public's right to know. Journalists should:

- Avoid conflicts of interest, real or perceived.
- Remain free of associations and activities that may compromise integrity or damage credibility.
- Refuse gifts, favors, fees, free travel and special treatment, and shun secondary employment, political involvement, public office and service in community organizations if they compromise journalistic integrity.
- Disclose unavoidable conflicts.
- Be vigilant and courageous about holding those with power accountable.
- Deny favored treatment to advertisers and special interests and resist their pressure to influence news coverage.
- Be wary of sources offering information for favors or money; avoid bidding for news.

Be Accountable

Journalists are accountable to their readers, listeners, viewers, and each other. Journalists should:

- Clarify and explain news coverage and invite dialogue with the public over journalistic conduct.
- Encourage the public to voice grievances against the news media.
- Admit mistakes and correct them promptly.
- Expose unethical practice of journalists and the news media.
- Abide by the same high standards to which they hold others.

Web sites that focus on media ethics are many and cut across all of the individual media industries for the benefit of executives, employees, and the public. The *OJR* (for *Online Journalism Review*), produced at the Annenberg School for Communication at the University of Southern California, is a lively digital media review with frequent assessments of ethical and unethical performance and content.

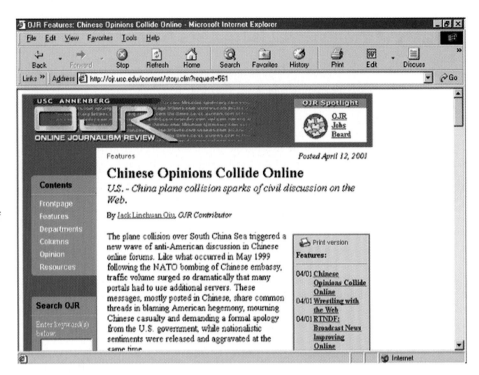

work for accuracy, and act as professionals at all times. Typically, this meant keeping a distance from such newsmakers as politicians and not mixing one's personal views with the news. On the other hand, publishers and other business-side personnel faced no such prohibitions. They could seek public office and otherwise participate in community affairs without being considered guilty of conflict of interest or unprofessional behavior.

This situation would later be challenged, largely unsuccessfully, by such scholar-critics as Philip Meyer, who wrote a book titled *Ethical Journalism* that urged an institutional model for media ethics wherein all employees would have the same high standards. To Meyer, it was unthinkable that reporters and editors should be held to one standard for conflict of interest, while advertising managers, publishers, and others were not.[11]

As noted earlier, most of what is written about media ethics has to do with the behavior of media people or the content they produce. On occasion, the owners of the media also come under fire. That was the basis of much of the criticism of media critic George Seldes who from the 1920s to the 1990s railed against corrupt ownerships. The ethics of a media baron was at issue when a controversy arose over a $5 million book advance that was offered to former House Speaker Newt Gingrich by a publisher owned by Rupert Murdoch, who was lobbying Congress in connection with reform of the Communications Act. Gingrich eventually turned down the advance as criticism mounted. Hillary Clinton faced similar criticism for an $8 million advance in 2000, prior to entering the U.S. Senate. The Hutchins Commission Report, whose fiftieth anniversary was commemorated at conferences at the University of Illinois and Southern Methodist University in 1997, specifically pointed to the transgressions of owners like William Randolph Hearst and Frank Gannett.

At times virtually all media functions are scrutinized for ethical breaches, whether this involves a movie that misrepresents or overstates (for example, Oliver Stone's films about John F. Kennedy and Richard Nixon); a radio talk show host who is accused of lying; a rock video that panders to sexual misbehavior; a novelist who appropriates the work of others; or an Internet hacker who perpetuates a cruel hoax.

THE LINK TO INDIVIDUALS AND CONTENT

Media ethics is rarely concerned with abstract institutional behavior, but is instead tied to the "blood and guts" of daily decision making and various disputes that later come to the attention of the public. Although journalistic inventions and fakery are not unknown in our history, the public was shocked in 1980 when it learned that *Washington Post* reporter Janet Cooke had faked a gripping story about "little Jimmy," an eight-year-old heroin addict in Washington, D.C.'s African-American community. No such person existed. Cooke claimed that it was a "composite." To its considerable embarrassment, the *Post* (which won a Pulitzer Prize for the story) had to admit the deception. The prize was returned, and the newspaper, to its credit, launched a major internal investigation of the ruse and released its findings to the public.

Later, the then-existing National News Council, with a grant from the Twentieth Century Fund, produced a book about the "little Jimmy" controversy and its impact on American journalism and journalistic ethics in general. The deception shook the roots of American journalism as people worried about the accuracy of stories in the press and the ethical standards of reporters. Commentators scrutinized the press's institutional responsibility to prevent this kind of behavior in the future, calling for routine personnel procedures and checking of resumes (which had also been faked in part).

The same issue of public deception arose years later when ABC News aired a piece of news footage allegedly showing a U.S. diplomat passing secrets to the Russians. The grainy and authentic-looking footage was actually staged and featured actors as reporters! The story was based on allegations in news reports, but anchor Peter Jennings later apologized to the American people for the newscast, which was a deliberate deception. By the 1990s, simulations on network news were mostly a thing of the past, though they are still common on other TV shows, especially in tabloid fare.

Of course, the fakery of Benjamin Franklin differs greatly from that of ABC News or Matt Drudge because news standards and social values have changed since the age of the early printing press. The press was a primitive instrument in Franklin's day; now it is a large and powerful enterprise that has considerable influence over all of its information, opinion, and entertainment functions.

DIMENSIONS OF ETHICS FOR THE MEDIA

Typically, media ethics have centered on three major issues: (1) *accuracy* and *fairness* in reporting and other activities, (2) the *behavior of reporters,* especially in relation to their sources, and (3) avoidance of *conflicts of interest.*

ACCURACY AND FAIRNESS

It is often said that the first rule of journalism is "accuracy, accuracy, accuracy." Burton Benjamin, a longtime producer at CBS News, got caught up in an accuracy and fair play conflict in the 1980s when CBS was accused of deliberately distorting information about the Vietnam War and General William Westmoreland in a news documentary.

Criticism from outside circles as well as media people themselves was so fierce that CBS executives commissioned Benjamin to investigate the charges and deliver a report. He found his network colleagues guilty of violating their own stated (and written) news standards and later wrote a book about the incident titled *Fair Play.*[12]

Insider reports like Benjamin's (which are rare) and other critiques of media performance, both good and bad, constitute a kind of common law of ethics. For almost every ethical dilemma in the press, there is a history and context, but unfortunately the press has little "institutional memory" and often ignores the past or "reinvents the wheel."

THE BEHAVIOR OF REPORTERS

The second area of ethical concern, the behavior of reporters, has to do with an important aspect of professionalism—whether reporters and other media personnel conduct themselves honestly and with integrity. This usually means being honest and aboveboard to *sources* about the purposes of gathering information. For many years, it was thought to be unethical to misrepresent oneself deliberately to obtain information—for example, by claiming to be someone else such as a lawyer or police officer. Yet, the precise relationship that should exist between journalists and sources has never been fully understood or established. In a now famous article in the *New Yorker,* Janet Malcolm blasted her fellow journalist Joe McGinniss for misleading a famous news source, Dr. Jeffrey MacDonald, who was convicted of murdering his wife and children. As Malcolm wrote:

> Every journalist who is not too stupid or too full of himself to notice what is going on knows that what he does is morally indefensible. He is a kind of confidence man, preying on people's vanity, ignorance, or loneliness, gaining their trust and betraying them without remorse. Like the credulous widow who wakes up one day to find the charming young man and all her savings gone, so the consenting subject of a piece of nonfiction writing learns—when the article or book appears—his hard lesson. Journalists justify their treachery in various ways according to their temperaments. The more pompous talk about freedom of speech and "the public's right to know"; the least talented talk about Art; the seemliest murmur about earning a living.[13]

The cause for Malcolm's agitation was that she felt McGinniss had convinced MacDonald that he was his friend and would actually do a book that was beneficial for his case. The issue of whether a journalist seeking full cooperation from a news source is prone to deceiving the source was widely discussed at the time. People joined from both sides, some condemning McGinniss and others accusing Malcolm of having committed in the past similar breaches herself. Malcolm's observations led to a lively nationwide debate in the journalistic community wherein the obligations, if any, of reporters to sources were thoroughly discussed. However, there was no clear resolution.

CONFLICT OF INTEREST

Conflict of interest is a third area of ethical concern. The term typically refers to engaging in activity that compromises one's integrity in the performance of one's professional or public duties. It is, for example, difficult to be engaged in partisan politics while writing impartially about politics. By the same token, media people have been urged to avoid cronyism, nepotism, and other conflicts that can compro-

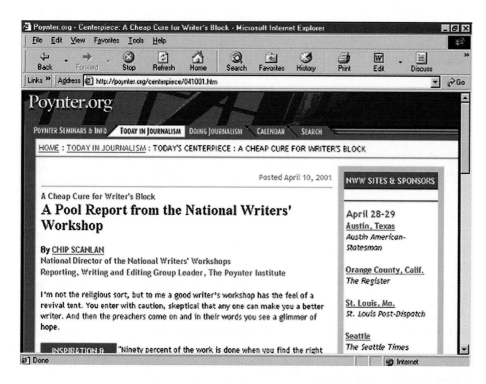

The respected Poynter Institute in St. Petersburg, Florida, offers regular instruction and information services as noted on its Web site, which also includes the popular Jim Romenesko media gossip home page.

mise their integrity or give the appearance of such compromise. A closely related area has been *checkbook journalism,* wherein news organizations pay sources to give interviews. This is a violation of journalistic norms, although there are times when media people do it and defend the practice. In the case of news people, conflict of interest usually involves a reporter or editor covering a topic in which he or she has a personal stake—a family member may be involved, the reporter may do work on the side for a company being scrutinized, and so forth. This sort of thing is strongly discouraged, even to the point where some reporters are fired for conflict of interest.

ALTERNATIVE APPROACHES TO ETHICS

Standardized codes of media ethics are difficult to establish because there are few ethical imperatives that work in all situations. Also, most codes of ethics and guidelines are so general that they are not always applicable to specific circumstances. For these reasons and others, a system of *situational ethics* has long been advocated for the media.

SITUATIONAL ETHICS

In a situation covered by situational ethics, each decision is made, not with respect to a universal or "one-size-fits-all" code, but within the context of a specific situation. In other words, it is argued, a decision about ethics "depends" on many time- and place-specific situations. Within this perspective, media ethics, like all other ethical considerations, is linked to human choices that involve doing the right thing at the right time. For example, in following up on a report on a political candidate's secret sex life, a reporter may invoke "the people's right to know" (about the character of their public servants) as an ethical reason for violating privacy and digging deeply into the individual's private affairs. In the case of a private citizen with similar secrets, however, that standard may not make sense. Publicizing details about such a person's private life may simply be unethical snooping.

THE CONTINUING SEARCH

The search for alternative answers has been a topic of lively debate among journalists for a long time. One thing is certain: the issue of media ethics remains on the agenda and is often discussed both within and outside the communications industry. Many industry seminars probe ethical issues and dilemmas. Electronic media deal with media ethics in such programs as "On the Media" on NPR, "Reliable Sources" on CNN, and "Media Matters" on PBS. Journalism schools have taught journalistic ethics intermittently, since the 1920s, and have established scores of new courses. One—the University of Oregon—even gives an annual ethics award to media firms, individuals, and students. There are at least ten relatively new texts on the topic. Various study centers and think tanks are working on media ethics issues, and some are single-mindedly devoted to this topic. There is a *Journal of Media Ethics,* which takes up important issues and seeks resolution as well as several ethics Web sites.

Most of the efforts to encourage media ethics have been less intellectual and more action oriented. Earlier, we mentioned press councils—small groups of responsible citizens organized at the local, state, and national levels as feedback mechanisms. While only partially successful, these efforts nonetheless represent models for accountability and ethical pursuit.

In one form or another, various codes of ethics have spread to virtually every part of the communications industry. Once mainly in the purview of journalism, there are now formalized ethical standards in advertising, public relations, opinion polling, market research, sports writing, and other areas. The fact that they exist, however, does not mean that they will be followed. These are generalized documents and not usually enforceable, but they still represent a serious concern for ethics.

CREDIBILITY STUDIES AND MARKET RESEARCH

Perhaps the most important efforts to promote media ethics have been *credibility studies* that probe public attitudes about the news media and dredge up concerns and problems ranging from sensationalism to reporter rudeness. A media credibility movement emerged in the 1980s because it was felt that news organizations, in particular, were losing ground as believable and trustworthy agencies. This probably stemmed from worry that a loss of credibility would both impair the media's moral authority and undermine its economic might. At a time of feverish competition among print and broadcast media for audiences and advertising, there was a real reason to deal with matters of credibility and ethics.

Market research is also a force that, perhaps unwittingly, promotes media ethics. Market and audience research provides media organizations and others in the communications industry with certain kinds of feedback about public tastes, preferences, and concerns. Often this feedback centers on matters that have an ethical connection and are therefore appropriate for discussion.

As we suggested, a concern with ethics now stretches across all media fields. Opinion makers—whether talk show hosts, media consultants, advertising executives, or entertainment producers—have standards and codes of conduct. Authors have ethical concerns and so do those who produce and manufacture their work. It is still most common to tie ethics to professional, rather than to technical functions, but even that distinction has broken down. Television camera operators had better have ethical standards, or the work they direct will be tainted. The same is true with printers, operators of desktop publishing systems, cartoonists, and others. It is true that the ethics of each of these categories of people may differ, reflecting varied concerns and values but, to be sure, they are all connected in some way with the current media ethics debate.

ETHICS, TECHNOLOGY, AND THE FUTURE

New technologies of communication, especially in the last ten years, have raised a variety of ethical questions and controversies. In 2000, a fake press release about the resignation of a corporate CEO led to a precipitous drop of that firm's stock value. Another misfired mock news story on the Internet accused Vice President Al Gore of murdering a child in the midst of his presidential campaign.

Ethical breaches using technology are often linked to privacy, including hidden cameras and microphones and the use of databases to mine personal information about individuals. For example, through distant-sensing cameras, it is easy to "spy" on news sources. Various audio and video recorders make this even easier. Some Internet sites have sought and misused personal information such as social security card numbers.

Satellite communication allows for easy movement over national boundaries into the midst of world crises and conflicts. This can result in ethical chaos. In December 1992, a circuslike atmosphere occurred when U.S. Marines waded ashore in an amphibious landing at Mogadishu, Somalia, to begin their campaign of moving food to the starving. While the marines were following their carefully rehearsed procedures for large-scale assault landings, they were met on the beach by one hundred or more journalists with bright TV lights and a forest of microphones that were shoved into the faces of the landing party. The whole event was ridiculed by elements of the press, even though both the journalists and the marines were carrying on their normal activities.

Because it is now relatively simple to capture news events on video cameras, many people have footage for sale. They range from amateur local "news hounds" who tape news events and try to hawk their footage to TV stations, to more professional freelancers who are not under the control of an established news organization. Determining the veracity of this material and the qualifications and proficiency of the person who presents it is not easy.

This has led to various deliberate or inadvertent problems for television. Just after the nuclear accident at Chernobyl, for example, American networks bought taped reports purportedly showing the crippled Ukrainian plant. Actually, it was a nuclear power plant in Italy. It was also alleged in 1989 that CBS anchor Dan Rather had broadcast freelance footage from Afghanistan that was faked and done in another country. Such examples in both print and electronic media abound, and technology enhances the deceiver's ability. A device called the "electronic darkroom" makes it possible to create authentic-looking pictures of individuals embracing, although they have never met each other.

These are only a few examples of ethical problems raised by new communications technologies. The speed of these new tools and their reach makes them both liberating and dangerous devices that warrant discussion. Again, they affect virtually all aspects of the media industries and much of society.

At its headquarters at the University of Maryland, the *American Journalism Review* (once the *Washington Journalism Review*) has a Web site and also publishes a magazine, which mostly focuses on journalism and the news media.

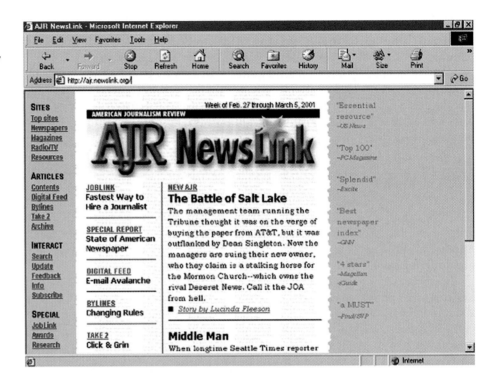

At the dawn of a new century, much of the discussion of media ethics is still locked firmly in the matrix of the past. However, it is also clear that much of the debate charts new ground and moves beyond established rules. Considerable thought, therefore, must go into determining (1) what should be codified as a lasting part of institutional and individual rules carried over from the past, (2) what should be left to the imagination of situational decision making in order to maximize freedom of expression, and (3) how ethical considerations need to be reevaluated to take into account the technologies of the future. Whatever those decisions, any system of accountability, no matter how modest, always impinges on freedom of choice. Of course, sometimes that infringement is warranted and even desirable.[14]

An important principle for the future is that voluntary methods of resolving ethical dilemmas are typically preferable to those that eventually end up in the courts. Although many ethical matters are not immediately legal concerns, in our litigious society one might guess that if they are not, they soon might be. To date, most of the impetus for media ethics has come internally from the media industries themselves and from communications education. This might not always be the case. It is easy to imagine courts or legislative bodies mandating a system of ethics that would be onerous, especially during a period of unpopularity for the media. In fact, the idea of licensing journalists and giving them a required code of ethics has actually been proposed. It was quickly dismissed, however, because of the seeming violation of the First Amendment.

Today, media ethics is something of a cottage industry and the subject of scores of professional seminars held for journalists, broadcasters, public relations people, and others. Many universities now offer courses in media ethics and have a rich literature on which to draw—not only many treatises, books, and articles, but also case studies—that point to the dilemmas and decisions that people must make in a modern society, many of them coping directly with ethics.

That cottage industry may be leading to significant changes in media ethics. Communications law scholar Donald Gillmor has written that such changes come in cycles. From the 1920s forward, there has been an ethics movement in the media that wanes and later resurfaces. Perhaps with a continually improving system of information storage and retrieval, that will not happen again. Ethical dilemmas abound, and they seem to compel enough human attention both from media professionals and from the consumers of communication that we can likely look forward to a period of maturation and development for this new and still uncharted territory.

Chapter Review

- Some critics ridicule the idea that competitive and profit-driven media can operate within an ethical framework. But most people disagree, saying that no media system can exist very long without public confidence, and that requires accurate, honest, and believable communication.

- Ethical behavior in a general sense simply means that people should not lie, steal, cheat, or commit other antisocial acts. Ethics is doing what is "right," but the problem is that "right" is defined differently by different people. Thus, the need exists for serious attention to media ethics in a society that is increasingly concerned about the ethics of all occupational groups and professionals.

- Media ethics is not an obscure or irrelevant topic, but something that arises daily as citizens observe the way media institutions relate to their communities as participants, observers, and critics. Ethical dilemmas also arise over the content of the media—whether it is entertainment, news, opinion, or advertising—as well as over the behavior of media people.

- Under the First Amendment to the Constitution of the United States, there is no requirement that the media be fair, responsible, or accurate. The courts have stated this quite explicitly, yet increasingly there is a higher standard of media performance evident in libel cases and other legal action against the mass and specialized media.

- Institutional media ethics have evolved considerably since the press of the early years of American journalism. During that time, the press was often scurrilous, making unwarranted partisan attacks on political figures with little regard for truth or accuracy. Later, a sensational press played on the public's morbid curiosity to stir up the audience and attract readers.

- A consistent thread promoting media ethics over the years has been media *criticism,* which dates back to the nineteenth century. Critics typically charged the press with violating common decency and obscuring the truth. This has kept public attention focused on the need for ethical standards.

- Typically, media ethics have centered on three major issues: (1) *accuracy* and *fairness* in reporting and other activities, (2) the *behavior of reporters,* especially in relation to their sources, and (3) avoidance of *conflicts of interest.*

- Standardized codes of media ethics are difficult to establish because there are few ethical imperatives that work in all situations. Also, most codes of ethics and guidelines are so general that they are not always applicable to specific circumstances. For these reasons and others, a system of *situational ethics* has long been advocated for the media.

- In one form or another, various codes of ethics have spread to virtually every part of the communications industry. Once mainly in the purview of journalism, there are now formalized ethical standards in advertising, public relations, opinion polling, market research, sports writing, and other areas. The fact that they exist, however, does not mean that they will be followed.

- New technologies of communication, especially in the last ten years, have raised a variety of ethical questions and controversies. The speed of these new tools and their reach makes them both liberating as well as dangerous devices that warrant discussion. They affect virtually all aspects of the media industries and much of society.

- An important principle for the future is that voluntary methods of resolving ethical dilemmas are typically preferable to those that eventually end up in the courts. To date most of the impetus for media ethics has come internally from the media industries themselves and from communications education. This might not always be the case.

Notes and References

1. Claude-Jean Bertrand, *Media Ethics and Accountability Systems* (New Brunswick, N.J.: Transaction Books, 2000). Also see Everette E. Dennis and Robert Snyder, eds., *Media and Public Life* (New Brunswick, N.J.: Transaction Books, 1997) and Louis A. Day, *Ethics in Mass Communication: Cases and Controversies* (Belmont, Calif.: Wadsworth Publishing, 1999).
2. David Pritchard, ed., *Holding the Media Accountable: Citizens, Ethics, and the Law* (Bloomington, Ind.: Indiana University Press, 2000).
3. Mark Fitzgerald, "Why They Do It—Desperation?, Kleptomania?, Stupidity?, or Just Plain Lazy," *Editor & Publisher*, August 7, 2000, p. 23, offers a discussion of recent plagiarism cases in the media and why they happened. A useful and standard text that offers context for this and other ethical dilemmas is Clifford G. Christians, et al., *Media Ethics: Cases and Moral Reasoning*, 6th ed. (New York: Longman, 2000).
4. Lawrence K. Grossman, "To Err Is Human, to *Admit* It Divine," *Columbia Journalism Review* (March/April 1997), p. 16.
5. Everette E. Dennis, Donald M. Gillmor, and Theodore Glasser, eds., *Media Freedom and Accountability* (Westport, Conn.: Greenwood, 1990).
6. Bill Kovach and Tom Rosenstiel, *Warp Speed: America in the Age of Mixed Media* (New York: Century Foundation, 1999). See also, Colin Sparks, et al., *Tabloid Tales: Global Debates Over Media Standards* (London: Rowman and Littlefield, 2000).
7. Kovach and Rosenstiel supplied the characteristics, but the explanation and examples are those of the authors.
8. Paul K. Lester, ed., *Images That Injure, Pictorial Stereotypes in the Media* (Westport, Conn.: Praeger, 1996).
9. Richard Bernstein, *Dictatorship of Virtue, Multiculturalism and the Battle for America's Future* (New York: Knopf, 1994).

10. Edmund B. Lambeth, *Committed Journalism: An Ethic for the Profession* (Bloomington, Ind.: Indiana University Press, 1986).

11. Philip Meyer, *Ethical Journalism* (White Plains, N.Y.: Longman, 1987).

12. Burton Benjamin, *Fair Play* (New York: Harper & Row, 1988).

13. Janet Malcolm's work appeared in *The New Yorker,* March 13 and March 20, 1989. It was later published as *The Journalist and the Murderer* (New York: Knopf, 1990).

14. John C. Merrill, *The Dialectic in Journalism: Toward a Responsible Use of Press Freedom* (Baton Rouge: Louisiana State University Press, 1989). Also see John C. Merrill, *Journalism Ethics, Philosophical Foundations for News Media* (New York: St. Martin's Press, 1997).

Appendix

MEDIA AND COMMUNICATION INDUSTRY WEB SITES

An Annotated Digitology

Jim Romenesko's Media News (www.poynter.org/medianews): This is an excellent portal for entry to a mix of journalism and media industry sites with links to key information on the comings and goings of top news media and other leaders and executives. This site includes pieces by thoughtful media columnists and commentators as well as the sometimes quirky, alternative weeklies. Funded by the Poynter Institute, this site is a brisk read—well-focused, critical, and always readable. It is a past winner of a Webby Award for the Best Media Site.

Inside (www.inside.com/front/index): The lively and authoritative digital presence of *Inside Magazine* covers the book, film, music, TV, digital, and other media and entertainment industries. It also offers an insider's perspective on "inside dope," "the latest deals," "job changes," and more. Respected editor-commentator-entrepreneur Kurt Anderson is co-chair for the site.

The Standard (www.thestandard.com): This is the Web presence of *The Industry Standard,* which rightly calls itself "intelligence for the Internet economy." There is daily news from *The Industry Standard,* opinion pieces and special reports as well as coverage of e-commerce, culture, ideas and strategies, jobs and the workplace, media and marketing, money and markets, policy and reports, tech and telecom, world news, and more. Extensive coverage of research and even a useful roster of conferences and events are included. This site is authoritative, respected, and frequently quoted by other media.

The Deal (www.thedeal.com): This site tracks "media maneuvers" and deals and bills itself as a "report on current changes in corporate control." This site provides information about who owns what and how much they paid for it. With its cheeky tone, the Deal offers early intelligence on IPOs (initial public offerings), ventures, movers and shakers, and trends as well as "rules of the road," which looks for predictable cues for corporate ownership shifts. This site is often critical of other media sites and publications.

min online (www.minonline.com): This is a Web site for the *min* (Media Industry Newsletter) magazine, which offers strategic news and proprietary data for magazine, newspaper, broadcast, and online publishers. This site is for publishers, and it has an executive tone. It offers box scores on performance in ad pages, other revenues, as well as news of new site launches, industry people, and even a roster of contests and awards.

mediachannel (www.mediachannel.org): This site offers an "eye on global media" with a mix of media news, issue and subject coverage (pubcasting, hip-hop media, books, etc.), and opinion pieces. It is especially strong on European and North American media, but other global players are monitored as well. This site provides links to five hundred media issues groups worldwide. It is produced by Global Vision New Media, New York City.

Brill's Content (www.brillscontent.com): This is the lively site *Brill's Content,* the *Fortune* of media industry rags, with long interpretative articles about media personalities that incorporate a *Vanity Fair* breathiness as well as a gossipy tone, but it is still a source for useful insights that give visitors a feel for the blood and guts of the media not present in the breezier newsletters and news sites. While criticizing others, *Brill's Content* is the only magazine in the business that has its own independent ombudsman, who often bites the hand that feeds him.

Media Research Center (www.mediaresearchcenter.com): For a view from the political right, this site, conducted by conservative critic and analyst Brent Bozell, scores liberal media and offers a somewhat conspiratorial view of big media outlets, most of which Bozell thinks are too liberal, if not downright dishonest and manipulative. This site often goes over the top and strains credulity.

FAIR (Fairness & Accuracy in Reporting) (www.fair.org): What the Media Research Center does for the right, FAIR does for the left. This site surveys the media, mostly the news media, with a leftist lens and finds conservative, right-wing conspiracies almost everywhere. There is little outside the alternative media with which FAIR agrees, and like other ideological sites, it tries to keep score on who is doing what to whom. This site is also frequently over the top with its use of shrill criticism.

Mediaweek (www.mediaweek.com): This site provides the most comprehensive treatment of media industries, especially the traditional general-circulation media, with less attention to the digital media economy. One finds a business-oriented perspective on the performance of newspapers, magazines, electronic media, and more with some analysis of corporate strategies and the people fashioning them. This site includes some analysis, but is mostly descriptive.

The Freedom Forum (www.freedomforum.org): This is the site of the Freedom Forum, formerly the Gannett Foundation, which covers freedom of expression issues, though narrowly and in a self-promotional fashion. This site offers a pro-industry perspective with an absolutist slant on First Amendment issues, but it rarely speaks well of media critics. It is useful for its treatment of freedom of expression controversies in the United States and overseas.

Poynter Institute (www.poynter.org): Another media foundation site, but it includes more emphasis on practical training and tips for journalists and media managers. It also offers analysis of media controversies and coverage and is tied to Poynter's extensive program of professional training seminars. This site provides a mainstream media view with an emphasis on professionalism.

Yahoo! (www.yahoo.com): This popular portal has scores of well-organized links to media industries, news and media, journalism, accountability, and almost any mix of subjects and buzz words desired. It is the most user friendly point of entry to each of the industries, media outlets themselves, and much more.

Credits

TEXT CREDITS

Chapter 1

The Nature and Uses of Theory; Adoption of Innovation Theory; Shannon and Weaver's Information Theory. Developed by Margaret N. DeFleur, *Fundamentals of Mass Communication Theory: Processes and Effects.* Reprinted by permission of the author.

Chapter 2

Figure 2.1: U.S. Census Bureau: Statistical Abstracts of the U.S. by year. Table 2.1: "Types of Book." From Datus Smith, *A Guide to Book Publishing,* Revised Edition, pp. 128–129. Used by permission. Figure 2.2: "Estimated Book Sales by Category, 2000." From *Communications Industry Forecast.* Used by permission of Veronis, Suhler & Associates, Communications Industry Forecast, New York, NY, Tel (212) 935-4990.

Chapter 3

Gatekeeping Theory; A Theory of Unintentional News Distortion; The Agenda-Setting Theory of the Press. Developed by Margaret N. DeFleur, *Fundamentals of Mass Communication Theory: Processes and Effects.* Reprinted by permission of the author. Figure 3.1: U.S. Bureau of the Census. Figure 3.2: Statistical Abstract of the U.S.; Newspaper Association of America, 2001.

Chapter 4

Table 4.1: U.S. Bureau of the Census; U.S. Department of Health, Education, and Welfare; Statistics of the School Systems, 1986–1987; U.S. Department of Education, Mini-Digest of Education Statistics: Enrollments, 1999. Table 4.3: National Directory of Magazines, 1999, Oxbridge Communications.

Chapter 5

The Creeping Cycle of Desensitization Theory. Developed by Margaret N. DeFleur, *Fundamentals of Mass Communication Theory: Processes and Effects.* Reprinted by permission of the author. Table 5.1: Motion Picture Association of America, 1999. Table 5.2: "Movie Admission by Age Group, 1996–1999." Copyright © 1994. Used by permission of Motion Picture Association of America.

Chapter 6

Figure 6.1: U.S. Bureau of the Census; Radio Advertising Bureau Reports. Figure 6.2: U.S. Census Bureau: Statistical Abstracts of the U.S. by year.

Chapter 7

Figure 7.1: U.S. Census Bureau: Statistical Abstracts of the U.S. by year. Figure 7.2: Television Bureau of Advertising, Inc.; A. C. Nielsen; Corbet S. Steinberg, TV Facts, 1980; Motion Picture Association of America, 2000. Figure 7.3: Nielsen Media Research; Television Bureau of Advertising, Inc.; U.S. Census Bureau. Figure 7.4: Veronis Suhler Media Merchant Bank; Paul Kagan and Associates; Nielsen Media Research, 2000.

Chapter 8

Table 8.1: Nielsen Net Ratings, March 2000. Table 8.2: Webby Awards, 2000. Figure 8.2: "Percentage of U.S. Households Online, 1998–2002." Veronis Suhler Communications Industry Forecast, 15th Edition, 2001. Figure 8.3: "Growth of Internet Households (in millions), 1997–2004." Veronis Suhler Communications Industry Forecast, 15th Edition, 2001.

Chapter 9

Cultural Imperialism Theory. Developed by Margaret N. DeFleur, *Fundamentals of Mass Communication Theory: Processes and Effects.* Reprinted by permission of the author.

Chapter 10

A Theory of the Negative Effects of Kitsch; Critical Cultural Theory. Developed by Margaret N. DeFleur, *Fundamentals of Mass Communication Theory: Processes and Effects.* Reprinted by permission of the author. Table 10.1: "Top Ten Selling Albums in 2000." Veronis Suhler Communications Industry Forecast, 15th Edition, 2001.

Chapter 11

Table 11.1: "Rankings of Advertising Agencies by Income (in millions)." Reprinted with permission from the April 24, 2000 issue of *Advertising Age.* Copyright, Crain Communications, Inc., 2000. Figure 11.2: Veronis Suhler Communications Industry Forecast, Industry Spending Projections, 2000–2004, 14th Annual Edition, July 2000. Figures based on estimates for 2000. Table 11.2: "Top Ten National Advertisers." Reprinted with permission from the September 27, 1999 issue of *Advertising Age.* Copyright, Crain Communications, Inc., 1999. Table 11.3: "Prime-Time Media Buys." Reprinted with permission from the October 2, 2000 issue of *Advertising Age.* Copyright, Crain Communications, Inc., 2000.

Chapter 12

Definition of "lobbyists." Copyright © 1981 by Houghton Mifflin Company. Reproduced by permission from *The American Heritage Dictionary of the English Language.*

Chapter 13

Figure 13.1: U.S. Census: Statistical Abstracts of the U.S. by year. Table 13.1: U.S. Census: Statistical Abstract of the U.S., 111th ed. (Washington, D.C., 1991). Figure 13.2: U.S. Census: Statistical Abstracts of the U.S. by year. Figure 13.3: U.S. Census: Statistical Abstracts of the U.S. by year. Table 13.2: U.S. Census: Statistical Abstract of the U.S., 1996. Table 13.3: U.S. Census: Statistical Abstract of the U.S., 1996. Figure 13.4: U.S. Census: Statistical Abstracts of the U.S. by year.

Chapter 15

The Magic Bullet Theory; Two-Step Flow of Communication Theory; Selected and Limited Influences Theory; Uses for Gratification Theory; Media Information Utility Theory; Modeling Theory; The Theory of Accumulation of Minimal Effects; Social Expectations Theory. Developed by Margaret N. DeFleur, *Fundamentals of Mass Communication Theory: Processes and Effects.* Reprinted by permission of the author.

Chapter 16

Society of Professional Journalists Code of Ethics reprinted by permission of the Society of Professional Journalists.

PHOTO CREDITS

Chapter 1

page 3: Bill Aron/PhotoEdit; *page 4:* Copyright © 2001, Ward Associates. Stephen Ward, Creator. Reprinted by permission of Ward Associates, www.wardassoc.com; *page 9:* Peter Vandermark/Stock, Boston; *page 11:* Michael Newman/PhotoEdit; *page 16:* Tom Benton/Impact Visuals; *page 17:* M. Schwartz/Image Works; *page 19:* M. J. Stroud/Archive Photos; *page 22:* Everett Collection; *page 23:* Chris Hondros/Liaison Agency.

Chapter 2

page 29: Archivo Iconografico, S.A./Corbis; *page 31:* Eric Meola/Image Bank; *page 35:* The Granger Collection, New York; *page 37:* The Bettmann Archive; *page 39:* Culver Pictures, Inc.; *page 43:* Spencer Grant/PhotoEdit; *page 48:* Reuters/Ian Waldie/Archive Photos; *page 49:* Chuck Nacke/Woodfin Camp & Associates; *page 51:* Copyright © 2000 Amazon.com, Inc. All rights reserved. Reprinted with permission; *page 52:* Copyright © 2000 by Houghton Mifflin Company. Reproduced by permission from *The American Heritage Dictionary of the English Language,* Fourth Edition.

Chapter 3

page 59: MPI/Archive Photos; *page 60:* Library of Congress; *page 65:* (top) Corbis; Corbis; *page 66:* The Hayden Collection. Charles Henry Hayden Fund. Courtesy, Museum of Fine Arts, Boston. *page 70:* John Neubauer/PhotoEdit; *page 71:* Barbara Alper/Stock, Boston; *page 80:* Los Angeles Times Syndicate; *page 81:* With permission of the artist, © Ann Telnaes/Ann Telnaes; *page 89:* SuperStock International; *page 90:* Richard Ellis/Liaison Agency.

Chapter 4

page 99: Michael A. Dwyer/Stock, Boston; *page 102:* Hulton Getty Picture Collection; *page 105:* The Granger Collection; *page 110:* (clockwise) Culver Pictures; Underwood & Underwood/Corbis; Bettman Archive/Edward Weston/Corbis; *page 117:* Antoine Verglas/E. Jean Carroll; *page 121:* AP/Wide World Photos.

Chapter 5

page 127: Bettmann/Corbis; *page 130:* Hulton Getty Picture Collection; *page 132:* The Granger Collection; *page 133:* Everett Collection; *page 135:* RKO/Kobal Collection; *page 140:* ST. NICHOLAS, RANDEE/20TH CENTURY FOX/Kobal Collection; *page 141:* FLAHERTY/Kobal Collection; *page 148:* Michele Burgess/Stock, Boston; *page 153:* LIVE ENTERTAIN-

MENT/Kobal Collection; *page 155:* Everett Collection; *page 156:* AP/Wide World Photos.

Chapter 6

page 161: Lucien Aigner/Corbis; *page 166:* Culver Pictures, Inc.; *page 176:* The Bettmann Archive; *page 178:* UPI/Corbis-Bettmann; *page 180:* RICHARD HOWARD/TimePix; *page 182:* Ethan Miller/Corbis; *page 183:* Aaron Mayes/Las Vegas Sun/AP/Wide World Photos; *page 184:* Screenshot from 1047kcld.com. Reprinted by permission.

Chapter 7

page 189: Schenectady Museum; Hall of Electrical History Foundation/Corbis; *page 193:* UPI/Corbis-Bettmann; *page 196:* Archive Photos; *page 198:* AP/Wide World Photos; *page 201:* AP Photo/Rick Bowmer; *page 206:* Tivo.com; *page 207:* Nielsen Media Research; *page 209:* Jeff Greenberg/PhotoEdit; *page 210:* Fox.com.

Chapter 8

page 215: Copyright by John Carey, Greystone Communications; *page 216:* SuperStock International; *page 217:* AP/Wide World Photos; *page 222:* AP/Wide World Photos; *page 229:* Gail Albert Halaban/Corbis/SABA Press Photos; *page 231:* Reprinted with permission of AtomShockwave Corp. Copyright © 1999–2000 AtomShockwave Corp. All rights reserved. Atom Films and Atom Films and logo are trademarks or registered trademarks of AtomShockwave Corp.; *page 232:* Bettmann/Corbis.

Chapter 9

page 241: AP/Wide World Photos; *page 245:* NBC News; *page 248:* AP/Wide World Photos; *page 250:* Ulrike Welsch/Stock, Boston.

Chapter 10

page 257: AFP/Corbis; *page 259:* C. Topham/The Image Works; *page 262:* White/Packert/Image Bank; *page 265:* Reuters/Greg Bos/Archive Photos; *page 269:* Reuters/Colin Braley/Hulton/Archive; *page 277:* AP/Wide World Photos; *page 281:* Bernie Nunez/Liaison Agency; *page 283:* AFP/Corbis; *page 286:* Screenshot from www.davematthewsband.com. Reprinted with the permission of Bama Rags, Inc.

Chapter 11

page 291: Leagas Delaney, San Francisco; *page 297:* Dana White/PhotoEdit; *page 302:* Leo Burnett U.S.A.; *page 304:* Jordan Harris/PhotoEdit; *page 318:* Reprinted by permission of Scholastic, Inc.

Chapter 12

page 325: AP/Wide World Photos; *page 330:* MediaMap; *page 335:* White Eagle Studio; *page 338:* Reuters NewMedia, Inc./Corbis; *page 341:* Gregg Mancuso/Stock, Boston, Inc./PictureQuest (PNI); *page 350:* Screenshot from devonpr.com. Reprinted with permission.

Chapter 13

page 355: SuperStock International; *page 362:* Rudi Von Briel/PhotoEdit; *page 373:* Mark Richards/PhotoEdit; *page 380:* Courtesy/Arbitron Company; *page 383:* BET.

Chapter 14

page 389: Reuters/POOL/Archive Photos; *page 392:* AP/Wide World Photos; *page 402:* AP/Wide World Photos; *page 404:* Reuters/Vince Bucci/Archive Photos; *page 412:* AP/Wide World Photos.

Chapter 15

page 423: Bob Daemmrich/Stock Boston; *page 430:* Archive Photos; *page 435:* Robert King/Liaison Agency; *page 440:* Donna Barstow; *page 443:* AFP/Stephen Jaffe/Corbis; *page 457:* SW Production/Index Stock Imagery.

Chapter 16

page 461: Mike Stocker/South Florida Sun Sentinel; *page 464:* Damian Dovarganes/AP/Wide World Photos; *page 466:* AP/Wide World Photos; *page 468:* Corbis; *page 470:* AP/Wide World Photos; *page 474:* Screenshot from ojr.usc.edu/content/story.cfm?request=561. The *Online Journalism Review* is a publication of the USC-Annenberg School for Communication. Reprinted with permission; *page 477:* Screenshot reprinted with permission from www.poynter.org; *page 480:* Screenshot from ajr.newllink.org. Reprinted with permission.

Index